INTERNATIONAL
ENVIRONMENTAL
LAW REPORTS

Volume 5

INTERNATIONAL ENVIRONMENTAL LAW
IN INTERNATIONAL TRIBUNALS

The fifth and final volume of the *International Environmental Law Reports* collects together eighteen decisions from international tribunals. As well as decisions of the International Court of Justice, the volume includes decisions from the International Tribunal for the Law of the Sea, various arbitral tribunals and the United Nations Compensation Commission. The comprehensive case summaries are backed up by detailed cross-references to original sources. Covering four decades of legal proceedings, this volume brings the 'classic' decisions up to date with the major modern decisions of international tribunals.

International Environmental Law Reports

Volume 1: Early Decisions
ISBN 978 0521 643474 HB
    978 0521 643979 PB

Volume 2: Trade and Environment
ISBN 978 0521 650359 HB
    978 0521 659673 PB

Volume 3: Human Rights and Environment
ISBN 978 0521 650366 HB
    978 0521 659666 PB

Volume 4: International Environmental Law in National Courts
ISBN 978 0521 650373 HB
    978 0521 659659 PB

Volume 5: International Environmental Law in International Tribunals
ISBN 978 0521 650380 HB
    978 0521 659642 PB

Set volumes 1–5
ISBN 978 0521 650342 HB
    978 0521 659680 PB

INTERNATIONAL ENVIRONMENTAL LAW REPORTS

Volume 5

INTERNATIONAL ENVIRONMENTAL LAW
IN INTERNATIONAL TRIBUNALS

Edited by

KAREN LEE
Lauterpacht Research Centre for International Law
University of Cambridge

Series editor

CAIRO A. R. ROBB

General editors

DANIEL BETHLEHEM

JAMES CRAWFORD

PHILIPPE SANDS

CAMBRIDGE
UNIVERSITY PRESS

CAMBRIDGE UNIVERSITY PRESS
Cambridge, New York, Melbourne, Madrid, Cape Town, Singapore, São Paulo

Cambridge University Press
The Edinburgh Building, Cambridge CB2 8RU, UK

Published in the United States of America by Cambridge University Press, New York

www.cambridge.org
Information on this title: www.cambridge.org/9780521659642

© Lauterpacht Research Centre for International Law 2007

First published 2007

Printed in the United Kingdom at the University Press, Cambridge

A catalogue record for this publication is available from the British Library

Library of Congress Catalog card number 00–551531

ISBN   978-0-521-65038-0 hardback
ISBN   978-0-521-65964-2 paperback

Contents

Preface

This is the fifth and final volume in this series of *International Environmental Law Reports*. As stated in the Preface to volume 1 (1999), it was intended 'to present [the] considerable and growing body of relevant jurisprudence' concerning international environmental law.

Volume 5 is in a sense a companion to volume 1 which began the series. Volume 1 covered in accessible form twenty-eight 'classic' decisions, many of them still cited as foundational to the subject: for example, *Behring Fur Seals*, *Trail Smelter, Diversion of Waters from the Meuse, Lac Lanoux*. The present volume brings the classics up to date, so to speak, with the major modern decisions of the International Court and the various tribunals which exercise jurisdiction under the 1982 UN Convention on the Law of the Sea. These cases – from *Fisheries Jurisdiction* through *Gabčíkovo–Nagymaros* and *Southern Bluefin Tuna* to *MOX Plant* and *Land Reclamation* – are now central to the subject. It is curious that none of them have yet generated, or perhaps are likely to generate, the immediate name recognition of *Trail Smelter*, and that none have associated with them a general principle of the *sic utere tuo* kind for which *Trail Smelter* is cited in a thousand academic articles and a million undergraduate essays. This prompts two questions – why do there seem to be no 'modern classics' of environmental law, and is this situation to be regretted?

As to the first question, the answer may simply be that name recognition takes time and repetition – often, it must be said, rather thoughtless repetition, of the kind that has for so long treated the *Corfu Channel* case as if it concerned an issue of environmental law or involved the application of the *sic utere tuo* principle, which it did not. Even with decisions which do involve issues of international environmental law, with time the case may come to stand straightforwardly for a proposition which tells only part of the story: the complex proceedings in *Trail Smelter* itself (set out in 1 *IELR* 231–331) provide an example. No doubt the modern cases may eventually acquire the status of 'classics', perhaps because they too will come to be treated as icons rather than as complex events. For – and this brings us to the second question – international environmental law is almost always about complexity and uncertainty, about striking a balance between conflicting uses and potentially conflicting rights and interests, in which issues of fact and appreciation are dominant and there is no trump card. Issues concerning the environment have to be worked through, understood in a measure of detail, lived rather than encapsulated. That is yet another reason why *Corfu Channel*, with the trump card of Article 2(4) of the United Nations Charter and the prohibition of forcible intervention, is very far from the present field.

At any rate, the modern decisions show clearly enough the processes by which international courts and tribunals, often at an interlocutory stage, are confronted with environmental issues and with conflicting assertions of right as between States. There can be little doubt that the frequency with which these issues come before international courts has increased. The substantial jurisprudence of the WTO and of international human rights tribunals was presented in volumes 2 and 3, and here we have, as it were, the remainder or residue – the international claims dealt with on an interstate basis by courts applying general international law. They present a fascinating picture of a still emerging jurisprudence, filling out (with nuances and occasional backslidings) the law so prolifically set out in the great number of treaties.

Thanks are due to many people for their assistance in the preparation of this volume. We are particularly grateful to Dapo Akande, Susan Breau, Joshua Brien, Kylie Evans, Professor Christopher Greenwood CMG, QC, Edward Helgeson and Samuel Wordsworth for writing the summaries and to the Editors of the *International Law Reports* for their kind permission to adapt those summaries that were originally written for the *ILR*. Our thanks also go to Tara Grant for her invaluable general and secretarial assistance, to Miss Maureen MacGlashan CMG, for her thorough preparation of the index and the table of treaties, to Diane Ilott for her patience and attention to detail in copy-editing this volume and to Finola O'Sullivan and everyone else at Cambridge University Press who has helped to publish this volume.

James Crawford
Karen Lee
Lauterpacht Research Centre for International Law
University of Cambridge

2006

Editorial note

The five volumes of *International Environmental Law Reports* contain significant decisions pertaining to the field of international environmental law rendered by various national and international tribunals. The decisions have been reproduced to the greatest extent possible in the form in which they were originally reported or handed down. Some old punctuation has been modernised, and efforts have been made to standardise typefaces; otherwise the texts are as originally published. For this reason the reader will find that spellings, especially of place names, may vary.

For reasons of space, the texts of the decisions of the International Court of Justice and other international tribunals in this volume have been heavily dissected and only relevant extracts relating to environmental issues broadly conceived are included. Report citations for omitted material are given in editorial footnotes in the list of documents following the summary where possible. Within the text omitted material is indicated by an ellipsis in square brackets. The report from which the decision has been reproduced is cited at the end of each decision, and the bold page numbers in square brackets throughout a decision refer to the pagination of that report.

Each case has been summarised. Although only relevant extracts of the texts of decisions are reproduced, the summary sums up the facts and decision(s) in the case as a whole so that the highlighted points of environmental interest can be understood in the context of the case. Each summary is preceded by italicised digest entries. The digest entries are collected together in the Digest at the beginning of the volume to give the reader an overview of the issues covered in the volume.

Immediately after the summary is a list of the documents that follow, and the pages on which they commence. In addition to the decision(s) being reported this may include any relevant special agreement or related decision. Occasionally an editorial note concerning subsequent or related events or decisions is included at the end of a case.

Footnotes in the summary cross-refer to other cases in the *Reports* or in the *International Law Reports* and provide other useful information. The original footnotes in the texts of the decisions have been renumbered for reasons of text extraction and every effort has been made to adapt the reproduced footnotes where appropriate. Any editorial footnotes in the texts of the decisions appear in square brackets.

For the reader's convenience the volume contains tables of cases reported, a digest, a table of treaties and an index.

The cases reported here may be cited as 5 *IELR* followed by the relevant page number, e.g. 5 *IELR* 1.

Editorial Advisory Board

Abbreviations

ADL	Arthur D. Little, consultancy
AFMA	Australian Fisheries Management Authority
BNFL	British Nuclear Fuels plc
BPC	British Phosphate Commissioners
CCAMLR	Commission for the Conservation of Antarctic Marine Living Resources
CCSBT	Convention for the Conservation of Southern Bluefin Tuna
CMLR	Common Market Law Reports
DEFRA	Department of the Environment, Food and Rural Affairs (UK)
DETR	Department of the Environment, Transport and the Regions (UK)
EA	Euratom Treaty
EAEC	European Atomic Energy Community
EC	European Community
ECE	Economic Commission for Europe
ECR	European Court Reports
EEZ	exclusive economic zone
EFP	experimental fishing programme
EFPWG	Experimental Fishing Programme Working Group
EIA	environmental impact assessment
EIS	environmental impact statement
ESSD	environmentally and socially sustainable development
EU	European Union
EURATOM	Treaty Establishing the European Atomic Energy Community
FAO	United Nations Food and Agriculture Organization
FMA	Australian Fisheries Management Act 1991

GIS	Geographic Information System
GOE	group of experts
HAST	highly active storage tank
IBRD	International Bank for Reconstruction and Development
ICAO	International Civil Aviation Organization
ICJ	International Court of Justice
ICSID	International Centre for the Settlement of Investment Disputes
ICSU	International Council of Scientific Unions
ILC	International Law Commission
ILM	International Legal Materials
ILO	International Labour Organization
ILR	International Law Reports
IPPNW	International Physicians for the Prevention of Nuclear War
ITLOS	International Tribunal for the Law of the Sea
IUU	illegal, unreported and unregulated [fishing]
JCP	Joint Contractual Plan
KOC	Kuwaiti Oil Company
KPC	Kuwait Petroleum Corporation
KPI	Kuwait Petroleum International Limited
LOS	Law of the Sea
MAFF	Ministry of Agriculture, Fisheries and Food (UK)
MOX	mixed oxide fuel
MSJCE	Malaysia–Singapore Joint Committee on the Environment
NAFO	North Atlantic Fisheries Organisation
NAFTA	North Atlantic Free Trade Agreement
NATO	North Atlantic Treaty Organisation
NLGC	Nauru Local Government Council
OECD	Organization for Economic Co-operation and Development
OEEC	Organization for European Economic Co-operation
OJ	Official Journal (of the European Union)
OSPAR Convention	Convention for the Protection of the Marine Environment of the North East Atlantic, 1992
PA	PA Consulting Group, London
PCA	Permanent Court of Arbitration
PCIJ	Permanent Court of International Justice

PNEs	peaceful nuclear explosions
RIAA	Reports of International Arbitral Awards
ROPME	Regional Organization for the Protection of the Marine Environment
SAR Zone	search and rescue zone
SBT	southern bluefin tuna
SCOPE	Scientific Committee on Problems of the Environment
SMP	Sellafield MOX Plant
TAC	total allowable catch
THORP	Thermal Oxide Reprocessing Plant
TTAPS	Turco, Toon, Ackerman, Pollack and Sagan
UNCC	United Nations Compensation Commission
UNCLOS	United Nations Convention on the Law of the Sea
UNDP	United Nations Development Programme
UNEP	United Nations Environment Programme
UNIDIR	United Nations Institute of Disarmament Research
UNIDO	United Nations Industrial Development Organization
UNSC	United Nations Security Council
UNSCEAR	United Nations Scientific Committee on the Effects of Atomic Radiation
UNSCR	United Nations Security Council Resolution
UNTS	United Nations Treaty Series
USD	United States Dollars
USSR	Union of Soviet Socialist Republics
VMS	Vessel Management System
WBC Claim	Well Blowout Control Claim
WHA	World Health Assembly
WHO	World Health Organization
WTO	World Trade Organization

Tables of cases reported

The tables of cases are arranged alphabetically and chronologically by tribunal.

Digest

(Those headings for which there are entries in the present volume are printed in italics.)

Air

Pollution – transport and dispersion of air pollution – whether claims for reasonable monitoring and assessment activities compensable – United Nations Compensation Commission

Report and Recommendations Made by the Panel of Commissioners Concerning the First Instalment of 'F4' Claims **5** 626

Claims

Large claims – United Nations Compensation Commission – claim by the Kuwait Oil Company for the cost of extinguishing fires at the oil well-heads

in Kuwait – evidence of cause of damage – costs – evidence that costs actually incurred – attribution of costs to particular claims – use of expert accountancy reports to verify costs – United Nations Compensation Commission
Report and Recommendations Made by the Panel of Commissioners Appointed to Review the Well Blowout Control Claim **5** 607

Compliance

International environmental law norms – Treaty-based obligation to apply evolving environmental standards to protect water quality, nature and fishing interests – International Court of Justice
Case Concerning the Gabčíkovo–Nagymaros Project (Hungary/Slovakia) **5** 272

Conservation

Management of fish stocks – marine environment – precautionary principle – whether part of customary international law – whether different from a precautionary approach – Convention for the Conservation of Southern Bluefin Tuna, 1993 – Straddling Stocks Agreement, 1995 – relevance for application of the Law of the Sea Convention – International Tribunal for the Law of the Sea
Southern Bluefin Tuna Cases (New Zealand v. Japan) (Australia v. Japan) (Provisional Measures) **5** 393

Patagonian toothfish – vessel illegally fishing Patagonian toothfish in exclusive economic zone of Australia – international concern over illegal, unregulated and unreported fishing in the Southern Ocean – Commission for the Conservation of Antarctic Marine Living Resources ('CCAMLR') – International Tribunal for the Law of the Sea
The 'Volga' Case (Russian Federation v. Australia) **5** 445

Southern bluefin tuna – United Nations Convention on the Law of the Sea, 1982 – Convention for the Conservation of Southern Bluefin Tuna, 1993 – Arbitral Tribunal
Southern Bluefin Tuna Case (Australia and New Zealand v. Japan) (Award) **5** 495

Damage and compensation

Damages – principles – claim by the Kuwait Oil Company for the cost of extinguishing fires at the oil well-heads in Kuwait – heads of damage – general principles of international law – mitigation of damages – interest – date from which interest to be awarded – date taken to be 19 October

1991 – use of different date for calculating interest in other claims – United Nations Compensation Commission

> *Report and Recommendations Made by the Panel of Commissioners Appointed to Review the Well Blowout Control Claim* **5** 607

Ex injuria jus non oritur – objectives of Treaty – whether purpose and intention of parties in concluding Treaty prevail over literal interpretation – Treaty obligations overtaken by events – recognition of positions adopted by the parties after conclusion of Treaty – good faith negotiations – joint regime – reparation for acts committed by both Parties – intersecting wrongs – settlement of accounts for the construction – International Court of Justice

> *Case Concerning the Gabčíkovo–Nagymaros Project (Hungary/Slovakia)* **5** 272

Iraq's invasion and occupation of Kuwait, 1991 – assessment and monitoring claims by six governments – claims for environmental damage – depletion of natural resources – impacts on marine and coastal environment – impacts on terrestrial environment – cultural heritage – public health – impact on environment of influx of refugees and involuntary migration – reasonable monitoring and assessment activities compensable – United Nations Compensation Commission

> *Report and Recommendations Made by the Panel of Commissioners Concerning the First Instalment of 'F4' Claims* **5** 626

Nauru – phosphate mining – rehabilitation of lands worked out during period of trusteeship – liability of former trustees – Nauru Trusteeship Agreement, 1947 – Nauru Island Agreement, 1919 – effect of transfer of phosphate industry to Nauru on independence – International Court of Justice

> *Case Concerning Certain Phosphate Lands in Nauru (Nauru v. Australia)* **5** 124

Submission of Germany that Iceland under an obligation to make compensation for interference with German fishing vessels – jurisdiction of International Court to award compensation – need for concrete submission as to existence and amount of damage – relief denied – International Court of Justice

> *Fisheries Jurisdiction Case (Federal Republic of Germany v. Iceland)* **5** 71

Hazardous activities and substances

Alleged radioactive contamination arising from French underground nuclear weapons tests in South Pacific – whether unlawful to undertake tests before conducting an environmental impact assessment – Court's ruling in 1974 that object of dispute had disappeared because of France's undertaking in 1974 to cease atmospheric tests – assumption in 1974 that no risk of contamination

from underground testing – whether earlier proceedings and judgment limited to atmospheric nuclear testing or concerning all radioactive contamination caused by whatever means of testing – developments in scientific knowledge and international environmental law since 1974 – International Court of Justice
> *Request for an Examination of the Situation in Accordance with Paragraph 63 of the Court's Judgment of 20 December 1974 in the* Nuclear Tests (New Zealand v. France) Case **5** 149

Atmospheric nuclear tests conducted by France in South Pacific causing deposit of radioactive fallout on territory of other States and on high seas – Court requested to declare tests unlawful and order France to cease conducting them – whether tests lawful – International Court of Justice
> *Nuclear Tests Case (New Zealand v. France)* **5** 88

Nuclear weapons – effect of use of nuclear weapons upon the environment – International Court of Justice
> *Legality of the Threat or Use of Nuclear Weapons* **5** 238

Nuclear weapons – whether use of nuclear weapons prohibited by international humanitarian law – protection of health and the environment in war and armed conflict – International Court of Justice
> *Legality of the Use by a State of Nuclear Weapons in Armed Conflict* **5** 212

Human rights

War – nuclear weapons – whether human rights treaties applicable to military operations in time of armed conflict – right to life – International Covenant on Civil and Political Rights, 1966 – relationship between the law of human rights and international humanitarian law – International Court of Justice
> *Legality of the Threat or Use of Nuclear Weapons* **5** 238

International cooperation

Duty to cooperate to prevent pollution of marine environment – Law of the Sea Convention, Part XII – International Tribunal for the Law of the Sea
> *Case Concerning Land Reclamation by Singapore in and around the Straits of Johor (Malaysia v. Singapore)* **5** 466

International humanitarian law

Relationship between international environmental law and international humanitarian law – Principle 24, Rio Declaration – United Nations

International organisations

Jurisdiction

to be applied in interpretation of declaration and reservations – intention of State making declaration – principle of good faith – International Court of Justice

Locus standi – whether *actio popularis* exists in international law – International Court of Justice

Provision for recourse to arbitration – United Nations Convention on the Law of the Sea, 1982 ('UNCLOS'), Article 281 – Convention for the Conservation of Southern Bluefin Tuna, 1993, Article 16 – whether 1993 Convention excludes recourse to UNCLOS dispute settlement provisions – Arbitral Tribunal

Request to International Court of Justice by New Zealand for resumption of proceedings begun in 1973 challenging legality of France's nuclear tests – whether Request was outside scope of paragraph 63 of 1974 Judgment – paragraph 63 related exclusively to atmospheric nuclear tests – whether jurisdiction for Court to consider underground testing or developments in international environmental law since 1974 – International Court of Justice

Territorial jurisdiction over fisheries – whether limited to 12 miles – whether extension to 50 miles permissible – Icelandic claim – whether opposable to United Kingdom – adjacent waters – rights of the coastal State – exceptional dependence upon fisheries – conservation of fish stocks – preferential rights of coastal State – historic rights of other States – duty of States to negotiate equitable balance between rights – Anglo-Icelandic Exchange of Notes 1961 – International Court of Justice

Pollution

Environmental damage resulting from Iraq's invasion and occupation of Kuwait – Security Council Resolution 687 – Iraq responsible for such damage – provision for claims by States and international organisations in respect of environmental damage – threat to environment caused by fires at oil well-heads

in Kuwait – claim by corporation – whether admissible – United Nations Compensation Commission
  Report and Recommendations Made by the Panel of Commissioners Appointed to Review the Well Blowout Control Claim **5** 607

Powers and procedures of tribunals

International Court of Justice – interim measures of protection – declaration that Icelandic Government not enforce new exclusive fishing zone against United Kingdom vessels by action inside disputed area or by measures in Icelandic waters against vessels fishing in the disputed area – limits on metric tons of fish permitted to be taken by British vessels in disputed area – whether measures sought were for protection of economic interests of private enterprises – interim measures granted – International Court of Justice
  Fisheries Jurisdiction Case (United Kingdom v. Iceland) **5** 3

International Tribunal for the Law of the Sea – jurisdiction – United Nations Convention on the Law of the Sea, 1982 – Article 292 of Convention – whether Russian Federation and Australia both State Parties to the Convention – whether jurisdiction established under Article 292 of Convention – International Tribunal for the Law of the Sea
  The 'Volga' Case (Russian Federation v. Australia) **5** 445

International Tribunal for the Law of the Sea – provisional measures – legal effects – provisional measures granted pending arbitration – Arbitral Tribunal subsequently holding that it lacked jurisdiction – discharge of provisional measures – Arbitral Tribunal
  Southern Bluefin Tuna Case (Australia and New Zealand v. Japan) (Award) **5** 495

International Tribunal for the Law of the Sea – provisional measures – United Nations Convention on the Law of the Sea, 1982, Article 290 – requirements for order of provisional measures – jurisdiction – Article 288 of Convention – Article 283 of Convention – obligation to exchange views regarding settlement of dispute by negotiation or other peaceful means – whether precondition of exhaustion of diplomatic negotiations before referring dispute to Tribunal – International Tribunal for the Law of the Sea
  Case Concerning Land Reclamation by Singapore in and around the Straits of Johor (Malaysia v. Singapore) **5** 466

International Tribunal for the Law of the Sea – provisional measures of protection – binding character – purpose – jurisdiction – Law of the Sea Convention,

Relationship between international law and national law

OSPAR Convention – Article 9(1) of Convention – obligation on Contracting Parties to ensure disclosure of information – international obligation – meaning of obligation – obligation of result rather than provision of access to domestic regime obtaining result – no exclusion of responsibility for inadequacy of national system or failure of competent authorities to act as prescribed by international obligation – Arbitral Tribunal

Dispute Concerning Access to Information under Article 9 of the OSPAR Convention (Ireland v. United Kingdom) **5** 552

Responsibility and liability

In general – atmospheric nuclear tests leading to deposit of radioactive fallout on territory of other States and on high seas – whether tests lawful – whether absolute responsibility for damage caused – International Court of Justice

Nuclear Tests Case (New Zealand v. France) **5** 88

Phosphate mining on Nauru – responsibility for rehabilitation of worked-out lands – administration of Nauru by Australia on behalf of itself, New Zealand and the United Kingdom – whether three States responsible for full extent of rehabilitation of worked-out lands – International Court of Justice

Case Concerning Certain Phosphate Lands in Nauru (Nauru v. Australia) **5** 124

State of necessity as a ground for precluding wrongfulness – Article 33 of the Draft Articles on State Responsibility – essential interest – circumstances constituting an essential interest – whether safeguarding the ecological balance an essential interest of all States – grave and imminent peril – act having to constitute the only means of safeguarding the interest threatened – party having contributed to the occurrence of the state of necessity – International Court of Justice

Case Concerning the Gabčíkovo–Nagymaros Project (Hungary/Slovakia) **5** 272

State responsibility – losses occasioned by invasion of another State – Iraqi invasion of Kuwait – Iraqi responsibility for losses resulting directly from invasion and occupation – proof of causation – damage to oil wells – allegation by Iraq that damage caused by Coalition armed forces – whether relieving Iraq of responsibility – application of general principles of State responsibility by United Nations Compensation Commission

Report and Recommendations Made by the Panel of Commissioners Appointed to Review the Well Blowout Control Claim **5** 607

Rights and interests

OSPAR Convention – right to information – Article 9(2) of Convention – scope of Article 9(2) – information sought not within scope – Arbitral Tribunal

> *Dispute Concerning Access to Information under Article 9 of the OSPAR Convention (Ireland v. United Kingdom)* **5** 552

Right to natural resources within territorial sea – estuary – semi-enclosed sea – right to integrity of marine environment – right to be consulted with respect to major land reclamation works – possible impact on maritime transit rights – International Tribunal for the Law of the Sea

> *Case Concerning Land Reclamation by Singapore in and around the Straits of Johor (Malaysia v. Singapore)* **5** 466

Sources of international law

Custom – conditions for existence of rule of custom – the law of the sea – 12-mile fishing limit – concept of preferential rights for coastal States outside 12-mile limit – underlying purpose of conservation – evolution into rules of customary international law since 1960 – difference between preferential rights and exclusive rights – Iceland failed to have reasonable regard for interests of other States – International Court of Justice

> *Fisheries Jurisdiction Case (United Kingdom v. Iceland)* **5** 3

Custom – requirements of custom – importance of actual State practice – persistent objector principle – *opinio juris* – United Nations General Assembly resolutions – normative significance – resolutions on the use of nuclear weapons – International Court of Justice

> *Legality of the Threat or Use of Nuclear Weapons* **5** 238

OSPAR Convention – general international law – sources applicable to extent *lex specialis* created by Parties – unilateral declarations – whether create binding obligations – Sintra Ministerial Statement of 1998 – not relevant to access to information – Rio Declaration, Principle 10 – Aarhus Convention on Access to Information, Public Participation in Decision-making and Access to Justice in Environmental Matters, 1998 – concept of 'environmental information' – evolving international law – not applicable by Tribunal – Arbitral Tribunal

> *Dispute Concerning Access to Information under Article 9 of the OSPAR Convention (Ireland v. United Kingdom)* **5** 552

Territory

Nature of territorial sovereignty – atmospheric nuclear tests causing deposit of radioactive fallout on territory of other States – whether an infringement of territorial sovereignty – International Court of Justice
  Nuclear Tests Case (New Zealand v. France) **5** 88

Treaties

Effect on third parties – treaty allegedly giving rise to rule of customary international law – Nuclear Test Ban Treaty, 1963 – International Court of Justice
  Nuclear Tests Case (New Zealand v. France) **5** 88

In general – form of international agreements – unilateral declaration – whether capable of amounting to assumption of legal obligation – French declaration that atmospheric nuclear tests would cease – International Court of Justice
  Nuclear Tests Case (New Zealand v. France) **5** 88

Successive treaties – priority – *lex specialis* – *lex posterior* – whether specialised agreement supersedes general agreement – Arbitral Tribunal
  Southern Bluefin Tuna Case (Australia and New Zealand v. Japan) (Award) **5** 495

Treaties for the protection of the environment – whether applicable to military operations in time of armed conflict – International Court of Justice
  Legality of the Threat or Use of Nuclear Weapons **5** 238

Treaty between Hungary and Czechoslovakia, 16 September 1977 – termination – fundamental change of circumstances – progress of environmental knowledge – development of new norms of international environmental law – changes not unforeseen – treaty allowing Parties to take account of and apply new developments – whether radical transformation of Treaty obligations – International Court of Justice
  Case Concerning the Gabčíkovo–Nagymaros Project (Hungary / Slovakia) **5** 272

War and armed conflict

Consequences – responsibility for damage occasioned by armed conflict – liability of aggressor – Iraqi invasion and occupation of Kuwait – responsibility of Iraq for losses resulting directly from invasion and occupation – damage to oil well-heads in Kuwait – whether attributable to sabotage by Iraqi forces –

whether caused by Coalition armed forces' bombing campaign – whether Iraq responsible if damage caused by military operations of Coalition – United Nations Compensation Commission

Iraq's invasion and occupation of Kuwait, 1991 – environmental damage caused by setting light to oil wells and spilling oil into Persian Gulf – impact on environment of influx of refugees and involuntary migration caused by war – United Nations Compensation Commission

Nuclear weapons – whether use of nuclear weapons prohibited in international humanitarian law – protection of health and the environment in war and armed conflict – International Court of Justice

Nuclear weapons – whether use or threat of use of nuclear weapons lawful – applicable law – relevance of law on the environment and human rights – International Court of Justice

Waters

Depletion of water resources – damage to groundwater – damage to marine and coastal environment – whether claims for reasonable monitoring and assessment activities compensable – United Nations Compensation Commission

Irish Sea – protection of the marine environment – United Nations Convention on the Law of the Sea, 1982 – environmental effects of the MOX plant and of international movements of radioactive materials – Arbitral Tribunal

Irish Sea – protection of the marine environment – United Nations Convention on the Law of the Sea, 1982 – environmental effects of the MOX plant and of international movements of radioactive materials – obligation to cooperate in taking measures to protect and preserve the Irish Sea – precautionary principle – International Tribunal for the Law of the Sea

Table of treaties

This table lists, in chronological order according to the date of signature, the treaties and other international agreements referred to in the decisions reported in this volume. It has not been possible to draw a distinction between treaties judicially considered and treaties that are merely cited.

I

DECISIONS OF THE INTERNATIONAL COURT OF JUSTICE

Fisheries Jurisdiction Case
(United Kingdom v. Iceland)[1]

International Court of Justice, The Hague

17 August 1972 (Sir Muhammad Zafrulla Khan, *President*; Ammoun, *Vice-President*; Sir Gerald Fitzmaurice, Padilla Nervo, Forster, Gros, Bengzon, Petrén, Lachs, Onyeama, Dillard, Ignacio-Pinto, de Castro, Morozov and Jiménez de Aréchaga, *Judges*)

2 February 1973 (Sir Muhammad Zafrulla Khan, *President*; Ammoun, *Vice-President*; Sir Gerald Fitzmaurice, Padilla Nervo, Forster, Gros, Bengzon, Petrén, Lachs, Onyeama, Dillard, Ignacio-Pinto, de Castro, Morozov and Jiménez de Aréchaga, *Judges*)

12 July 1973 (Lachs, *President*; Ammoun, *Vice-President*; Forster, Gros, Bengzon, Petrén, Onyeama, Ignacio-Pinto, de Castro, Morozov, Jiménez de Aréchaga, Sir Humphrey Waldock, Nagendra Singh and Ruda, *Judges*)

25 July 1974 (Lachs, *President*; Forster, Gros, Bengzon, Petrén, Onyeama, Dillard, Ignacio-Pinto, de Castro, Morozov, Jiménez de Aréchaga, Sir Humphrey Waldock, Nagendra Singh and Ruda, *Judges*)

Jurisdiction – territorial jurisdiction over fisheries – whether limited to 12 miles – whether extension to 50 miles permissible – Icelandic claim – whether opposable to United Kingdom – adjacent waters – rights of the coastal State – exceptional dependence upon fisheries – conservation of fish stocks – preferential rights of coastal State – historic rights of other States – duty of States to

---

[1] Comparable proceedings were also commenced against Iceland by the Federal Republic of Germany and appear at p. 71 below. The full Judgment of the International Court of Justice on the merits in those proceedings appears in *ICJ Reports 1974* at p. 175; also 56 *ILR* 146. On 17 January 1974, the Court decided that, despite the similarity of the issues in the two cases, it would not join them.

The United Kingdom was represented by the Rt Hon. Sir Peter Rawlinson QC, MP, Dr D. W. Bowett, Professor D. H. N. Johnson, Mr J. L. Simpson CMG TD, Mr G. Glynn and Mr P. Langdon-Davies.

negotiate equitable balance between rights – Anglo-Icelandic Exchange of Notes 1961

Powers and procedures of tribunals – International Court of Justice – interim measures of protection – declaration that Icelandic Government not enforce new exclusive fishing zone against United Kingdom vessels by action inside disputed area or by measures in Icelandic waters against vessels fishing in the disputed area – limits on metric tons of fish permitted to be taken by British vessels in disputed area – whether measures sought were for protection of economic interests of private enterprises – interim measures granted

Sources of international law – custom – conditions for existence of rule of custom – the law of the sea – 12-mile fishing limit – concept of preferential rights for coastal States outside 12-mile limit – underlying purpose of conservation – evolution into rules of customary international law since 1960 – difference between preferential rights and exclusive rights – Iceland failed to have reasonable regard for interests of other States

SUMMARY   *The facts*   In 1958, Iceland proclaimed a 12-mile exclusive fishing zone. This proclamation was part of a wider policy reflected in a resolution of the Icelandic Parliament (the *Althing*), adopted on 5 May 1959. This stated:

...the Althing declares that it considers that Iceland has an indisputable right to fishery limits of 12 miles, that recognition should be obtained of Iceland's right to the entire continental shelf area in conformity with the policy adopted by the Law of 1948, concerning the Scientific Conservation of the Continental Shelf Fisheries, and that fishery limits of less than 12 miles from base-lines around the country are out of the question.

These measures resulted in a dispute with the United Kingdom, whose vessels had traditionally fished in the area. The dispute was ended by the conclusion of an Exchange of Notes of 11 March 1961[2] between the two governments. The United Kingdom recognised, subject to certain transitional arrangements, Iceland's exclusive fisheries jurisdiction within the 12-mile limit. With regard to the more extensive Icelandic claims, the 1961 Exchange of Notes provided that:

The Icelandic Government will continue to work for the implementation of the *Althing* Resolution of 5 May 1959, regarding the extension of fisheries jurisdiction around Iceland, but shall give to the United Kingdom Government six months' notice of such extension, and, in case of a dispute in relation to such extension, the matter shall, at the request of either party, be referred to the International Court of Justice.

---

[2] UKTS No. 17 (1961), Cmnd 1328.

In 1971, Iceland notified the United Kingdom that it intended to extend its exclusive fishing zone 'to include the areas of sea covering the continental shelf'. It declared also that it regarded the 1961 Exchange of Notes as having achieved its purpose and thus as having ceased to be effective. The United Kingdom replied that such an extension would have no basis in international law and reserved its rights under the 1961 Exchange of Notes.

Following the failure of negotiations, the United Kingdom applied on 14 April 1972 to the International Court of Justice for declarations that:

(1)   there was no foundation in international law for Iceland's extension of her fisheries jurisdiction; and

(2)   international law did not permit Iceland to determine the question of conservation of fish stocks by unilateral action of this nature.

Iceland did not appear and did not appoint an agent, but in a number of communications to the Court contended, *inter alia,* that the 1961 Exchange of Notes was no longer in force and, hence, that the Court did not have jurisdiction. On 14 July 1972, Iceland issued new fishery regulations establishing fishing limits of 50 miles and prohibiting fishing by foreign vessels within those limits.

Decision on Request for Interim Measures of Protection, 17 August 1972
On 19 July 1972, the United Kingdom asked the Court to indicate interim measures of protection. The measures requested were that the Icelandic Government should not seek to enforce the new limits against United Kingdom vessels either by action inside the disputed area or by taking measures within Icelandic waters against vessels which had been fishing in the disputed area. British vessels were to be allowed to take not more than 185,000 metric tons of fish in any one year from the disputed area and both parties were to avoid measures which might aggravate the dispute or prejudice the other party's rights. The Icelandic Government did not appear, but in a telegram of 28 July 1972 repeated its argument that the Court lacked jurisdiction and objected to the indication of interim measures on that ground. It objected also on the ground that the interim measures sought were for the protection of the economic interests of various private enterprises and so lacked the necessary connection with the United Kingdom's Application (which concerned a dispute between States).

Held by the International Court of Justice (by fourteen votes to one)   (1)   The United Kingdom's Application for a declaration that Iceland's extension of fishing limits was invalid was, in substance, a request for a declaration that this extension could not be opposed to United Kingdom vessels. It therefore had a sufficient connection with the interim measures sought. The Applicant's contention that its vessels were entitled to continue fishing within the zone of 50 nautical miles was part of the subject matter of the dispute. The request for provisional measures designed to protect such rights was therefore directly connected with the Application.

(2)   On a request for interim measures it was not necessary for the Court finally to satisfy itself that it had jurisdiction. However, it should not indicate interim measures if the absence of jurisdiction was manifest. In the present case, the compromissory clause in the 1961 Exchange of Notes, *prima facie,* gave jurisdiction. The Icelandic contention that the compromissory clause had been terminated would fall to be decided at a later stage.

(3)   For the purposes of interim measures the calculation of the average catch by UK vessels ought to be based on the available statistical data before the Court for the preceding five years.

(4)   The immediate implementation of Iceland's new fishery regulations would prejudice the rights claimed by the United Kingdom and would affect the possibility of their full restoration in the event of a judgment in its favour. It was also necessary to bear in mind the exceptional dependence of the Icelandic nation upon coastal fisheries for its livelihood and economic development and from that point of view, the need for the conservation of fish stocks in the Iceland area. Accordingly, the Court indicated interim measures substantially similar to those sought by the United Kingdom, with the qualification that the annual catch by United Kingdom vessels in the disputed area should be limited to 170,000 metric tons and not 185,000 tons as requested.

Vice-President Ammoun and Judges Forster and Jiménez de Aréchaga appended a brief declaration in support of the decision to the effect that interim measures should only be indicated by the Court where there was a likelihood of irremediable damage to the rights claimed and over which the Court would adjudicate in subsequent proceedings.

Dissenting Opinion of Judge Padilla Nervo   The arguments developed in the request for interim measures appeared to have as their real object the protection of economic interests of private fishing enterprises rather than the 'rights' of the United Kingdom. The existence of those rights could not, in any event, be taken for granted at the preliminary stage of proceedings. Moreover, the claim of immediate and irreparable damage to the Applicant had not been proved but was based on the unfounded assumption that the dispute would not be settled by the Court for many years. Allegations that fishing enterprises would suffer financial losses and that eating habits would be disturbed could not be opposed to the sovereign rights of Iceland over its exclusive jurisdiction and the protection of the living resources of the sea covering its continental shelf. The Court should not indicate interim measures of protection without making at least a provisional determination that it had jurisdiction to hear the case on the merits. Moreover, it was not at all clear that Iceland had acted contrary to international law and its extension of its fishery limits was the exercise of a right impliedly recognised by the United Kingdom in the 1961 Exchange of Notes. By indicating interim measures which gave the United Kingdom almost everything for which it had asked, the Court had failed to maintain a proper balance between the parties.

On 18 August 1972, the Court decided, by nine votes to six, that the first pleadings should be devoted solely to the question of jurisdiction. It then fixed the time-limits for the written pleadings.[3]

Judgment on Jurisdiction, 2 February 1973
The United Kingdom claimed that the Court had jurisdiction by virtue of the compromissory clause in the 1961 Exchange of Notes. In its letter and telegrams to the Court, Iceland denied this claim on the grounds that:
(1)　the clause did not apply to this particular dispute;
(2)　the 1961 Exchange of Notes had been concluded after British warships had used force to protect trawlers;
(3)　the Exchange of Notes was not a permanent agreement and Iceland had exercised her right to terminate it;
(4)　since Iceland was now entitled to a 12-mile fisheries limit as of right, the United Kingdom was no longer providing consideration for Iceland's promises;
(5)　changes in the law of the sea and in fishing techniques constituted a fundamental change of circumstances which rendered the 1961 Exchange of Notes inoperative.

Held by the International Court of Justice (by fourteen votes to one)　　　The Court had jurisdiction under the 1961 Exchange of Notes which remained a valid and effective treaty.

---

[3]　The Order fixing time-limits is not reproduced in this volume but can be found at *ICJ Reports 1972*, p. 181.

(1)   *Prima facie* this was exactly the type of dispute envisaged by the compromissory clause, so that there was no need to examine the *travaux préparatoires* of the 1961 Exchange of Notes. Nevertheless, a brief examination of them, undertaken because of the peculiar features of the case, made it clear that the clause was intended to cover the present dispute.

(2)   Iceland's vague allegation that it had entered into the 1961 Exchange of Notes because of force used by the United Kingdom was rejected. However, had the Exchange of Notes been concluded under duress, it was clear from the United Nations Charter and Article 52 of the Vienna Convention on the Law of Treaties that the agreement would have been void.

(3)   The Exchange of Notes was not a permanent agreement but it would only come to an end when Iceland had implemented the *Althing* Resolution or abandoned the intention of doing so. While Iceland's intention to implement the Resolution remained, so did the United Kingdom's right to refer the matter to the Court.

(4)   The fact that Iceland was now entitled by law to claim a 12-mile limit, so that it was gaining nothing from the United Kingdom's promise to respect such a limit, did not render the 1961 Exchange of Notes inoperative. The purpose of the Exchange of Notes was far wider than the mere recognition of the 12-mile limit. Moreover, Iceland, having had the benefit of the United Kingdom's promises in the past, could not now fail to perform its side of the bargain.

(5)   Alterations in fishing techniques could be an important consideration on the merits but were not a change of circumstances so fundamental as to affect the obligation to submit disputes to the Court.

President Sir Muhammad Zafrulla Khan appended a brief declaration in support of the decision agreeing that any consideration of the validity or otherwise of Iceland's action was irrelevant at this stage of the proceedings.

Separate Opinion of Judge Sir Gerald Fitzmaurice   The question of fishery conservation had no relevance to the jurisdictional issue before the Court which involved its competence to adjudicate upon a dispute occasioned by Iceland's claim unilaterally to assert exclusive jurisdiction for fishery purposes up to a distance of 50 nautical miles from and around her coasts.

Dissenting Opinion of Judge Padilla Nervo   The Judge repeated the comments which he had made at the Interim Measures stage, adding that Iceland's action was legitimate and that in this case questions of jurisdiction and merits were intertwined. The Exchange of Notes was no longer in force since there had been a fundamental change of circumstances.

Continuance of Interim Measures of Protection, 12 July 1973
The United Kingdom Government applied to the Court to continue the order for interim measures, which was due to be reviewed by 15 August 1973.

Held by the International Court of Justice (by eleven votes to three)   The indication of interim measures of protection did not preclude the parties from negotiating interim arrangements but, in the absence of a negotiated arrangement, the interim measures indicated by the Court must continue. The interim measures indicated on 17 August 1972 would therefore remain operative until the Court gave judgment on the merits.

Declaration of Judge Ignacio-Pinto   Circumstances had changed since the interim measures had first been indicated and the serious clashes between British and Icelandic vessels meant that different interim measures should have been indicated.

Dissenting Opinion of Judge Gros   The Court's decision should have been preceded by an examination of all the prevailing circumstances with the help of the Applicant so as to verify any argument and allow the opportunity to decide whether a new time limit ought to be fixed for the merits proceedings. Paragraphs 7 and 8 of Article 61 of the 1946 Rules of Court, concerning the modification of existing provisional measures, should have been differently applied.

Dissenting Opinion of Judge Petrén   In the light of negotiations between the Parties leading up to and during the dispute and of the interim measures, it was evident that the dispute between the Parties included disagreements as to the extent and scope of their respective rights in the fishery resources and the adequacy of measures to conserve them. Such disagreements were an element of the 'dispute in relation to the extension of fisheries jurisdiction around Iceland'.

Judgment on the Merits, 25 July 1974
On 13 November 1973, the parties concluded an interim agreement (the 1973 Exchange of Notes)[4] which provided that British vessels would be entitled, for a period of two years, to catch not more than 130,000 metric tons of fish a year in the disputed area. The agreement was expressed to be without prejudice to the legal rights of either party on its termination.

---

[4] UKTS No. 122 (1973), Cmnd 5484.

The United Kingdom therefore proceeded with its application for judgment on the merits, asking the Court to declare in its favour on four points:

(1) that Iceland's claim to a 50-mile fishing limit was without foundation in international law;

(2) that, as against the United Kingdom, Iceland was not entitled unilaterally to assert an exclusive fisheries jurisdiction beyond the limits agreed to in the 1961 Exchange of Notes;

(3) that Iceland could not therefore exclude United Kingdom fishing vessels from the disputed area;

(4) that the parties were under a duty to examine together the need for restrictions on fishing on conservation grounds and, if such a need was proved, to negotiate a regime which recognised both the preferential rights of Iceland, as a coastal State dependent on fishing, and the rights of the United Kingdom and other interested States.

Held by the International Court of Justice (by ten votes to four)   (1)   *Procedure in Iceland's absence*   The Court was entitled to give judgment under Article 53 of the Statute but must first satisfy itself that the British claim was well founded in fact and law and to that end it must ascertain all the relevant rules of international law.

(2)   *The effect of the interim agreement*   The 1973 Exchange of Notes was stated to be without prejudice to the rights of the parties and did not affect the existence of the dispute. The Court was competent to pronounce upon the present legal position of the parties, although that legal position would be subject to the interim agreement so long as that remained in force. However, the Court could not anticipate what the legal position would be when the 1973 Exchange of Notes expired.

(3)   *Competence of the Court*   The Court was competent to pronounce upon issues of conservation of fisheries resources and of preferential fishing rights as raised in the United Kingdom's fourth claim. The Court had already considered such matters in its order indicating interim measures of protection.

(4)   *The rules of international law*   Since 1960 two concepts had evolved into rules of customary international law – the 12-mile fishing limit and the concept of preferential rights for the coastal State in adjacent waters outside those limits. Preferential rights came into being where the need for conservation necessitated some form of catch limitation and the coastal State was exceptionally dependent upon fisheries. Both requirements seemed to be satisfied in this case. However, the Icelandic regulations of 1972 claimed not preferential but exclusive rights in

the disputed area, thus disregarding the historic interests of the United Kingdom and the dependence of part of its economy upon fishing in the disputed area. These interests gave rise to legal rights just as much as did Iceland's interests. Consequently, the Court held that the Icelandic regulations were:

(a) a breach of the general principle, enshrined in Article 2 of the 1958 Geneva Convention on the High Seas, that all States in exercising their right of fishing must have reasonable regard for the interests of other States; and

(b) a violation of the United Kingdom's rights under the 1961 Exchange of Notes.

The Court therefore held that the regulations were not opposable to the United Kingdom and that Iceland was not entitled to exclude United Kingdom vessels from the disputed area (points (2) and (3) of the United Kingdom submissions). The Court did not, however, make a decision on point (1) of the United Kingdom submissions.

The Court then held that it was necessary to achieve an equitable balance between the preferential rights of Iceland (the coastal State) and those of the United Kingdom and other interested States. Accordingly, the Court found in favour of the United Kingdom on point (4), holding that the parties were under a duty to negotiate an equitable solution "derived from the existing law". In seeking to do so, they were to take into account: (a) Iceland's preferential rights; (b) the special interests of the United Kingdom; (c) the interests of other States in conservation and equitable exploitation of the resources; (d) the need to give effect to the above rights and interests to the extent compatible with conservation and equitable exploitation of fish stocks; and (e) the obligation to keep the state of these resources under review.

Though the Court was aware of proposals made at the United Nations Conference on the Law of the Sea for progressive development of the law and the claims made by certain States, it had to decide the case on the basis of the present law and could not anticipate future developments.

President Lachs appended a short declaration in support of the reasoning and conclusions of the Court.

Declaration of Judge Ignacio-Pinto The Court should have given a decision on the first United Kingdom submission – that Iceland's actions were without foundation in international law – a submission which was well founded. By concentrating on questions of preferential rights and seeking to prescribe the guiding principles for negotiations between the parties, it had avoided the chief issue.

Declaration of Judge Nagendra Singh   It had not been necessary for the Court to consider the first United Kingdom submission as the United Kingdom had made clear that its other submissions were not dependent upon it. The recognition in the judgment of preferential rights, the need for conservation and the duty to have regard to the rights of other States was a positive contribution to the development of the law. The Court should, as it had done here, encourage negotiation between parties to a dispute and not regard it as inconsistent with its judicial function.

Joint Separate Opinion of Judges Forster, Bengzon, Jiménez de Aréchaga, Nagendra Singh and Ruda   The five Judges had supported the Judgment because it decided only that the Icelandic fishery limits were not opposable to the United Kingdom and had not decided whether the fishery limits were without foundation in international law. There was no general rule of customary international law that fishery limits might not exceed 12 miles. There was insufficient State practice to support such a rule.

Separate Opinion of Judge Dillard   Although there was at least persuasive evidence of a rule of customary international law that fishery limits might not exceed 12 miles, the Court was justified in not pronouncing upon this difficult issue, since the decision that Iceland's limits were not opposable to the United Kingdom was sufficient to decide the case. The Court was also justified in deciding on the questions of equity and preferential rights raised in the fourth United Kingdom submission, since disputes on such matters were within the scope of the 1961 Exchange of Notes. Moreover, the decision that the parties were under a duty to negotiate was correct; there was strong evidence of a rule of customary international law imposing such a duty.

Separate Opinion of Judge de Castro   There was no rule of customary international law restricting fishing limits to 12 miles. However, that did not mean that international law left the extent of fisheries jurisdiction to be determined solely by municipal law. All States were free to fish in the high seas but that freedom was now subject to the preferential rights of the coastal State and historic rights of other States. In dealing with this network of rights and interests, international law imposed a duty to arrive at an equitable arrangement, rather than prescribing a rigid rule of law.

Separate Opinion of Judge Sir Humphrey Waldock   (i) The Judgment of the Court, while arriving at the correct conclusion, did not place sufficient emphasis upon the 1961 Exchange of Notes. That agreement governed the dispute since it was clear from the terms of the agreement that Iceland had undertaken not to extend its fishing limits beyond 12 miles as against the

United Kingdom, except in accordance with the compromissory clause of the 1961 Exchange of Notes. By refusing to appear before the Court, Iceland had manifestly failed to comply with the compromissory clause and, for that reason, its extended fishing limits were not opposable to the United Kingdom. (ii) It was not necessary to consider the United Kingdom's first submission – that the extended limits were invalid *erga omnes*. In any event, that was not the real issue in this area of the law, for the absence of clearly established general rules meant that the real issue was whether such limits could be opposed to any given State. The United Kingdom had always protested at Iceland's extended limits, with the result that the limits could not be opposed to it. (iii) The question of preferential rights formed an integral part of this dispute and the Court was competent to pronounce upon it.

Dissenting Opinion of Judge Gros　　(i) The purpose of the compromissory clause in the 1961 Exchange of Notes was to refer to the Court any dispute concerning a future extension of Iceland's fishing limits so that the Court could decide whether that extension was permitted by international law. The Court had erred by failing to decide on that central question. The extended limits were contrary to international law and were not opposable to any State. (ii) The Court was also wrong to hold that the parties were under a duty to negotiate an equitable settlement. Questions of preferential rights and conservation were not within the compromissory clause of the 1961 Exchange of Notes and the Court therefore had no jurisdiction to decide upon them. (iii) The decision on the duty to negotiate was also illusory, since the 1973 Exchange of Notes had effectively suspended any duty to negotiate.

Dissenting Opinion of Judge Petrén　　The Court had failed to answer the most important question and, by deciding that the parties were under a duty to achieve an equitable settlement by negotiation, had exceeded its jurisdiction. Moreover, since the Judgment could not take effect until the expiry of the interim agreement contained in the 1973 Exchange of Notes, the Court was being asked to decide what the law between the parties would have been had the interim agreement not been concluded. That was inconsistent with the judicial function and the submissions of the United Kingdom should therefore have been rejected as being pointless, except in respect of the period between the imposition of Iceland's new regulations and the entry into force of the 1973 Exchange of Notes. As Iceland's new regulations and extended limits were without foundation in international law, her action during this period had been unlawful.

Dissenting Opinion of Judge Onyeama　　The Court should have decided that Iceland's extended fishing limits were without foundation in international law. The Court exceeded its jurisdiction by considering the question of preferential rights.

Order of International Court of Justice on Request for the Indication of Interim Measures of Protection, 17 August 1972 (extract)

[13][. . .] 1. Having regard to the request dated 19 July 1972 and filed in the Registry the same day, whereby the Government of the United Kingdom, relying on Article 41 of the Statute and Article 61 of the Rules of Court, asks to the Court to indicate,

---

[5] Vice-President Ammoun and Judges Forster and Jiménez de Aréchaga issued a joint declaration which is not reproduced in this volume but can be found at *ICJ Reports 1972*, p. 18.

[6] President Sir Muhammad Zafrulla Khan made a declaration which is not reproduced in this volume but can be found at *ICJ Reports 1973*, p. 22.

[7] Judge Ignacio-Pinto made a declaration which is not reproduced in this volume but can be found at *ICJ Reports 1973*, p. 304. Judge Gros appended a dissenting opinion which is not reproduced here but can be found at *ICJ Reports 1973*, p. 306.

[8] The individual declarations of President Lachs and Judge Ignacio-Pinto are not reproduced in this volume but can be found at *ICJ Reports 1974*, p. 35. The joint separate opinion of Judges Forster, Bengzon, Jiménez de Aréchaga, Nagendra Singh and Ruda is not reproduced here but can be found at *ICJ Reports 1974*, p. 45.

pending the final decision in the case brought before it by the Application of 14 April 1972, the following interim measures of protection:

(a) The Government of Iceland should not seek to enforce the regulations referred to in paragraph 4 [of the request] against, or otherwise interfere or threaten to interfere with, vessels registered in the United Kingdom fishing outside the 12-mile limit agreed on by the parties in the Exchange of Notes between the Government of the United Kingdom and the Government of Iceland dated 11 March 1961 (as set out in Annex A to the said Application);

(b) the Government of Iceland should not take or threaten to take in their territory (including their ports and territorial waters) or inside the said 12-mile limit or elsewhere measures of any kind against any vessels registered in the United Kingdom, or against persons connected with such vessels, being measures which have as their purpose or effect the impairment of the freedom of such vessels to fish outside the said 12-mile limit;

(c) in conformity with sub-paragraph (a) above, vessels registered in the United Kingdom should be free, save in so far as may be provided for by arrangements between the Government of the United Kingdom and the Government of Iceland such as are referred to in paragraph 21 (b) of the said Application, to fish as heretofore in all parts of the high seas outside the said 12-mile limit, but the Government of the United Kingdom should ensure that such vessels do not take more than 185,000 metric tons of fish in any one year from the sea area of Iceland, that is to say, the area defined by the International Council for the Exploration of the Sea as area Va and so marked on the map attached [to the request] at Annex B2;

(d) the Government of the United Kingdom and the Government of Iceland should each seek to avoid circumstances arising which are inconsistent with the foregoing measures and which [14] are capable of aggravating or extending the dispute submitted to the Court; and

(e) in conformity with the foregoing measures, the Government of the United Kingdom and the Government of Iceland should each ensure that no action is taken which might prejudice the rights of the other party in respect of the carrying out of whatever decision on the merits the Court may subsequently render;

[. . .]

[15] [. . .] 15. Whereas on a request for provisional measures the Court need not, before indicating them, finally satisfy itself that it has jurisdiction on the merits of the case, yet it ought not to act under Article 41 of the Statute if the absence of jurisdiction on the merits is manifest;

[16] 16. Whereas the penultimate paragraph of the Exchange of Notes between the Governments of Iceland and of the United Kingdom dated 11 March 1961 reads as follows:

> The Icelandic Government will continue to work for the implementation of the Althing Resolution of May 5, 1959, regarding the extension of fisheries jurisdiction around Iceland, but shall give to the United Kingdom Government six months' notice of such extension and, in case of a dispute in relation to such extension, the matter shall, at the request of either party, be referred to the International Court of Justice;

17. Whereas the above-cited provision in an instrument emanating from both Parties to the dispute appears, prima facie, to afford a possible basis on which the jurisdiction of the Court might be founded;

18. Whereas the complaint outlined in the United Kingdom Application is that the Government of Iceland has announced its intention, as from 1 September 1972, to extend unilaterally its exclusive jurisdiction in respect of the fisheries around Iceland to a distance of 50 nautical miles from the baselines mentioned in the 1961 Exchange of Notes; and whereas on 14 July 1972 the Government of Iceland issued Regulations to that effect;

19. Whereas the contention of the Government of Iceland, in its letter of 29 May 1972, that the above-quoted clause contained in the Exchange of Notes of 11 March 1961 has been terminated, will fall to be examined by the Court in due course;

20. Whereas the decision given in the course of the present proceedings in no way prejudges the question of the jurisdiction of the Court to deal with the merits of the case or any questions relating to the merits themselves and leaves unaffected the right of the Respondent to submit arguments against such jurisdiction or in respect of such merits;

21. Whereas the right of the Court to indicate provisional measures as provided for in Article 41 of the Statute has as its object to preserve the respective rights of the Parties pending the decision of the Court, and presupposes that irreparable prejudice should not be caused to rights which are the subject of dispute in judicial proceedings and that the Court's judgment should not be anticipated by reason of any initiative regarding the measures which are in issue;

22. Whereas the immediate implementation by Iceland of its Regulations would, by anticipating the Court's judgment, prejudice the rights claimed by the United Kingdom and affect the possibility of their full restoration in the event of a judgment in its favour;

23. Whereas it is also necessary to bear in mind the exceptional dependence of the Icelandic nation upon coastal fisheries for its livelihood and economic development as expressly recognized by the United Kingdom in its Note addressed to the Foreign Minister of Iceland dated 11 March 1961;

[17] 24. Whereas from this point of view account must be taken of the need for the conservation of fish stocks in the Iceland area;

25. Whereas the total catch by United Kingdom vessels in that area in the year 1970 was 164,000 metric tons and in the year 1971 was 207,000 metric tons; and whereas the figure of 185,000 metric tons mentioned in the United Kingdom request for interim measures was based on the average annual catch for the period 1960–1969;

26. Whereas in the Court's opinion the average of the catch should, for purposes of interim measures, and so as to reflect the present situation concerning fisheries of different species in the Iceland area, be based on the available statistical information before the Court for the five years 1967–1971, which produces an approximate figure of 170,000 metric tons,

Accordingly,

THE COURT,

by fourteen votes to one,

(1) Indicates, pending its final decision in the proceedings instituted on 14 April 1972 by the Government of the United Kingdom against the Government of Iceland, the following provisional measures:

(a) the United Kingdom and the Republic of Iceland should each of them ensure that no action of any kind is taken which might aggravate or extend the dispute submitted to the Court;

(b) the United Kingdom and the Republic of Iceland should each of them ensure that no action is taken which might prejudice the rights of the other Party in respect of the carrying out of whatever decision on the merits the Court may render;

(c) the Republic of Iceland should refrain from taking any measures to enforce the Regulations of 14 July 1972 against vessels registered in the United Kingdom and engaged in fishing activities in the waters around Iceland outside the 12-mile fishery zone;

(d) the Republic of Iceland should refrain from applying administrative, judicial or other measures against ships registered in the United Kingdom, their crews or other related persons, because of their having engaged in fishing activities in the waters around Iceland outside the 12-mile fishery zone;

(e) the United Kingdom should ensure that vessels registered in the United Kingdom do not take an annual catch of more than 170,000 metric tons of fish from the 'Sea Area of Iceland' as defined by the International Council for the Exploration of the Sea as area Va;

[18] (f) the United Kingdom Government should furnish the Government of Iceland and the Registry of the Court with all relevant information, orders issued and arrangements made concerning the control and regulation of fish catches in the area.

(2) Unless the Court has meanwhile delivered its final judgment in the case, it shall, at an appropriate time before 15 August 1973, review the matter at the request of either Party in order to decide whether the foregoing measures shall continue or need to be modified or revoked.

[. . .]

[20] DISSENTING OPINION OF JUDGE PADILLA NERVO (EXTRACT)

I am unable to concur in the Order of the Court and therefore I voted against its adoption.

In my view, the Court should not have indicated measures of protection. Notwithstanding contrary opinion, the special features of this case do not justify such measures against a State which denies the jurisdiction of the Court, which is not a party to these proceedings and whose rights as a sovereign State are thereby interfered with.

The claim of the Republic of Iceland to extend its fisheries jurisdiction to a zone of 50 nautical miles around Iceland, has not been proved to be contrary to international law.

The question regarding the jurisdiction of the Court has not been fully explored. It relies mainly as a source of its jurisdiction on the Exchange of Notes of 11 March 1961, an agreement which the Republic of Iceland contends has fully achieved its purpose and object, and the provisions of which it considers no longer to be applicable and, consequently, terminated.

The Minister for Foreign Affairs of Iceland sent to the Registrar on 29 May 1972 a letter regarding the filing on 14 April 1972 of an Application by the Government of the United Kingdom, instituting proceedings against Iceland.

With that letter were sent several documents dealing with the background and termination of the Agreement of 11 March 1961, and 'with the changed circumstances resulting from the ever-increasing exploitation of the fishery resources in the seas surrounding Iceland'.

The letter refers to the dispute with the United Kingdom who opposed the 12-mile fishery limit established by the Icelandic Government in 1958, and to the 1961 Exchange of Notes.

Iceland states that 'the 1961 Exchange of Notes took place under extremely difficult circumstances, when the British Royal Navy had been using force to oppose the 12-mile fishery limit'.

In paragraph 4 of the United Kingdom Application instituting proceedings, it is said:

> The validity of this action was not accepted by the United Kingdom and fishing vessels from the United Kingdom continued to fish inside the 12-mile limit. There then ensued a number of incidents involving, on the one hand, Icelandic coastguard vessels and, on the [21] other hand, British fishing vessels and fisheries protection vessels of the Royal Navy.

It appears from the above-quoted statements, that such circumstances were not the most appropriate to negotiate and conclude the 1961 Agreement.

The Foreign Minister of Iceland further indicates:

> The Agreement by which that dispute was settled, and consequently the possibility of such recourse to the Court (to which the Government of Iceland was consistently opposed as far as concerns disputes over the extent of its exclusive fisheries jurisdiction, as indeed the United Kingdom recognizes) was not of a permanent nature. In particular, an undertaking for judicial settlement cannot be considered to be of a permanent nature. There is nothing in that situation, or in any general rule of contemporary international law, to justify any other view . . .

... After the termination of the agreement recorded in the Exchange of Notes of 1961, there was on 14 April 1972 no basis under the Statute for the Court to exercise jurisdiction in the case to which the United Kingdom refers.

The Government of Iceland, considering that the vital interests of the people of Iceland are involved, respectfully informs the Court that it is not willing to confer jurisdiction on the Court in any case involving the extent of the fishery limits of Iceland, and specifically in the case sought to be instituted by the Government of the United Kingdom of Great Britain and Northern Ireland on 14 April 1972.

In the *Anglo-Iranian Oil Co.* case, Judges Winiarski and Badawi Pasha gave the following reasons for their dissenting opinions which – in my view – are applicable and valid in the present case:

> The question of interim measures of protection is linked, for the Court, with the question of jurisdiction; the Court has power to indicate such measures only if it holds, should it be only provisionally, that it is competent to hear the case on its merits. (*ICJ Reports 1951*, p. 96).
>
> In international law it is the consent of the parties which confers jurisdiction on the Court; the Court has jurisdiction only in so far as that jurisdiction has been accepted by the parties. The power given to the Court by Article 41 is not unconditional; it is given for the purposes of the proceedings and is limited to those proceedings. If there is no jurisdiction as to the merits, there can be no jurisdiction to indicate interim measures of protection. Measures of this kind in international law are exceptional in character to an even greater extent than they are in municipal law; they may easily be considered [22] a scarcely tolerable interference in the affairs of a sovereign State. (*Ibid.*, p. 97.)
>
> We find it difficult to accept the view that if *prima facie* the total lack of jurisdiction of the Court is not patent, that is, if there is a possibility, however remote, that the Court may be competent, then it may indicate interim measures of protection. This approach, which also involves an element of judgment, and which does not reserve to any greater extent the right of the Court to give a final decision as to its jurisdiction, appears however to be based on a presumption in favour of the competence of the Court which is not in consonance with the principles of international law. In order to accord with these principles, the position should be reversed: if there exist weighty arguments in favour of the challenged jurisdiction, the Court may indicate interim measures of protection; if there exist serious doubts or weighty arguments against this jurisdiction such measures cannot be indicated. (*Ibid.*, p. 97.)

In my opinion such doubts do exist in the present case.

The Exchange of Notes on which the Application founds the jurisdiction of the Court, dated 11 March 1961, makes reference to the Resolution of the Parliament of Iceland of 5 May 1959, which declared that a recognition of the rights of Iceland to fisheries limits *extending to the whole continental shelf* 'should be sought'.

In the Note of 11 March 1961 it is stated that: 'The Icelandic Government will continue to work for the *implementation* of the Althing Resolution of 5 May 1959, regarding the *extension* of fisheries jurisdiction around Iceland . . .'

The claim of Iceland that its continental shelf must be considered to be a part of the country itself, has support in the Convention on this subject, done at Geneva on 29 April 1958.

This Court, in its Judgment of 20 February 1969, stated:

> ... the most fundamental of all the rules of law relating to the continental shelf, en-shrined in Article 2 of the 1958 Geneva Convention, ... namely that the rights of the coastal State in respect of the area of continental shelf that constitutes a natural prolon-gation of its land territory into and under the sea exist *ipso facto* and *ab initio*, by virtue of its sovereignty over the land, and as an extension of it in an exercise of sovereign rights for the purpose of exploring the seabed and exploiting its natural resources. In short, there is here an inherent right. In order to exercise it, no special legal process has to be gone through, nor have any special legal acts to be performed. Its existence can be declared (and many States have done this) but does not need to be constituted. Furthermore, the right does not depend on its being exercised. To echo the language of the Geneva Convention, it is 'exclusive' in the sense that if the coastal State does not choose to explore or exploit the areas of shelf appertaining to it, that is its [23] own affair, but no one else may do so without its express consent. (*ICJ Reports 1969*, p. 22, para. 19.)

The Government of Iceland in its information and documents sent to the Court, has given well-founded reasons and explanations of its sovereign right to extend its fisheries jurisdiction to the entire continental shelf area.

The coastal fisheries in Iceland have always been the foundation of the country's economy.

The coastal fisheries are the *conditio sine qua non* for the Icelandic economy; without them the country would not have been habitable.

Iceland rests on a platform or continental shelf whose outlines follow those of the country itself. In these shallow underwater terraces, ideal conditions are found for spawning areas and nursery grounds upon whose preservation and utilization the livelihood of the nation depends. It is increasingly being recognized that coastal fisheries are based on the special conditions prevailing in the coastal areas which provide the necessary environment for the fishstocks. This environment is an integral part of the natural resources of the coastal State.

The continental shelf is really the platform of the country and must be considered to be a part of the country itself.

The vital interests of the Icelandic people are therefore at stake. They must be protected.

The priority position of the coastal State has then always been recognized through the system of fishery limits. In the past these limits have to a great extent not been established with any regard to the interests of the coastal State. They owe their origin rather to the preponderant influence of distant water fishery nations, who wished to fish as close as possible to the shores of other nations, frequently destroying one area and then proceeding to another.

In a system of progressive development of international law the question of fishery limits has to be reconsidered in terms of the protection and utilization of coastal resources regardless of other considerations which apply to the extent of the territorial sea. The international community has increasingly recognized that the coastal fishery resources are to be considered as a part of the natural resources of the coastal State. The special situation of countries who are overwhelmingly dependent on coastal fisheries, was generally recognized at both Geneva Conferences in 1958 and 1960. Since then this view has found frequent expression both in the legislation of various countries and in important political statements. The course of events is decidedly progressing in this direction.

Reiterating the considerations which lead the Government of Iceland to issue new regulations relating to exclusive fisheries jurisdiction in the [24] continental shelf area, it stated the following:

> In the *aide-mémoire* of 31 August, 1971, it was intimated that 'in order to strengthen the measures of protection essential to safeguard the vital interests of the Icelandic people in the seas surrounding its coasts, the Government of Iceland now finds it essential to extend further the zone of exclusive fisheries jurisdiction around its coasts to include the areas of sea covering the continental shelf'. It was further stated that in the opinion of the Icelandic Government, the object and purpose of the provisions in the 1961 Exchange of Notes for recourse to judicial settlement in certain eventualities have been fully achieved. The Government of Iceland, therefore, considers the provisions of the Notes exchanged no longer to be applicable and consequently terminated. (Government of Iceland's *aide-mémoire* of 24 February 1972, Annex H to United Kingdom Application.)
>
> . . . In the period of ten years which has elapsed, the United Kingdom Government enjoyed the benefit of the Icelandic Government's policy to the effect that further extension of the limits of exclusive fisheries jurisdiction would be placed in abeyance *for a reasonable and equitable period*. Continuation of that policy by the Icelandic Government, in the light of intervening scientific and economic evolution (including the ever greater threat of increased diversion of highly developed fishing effort to the Icelandic area) has become excessively onerous and unacceptable, and is harmful to the maintenance of the resources of the sea on which the livelihood of the Icelandic people depends. (Government of Iceland's *aide-mémoire* of 31 August 1971, Annex C to United Kingdom Application.)

In the Request by the Government of the United Kingdom for the indication of interim measures of protection the grounds of the request are stated at length.
[. . .]
[25] [. . .] Not only Iceland but many coastal States in all regions of the world, know by experience the harmful effects of the ever greater threat of highly developed fishing effort near their shores, by foreign fishing fleets equipped – like the modern trawlers of the United Kingdom – with *sophisticated technical gear.*

The arguments developed in the request for measures of protection and in the oral hearing of 1 August 1972 appear, in my view, to have as their real object the protection of the interests, financial or economic, of private fishing enterprises rather than the 'rights' of the United Kingdom.

Furthermore, the existence of those rights cannot be taken for granted. This matter belongs to the merits of the case, to be decided when the Court deals with them.

[. . .]

[**27**] [. . .] The most essential asset of coastal States is to be found in the living resources of the sea covering their continental shelf and in the fishing zone contiguous to their territorial sea.

The progressive development of international law entails the recognition of the concept of the *patrimonial* sea, which extends from the territorial waters to a distance fixed by the coastal State concerned, in exercise of its sovereign rights, for the purpose of protecting the resources on which its economic development and the livelihood of its people depends.

This concept is not a new one. It has found expression in declarations by many governments proclaiming as their international maritime policy, their sovereignty and exclusive fisheries jurisdiction over the sea contiguous to their shores.

There are nine States which have adopted a distance of 200 nautical miles from their shores as their exclusive fisheries jurisdiction. Some of them have enacted and enforced regulations to that effect since 20 years ago, when the 'Santiago Declaration' was signed by the Governments of Chile, Ecuador and Peru in August 1952.

My last observation is the following. The claim of irremediable damages to the Applicant has not, in my opinion, been proved. They are only allegations that the fishing enterprises would suffer financial losses and also allegations that the eating habits of people in the countries concerned will be disturbed. Such an argument cannot, in my opinion, be opposed to the sovereign rights of Iceland over its exclusive jurisdiction and the protection of the living resources of the sea covering its continental shelf. The Order does not strike, in my view, a fair balance between the two sides as required by the relevant article of the Statute. The restrictions indicated in the Order are obviously against Iceland, interfering with its indisputable rights to legislate over its own territory as it considers essential (cf. para. 1, sub-para. *(d)*, of the operative clause of the Court's [**28**] Order). In the measures indicated in that Order the only substantial restriction to the Applicant consists in limiting the amount of its annual catch to 170,000 metric tons instead of its claim to 185,000 metric tons, 15,000 metric tons less than the Applicant had asked for in its request for measures of protection. All the other measures of protection requested in the Application the Court has accepted. On this aspect also I am not able to agree with the indication of measures in the Order of the Court.

[Reports: *ICJ Reports 1972*, p. 12; *55 ILR* 160]

Judgment of International Court of Justice on Jurisdiction, 2 February 1973 (extract)

[**18**][. . .] 35. In his letter of 29 May 1972 to the Registrar, the Minister for Foreign Affairs of Iceland refers to 'the changed circumstances resulting from the ever-increasing

exploitation of the fishery resources in the seas surrounding Iceland'. Judicial notice should also be taken of other statements made on the subject in documents which Iceland has brought to the Court's attention. Thus, the resolution adopted by the Althing on 15 February 1972 contains the statement that 'owing to changed circumstances the Notes concerning fishery limits exchanged in 1961 are no longer applicable'.

36. In these statements the Government of Iceland is basing itself on the principle of termination of a treaty by reason of change of circumstances. International law admits that a fundamental change in the circumstances which determined the parties to accept a treaty, if it has resulted in a radical transformation of the extent of the obligations imposed by it, may, under certain conditions, afford the party affected a ground for invoking the termination or suspension of the treaty. This principle, and the conditions and exceptions to which it is subject, have been embodied in Article 62 of the Vienna Convention on the Law of Treaties, which may in many respects be considered as a codification of existing customary law on the subject of the termination of a treaty relationship on account of change of circumstances.

37. One of the basic requirements embodied in that Article is that the [19] change of circumstances must have been a fundamental one. In this respect the Government of Iceland has, with regard to developments in fishing techniques, referred in an official publication on *Fisheries Jurisdiction in Iceland*, enclosed with the Foreign Minister's letter of 29 May 1972 to the Registrar, to the increased exploitation of the fishery resources in the seas surrounding Iceland and to the danger of still further exploitation because of an increase in the catching capacity of fishing fleets. The Icelandic statements recall the exceptional dependence of that country on its fishing for its existence and economic development. In his letter of 29 May 1972 the Minister stated:

> The Government of Iceland, considering that the vital interests of the people of Iceland are involved, respectfully informs the Court that it is not willing to confer jurisdiction on the Court in any case involving the extent of the fishery limits of Iceland . . .

In this same connection, the resolution adopted by the Althing on 15 February 1972 had contained a paragraph in these terms:

> That the Governments of the United Kingdom and the Federal Republic of Germany be again informed that because of the vital interests of the nation and owing to changed circumstances the Notes concerning fishery limits exchanged in 1961 are no longer applicable and that their provisions do not constitute an obligation for Iceland.

38. The invocation by Iceland of its 'vital interests', which were not made the subject of an express reservation to the acceptance of the jurisdictional obligation under the 1961 Exchange of Notes, must be interpreted, in the context of the assertion of changed circumstances, as an indication by Iceland of the reason why it regards as fundamental the changes which in its view have taken place in previously existing fishing techniques. This interpretation would correspond to the traditional view that

the changes of circumstances which must be regarded as fundamental or vital are those which imperil the existence or vital development of one of the parties.

39. The Applicant, for its part, contends that the alterations and progress in fishing techniques have not produced in the waters around Iceland the consequences apprehended by Iceland and therefore that the changes are not of a fundamental or vital character. In its Memorial, it points out that, as regards the capacity of fishing fleets, increases in the efficiency of individual trawlers have been counter-balanced by the reduction in total numbers of vessels in national fleets fishing in the waters around Iceland, and that the statistics show that the total annual catch of demersal species has varied to no great extent since 1960.

40. The Court, at the present stage of the proceedings, does not need [20] to pronounce on this question of fact, as to which there appears to be a serious divergence of views between the two Governments. If, as contended by Iceland, there have been any fundamental changes in fishing techniques in the waters around Iceland, those changes might be relevant for the decision on the merits of the dispute, and the Court might need to examine the contention at that stage, together with any other arguments that Iceland might advance in support of the validity of the extension of its fisheries jurisdiction beyond what was agreed to in the 1961 Exchange of Notes. But the alleged changes could not affect in the least the obligation to submit to the Court's jurisdiction, which is the only issue at the present stage of the proceedings. It follows that the apprehended dangers for the vital interests of Iceland, resulting from changes in fishing techniques, cannot constitute a fundamental change with respect to the lapse or subsistence of the compromissory clause establishing the Court's jurisdiction.

41. It should be observed in this connection that the exceptional dependence of Iceland on its fisheries for its subsistence and economic development is expressly recognized in the 1961 Exchange of Notes, and the Court, in its Order of 17 August 1972, stated that 'it is also necessary to bear in mind the exceptional dependence of the Icelandic nation upon coastal fisheries for its livelihood and economic development as expressly recognized by the United Kingdom in its Note addressed to the Foreign Minister of Iceland dated 11 March 1961'. The Court further stated that 'from this point of view account must be taken of the need for the conservation of fish stocks in the Iceland area' (*ICJ Reports 1972*, pp. 16 and 17). This point is not disputed.[9]

42. Account must also be taken of the fact that the Applicant has contended before the Court that to the extent that Iceland may, as a coastal State specially dependent on coastal fisheries for its livelihood or economic development, assert a need to procure the establishment of a special fisheries conservation régime (including such a régime under which it enjoys preferential rights) in the waters adjacent to its coast but beyond the exclusive fisheries zone provided for by the 1961 Exchange of Notes, it can legitimately pursue that objective by collaboration and agreement with the other countries concerned, but not by the unilateral arrogation of exclusive rights within

[9 See pp. 15–16 above.]

those waters. The exceptional dependence of Iceland on its fisheries and the principle of conservation of fish stocks having been recognized, the question remains as to whether Iceland is or is not competent unilaterally to assert an exclusive fisheries jurisdiction extending beyond the 12-mile limit. The issue before the Court in the present phase of the proceedings concerns solely its jurisdiction to determine the latter point.

*   *

[21] 43. Moreover, in order that a change of circumstances may give rise to a ground for invoking the termination of a treaty it is also necessary that it should have resulted in a radical transformation of the extent of the obligations still to be performed. The change must have increased the burden of the obligations to be executed to the extent of rendering the performance something essentially different from that originally undertaken. In respect of the obligation with which the Court is here concerned, this condition is wholly unsatisfied; the change of circumstances alleged by Iceland cannot be said to have transformed radically the extent of the jurisdictional obligation which is imposed in the 1961 Exchange of Notes. The compromissory clause enabled either of the parties to submit to the Court any dispute between them relating to an extension of Icelandic fisheries jurisdiction in the waters above its continental shelf beyond the 12-mile limit. The present dispute is exactly of the character anticipated in the compromissory clause of the Exchange of Notes. Not only has the jurisdictional obligation not been radically transformed in its extent; it has remained precisely what it was in 1961.

*   *

44. In the United Kingdom Memorial it is asserted that there is a flaw in the Icelandic contention of change of circumstances: that the doctrine never operates so as to extinguish a treaty automatically or to allow an unchallengeable unilateral denunciation by one party; it only operates to confer a right to call for termination and, if that call is disputed, to submit the dispute to some organ or body with power to determine whether the conditions for the operation of the doctrine are present. In this connection the Applicant alludes to Articles 65 and 66 of the Vienna Convention on the Law of Treaties. Those Articles provide that where the parties to a treaty have failed within 12 months to achieve a settlement of a dispute by the means indicated in Article 33 of the United Nations Charter (which means include reference to judicial settlement) any one of the parties may submit the dispute to the procedure for conciliation provided in the Annex to the Convention.

45. In the present case, the procedural complement to the doctrine of changed circumstances is already provided for in the 1961 Exchange of Notes, which specifically calls upon the parties to have recourse to the Court in the event of a dispute relating to Iceland's extension of fisheries jurisdiction. Furthermore, any question as to the jurisdiction of the Court, deriving from an alleged lapse through changed circumstances, is resolvable through the accepted judicial principle enshrined in Article 36,

paragraph 6, of the Court's Statute, which provides that 'in the event of a dispute as to whether the Court has jurisdiction, the matter shall be settled by the decision of the Court'. In this case such a dispute obviously exists, as can be seen from Iceland's communications to the Court, and [22] to the other Party, even if Iceland has chosen not to appoint an Agent, file a Counter-Memorial or submit preliminary objections to the Court's jurisdiction; and Article 53 of the Statute both entitles the Court and, in the present proceedings, requires it to pronounce upon the question of its jurisdiction. This it has now done with binding force.

*

*   *   *   *

46. For these reasons,

THE COURT,

by fourteen votes to one,

finds that it has jurisdiction to entertain the Application filed by the Government of the United Kingdom of Great Britain and Northern Ireland on 14 April 1972 and to deal with the merits of the dispute.

[. . .]

SEPARATE OPINION OF JUDGE SIR GERALD FITZMAURICE (EXTRACT)

[26] [. . .] 6. The question of fishery conservation was separately dealt with by the 1958 Geneva Conservation Convention, and by the subsequent North-East Atlantic Fisheries Convention concluded in London on 24 January 1959, of which Iceland, the Federal Republic and the United Kingdom were all signatories, and the object of which, according to its preamble, was 'to ensure the conservation of the fish stocks and the rational exploitation of the fisheries of the North-East Atlantic Ocean and adjacent waters, *which are of common concern to them*' (my italics).[10] But agreed measures of conservation on the high seas for the preservation of common fisheries in which all have a right to participate, is of course a completely different matter from a unilateral claim by a coastal State to prevent fishing by foreign vessels entirely, or to allow it only at the will and under the control of that State. The question of conservation has therefore no relevance to the jurisdictional issue now before the Court, which involves its competence to adjudicate upon a dispute occasioned by Iceland's [27] claim unilaterally to assert exclusive jurisdiction for fishery purposes up to a distance of 50 nautical miles from and around her coasts.

[. . .]

[36] DISSENTING OPINION OF JUDGE PADILLA NERVO (EXTRACT)

I cannot concur in the Judgment of the Court in the present proceedings.

---

[10] The phrase here italicized was intended to relate to all the waters covered by the Convention, including – and above all – those of the north-east Atlantic.

I am unable to agree with the manner and reasoning through which the Court easily disposed of and rejected the objections and *arguments* raised against its jurisdiction to deal with the merits of the Application.

The Court might give the impression by the development of too dogmatic and formalistic assertions that its main concern has been the search for juridical foundations to justify a previously admitted premise of somewhat axiomatic character.

That of course is not the case, but, in my view, the objections raised have not been answered convincingly.

The formulation of general principles and the invocation of a settled practice of the Court regarding certain issues in former decisions, do not necessarily solve the problem in a case like the present one, which has exceptional characteristics and very special features, and where jurisdiction and merits are interdependent from several points of view.

[...]

[41] [...] If the *object* and purpose of the provision to recourse to judicial settlement has been fully achieved and validly terminated, there would be no basis in that provision for the jurisdiction of the Court – and that is in my opinion the case.

There are many valid arguments and reasons in favour of the Icelandic thesis to the effect that the Exchange of Notes has *lapsed*.

Since the Exchange of Notes was negotiated, a fundamental change of circumstances has taken place, and new customary international rules and norms have emerged and developed, permitting coastal States to claim fisheries jurisdiction over the waters covering their continental shelves.

[...]

[43] [...] It may be concluded, therefore, that the circumstances existing in 1961 when the Exchange of Notes took place, have changed in many fundamental respects, which Iceland has validly invoked to sustain that the agreement is no longer is force.

In the last decades great changes have taken place in the political, social, economic and technical fields. The need to strike a fair balance between strong and weak nations, between industrial countries and those in the course of development, is each day more urgent.

The struggle for freedom and self-determination of dependent peoples has been successful. Many new States are now giving fresh views, force and co-operation to the community of nations.

The struggle to assert their sovereign rights over the natural resources belonging to them is a common denominator among the coastal States the world over.

Old practices and unfair so-called traditional situations have already ended or will soon disappear. The need and the will to liquidate the unjust privileges obtained through the assertion of superior strength, is each day more pressing. These facts have created new circumstances producing new changes.

Emerging customary laws on the problems of the sea have found expression in many political statements, in declarations of governments, [44] in laws and regulations implemented by coastal States in many parts of the world, for the purpose of asserting their sovereign rights and jurisdiction not only over their territorial sea but over the waters covering their continental shelves.

In international regional conferences, important declarations of principles were proclaimed, which advance the progressive development of the law of the sea.

The concepts and ideas which found new expression in the adoption of such principles were prevalent among jurists and statesmen in America more than two decades ago. Those principles apply to the situation of other coastal States in other continents as well, and Iceland could not be excluded.

The Specialized Conference of the Caribbean Countries formulated a Declaration of Principles; some of them are quoted below because of their relevance to the points in issue:

> *Recalling:* That the International American Conferences held in Bogotà in 1948, and in Caracas in 1954, recognized that the peoples of the Americas depend on the natural resources as a means of subsistence, and proclaimed the right to protect, conserve and develop those resources, as well as the right to ensure their use and utilization.
>
> That the 'Principles of Mexico on the Legal Régime of the Sea' which were adopted in 1956 and which were recognized 'as the expression of the juridical conscience of the Continent and as applicable, by the American States', established the basis for the evolution of the Law of the Sea which culminated, that year, with the annunciation by the Specialized Conference in the Capital of the Dominican Republic, of concepts which deserved endorsement by the United Nations Conference on the Law of the Sea, Geneva, 1958.
>
> *Considering* . . . That the renewable and non-renewable resources of the sea contribute to improve the standard of living of the developing countries and to stimulate and accelerate their progress;
>
> That such resources are not inexhaustible since even the living species may be depleted or extinguished as a consequence of irrational exploitation or pollution; . . .
>
> Formulate the following Declaration of Principles:
>
> *Territorial Sea* . . . The breadth of the territorial sea and the manner of its delimitation should be the subject of an international agreement, preferably of a worldwide scope. In the meantime, each State has the right to establish the breadth of its territorial sea up to a limit of 12 nautical miles to be measured from the applicable baseline . . .
>
> *Patrimonial Sea.* The coastal State has sovereign rights over [45] the renewable and non-renewable natural resources, which are found in the waters, in the seabed and in the subsoil of an area adjacent to the territorial sea called the *patrimonial sea.*
>
> The coastal State has the duty to promote and the right to regulate the conduct of scientific research within the patrimonial sea, as well as the right to adopt the necessary measures to prevent marine pollution and *to ensure its sovereignty over the resources of the area.*
>
> The breadth of this zone should be the subject of an international agreement, preferably of a worldwide scope. The whole of the area of both the territorial sea and the patrimonial sea, taking into account geographic circumstances, should not exceed a maximum of 200 nautical miles . . .
>
> *Continental Shelf.* The coastal State exercises over the continental shelf sovereign rights for the purpose of exploring it and exploiting its natural resources.

The continental shelf includes the sea-bed and subsoil of the submarine areas adjacent to the coast, but outside the area of the territorial sea, to a depth of 200 metres or, beyond that limit, to where the depth of the superjacent waters admits the exploitation of the natural resources of the said areas.

In addition, the States participating in this Conference consider that the Latin American Delegations in the Committee on the Sea-bed and Ocean Floor of the United Nations should promote a study concerning the advisability and timing for the establishment of precise outer limits of the continental shelf taking into account the outer limits of the continental rise.

In that part of the continental shelf covered by the patrimonial sea the legal régime provided for this area shall apply. With respect to the part beyond the patrimonial sea, the régime established for the continental shelf by International Law shall apply. (Italics added.)

[. . .]

[Reports: *ICJ Reports 1973*, p. 3; 55 ILR 183]

Order of International Court of Justice on Continuance of Interim Measures of Protection, 12 July 1973

[**303**] [*The Court*] [*m*]*akes the following Order:*
[. . .]

8. Whereas the Court, pending the final decision, and in the absence of such interim arrangement, must remain concerned to preserve, by the indication of provisional measures, the rights which may subsequently be [**304**] adjudged by the Court to belong respectively to the Parties;

Accordingly,
THE COURT,
by 11 votes to 3,

Confirms that the provisional measures indicated in operative paragraph (1) of the Order of 17 August 1972 should, subject to the power of revocation or modification conferred on the Court by paragraph 7 of Article 61 of the 1946 Rules, remain operative until the Court has given final judgment in the case.

[. . .]

[**310**] DISSENTING OPINION OF JUDGE PETRÉN

[Translation]
Having voted against the Order, I append thereto this dissenting opinion.

There is an evident possibility that the circumstances in which the Court, on 17 August 1972, indicated interim measures of protection might have undergone such changes as could justify some modification of those measures. One of the factors which ought to be taken into account in that respect is the evolution of fish-stocks. In its telegram protesting against the continuation of interim measures, the Government of Iceland maintained that British and Icelandic catches continue to decrease per unit effort and that small immature fish of the 1970 year-class, which is the only known sizeable year-class and should constitute the main source of supply in 1976–1978 and the necessary 'recruitment', are now increasingly being landed in United Kingdom ports. To my mind, these indications gave rise to questions which were serious enough to warrant inviting the Parties, before the Court took up any position on the continuance of interim measures, to furnish it with the relevant information, available from specialized organizations and institutions, as to the evolution and exploitation of fish-stocks in the fishing-waters concerned.

The many incidents that have occurred at the fishing-grounds have shown that the interim measures of protection indicated on 17 August 1972 have not been fulfilling their purpose, and there I see another reason for re-appraisal of those measures.

Another element which, as I see it, would have merited being taken into consideration is the way the Court recently founded the indication of interim measures on the possible existence of a new rule of international law. By the Orders made on 22 June 1973 in the cases concerning *Nuclear Tests (Australia* v. *France; New Zealand* v. *France)* the Court indicated in particular that the French Government should avoid nuclear tests causing the deposit of radio-active fall-out on Australian and New Zealand territory. This indication of interim measures was apparently founded on the possible existence of a new general rule of international law prohibiting States from carrying out atmospheric nuclear tests causing the deposit of radio-active fall-out, however slight, on the territory of other States. Nevertheless this general rule of international law, if it exists, has not yet been given codified expression. Its existence, therefore, could only be proved with the aid of other sources of law representing an evolution which is still in progress.

[311] Now, in claiming the fishing-rights contested by the British Government in the present case, the Government of Iceland has sought to draw authority from an evolution of international law which is upheld by an ever-increasing number of declared attitudes and is less hypothetical in character than the putative right on the basis of which the Court indicated interim measures in favour of Australia and New Zealand.

I therefore feel that the question of interim measures of protection in the present case ought also to be re-examined in the light of this recent precedent.

In view of the foregoing, and as the Court, in accordance with Article 53 of its Statute, is under a duty also to take into consideration such indications as it may have which militate in favour of a party that fails to appear, I am of the opinion that the interim measures should have been subjected to re-appraisal. That, in accordance with Article 61, paragraph 8, of the 1946 Rules, would have required the Court to invite the Parties to present their observations on the subject. The majority having opposed this course, I was obliged to vote against the Order.

[Reports: *ICJ Reports 1973*, p. 302; *55 ILR 228*]

Judgment of International Court of Justice on Merits, 25 July 1974 (extract)

[20] [. . .] 42. The question has been raised whether the Court has jurisdiction to pronounce upon certain matters referred to the Court in the last paragraph of the Applicant's final submissions (paragraphs 11 and 12 above)[11] to the effect that the parties are under a duty to examine together the existence and extent of the need for restrictions of fishing activities in Icelandic waters on conservation grounds and to negotiate for the establishment of such a régime as will, *inter alia*, ensure for Iceland a preferential position consistent with its position as a State specially dependent on its fisheries.

43. In its Judgment of 2 February 1973, pronouncing on the jurisdiction of the Court in the present case, the Court found 'that it has jurisdiction to entertain the Application filed by the Government of the United Kingdom of Great Britain and Northern Ireland on 14 April 1972 and to deal with the merits of the dispute' (*ICJ Reports 1973*, p. 22, para. 46).[12] The Application which the Court found it had jurisdiction to entertain contained a submission under letter *(b)* (cf. paragraph 11 above) which in its second part raised the issues of conservation of fishery resources and of preferential fishing rights. These questions, among others, had previously been discussed in the negotiations between the parties referred to in paragraphs 27 to 32 above[13] and were also extensively examined in the pleadings and hearings on the merits.

44. The Order of the Court indicating interim measures of protection (*Fisheries Jurisdiction (United Kingdom v. Iceland), Interim Protection, Order of 17 August 1972, ICJ Reports 1972*, p. 12)[14] implied that the case before the Court involved questions of fishery conservation and of preferential fishing rights since, in indicating a catch-limitation figure for the Applicant's fishing, the Court stated that this measure was based on 'the exceptional dependence of the Icelandic nation upon coastal **[21]** fisheries' and 'of the need for the conservation of fish stocks in the Iceland area' (*loc. cit.*, pp. 16–17, paras. 23 and 24).[15]

45. In its Judgment of 2 February 1973, pronouncing on its jurisdiction in the case, the Court, after taking into account the aforesaid contentions of the Applicant concerning fishery conservation and preferential rights, referred again to 'the exceptional dependence of Iceland on its fisheries and the principle of conservation of fish stocks' (*ICJ Reports 1973*, p. 20, para. 42).[16] The judicial notice taken therein of the recognition given by the Parties to the exceptional dependence of Iceland on its fisheries and to the need of conservation of fish stocks in the area clearly implies that such questions are before the Court.

46. The Order of the Court of 12 July 1973 on the continuance of interim measures of protection referred again to catch limitation figures and also to the question

[11] Not reproduced in this volume.]
[12] See p. 26 above.]
[13] Not reproduced in this volume.]
[14] See p. 14 above.]
[15] See p. 16 above.]
[16] See p. 25 above.]

of 'related restrictions concerning areas closed to fishing, number and type of vessels allowed and forms of control of the agreed provisions' (*ICJ Reports 1973*, p. 303, para. 7). Thus the Court took the view that those questions were within its competence. As the Court stated in its Order of 17 August 1972, there must be a connection 'under Article 61, paragraph 1, of the Rules between a request for interim measures of protection and the original Application filed with the Court' (*ICJ Reports 1972*, p. 15, para. 12).

47. As to the compromissory clause in the 1961 Exchange of Notes, this gives the Court jurisdiction with respect to 'a dispute in relation to such extension', i.e., 'the extension of fisheries jurisdiction around Iceland'. The present dispute was occasioned by Iceland's unilateral extension of its fisheries jurisdiction. However, it would be too narrow an interpretation of the compromissory clause to conclude that the Court's jurisdiction is limited to giving an affirmative or a negative answer to the question of whether the extension of fisheries jurisdiction, as enacted by Iceland on 14 July 1972, is in conformity with international law. In the light of the negotiations between the Parties, both in 1960 (paragraph 25 above)[17] and in 1971–1972 (paragraphs 28 to 32 above),[18] in which the questions of fishery conservation measures in the area and Iceland's preferential fishing rights were raised and discussed, and in the light of the proceedings before the Court, it seems evident that the dispute between the Parties includes disagreements as to the extent and scope of their respective rights in the fishery resources and the adequacy of measures to conserve them. It must therefore be concluded that those disagreements are an element of the 'dispute in relation to the extension of fisheries jurisdiction around Iceland'.

48. Furthermore, the dispute before the Court must be considered in all its aspects. Even if the Court's competence were understood to be confined to the question of the conformity of Iceland's extension with the rules of international law, it would still be necessary for the Court to [22] determine in that context the role and function which those rules reserve to the concept of preferential rights and that of conservation of fish stocks. Thus, whatever conclusion the Court may reach in regard to preferential rights and conservation measures, it is bound to examine these questions with respect to this case. Consequently, the suggested restriction on the Court's competence not only cannot be read into the terms of the compromissory clause, but would unduly encroach upon the power of the Court to take into consideration all relevant elements in administering justice between the Parties.

*

*   *

49. The Applicant has challenged the Regulations promulgated by the Government of Iceland on 14 July 1972, and since the Court has to pronounce on this challenge, the ascertainment of the law applicable becomes necessary. As the Court stated in the *Fisheries* case:

[17 Not reproduced in this volume.]
[18 Not reproduced in this volume.]

> The delimitation of sea areas has always an international aspect; it cannot be dependent merely upon the will of the coastal State as expressed in its municipal law. Although it is true that the act of delimitation is necessarily a unilateral act, because only the coastal State is competent to undertake it, the validity of the delimitation with regard to other States depends upon international law. (*ICJ Reports 1951*, p. 132.)

The Court will therefore proceed to the determination of the existing rules of international law relevant to the settlement of the present dispute.

50. The Geneva Convention on the High Seas of 1958, which was adopted 'as generally declaratory of established principles of international law', defines in Article 1 the term 'high seas' as 'all parts of the sea that are not included in the territorial sea or in the internal waters of a State'. Article 2 then declares that 'The high seas being open to all nations, no State may validly purport to subject any part of them to its sovereignty' and goes on to provide that the freedom of the high seas comprises, *inter alia*, both for coastal and non-coastal States, freedom of navigation and freedom of fishing. The freedoms of the high seas are however made subject to the consideration that they 'shall be exercised by all States with reasonable regard to the interests of other States in their exercise of the freedom of the high seas'.

51. The breadth of the territorial sea was not defined by the 1958 Convention on the Territorial Sea and the Contiguous Zone. It is true that Article 24 of this Convention limits the contiguous zone to 12 miles 'from the baseline from which the breadth of the territorial sea is measured'. At the 1958 Conference, the main differences on the breadth [23] of the territorial sea were limited at the time to disagreements as to what limit, not exceeding 12 miles, was the appropriate one. The question of the breadth of the territorial sea and that of the extent of the coastal State's fishery jurisdiction were left unsettled at the 1958 Conference. These questions were referred to the Second Conference on the Law of the Sea, held in 1960. Furthermore, the question of the extent of the fisheries jurisdiction of the coastal State, which had constituted a serious obstacle to the reaching of an agreement at the 1958 Conference, became gradually separated from the notion of the territorial sea. This was a development which reflected the increasing importance of fishery resources for all States.

52. The 1960 Conference failed by one vote to adopt a text governing the two questions of the breadth of the territorial sea and the extent of fishery rights. However, after that Conference the law evolved through the practice of States on the basis of the debates and near-agreements at the Conference. Two concepts have crystallized as customary law in recent years arising out of the general consensus revealed at that Conference. The first is the concept of the fishery zone, the area in which a State may claim exclusive fishery jurisdiction independently of its territorial sea; the extension of that fishery zone up to a 12-mile limit from the baselines appears now to be generally accepted. The second is the concept of preferential rights of fishing in adjacent waters in favour of the coastal State in a situation of special dependence on its coastal fisheries, this preference operating in regard to other States concerned in the exploitation of the same fisheries, and to be implemented in the way indicated in paragraph 57 below.

53. In recent years the question of extending the coastal State's fisheries jurisdiction has come increasingly to the forefront. The Court is aware that a number of States [have] asserted an extension of fishery limits. The Court is also aware of present endeavours, pursued under the auspices of the United Nations, to achieve in a third Conference on the Law of the Sea the further codification and progressive development of this branch of the law, as it is of various proposals and preparatory documents produced in this framework, which must be regarded as manifestations of the views and opinions of individual States and as vehicles of their aspirations, rather than as expressing principles of existing law. The very fact of convening the third Conference on the Law of the Sea evidences a manifest desire on the part of all States to proceed to the codification of that law on a universal basis, including the question of fisheries and conservation of the living resources of the sea. Such a general desire is understandable since the rules of international maritime law have been the product of mutual accommodation, reasonableness and co-operation. So it was in the past, and so it necessarily is today. In the circumstances, the Court, as a court of law, cannot render judgment *sub* [24] *specie legis ferendae*, or anticipate the law before the legislator has laid it down.

54. The concept of a 12-mile fishery zone, referred to in paragraph 52 above, as a *tertium genus* between the territorial sea and the high seas, has been accepted with regard to Iceland in the substantive provisions of the 1961 Exchange of Notes, and the United Kingdom has also applied the same fishery limit to its own coastal waters since 1964; therefore this matter is no longer in dispute between the Parties. At the same time, the concept of preferential rights, a notion that necessarily implies the existence of other legal rights in respect of which that preference operates, has been admitted by the Applicant to be relevant to the solution of the present dispute. Moreover, the Applicant has expressly recognized Iceland's preferential rights in the disputed waters and at the same time has invoked its own historic fishing rights in these same waters, on the ground that reasonable regard must be had to such traditional rights by the coastal State, in accordance with the generally recognized principles embodied in Article 2 of the High Seas Convention. If, as the Court pointed out in its dictum in the *Fisheries* case, cited in paragraph 49 above, any national delimitation of sea areas, to be opposable to other States, requires evaluation in terms of the existing rules of international law, then it becomes neccessary for the Court, in its examination of the Icelandic fisheries Regulations, to take those elements into consideration as well. Equally it has necessarily to take into account the provisions of the Exchange of Notes of 1961 which govern the relations between the Parties with respect to Iceland's fishery limits. The said Exchange of Notes, which was concluded within the framework of the existing provisions of the law of the sea, was held by the Court, in its Judgment of 2 February 1973, to be a treaty which is valid and in force.

*
*   *

55. The concept of preferential rights for the coastal State in a situation of special dependence on coastal fisheries originated in proposals submitted by Iceland at the Geneva Conference of 1958. Its delegation drew attention to the problem which would arise when, in spite of adequate fisheries conservation measures, the yield ceased to be sufficient to satisfy the requirements of all those who were interested in fishing in a given area. Iceland contended that in such a case, when a catch-limitation becomes necessary, special consideration should be given to the coastal State whose population is overwhelmingly dependent on the fishing resources in its adjacent waters.

56. An Icelandic proposal embodying these ideas failed to obtain the majority required, but a resolution was adopted at the 1958 Conference [25] concerning the situation of countries or territories whose people are overwhelmingly dependent upon coastal fisheries for their livelihood or economic development. This resolution, after 'recognizing that such situations call for exceptional measures befitting particular needs' recommended that:

> ... where, for the purpose of conservation, it becomes necessary to limit the total catch of a stock or stocks of fish in an area of the high seas adjacent to the territorial sea of a coastal State, any other States fishing in that area should collaborate with the coastal State to secure just treatment of such situation, by establishing agreed measures which shall recognize any preferential requirements of the coastal State resulting from its dependence upon the fishery concerned while having regard to the interests of the other States.

The resolution further recommended that 'appropriate conciliation and arbitral procedures shall be established for the settlement of any disagreement'.

57. At the Plenary Meetings of the 1960 Conference the concept of preferential rights was embodied in a joint amendment presented by Brazil, Cuba and Uruguay which was subsequently incorporated by a substantial vote into a joint United States–Canadian proposal concerning a 6-mile territorial sea and an additional 6-mile fishing zone, thus totalling a 12-mile exclusive fishing zone, subject to a phasing-out period. This amendment provided, independently of the exclusive fishing zone, that the coastal State had:

> ... the faculty of claiming preferential fishing rights in any area of the high seas adjacent to its exclusive fishing zone when it is scientifically established that a special situation or condition makes the exploitation of the living resources of the high seas in that area of fundamental importance to the economic development of the coastal State or the feeding of its population.

It also provided that:

> A special situation or condition may be deemed to exist when:
>
> (a) The fisheries and the economic development of the coastal State or the feeding of its population are so manifestly interrelated that, in consequence, that State is greatly dependent on the living resources of the high seas in the area in respect of which preferential fishing is being claimed;

(b)   It becomes necessary to limit the total catch of a stock or stocks of fish in such areas . . .

The contemporary practice of States leads to the conclusion that the [26] preferential rights of the coastal State in a special situation are to be implemented by agreement between the States concerned, either bilateral or multilateral, and, in case of disagreement, through the means for the peaceful settlement of disputes provided for in Article 33 of the Charter of the United Nations. It was in fact an express condition of the amendment referred to above that any other State concerned would have the right to request that a claim made by a coastal State should be tested and determined by a special commission on the basis of scientific criteria and of evidence presented by the coastal State and other States concerned. The commission was to be empowered to determine, for the period of time and under the limitations that it found necessary, the preferential rights of the coastal State, 'while having regard to the interests of any other State or States in the exploitation of such stock or stocks of fish'.

58. State practice on the subject of fisheries reveals an increasing and widespread acceptance of the concept of preferential rights for coastal States, particularly in favour of countries or territories in a situation of special dependence on coastal fisheries. Both the 1958 Resolution and the 1960 joint amendment concerning preferential rights were approved by a large majority of the Conferences, thus showing overwhelming support for the idea that in certain special situations it was fair to recognize that the coastal State had preferential fishing rights. After these Conferences, the preferential rights of the coastal State were recognized in various bilateral and multilateral international agreements. The Court's attention has been drawn to the practice in this regard of the North-West and North-East Atlantic Fisheries Commissions, of which 19 maritime States altogether, including both Parties, are members; its attention has also been drawn to the Arrangement Relating to Fisheries in Waters Surrounding the Faroe Islands, signed at Copenhagen on 18 December 1973 on behalf of the Governments of Belgium, Denmark, France, the Federal Republic of Germany, Norway, Poland and the United Kingdom, and to the Agreement on the Regulation of the Fishing of North-East Arctic (Arcto-Norwegian) Cod, signed on 15 March 1974 on behalf of the Governments of the United Kingdom, Norway and the Union of Soviet Socialist Republics. Both the aforesaid agreements, in allocating the annual shares on the basis of the past performance of the parties in the area, assign an additional share to the coastal State on the ground of its preferential right in the fisheries in its adjacent waters. The Faroese agreement takes expressly into account in its preamble 'the exceptional dependence of the Faroese economy on fisheries' and recognizes 'that the Faroe Islands should enjoy preference in waters surrounding the Faroe Islands'.

59. There can be no doubt of the exceptional dependence of Iceland on its fisheries. That exceptional dependence was explicitly recognized by the Applicant in the Exchange of Notes of 11 March 1961, and the Court [27] has also taken judicial notice of such recognition, by declaring that it is 'necessary to bear in mind the exceptional

dependence of the Icelandic nation upon coastal fisheries for its livelihood and economic development' (*ICJ Reports 1972*, p. 16, para. 23).[19]

60. The preferential rights of the coastal State come into play only at the moment when an intensification in the exploitation of fishery resources makes it imperative to introduce some system of catch-limitation and sharing of those resources, to preserve the fish stocks in the interests of their rational and economic exploitation. This situation appears to have been reached in the present case. In regard to the two main demersal species concerned – cod and haddock – the Applicant has shown itself aware of the need for a catch-limitation which has become indispensable in view of the establishment of catch-limitations in other regions of the North Atlantic. If a system of catch-limitation were not established in the Icelandic area, the fishing effort displaced from those other regions might well be directed towards the unprotected grounds in that area.

*
*   *

61. The Icelandic regulations challenged before the Court have been issued and applied by the Icelandic authorities as a claim to exclusive rights thus going beyond the concept of preferential rights. Article 2 of the Icelandic Regulations of 14 July 1972 states:

> Within the fishery limits all fishing activities by foreign vessels shall be prohibited in accordance with the provisions of Law No. 33 of 19 June 1922, concerning Fishing inside the Fishery Limits.

Article 1 of the 1922 Law provides: 'Only Icelandic citizens may engage in fishing in the territorial waters of Iceland, and only Icelandic boats or ships may be used for such fishing.' The language of the relevant government regulations indicates that their object is to establish an exclusive fishery zone, in which all fishing by vessels registered in other States, including the United Kingdom, would be prohibited. The mode of implementation of the regulations, carried out by Icelandic governmental authorities vis-à-vis United Kingdom fishing vessels, before the 1973 interim agreement, and despite the Court's interim measures, confirms this interpretation.

62. The concept of preferential rights is not compatible with the exclusion of all fishing activities of other States. A coastal State entitled to preferential rights is not free, unilaterally and according to its own uncontrolled discretion, to determine the extent of those rights. The characterization of the coastal State's rights as preferential implies a certain priority, but cannot imply the extinction of the concurrent rights of other **[28]** States, and particularly of a State which, like the Applicant, has for many years been engaged in fishing in the waters in question, such fishing activity being important to the economy of the country concerned. The coastal State has to take into account and pay regard to the position of such other States, particularly when they

[19 See p. 16 above.]

have established an economic dependence on the same fishing grounds. Accordingly, the fact that Iceland is entitled to claim preferential rights does not suffice to justify its claim unilaterally to exclude the Applicant's fishing vessels from all fishing activity in the waters beyond the limits agreed to in the 1961 Exchange of Notes.

*
*   *

63. In this case, the Applicant has pointed out that its vessels have been fishing in Icelandic waters for centuries and that they have done so in a manner comparable with their present activities for upwards of 50 years. Published statistics indicate that from 1920 onwards, fishing of demersal species by United Kingdom vessels in the disputed area has taken place on a continuous basis from year to year, and that, except for the period of the Second World War, the total catch of those vessels has been remarkably steady. Similar statistics indicate that the waters in question constitute the most important of the Applicant's distant-water fishing grounds for demersal species.

64. The Applicant further states that in view of the present situation of fisheries in the North Atlantic, which has demanded the establishment of agreed catch-limitations of cod and haddock in various areas, it would not be possible for the fishing effort of United Kingdom vessels displaced from the Icelandic area to be diverted at economic levels to other fishing grounds in the North Atlantic. Given the lack of alternative fishing opportunity, it is further contended, the exclusion of British fishing vessels from the Icelandic area would have very serious adverse consequences, with immediate results for the affected vessels and with damage extending over a wide range of supporting and related industries. It is pointed out in particular that wide-spread unemployment would be caused among all sections of the British fishing industry and in ancillary industries and that certain ports – Hull, Grimsby and Fleetwood – specially reliant on fishing in the Icelandic area, would be seriously affected.

65. Iceland has for its part admitted the existence of the Applicant's historic and special interests in the fishing in the disputed waters. The Exchange of Notes as a whole and in particular its final provision requiring Iceland to give advance notice to the United Kingdom of any extension of its fishery limits impliedly acknowledged the existence of United Kingdom fishery interests in the waters adjacent to the 12-mile limit. The discussions which have taken place between the two countries also imply an acknowledgement by Iceland of the existence of such [29] interests. Furthermore, the Prime Minister of Iceland stated on 9 November 1971:

> ... the British have some interests to protect in this connection. For a long time they have been fishing in Icelandic waters ... The well-being of specific British fishing towns may nevertheless to some extent be connected with the fisheries in Icelandic waters ...

66. Considerations similar to those which have prompted the recognition of the preferential rights of the coastal State in a special situation apply when coastal populations in other fishing States are also dependent on certain fishing grounds. In both instances the economic dependence and the livelihood of whole communities are

affected. Not only do the same considerations apply, but the same interest in conservation exists. In this respect the Applicant has recognized that the conservation and efficient exploitation of the fish stocks in the Iceland area are of importance not only to Iceland but also to the United Kingdom.

67. The provisions of the Icelandic Regulations of 14 July 1972 and the manner of their implementation disregard the fishing rights of the Applicant. Iceland's unilateral action thus constitutes an infringement of the principle enshrined in Article 2 of the 1958 Geneva Convention on the High Seas which requires that all States, including coastal States, in exercising their freedom of fishing, pay reasonable regard to the interests of other States. It also disregards the rights of the Applicant as they result from the Exchange of Notes of 1961. The Applicant is therefore justified in asking the Court to give all necessary protection to its own rights, while at the same time agreeing to recognize Iceland's preferential position. Accordingly, the Court is bound to conclude that the Icelandic Regulations of 14 July 1972 establishing a zone of exclusive fisheries jurisdiction extending to 50 nautical miles from baselines around the coast of Iceland, are not opposable to the United Kingdom, and the latter is under no obligation to accept the unilateral termination by Iceland of United Kingdom fishery rights in the area.

68. The findings stated by the Court in the preceding paragraphs suffice to provide a basis for the decision of the present case, namely: that Iceland's extension of its exclusive fishery jurisdiction beyond 12 miles is not opposable to the United Kingdom; that Iceland may on the other hand claim preferential rights in the distribution of fishery resources in the adjacent waters; that the United Kingdom also has established rights with respect to the fishery resources in question; and that the principle of reasonable regard for the interests of other States enshrined in Article 2 of the Geneva Convention on the High Seas of 1958 requires Iceland and the United Kingdom to have due regard to each other's interests, and to the interests of other States, in those resources.

*

*   *

[30] 69. It follows from the reasoning of the Court in this case that in order to reach an equitable solution of the present dispute it is necessary that the preferential fishing rights of Iceland, as a State specially dependent on coastal fisheries, be reconciled with the traditional fishing rights of the Applicant. Such a reconciliation cannot be based, however, on a phasing-out of the Applicant's fishing, as was the case in the 1961 Exchange of Notes in respect of the 12-mile fishery zone. In that zone, Iceland was to exercise exclusive fishery rights while not objecting to continued fishing by the Applicant's vessels during a phasing-out period. In adjacent waters outside that zone, however, a similar extinction of rights of other fishing States, particularly when such rights result from a situation of economic dependence and long-term reliance on certain fishing grounds, would not be compatible with the notion of preferential rights as it was recognized at the Geneva Conferences of 1958 and 1960, nor would

it be equitable. At the 1960 Conference, the concept of preferential rights of coastal States in a special situation was recognized in the joint amendment referred to in paragraph 57 above, under such limitations and to such extent as is found 'necessary by reason of the dependence of the coastal State on the stock or stocks of fish, while having regard to the interests of any other State or States in the exploitation of such stock or stocks of fish'. The reference to the interests of other States in the exploitation of the same stocks clearly indicates that the preferential rights of the coastal State and the established rights of other States were considered as, in principle, continuing to co-exist.

70. This is not to say that the preferential rights of a coastal State in a special situation are a static concept, in the sense that the degree of the coastal State's preference is to be considered as fixed for ever at some given moment. On the contrary, the preferential rights are a function of the exceptional dependence of such a coastal State on the fisheries in adjacent waters and may, therefore, vary as the extent of that dependence changes. Furthermore, as was expressly recognized in the 1961 Exchange of Notes, a coastal State's exceptional dependence on fisheries may relate not only to the livelihood of its people but to its economic development. In each case, it is essentially a matter of appraising the dependence of the coastal State on the fisheries in question in relation to that of the other State concerned and of reconciling them in as equitable a manner as is possible.

71. In view of the Court's finding (paragraph 67 above) that the Icelandic Regulations of 14 July 1972 are not opposable to the United Kingdom for the reasons which have been stated, it follows that the Government of Iceland is not in law entitled unilaterally to exclude United Kingdom fishing vessels from sea areas to seaward of the limits agreed to in the 1961 Exchange of Notes or unilaterally to impose restrictions on their activities in such areas. But the matter does not end there; [31] as the Court has indicated, Iceland is, in view of its special situation, entitled to preferential rights in respect of the fish stocks of the waters adjacent to its coasts. Due recognition must be given to the rights of both Parties, namely the rights of the United Kingdom to fish in the waters in dispute, and the preferential rights of Iceland. Neither right is an absolute one: the preferential rights of a coastal State are limited according to the extent of its special dependence on the fisheries and by its obligation to take account of the rights of other States and the needs of conservation; the established rights of other fishing States are in turn limited by reason of the coastal State's special dependence on the fisheries and its own obligation to take account of the rights of other States, including the coastal State, and of the needs of conservation.

72. It follows that even if the Court holds that Iceland's extension of its fishery limits is not opposable to the Applicant, this does not mean that the Applicant is under no obligation to Iceland with respect to fishing in the disputed waters in the 12-mile to 50-mile zone. On the contrary, both States have an obligation to take full account of each other's rights and of any fishery conservation measures the necessity of which is shown to exist in those waters. It is one of the advances in maritime international law, resulting from the intensification of fishing, that the former *laissez-faire* treatment of

the living resources of the sea in the high seas has been replaced by a recognition of a duty to have due regard to the rights of other States and the needs of conservation for the benefit of all. Consequently, both Parties have the obligation to keep under review the fishery resources in the disputed waters and to examine together, in the light of scientific and other available information, the measures required for the conservation and development, and equitable exploitation, of those resources, taking into account any international agreement in force between them, such as the North-East Atlantic Fisheries Convention of 24 January 1959, as well as such other agreements as may be reached in the matter in the course of further negotiation.

*
*   *

73. The most appropriate method for the solution of the dispute is clearly that of negotiation. Its objective should be the delimitation of the rights and interests of the Parties, the preferential rights of the coastal State on the one hand and the rights of the Applicant on the other, to balance and regulate equitably questions such as those of catch-limitation, share allocations and 'related restrictions concerning areas closed to fishing, number and type of vessels allowed and forms of control of the agreed provisions' (*Fisheries Jurisdiction (United Kingdom v. Iceland), Interim Measures, Order of 12 July 1973, ICJ Reports 1973*, p. 303, [**32**] para. 7). This necessitates detailed scientific knowledge of the fishing grounds. It is obvious that the relevant information and expertise would be mainly in the possession of the Parties. The Court would, for this reason, meet with difficulties if it were itself to attempt to lay down a precise scheme for an equitable adjustment of the rights involved. It is thus obvious that both in regard to merits and to jurisdiction the Court only pronounces on the case which is before it and not on any hypothetical situation which might arise in the future.

74. It is implicit in the concept of preferential rights that negotiations are required in order to define or delimit the extent of those rights, as was already recognized in the 1958 Geneva Resolution on Special Situations relating to Coastal Fisheries, which constituted the starting point of the law on the subject. This Resolution provides for the establishment, through collaboration between the coastal State and any other State fishing in the area, of agreed measures to secure just treatment of the special situation.

75. The obligation to negotiate thus flows from the very nature of the respective rights of the Parties; to direct them to negotiate is therefore a proper exercise of the judicial function in this case. This also corresponds to the Principles and provisions of the Charter of the United Nations concerning peaceful settlement of disputes. As the Court stated in the *North Sea Continental Shelf* cases:

> . . . this obligation merely constitutes a special application of a principle which underlies all international relations, and which is moreover recognized in Article 33 of the Charter of the United Nations as one of the methods for the peaceful settlement of international disputes (*ICJ Reports 1969*, p. 47, para. 86).

76. In this case negotiations were initiated by the Parties from the date when Iceland gave notice of its intention to extend its fisheries jurisdiction, but these negotiations reached an early deadlock, and could not come to any conclusion; subsequently, further negotiations were directed to the conclusion of the interim agreement of 13 November 1973. The obligation to seek a solution of the dispute by peaceful means, among which negotiations are the most appropriate to this case, has not been eliminated by that interim agreement. The question has been raised, however, on the basis of the deletion of a sentence which had been proposed by the United Kingdom in the process of elaboration of the text, whether the parties agreed to wait for the expiration of the term provided for in the interim agreement without entering into further negotiations. The deleted sentence, which would have appeared in paragraph 7 of the 1973 Exchange of Notes, read: 'The Governments will reconsider the position before that term expires unless they have in the meantime agreed to a settlement of the substantive dispute.'

77. The Court cannot accept the view that the deletion of this sentence which concerned renegotiation of the interim régime warrants the inference [33] that the common intention of the Parties was to be released from negotiating in respect of the basic dispute over Iceland's extension to a 50-mile limit throughout the whole period covered by the interim agreement. Such an intention would not correspond to the attitude taken up by the Applicant in these proceedings, in which it has asked the Court to adjudge and declare that the Parties are under a duty to negotiate a régime for the fisheries in the area. Nor would an interpretation of this kind, in relation to Iceland's intention, correspond to the clearly stated policy of the Icelandic authorities to continue negotiations on the basic problems relating to the dispute, as emphasized by paragraph 3 of the Althing Resolution of 15 February 1972, referred to earlier, which reads: 'That efforts to reach a solution of the problems connected with the extension be continued through discussions with the Governments of the United Kingdom and the Federal Republic of Germany.' Taking into account that the interim agreement contains a definite date for its expiration, and in the light of what has been stated in paragraph 75 above, it would seem difficult to attribute to the Parties an intention to wait for that date and for the reactivation of the dispute, with all the possible friction it might engender, before one of them might require the other to attempt a peaceful settlement through negotiations. At the same time, the Court must add that its Judgment obviously cannot preclude the Parties from benefiting from any subsequent developments in the pertinent rules of international law.

78. In the fresh negotiations which are to take place on the basis of the present Judgment, the Parties will have the benefit of the above appraisal of their respective rights, and of certain guidelines defining their scope. The task before them will be to conduct their negotiations on the basis that each must in good faith pay reasonable regard to the legal rights of the other in the waters around Iceland outside the 12-mile limit, thus bringing about an equitable apportionment of the fishing resources based on the facts of the particular situation, and having regard to the interests of other States which have established fishing rights in the area. It is not a matter of finding

simply an equitable solution, but an equitable solution derived from the applicable law. As the Court stated in the *North Sea Continental Shelf* cases:

> ... it is not a question of applying equity simply as a matter of abstract justice, but of applying a rule of law which itself requires the application of equitable principles (*ICJ Reports 1969*, p. 47, para. 85).

*
*   *

[34] 79. For these reasons,

THE COURT,

by ten votes to four,

(1) finds that the Regulations concerning the Fishery Limits off Iceland (*Reglugerð um fiskveiðilandhelgi Íslands*) promulgated by the Government of Iceland on 14 July 1972 and constituting a unilateral extension of the exclusive fishing rights of Iceland to 50 nautical miles from the baselines specified therein are not opposable to the Government of the United Kingdom;

(2) finds that, in consequence, the Government of Iceland is not entitled unilaterally to exclude United Kingdom fishing vessels from areas between the fishery limits agreed to in the Exchange of Notes of 11 March 1961 and the limits specified in the Icelandic Regulations of 14 July 1972, or unilaterally to impose restrictions on the activities of those vessels in such areas;

by ten votes to four,

(3) holds that the Government of Iceland and the Government of the United Kingdom are under mutual obligations to undertake negotiations in good faith for the equitable solution of their differences concerning their respective fishery rights in the areas specified in subparagraph 2;

(4) holds that in these negotiations the Parties are to take into account, *inter alia*:

(a) that in the distribution of the fishing resources in the areas specified in subparagraph 2 Iceland is entitled to a preferential share to the extent of the special dependence of its people upon the fisheries in the seas around its coasts for their livelihood and economic development;

(b) that by reason of its fishing activities in the areas specified in subparagraph 2, the United Kingdom also has established rights in the fishery resources of the said areas on which elements of its people depend for their livelihood and economic well-being;

(c) the obligation to pay due regard to the interests of other States in the conservation and equitable exploitation of these resources;

(d) that the above-mentioned rights of Iceland and of the United Kingdom should each be given effect to the extent compatible with the conservation and development of the fishery resources in the areas

specified in subparagraph 2 and with the interests of other States in
their conservation and equitable exploitation;

(e)   their obligation to keep under review those resources and to examine together, in the light of scientific and other available information,
such measures as may be required for the conservation [35] and development, and equitable exploitation, of those resources, making
use of the machinery established by the North-East Atlantic Fisheries
Convention or such other means as may be agreed upon as a result
of international negotiations.

[...]

DECLARATION OF JUDGE NAGENDRA SINGH (EXTRACT)

[40] [...] II

The contribution which the Judgment makes towards the development of the Law
of the Sea lies in the recognition which it gives to the concept of preferential rights
of a coastal State in the fisheries of the adjacent waters particularly if that State is in
a special situation with its population dependent on those fisheries. Moreover, the
Court proceeds further to recognize that the law pertaining to fisheries must accept
the primacy for the need of conservation based on scientific data. This aspect has been
properly emphasized to the extent needed to establish that the exercise of preferential
rights of the coastal State as well as the historic rights of other States dependent on
the same fishing grounds, have all to be subject to the over-riding consideration of
proper conservation of the fishery resources for the benefit of all concerned. This
conclusion would appear warranted if this vital source of man's nutrition is to be
preserved and developed for the community.

In addition there has always been the need for accepting clearly in maritime matters
the existence of the duty to 'have reasonable regard to the interests of other States' –
a principle enshrined in Article 2 of the Geneva Convention of the High Seas 1958
which applies even to the four freedoms of the seas and has weighed with the Court
in this case. Thus the rights of the coastal State which must have preference over the
rights of other States in the coastal fisheries of the adjacent waters have nevertheless
to be exercised with due regard to the rights of other States and the claims and
counter-claims in this respect have to be resolved on the basis of considerations of
equity. There is, as yet, no specific conventional law governing this aspect and it is the
evolution of customary law which has furnished the basis of the Court's Judgment
in this case.

[...]

[43] IV

For purposes of administering the law of the sea and for proper understanding of
matters pertaining to fisheries as well as to appreciate the facts of this case, it is of
some importance to know the precise content of the expression 'fisheries jurisdiction'

and for what it stands and means. The concept of fisheries jurisdiction does cover aspects such as enforcement of conservation measures, exercise of preferential rights and respect for historic rights since each one may involve an element of jurisdiction to implement them. Even the reference to 'extension' in relation to fisheries jurisdiction which occurs in the compromissory clause of the 1961 treaty could not be confined to mean merely the extension of a geographical boundary line or limit since such an extension would be meaningless without a jurisdictional aspect which constitutes, as it were, its juridical content. It is significant, therefore, that the preamble of the Truman Proclamation of 1945 respecting United States coastal fisheries refers to a 'jurisdictional' basis for implementing conservation measures in the adjacent sea since such measures have to be enforced like any other regulations in relation to a particular area. This further supports the Court's conclusion that it had jurisdiction to deal with aspects relating to conservation and preferential rights since the 1961 treaty by the use of the words 'extension of fisheries jurisdiction' must be deemed to have covered those aspects.

[...]

[53] SEPARATE OPINION OF JUDGE DILLARD (EXTRACT)

I concur in the Judgment of the Court. I am moved to write a separate opinion first to elaborate on a few possibly controversial aspects of the Judgment and second to put it in a broader perspective.

[...]

[62] [...] The jurisdiction of the Court to entertain the merits of the dispute was, as previously noted, definitively established by its Judgment of 2 February 1973. But the endowment of jurisdiction in the sense of the *general power* to deal with the merits is one thing; the nature and scope of that power is quite another.

It is precisely with reference to the third and fourth subparagraphs of the *dispositif* that questions of the latter kind have been raised concerning the extent of the Court's assumption of jurisdiction.

The third subparagraph states that the two Parties are under mutual obligations to undertake negotiations in good faith for the equitable solution of their differences concerning their respective fishery rights in the areas around Iceland to seaward of the fishery limits agreed to in the Exchange of Notes of 1961. The fourth subparagraph indicates the guidelines for doing so. Briefly summarized it specifies that in the distribution of the fishery resources, account be taken of the preferential share to which Iceland is entitled to the extent that she qualifies as a State in a condition of special dependence on coastal fisheries; that account also be taken of the established rights of the United Kingdom; that the rights of both States should be given effect to the extent compatible with the conservation and development of the fishing resources in the area; that regard also be paid to the interests of other States in the conservation and equitable exploitation of the resources and that the two States keep under review the measures required for the conservation, development and equitable exploitation of the resources in light of scientific and other available information.

[. . .]

[63] [. . .] As I understand it, the argument questioning the Court's power to deal with the above issues rests on the following chain of reasoning. Both the existence and scope of the Court's jurisdiction [are] confined to the Exchange of Notes of 1961. The reference in the Exchange of Notes to a 'dispute' must be strictly confined to the kind of dispute contemplated by the parties in negotiating and framing the Exchange of Notes. This, and this alone, constitutes the *subject-matter* to which the Court's jurisdiction attaches. At no relevant time was there a dispute concerning preferential rights or conservation. Quite the contrary, it concerned only the extension itself and whether it could be held well founded under international law. The Court is not privileged to change the nature of the dispute without doing violence to its endowment of limited power in the Exchange of Notes.

[. . .]

[64] Indeed at the very first discussion on 1 October 1960 Sir Patrick Reilly in his opening remarks conceded that there may be areas both inside and outside the 6–12-mile zone 'which on the scientific principle of conservation should be reserved from trawling'. Mr Andersen of Iceland countered with the assertion that 'conservation measures applicable to all alike were not sufficient to safeguard Iceland's coastal fisheries' (Records of the Anglo-Icelandic Discussions, 1 October 1960 to 4 December 1960, at pp. 1 and 5). Furthermore it should be recognized that a certain ambiguity attends the meaning of the term 'exclusive', a point to be alluded to later and revealed in some of the diplomatic exchanges subsequent to the adoption of the Exchange of Notes, as, for instance, in the Government of Iceland's Note of 11 August 1972 in which preferential rights are expressly mentioned (United Kingdom Memorial on the merits, Annex 10, p. 125). But the more important point, in my view, is the larger context in which the dispute itself is located.

[. . .]

SEPARATE OPINION OF JUDGE DE CASTRO (EXTRACT)

[Translation]

[. . .] III. *The development of the law of the sea*

[87] [. . .] The seed sown by the Truman Proclamations is still bearing fruit, and it is from them that innovating ideas continue to spring concerning the law of the sea.[20]

---

[20] The tendency to extend fisheries zones in the interest of coastal populations may also be observed in countries of the Western group.

The Senate and House of Representatives of Massachusetts, assembled in General Court, authorized the Director of the Division of Marine Fisheries, with the approval of the Governor, to extend jurisdiction up to 200 miles for the purposes of conservation and protection of maritime resources (Massachusetts, *An Act Relative to the Territorial Waters of the Commonwealth*). In 1972,

The recognition of a third maritime zone, inserted between the territorial sea and the high seas, is the basis of a new concept, that of the patrimonial sea or economic zone. According to the Declaration of Santo Domingo, the coastal State has sovereign rights over the renewable and non-renewable natural resources which are found in the waters, in the sea-bed and in the subsoil of an area adjacent to the territorial sea called [**88**] the patrimonial sea; the area of the territorial sea and the patrimonial sea, taking into account geographic circumstances, should not exceed a maximum of 200 sea-miles.

In the Truman Proclamation, and at the 1958 Conference, reference was made to the natural resources of the continental shelf over which it was recognized that the coastal State had an exclusive right, in order to define the scope thereof, with a view to respecting the freedom of fishing in the high seas. At the present time, the reference to rights over natural resources is taking a new turn. A point has been reached at which the right of States is reaffirmed to permanent sovereignty over all the natural resources of the sea-bed and subsoil within their national jurisdiction, and in the superjacent waters. This is also what was said in General Assembly resolution 3016 (XXVII), in a recommendation adopted by the Committee on Natural Resources of the Economic and Social Council (Session of February 1973) and in a resolution of the Economic and Social Council (April–May 1973).[21]

It seems to me that with its Resolution of 1972, Iceland followed the same tactics as those which had previously brought it success. It faced the defendant State with a *fait accompli*, and did so in the conviction that the development of the law of the sea is moving towards a justification of its decision. Iceland may cherish the hope that the trends in favour of extension of fisheries zones will obtain the support of the greater number of States at the Caracas conference.[22]

Congress of the State of Maine requested the Secretary of State and the delegation to the United States Congress to extend jurisdiction over fisheries to the whole extent of the continental shelf (J. H. Samet and R. L. Fuerst, *The Latin-American Approach to the Law of the Sea*, University of North Carolina, Sea Grant Publication, March 1973, App. A and B, pp. 150–1). In the United States, there are conflicts between the states and the Federal Government. New England is in favour of an extension of jurisdiction to protect coastal fisheries. California favours limiting jurisdiction, taking account of cod fishing in the high seas. Military interests operate in favour of the 12-mile limit (Hjertonsson, *The New Law of the Sea*, 'Influence of the Latin American States on Recent Developments of the Law of the Sea', Leiden–Stockholm, 1973, p. 96).

In Canada, the Governor is authorized to prescribe by Order in Council fishing zones in areas of the sea adjacent to the coast of Canada (Law of 16 June 1970 amending the Law on the Territorial Sea and Fishery Zones, new paras. 4 and 5A).

[21] The *travaux préparatoires* of the Caracas Conference should be taken into account, though *cum grano salis*, as of assistance in ascertaining the present tendencies amongst States; in addition they reveal the taking up of positions with a view to the discussions during the Conference.

[22] The Government of the United Kingdom has explained, in its reply to a question by a Member of the Court, that in para. 297 of its Memorial it intended to make the point 'that the forthcoming Third United Nations Conference on the Law of the Sea may reveal whether a consensus can be reached which will bring about a development in the law so as to permit the kind of claim which Iceland is now making'.

IV. The law to be applied

[...]

[94] [...] 5. I cannot see that there is any other customary rule fixing the extent of the fishery zone. The 200-mile rule cannot be regarded as an accepted one, and as thus conferring on States the right to extend their jurisdiction to that extent. Despite the progress which it has made in recent years, it is not marked either by the uniformity or the general acceptance which it would require in order to be regarded as a customary rule, even of regional extent.[23]

Against the contentions of the Applicant, Judge Padilla Nervo has argued that:

> The progressive development of international law entails the recognition of the con-
> cept of the *patrimonial* sea, which extends from the territorial waters to a distance fixed
> by the coastal State concerned, in exercise of its sovereign rights, for the purpose of
> protecting the resources on which its economic development and the livelihood of its
> people depends. (Dissenting opinion, *ICJ Reports 1973*, p. 41.)

The view of Judge Padilla Nervo must be rejected for several reasons. The patrimonial sea is a compromise concept, which is worthy of consideration but which
does not meet the conditions required of a rule of law. The countries represented at
Santo Domingo did not claim that their proposal concerning a zone of patrimonial
sea should be applicable to all Latin American States, or that it was generally favoured
by them, but they regarded it as a contribution to the working out of an eventual
joint Latin American formula.[24]

[...]

[97] It is generally conceded, even by the Latin American States, that the high seas
are free, and that freedom of fishing is one of the four freedoms of the seas.[25]

The high seas are not *res nullius* to be appropriated by the first-comer, nor by the
most powerful.[26] They belong to the community of peoples, or to mankind.[27] The
high seas are regarded as *res omnium communis*, and the use of them belongs equally
to all peoples. The appropriation of an exclusive fisheries zone in an area hitherto
considered as part of the free seas is equivalent to deprivation of other peoples

---

[23] García Amador observes that the differences relate to the very nature of the claims, *Latin-America and the Law of the Sea*, University of Rhode Island, Occasional Paper No. 14, 1972, p. 1. On the protests of States and of writers, see Rojahn, 'Zur zukünftigen Rechtsordnung des Festlandsockels und der Fischerei auf dem Hohen Meer', *Jahrbuch für internationales Recht*, Vol. XV, 1971, p. 407.

[24] Castañeda, 'The Concept of Patrimonial Sea in International Law', *Indian Journal of International Law*, Vol. 12, No. 4, October 1972, p. 538.

[25] This is the principle enshrined in Articles 1 and 2 of the 1958 Geneva Convention on the High Seas. This Convention lays down on this point general principles of international law established long before their formulation in the Convention (*ICJ Reports 1969*, p. 39, para. 65).

[26] This is, I think, the general opinion. On the question of the nature of the high seas, see Jenisch, *Das Recht zur Vornahme militärischer Übungen und Versuche auf Hoher See in Friedenszeiten*, Hamburg, 1970, pp. 43–52.

[27] General Assembly resolution 2749 (XXV) of 17 December 1970 refers in paragraph 1 to the common heritage of mankind. On the idea of fishing zones as 'property devoted to a purpose' (*Zweckvermögen*) and relevant references, see Rojahn, *Die Ansprüche*, p. 171; on the concept of coastal nations as trustees for the international community, see President Nixon's statement of 23 May 1970, quoted by Rojahn in 'Zur zukünftigen', p. 425.

of their rights. The extension of its jurisdiction over the adjacent sea by a coastal State presupposes a reduction of the freedom of fishing of other States, and such respective increase and loss of power calls for legal justification. At all times, States have endeavoured to justify their claims in one way or another. According to Vattel [. . .], there must be 'some lawful end' for the appropriation of something which is common property. Judge Alvarez contended that States might alter the extent of the territorial sea 'provided that they furnish adequate grounds to justify the change' (individual opinion, *ICJ Reports 1951*, p. 150).[28]

7. I think that the principle of the freedom of the high seas is as valid as ever it was, but it does not operate in isolation, it must be applied in accordance with existing circumstances and the views currently held. In the time of Grotius, and up to the end of the Second World War, the principle could be expressed in absolute terms; today, reality is otherwise, and compels us to express it more moderately, and to harmonize it with other secondary principles.

The case before the Court requires a just solution to be found to the conflict which is emerging between the principle of the freedom of the high seas with regard to fisheries, and the trends in favour of extension of the zone of jurisdiction of coastal States. But for this purpose it should be borne in mind that the Court does not have to decide a general and [98] abstract question, but a dispute between two countries, for the settlement of which the positions and relationships of the Parties should primarily be considered.

The consideration of 'the close dependence of the territorial sea upon the land domain' (*ICJ Reports 1951*, p. 133) also underlies the recognized extent of the new zone of fisheries jurisdiction. But the establishment of jurisdiction over the fishing zones must be justified by the special interest of the coastal State, and by the existence of reasons permitting of the recognition that that State has preferential or priority rights.

The 1958 Conference recognized the concepts of 'special interest', 'preferential requirements' and 'just treatment' (Convention on Fishing and Conservation of the Living Resources of the High Seas, Art. 6; Resolution on Special Situations Relating to Coastal Fisheries). The scope of these concepts is limited to fishery conservation, and the situation of countries whose coastal population depends on fishing. At the 1960 Conference, Brazil, Cuba and Uruguay proposed a text in which it was said that 'the coastal State has the faculty of claiming preferential fishing rights in any area of the high seas adjacent to its exclusive fishing zone . . . '; this draft furthermore almost obtained unanimity, but as has already been stated, it failed to be adopted, along with the proposal by Canada and the United States.

Although these concepts have not been enshrined in a convention, and despite the restrictions subject to which they were advanced, in fact what is happening to them

---

[28] Quotations on the criterion of what is reasonable will be found in Brownlie, pp. 196 and 215. The Prime Minister of Iceland has referred to what is 'reasonable' (Memorial of the Federal Republic of Germany, Part IV, para. 58). See also *ICJ Reports 1951*, p. 131 'moderate and reasonable'; *ICJ Reports 1969*, pp. 52 and 54, paras. 98 and 101 (D) (3): 'reasonable degree of proportionality'. But the criterion of what is reasonable should be determined objectively.

is what happened to the Truman Proclamations, they are the 'starting point of the positive law on the subject' (*ICJ Reports 1969*, pp. 32–3). They are accepted as something natural. As examples of this development, one might mention the recommendation of the American Bar Association of August 1964 (para. 1 *(b)*, quoted by Johnston, [. . .]), the draft of the Inter-American Committee of 1956, the Statement by President Nixon of 23 May 1970 (quotations in Rojahn, 'Zur zukünftigen', p. 412), and the proposal of the United States according to Stevenson [. . .]. In United Nations General Assembly resolution 2750 C (XXV) of 17 December 1970, in which the subjects to be dealt with by the Conference on the Law of the Sea are laid down, is included the question of the preferential rights of coastal States. The Government of the United Kingdom 'accepts that the concept of preferential fishing rights of coastal States and the spirit of the proposals embodied in the three-Power amendment are applicable, are relevant, to the solution of the present dispute' (CR 74/3, pp. 16–17).[29]

Along with the special interest and the preferential rights of the coastal State, account should be taken of the historic rights of the countries concerned with high sea fishing. The acquisition of rights over the sea by prescription is not admitted, but long usage should be respected, and [99] that for the same reasons as for the interests of the coastal State. It is contrary to the concept of justice to disregard situations which have been established for years, the capital invested, the establishment of industries, the protein needs of populations, and above all the confidence inspired by a respect for the status quo concerning the use of the high seas as common property.

8. The difficulties in the way of harmonizing these interests are not insurmountable. This practical possibility of effecting a delimitation of the respective rights is well demonstrated, for example, in the negotiations with a view to fixing the different countries' fishing quotas in the North-West Atlantic, and the agreements concerning fisheries in the region of the Faroe Isles (CR 74/3, pp. 48–55).

The conduct of the parties results from recognition of their respective interests. Study of the Exchanges of Notes of 1961, and the documents supplementary thereto (the Resolutions of 1948 and 1959), shows that the right unilaterally to declare an extension of jurisdiction, as reserved by Iceland, is not an absolute right. It requires justification. Extension is contemplated if it becomes necessary for reasons relating both to the conservation of fisheries and the needs of the Icelandic people. That reservation was accepted by the Applicant. Iceland for its part tacitly recognized the historical rights of the Applicant in 1961 and in 1972. There is thus mutual recognition of preferential rights and historic rights, coinciding with the present trends in practice, and with what writers have argued to be desirable.

In the *North Sea Continental Shelf* cases, the Court was in a situation which was to some extent analogous to the present situation, inasmuch as there was no mathematical rule to be applied to the delimitation of adjacent zones of the continental shelf. It did not follow from a denial that the equidistance rule was a legal rule that another 'single equivalent rule' had to be found. Failing a single rule enabling the areas to be

---

[29]   See also CR 74/1, pp. 82–3.

delimited, the Court stated that nonetheless 'there are still rules and principles of law to be applied' (*ICJ Reports 1969*, p. 46, para. 83).

When the General Assembly decided to convene the Conference on the Law of the Sea, it said that its purpose would be 'the establishment of an equitable international régime' (resolution 2750 C (XXV) of 17 December 1970). The Court applies 'equitable principles', which 'on a foundation of very general precepts of justice and good faith' lead to actual rules of law.

> It is not a question of applying equity simply as a matter of abstract justice, but of applying a rule of law which itself requires the application of equitable principles, in accordance with the ideas which have always underlain the development of the legal régime of the continental shelf in this field . . . (*ICJ Reports 1969*, pp. 46–7, para. 85.)

There is no need to demonstrate and prove what is a matter of general [100] knowledge and general recognition, namely the changes which have occurred in fishing techniques, the risk of exhaustion of fish stocks resulting therefrom, and the increasing protein requirements of ever more numerous populations.

9. It cannot be concealed that it is difficult to see how the concepts of special rights, preferential rights and historic rights can be brought under the heading of one of the sources of international law. It is not easy to prove the existence of a general practice accepted as law, nor would these concepts appear to form part of the general principles of law recognized by civilized nations. But it does appear possible to overcome the difficulty resulting from the unfortunate drafting of Article 38 of the Statute with the assistance of the teachings of the most highly qualified writers. One cannot make a sharp division between customary law and the principles of law. At the origin of the modern doctrine, in the historical school to which legal science owes the foundations of the theory of custom, they can be seen to be closely united. Savigny teaches us that practice (usages) is not the foundation of customary law, but that it is the sign by which the existence of a custom may be known. The custom is produced by the community of conviction, not by the will of men, whose acts only manifest this community of ideas.[30] This observation is still of assistance. In order to be binding as a legal rule, the general conviction (*opinio communis*) does not have to fulfil all the conditions necessary for the emergence of a custom. This is what explains the value of *opinio juris*, and why it may confer on one single act the possibility of becoming 'the starting point of the positive law' (*ICJ Reports 1969*, pp. 32–3).

[. . .]

---

[30] Savigny, *System des heutigen römischen Rechts* (1840), I, paras. 12 and 18. Puchta, *Pandekten*, para. 12, Fifth Edition (1850), p. 19; *Cursus der Institutionen*, I, para. 13, Ninth Edition (1881), pp. 18 and 19. The Court has referred to usages accepted as expressing principles of law: *PCIJ, Series A, No. 10* (1927), p. 18.

[103] *VI. Equitable solution*

[...]

[104] [...] For the purposes of the case now before the Court, no mathematical rule can be found which would enable the zone of exclusive fisheries jurisdiction to be delimited, but it should be observed that guidelines do exist for reaching an equitable delimitation. The special interest of Iceland in the adoption of measures for conservation of fish in the zone of the continental shelf, and in consideration being given in priority to the needs of its population and its industry, is recognized. On the other hand, so far as possible these rights must be reconciled with the historic interests or rights of the Applicant. The actual catch potential of each Party, without risk of exhaustion of the stock, must be considered. Provision should therefore be made for reserved zones, catch quotas, limitation on number of vessels, types of permitted vessels, size of mesh of nets, times of fishing, transition period, periodic revision of agreements, etc.

[...]

SEPARATE OPINION OF JUDGE SIR HUMPHREY WALDOCK (EXTRACT)

[...]

[109] 9. Similarly, the Convention on Fishing and Conservation of the Living Resources of the High Seas took a different approach to the conservation of fishery resources outside the territorial sea from that of the Law of 1948. Reflecting the approach of President Truman's fishery Proclamation rather than of the Icelandic Law, the Geneva Conference recognized that 'a coastal State has a special interest in the maintenance of the productivity of the living resources in any area of the high seas adjacent to its territorial sea', but did not allow any exclusive rights of jurisdiction to coastal States outside their territorial sea. Instead, it placed a general obligation on non-coastal States to enter into negotiations with the coastal State, at the latter's request, 'with a view to prescribing *by agreement* the measures necessary for the conservation of the living resources of the high seas in that area' (emphasis added). True, if such negotiations were requested by a coastal State and had not led to an agreement within six months, the Convention empowered the coastal State to adopt unilateral measures of conservation; but it did so only under strictly circumscribed conditions and pending the settlement of any disagreement as to their validity by a special commission. Thus, in this Convention the 1958 Conference left fishery conservation in waters outside the territorial sea essentially a matter to be agreed between the coastal State and any other States concerned and, in the event of disagreement, to be decided by an independent commission. In consequence, Iceland's Law of 1948 could equally not find its justification in the Convention on Fishing and Conservation of the Living Resources of the High Seas.

[...] 11. Two other developments at the 1958 Conference require to be noticed, since they contributed to shaping the course of the present dispute. The first is the emergence at the Conference of the concept of the preferential position of a coastal State whose people are specially dependent upon coastal fisheries. As paragraph

56 of the Judgment recalls, [110] although an Icelandic proposal embodying this concept failed to obtain the necessary majority, the Conference adopted a resolution concerning 'the situation of countries or territories whose people are overwhelmingly dependent on coastal fisheries for their livelihood or economic development'. This resolution, entitled 'Special Situations relating to Coastal Fisheries', recognized that 'such situations call for exceptional measures befitting particular needs', and made the recommendations which are set out in that paragraph of the Judgment. In such 'special situations' the resolution in effect advocated that, if catch-limitation becomes necessary for the purpose of conservation, non-coastal States should collaborate with the coastal State to establish agreed conservation measures which recognize such preferential requirements of the latter as result from its dependence on the fishery in question. Thus, even in the case of a State specially dependent on coastal fisheries, like Iceland, the resolution did not envisage the unilateral assumption of exclusive rights by the coastal State. On the other hand, it clearly did envisage that they should have a certain preference in the exploitation of the fisheries in adjacent areas of the high seas.

[. . .]

[111] [. . .] 15. The period between the 1958 and 1960 Conferences also saw the conclusion of a fishery conservation convention by 14 States interested in the fisheries of the North-East Atlantic. This was the North-East Atlantic Fisheries Convention of 24 January 1959, which embraced the Icelandic area and to which Iceland and the United Kingdom are parties.[31] The Convention set up for the North-East Atlantic Area a régime for the conservation and exploitation of fisheries, operated by a Fishery Commission and by Regional Committees and similar to the régime created a decade earlier for the North-West Atlantic by the North-West Atlantic Fishery Convention of 8 February 1949. The 1959 Convention is expressed to apply to all the waters situated within the North-East Atlantic area, but under Article 2 nothing in the Convention is to be 'deemed to affect the rights, claims or views of any contracting State in regard to the extent of jurisdiction over fisheries'.

[. . .]

[113] [. . .] 20. The negotiations continued with proposals and counter-proposals from each side. The Icelandic delegates insistently pressed for the reservation to Icelandic fishermen of certain areas even outside the 12-mile limit as being essential, in their view, to solve the problem of densely fished areas. The United Kingdom delegation no less insistently contested that view and objected that in the light of the scientific evidence concerning the fisheries, the reservation of areas outside the 12-mile limit could not be justified on grounds of conservation; while offering to examine together with the Icelandic delegation any proposals for conservation measures in particular areas or for policing regulations to avoid difficulties in any areas of more dense fishing, they declined to accede to Iceland's demand for reserved areas outside the 12-mile limit.

[. . .]

---

[31] As also is the Federal Republic of Germany, Applicant in the other *Fisheries Jurisdiction* case now before the Court.

[122] [. . .] 41. Although Iceland's primary objective has, no doubt, been to extend her exclusive fishery rights over more and more areas of the continental shelf, it does not seem to me justifiable to regard either the Law of 1948 or the Althing Resolution of 1959 as relating only to extensions of Iceland's exclusive fishery *limits* as the means for expanding her claims to the fishery resources of the continental shelf. Quite apart from the express reference to 'conservation' as the *motif* for the Law of 1948, it is clear not only from the proceedings of the 1958 and 1960 Conferences but also from the records of the 1960 negotiations that Iceland was ready to make use of any concept, and especially those of 'preferential rights' and 'conservation zones', as a means of furthering her fisheries objectives. Consequently, in my opinion, it would be altogether too narrow an interpretation of the compromissory clause to interpret the reference in it to the Althing Resolution of 1959 as confining the Court's competence to a dispute in relation to an extension of Iceland's exclusive fishery limits and nothing else. The compromissory clause itself does not refer to an extension of fishery *limits* but to an extension of fishery *jurisdiction*, a term apt to cover any form of an attempt by Iceland to extend her authority over fisheries outside the 12-mile limit.

[123] 42. In addition, as I have indicated, such a narrow interpretation does not seem consistent with the *travaux préparatoires* of the compromissory clause. Equally, it does not seem to me consistent with the Court's conclusion, in its Judgment of 2 February 1973, that:

> . . . the real intention of the parties was to give the United Kingdom Government an *effective* assurance . . . : namely, the right to challenge before the Court the validity of *any further extension of Icelandic fisheries jurisdiction in the waters above its continental shelf* . . . (*ICJ Reports 1973*, p. 13, para. 23; emphasis added).

If, instead of extending her exclusive fishery limit pure and simple, Iceland had introduced measures greatly to restrict, or render unprofitable, foreign fishing but in the guise of a 'preferential' or 'conservation' régime, it would make nonsense of the 'effective assurance' – the '*sine qua non* of the whole agreement' in the Exchange of Notes – to interpret it as not covering such measures. Nor should it be overlooked that the 'extension of fisheries jurisdiction' effected by Iceland's 1972 Regulations was in fact expressed in those Regulations to be an application of the Law of 1948 concerning '*Scientific Conservation* of the Continental Shelf Fisheries'. Consequently, it seems to me evident that the Court's competence must be understood as covering questions of preferential rights and conservation, and more especially when raised in direct connection with a dispute in relation to an extension of Iceland's zone of exclusive fisheries.

*

43. There remains, however, the question whether the present 'dispute' does involve the questions of preferential rights and conservation. I share the view of the Court that, although occasioned by Iceland's unilateral extension of her fishery jurisdiction, the present dispute at the same time clearly includes differences regarding those matters. This seems to me sufficiently established by the account of the dispute given

in paragraphs 17–29 of the United Kingdom's Memorial on the merits which show that the differences between the Parties were not limited to the question of the validity of the extension of the exclusive fishery zone, as such, but involved Iceland's claims to exclusive fishery limits *by reason of her right to preferential treatment* and her claims to be entitled to take *unilateral* conservation measures.

[. . .]

[125] [. . .] 45. A 'dispute', as has frequently been said both by the Permanent Court of International Justice and by this Court,[32] is: 'a disagreement on a point of law or fact, a conflict of legal views or of interests between two persons'. In the present instance it seems to me clear that the 'disagreement on a point of law' and the 'conflict of legal views or of interests', though occasioned by Iceland's extension of her fishery limit, included disagreements and conflicts as to whether Iceland's right to preferential treatment entitled her to exclusive fishery rights, whether exclusive rights may be claimed in the name of conservation, whether conservation measures may be taken unilaterally and whether Iceland's claims should prevail over the United Kingdom's traditional rights in the waters in dispute. Accordingly, I think the Court fully justified in concluding that these issues form an integral part of a dispute *in relation to an extension of fisheries jurisdiction around Iceland* within the meaning of the compromissory clause.

[. . .]

DISSENTING OPINION OF JUDGE GROS (EXTRACT)

[*Translation*]

[136] [. . .] 16. Going beyond the events of 1961, it should be added that analysis of Iceland's position on the fisheries problem for the last quarter-century and more leads to the conclusion that that State has unremittingly advanced, and secured recognition of, the view that claims as to the extent of the fishery zone were entirely distinct from problems of conservation. Thus under the North-West Atlantic Fisheries Convention of 8 February 1949 (Art. I, para. 2), and then under the North-East Atlantic Fisheries Convention of 24 January 1959, Iceland was to be one of the parties which attached the greatest importance to the formal reservation that those conventions did not affect the rights, claims, or views of any contracting State in regard to the extent of jurisdiction over fisheries.

[. . .]

17. Subparagraph 3 of the operative clause of the Judgment contains a decision that there is an obligation to negotiate between Iceland and the United Kingdom 'for the equitable solution of their differences concerning their respective fishery rights . . . ', and subparagraph 4 indicates various considerations as guidelines for such negotiations. I consider that the role of the Court does not permit of it giving a

---

[32] E.g., *Mavrommatis Palestine Concessions* case, *PCIJ Series A, No. 2*, at p. 11; *Right of Passage over Indian Territory* case, *ICJ Reports 1960* at p. 34.

pronouncement on these two points, and that by doing so, the Court has exceeded the bounds of its jurisdiction.

[**137**] 18. Subparagraph 3 refers to differences concerning the 'respective' fishery rights of the two States. There are of course differences, since Iceland is claiming to exclude the United Kingdom finally from the area up to 50 miles, but this claim is made *erga omnes*, and it is somewhat unreal to treat as a bilateral problem, capable of being bilaterally resolved, the effects of the Icelandic Regulations of 14 July 1972 asserting exclusive jurisdiction over the superjacent waters of the continental shelf, after having declined to reply to the question raised as to the unlawfulness of such Regulations in international law. Although in subparagraph 4 there are formal safeguards for the position of the other States, the Court has regarded it as possible, to isolate, as it were, the bilateral differences and settle them by the Judgment. This is the first point that I should deal with before turning to the substance of subparagraphs 3 and 4 of the operative clause of the Judgment.

19. The origin of these subparagraphs 3 and 4 of the operative clause is in the last part of the United Kingdom's submissions (final submission *(d)*) which gave the dispute a wider dimension than the sole question of the lawfulness of the unilateral extension of jurisdiction, and on the basis of that submission problems of conservation have been extensively discussed in argument. But the bounds of a judgment are not fixed by a party in its Application, nor in its final submissions, nor, *a fortiori*, in its argument, when the jurisdiction being exercised is one specially laid down by a treaty, with a view to bringing before the Court a precise question of law. Particularly when the other Party is absent from the proceedings, the Court cannot simultaneously decline to reply to the joint request for a declaratory judgment which was indisputably made in the 1961 agreement, and decide what the conditions shall be of negotiations over conservation as to which no-one but the Applicant has ever asked its opinion, since it should be remembered that according to Iceland there are 11 States regularly fishing in the waters around Iceland (cf. *Fisheries Jurisdiction in Iceland*, Reykjavik, February 1972, table 1, p. 14). As for the United Kingdom, its counsel, in reply to a question on 29 March 1974, stated that in the United Kingdom's pleadings, the only States which were regarded as interested or affected or concerned by the question of fisheries around Iceland were those which have in the past fished in that area, that is to say, apart from the United Kingdom and Iceland, the Federal Republic of Germany, the Faroes, Belgium and Norway. Thus questions also arose as to the nature of the interest in the fisheries of the geographical area in question, which the Judgment neither takes into account nor resolves.

20. It is now some considerable time ago that attention was drawn to the difficulties which result from submissions being drafted both as a restatement of the arguments in support of the claim and as the final definition of what the Court is asked to decide (cf. 'Quelques mots sur les "conclusions" en procédure internationale', J. Basdevant, *Mélanges Tomaso Perassi*, p. 175). The present case affords a fresh example of this. The Court, which is the sole judge of its jurisdiction, must therefore sort [**138**] out what in the submissions is a statement of arguments and what is the precise statement

of the claim; the claim cannot go beyond the subject of the jurisdiction conferred upon the Court, and that jurisdiction was limited to a declaratory decision as to the conformity of Iceland's unilateral extension of jurisdiction from 12 to 50 miles with existing international law on 1 September 1972, the date on which the Icelandic Regulations were brought into force.

21. If one reads the second submission in the United Kingdom's Application it is apparent that the second part thereof was so drafted that it could not constitute a claim, but merely an argument in support of the first part of that submission, by which the Court was asked to declare that questions of conservation cannot be regulated by a unilateral extension of limits to 50 miles, as a sort of consequence of the declaration asked for as to the non-conformity of the Icelandic regulations with general international law, in the first submission of the United Kingdom. The submission continues with the following:

> [questions of conservation] are matters that may be regulated, as between Iceland and the United Kingdom, by arrangements agreed between those two countries, *whether or not together with other interested countries* and whether in the form of arrangements reached in accordance with the North-East Atlantic Fisheries Convention of 24 January, 1959, or in the form of arrangements for collaboration in accordance with the Resolution on Special Situations relating to Coastal Fisheries of 26 April, 1958, *or otherwise in the form of arrangements agreed between them* that give effect to the continuing rights and interests of both of them in the fisheries of the waters in question (Application, para. 21; emphasis added).

A further version of this submission was given in the Memorial on the merits (reproduced in para. 11 of the Judgment) where the obligation to negotiate appears formally expressed, and was to be maintained as a final submission. The Court would have exhausted its jurisdiction by saying, in reply to the first part of the submission, that questions of conservation cannot be regulated by a unilateral extension of limits to 50 miles and a claim by Iceland to exclusive jurisdiction in that zone.

How could such a general question of law as conservation involving at least 11 fishing States be judicially settled 'between Iceland and the United Kingdom ... whether or not together with other interested countries'? While it was possible in 1961 for Iceland and the United Kingdom to agree on an assurance against any fresh extension of jurisdiction, the effect of which would be suspended as between those two States by recourse to the Court, it is not reasonable to imagine that a system of conservation of marine resources concerning 11 States could be worked out by two of them. The importance of the United Kingdom's interest in the fisheries around Iceland is recognized. But the question put to the Court is not the equitable sharing of the resources of these fisheries, a suggestion analogous to that which the Court rejected in its [139] Judgment with regard to the delimitation of the continental shelf of the North Sea (*ICJ Reports 1969*, p. 13, para. 2, and pp. 21 to 23, paras. 18 to 20), from which Judgment I would adopt the expression that in the present case, there is nothing 'undivided to share out' between the United Kingdom and Iceland. The idea of the 'respective' fishing rights is not a correct description of the position in fact and in law. The legal status of the fisheries between 12 and 50 miles from Iceland can only be an objective status, which takes account of the interests of all States fishing in those waters. Further, the problems of 'fishing rights' in the waters around Iceland have been under study for a considerable time with the States concerned, and Iceland has recognized the need to resolve those problems with such States, as has also the United Kingdom.

22. On 22 July 1972 – at the height of the Iceland fishery crisis and one week after the promulgation of the Icelandic Regulations of 14 July 1972 which constitute the act impugned in the United Kingdom Application – there was signed in Brussels an agreement between the European Economic Community and Iceland in order to 'consolidate and to extend . . . the economic relations existing between the Community and Iceland'. The first article relates that 'the aim is to foster in the Community and in Iceland the advance of economic activity [and] the improvement of living and employment conditions'. The agreement applies to fish products (Art. 2), to which a Protocol No. 6 is specially devoted; Article 2 of that Protocol provides:

> The Community reserves the right not to apply the provisions of this Protocol *if a solution satisfactory to the Member States of the Community and to Iceland has not been found for the economic problems arising from the measures adopted by Iceland concerning fishing rights.* (Emphasis added.)

In application of this Article 2 of Protocol No. 6, and at the request or with the approval of member States of the Community (including the United Kingdom and the Federal Republic of Germany), although the agreement with Iceland had come into force on 1 April 1973, the implementation of the Protocol on Icelandic fish products has already been postponed five times, the last time on 1 April 1974. To prevent Iceland from benefiting from a customs arrangement granted it by a treaty because there is an unsettled dispute over 'fishing rights' is, to say the least, to declare oneself concerned or affected by that dispute. Thus the European Economic Community has five times declared its direct interest in coming to a settlement regarding fishing rights in the waters round Iceland by refusing to grant Iceland the implementation of the special tariff provisions laid down in the agreement of 22 July 1972. This agreement is moreover mentioned in the *White Book* on the fishing dispute published by the British Government in June 1973 (*Cmnd 5341*): the reference occurs in paragraph 22, immediately following a paragraph on Anglo-German co-operation, and we read:

> [140] It will be for the Community to declare when a satisfactory solution to the fisheries dispute has been achieved and, consequently, when to decide that the terms of the Protocol should take effect.

23. The common interest evinced by the member States of the European Economic Community, and the terms of Article 2, paragraph 1, of the above-cited Protocol No. 6, alike show that these States are not indifferent to the elaboration of a régime for fisheries in the waters round Iceland. For its part, Iceland, by accepting the agreement and Protocol No. 6, has recognized the interest of the European Economic Community

in the settlement of the question of fishing rights. Thus the memorandum explaining the grounds of the first proposal to postpone implementation of Protocol No. 6, submitted by the Commission to the Council on 20 March 1973, refers to the 'economic problems arising from the measures adopted by Iceland concerning fishing rights' for the member States of the Community. This position of Iceland vis-à-vis the EEC may usefully be compared with that of Norway in its agreement of 14 May 1973 with the EEC, which came into force on 1 July 1973: the concessions granted therein by the EEC will only be valid provided Norway respects 'fair conditions of competition'; on 16 April 1973, the date when the agreement was initialled, the Commission indicated that all the tariff-reductions granted on certain fish products of Norwegian origin had been agreed to subject to the continued observance of the existing conditions of overall competition in the fishing sector, which covers the eventuality of any unilateral extension of the fishery zone.

As is well known, the member States of the European Community constitute a majority in the North-East Altantic Fisheries Commission; what is more, an observer of the Community as such takes part in its work, as is also the case of the North-West Atlantic Fisheries Commission. The catch-quotas of the participant Community members could, according to a proposal made by the Commission of the Communities to the Council, be negotiated and administered on a Community basis.

24. Now an agreement whereby Iceland formally accepts that treaty provisions of undoubted economic importance for that country should be suspended for so long as the problem of the economic difficulties arising out of the measures it has taken in respect of fishing rights remains unresolved would appear to constitute a recognition by Iceland and the EEC of an obligation to negotiate. The negotiations concern the economic consequences of Iceland's claim to exclusive fisheries jurisdiction, and the context of the negotiations is no longer, directly, fishing rights; but what the EEC understood in an analogous situation has been seen in the instance of Norway, and the distinction should not be over-nicely drawn. The question of fishing rights is necessarily affected by any decision regarding the economic consequences, whatever solution is reached for dealing with the economic consequences and whatever the chosen method; but the debate is one of wider scope, and extends to [141] general economic relations between all the countries concerned. While the Court, in sub-paragraph 4 of the operative part of the Judgment, has not sought to define more than the conservation aspect of fishing rights in the prescriptions directed to the United Kingdom and Iceland, the working-documents of the Community accurately convey an all-round picture of the various aspects of the problem of fishing in the waters round Iceland. One more example: a Danish memorandum on fishing submitted to the Council on 20 March 1973 recommends, after reviewing the problem of regions almost wholly dependent on fishing (Greenland, the Faroes), special measures of both a structural and a regional nature.

By finding, in the Judgment, that there is a bilateral obligation to negotiate concerning 'respective' rights of a bilateral character, when Iceland has accepted a multilateral obligation to negotiate on much wider bases in institutions and international bodies which do not come within the purview of the Court's jurisdiction, the Court has formulated an obligation which is devoid of all useful application.

25. The necessity of dealing with the problem of fisheries in the waters round Iceland comprehensively and with those States particularly interested is also accentuated by the fact that certain States have concluded agreements of an interim character with Iceland, as the United Kingdom did on 13 November 1973, in order to mitigate the difficulties caused them by the application of the Icelandic Regulations of 14 July 1972. The first negotiations were conducted with the local government of the Faroe Islands and enabled fishermen from these islands to fish within the 50-mile limit (Reykjavik agreements of 15–16 August on bottom-line and handline fishing and of 19 September 1972 on trawl fishing). A Danish *Note verbale* of 23 August 1972 states that 'questions concerning fishing in the North Atlantic should ... be settled in an international context' and expresses the hope that negotiations 'with the Parties whose interests are threatened by the new Icelandic regulations may be resumed as quickly as possible' (cited in *Revue générale de droit international public*, 1974, pp. 343 f.).[33]

Belgium, on 7 September 1972, concluded with Iceland an agreement which was renewed for 18 months in March 1974; Article 1 reserves the position of the parties on the extent of fisheries jurisdiction, but when the text was transmitted to the Council of the European Communities, the following indication was given: 'the Belgian Government considers that so far as Belgium is concerned, this agreement constitutes a satisfactory, albeit temporary solution within the meaning of Article 2 of Protocol No. 6 to the EEC–Icelandic Agreement of 22 July 1972'. Another agreement was concluded with Norway on 10 July 1973. These agreements, even when they reserve the legal position of each of the States vis-à-vis Iceland, necessarily take account of the 1972 Regulations which are the source of the dispute, and Iceland doubtless views them as provisional accommodations of very limited duration which have been made pending [142] the general acceptance of its claim. (The agreement of 19 September 1972 concluded with the Faroes is subject to denunciation by Iceland at any time, while it may denounce that of 15–16 August at six months' notice.) Hence all one may deduce therefrom is an affirmation of the interest of those States in reaching an objective solution of the problem. These agreements, added to the treaty with the EEC which one of them mentions, give concrete support to the dual conclusion that there exists a group of specially interested States concerning which the Court has no means of knowing what intentions they may have of negotiating with a view to establishing an objective fisheries régime, and that it has no jurisdiction to lay down the law to them, not even by way of directions for negotiation. The failure of all these bilateral negotiations to arrive at anything other than phasing-out agreements which leave the substantive problem aside shows that the situation will be resolved solely by a multilateral agreement corresponding to the objective character of the régime desired.

---

[33] Quotations translated from French by the Registry.

26. It was not a series of accidents which caused these problems to be considered successively under the auspices of the OEEC (in 1956, in order to put an end to the difficulties of landing Icelandic fish catches in British ports) and of NATO (informal talks in 1958 between representatives of Iceland, the United Kingdom, the Federal Republic of Germany and France), before being raised in the framework of the European Economic Community and the treaty of 1972, but the recognition of the objective character of the régime of these fisheries.

If a bilateral agreement with Iceland was possible in 1961, that was because the essential content of that agreement consisted of the United Kingdom's recognition of the 12-mile limit; but in the last portion of the operative part of its Judgment the Court passes upon a question regarding a fisheries régime for the conservation of resources, and there is nothing bilateral about that. Iceland pointed this out in clear terms to the United Kingdom during the London conversations of 3 and 4 November 1971 (United Kingdom Memorial on the merits, para. 23) before enacting its 1972 Regulations: Iceland's purpose was to protect its fishing industry against massive competition by 'super-trawlers' from Spain, Portugal, Poland, the USSR and Japan and to facilitate the planned expansion of Iceland's own fishing industry (it will be noted that Iceland here adds three States, to the eleven listed in paragraph 19 above, but, in any event, the circle of States concerned is not unlimited even if such variations are to be found; it is thus wholly irrelevant to look into the claims of States which are equally far removed from the Iceland fishery area and Iceland's preoccupations). Iceland has wider aims than conservation. A review of Iceland's economic problems seen in relation to an extension of fisheries jurisdiction is to be found in the already-quoted OECD report of 1972 (in particular, pp. 32–9). As the Court did not touch upon this aspect of the situation, I will simply say that any tribunal that wished to study the régime of Iceland's fisheries would have found it indispensable to consider these problems; it is not sufficient to say in general [143] terms that Iceland is dependent on its coastal fisheries 'for its livelihood, and economic development' if no attempt is made to grasp the economic realities underlying the phrase. Indeed, for want of all research on the point, the Court's pronouncement constitutes simply an abstract reply to an abstract question. Even from the standpoint adopted by the Court, whereby a problem of objective régime may purportedly be resolved by means of bilateral negotiations, the question should have been placed within its true dimensions, these being of wider scope than conservation procedure, which, in the unique case of Iceland, is probably not the only factor capable of reconciling the legitimate interests that stand confronted (cf. para. 31 below).

27. The obligation to negotiate in the present case does not originate in a kind of general undertaking drawn from Article 33 of the Charter, which is above all a list of means of settlement; this theory makes of the obligation to negotiate a universal but an uncertain remedy, since when negotiations take place without a specific objective the Parties necessarily remain free to appraise their desirability and the necessity of their success. [. . .]

The source of the obligation to negotiate in this case is the legal nature of the fisheries régime which is the subject of the dispute, and that can only be actualized by means of negotiation among all the States concerned; it is there, solely, that the Court could have found the answer to the question it had chosen to ask itself and discovered that it could not incorporate it into its decision but at most give it a place in the reasoning of the judgment.

28. To conclude my observations on subparagraphs 3 and 4 of the operative part: by virtue of the interpretation placed on the 1961 agreement and the negotiations that enabled it to be concluded (see in particular [**144**] paras. 25 and 47 of the Judgment) the Court considers that Iceland has agreed to the inclusion of problems of conservation (zones and methods), preferential rights and historic rights within the categories of dispute which it might find the Court adjudicating. I have already indicated that it appeared to me to be an unwavering constant of Icelandic policy always to distinguish problems of conservation and preferential rights from the problem of the extension of fisheries jurisdiction (para. 16 above) and that the 1961 agreement was one of the proofs of this. If this position had shifted in 1961, why is there nothing in the records to reveal as much? Yet what would have been the concession in point? – the recognition that, in relation to any extension beyond the 12-mile limit of the exclusive fishery zone, any problems of conservation or preferential and historic rights might also be referred to adjudication as elements of a dispute over the extension of the zone. I must say that I find this improbable in the absence of any formal admission on the part of Iceland and considering its constant attitude of opposition to all confusion of problems concerning the breadth of the exclusive fishery zone with problems of the fishery régime beyond that zone.

[...]

[**146**] [...] 31. Since a dissenting or separate opinion should be kept within limits, I will not deal with other points on which I also disagree with the Judgment, – with the exception of one of these. The invocation of the Judgment in the *North Sea Continental Shelf* cases to support the present decision, with regard to the recognition of a bilateral obligation to negotiate and the reference to equity in paragraphs 75 and 78 of the Judgment and in the final part of the operative clause, is unjustified. The present legal position is quite distinct, since it was the special agreements which had decided that the task of actually fixing the boundaries should be reserved to the Parties, who undertook to do so 'on the basis of, and in accordance with, the principles and rules of international law found by the Court to be applicable' (*ICJ Reports 1969*, p. 13, para. 2 of the Judgment). Thus in 1969 the Court did exactly the opposite of what it has done today, when instead of giving a judicial statement of the state of international law on the subject, and leaving the application thereof to the Parties, the Judgment disregards the obligation to state the law, and falls back on an obligation to negotiate which was not provided for in the 1961 agreement by the two States. Furthermore, in 1969 the delimitation of the continental shelf only concerned the three States which were Parties before the Court, and they alone were competent to effect it. That is not the case here for the matters which the Court has sought to resolve in subparagraph

4 of the operative clause: that is, the bilateral organization of a fishery conservation régime while there is a multilateral obligation to negotiate.

Since I also attach particular importance to the question of equity, I would recall that the Court on that occasion took the greatest possible precautions in its drafting specifically in order to prevent its observations being treated as of general application. The inequity of the geographical [147] situation was simple, and was the result of the natural configuration of the coast; the adjustment involved a single operation, which was also simple, namely, as just a modification as possible of the boundary. The fisheries situation of Iceland is quite unrelated to this, since it involves interests which are of their nature extremely diverse; to inject the concept of equity into a recommendation of negotiations is not sufficient to make it applicable, because of the circumstance, which is unique in the world, of the absolute economic dependence of a State on fisheries. 'Equality is to be reckoned within the same plane, and it is not such natural inequalities as these that equity could remedy' (*ICJ Reports 1969*, p. 50, para. 91). To hold the balance between the economic survival of a people and the interests of the fishing industry of other States raises a problem of the balanced economic development of all, according to economic criteria, in which fishing is only one of the elements taken into account, and of which the bases are international interdependence and solidarity. The concepts of rate of economic growth, industrial diversification, vulnerability of an economy faced with the 'caprices' of nature, population structure and growth, use of energy, investment needs, development of external markets for fish products, regularization of such markets, foreign participation in Icelandic undertakings, industrial development funds, among many others, define the economic interests of Iceland in obtaining a certain settlement of the fisheries problem. Not merely have these expressions never been used, but it is clear that differences of views on these questions do not give rise to justiciable disputes, since these are problems of economic interests which are not the concern of the Court. But the Court cannot make them disappear by refusing to see anything but a conservation problem; the balance of facts and interests is broken.

32. In effect the Judgment decides that Iceland did not have the right to extend its fisheries limits from 12 to 50 miles on grounds of conservation, which will be generally conceded, but this is to choose a ground which is not that of Iceland, after having avoided deciding that, in the present state of existing law, the extension to 50 miles is not opposable to the fishing States, whatever ground may be relied on for such an extension, including the interests of Iceland as it has explained them; but to disregard a line of argument amounts to rejecting it. Then, sticking to this single theme of conservation, the Court constructs for the two parties to a dispute a system of consultation on conservation problems as if the solution of these could take the place of the only decision which was contemplated in 1961, namely that on the lawfulness of any fresh extension of limits beyond 12 miles. To respond to a

dispute over a claim to exclusive jurisdiction by giving guidelines for a conservation agreement is not a fulfilment of the Court's task; even if the Court thought that the question raised under the agreement was too narrow, it is the question which was [**148**] defined by the parties. An agreement can never define anything other than what was subject to negotiation at the appropriate time between the parties who concluded it; as the Court has said: 'no party can impose its terms on the other party' *(ICJ Reports 1950*, p. 139). Nor can a court impose its interpretation of an agreement on the States which concluded it, so as to make it say something more than, or something different from, what it says. Here again the Court has already spoken:

> ... though it is certain that the Parties, being free to dispose of their rights, might ... embody in their agreement any provisions they might devise ..., it in no way follows that the Court enjoys the same freedom; as this freedom, being contrary to the proper functions of the Court, could in any case only be enjoyed by it if such freedom resulted from a clear and explicit provision ... *(Free Zones of Upper Savoy and the District of Gex, Order of 6 December 1930, PCIJ, Series A, No. 24*, p. 11).

33. By centring its decision around problems of conservation which are not the subject of the dispute which arose in 1972 as a result of Iceland's extension of its fisheries jurisdiction from 12 to 50 miles, the Court has raised an abstract question to which it has given, in the last part of the operative clause of the Judgment, an abstract reply. In contentious cases, the Court is bound by what it is asked to adjudge; when it applies Article 53 of the Statute, the rule is still stricter, since the Court must satisfy itself that it is not going further or in a direction other than what was agreed to by the State which is absent from the proceedings, in the instrument which established the competence of the tribunal. Thus the Court observed in the *Ambatielos* case that: 'in the absence of a clear agreement between the Parties ... the Court has no jurisdiction to go into all the merits of the present case' *(ICJ Reports 1952*, p. 39); the least that can be said is that the problems of conservation were not the subject of such discussion in 1960 between the United Kingdom and Iceland, and that it is difficult to see by what unequivocal agreement it could have become a dispute in itself under the Exchange of Notes of 1961.

34. The Court has not fulfilled its mission in the present case, since it has not decided the legal question which the Parties to the 1961 agreement had envisaged laying before it, for purposes which they were free to decide upon, and since it has dealt with the problem of the conservation of Icelandic fisheries as being the substance of the dispute. Such a judgment cannot therefore be effective for the settlement of the real substantive dispute, even if there were an intention to achieve this, as appears from paragraph 48 and from certain covert allusions in the text.

The real task of the Court is still to 'decide in accordance with international law such disputes as are submitted to it' (Art. 38 of the Statute). To introduce into international relations an idea that the decisions of the Court may be given according to what on each occasion the majority thought to be both just and convenient, would be to effect a profound transformation. It will be sufficient to quote the Court itself:

[149] Having thus defined ... the legal relations between the Parties ..., the Court has completed its task. It is unable to give any practical advice as to the various courses which might be followed with a view to terminating the asylum, since, by doing so, it would depart from its judicial function. But it can be assumed that the Parties, now that their mutual legal relations have been made clear, will be able to find a practical ... solution ... (*ICJ Reports 1951*, p. 83.)

That this new concept must be rejected as in contradiction with the role of an international tribunal appears to me to be clear, simply from the observation that an international court is not a federal tribunal; the States – of which there are now not many – which come before the Court do not do so to receive advice, but to obtain judicial confirmation of the treaty commitments which they have entered into, according to established international law, in relation to a situation with which they are well acquainted. The Court saw all this in the Judgment in the *Fisheries* case, in which the special nature of the situation was the dominant feature in the decision (*ICJ Reports 1951, Judgment of 18 December 1951*); by seeking to effect, under cover of a case limited to Icelandic fisheries, a pronouncement of universal effect, the Court contradicts its whole previous attitude. As long ago as 1963, Charles De Visscher wrote in his commentary on judicial interpretation:

> The function of interpretation is not to perfect a legal instrument with a view to adapting it more or less precisely to what one may be tempted to envisage as the full realisation of an objective which was logically postulated, but to shed light on what was in fact the will of the Parties.

There could be no better response to the philosophy which inspires the Judgment and the postulates it contains (particularly paras. 44–8).

DISSENTING OPINION OF JUDGE PETRÉN (EXTRACT)

[*Translation*]
[151] [...] While the documentation placed at the Court's disposal shows that the dispute concerns the breadth of fishery zone which Iceland is entitled to claim, there is on the other hand nothing to indicate any disagreement between the Parties as to the principles which should govern the regulation, in the waters adjacent to the fishery zone and in a framework of agreed conservation measures, of the relationships between the preferential rights of Iceland as the coastal State and the rights of other States whose vessels fish in the same region. [...]

[152] [...] [I]t is not in my view possible to say that recognition of the United Kingdom's historic rights in the area now in dispute was covered by the agreement of 1961, where they are not even mentioned. [...] But there is no basis in the 1961 agreement for the Court to broach questions concerning certain historic rights of the United Kingdom and measures of conservation without first settling the question of the limits of Iceland's fishery zone.

[...]

[154] [. . .] Without settling the question whether the recent extension by Iceland of its fishery zone is in conformity with international law, the Court finds that it is not opposable to the United Kingdom on account of the latter's historic rights, and that it is necessary to establish, within a framework of agreed measures of conservation, a régime wherein these historic rights will be balanced against the preferential rights of Iceland as the coastal State. The Court therefore considers itself competent to pronounce upon questions of preferential and historic rights and measures of conservation in the disputed waters independently of any consideration of the basis, if any, in international law of an extension of Iceland's fishery zone. At the same time the Court creates an obligation upon the Parties to undertake negotiations on these points while taking into consideration a series of recommendations enunciated in the Judgment. Yet these are matters which, if they concern waters outside the fishery zones of coastal States, require by their very nature to be regulated on a multilateral basis with the participation of all those States whose interests are at stake. There are international instruments which provide procedures to that end without envisaging reference to the Court. So far as the North-East Atlantic is concerned, the Federal Republic of Germany is the only State, apart from the United Kingdom, to have expressed any desire that the Court should deal with such questions, but the Court, by deciding not to join the parallel cases instituted by these two States, deprived itself of the possibility of prescribing joint negotiations between them and Iceland.

In its Judgment of 2 February 1973 the Court found that the 1961 agreement was still in force. Iceland will doubtless be inclined to maintain the extension of its fishery zone, since the Court has declared it unlawful only vis-à-vis the United Kingdom and – by its Judgment in the other case – the Federal Republic of Germany. Hence the possibility must be foreseen of further disputes between the Parties over the exercise of their rights in the belt between the 12-mile and the 50-mile limit. It is also possible that disputes may arise between the Parties over the interpretation or application of the guidelines laid down by the Court for the conduct of the negotiations it has directed them to undertake. As the Judgment shows that the Court, by considering it could leave aside the question of the conformity with international law of Iceland's extension of its fishery zone, regards itself as competent to deal with questions of fishing rights and conservation measures beyond the 12-mile limit, there is no escaping the conclusion that, according to the logic of the Judgment, a [155] whole series of disputes born of the situation created by the Judgment would be referable to the Court.

In the light of the foregoing considerations, I am of the view that in the present Judgment the Court has considerably exceeded the jurisdiction conferred upon it by the 1961 agreement.

[. . .]

[159][. . .] However, in subparagraphs 3 and 4 of the operative part of the Judgment, the Court finds that the Parties are under mutual obligations to undertake negotiations concerning their respective fishery rights in the disputed area, negotiations in which

they must take into account *inter alia* certain preferential rights attributable to Iceland. As the Court's jurisdiction to deal with the present case is founded solely on the jurisdictional clause of the 1961 Exchange of Notes, and as that clause concerns only the question whether a future extension by Iceland of its zone of exclusive fisheries jurisdiction would be in conformity with international law, I consider that the Court, by imposing on the Parties an obligation to negotiate in respect of something else, has exceeded the limits of its jurisdiction.

But that is not the only reason why I consider that the Court is not competent to prescribe negotiations between the Parties.

[. . .]

[162] [. . .] For the foregoing reasons I consider that the submissions put forward and maintained by the United Kingdom should have been rejected as without object, except in relation to the period between Iceland's implementation of the extension of its zone of exclusive fisheries jurisdiction up to the 50-mile limit (1 September 1972) and the coming into force of the interim agreement between the Parties (13 November 1973). Considering as I do that the measure decided by Iceland was without foundation in international law, I find that its application to British fishing vessels during the above-mentioned period constituted an infringement of international law vis-à-vis the United Kingdom. In the light of the considerations I have put forward above, this finding does not mean that, on the termination of the interim agreement concluded between the Parties on 13 November 1973, the extension of Iceland's fishery zone should automatically be considered as still inconsistent with international law.

[. . .]

[164] DISSENTING OPINION OF JUDGE ONYEAMA (EXTRACT)

1. Although I agree that the Regulations concerning the Fishery Limits off Iceland (*Reglugerð um fiskveiðilandhelgi Íslands*) promulgated by the Government of Iceland on 14 July 1972, and constituting a unilateral extension of the exclusive fishing rights of Iceland to 50 nautical miles from the baselines specified therein are not opposable to the Government of the United Kingdom; and, although I agree also that, in consequence, the Government of Iceland is not entitled unilaterally to exclude United Kingdom fishing vessels from areas to seaward of the fishery limits agreed to in the Exchange of Notes of 11 March 1961 or unilaterally to impose restrictions on the activities of those vessels in such areas, my reasons for reaching these conclusions are so fundamentally different from those of the Court that I feel unable to vote for the first part of the operative clause of the Judgment for the reasons given by the Court. For the rest of the Judgment, it is my view that the Court settled an issue on which the Parties were not in dispute. In my view the Court's approach to the entire case has led it to refrain from deciding the sole dispute before it, and to consider and settle an issue on which the Parties were not shown to be in difference and on which the Court's jurisdiction is very much in doubt.

[. . .]

[166] [. . .] 6. Throughout these negotiations the question of Iceland's preferential rights or of conservation was not discussed, although the United Kingdom delegation, on a number of occasions, suggested that it might consider restrictions on fishing by the United Kingdom outside the 12-mile zone during the phasing-out period yet to be agreed on, if such restrictions were shown to be necessary in the interests of conservation. The Icelandic delegation did not take up these suggestions, and left no doubt that outside the 12-mile zone its long-term aim remained the extension of Iceland's exclusive fishery jurisdiction. [. . .]

[167] [. . .] 9. In these negotiations preceding the Exchange of Notes, no mention was made of the need for conservation of the fish-stocks around Iceland nor of Iceland's preferential rights as matters on which either of the parties required assurances then or thereafter. These matters were not discussed at all as they were not the problems created by the proposed extension of Iceland's exclusive fishery jurisdiction from 4 miles to 12 miles in 1958.

[. . .]

[169] [. . .] 13. The discussions which followed between the United Kingdom and Iceland in an effort to find a 'practical solution to the problem' did not alter the nature of the claim Iceland was making nor the nature of the dispute. The suggestions by the United Kingdom for mutually agreed conservation measures as a solution to the problem of possible injury to fish stocks in the area, and for limitation of the catch of demersal fish as an interim measure pending the elaboration of a multilateral agreement within the North-East Atlantic Fisheries Commission, were not accepted by Iceland which was concerned to maintain the exclusive character of its **[170]** claim to the fishery in the area, while it remained ready to consider practical arrangements under which British ships might be permitted, subject to certain conditions, to continue to fish in the area in question for a limited phase-out period. It evinced no interest in the question of its preferential rights or conservation measures in the area as a possible answer to its claim.

14. In the jurisdiction phase of the present case, the Court considered what the issue before it was, and said:

> Account must also be taken of the fact that the Applicant has contended before the Court that to the extent that Iceland may, as a coastal State specially dependent on coastal fisheries for its livelihood or economic development, assert a need to procure the establishment of a special fisheries conservation régime (including such a régime under which it enjoys preferential rights) in the waters adjacent to its coast but beyond the exclusive fisheries zone provided for by the 1961 Exchange of Notes, it can legitimately pursue that objective by collaboration and agreement with the other countries concerned, but not by the unilateral arrogation of exclusive rights within those waters. *The exceptional dependence of Iceland on its fisheries and the principle of conservation of fish stocks having been recognized, the question remains as to whether Iceland is or is not competent unilaterally to assert an exclusive fisheries jurisdiction extending beyond the 12-mile limit. The issue before the Court in the present phase of the proceedings concerns solely its jurisdiction to determine the latter point.* (Emphasis added.) (*ICJ Reports 1973*, p. 20, para. 42.)[34]

[34 See pp. 24–5 above.]

This 'latter point' was covered in the first submission of the United Kingdom in its Application.

15. Regarding the second submission in the Application the Court, in the jurisdiction phase, dealt with it in paragraphs 41 and 42 of the Judgment. Paragraph 41 is as follows:

> It should be observed in this connection that the exceptional dependence of Iceland on its fisheries for its subsistence and economic development is expressly recognized in the 1961 Exchange of Notes, and the Court, in its Order of 17 August 1972, stated that 'it is also necessary to bear in mind the exceptional dependence of the Icelandic nation upon coastal fisheries for its livelihood and economic development as expressly recognized by the United Kingdom in its Note addressed to the Foreign Minister of Iceland dated 11 March 1961'. The Court further stated that 'from this point of view account must be taken of the need for the conservation of fish stocks in the Iceland area'. (*ICJ Reports 1972*, pp. 16 and 17.) This point is not disputed. (*ICJ Reports 1973*, p. 20, para. 41.)[35]

[171] It is to be noted with reference to this second submission, which is repeated in more elaborate form in the Memorial and in the submissions at the end of the oral proceedings, that it is hypothetical, and based on the assumption that Iceland, as a coastal State in a special situation, raises questions concerning conservation of fish stocks and preferential rights; but Iceland has not raised these questions in any of the negotiations or in any of the documents it saw fit to transmit to the Court. I understand the statements of the Court cited above to mean that the exceptional dependence of Iceland on its fisheries for its subsistence and economic development, and the principle of conservation (including a conservation régime under which Iceland enjoys preferential rights) were recognized by the United Kingdom, and were, therefore, not in issue. The issue before the Court was whether it had jurisdiction to determine whether Iceland was competent unilaterally to assert an exclusive fisheries jurisdiction extending beyond the 12-mile limit. It was on this dispute, about the validity of the extension, that the Court decided it had jurisdiction.

[. . .]

[173] [. . .] 21. Iceland has not, so far as I can see, asserted any claim to preferential rights in the area in question; on the other hand, the United Kingdom has always stood ready to concede such rights if they were asserted on conservation grounds and in circumstances of catch-limitations. It does not appear to me to be possible to have a dispute where there is no difference on a common issue between the parties, or where a right is conceded. The Permanent Court of International Justice defines a dispute as 'a disagreement on a point of law or fact, a conflict of legal views or of interests between two persons'.[36] As I understand it, for a dispute to exist, it should clearly appear that the claim of one party is positively opposed by the other, and it is not sufficient merely for it to appear that the interests of the two parties are in conflict.

[35 See p. 24 above.]
36 *PCIJ, Series* A, No. 2, p. 11.

22. The claim clearly put forward and positively opposed in this case is Iceland's entitlement under international law to extend its exclusive fishery jurisdiction to 50 miles from the baselines around its coast; that was the point which this Court decided it had jurisdiction to determine.

23. The Court derives its jurisdiction in this case from the compromissory clause of the Exchange of Notes of 1961. I think the words 'in relation to such extension' in that clause cannot reasonably be interpreted as including disputes about conservation, catch-limitations and preferential rights (which are not susceptible of unilateral delimitation) within the range of disputes the Parties agreed to refer to the Court; and in deciding that the Parties were obliged to negotiate these matters, the Court, to my mind, exceeded the jurisdiction conferred on it by the Exchange of Notes and settled a non-existent dispute.

[Reports: *ICJ Reports 1974*, p. 3; 55 ILR 238]

Fisheries Jurisdiction Case
(Federal Republic of Germany *v*. Iceland)[1]

International Court of Justice, The Hague

25 July 1974 (Lachs, *President*; Forster, Gros, Bengzon, Petrén, Onyeama, Dillard, Ignacio-Pinto, de Castro, Morozov, Jiménez de Aréchaga, Sir Humphrey Waldock, Nagendra Singh and Ruda, *Judges*)

Damage and compensation — submission of Germany that Iceland under an obligation to make compensation for interference with German fishing vessels — jurisdiction of International Court to award compensation — need for concrete submission as to existence and amount of damage — relief denied

SUMMARY   *The facts*   On 26 May 1972, the Federal Republic of Germany commenced proceedings against Iceland in respect of a dispute concerning the proposed extension by Iceland of its fisheries jurisdiction. Comparable proceedings were commenced against Iceland by the United Kingdom (reported in this volume at p. 3).[2] The International Court of Justice decided not to join the two cases.

An important difference between the two cases concerned the relief sought by the two applicant States. In its Memorial, Germany listed a large number of incidents involving its vessels and Icelandic coastal patrol boats. In its fourth submission, it asked the International Court to declare, *inter alia*:

> ... that the acts of interference by Icelandic coastal patrol boats with fishing vessels registered in the Federal Republic of Germany or with their fishing operations by the threat or use of force are unlawful under international law, and that Iceland is under an obligation to make compensation ... to the Federal Republic of Germany.[3]

---

[1] The Federal Republic of Germany was represented by Dr G. Jaenicke, Dr D. von Schenck, Mr G. Möcklinghoff, Dr C. A. Fleischhauer, Dr D. Booss, Dr Kaufmann-Bühler and Dr Arno Meyer. Iceland did not appear before the International Court of Justice in the proceeding.

[2] The full Judgment of the International Court of Justice on the merits in the *United Kingdom* v. *Iceland Fisheries Jurisdiction Case* is reported at *ICJ Reports 1974*, p. 3 and reproduced at 55 ILR 238.

[3] The full relief sought by the Federal Republic of Germany is outlined in paragraph 12 of the Judgment (see pp. 73–5 below).

The case between Germany and Iceland is extracted in this volume only in respect of this submission.

Held by the International Court of Justice (by ten votes to four)   The Court rejected Germany's fourth submission request for a declaration that Iceland was under an obligation to compensate Germany for allegedly having harassed its fishing vessels. The Court held that it had jurisdiction to consider the claim but that the submission had been made in too abstract a form for the Court to be able to accept it. Germany had not produced the necessary evidence of the existence and amount of each head of damage. The Court could only make a general declaration that compensation was due in a case where it would be asked to assess the amount of damages in a subsequent phase of the proceedings. That was not so in the present case.

President Lachs appended a brief declaration in support of the Judgment.

Declaration of Judge Dillard   Although the Court's decision on Germany's request was supported, it was nevertheless regrettable that the Court had not granted a declaration that Iceland's acts of harassment were unlawful and that, in principle, Iceland was obliged to pay compensation.

Declaration of Judge Ignacio-Pinto   Before considering questions of preferential rights, the Court should have given a decision that Iceland's acts were contrary to international law and, therefore, not opposable to Germany. By concentrating upon equitable principles which should guide the Parties in their negotiations, the Court had avoided the chief issue.

Declaration of Judge Nagendra Singh   Having decided that the Icelandic regulations were not opposable to Germany, it was unnecessary for the Court to consider whether they were invalid *erga omnes.* The recognition in the Judgment of preferential rights, the need for conservation and the duty to have regard to the rights of other States were a positive contribution to the development of the law. The Court should, as it had done here, encourage negotiation between parties to a dispute and not regard it as inconsistent with its judicial function.

Joint Separate Opinion of Judges Forster, Bengzon, Jiménez de Aréchaga, Nagendra Singh and Ruda   The Judgment was supported because it decided only that the Icelandic fishery limits were not opposable to Germany and did not decide whether the fishery limits were without foundation in international law. There was no general rule of customary international law that fishery limits might not exceed 12 miles. There was not sufficient State practice to support such a rule today.

Separate Opinion of Judge de Castro   Germany's fourth submission was too abstract to be answered. Whether the Court had jurisdiction to consider it was also doubted.

Separate Opinion of Judge Sir Humphrey Waldock   The Court had jurisdiction to consider Germany's fourth submission because it was within the scope of the compromissory clause in the 1961 Exchange of Notes; and the addition of this submission in the Memorial on the merits was a permissible amendment to Germany's application. The Court should have granted a declaration that Iceland's acts were unlawful and that, in principle, there was a duty to pay compensation.

Dissenting Opinion of Judge Gros   Germany's fourth submission was outside the scope of the compromissory clause in the 1961 Exchange of Notes. The Court therefore lacked jurisdiction to consider it.

Dissenting Opinion of Judge Petrén   The Court had no jurisdiction to consider Germany's fourth submission as, aside from the procedural considerations, the claim did not fall within the scope of the jurisdictional clause of the 1961 agreement.

Dissenting Opinion of Judge Onyeama   The Court should have granted a declaration that Iceland's acts were unlawful and that, in principle, there was a duty to pay compensation or it should have requested more detailed evidence. The Court was wrong to reject the submission out of hand.

There follows

Judgment of International Court of Justice on Merits, 25 July 1974 (extract)

[178][. . .] 12. In the course of the written proceedings, the following submissions were presented on behalf of the Government of the Federal Republic of Germany:

in the Application:

---

[4] President Lachs and Judges Ignacio-Pinto and Nagendra Singh each issued a declaration which is not reproduced in this volume but can be found at *ICJ Reports 1974*, pp. 206, 208 and 211 respectively. The joint separate opinion of Judges Forster, Bengzon, Jiménez de Aréchaga, Nagendra Singh and Ruda is also not reproduced in this volume but can be found at *ICJ Reports 1974*, p. 217.

The Federal Republic of Germany asks the Court to adjudge and declare:

(a)   That the unilateral extension by Iceland of its zone of exclusive fisheries jurisdiction to 50 nautical miles from the present baselines, to be effective from 1 September 1972, which has been decided upon by the Parliament (Althing) and the Government of Iceland and communicated by the Minister for Foreign Affairs of Iceland to the Federal Republic of Germany by aide-mémoire handed to its Ambassador in Reykjavik on 24 February 1972, would have no basis in international law and could therefore not be opposed to the Federal Republic of Germany and to its fishing vessels.

(b)   That if Iceland, as a coastal State specially dependent on coastal fisheries, establishes a need for special fisheries conservation measures in the waters adjacent to its coast but beyond the exclusive fisheries zone provided for by the Exchange of Notes of 1961, such conservation measures, as far as they would affect fisheries of the Federal Republic of Germany, may not be taken, under international law, on the basis of a unilateral extension by Iceland of its fisheries jurisdiction, but only on the basis of an agreement between the Federal Republic of Germany and Iceland concluded either bilaterally or within a multilateral framework.

[179] in the Memorial on the merits:

May it please the Court to adjudge and declare:

1.   That the unilateral extension by Iceland of its zone of exclusive fisheries jurisdiction to 50 nautical miles from the present baselines, put into effect by the Regulations No. 189/1972 issued by the Icelandic Minister for Fisheries on 14 July 1972, has, as against the Federal Republic of Germany, no basis in international law and can therefore not be opposed to the Federal Republic of Germany and the fishing vessels registered in the Federal Republic of Germany.

2.   That the Icelandic Regulations No. 189/1972 issued by the Icelandic Minister for Fisheries on 14 July 1972, and any other regulations which might be issued by Iceland for the purpose of implementing Iceland's claim to a 50-mile exclusive fisheries zone, shall not be enforced against the Federal Republic of Germany, vessels registered in the Federal Republic of Germany, their crews and other persons connected with fishing activities of such vessels.

3.   That if Iceland, as a coastal State specially dependent on its fisheries, establishes a need for conservation measures in respect to fish stocks in the waters adjacent to its coast beyond the limits of Icelandic jurisdiction agreed to by the Exchange of Notes of 19 July 1961, such conservation measures, as far as they would affect fishing activities by vessels registered in the Federal Republic of Germany, may not be taken on the basis of a unilateral extension by Iceland of its fisheries jurisdiction but only on the basis of an agreement between the Parties, concluded either bilaterally or within a multilateral framework, with due regard to the special dependence of Iceland on its fisheries and to the traditional fisheries of the Federal Republic of Germany in the waters concerned.

4.   That the acts of interference by Icelandic coastal patrol boats with fishing vessels registered in the Federal Republic of Germany or with their fishing operations by

the threat or use of force are unlawful under international law, and that Iceland is under an obligation to make compensation therefor to the Federal Republic of Germany.

[. . .]

[203] [. . .] 71. By the fourth submission in its Memorial, maintained in the oral proceedings, the Federal Republic of Germany raised the question of compensation for alleged acts of harassment of its fishing vessels by Icelandic coastal patrol boats; the submission reads as follows:

> That the acts of interference by Icelandic coastal patrol boats with fishing vessels registered in the Federal Republic of Germany or with their fishing operations by the threat or use of force are unlawful under international law, and that Iceland is under an obligation to make compensation therefor to the Federal Republic of Germany.

72. The Court cannot accept the view that it would lack jurisdiction to deal with this submission. The matter raised therein is part of the controversy between the Parties, and constitutes a dispute relating to Iceland's extension of its fisheries jurisdiction. The submission is one based on facts subsequent to the filing of the Application, but arising directly out of the question which is the subject-matter of that Application. As such it falls within the scope of the Court's jurisdiction defined in the compromissory clause of the Exchange of Notes of 19 July 1961.

73. In its Memorial, and in the oral proceedings, when presenting its submission on compensation, the Federal Republic of Germany stated that:

> . . . [it] reserves all its rights to claim full compensation from the Government of Iceland for all unlawful acts that have been committed, or may yet be committed . . . [it] does not, at present, submit a claim against the Republic of Iceland for the payment of a certain amount of money as compensation for the damage already inflicted upon the fishing vessels of the Federal Republic. [It does] however, request the Court to adjudge and declare that the Republic of Iceland is, in principle, responsible for the damage inflicted upon German fishing vessels . . . and under an obligation to pay full compensation for all the damage which the Federal Republic of Germany and its nationals have actually suffered thereby.

74. The manner of presentation of this claim raises the question whether the Court is in a position to pronounce on a submission maintained **[204]** in such an abstract form. The submission does not ask for an assessment of compensation for certain specified acts but for a declaration of principle that Iceland is under an obligation to make compensation to the Federal Republic in respect of all unlawful acts of interference with fishing vessels of the Federal Republic. The Applicant is thus asking for a declaration adjudicating, with definitive effect, that Iceland is under an obligation to pay full compensation for all the damage suffered by the Applicant as a consequence of the acts of interference specified in the proceedings. In its Memorial the Federal Republic has listed a large number of incidents involving its vessels and Icelandic coastal patrol boats, and continues:

> The Government of the Federal Republic does ... request the Court to adjudge and declare that the Republic of Iceland is, in principle, responsible for the damage inflicted upon German fishing vessels by the illegal acts of the Icelandic coastal patrol boats *described in the preceding paragraphs*, and under an obligation to pay full compensation for *all the damage* which the Federal Republic of Germany and its nationals have actually suffered *thereby*. (Emphasis added.)

The final submission, which refers to 'the acts of interference' and the 'obligation to make compensation therefor', confirms the above interpretation.

75. Part V of the Memorial on the merits contains a general account of what the Federal Republic describes as harassment of its fishing vessels by Iceland, while Annexes G, H, I and K give some further details in diplomatic Notes and Annex L lists the incidents, with a statement of the kind of each incident. Some information concerning incidents is also to be found in the Federal Republic's reports regarding the implementing of the Court's Order for provisional measures.

76. The documents before the Court do not however contain in every case an indication in a concrete form of the damages for which compensation is required or an estimation of the amount of those damages. Nor do they furnish evidence concerning such amounts. In order to award compensation the Court can only act with reference to a concrete submission as to the existence and the amount of each head of damage. Such an award must be based on precise grounds and detailed evidence concerning those acts which have been committed, taking into account all relevant facts of each incident and their consequences in the circumstances of the case. It is only after receiving evidence on these matters that the Court can satisfy itself that each concrete claim is well founded in fact and in law. It is possible to request a general declaration establishing the principle that compensation is due, provided the claimant asks the Court to receive evidence and to determine, in a subsequent phase of the same proceedings, the amount of damage to be assessed. Moreover, while the Applicant has reserved all its rights 'to claim compensation', it has not [205] requested that these damages be proved and assessed in a subsequent phase of the present proceedings. It would not be appropriate for the Court, when acting under Article 53 of the Statute, and after the Applicant has stated that it is not submitting a claim for the payment of a certain amount of money as compensation, to take the initiative of requesting specific information and evidence concerning the indemnity which, in the view of the Applicant, would correspond to each incident and each head of damage. In these circumstances, the Court is prevented from making an all-embracing finding of liability which would cover matters as to which it has only limited information and slender evidence. Accordingly, the fourth submission of the Federal Republic of Germany as presented to the Court cannot be acceded to.

*

*   *

77. For these reasons,

THE COURT,

by ten votes to four,

(1) finds that the Regulations concerning the Fishery Limits off Iceland (*Reglugerð um fiskveiðilandhelgi Íslands*) promulgated by the Government of Iceland on 14 July 1972 and constituting a unilateral extension of the exclusive fishing rights of Iceland to 50 nautical miles from the baselines specified therein are not opposable to the Government of the Federal Republic of Germany;

(2) finds that, in consequence, the Government of Iceland is not entitled unilaterally to exclude fishing vessels of the Federal Republic of Germany from areas between the fishery limits agreed to in the Exchange of Notes of 19 July 1961 and the limits specified in the Icelandic Regulations of 14 July 1972, or unilaterally to impose restrictions on the activities of those vessels in such areas;

by ten votes to four,

(3) holds that the Government of Iceland and the Government of the Federal Republic of Germany are under mutual obligations to undertake negotiations in good faith for the equitable solution of their differences concerning their respective fishery rights in the areas specified in subparagraph 2;

(4) holds that in these negotiations the Parties are to take into account, *inter alia:*

(a) that in the distribution of the fishing resources in the areas specified in subparagraph 2 Iceland is entitled to a preferential share to the extent of the special dependence of her people upon [**206**] the fisheries in the seas around her coasts for their livelihood and economic development;

(b) that by reason of its fishing activities in the areas specified in subparagraph 2, the Federal Republic of Germany also has established rights in the fishery resources of the said areas on which elements of its people depend for their livelihood and economic well-being;

(c) the obligation to pay due regard to the interests of other States in the conservation and equitable exploitation of these resources;

(d) that the above-mentioned rights of Iceland and of the Federal Republic of Germany should each be given effect to the extent compatible with the conservation and development of the fishery resources in the areas specified in subparagraph 2 and with the interests of other States in their conservation and equitable exploitation;

(e) their obligation to keep under review those resources and to examine together, in the light of scientific and other available information, such measures as may be required for the conservation and development, and equitable exploitation of those resources, making use of the machinery established by the North-East Atlantic Fisheries Convention or such other means as may be agreed upon as a result of international negotiations,

by ten votes to four,

> (5) finds that it is unable to accede to the fourth submission of the Federal Republic of Germany.

[...]

[207] DECLARATION OF JUDGE DILLARD

I concur in the findings of the Court indicated in the first four subparagraphs of the *dispositif.* My reasons for concurrence are set out in my separate opinion in the companion case of the *United Kingdom of Great Britain and Northern Ireland v. Iceland.* I consider these reasons applicable *mutatis mutandis* to the present case.

While I concurred in the finding in the fifth subparagraph that the Court 'is unable to accede to the fourth submission of the Federal Republic of Germany', I am impelled to add the following reservation.[5]

The Court has held, in paragraph 72, that it is competent to entertain this particular submission. Although, for obvious reasons, the submission was not included in the Application filed on 5 June 1972 since the acts of harassment and interference occurred thereafter, it was included in the Memorial on the merits and in the final submissions. The delay therefore should not be a bar. The Court's construction of the nature and scope of the Exchange of Notes of 1961, revealed in its analysis of the other submissions, is clearly consistent with its finding that the compromissory clause is broad enough to cover this submission as well. In my view the conclusion that the Court is competent to entertain it, is thus amply justified.

The Court, however, has interpreted this submission as one asking the Court to adjudicate with definitive effect that Iceland is under an obligation *to pay full compensation* for *all* the damages suffered by the Applicant as a consequence of the acts of interference specified in the proceedings (para. 74). In keeping with this interpretation it considers the submission to fall outside its province under Article 53 of its Statute since it considers there is insufficient evidence to satisfy itself that *each concrete claim* is well founded in fact and law (para. 76). If the Court's interpretation of the submission were the only permissible one, I would concur without reservation in its conclusion.

But, in my view, it is not the only permissible one and it may not be the most desirable one. The Applicant both in its Memorial on the merits and in the oral proceedings has stressed the point that it is not at present submitting any claim for the payment of a certain amount of money. The submission itself only requests that the Court should declare that the acts of harassment and interference were unlawful and in consequence Iceland, as a matter of principle, is under a duty to make compensation. True the submission is couched in a form that is abstract but the question is whether this should deter the Court from passing upon it. I am not altogether persuaded that it is.

[5] All of the Applicant's submissions are set out in para. 12 of the Judgment and the fourth submission is also set out in para. 71.

That Iceland's acts of harassment and interference (indicated in considerable detail in the proceedings) were unlawful hardly admits of doubt. **[208]** They were committed *pendente lite* despite the obligations assumed by Iceland in the Exchange of Notes of 1961 which the Court had declared to be a treaty in force. That their unlawful character engaged the international responsibility of Iceland is also clear. In the *Phosphates in Morocco* case (*PCIJ, Series A/B, No. 74,* p. 28) the Court linked the creation of international responsibility with the existence of an 'act being attributable to the State and described as contrary to the treaty right of another State'. It is hardly necessary to marshal authority for so elementary a proposition. It follows that, in effect, the Court was merely asked to indicate the unlawful character of the acts and to take note of the consequential liability of Iceland to make reparation. It was not asked to assess damages.

The Court recognized this point in paragraph 74 of the Judgment but instead of stressing the limited nature of the submission it preferred to attribute to it a more extensive character. As indicated above, its interpretation led naturally to the conclusion that it could not accede to the submission in the absence of detailed evidence bearing on each concrete claim. While conceding the force of the Court's reasoning, I would have preferred the more restrictive interpretation.

I wish to add that on this matter I associate myself with the views expressed by Judge Sir Humphrey Waldock in his separate opinion.

[225] SEPARATE OPINION OF JUDGE DE CASTRO

[*Translation*]

I voted with the majority, and I have explained the reasons for my vote in my separate opinion in the case of *Fisheries Jurisdiction (United Kingdom v. Iceland)*, and these reasons apply *mutatis mutandis* to the present case. I would like however to add the following observations.

During the oral proceedings, the Government of the Federal Republic requested the Court, in its last submission, to adjudge and declare that Iceland is under an obligation to make compensation for the acts of interference by Icelandic coastal patrol boats with the German fishing vessels by the threat or use of force (hearing of 28 March 1974, p. 92). In the German Memorial its request is clearer, namely that the Court should declare:

> That the Republic of Iceland is, in principle, responsible for the damage inflicted upon German fishing vessels by the illegal acts of the Icelandic coastal patrol boats described in the preceding paragraphs, and under an obligation to pay full compensation for all damage which the Federal Republic of Germany and its nationals have actually suffered thereby. (Part V, para. 18.)

This claim by the Federal Republic raises two preliminary questions for the Court, which should be examined separately.

I do not see how the Court can agree to this claim by the Federal Republic. In its judgment on a case the Court does not have to make declarations of principle. To say that an illegal act which has caused injury gives rise to an obligation to make reparation is a mere truism, and there is therefore no point in saying it. But for that very reason, to say as much would suggest that the Court has, at least prima facie, accepted the existence of illegal acts and of damage.

A claim for reparation, if it is to be admissible before a court, must include an offer of evidence, as to the fault of the defendant, and as to the existence and the amount of each head of damage; the possibility must also be considered of balancing of fault on each side, or set-off of damages. It is after hearing evidence that the Court can satisfy itself that the submissions as to reparation are well founded in fact and in law.

The other question to be examined concerns the Court's jurisdiction to entertain the claim for reparation.

I should observe first of all that I do not consider that the Court has to settle the question of jurisdiction before stating that the claim is inadmissible. It is open to the Court to take no action on the claim because it is not properly made. The Court always has jurisdiction to [226] decide that a claim is inadmissible because its formulation is wholly defective.

I think also that I should make no secret of my doubts as to the Court's jurisdiction to examine the question of reparation. My hesitation arises from the fact that I do not see how it can be argued from the compromissory clause that the task entrusted to the Court includes the question of reparation. The clause was accepted unwillingly by Iceland, and it would appear that there is nothing to justify its being interpreted extensively. The 1961 agreement is confined to the establishment of fishing zones; the compromissory clause relates to 'the matter' of the extension. The Court can and must give a decision on the extension. Can it do so also on connected questions? In my view, the damage and injury relied on by the Federal Republic derive from something other than the extension. The unlawfulness of the activities of the Iceland coastal patrol boats which has been asserted might be deduced from the fact that they occurred either *pendente lite* or in disregard of the Court's Order as to interim measures; they would thus arise not from non-compliance with contractual obligations (arising from the same treaty) but *ex delicto*.

It is not easy to interpret the compromissory clause so extensively. The extension of fisheries jurisdiction is not the cause of the damage; the acts of the coastal patrol boats are new facts, not foreseen at the time of conclusion of the agreement.

The old saying that *boni judicis est ampliare jurisdictionem* is not applicable to the Court's jurisdiction (United Nations Charter, Art. 2, para. 7). I consider that the compromissory clause in the 1961 Exchange of Notes should not be interpreted restrictively, but should not be interpreted extensively either; it should be read in accordance with the ordinary meaning to be given to the terms of the Notes in their context and in the light of their object and purpose (Vienna Convention on the Law of Treaties, Art. 31).

SEPARATE OPINION OF JUDGE SIR HUMPHREY WALDOCK (EXTRACT)

[229] [. . .] 6. The Federal Republic, unlike the United Kingdom in the other case before the Court, has maintained its claim, set out in its fourth submission, to

compensation for alleged acts of harassment of its vessels by Icelandic coastal patrol vessels. I concur in the Court's view, stated in paragraph 72 of the Judgment, that this submission falls within its competence in the present proceedings. Although the Court does not develop its grounds for so holding and I myself entertain no doubt upon the point, I wish to indicate briefly the reasons which lead me to share the Court's view.

[**230**] 7. The claim to compensation raises two points as to the Court's competence to entertain it, the first of which is whether the claim falls within the terms of the compromissory clause: 'in case of a dispute in relation to such extension, the matter shall, at the request of either party, be referred to the International Court of Justice'. It seems to me too narrow an interpretation of those words to regard them as confining the competence conferred on the Court to the question of the extension of jurisdiction as such. In my view, incidents arising out of Iceland's extension of her fishery limit and claims in respect of such incidents clearly form part of 'a dispute *in relation to* such extension' – words of a quite general character. Indeed, every act enforcing Iceland's jurisdiction outside the 12-mile limit is in a very real sense an extension of her jurisdiction beyond the agreed limit. Furthermore, as the Court itself emphasized in paragraphs 21–2 of its Judgment of 2 February 1973 on its jurisdiction in the case of the United Kingdom *v.* Iceland, the very object of the compromissory clause was to provide an assurance that 'if there was a dispute, *no measure to apply an extension* on fishery limits would be taken pending reference to the International Court' *(ICJ Reports 1973,* at p. 13; emphasis added). It therefore seems entirely justifiable to consider that the Federal Republic's claim to compensation must, in principle, fall within the general competence conferred on the Court in the case of a dispute in relation to an extension of fishery jurisdiction.

8. Moreover, as Judge Jiménez de Aréchaga pointed out in the *ICAO Council* case *(ICJ Reports 1972,* p. 147) both this Court and the Permanent Court of International Justice have held that, if a jurisdictional clause provides for the reference to an international tribunal of disagreements relating to the interpretation or application of a treaty, the competence given to the tribunal embraces questions arising out of the performance or non-performance of the treaty. Thus, in the Advisory Opinion on *Interpretation of Peace Treaties* the Court considered that disputes relating to the question of the performance or non-performance of the obligations provided for in treaties 'are clearly disputes concerning the interpretation or execution' of the treaties in question *(ICJ Reports 1950,* p. 75). Even more specific, for present purposes, is the dictum of the Permanent Court in the *Factory at Chorzów* case *(PCIJ, Series A, No. 9,* p. 21):

> It is a principle of international law that the breach of an engagement involves an obligation to make reparation in an adequate form. Reparation therefore is the indispensable complement of a failure to apply a convention and there is no necessity for this to be stated in the convention itself. *Differences relating to reparations, which may be due by reason of failure to apply a convention, are* [**231**] *consequently differences relating to its application.* (Emphasis added.)

In my view, as I have indicated above, the present dispute in relation to an extension of Iceland's fishery jurisdiction is at the same time a dispute in relation to the application of the 1961 Exchange of Notes. But in any event, by parity of reasoning, it seems to me clear that a jurisdictional clause conferring competence on the Court to determine the validity of an extension of fishery jurisdiction embraces differences relating to reparations which may be due by reason of the invalidity of an extension.

*

9. The second point concerns the question whether the claim comes within the scope of the case referred to the Court by the Federal Republic's Application of 5 June 1972. The Application contained only two submissions: one concerning the alleged unlawfulness of the unilateral extension of the fishery limit, and the other concerning the need for agreement in regard to conservation measures. The Application did not deal with acts of harassment or compensation in respect of them for the very good reason that it was filed before the new Icelandic Regulations came into force on 1 September 1972 and before any acts of harassment had occurred. Indeed, soon after filing the Application, the Federal Republic sought to obviate any risk of harassment by requesting and obtaining an Order for provisional measures. True, the Federal Republic's Memorial on jurisdiction, which was filed on 5 October 1972 after some acts of harassment had occurred, also made no mention of them. But the Court had ordered that the Federal Republic's first Memorial should be directed specifically to the question of its jurisdiction to entertain the Application, and the question of harassment was not germane to that issue. Consequently, it was in the Memorial on the merits that acts of harassment were first made a cause of action and a claim to compensation was first included among the submissions.

10. The question then is whether the Federal Republic's claim to compensation, formulated in the Memorial on the merits and again in the final submissions, is a permissible modification of the submissions formulated in the Application. In other words, is the addition of the claim to compensation such a modification of the submissions in the Application as is permissible under Article 40 of the Statute and Article 32 (2) of the Rules? Under the practice of the Permanent Court of International Justice the parties to proceedings begun by a unilateral Application were allowed a certain freedom to amend their submissions so long as the amendments did not have the effect of altering the subject of the dispute. [. . .]

[232][. . .] 11. In the present case, Iceland had the opportunity, by filing a Counter-Memorial, to reply to the Federal Republic's claim to compensation and, if she considered it to be outside the scope of the Application, to object to its admissibility. But she decided not to appear in the proceedings. As to the claim itself, this seems to me related to the subject of the Application more directly than was the restoration of the Temple objects in the *Temple of Preah Vihear* case: the relief for which it asks is consequential upon and implied in the Federal Republic's first submission. True, the facts on which it is based occurred subsequently to the Application and the claim therefore introduces a new element into the case. But it does not seem to me to 'transform the dispute' brought before the Court in the Application into 'another dispute which is different in character'. On the contrary, it arose directly out of the matter which is the

subject of the first submission in the Application and was the direct result of Iceland's own actions with respect to that matter when it was already before the Court. The very fact that the new claim concerns matters explicitly dealt with in the Court's Order for provisional measures seems to me to make it difficult to treat that claim as an impermissible modification of the submissions in the Application. Consequently, in my view, the claim to compensation ought not to be ruled out on the ground that it had no place in the Application.

*   *

[233] 12. My reservation regarding subparagraph 5 of the operative clause arises from a doubt as to whether the Court should simply state that it is unable to accede to the Federal Republic's fourth submission and thus, in effect, to dismiss outright the claim to compensation. In so far as this submission may be considered as asking the Court for a final decision pronouncing upon Iceland's obligation to make compensation for particular specified acts of interference, I agree with the Court that, as the case now stands, it is not in a position to give such a decision because the evidence is scarcely sufficient. The Federal Republic appears, moreover, to be asking for final judgment in the case without requesting further proceedings to deal with its claim to compensation or requesting the Court to reserve for the Federal Republic the liberty to apply to the Court on the question of compensation in the event that no agreement is arrived at between the Parties on this question. In consequence, it may be doubtful whether it would be appropriate for the Court, *proprio motu*, to reserve the question of compensation to be dealt with in further proceedings.

13. In so far, however, as the fourth submission may be understood as merely claiming a declaration of principle that Iceland is under an obligation to make reparation for any acts of interference established as unlawful under subparagraphs 1 and 2 of the operative clause of the Court's Judgment, I do not myself see the same difficulty in the Court's acceding to the claim. The Court has held that Iceland's unilateral extension of her exclusive fishing rights to 50 miles is not opposable to the Federal Republic and that Iceland is not entitled unilaterally to exclude the Federal Republic's fishing vessels from the waters to seaward of the fishery limits agreed to in the 1961 Exchange of Notes. It then really follows automatically that acts enforcing that extension against fishing vessels of the Federal Republic are unlawful and engage Iceland's international responsibility to the Federal Republic with respect to such acts. Since it is a well-established principle of international law that every violation of an international obligation entails a duty to make reparation, the right to reparation also follows without even being stated. Accordingly, it may be said, as was indeed said in the *Corfu Channel* case *(ICJ Reports 1949*, pp. 23–4), that to make the claim to reparation is superfluous; if the claim to a declaration of the unlawful character of acts is upheld, the consequence is that as a matter of law, reparation is due. Nevertheless, an Applicant may think it important to obtain from the Court, as a form of satisfaction, an express declaration in the operative part of the Judgment that reparation is due, and I see no obstacle to the Court's acceding to such a submission.

DISSENTING OPINION OF JUDGE GROS (EXTRACT)

[*Translation*]

[**236**][. . .] 3. The point which is peculiar to the present Judgment concerns the fourth submission of the Federal Republic, which is dealt with in the last subparagraph of the operative clause. The Court has decided that it is unable to accede to this fourth submission of the Federal Republic of Germany – which was a claim for reparation for the consequences of action taken against its fishing vessels – exclusively on the grounds of the way in which the submission has been presented: 'The fourth submission . . . as presented to the Court cannot be acceded to' (para. 76 of the Judgment). It may be deduced from this that in another form the claim could be acceded to by the Court; but it might be contended, on the basis of the continuance in force of the 1961 agreement, that further action would be possible, particularly should the negotiations which the Court recommends break down. Since there is between Iceland and the Federal Republic no interim agreement, like the agreement of 13 November 1973 with the United Kingdom, there is therefore nothing to prevent the Federal Republic from immediately re-presenting this part of its claim. Since I am unable to accept the implications of the Judgment on this point, and for other reasons also, I voted against subparagraph 5 of the operative clause, as I did in respect of the Judgment as a whole.

[. . .]

[**237**][. . .] 5. The Court is bound to satisfy itself that the Applicant's claim is well founded in fact and law; I consider that the two identical agreements of 1961 do not provide for any proceedings to establish responsibility (*contentieux de responsabilité*), but only proceedings to establish lawfulness (*contentieux de légalité*), directed to obtaining a declaratory judgment on a limited point of law, and nothing more. It is therefore because the fourth submission of the Federal Republic fell outside the subject-matter of the compromissory clause, and therefore of the Court's jurisdiction, that it should have been rejected in the Judgment, and not by means of an argument based on the way in which the submission was presented. As to certain arguments concerning the law of responsibility in general, since the Court has not given its decision on this aspect of the matter, but may be seised of it again, I do not consider it possible to discuss the point.

[. . .]

DISSENTING OPINION OF JUDGE PETRÉN (EXTRACT)

[*Translation*]

[**242**][. . .] There remains the third and last part of the operative clause, subparagraph 5, concerning the fourth final submission requesting the Court to adjudge and declare that the acts of interference by Icelandic coastal patrol boats with fishing vessels registered in the Federal Republic of Germany or with their fishing operations by the threat or use of force are unlawful under international law, and that Iceland is under an obligation to make compensation therefor to the Federal Republic of Germany.

This claim, which appeared in the Federal Republic's Memorial on the merits, was not included in the Application instituting proceedings filed in the Registry on 5 June 1972. In its Judgment of 2 February 1973, the Court found that it had jurisdiction to entertain the Application and to deal with the merits of the case. That Judgment was based entirely upon paragraph 5 of the Exchange of Notes of 1961, which reads as follows:

> The Government of the Republic of Iceland shall continue to work for the implementation of the Althing Resolution of 5 May 1959, regarding the extension of the fishery jurisdiction of Iceland. However, it shall give the Government of the Federal Republic of Germany six months' notice of any such extension; in case of a dispute relating to such an extension, the matter shall, at the request of either party, be referred to the International Court of Justice.

The point at issue is therefore whether the phrase 'a dispute relating to such an extension' signifies that it is not only the question whether a future extension of Iceland's fishery jurisdiction is in conformity with international law that may be referred to the Court, but also such supplementary questions as the present compensation claim. Even in the affirmative, it would still be necessary that the Court's finding that it possessed jurisdiction to entertain the Application and deal with the merits of the dispute should further imply that the Court may adjudicate upon an additional claim concerning incidents subsequent to the filing of the Application. This question is all the more delicate in the present case because the respondent Party has chosen not to be represented before the Court and the situation calls for the application of Article 53 of the Statute.

Iceland's acceptance of the Court's jurisdiction was exceptional in character. It is plain that the Government of Iceland meant it to be strictly limited to the question of whether the next step in the extension of Iceland's fishery zone would be in conformity with international law. Considering the atmosphere in which the 1961 agreement was negotiated, [243] it may be supposed that the Government of the Federal Republic was conscious of the Icelandic Government's attitude in this respect. It was at a moment when memories of the first 'cod war' were still fresh that the Althing approved the two 1961 agreements with the United Kingdom and the Federal Republic respectively. Would it have done so if it had believed that it was at the same time accepting that any pecuniary dispute arising out of a future extension of the Iceland fishery zone should be referred to the Court? I think not, and therefore consider that the Federal Republic's compensation claim does not fall within the scope of the jurisdictional clause of the 1961 agreement. That being so, it is scarcely necessary for me to consider the consequences of the fact that this claim was mentioned neither in the Application instituting proceedings nor in the Judgment on jurisdiction.

The Court finds that it has jurisdiction to deal with the compensation claim, but finds that it is unable to 'accede' to it for want of sufficient evidence. In my view, the Court ought not to have dismissed the submission in this way, for it did not afford the Federal Republic the opportunity to complete its documentation in the course of the oral proceedings, in conformity with Article 54 of the 1946 Rules of Court. The oral proceedings enable the Court, *inter alia*, to lead litigants by its questions to fill in the gaps in the presentation of their arguments, or even to withdraw part of their claims.

The last sentence of paragraph 76 of the Judgment seems to imply that if the Federal Republic revived its compensation claim the Court would be ready to consider it. Leaving aside all considerations of procedural law, I will confine myself to stating that, according to my interpretation of the 1961 agreement, it cannot be accorded so prolonged an effect.

It follows from the foregoing that I found it necessary to vote against the last part of the operative clause.

DISSENTING OPINION OF JUDGE ONYEAMA (EXTRACT)

[**250**] [. . .] Regarding the fourth submission of the Federal Republic of Germany that the acts of interference by Icelandic coastal patrol boats with fishing vessels registered in the Federal Republic of Germany or with their fishing operations by the threat or use of force are unlawful under international law, and that Iceland is under an obligation to make compensation therefor to the Federal Republic of Germany, I am of the opinion that the Court is competent to entertain the claim grounded on the submission, since the acts of interference complained of arose directly out of Iceland's attempt to enforce its extension of its fisheries jurisdiction before the validity of such extension had been decided by the Court as agreed in the Exchange of Notes of 1961. In my view, claims for compensation for acts done in breach of the agreement constituted by the Exchange of Notes must be deemed to be in the contemplation of the Parties when they conferred jurisdiction on the Court, and the particular acts in this case appear to me to form part of what the Exchange of Notes referred to as 'a dispute in relation to such extension'.

If, as I believe, the Court has jurisdiction to entertain the claim for compensation, I consider its reasons for rejecting the claim wholly inadequate. In the first place, the Federal Republic of Germany was not asking for quantified compensation but for a declaration of principle as follows:

(a)   that the acts of interference by Icelandic coastal patrol boats with fishing vessels registered in the Federal Republic of Germany were illegal;

(b)   that Iceland is responsible for the damage inflicted;

(c)   that Iceland is under an obligation to pay full compensation for all the damage which the Federal Republic and its nationals have actually suffered as a result of the acts of interference.

In the second place, even if a claim for a specific sum was made, the Court is not without means of calling for further information on any issue in the claim if it considers that course necessary in the interest of justice.[6]

---

[6]   See, for example, Art. 57, paras. 1 and 2 of the Rules of Court.

[251] The decision that the Regulations whereby Iceland sought to extend its fisheries jurisdiction beyond the limit agreed in the Exchange of Notes are not opposable to the Federal Republic of Germany, appears to me to carry the necessary implication that acts done in enforcement of the Regulations against German fishing vessels are contrary to law. Consistently with its Judgment, the Court should have made a general declaration of principle along the lines set out in the submission in the Memorial on the merits of the Federal Republic of Germany.

[Reports: *ICJ Reports 1974*, p. 175; 56 *ILR* 146]

Nuclear Tests Case
(New Zealand *v.* France)[1]

International Court of Justice, The Hague

22 June 1973 (Ammoun,*Vice-President*; Forster, Gros, Bengzon, Petrén, Onyeama, Ignacio-Pinto, de Castro, Morozov, Jiménez de Aréchaga, Sir Humphrey Waldock, Nagendra Singh and Ruda, *Judges*; Sir Garfield Barwick, *Judge* ad hoc)

12 July 1973 (Lachs, *President*; Ammoun,*Vice-President*; Forster, Gros, Bengzon, Petrén, Onyeama, Ignacio-Pinto, Morozov, Jiménez de Aréchaga, Sir Humphrey Waldock and Ruda, *Judges*; Sir Garfield Barwick, *Judge* ad hoc)

20 December 1974 (Lachs, *President*; Forster, Gros, Bengzon, Petrén, Onyeama, Dillard, Ignacio-Pinto, de Castro, Morozov, Jiménez de Aréchaga, Sir Humphrey Waldock, Nagendra Singh and Ruda, *Judges*; Sir Garfield Barwick, *Judge* ad hoc)

20 December 1974 (Lachs, *President*; Forster, Gros, Bengzon, Petrén, Onyeama, Dillard, Ignacio-Pinto, de Castro, Morozov, Jiménez de Aréchaga, Sir Humphrey Waldock, Nagendra Singh and Ruda, *Judges*; Sir Garfield Barwick, *Judge* ad hoc)

Hazardous activities and substances – atmospheric nuclear tests conducted by France in South Pacific causing deposit of radioactive fallout on territory of other States and on high seas – Court requested to declare tests unlawful and order France to cease conducting them – whether tests lawful

Jurisdiction – locus standi *– whether* actio popularis *exists in international law*

Treaties – in general – form of international agreements – unilateral declaration – whether capable of amounting to assumption of legal obligation – French declaration that atmospheric nuclear tests would cease

[1] Professor R. Q. Quentin-Baxter, Hon. Dr A. M. Finlay QC, Mr R. C. Savage QC, Professor K. J. Keith, Mr C. D. Beeby and Mrs A. B. Quentin-Baxter acted as Counsel for New Zealand.

Treaties – effect on third parties – treaty allegedly giving rise to rule of customary international law – Nuclear Test Ban Treaty, 1963

Responsibility and liability – in general – atmospheric nuclear tests leading to deposit of radioactive fallout on territory of other States and on high seas – whether tests lawful – whether absolute responsibility for damage caused

Territory – nature of territorial sovereignty – atmospheric nuclear tests causing deposit of radioactive fallout on territory of other States – whether an infringement of territorial sovereignty

SUMMARY   *The facts*   Between 1966 and 1972, the French Government carried out a number of atmospheric tests in the territory of French Polynesia in the South Pacific. The main firing point for the nuclear tests was Mururoa atoll, located approximately 2,500 nautical miles from the nearest point of the North Island of New Zealand. The New Zealand Government had asserted that these tests had led to the deposit of radioactive fallout on New Zealand territory. Following reports that a further series of atmospheric nuclear tests were planned to commence in 1973, New Zealand protested to France. However, the French Government indicated that it would continue with the tests.

On 9 May 1973, New Zealand commenced proceedings in the International Court of Justice against France. New Zealand sought a declaration that further atmospheric nuclear tests in the South Pacific would be contrary to international law and an order that the French Government should not carry out any further such tests. On the same day, Australia also commenced proceedings against France in relation to its atmospheric nuclear testing in the South Pacific.[2] In their dissenting opinions at the interim measures phase, Judges Forster, Gros and Ignacio-Pinto stated that the two cases should have been joined. However, this did not occur.

There were certain differences between the applications brought by Australia and New Zealand. In the merits phase of the New Zealand case, the joint dissenting opinion of Judges Onyeama, Dillard, Jiménez de Aréchaga and Sir Humphrey Waldock and the dissenting opinion of Judge *ad hoc* Sir Garfield Barwick took the view that the Court's decision was even less justifiable in the case of *New Zealand v. France* than it was in *Australia v. France,* since the only New Zealand claim was for a declaratory judgment.[3] Another difference between the two applications was the

---

[2] The Judgment in *Nuclear Tests Case (Australia v. France)* is not reproduced in this volume but can be found at *ICJ Reports 1974*, p. 253 and 57 ILR 348.

[3] See especially *ICJ Reports 1974*, pp. 494–6 and 525–8.

ways in which the States referred to the subject matter of their claims. Australia referred specifically to atmospheric nuclear testing, whereas New Zealand referred only to nuclear testing in general.

The judgments and orders of the Court in both cases are substantially the same. The potential differences were however explored in the resumed proceedings in 1995.[4]

In its application to the Court, New Zealand asked the Court to adjudge and declare:

That the conduct by the French Government of nuclear tests in the South Pacific region that give rise to radio-active fall-out constitutes a violation of New Zealand's rights under international law, and that these rights will be violated by any further such tests.

New Zealand submitted in respect of the French conduct of nuclear tests that:

(a) it violates the rights of all members of the international community, including New Zealand, that no nuclear tests that give rise to radio-active fall-out be conducted;

(b) it violates the rights of all members of the international community, including New Zealand, to the preservation from unjustified artificial radio-active contamination of the terrestrial, maritime and aerial environment and, in particular, of the environment of the region in which the tests are conducted and in which New Zealand, the Cook Islands, Niue and the Tokelau Islands are situated;

(c) it violates the right of New Zealand that no radio-active material enter the territory of New Zealand, the Cook Islands, Niue or the Tokelau Islands, including their air space and territorial waters, as a result of nuclear testing;

(d) it violates the right of New Zealand that no radio-active material, having entered the territory of New Zealand, the Cook Islands, Niue or the Tokelau Islands, including their air space and territorial waters, as a result of nuclear testing, cause harm, including apprehension, anxiety and concern, to the people and Government of New Zealand and of the Cook Islands, Niue and the Tokelau Islands;

(e) it violates the right of New Zealand to freedom of the high seas, including freedom of navigation and overflight and the freedom to explore and exploit the resources of the sea and the seabed, without interference or detriment resulting from nuclear testing.

In claiming on behalf of the Cook Islands, Niue and the Tokelau Islands, New Zealand invoked its special legal responsibility for these territories.

---

[4] The *Request for an Examination of the Situation in accordance with Paragraph 63 of the Court's Judgment of 20 December 1974 in the Nuclear Tests (New Zealand v. France) Case* is reported in this volume at p. 149 below.

In an annex to a letter of 16 May 1973 to the Court, the French Government stated that the Court manifestly lacked jurisdiction in the case. The French Government maintained that the General Act of 1928 had been an integral part of the League of Nations system and had thus become ineffective upon the dissolution of the League. As regarded Article 36(2) of the Statute, the French Government pointed out that its acceptance of the compulsory jurisdiction of the Court, by its declaration of 20 May 1966, specifically excluded 'disputes concerning activities connected with national defence', into which category the present dispute fell. The French Government also contended that, as between France and New Zealand, the General Act could not prevail over the more recent and more specific French acceptance of the Optional Clause and could not, therefore, provide an alternative basis for the compulsory jurisdiction of the Court. France accordingly declined to appoint an agent or to appear in the case and requested that the Court strike the case from the list.

Order on Request for Interim Measures of Protection, 22 June 1973
Pending judgment in the case, New Zealand asked the Court to indicate interim measures of protection requiring the French Government 'to refrain from conducting any further nuclear tests that give rise to radioactive fall-out while the Court is seized of the case'. New Zealand based this claim on Articles 41 and 48 of the Statute of the Court and on Article 33 of the General Act, both of which provided for the indication of interim measures by the Court.

Held by the International Court of Justice (by eight votes to six) Interim measures were indicated.

(1)   France's failure to appear could not, by itself, constitute an obstacle to the indication of interim measures of protection.

(2)   On a request for the indication of interim measures, it was not necessary for the Court finally to satisfy itself that it had jurisdiction in the dispute. Nevertheless, the Court should not indicate interim measures unless there appeared, *prima facie*, to be a basis for jurisdiction. The provisions invoked by New Zealand satisfied this requirement. The Court noted the French request that the case be struck from the list and decided to consider that request, together with the question of jurisdiction, in the next phase of the proceedings.

(3)   It could not be assumed that the claims put forward by New Zealand in its application fell completely outside the jurisdiction of the Court or that New Zealand would fail to establish a legal interest in respect

of those claims. The information submitted to the Court did not exclude the possibility that the deposit of radioactive fallout on New Zealand territory might have harmful effects. The Court would, therefore, indicate interim measures of protection in order to protect the right claimed by New Zealand in respect of the deposit of such fallout on her territory. It followed that it was not necessary to consider at this stage the other rights claimed by New Zealand. The Court therefore indicated interim measures of protection which required both parties to abstain from any action which might aggravate the dispute and, in particular, required the French Government to avoid nuclear tests which would cause radioactive fallout to be deposited on New Zealand territory.[5]

Declaration of Judge Jiménez de Aréchaga   Before indicating interim measures of protection, the Court should give the fullest attention possible, in light of the time and information available, to the question of jurisdiction, even though it would subsequently examine the question afresh. The question whether New Zealand had a legal interest in the claims which it advanced was relevant to the merits and not really to the issue of jurisdiction which fell to be decided in the next phase of the case.

Declaration of Judge Nagendra Singh   The Court had to be satisfied before it indicated interim measures that there was at least a possibility that it had jurisdiction. However, the decision to indicate interim measures of protection did not prejudge the question of jurisdiction.

Judge Sir Humphrey Waldock and Judge ad hoc *Sir Garfield Barwick* appended brief declarations of their support for the decision.

Dissenting Opinion of Judge Forster   The Court had no power to indicate interim measures until it had decided that it had jurisdiction in the case. The interim measures requested by New Zealand were practically indistinguishable from the substance of the case and should not, therefore, have been the subject of a provisional Order. By not protecting the rights of France, the Court had failed to maintain equality between the parties.

Dissenting Opinion of Judge Gros   The majority opinion was based upon a misinterpretation of Article 53 of the Statute of the Court. In the event of a State's failure to appear, Article 53 required the Court to satisfy itself that it had jurisdiction and that the claim before it was well founded in fact and law. The Court should, therefore, have decided whether it had jurisdiction before it indicated interim measures. The indication of interim measures in the present case necessarily prejudged the question

---

[5] The Order of the Court is set out in full at p. 103 below.

of jurisdiction, which had not received proper consideration. Moreover, the interim measures which had been indicated were too close to the substance of the New Zealand claim.

Dissenting Opinion of Judge Petrén   The arguments advanced by New Zealand did not appear, *prima facie,* to provide a basis on which the Court could found jurisdiction in the case.

Dissenting Opinion of Judge Ignacio-Pinto   The Court did not have jurisdiction in the case. Moreover, the existence of the rights claimed by New Zealand was a matter for grave doubt and, on that ground also, the Court should have refused to indicate interim measures of protection.

Order on Application by Fiji for Permission to Intervene, 12 July 1973
Fiji applied under Article 62 of the Statute of the Court for permission to intervene in both cases on the grounds that it would also be affected by the French tests.

Held by the International Court of Justice (by eight votes to five)   The Fijian application presupposed that the Court had jurisdiction in the case and consideration of it would therefore be deferred until the Court had decided the question of jurisdiction.

Judges Gros, Petrén, Onyeama and Ignacio-Pinto appended brief individual declarations against the Court's decision to defer consideration of Fiji's application to intervene.

Judgment, 20 December 1974
During 1973 and 1974, the French Government conducted two series of atmospheric nuclear tests at Mururoa, in French Polynesia, which New Zealand alleged were violations of the Court's Order of 22 June 1973 indicating interim measures of protection. The French Government declined to stop the programme of tests. However, on 8 June 1974, the Office of the President of the French Republic issued a communiqué stating that, following the 1974 atmospheric tests, France would be in a position to proceed to underground testing. In addition, a Note of 10 June 1974 from the French Embassy in Wellington to the New Zealand Ministry of Foreign Affairs stated that the atmospheric tests of 1974 would, in the normal course of events, be the last. Both statements were referred to in oral proceedings before the International Court.

After the oral proceedings had concluded, further statements were made, at press conferences, by the French President and the Minister of Defence, and to the United Nations General Assembly by the Minister for Foreign Affairs. These statements categorically stated that there would be no further atmospheric tests.

Held by the International Court of Justice (by nine votes to six)   The New Zealand claim no longer had any object so the Court was therefore not required to give a decision on it.

(1)   It would not be appropriate for the Court to exercise its power summarily to remove the case from the list.

(2)   The refusal of France to appear was regrettable but could not relieve the Court of the responsibility of considering the case and, in particular, of deciding whether it had jurisdiction.

(3)   Since the present stage of the proceedings was devoted to the questions of jurisdiction and admissibility, the merits of the case could not be considered. However, the Court had a duty to consider any matter which of its nature required prior examination and, in particular, any matter which might call in question the judicial character of the Court. It would be contrary to the judicial function for the Court to proceed to judgment on the merits if no dispute existed between the parties. Therefore, it became necessary, even at this preliminary stage, for the Court to examine the case in order to determine whether a justiciable dispute in fact existed.

(4)   Statements by the New Zealand Government, including a number of statements made in the course of the oral proceedings, indicated that New Zealand's concern was to put an end to French atmospheric nuclear tests in the South Pacific. This issue, and not the legality of atmospheric tests, was the essence of the dispute between the parties. Although the Application asked the Court to adjudge and declare that further atmospheric nuclear tests in the South Pacific would be contrary to international law, the substance of the New Zealand claim was the request for an order prohibiting further tests. New Zealand was not seeking compensation and the request that the Court adjudge and declare the tests to be unlawful was merely the reason advanced for the claim for an order and not a separate claim for a declaratory judgment.

(5)   The statements of the French President and French ministers that France would conduct no further atmospheric tests in the South Pacific amounted to a binding undertaking to refrain from such tests. A unilateral declaration made on behalf of a State by a competent authority could create an obligation under international law to comply with that declaration, if at the time of making the declaration the State had had an intention to be bound. International law contained no formal requirements, such as that the declaration should be in writing or should be communicated to a particular State. In the present case, there could be no doubt as to the authority of those making the statements to enter into

binding obligations on behalf of France. In making those statements, the French Government must have assumed that other States would rely upon them. In the circumstances, it must be presumed that the French Government had intended to be bound by the declarations. Although the New Zealand Government had not interpreted the French statements as binding and had pointed to the qualification inherent in the phrase 'in the normal course of events', this phrase was not included in the later statements and, taken as a whole, the statements amounted to a binding undertaking not to conduct further atmospheric tests. It followed that there was no longer any dispute for the Court to decide.

(6)   Although a number of the French statements had been made after the conclusion of the oral proceedings, the interests of justice had not required the Court to re-open those proceedings. The later statements did not raise any new issue on which the Court had not heard argument from New Zealand. They merely supplemented the earlier statements which New Zealand itself had drawn to the attention of the Court and about which New Zealand had presented submissions.

Separate Opinion of Judge Forster   Both the Australian and the New Zealand claims had been without object from the start and not merely since the recent French statements.

Separate Opinion of Judge Gros (with reference to the Separate Opinion in the Australia case)   The question of whether there was a legal dispute was one which the Court should have considered at the beginning. Where the Respondent State failed to appear, Article 53 of the Statute of the Court required the Court to consider at the outset whether the claim was well founded in fact and in law. Since Australia and New Zealand's own conduct in respect of nuclear tests showed that there was no rule of international law, opposable to France, which prohibited atmospheric nuclear tests, the dispute was of a political rather than a legal character. Moreover, the reliance by Australia and New Zealand upon the General Act was misconceived, as it had fallen into desuetude.

Separate Opinion of Judge Petrén   The Court had a duty to decide on the admissibility of the Application at the earliest possible moment. The crucial question in relation to admissibility was whether the dispute was about a matter governed by international law. The absence of any rule of international law governing the conduct of nuclear tests meant that this was a political dispute and therefore that the Application was not admissible.

Separate Opinion of Judge Ignacio-Pinto   The case was a political one and had been inadmissible from the outset. Although the reasoning of the judgment produced a satisfactory result, it was regrettable that jurisdictional questions such as the status of the General Act should have remained unanswered.

Joint Dissenting Opinion of Judges Onyeama, Dillard, Jiménez de Aréchaga and Sir Humphrey Waldock   (1)   *Reasons for Dissent*   The Court had erred in interpreting the Application as a claim solely for an Order prohibiting further French atmospheric nuclear tests. The request that the Court declare such tests to be illegal was a claim for a declaratory judgment which was quite distinct from the claim for a prohibiting Order. The Court's decision amounted to an impermissible reformulation of the Application.

New Zealand was concerned not merely with tests which might take place after the date of the judgment but also with those which had taken place between the filing of the Application and the judgment. A declaration of the illegality of those tests would be highly relevant to any future claim for compensation. Moreover, the decision that France had unilaterally undertaken an obligation not to conduct further tests did not give New Zealand the legal security which it had sought in its request for a declaratory judgment. In attributing to itself an 'inherent jurisdiction' to determine, not whether there had, from the outset, been any legal dispute, but whether there remained such a dispute, the Court had exceeded its powers, especially in view of its failure to give the Applicant an opportunity to be heard on this question.

(2)   *The Jurisdiction of the Court*   It was, therefore, necessary for the Court to consider the question of jurisdiction. The General Act of 1928, together with Articles 36(1) and 37 of the Statute of the Court, provided a basis for the Court's jurisdiction. Although concluded under the auspices of the League of Nations, the General Act was not so closely bound up with the League's institutions or ideology as to have been terminated by the dissolution of the League. Nor had it ceased to be effective for reasons of desuetude. Desuetude was not an independent ground for the termination of treaties and there was no evidence that the parties to the General Act had agreed to abandon it. On the contrary, there was sufficient State practice to show that the General Act was still in force. France's 1966 declaration, by which she accepted, subject to reservations, the compulsory jurisdiction of the Court under Article 36(2) of the Statute, neither amended nor superseded the provisions of the General Act of 1928, which remained applicable between New Zealand and France. New Zealand's alleged breach of the General Act in 1939 was immaterial.

(3)   *Article 17 of the General Act and Admissibility of the Application*   Article 17 of the General Act therefore conferred jurisdiction in respect of

any 'legal dispute' between New Zealand and France. The present dispute was clearly of a legal, rather than a political, character. It was necessary to distinguish between genuine preliminary questions and questions relating to the merits. The question whether New Zealand's claims were well founded in international law was not a preliminary question, except in so far as it was necessary for the Court to ensure that there was a reasonably arguable legal claim. This requirement was clearly satisfied and the Court should have deferred consideration of other matters to the merits phase.

Dissenting Opinion of Judge de Castro The reasoning set forth in the parallel *Australia* v. *France* case was applicable in this case in view of the practically identical nature of the cases.

(1) The French statements of intention regarding future nuclear tests did not amount to a binding undertaking to conduct no further atmospheric nuclear tests. The New Zealand claim was not, therefore, without object.

(2) It was clear that the Court did not possess jurisdiction by virtue of the 1966 French declaration under Article 36(2). The French reservation of matters relating to national defence was not self-judging but it clearly applied to the present case. Even if it had been self-judging, and hence void, the result would have been that the whole declaration was void. Jurisdiction existed only under the General Act on which the 1966 French declaration and reservation had had no effect.

(3) On the question of admissibility, the Applicant had no *locus standi* to seek a declaration that atmospheric nuclear tests in general were unlawful, since in doing so it would not be protecting a legal interest of its own but rather purporting to represent the international community. However, New Zealand was clearly entitled to claim in respect of the pollution of her own territory. As regards the claim in respect of the alleged infringement of the freedom of the high seas, New Zealand was not entitled to present the claim in the abstract form in which it had been presented, since New Zealand was not there relying on a right of her own.

Dissenting Opinion of Judge ad hoc *Sir Garfield Barwick* The reasons given in his dissenting opinion in the Australian proceeding applied with equal force in respect of New Zealand. In the Australian proceeding, Sir Garfield Barwick said the Court had jurisdiction in the case by virtue of the General Act of 1928. The Act remained in force between Australia and France and between New Zealand and France, notwithstanding the dissolution of the League of Nations, and the 1966 French declaration under Article 36(2) of the Statute of the Court neither amended nor superseded its obligations under the General Act. The reservation to the French declaration also had no effect upon the General Act. On the subject of admissibility, in so far as this was separable from the question of jurisdiction, there were two questions for the Court to decide: whether there was a dispute as to legal rights, and whether New Zealand had a legal interest sufficient to entitle it to bring the claim. In deciding the first question it was unnecessary to consider the validity of Australia's claim, i.e. whether international law imposed restrictions upon atmospheric nuclear testing. There was a dispute between the parties about the existence and application of rules of law and that gave the case a legal character. As regarded the second question, Australia's interest in her own territory and in the high seas was clearly sufficient to entitle her to claim in respect of alleged infringements of her territorial sovereignty and the freedom of the high seas. The question of Australia's *locus standi* to claim that atmospheric nuclear tests were *per se* unlawful was more difficult but was inseparable from the merits of the case.

The action of the Court in deciding the case on grounds on which the parties had had no opportunity to present submissions and on evidence largely considered *proprio motu* was incompatible with the judicial function. Moreover, the decision that the object of the Application was to secure the cessation of atmospheric tests in the South Pacific was the result of erroneously equating the relief claimed in the Application with the Applicant's motives in instituting the litigation. Even if the French statements amounted to the assumption of a binding undertaking not to conduct further atmospheric tests, which was unlikely, the Court was not entitled to decide that France was bound without first finding that it had jurisdiction in respect of France. The claim for a declaratory judgment was far from being without object since a declaration would settle the dispute as to the rights of the parties and there might be an ancillary claim for compensation in respect of the 1973 and 1974 tests to which such a declaration would be highly relevant. According to Sir Garfield Barwick's opinion in the Australian case, '[a] voluntary promise, even if binding, not to exercise what the Respondent still maintained was its right cannot be the equivalent or substitute for such an adjudication in these proceedings'.

Application by Fiji for Permission to Intervene, 20 December 1974

Held by the International Court of Justice (unanimously)   Since the New Zealand claim no longer had any object and the Court was not called upon to pronounce upon it, the Fijian application had lapsed.

Individual Declarations of Judges Gros, Onyeama, Jiménez de Aréchaga and Judge ad hoc Sir Garfield Barwick   The Fijian application should have been dismissed on the ground that the Court lacked jurisdiction as between Fiji and France and Fiji could not circumvent this difficulty by intervening in proceedings brought by another State.

Joint Declaration of Judges Dillard and Sir Humphrey Waldock   The decision was a natural result of the decision in *Australia v. France* from which they had dissented.

There follows

---

[6] The individual declarations of Judges Jiménez de Aréchaga, Sir Humphrey Waldock and Nagendra Singh are not reproduced in this volume but can be found at *ICJ Reports 1974*, pp.143, 144 and 145 respectively. A translation of the dissenting opinion of Judge Forster is similarly not reproduced in this volume but can be found at *ICJ Reports 1974*, p. 148.

[7] The individual declarations of Judges Gros, Petrén, Onyeama and Ignacio-Pinto are not reproduced in this volume but can all be found at *ICJ Reports 1974*, p. 326.

[8] Translations of the separate opinions of Judges Forster, Gros and Ignacio-Pinto can be found at *ICJ Reports 1974*, pp. 479, 480 and 493 respectively. A translation of the dissenting opinion of Judge de Castro can be found at *ICJ Reports 1974*, p. 524.

[9] The individual declarations of Judges Gros and Onyeama are not reproduced in this volume but can be found at *ICJ Reports 1974*, p. 536. The joint declaration of Judges Dillard and Sir Humphrey Waldock and the declaration of Judge Jiménez de Aréchaga are also not reproduced in this volume but can be found at *ICJ Reports 1974*, p. 537. The declaration of Judge *ad hoc* Sir Garfield Barwick is also not reproduced in this volume but can be found at *ICJ Reports 1974*, p. 538.

Order of International Court of Justice on Request for the Indication of Interim Measures of Protection, 22 June 1973 (extract)

[136] [. . .] 1. Having regard to the request dated 14 May 1973 and filed in the Registry the same day, whereby the Government of New Zealand, relying on Article 33 of the General Act of 1928 for the Pacific Settlement of International Disputes and on Articles 41 and 48 of the Statute and Article 66 of the Rules of Court, asks the Court to indicate, pending the final decision in the case brought before it by the Application of the same date, the following interim measures of protection:

> The measure which New Zealand requests . . . is that France refrain from conducting any further nuclear tests that give rise to radio-active fall-out while the Court is seized of the case.

[. . .]

[138] [. . .] 19. Whereas the request of the Government of New Zealand for the indication of provisional measures is based on Article 33 of the General Act of 1928, as well as on Article 41 of the Statute of the Court; and whereas the Government of New Zealand in its final submission asks the [139] Court to indicate such measures under Article 33 of the General Act or, alternatively, under Article 41 of the Statute;

20. Whereas the Court considers that it should not exercise its power to indicate provisional measures under Article 33 of the General Act of 1928 until it has reached a final conclusion that the General Act is still in force; whereas the Court is not in a position to reach a final conclusion on this point at the present stage of the proceedings, and will therefore examine the request for the indication of interim measures only in the context of Article 41 of the Statute;

21. Whereas the power of the Court to indicate interim measures under Article 41 of the Statute has as its object to preserve the respective rights of the Parties pending the decision of the Court, and presupposes that irreparable prejudice should not be caused to rights which are the subject of dispute in judicial proceedings and that the Court's judgment should not be anticipated by reason of any initiative regarding the matters in issue before the Court;

22. Whereas it follows that the Court in the present case cannot exercise its power to indicate interim measures of protection unless the rights claimed in the Application, prima facie, appear to fall within the purview of the Court's jurisdiction;

23. Whereas it is claimed by the Government of New Zealand in its Application that rules and principles of international law are now violated by nuclear testing undertaken by the French Government in the South Pacific region, and that, *inter alia*,

> (a) it violates the rights of all members of the international community including New Zealand, that no nuclear tests that give rise to radioactive fall-out be conducted;

(b) it violates the rights of all members of the international community, including New Zealand, to the preservation from unjustified artificial radioactive contamination of the terrestrial, maritime and aerial environment
and, in particular, of the environment of the region in which the tests are
conducted and in which New Zealand, the Cook Islands, Niue and the
Tokelau Islands are situated;

(c) it violates the right of New Zealand that no radio-active material enter the
territory of New Zealand, the Cook Islands, Niue or the Tokelau Islands,
including their air space and territorial waters, as a result of nuclear testing;

(d) it violates the right of New Zealand that no radio-active material, having
entered the territory of New Zealand, the Cook Islands, Niue or the
Tokelau Islands, including their air space and territorial waters, as a result of
nuclear testing, cause harm, including apprehension, anxiety and concern,
to the people and Government of New Zealand and of the Cook Islands,
Niue and the Tokelau Islands;

(e) it violates the right of New Zealand to freedom of the high seas, including
freedom of navigation and overflight and the freedom to [**140**] explore and
exploit the resources of the sea and the seabed, without interference or
detriment resulting from nuclear testing;

and whereas New Zealand invokes its moral and legal responsibilities in relation to
the Cook Islands, Niue and the Tokelau Islands;

24. Whereas it cannot be assumed *a priori* that such claims fall completely outside
the purview of the Court's jurisdiction, or that the Government of New Zealand may
not be able to establish a legal interest in respect of these claims entitling the Court
to admit the Application;

25. Whereas by the terms of Article 41 of the Statute the Court may indicate
interim measures of protection only when it considers that circumstances so require
in order to preserve the rights of either party;

26. Whereas the Government of New Zealand alleges, *inter alia*, that during the
period from 1966 to 1972 the French Government has carried out a series of atmospheric nuclear tests centred on Mururoa in the South Pacific; that the French
Government has refused to give an assurance that its programme of atmospheric
nuclear testing in the South Pacific is at an end, and that on 2 May 1973 the French
Government announced that it did not envisage cancelling or modifying the programme originally planned; that from official pronouncements it is clear that some
further tests are envisaged with the likelihood of deploying a thermonuclear war-
head by 1976; that the French Government has also reserved its options on the
development of yet another generation of nuclear weapons after 1976 which would
require further tests; that in previous years the nuclear testing series conducted
by France have begun on dates between 15 May and 7 July; that on the basis of
the pronouncements referred to above and the past practice of the French Government, there are strong grounds for believing that the French Government will
carry out further testing of nuclear devices and weapons in the atmosphere at

Mururoa Atoll before the Court is able to reach a decision on the Application of New Zealand;

27. Whereas these allegations give substance to the New Zealand Government's contention that there is an immediate possibility of a further atmospheric nuclear test being carried out by France in the Pacific;

28. Whereas the Government of New Zealand also alleges that each of the series of French nuclear tests has added to the radio-active fall-out in New Zealand territory; that the basic principles applied in this field by international authorities are that any exposure to radiation may have irreparable, and harmful, somatic and genetic effects and that any additional exposure to artificial radiation can be justified only by the benefit which results; that, as the New Zealand Government has repeatedly pointed out in its correspondence with the French Government, the radio-active fall-out which reaches New Zealand as a result of French nuclear tests is inherently harmful, and that there is no compensating benefit to justify New Zealand's exposure to such harm; that the uncertain [141] physical and genetic effects to which contamination exposes the people of New Zealand causes them acute apprehension, anxiety and concern; and that there could be no possibility that the rights eroded by the holding of further tests could be fully restored in the event of a judgment in New Zealand's favour in these proceedings;

29. Whereas the French Government, in a diplomatic Note addressed to the Government of New Zealand and dated 10 June 1966, the text of which was annexed to the Application in this case, emphasized that every precaution would be taken with a view to ensuring the safety and the harmlessness of the French nuclear tests, and observed that the French Government, in taking all appropriate steps to ensure the protection of the populations close to the test zone, had sought *a fortiori* to guarantee the safety of populations considerably further distant, such as New Zealand or the territories for which it is responsible; and whereas in a letter dated 19 February 1973 to the Prime Minister of New Zealand from the French Ambassador to New Zealand, the text of which was also annexed to the Application in this case, the French Government called attention to Reports of the New Zealand National Radiation Laboratory, and of the Australian National Radiation Advisory Committee, which reached the conclusion that the fall-out from the French tests had never involved any danger to the health of the populations of those two countries, and observed that the concern which had been expressed as to the long-term effects of testing could not be based on anything other than conjecture;

30. Whereas for the purpose of the present proceedings it suffices to observe that the information submitted to the Court, including Reports of the United Nations Scientific Committee on the Effects of Atomic Radiation between 1958 and 1972, does not exclude the possibility that damage to New Zealand might be shown to be caused by the deposit on New Zealand territory of radio-active fall-out resulting from such tests and to be irreparable;

31. Whereas in the light of the foregoing considerations the Court is satisfied that it should indicate interim measures of protection in order to preserve the right claimed

by New Zealand in the present litigation in respect of the deposit of radio-active fall-out on the territory of New Zealand, the Cook Islands, Niue or the Tokelau Islands;

32. Whereas the circumstances of the case do not appear to require the indication of interim measures of protection in respect of other rights claimed by New Zealand in the Application;

*

33. Whereas the foregoing considerations do not permit the Court to accede at the present stage of the proceedings to the request made by the [142] French Government in its letter dated 16 May 1973 that the case be removed from the list;

34. Whereas the decision given in the present proceedings in no way prejudges the question of the jurisdiction of the Court to deal with the merits of the case, or any questions relating to the admissibility of the Application, or relating to the merits themselves, and leaves unaffected the right of the French Government to submit arguments in respect of those questions;

35. Having regard to the position taken by the French Government in its letter dated 16 May 1973 that the Court was manifestly not competent in the case and to the fact that it was not represented at the hearings held on 24 and 25 May on the question of the indication of interim measures of protection;

36. Whereas, in these circumstances, it is necessary to resolve as soon as possible the questions of the Court's jurisdiction and of the admissibility of the Application;

Accordingly,

THE COURT

Indicates, by 8 votes to 6, pending its final decision in the proceedings instituted on 9 May 1973 by New Zealand against France, the following provisional measures:

> The Governments of New Zealand and France should each of them ensure that no action of any kind is taken which might aggravate or extend the dispute submitted to the Court or prejudice the rights of the other Party in respect of the carrying out of whatever decision the Court may render in the case; and, in particular, the French Government should avoid nuclear tests causing the deposit of radioactive fall-out on the territory of New Zealand, the Cook Islands, Niue or the Tokelau Islands;

Decides that the written proceedings shall first be addressed to the questions of the jurisdiction of the Court to entertain the dispute, and of the admissibility of the Application;

Fixes as follows the time-limits for the written proceedings:

21 September 1973 for the Memorial of the Government of New Zealand;

21 December 1973 for the Counter-Memorial of the French Government;

And reserves the subsequent procedure for further decision.

[...]

DECLARATION OF JUDGE *AD HOC* SIR GARFIELD BARWICK (EXTRACT)

[146] [. . .] Lastly, the material before the Court, particularly that appearing in the UNSCEAR reports, provides reasonable grounds for concluding that further deposit in the New Zealand territorial environment and that of [147] the Cook Islands of radio-active particles of matter is likely to do harm for which no adequate compensatory measures could be provided.

These conclusions are sufficient to warrant the indication of interim measures.

I agree with the form of the provisional measures indicated, understanding that the action proscribed is action on the part of governments and that the measures are indicated in respect only of the New Zealand Government's claim to the inviolability of its territory, and of that of the Cook Islands.

DISSENTING OPINION OF JUDGE GROS (EXTRACT)

[Translation]

[156] [. . .] A certain tendency has arisen to consider that the Orders of 17 August 1972 in the *Fisheries Jurisdiction* cases have, as it were, consolidated the law concerning provisional measures. But each case must be examined according to its own merits and, as Article 41 says, according to 'the circumstances'. Now the case of Iceland was entirely different in circumstances. The Court had developed an awareness of the existence of its own jurisdiction, the urgency was admitted, the reality and the precise definition of the dispute were not contested; finally, the right of the Applicant States which was protected by the Orders was recognized as being a right currently exercised, whereas the claim of Iceland constituted a modification of existing law. It suffices to enumerate these points to show that the situation is entirely different today; so far as the last point is concerned, the situation is now even the reverse, since the Applicants stand upon a claim to the modification of existing positive law when [157] they ask the Court to recognize the existence of a rule forbidding the overstepping of a threshold of atomic pollution.

[. . .]

DISSENTING OPINION OF JUDGE PETRÉN (EXTRACT)

[Translation]

[159] Having voted against the adoption of the Order, I append a dissenting opinion.

Considering the identity of claims and submissions between this case and the *Nuclear Tests* case *(Australia v. France)*, as well as the coincident circumstances of fact and law, I was of the opinion that the two cases should have been joined even at the present stage of the proceedings. The Court having rejected that proposal, it only remains for me to express the same opinion here as in the other case.

I am unable to concur in the opinion of the majority either with regard to the defer-ment, to a later stage in the proceedings, of the questions of the Court's jurisdiction and the admissibility of the Application, or with regard to the indication of provisional measures.

In my view, the questions of the Court's jurisdiction and of the admissibility of the Application, and also the question of the indication of provisional measures, fall into a common framework as follows:

Before undertaking the examination of the merits of the case, the International Court of Justice, like any other court, has the duty of making sure as far as possible that it possesses jurisdiction and that the application is admissible. The absence of the State against which application is made does not alter this requirement in any way. On the contrary. Article 53 of the Statute lays an obligation on the Court to satisfy itself as to its possession of jurisdiction and the admissibility of the application on the basis of the elements at its disposal. Among the latter in the present case are the arguments put forward by France in the letter handed in by its Ambassador and by New Zealand in its Application and in its oral pleadings of 24–25 May 1973. It is, however, the Court's duty also to consider any other elements that it may find relevant. The fact that New Zealand has requested provisional measures does not dispense the Court from the obligation of beginning by an examination of the questions of its jurisdiction and of the admissibility of the Application: indeed, it makes that examination, if anything, more urgent.

[. . .]

[161] [. . .] Alongside the question of the Court's jurisdiction, there arises that of the admissibility of New Zealand's Application. As I understand that term, it includes the examination of every question that arises in connection with the ascertainment of whether the Court has been validly seised of the case. But what is first and foremost necessary from that point of view is to ask oneself whether atmospheric tests of nuclear weapons are, generally speaking, already governed by norms of international law, or whether they do not still belong to a highly political domain where the norms concerning their international legality or illegality are still at the gestation stage.

[162] Certainly, the existence of nuclear weapons and the tests serving to perfect and multiply them, are among the foremost subjects of dread for mankind today. To exorcise their spectre, is, however, primarily a matter for statesmen. One must hope that they will one day succeed in establishing a state of affairs, both political and legal, which will shield the whole of mankind from the anxiety created by nuclear arms. Meanwhile there is the question whether the moment has already come when an international tribunal is the appropriate recipient of an application like that directed in the present case against but one of the present nuclear Powers.

The Order defers the question of the admissibility of the Application, like that of the Court's jurisdiction, to a later stage in the proceedings. I am unable to concur in this decision, because I consider that the Court could and should have settled in its present session the whole of the preliminary and urgent questions which arise in the case and concerning which it is incumbent upon the Court to take up a position *proprio motu*.

[. . .]

[163] DISSENTING OPINION OF JUDGE IGNACIO-PINTO

[Translation]

I am opposed to the Order made this day by the Court, granting New Zealand the same interim measures of protection as were granted Australia a few hours before on this same date, in the latter's case against France.

My opposition to the present Order is based on the same considerations as I have already expounded at length in my dissenting opinion in the first *Nuclear Tests* case *(Australia* v. *France)*. I am therefore voting against it as I voted against the first Order, in the case of *Australia* v. *France*.

But before going farther, I venture to observe that the Court ought from the beginning to have pronounced a joinder of the two cases, as some judges had moreover requested.

For in fact, in the two requests for interim measures presented by the two States, Australia and New Zealand, there is more than a mere analogy between the two claims. They have indeed the same object, namely *to secure from the Court an indication that 'the French Government should avoid nuclear tests causing the deposit of radio-active fall-out' on the territory* (emphasis added):

    (1)   of Australia;

    (2)   of New Zealand, the Cook Islands, Niue or the Tokelau Islands.

There is therefore identity as to the object of the claim; the litigant cited as respondent, France, is also identical; finally there is, as nearly as makes no difference, an identity in the terms employed in the requests.

That being so, I think that there was every reason to order a joinder and to pronounce upon the two States' requests for the indication of interim measures in one and the same Order.

For that reason I am also voting against the Order made today by the Court in respect of the New Zealand request, and for the rest of the arguments I would adduce in support of my dissenting opinion in the present case, I will confine myself to referring to those I have already put forward in the case of *Australia* v. *France*.

But I wish to take this opportunity of modifying somewhat, in regard to New Zealand, what I said about the nuclear tests carried out by the United Kingdom at Maralinga in Australia in the years 1952–1957.

The same reasoning that I followed in order to deny that Australia was entitled to put forward its claims is likewise valid where New Zealand is [164] concerned. It is also necessary to refer in this connection to the tests carried out by the United Kingdom at Christmas Island – thermonuclear explosions, what is more – at a distance of 1,200 miles from the Tokelau Islands, under New Zealand administration.

If therefore New Zealand considered that the United Kingdom was acting acceptably in carrying out tests at Christmas Island, it is not entitled to request that the French Government be prevented from exploding nuclear devices at a site some 1,400 miles from New Zealand.

And so far as the effects of radio-activity are concerned – a subject on which there is such eagerness to sensitize public opinion –, it is interesting to note the following passage, taken from page 18 of *New Zealand and Nuclear Testing in the Pacific* by Nigel S. Roberts, Lecturer in Political Science, University of Canterbury, a work published at Wellington in 1972 by the Institute of International Affairs, of which Mr Allan Martyn Finlay, Attorney-General of New Zealand and counsel for his country in the present case, is the Vice-President:

> Before French testing began, a special report was presented to the Prime Minister and then to the House of Representatives in an attempt to assess the health hazards to New Zealand, as well as to other Pacific areas, from the proposed French tests of nuclear weapons. The report concluded that:
>
>> Testing of nuclear weapons up to the present time does not and will not present a significant health hazard to the people of New Zealand or the Pacific Territories with which it is associated. The proposed French tests will add *fractionally but not significantly* to the long-lived fall-out in these areas. The general levels of such radio-active contamination in the Southern hemisphere will remain *below those* already existing in the Northern hemisphere ... For New Zealand the chance of significant levels of contamination being reached is *even more unlikely* than for the islands in the Pacific. (Emphasis added.)

If that could be the unequivocal opinion of the experts in an undisputed official report addressed to the New Zealand Prime Minister and House of Representatives, that confirms my conviction that this second *Nuclear Tests* case is also political in character. Hence I remain strongly opposed to the Order indicating the interim measures requested by New Zealand. In making it, the Court has exceeded its competence and it should have rejected that request.

[Report: *ICJ Reports 1973*, p. 135]

Order of International Court of Justice on Application by Fiji for Permission to Intervene, 12 July 1973 (extract)

[**325**][...] 1. Whereas the application of Fiji by its very nature presupposes that the Court has jurisdiction to entertain the dispute between New Zealand and France and that New Zealand's Application against France in respect of that dispute is admissible;

2. Having regard to the position taken by the French Government in a letter dated 16 May 1973 from the Ambassador of France to the Netherlands, handed by him to the Registrar the same day, that the Court was manifestly not competent to entertain New Zealand's Application;

3. Having regard to the fact that by its Order dated 22 June 1973 the Court decided that the written proceedings in the case should first be addressed to the questions of the jurisdiction of the Court to entertain the dispute between New Zealand and France and of the admissibility of New Zealand's Application;

THE COURT,
by 8 votes to 5,

Decides to defer its consideration of the application of the Government of Fiji for permission to intervene in the proceedings instituted by New Zealand against France until it has pronounced upon the questions to which the pleadings mentioned in its Order dated 22 June 1973 are to be addressed.

[...]

[Report: *ICJ Reports 1973*, p. 324]

Judgment of International Court of Justice on Merits, 20 December 1974 (extract)

[**463**] [...] 25. The Court would recall that the submission made in the Application (paragraph 11 above)[10] is that the Court should adjudge and declare [**464**] 'that the conduct by the French Government of nuclear tests in the South Pacific region that give rise to radio-active fall-out constitutes a violation of New Zealand's rights under international law' – the alleged rights so violated being enumerated in the Application – and 'that these rights will be violated by any further such tests'.

26. The diplomatic correspondence between New Zealand and France over the past ten years reveals New Zealand's preoccupation with French nuclear tests in the atmosphere in the South Pacific region, and indicates that its objective was to bring about their termination. Thus in a letter from the Prime Minister of New Zealand to the French Ambassador in Wellington dated 19 December 1972, the Prime Minister said:

> My Government is committed to working through all possible means to bring the tests to an end, and we shall not hesitate to use the channels available to us in concert as appropriate with like-minded countries. It is my hope, however, Mr Ambassador, that you will convey to your Government while in Paris my earnest desire to see this one element of serious contention removed from what is in other respects an excellent relationship between our countries. For my part, I see no other way than a halt to further testing.

Furthermore in the Application of New Zealand, it is stated, in connection with discussions held in April 1973 between the two Governments that:

> Unfortunately, however, they [the discussions] did not lead to agreement. In particular, the French Government did not feel able to give the Deputy Prime Minister of New Zealand the assurance which he sought, namely that the French programme of atmospheric nuclear testing in the South Pacific had come to an end.

And in a letter to the President of the French Republic by the Prime Minister of New Zealand dated 4 May 1973, following those discussions, the Prime Minister said:

> Since France has not agreed to our request that nuclear weapons testing in the atmosphere of the South Pacific be brought to an end, and since the French Government

[10 Not reproduced in this volume.]

does not accept New Zealand's view that these tests are unlawful, the New Zealand Government sees no alternative to its proceeding with the submission of its dispute with France to the International Court of Justice.

I stress again that we see this as the one question at issue between us, and that our efforts are solely directed at removing it from contention.

27. Further light is thrown on the nature of the New Zealand claim by the reaction of New Zealand, both through its successive Prime Ministers and through its representatives before the Court, to the statements [465] referred to in paragraph 20 above,[11] made on behalf of France and relating to nuclear tests in the South Pacific region. In the course of the oral proceedings, the Attorney-General of New Zealand outlined the history of the dispute, and included in this review mention of diplomatic correspondence exchanged between 10 June and 1 July 1974 by France and New Zealand, which was communicated to the Court on 3 July by the Applicant, and of a communiqué issued by the Office of the President of the French Republic on 8 June 1974. The Attorney-General's comments on these documents, which are thus part of the record in the case, indicated that they merited analysis as possible evidence of a certain development in the controversy between the Parties, though at the same time he made it clear that this development was not, in his Government's view, of such a nature as to resolve the dispute to its satisfaction. More particularly, when referring to a Note of 10 June 1974 from the French Embassy in Wellington to the New Zealand Ministry of Foreign Affairs (quoted in paragraph 36 below) he stated: 'New Zealand has not been given anything in the nature of an unqualified assurance that 1974 will see the end of atmospheric nuclear testing in the South Pacific.' The Attorney-General continued:

> On 11 June the Prime Minister of New Zealand, Mr Kirk, asked the French Ambassador in Wellington to convey a letter to the President of France. Copies of that letter have been filed with the Registry. It urged among other things that the President should, even at that time, weigh the implications of any further atmospheric testing in the Pacific and resolve to put an end to an activity which has been the source of grave anxiety to the people of the Pacific region for more than a decade. (Hearing of 10 July 1974.)

It is clear from these statements, read in the light of the diplomatic correspondence referred to above, that if the Note of 10 June 1974 could have been construed by New Zealand as conveying 'an unqualified assurance that 1974 [would] see the end of atmospheric nuclear testing' by France 'in the South Pacific', or if the President of the Republic, following the letter of 11 June 1974, did 'resolve to put an end to [that] activity', the applicant Government would have regarded its objective as having been achieved.

28. Subsequently, on 1 November 1974, the Prime Minister of New Zealand, Mr W. E. Rowling, commented in a public statement on the indications given by France of its intention to put an end to atmospheric tests in the Pacific, and said:

[11 Not reproduced in this volume.]

> It should ... be clearly understood that nothing said by the French Government, whether to New Zealand or to the international community at large, has amounted to an assurance that there will [**466**] be no further atmospheric nuclear tests in the South Pacific. The option of further atmospheric tests has been left open. *Until we have an assurance that nuclear testing of this kind is finished for good, the dispute between New Zealand and France persists* ... (Emphasis added.)

Without commenting for the moment on the Prime Minister's interpretation of the French statements, the Court would observe that the passage italicized above clearly implies that an assurance that atmospheric testing is 'finished for good' would, in the view of New Zealand, bring the dispute to an end.

29. The type of tests to which the proceedings relate is described in the Application as 'nuclear tests in the South Pacific region that gave rise to radio-active fall-out', the type of testing contemplated not being specified. However, New Zealand's case has been argued mainly in relation to atmospheric tests; and the statements quoted in paragraphs 26, 27 and 28 above, particularly those of successive Prime Ministers of New Zealand, of 11 June and 1 November 1974, show that an assurance 'that nuclear testing of this kind', that is to say, testing in the atmosphere, 'is finished for good', would meet the object of the New Zealand claim. The Court therefore considers that, for purposes of the Application, the New Zealand claim is to be interpreted as applying only to atmospheric tests, not to any other form of testing, and as applying only to atmospheric tests so conducted as to give rise to radio-active fall-out on New Zealand territory.

[...]

[**467**] [...] 31. In the circumstances of the present case, as already mentioned, the Court must ascertain the true subject of the dispute, the object and purpose of the claim (cf. *Interhandel, Judgment, ICJ Reports 1959*, p. 19; *Right of Passage over Indian Territory, Merits, Judgment, ICJ Reports 1960*, pp. 33–4). In doing so it must take into account not only the submission, but the Application as a whole, the arguments of the Applicant before the Court, and other documents referred to above. If these clearly define the object of the claim, the interpretation of the submission must necessarily be affected. The Court is asked to adjudge and declare that French atmospheric nuclear tests are illegal, but at the same time it is requested to adjudge and declare that the rights of New Zealand 'will be violated by any further such tests'. The Application thus contains a submission requesting a definition of the rights and obligations of the Parties. However, it is clear that the *fons et origo* of the dispute was the atmospheric nuclear tests conducted by France in the South Pacific region, and that the original and ultimate objective of the Applicant was and has remained to obtain a termination of those tests. This is indeed confirmed by the various statements made by the New Zealand Government, and in particular by the statement made before the Court in the oral proceedings, on 10 July 1974, when, after referring to New Zealand's submission, the Attorney-General stated that 'My Government seeks a halt to a hazardous and unlawful activity.' Thus the dispute brought before the Court cannot be separated

from the situation in which it has arisen, and from further developments which may have affected it.

[...]

[**468**] [...] 33. At the hearing of 10 July 1974 the Court was presented by counsel for New Zealand with an interpretation of certain expressions of intention communicated to the New Zealand Government by the French Government and the French President. In particular he referred to a communiqué of 8 June 1974 (paragraph 35 below) and a diplomatic Note of 10 June 1974 (paragraph 36 below), and after quoting from that Note, he said:

> I emphasize two points: first, the most France is offering is that in her own time she will cease to disregard an existing Order of the Court; and second, even that offer is qualified by the phrase 'in the normal course of events'. New Zealand has not been given anything in the nature of an unqualified assurance that 1974 will see the end of atmospheric nuclear testing in the South Pacific.

Since that time, certain French authorities have made a number of consistent public statements concerning future tests which provide material facilitating the Court's task of assessing the Applicant's interpretation of the earlier documents, and which indeed require to be examined in order to discern whether they embody any modification of intention as to France's future conduct. It is true that these statements have not been made before the Court, but they are in the public domain, are known to the New Zealand Government, and were commented on by its Prime Minister in his statement of 1 November 1974. It will clearly be necessary to consider all these statements, both those drawn to the Court's attention in July 1974 and those subsequently made.

[...]

[**469**] [...] 35. It will be convenient to take the statements referred to above in chronological order. The first statement is contained in the communiqué issued by the Office of the President of the French Republic on 8 June 1974, shortly before the commencement of the 1974 series of French nuclear tests:

> The Decree reintroducing the security measures in the South Pacific nuclear test zone has been published in the Official Journal of 8 June 1974.
>
> The Office of the President of the Republic takes this opportunity of stating that in view of the stage reached in carrying out the French nuclear defence programme France will be in a position to pass on to the stage of underground explosions as soon as the series of tests planned for this summer is completed.

36. The second is contained in a Note of 10 June 1974 from the French Embassy in Wellington to the New Zealand Ministry of Foreign Affairs:

> It should ... be pointed out that the decision taken by the Office of the President of the French Republic to have the opening of the nuclear test series preceded by a press communiqué represents a departure from the practice of previous years. This procedure has been chosen in view of the fact that a new element has intervened in the development of the programme for perfecting the French deterrent force. This new

element is as follows: France, at the point which has been reached in the execution of its programme of defence [470] by nuclear means, will be in a position to move to the stage of underground firings as soon as the test series planned for this summer is completed.

Thus the atmospheric tests which will be carried out shortly will, in the normal course of events, be the last of this type.

The French authorities express the hope that the New Zealand Government will find this information of some interest and will wish to take it into consideration.

37. As indicated by counsel for the Applicant at the hearing of 10 July 1974, the reaction of the New Zealand Prime Minister to this second statement was expressed in a letter to the President of the French Republic dated 11 June 1974, from which the following are two extracts:

... I have noted that the terms of the announcement do not represent an unqualified renunciation of atmospheric testing for the future.

I would hope that even at this stage you would be prepared to weigh the implications of any further atmospheric testing in the Pacific and resolve to put an end to this activity which has been the source of grave anxiety to the people in the Pacific region for more than a decade.

Thus the phrase 'in the normal course of events' was regarded by New Zealand as qualifying the statement made, so that it did not meet the expectations of the Applicant, which evidently regarded those words as a form of escape clause. This is clear from the observations of counsel for New Zealand at the hearing of 10 July 1974. In a Note of 17 June 1974, the New Zealand Embassy in Paris stated that it had good reason to believe that France had carried out an atmospheric nuclear test on 16 June and made this further comment:

The announcement that France will proceed to underground tests in 1975, while presenting a new development, does not affect New Zealand's fundamental opposition to all nuclear testing, nor does it in any way reduce New Zealand's opposition to the atmospheric tests set down for this year: the more so since the French Government is unable to give firm assurances that no atmospheric testing will be undertaken after 1974.

38. The third French statement is contained in a reply made on 1 July 1974 by the President of the Republic to the New Zealand Prime Minister's letter of 11 June:

In present circumstances, it is at least gratifying for me to note the positive reaction in your letter to the announcement in the communiqué of 8 June 1974 that we are going over to underground [471] tests. There is in this a new element whose importance will not, I trust, escape the New Zealand Government.

39. These three statements were all drawn to the notice of the Court by the Applicant at the time of the oral proceedings. As already indicated, the Court will also have to consider the relevant statements subsequently made by the French authorities: on 25 July 1974 by the President of the Republic; on 16 August 1974 by the Minister

of Defence; on 25 September 1974 by the Minister for Foreign Affairs in the United Nations General Assembly; and on 11 October 1974 by the Minister of Defence.

40. The next statement to be considered, therefore, will be that made on 25 July at a press conference given by the President of the Republic, when he said:

> ... on this question of nuclear tests, you know that the Prime Minister had publicly expressed himself in the National Assembly in his speech introducing the Government's programme. He had indicated that French nuclear testing would continue. I had myself made it clear that this round of atmospheric tests would be the last, and so the members of the Government were completely informed of our intentions in this respect ...

41. On 16 August 1974, in the course of an interview on French television, the Minister of Defence said that the French Government had done its best to ensure that the 1974 nuclear tests would be the last atmospheric tests.

42. On 25 September 1974, the French Minister for Foreign Affairs, addressing the United Nations General Assembly, said:

> We have now reached a stage in our nuclear technology that makes it possible for us to continue our programme by underground testing, and we have taken steps to do so as early as next year.

43. On 11 October 1974, the Minister of Defence held a press conference during which he stated twice, in almost identical terms, that there would not be any atmospheric tests in 1975 and that France was ready to proceed to underground tests. When the comment was made that he had not added 'in the normal course of events', he agreed that he had not. This latter point is relevant in view of the Note of 10 June 1974 from the French Embassy in Wellington to the Ministry of Foreign Affairs of New Zealand (paragraph 36 above), to the effect that the atmospheric tests contemplated 'will, in the normal course of events, be the last of this type'. The Minister also mentioned that, whether or not other governments had been officially advised of the decision, they could become aware of it through the press and by reading the communiqués issued by the Office of the President of the Republic.

[472] 44. In view of the foregoing, the Court finds that the communiqué issued on 8 June 1974 (paragraph 35 above), the French Embassy's Note of 10 June 1974 (paragraph 36 above) and the President's letter of 1 July 1974 (paragraph 38) conveyed to New Zealand the announcement that France, following the conclusion of the 1974 series of tests, would cease the conduct of atmospheric nuclear tests. Special attention is drawn to the hope expressed in the Note of 10 June 1974 'that the New Zealand Government will find this information of some interest and will wish to take it into consideration', and the reference in that Note and in the letter of 1 July 1974 to 'a new element' whose importance is urged upon the New Zealand Government. The Court must consider in particular the President's statement of 25 July 1974 (paragraph 40 above) followed by the Defence Minister's statement of 11 October 1974 (paragraph 43). These reveal that the official statements made on behalf of France concerning

future nuclear testing are not subject to whatever proviso, if any, was implied by the expression 'in the normal course of events [*normalement*]'.

[. . .]

[**473**] [. . .] 50. Having examined the legal principles involved, the Court will now turn to the particular statements made by the French Government. The Government of New Zealand has made known to the Court its own interpretation of some of these statements at the oral proceedings (paragraph 27 above). As to subsequent statements, reference may be made to what was said by the Prime Minister of New Zealand on 1 November 1974 (paragraph 28 above). It will be observed that New Zealand has recognized the possibility of the dispute being resolved by a unilateral declaration, of the kind specified above, on the part of France. In the public statement of 1 November 1974, it is stated that 'Until we have an assurance that nuclear testing of this kind is finished for good, the dispute between New Zealand and France persists.' This is based on the view [**474**] that 'the option of further atmospheric tests has been left open'. The court must however form its own view of the meaning and scope intended by the author of a unilateral declaration which may create a legal obligation, and cannot in this respect be bound by the view expressed by another State which is in no way a party to the text.

51. Of the statements by the French Government now before the Court, the most essential are clearly those made by the President of the Republic. There can be no doubt, in view of his functions, that his public communications or statements, oral or written, as Head of State, are in international relations acts of the French State. His statements, and those of members of the French Government acting under his authority, up to the last statement made by the Minister of Defence (of 11 October 1974), constitute a whole. Thus, in whatever form these statements were expressed, they must be held to constitute an engagement of the State, having regard to their intention and to the circumstances in which they were made.

52. The unilateral statements of the French authorities were made outside the Court, publicly and *erga omnes*, even if some of them were communicated to the Government of New Zealand. As was observed above, to have legal effect, there was no need for these statements to be addressed to a particular State, nor was acceptance by any other State required. The general nature and characteristics of these statements are decisive for the evaluation of the legal implications, and it is to the interpretation of the statements that the Court must now proceed. The Court is entitled to presume, at the outset, that these statements were made [not] *in vacuo*, but in relation to the tests which constitute the very object of the present proceedings, although France has not appeared in the case.

53. In announcing that the 1974 series of atmospheric tests would be the last, the French Government conveyed to the world at large, including the Applicant, its intention effectively to terminate these tests. It was bound to assume that other States might take note of these statements and rely on their being effective. The validity of these statements and their legal consequences must be considered within the general framework of the security of international intercourse, and the confidence and trust which are so essential in the relations among States. It is from the actual

substance of these statements and from the circumstances attending their making, that the legal implications of the unilateral act must be deduced. The objects of these statements are clear and they were addressed to the international community as a whole, and the Court holds that they constitute an undertaking possessing legal effect. The Court considers that the President of the Republic, in deciding upon the effective cessation of atmospheric tests, gave an undertaking to the international community to which his words were addressed. It is true that the French Government has consistently maintained that its nuclear experiments [475] do not contravene any subsisting provision of international law, nor did France recognize that it was bound by any rule of international law to terminate its tests, but this does not affect the legal consequences of the statements examined above. The Court finds that the unilateral undertaking resulting from these statements cannot be interpreted as having been made in implicit reliance on an arbitrary power of reconsideration. The Court finds further that the French Government has undertaken an obligation the precise nature and limits of which must be understood in accordance with the actual terms in which they have been publicly expressed.

54. The Court will now confront the commitment entered into by France with the claim advanced by the Applicant. Though the latter has formally requested from the Court a finding on the rights and obligations of the Parties, it has throughout the dispute maintained as its final objective the termination of the tests. It has sought from France an assurance that the French programme of atmospheric nuclear testing would come to an end. While expressing its opposition to the 1974 tests, the Government of New Zealand made specific reference to an assurance that '1974 will see the end of atmospheric nuclear testing in the South Pacific' (paragraph 33 above). On more than one occasion it has indicated that it would be ready to accept such an assurance. Since the Court now finds that a commitment in this respect has been entered into by France, there is no occasion for a pronouncement in respect of rights and obligations of the Parties concerning the past – which in other circumstances the Court would be entitled and even obliged to make – whatever the date by reference to which such pronouncement might be made.

55. Thus the Court faces a situation in which the objective of the Applicant has in effect been accomplished, inasmuch as the Court finds that France has undertaken the obligation to hold no further nuclear tests in the atmosphere in the South Pacific.

56. This conclusion is not affected by a reference made by the New Zealand Government, in successive diplomatic Notes to the French Government from 1966 to 1974, to a formal reservation of 'the right to hold the French Government responsible for any damage or losses received by New Zealand ... as a result of any nuclear weapons tests conducted by France'; for no mention of any request for damages is made in the Application, and at the public hearing of 10 July 1974 the Attorney-General of New Zealand specifically stated: 'My Government seeks a halt to a hazardous and unlawful activity, and not compensation for its continuance.' The Court therefore finds that no question of damages in respect of tests already conducted arises in the present case.

57. It must be assumed that had New Zealand received an assurance, on one of the occasions when this was requested, which, in its interpretation, would have been satisfactory, it would have considered the dispute as concluded and would have discontinued the proceedings in [476] accordance with the Rules of Court. If it has not done so, this does not prevent the Court from making its own independent finding on the subject. It is true that 'the Court cannot take into account declarations, admissions or proposals which the Parties may have made during direct negotiations between themselves, when such negotiations have not led to a complete agreement' (*Factory at Chorzów (Merits), PCIJ, Series A, No. 17,* p. 51). However, in the present case, that is not the situation before the Court. The Applicant has clearly indicated what would satisfy its claim, and the Respondent has independently taken action; the question for the Court is thus one of interpretation of the conduct of each of the Parties. The conclusion at which the Court has arrived as a result of such interpretation does not mean that it is itself effecting a compromise of the claim; the Court is merely ascertaining the object of the claim and the effect of the Respondent's action, and this it is obliged to do. Any suggestion that the dispute would not be capable of being terminated by statements made on behalf of France would run counter to the unequivocally expressed views of the Applicant both before the Court and elsewhere.

58. The Court, as a court of law, is called upon to resolve existing disputes between States. Thus the existence of a dispute is the primary condition for the Court to exercise its judicial function; it is not sufficient for one party to assert that there is a dispute, since 'whether there exists an international dispute is a matter for objective determination' by the Court (*Interpretation of Peace Treaties with Bulgaria, Hungary and Romania (First Phase), Advisory Opinion, ICJ Reports 1950,* p. 74). The dispute brought before it must therefore continue to exist at the time when the Court makes its decision. It must not fail to take cognizance of a situation in which the dispute has disappeared because the final objective which the Applicant has maintained throughout has been achieved by other means. If the declarations of France concerning the effective cessation of the nuclear tests have the significance described by the Court, that is to say if they have caused the dispute to disappear, all the necessary consequences must be drawn from this finding.

59. It may be argued that although France may have undertaken such an obligation, by a unilateral declaration, not to carry out atmospheric nuclear tests in the South Pacific region, a judgment of the Court on this subject might still be of value because, if the Judgment upheld the Applicant's contentions, it would reinforce the position of the Applicant by affirming the obligation of the Respondent. However, the Court having found that the Respondent has assumed an obligation as to conduct, concerning the effective cessation of nuclear tests, no further judicial action is required. The Applicant has repeatedly sought from the Respondent an assurance that the tests would cease, and the Respondent has, on its own initiative, made a series of statements to the effect that they will cease. Thus the Court concludes that, the dispute having disappeared, the claim advanced by New Zealand no longer has any object. It follows that any further finding would have no *raison d'être.*

[. . .]

[477] [. . .] 61. [. . .] The Court therefore sees no reason to allow the continuance of proceedings which it knows are bound to be fruitless. While judicial settlement may provide a path to international harmony in circumstances of conflict, it is none the less true that the needless continuance of litigation is an obstacle to such harmony.

62. Thus the Court finds that no further pronouncement is required in the present case. It does not enter into the adjudicatory functions of the Court to deal with issues *in abstracto*, once it has reached the conclusion that the merits of the case no longer fall to be determined. The object of the claim having clearly disappeared, there is nothing on which to give judgment.

63. Once the Court has found that a State has entered into a commitment concerning its future conduct it is not the Court's function to contemplate that it will not comply with it. However, the Court observes that if the basis of this Judgment were to be affected, the Applicant could request an examination of the situation in accordance with the provisions of the Statute; the denunciation by France, by letter dated 2 January 1974, of the General Act for the Pacific Settlement of International Disputes, which is relied on as a basis of jurisdiction in the present case, cannot constitute by itself an obstacle to the presentation of such a request.

64. In its above-mentioned Order of 22 June 1973, the Court stated that the provisional measures therein set out were indicated 'pending its final decision in the proceedings instituted on 9 May 1973 by New [478] Zealand against France'. It follows that such Order ceases to be operative upon the delivery of the present Judgment, and that the provisional measures lapse at the same time.

65. For these reasons,
The Court,
by nine votes to six,
finds that the claim of New Zealand no longer has any object and that the Court is therefore not called upon to give a decision thereon.
[. . .]

[483] SEPARATE OPINION OF JUDGE PETRÉN (EXTRACT)

[Translation]
[. . .]
If I have been able to vote for the Judgment, it is because its operative paragraph finds that the claim is without object and that the Court is not called upon to give a

decision thereon. My examination of the case has led me to the same conclusion, but on grounds which do not coincide with the reasoning of the Judgment.

[. . .]

[**487**] [. . .] It is only an evolution subsequent to the Second World War which has made the duty of States to respect the human rights of all, including their own nationals, an obligation under international law towards all States members of the international community. [. . .]

[**488**] [. . .] We can see a similar evolution taking place today in an allied field, that of the protection of the environment. Atmospheric nuclear tests, envisaged as the bearers of a particularly serious risk of environmental pollution, are a source of acute anxiety for present-day mankind, and it is only natural that efforts should be made on the international plane to erect legal barriers against that kind of test. In the present case, the question is whether such barriers existed at the time of the filing of the New Zealand Application. That Application cannot be considered admissible if, at the moment when it was filed, international law had not reached the stage of applicability to the atmospheric testing of nuclear weapons. It has been argued that it is sufficient for two parties to be in dispute over a right for an application from one of them on that subject to be admissible. Such would be the situation in the present case, but to my mind the question of the admissibility of an application cannot be reduced to the observance of so simple a formula. It is still necessary that the right claimed by the applicant party should belong to a domain governed by international law. In the present case, the Application is based upon an allegation that France's nuclear tests in the Pacific have given rise to radio-active fall-out on the territory of New Zealand. The New Zealand Government considers that its sovereignty has thereby been infringed in a manner contrary to international law. As there is no treaty link between New Zealand and France in the matter of nuclear tests, the Application presupposes the existence of a rule of customary international law whereby States are prohibited from causing, through atmospheric nuclear tests, the deposit of radio-active fall-out on the territory of other States. It is therefore the existence or non-existence of such a customary rule which has to be determined.

[. . .]

[**489**] [. . .] As is clear from the foregoing, the admissibility of the Application depends, in my view, on the existence of a rule of customary international law which prohibits States from carrying out atmospheric tests of nuclear weapons giving rise to radio-active fall-out on the territory of other States. Now it is common knowledge, and is admitted by the New Zealand Government itself, that any nuclear explosion in the atmosphere gives rise to radio-active fall-out over the whole of the hemisphere where it takes place. New Zealand, therefore, is only one of many States on whose territory France's atmospheric nuclear tests, and likewise those of other States, have given rise to the deposit of radio-active fall-out. Since the Second World War, certain States have conducted atmospheric nuclear tests for the purpose of enabling them to pass from the atomic to the thermo-nuclear stage in the field of armaments. The conduct of these [**490**] States proves that their Governments have not been of the

opinion that customary international law forbade atmospheric nuclear tests. What is more, the Treaty of 1963 whereby the first three States to have acquired nuclear weapons mutually banned themselves from carrying out further atmospheric tests can be denounced. By the provision in that sense, the signatories of the Treaty showed that they were still of the opinion that customary international law did not prohibit atmospheric nuclear tests.

To ascertain whether a customary rule to that effect might have come into being, it would appear more important to learn what attitude is taken up by States which have not yet carried out the tests necessary for reaching the nuclear stage. For such States the prohibition of atmospheric nuclear tests could signify the division of the international community into two groups: States possessing nuclear weapons and States not possessing them. If a State which does not possess nuclear arms refrains from carrying out the atmospheric tests which would enable it to acquire them, and if that abstention is motivated not by political or economic considerations but by a conviction that such tests are prohibited by customary international law, the attitude of that State would constitute an element in the formation of such a custom. But where can one find proof that a sufficient number of States, economically and technically capable of manufacturing nuclear weapons, refrain from carrying out atmospheric nuclear tests because they consider that customary international law forbids them to do so? The example recently given by China when it exploded a very powerful bomb in the atmosphere is sufficient to demolish the contention that there exists at present a rule of customary international law prohibiting atmospheric nuclear tests. It would be unrealistic to close one's eyes to the attitude, in that respect, of the State with the largest population in the world.

To complete this brief outline, one may ask what has been the attitude of the numerous States on whose territory radio-active fall-out from the atmospheric tests of the nuclear Powers has been deposited and continues to be deposited. Have they, generally speaking, protested to these Powers, pointing out that their tests were in breach of customary international law? I do not observe that such has been the case. The resolutions passed in the General Assembly of the United Nations cannot be regarded as equivalent to legal protests made by one State to another and concerning concrete instances. They indicate the existence of a strong current of opinion in favour of proscribing atmospheric nuclear tests. That is a political task of the highest urgency, but it is one which remains to be accomplished. Thus the claim submitted to the Court by New Zealand belongs to the political domain and is situated outside the framework of international law as it exists today.

I consider, consequently, that the Application of New Zealand was, from the very institution of proceedings, devoid of any object on which the Court could give a decision, whereas the Judgment finds only that [491] such an object is lacking now. I concur with the Judgment so far as the outcome to be given the proceedings is concerned, i.e., that the Court is not called upon to give a decision, but that does not enable me to associate myself with the grounds on which the Judgment is based. [. . .]

[**494**] JOINT DISSENTING OPINION OF JUDGES ONYEAMA, DILLARD, JIMÉNEZ DE
ARÉCHAGA AND SIR HUMPHREY WALDOCK (EXTRACT)

[...]

Part I. Reasons for our dissent

2. Basically, the Judgment is grounded on the premise that the sole object of the
claim of New Zealand is 'to obtain a termination of' the 'atmospheric nuclear tests
conducted by France in the South Pacific region' (para. 31).

In our view the basic premise of the Judgment, which limits the Applicant's submissions to a single purpose, and narrowly circumscribes its objective in pursing the
present proceedings, is untenable. In consequence the Court's chain of reasoning
leads to an erroneous conclusion. This occurs, we think, partly because the Judgment fails to take account of the purpose and utility of a request for a declaratory
judgment and even more because its basic premise fails to correspond to and even
changes the nature and scope of New Zealand's formal submission as presented in
the Application.

3. In the Application New Zealand:

> ... asks the Court to adjudge and declare: That the conduct by the French Government of
> nuclear tests in the South Pacific region that give rise to radio-active fall-out constitutes
> a violation of New Zealand's rights under international law, and that these rights will
> be violated by any further such tests.

[...]

[**499**] [...] 12. In accordance with the above-mentioned basic principles, the true
nature of New Zealand's claim, and of the objectives sought by the Applicant, ought
to have been determined on the basis of the clear and natural meaning of the text
of its formal submission. The interpretation of that submission made by the Court
constitutes in our view not an interpretation but a complete revision of the text,
which ends in eliminating what constitutes the essence of that submission, namely the
request for a declaration of illegality of nuclear tests in the South Pacific Ocean giving
rise to radio-active fall-out. A radical alteration of an applicant's submission under the
guise of interpretation has serious consequences because it constitutes a frustration of
a party's legitimate expectations that the case which it has put before the Court will be
examined and decided. In this instance the serious consequences have an irrevocable
character because the Applicant is now prevented from resubmitting its Application
and seising the Court again by reason of France's denunciation of the instruments on
which it is sought to base the Court's jurisdiction in the present dispute.

13. The Judgment revises, we think, the Applicant's submission by bringing in other
materials such as diplomatic communications and statements made in the course of
the hearings and governmental press statements which are no part of the judicial
proceedings. These materials do not justify, however, the interpretation arrived at
in the Judgment. They refer to requests made repeatedly by the Applicant for an
assurance from France as to the cessation of tests. But these requests for an assurance

cannot have the effect attributed to them by the Judgment. While litigation is in progress an applicant may address requests to a respondent to give an assurance that it will not pursue the contested activity, but such requests cannot by themselves support the inference that an unqualified assurance, if received, would satisfy *all* the objectives the applicant is seeking through the judicial proceedings; still less can they restrict or [**500**] amend the claims formally submitted to the Court. According to the Rules of Court, this can only result from a clear indication by the applicant to that effect, through a withdrawal of the case, a modification of its submissions or an equivalent action. It is not for nothing that the submissions are required to be presented in writing and bear the signature of the Agent. It is a *non sequitur*, therefore, to interpret such requests for an assurance as constituting an implied renunciation, a modification or a withdrawal of the claim which is still maintained before the Court, asking for a judicial declaration of illegality of atmospheric tests. At the very least, since the Judgment attributes intentions and implied waivers to the Applicant, that Party should have been given an opportunity to explain its real intentions and objectives, instead of proceeding to such a determination *inaudita parte*.

*

* *

14. The Judgment, while it reiterates that the Applicant's objective has been to bring about the termination of atmospheric nuclear tests, fails to examine a crucial question, namely from what date the Applicant sought to achieve this objective. To answer this point it is necessary to take into account the date from which, according to New Zealand's submission, the legality of the French atmospheric tests is brought into question.

New Zealand's submission refers, in general terms, to nuclear tests 'that give rise to radio-active fall-out'. In making a declaration like the one requested, the Court might have had to pronounce generally on the legality of tests conducted by France in the South Pacific region, which gave rise to radio-active fall-out. The judicial declaration of illegality asked for in the submission would thus have implications not merely for future, but also for past tests, in respect of which the New Zealand Government reserved the right to hold the French Government responsible for any damage or losses. This would certainly include the tests conducted in 1973 and 1974 in disregard of the Court's interim order. There is not only occasion, but a duty of the Court, to pronounce on the legality of the tests which have taken place, since a request for a declaration of illegality covering atmospheric tests conducted in the past, could not be deprived of its object by statements of intention limited to tests to be conducted in 1975 or thereafter.

15. Such a view of the matter takes no account of the possibility of New Zealand seeking to claim compensation, particularly in respect of the tests conducted in 1973 and 1974. It is true that the Applicant has not asked for compensation for damage in the proceedings which are now before the Court. However, the New Zealand Government has since [**501**] 1966 consistently reserved 'the right to hold the French

Government responsible for any damages or losses incurred as a result of the tests by New Zealand or the Pacific Islands for which New Zealand has special responsibility or concern'. Such a reservation should have been taken into consideration in determining the Applicant's objectives in the proceedings. Account should also have been taken of the fact that counsel for the Applicant stated at the hearings that with respect to some of the damages allegedly caused, its Government intended to bring at a subsequent stage a claim related to the dispute before the Court but distinct from it (CR 74/10, p. 23). The possibility cannot therefore be excluded that the Applicant may intend to claim damages, at a later date, through the diplomatic channel or otherwise, in the event of a favourable decision furnishing it with a declaration of illegality. Such a procedure, which has been followed in previous cases before international tribunals, would have been particularly understandable in a case involving radio-active fallout in which the existence and extent of damage may not readily be ascertained before some time has elapsed.

[. . .]

[**502**] 18. The Judgment implies that there was a dispute between the Parties but asserts that such a dispute has now disappeared because 'the final objective which the Applicant has maintained throughout has been achieved by other means' (para. 58).

We cannot agree with this finding, which is based on the premise that the sole purpose of the Application was to obtain a cessation of tests as from the date of the Judgment. In our view the dispute between the Parties has not disappeared since it has concerned, from its origin, the question of the legality of the tests. [. . .]

[**525**] DISSENTING OPINION OF JUDGE SIR GARFIELD BARWICK (EXTRACT)

I have already expressed my reasons for being unable to join in the Judgment of the Court in the case of *Australia* v. *France*:[12] All those reasons apply with equal force in this case and need not be repeated.

[. . .]

Perhaps the emphasis respectively placed upon the unlawfulness of the testing of nuclear weapons and upon the infringement of sovereignty by the fall-out in New Zealand resulting from the detonation of nuclear devices, differs slightly in the two cases. This, in my opinion, does not require any special treatment in these reasons as the difference is not of any substantial importance.

The Applicant however, unlike Australia, did not seek an order of [**526**] injunction. Its only claim was for a declaration. Its claim is expressed in its Application as follows:

> *Accordingly, New Zealand asks the Court to adjudge and declare:* That the conduct by the French Government of nuclear tests in the South Pacific region that give rise to radio-active fall-out constitutes a violation of New Zealand's rights under international law, and that these rights will be violated by any further such tests.

[12] See *ICJ Reports 1974*, p. 253 at p. 391.

It is thus even more difficult in this case to support the view that the Applicant's request for a declaration was but as a reason or foundation for an order of injunction or, as it is put, was merely a means to an end and not an end in itself. Any suggestion that the claim must be regarded as either a claim for a declaration or a claim for an injunction would be a false dichotomy. In truth the claim could seek both, as in the case of Australia but the claim of the Applicant does not.

[. . .]

[**528**] [. . .] As in the case of *Australia* v. *France*, I am unable to join in the Judgment which follows from an unjust procedure and which produces a result which I cannot accept as right and proper in the circumstances.

[Report: *ICJ Reports 1974*, p. 457]

Order of International Court of Justice on Application by Fiji for Permission to Intervene, 20 December 1974 (extract)

[**535**] [. . .] 1. Whereas by a Judgment of 20 December 1974 in this case the Court finds that the claim of New Zealand no longer has any object and that the Court is therefore not called upon to give a decision thereon,

2. Whereas in consequence there will no longer be any proceedings before the Court to which the Application for permission to intervene could relate,

[**536**] THE COURT,

Unanimously,

Finds that the Application of the Government of Fiji for permission to intervene in the proceedings instituted by New Zealand against France lapses, and that no further action thereon is called for on the part of the Court.

[. . .]

[Report: *ICJ Reports 1974*, p. 535]

Case Concerning Certain Phosphate Lands in Nauru (Nauru v. Australia)[1]

International Court of Justice, The Hague

26 June 1992 (Sir Robert Jennings, *President*; Oda, *Vice-President*; Lachs, Ago, Schwebel, Bedjaoui, Ni, Evensen, Tarassov, Guillaume, Shahabuddeen, Aguilar Mawdsley and Ranjeva, *Judges*)

Damage and compensation – Nauru – phosphate mining – rehabilitation of lands worked out during period of trusteeship – liability of former trustees – Nauru Trusteeship Agreement, 1947 – Nauru Island Agreement, 1919 – effect of transfer of phosphate industry to Nauru on independence

Responsibility and liability – phosphate mining on Nauru – responsibility for rehabilitation of worked-out lands – administration of Nauru by Australia on behalf of itself, New Zealand and the United Kingdom – whether three States responsible for full extent of rehabilitation of worked-out lands

Jurisdiction – International Court of Justice – Australian declaration under Article 36(2) of Statute of International Court of Justice – reservation attached to declaration – whether dispute within reservation – whether agreement between Nauru and Australia for recourse to other dispute resolution mechanism

SUMMARY   *The facts*   At the end of the First World War, the Island of Nauru, in the South Pacific, was placed under a League of Nations mandate. The mandate was conferred upon 'His Britannic Majesty'. The Nauru Island Agreement, 1919 ('the 1919 Agreement'), between Australia, New Zealand and the United Kingdom, provided, *inter alia*, that the three States would administer Nauru through an Administrator. In practice, the Administrator was always appointed by the Government of

[1] The Republic of Nauru was represented by Mr V. S. Mani, Mr Leo D. Keke, HE Mr Hammer DeRoburt GCMG, OBE, MP, Mr Ian Brownlie QC, Mr Barry Connell and Mr James Crawford. Australia was represented by Mr Gavan Griffith QC, Mr Henry Burmester, Mr Eduardo Jiménez de Aréchaga, Mr Derek W. Bowett QC, Mr Alain Pellet and Ms Susan Kenny.

    The Settlement Agreement and Joint Declaration can be found at pp. 143 and 145 below.

Australia. In 1947, Nauru was placed under United Nations Trusteeship. The Trusteeship Agreement designated the Governments of Australia, New Zealand and the United Kingdom as the joint authority ('the Administering Authority') for the territory, although it provided that, in accordance with practice under the 1919 Agreement, the Government of Australia would exercise full powers of legislation, administration and jurisdiction over Nauru on behalf of the Administering Authority. In 1965, the three Governments agreed to the establishment of Nauruan Legislative and Executive Councils but the administration of the Territory remained vested in an Administrator appointed by the Government of Australia. This arrangement continued until Nauru became independent on 31 January 1968.

The 1919 Agreement also provided that the three States would establish the British Phosphate Commissioners ('the BPC') to extract phosphates from Nauru and to dispose of those phosphates 'for the purpose of the agricultural requirements' of the three States. The BPC was a partnership, not separately incorporated: it operated the Nauru phosphate industry as well as that on Ocean Island.[2] By an agreement concluded in 1967 ('the 1967 Agreement') between the three States and the Nauru Local Government Council ('the NLGC'), the industry was transferred to the NLGC. In 1987, an agreement between Australia, New Zealand and the United Kingdom ('the 1987 Agreement') wound up the BPC and distributed its overseas assets between the three States.

In 1989, Nauru instituted proceedings in the International Court of Justice against Australia in respect of 'a dispute . . . over the rehabilitation of certain phosphate lands worked out before Nauruan independence'. In its application, Nauru maintained that Australia had breached its trusteeship obligations under Article 76 of the United Nations Charter and Articles 3 and 5 of the Trusteeship Agreement, as well as its obligations under general international law. In particular, Nauru alleged that, by failing to make provision for the rehabilitation of those parts of Nauru from which phosphates had been extracted during the period of the trusteeship, Australia had failed to comply with the international standards generally recognised as applicable in the implementation of the principle of self-determination; the obligation to respect the right of the Nauruan people to permanent sovereignty over their natural wealth and resources; the obligation not to exercise powers of administration in such a way as to produce a denial of justice *lato sensu* or to constitute an abuse of rights; and the principle of general international law of a State responsible for

---

[2] See *Tito v. Waddell (No. 2)* [1977] 3 All ER 129.

the administration of a territory being under an obligation not to bring about changes in the condition of that territory which will cause irreparable damage to, or substantially prejudice the existing or contingent legal interest of, another State in respect of that territory.

In its Memorial, Nauru repeated these claims and sought to add a further claim that it was entitled to the share of the overseas assets of the BPC which Australia had received under the 1987 Agreement. Nauru asserted that the Court had jurisdiction by virtue of the fact that both Australia (13 March 1975) and Nauru (30 December 1987) had made declarations accepting the jurisdiction of the Court under Article 36(2) of the Statute of the Court.

Australia maintained that the Court lacked jurisdiction and that the application was inadmissible on the following grounds:

(1) Australia had attached a reservation to its acceptance of the Court's jurisdiction under Article 36(2), excluding disputes in relation to which the parties had agreed to have recourse to some other method of settlement, and this reservation was applicable in the present case because, *inter alia*, disputes between the people of Nauru and the Administering Authority under the Trusteeship Agreement fell within the exclusive jurisdiction of the United Nations Trusteeship Council and General Assembly;

(2) Nauru had waived any claims in respect of rehabilitation in the 1967 Agreement and by virtue of statements made by Nauruan representatives in the United Nations during the debates leading to the termination of the trusteeship over Nauru and to its independence;

(3) the termination of the trusteeship by United Nations General Assembly Resolution 2347 amounted to a complete discharge for the Administering Authority and precluded allegations of breach of that trusteeship being examined by the Court;

(4) Nauru's claim had not been submitted within a reasonable time;

(5) Nauru had failed to act consistently and in good faith and the Court should therefore exercise its discretion to decline to hear Nauru's claims;

(6) the claim was, in reality, a claim against the Administering Authority and, in the absence of New Zealand and the United Kingdom as parties to the proceedings, any judgment on the question of breach of the Trusteeship Agreement by Australia would involve the responsibility of third States which had not consented to the Court's jurisdiction in the present case.

In addition, Australia maintained that Nauru's claim in respect of the assets of the BPC was inadmissible and that the Court had no jurisdiction in respect of it on the grounds that, *inter alia*, it was an attempt to add an entirely new claim to those set out in the Nauruan application.

Held by the International Court of Justice

(*unanimously*) (1)   The dispute did not fall within the reservation to Australia's declaration accepting the jurisdiction of the Court. Declarations under Article 36(2) of the Statute could relate only to disputes between States, so that the question was whether, since Nauru became independent, Nauru and Australia had agreed to have recourse to some other mechanism for dispute settlement. No such agreement existed.

(*by twelve votes to one*) (2)   There had been no waiver by Nauru of its claims regarding rehabilitation. The 1967 Agreement was silent on the question of responsibility for rehabilitation which had been the subject of differences of opinion in the negotiations. In the absence of an express provision, the Agreement could not be read as a waiver by Nauru. Statements made in the United Nations by Nauruan representatives also fell far short of a clear and unequivocal waiver.

(*by twelve votes to one*) (3)   General Assembly Resolution 2347 did not give the Administering Authority a complete discharge in relation to rights which Nauru might have regarding rehabilitation. Although that resolution did not refer to rehabilitation or expressly reserve Nauru's rights, the differences of opinion between the NLGC and the Administering Authority regarding rehabilitation were well known in the United Nations at the time of its adoption and it referred back to earlier resolutions which had expressly called upon the Administering Authority to make provision for rehabilitation.

(*by twelve votes to one*) (4)   Although international law did not lay down any specific time-limits for the bringing of a claim, even in the absence of any applicable treaty provision delay on the part of a claimant State might render an application inadmissible. In the present case, however, the nature of Nauru's relations with Australia and the fact that Nauru had raised the question of rehabilitation on a number of occasions since independence meant that the application was not time-barred. It would be for the Court to ensure that Nauru's delay in bringing the matter before the Court did not cause prejudice to Australia with regard to the establishment of the facts and the determination of the applicable law.

(*by twelve votes to one*) (5)   Nauru's conduct did not amount to an abuse of process and the Australian argument that Nauru had not acted consistently and in good faith had to be rejected.

(*by nine votes to four*) (6)   The fact that New Zealand and the United Kingdom were not parties to the proceedings did not render the application inadmissible.

(a)   The Administering Authority did not have an international legal personality distinct from those of the three States of which it was composed. Of those three States, Australia had played a very special role, established by the Trusteeship Agreement of 1947, by the Agreements of 1919, 1923 and 1965, and by practice.

(b)   The question whether any liability on the part of the three States was joint and several, so that any one of them would be required to make full reparation, would be considered at the merits phase but it was separate from the question whether Australia could be sued alone. Australia had obligations under the Trusteeship Agreement in its capacity as one of the three States forming the Administering Authority and no reasons had been shown why a claim brought against Australia should be declared inadmissible merely because that claim raised questions of the administration of territory which was shared with New Zealand and the United Kingdom.

(c)   The present case differed from the *Monetary Gold*[3] case since the interests of New Zealand and the United Kingdom did not constitute the very subject matter of the judgment to be rendered on the merits of Nauru's application against Australia. A finding by the Court regarding the existence or the content of the responsibility attributed to Australia by Nauru might well have implications for the legal situation of the two other States concerned, but no finding in respect of that legal situation would be needed as a basis for the Court's decision on Nauru's claims against Australia. The interests of New Zealand and the United Kingdom were protected by Article 59 of the Statute, which provided that 'the decision of the Court had no binding force except between the parties and in respect of that particular case'.

(*unanimously*) (7)   The claim made in the Nauruan Memorial to the Australian share of the overseas assets of the BPC was a new claim that was different in character from the claims made in the application. Although there may have been links between the claims in the application and the claim to the BPC assets, the latter did not arise directly out of the question

---

[3]   21 *ILR* 399.

which was the subject matter of the application, and to entertain it would transform the subject of the dispute originally submitted to the Court. This claim was therefore inadmissible.

Separate Opinion of Judge Shahabuddeen (1) Australia's objection that the application was inadmissible in the absence of New Zealand and the United Kingdom was a preliminary objection and the Court was right to deal with it at this stage, rather than reserving it for consideration at the merits phase.

(2) It had to be assumed at the present stage that Australia had an obligation to ensure rehabilitation as alleged by Nauru. The question whether such an obligation existed was part of the merits and could not be determined in preliminary proceedings.

(3) The reality of the administration of Nauru under trusteeship was that, for all practical purposes, Australia had the exclusive authority to administer Nauru right up until Nauruan independence. New Zealand and the United Kingdom had no real part to play in the administration of Nauru.

(4) The obligations of the three States which comprised the Administering Authority were joint and several. Although there was little authority on the point, the better view was that a concept of joint and several liability existed in international law. It was therefore perfectly proper for Nauru to bring proceedings against only one of the three States.

(5) Even if the obligations were joint, rather than joint and several, that would not by itself prevent Australia from being sued alone. Once it was accepted that Australia could be sued alone, the question of the extent of Australia's liability became a matter for the merits phase. The question whether Australia had a right to require contributions from New Zealand and the United Kingdom constituted a separate dispute between those three States which would fall to be determined by appropriate methods of dispute resolution.

(6) A judgment against Australia would not amount to a judicial determination of the responsibility of New Zealand and the United Kingdom. While a possible judgment on the merits against Australia might be based on a course of reasoning which was capable of extension to New Zealand and the United Kingdom, that reasoning would operate only at the level of persuasive precedent in any case that might subsequently be brought by Nauru against those two States. There was, therefore, no question of the Court exercising jurisdiction in respect of States which were not party to the proceedings before it.

Dissenting Opinion of President Sir Robert Jennings   Australia, New Zealand and the United Kingdom together constituted the Administering Authority for Nauru and were the three members of the BPC. The legal interests of New Zealand and the United Kingdom were therefore inextricably bound up with those of Australia and would not only be affected by a decision of the Court but would constitute the very subject matter of that decision. Moreover, if there should be any question of assessing the reparation that might be due from Australia, in the case that Australia was liable jointly and severally or only for some proportion of the sum, the Court would unavoidably and simultaneously be making a decision in respect of the legal interests of New Zealand and the United Kingdom. For the Court to proceed in the absence of those two States would therefore be inconsistent with the consensual basis of the Court's jurisdiction.

Dissenting Opinion of Vice-President Oda   (1)   Australia's objection based on the absence of New Zealand and the United Kingdom was too closely connected with the merits for the present decision and could not be accepted without further examination.

(2)   The question of rehabilitation had been thoroughly discussed in the negotiations which preceded Nauru's independence. Nevertheless, the 1967 Agreement on the transfer of the phosphate industry made no mention of that issue. Considering that, at that critical point, Nauru failed to make an express reservation of its claims, the silence of the 1967 Agreement could be construed as an implied waiver.

(3)   The question of rehabilitation had also been repeatedly aired in the debates in the Trusteeship Council. Nevertheless, neither the Council, in recommending the termination of the trusteeship, nor the General Assembly, in acting upon that recommendation, took any position on that question. In the circumstances, General Assembly Resolution 2347 had to be regarded as having completely terminated the rights and duties of the Administering Authority and thus as having put an end to any claims arising from the implementation of the Trusteeship Agreement.

(4)   Even if Nauru had possessed a claim which could have been asserted against Australia at the time Nauru became independent, the fact that Nauru had remained silent on this question for some fifteen years made it inappropriate, on grounds of judicial propriety, for the Court to entertain such a claim now. Moreover, the fact that Nauru had taken no steps to rehabilitate the lands which had been worked since independence raised questions about its good faith.

(5)   The importance of the preservation of the environment from any damage that might be caused by the development or exploitation of resources, particularly in the developing regions of the world, could not be denied. It was to be hoped that some measures might well be considered by Australia for promoting rehabilitation of the worked-out lands in parallel with the efforts to be made by the State of Nauru itself in that direction.

Dissenting Opinion of Judge Ago   The Court should have upheld the Australian objection based upon the absence from the proceedings of New Zealand and the United Kingdom. The United Nations had conferred the trusteeship of Nauru upon the three States on a basis of legal equality. By ruling on Nauru's claims against Australia alone, the Court would inevitably affect the rights and obligations of the other two States. If the Court were to determine the share of the responsibility falling upon Australia, it would thereby indirectly establish that the remainder of the responsibility would fall upon the other two States. If, on the other hand, the Court were to determine, on what would be an extremely questionable basis, that Australia bore the full responsibility, that decision would also affect the legal situation of the other two States. The exercise by the Court of its jurisdiction would thus be deprived of its consensual basis.

Dissenting Opinion of Judge Schwebel   (1)   The basis of the Court's jurisdiction was consensual. Where more than one State was charged with joint (or joint and several) commission of a wrongful act under international law but only one such State was before the Court, the question was whether the Court might exercise jurisdiction over that State, even though its determination of the liability of that State might or would entail the effective determination of the liability of another. In dealing with that question, private law analogies were of little use, since jurisdiction was not consensual in national law.

(2)   If the legal interests of a third State would not merely be affected but effectively determined by the Court's judgment, the Court should not proceed to give judgment in the absence of that third State.

(3)   In the present case, Australia had administered Nauru on behalf of the three States. Moreover, Nauru had frequently asserted that all three States were under an obligation to rehabilitate the worked-out lands and had restated its claims in diplomatic notes to New Zealand and the United Kingdom at the time it filed its application against Australia. A judgment by the Court upon the responsibility of Australia would thus be tantamount to a judgment upon the responsibility of New Zealand and the United Kingdom. The protection afforded to those States by Article 59

of the Statute would be notional rather than real, and the application against Australia alone should have been held inadmissible.

Subsequent facts and settlement   Following the Judgment of the Court on Preliminary Objections, negotiations took place between Australia and Nauru with a view to settling the case. As a result, on 10 August 1993, Australia and Nauru concluded an agreement by which Australia agreed, *inter alia*, to pay to Nauru Au $107 million as a cash settlement and Nauru agreed to discontinue proceedings before the ICJ and to waive the right to make a claim in relation to the administration of Nauru during the mandate and trusteeship periods. The waiver was for the benefit of not only Australia but also the United Kingdom and New Zealand. At the same time as the settlement agreement was concluded, so also was a Joint Declaration of Principles Guiding Relations between Australia and the Republic of Nauru. The International Court of Justice removed the case from its list on 13 September 1993 (*ICJ Reports 1993*, p. 322).

There follows

Judgment of International Court of Justice on Preliminary Objections, 26 June 1992 (extract)

[245] [. . .] 7. The Court will first consider those of Australia's objections which concern the circumstances in which the dispute relating to rehabilitation of the phosphate lands worked out prior to 1 July 1967 arose between Nauru and Australia. It will then turn to the objection based on the fact that New Zealand and the United Kingdom are not parties to the proceedings. Lastly, it will rule on the objections to Nauru's submissions relating to the overseas assets of the British Phosphate Commissioners.

*   *

---

[4] The dissenting opinions of President Sir Robert Jennings and Judge Schwebel are not reproduced in this volume but can be found at *ICJ Reports 1992*, pp. 301 and 329 respectively.

8. The Court will begin by considering the question of its jurisdiction. In its Application, Nauru bases jurisdiction on the declarations whereby Australia and Nauru have accepted the jurisdiction of the Court under Article 36, paragraph 2, of the Statute. Those declarations were deposited with the Secretary-General of the United Nations on 17 March 1975 in the case of Australia and on 29 January 1988 in the case of Nauru. The declaration of Nauru stipulates that Nauru's acceptance of the Court's jurisdiction does not extend to 'any dispute with respect to which there exists a dispute settlement mechanism under an agreement between the Republic of Nauru and another State'. The declaration of Australia, for its part, specifies that it 'does not apply to any dispute in regard to which the parties thereto have agreed or shall agree to have recourse to some other method of peaceful settlement'.

[. . .]

[**246**] [. . .] 11. The Court does not consider it necessary to enter at this point into the details of the arguments thus advanced. Declarations made pursuant to Article 36, paragraph 2, of the Statute of the Court can only relate to disputes between States. The declaration of Australia only covers that type of dispute; it is made expressly 'in relation to any other State accepting the same obligation . . . '. In these circumstances, the question that arises in this case is whether Australia and the Republic of Nauru did or [**247**] did not, after 31 January 1968, when Nauru acceded to independence, conclude an agreement whereby the two States undertook to settle their dispute relating to rehabilitation of the phosphate lands by resorting to an agreed procedure other than recourse to the Court. No such agreement has been pleaded or shown to exist. That question has therefore to be answered in the negative. The Court thus considers that the objection raised by Australia on the basis of the above-mentioned reservation must be rejected.

*

12. Australia's second objection is that the Nauruan authorities, even before acceding to independence, waived all claims relating to rehabilitation of the phosphate lands. This objection contains two branches. In the first place, the waiver, it is said, was the implicit but necessary result of the above-mentioned Agreement of 14 November 1967. It is also said to have resulted from the statements made in the United Nations in the autumn of 1967 by the Nauruan Head Chief on the occasion of the termination of the Trusteeship. In the view of Australia, Nauru may not go back on that twofold waiver and its claim should accordingly be rejected as inadmissible.

[. . .]

14. The Parties are at one in recognizing that the Agreement of 14 November 1967 laid down the conditions under which the property in the capital assets of the phosphate industry on Nauru was to pass to the local authorities and the ways in which the phosphate would, in future, be worked and sold. They also recognize that that Agreement did not contain any express provision relating to rehabilitation of the phosphate lands previously worked out. However, the Parties disagree as to the significance of that silence. Australia maintains that 'the Agreement did represent a

comprehensive settlement of all claims by Nauru in relation to the phosphate industry', including rehabilitation of the lands, and that the Agreement was accordingly tantamount to a waiver by Nauru of its previous claims in that regard. Nauru, on the contrary, contends that the absence of any reference to that matter in the Agreement cannot be interpreted as implying a waiver.

[...]

[**250**] [...] 21. The Court concludes that the Nauruan local authorities did not, before independence, waive their claim relating to rehabilitation of the phosphate lands worked out prior to 1 July 1967. The second objection raised by Australia must in consequence be rejected.

*

22. Australia's third objection is that Nauru's claim is

> inadmissible on the ground that termination of the Trusteeship by the United Nations precludes allegations of breaches of the Trusteeship Agreement from now being examined by the Court.

[...]

[**251**] [...] 23. The Court notes that, by resolution 2347 (XXII) of 19 December 1967, the General Assembly of the United Nations resolved

> in agreement with the Administering Authority, that the Trusteeship Agreement for the Territory of Nauru ... shall cease to be in force upon the accession of Nauru to independence on 31 January 1968.

Such a resolution had 'definitive legal effect' (*Northern Cameroons, Judgment, ICJ Reports 1963*, p. 32). Consequently, the Trusteeship Agreement was 'terminated' on that date and 'is no longer in force' (*ibid.*, p. 37). In the light of these considerations, it might be possible to question the admissibility of an action brought against the Administering Authority on the basis of the alleged failure by it to comply with its obligations with respect to the administration of the Territory. However, the Court does not consider it necessary to enter into this debate and will confine itself to examining the particular circumstances in which the Trusteeship for Nauru was terminated.

[...]

[**253**] [...] 30. The facts set out above show that, when, on the recommendation of the Trusteeship Council, the General Assembly terminated the Trusteeship over Nauru in agreement with the Administering Authority, everyone was aware of subsisting differences of opinion between the Nauru Local Government Council and the Administering Authority with regard to rehabilitation of the phosphate lands worked out before 1 July 1967. Accordingly, though General Assembly resolution 2347 (XXII) did not expressly reserve any rights which Nauru might have had in that regard, the Court cannot view that resolution as giving a discharge to the Administering Authority with respect to such rights. In the opinion of the Court, the rights Nauru might have had in connection with rehabilitation of the lands remained unaffected. Regard

being had to the particular circumstances of the case, Australia's third objection must in consequence be rejected.

*

31. Australia's fourth objection stresses that Nauru achieved independence on 31 January 1968 and that, as regards rehabilitation of the lands, it was not until December 1988 that that State formally 'raised with Australia and the other former Administering Powers its position'. Australia therefore contends that Nauru's claim is inadmissible on the ground that it has not been submitted within a reasonable time. Nauru's delay in making its claim is alleged to be all the more prejudicial to Australia because the documentation relating to the Mandate and the Trusteeship may have been lost or dispersed in the interval, and because developments in the law during the interval render it more difficult to determine the legal obligations incumbent on the Administering Powers at the time of the alleged breaches of those obligations.

32. The Court recognizes that, even in the absence of any applicable treaty provision, delay on the part of a claimant State may render an application inadmissible. It notes, however, that international law does not lay [254] down any specific time-limit in that regard. It is therefore for the Court to determine in the light of the circumstances of each case whether the passage of time renders an application inadmissible.

[. . .]

36. [. . .] The Court considers that, given the nature of relations between Australia and Nauru, as well as the steps thus taken, Nauru's [255] Application was not rendered inadmissible by passage of time. Nevertheless, it will be for the Court, in due time, to ensure that Nauru's delay in seising it will in no way cause prejudice to Australia with regard to both the establishment of the facts and the determination of the content of the applicable law.

*

37. Australia's fifth objection is that 'Nauru has failed to act consistently and in good faith in relation to rehabilitation' and that therefore 'the Court in exercise of its discretion, and in order to uphold judicial propriety should . . . decline to hear the Nauruan claims'.

38. The Court considers that the Application by Nauru has been properly submitted in the framework of the remedies open to it. At the present stage, the Court is not called upon to weigh the possible consequence of the conduct of Nauru with respect to the merits of the case. It need merely note that such conduct does not amount to an abuse of process. Australia's objection on this point must also be rejected.

[. . .]

[262] [. . .] 57. For the reasons given, the Court considers that the fact that New Zealand and the United Kingdom are not parties to the case is no bar to the proceedings brought by Nauru against Australia. The objection put forward in this respect by Australia must be rejected.

[. . .]

[**267**] [. . .] 70. In the light of the foregoing, the Court concludes that the Nauruan claim relating to the overseas assets of the British Phosphate Commissioners is inadmissible inasmuch as it constitutes, both in form and in substance, a new claim, and the subject of the dispute originally submitted to the Court would be transformed if it entertained that claim.

71. The preliminary objection raised by Australia on this point is therefore well founded. It follows that it is not necessary for the Court to consider here the other objections of Australia with regard to the submissions of Nauru concerning the overseas assets of the British Phosphate Commissioners.

*
*   *

[**268**] 72. For these reasons,

THE COURT,

(1) (a) *rejects*, unanimously, the preliminary objection based on the reservation made by Australia in its declaration of acceptance of the compulsory jurisdiction of the Court;

(b) *rejects*, by twelve votes to one, the preliminary objection based on the alleged waiver by Nauru, prior to accession to independence, of all claims concerning the rehabilitation of the phosphate lands worked out prior to 1 July 1967;

    IN FAVOUR: *President* Sir Robert Jennings; *Judges* Lachs, Ago, Schwebel, Bedjaoui,
        Ni, Evensen, Tarassov, Guillaume, Shahabuddeen, Aguilar Mawdsley, Ranjeva;
    AGAINST: *Vice-President* Oda;

(c) *rejects*, by twelve votes to one, the preliminary objection based on the termination of the Trusteeship over Nauru by the United Nations;

    IN FAVOUR: *President* Sir Robert Jennings; *Judges* Lachs, Ago, Schwebel, Bedjaoui,
        Ni, Evensen, Tarassov, Guillaume, Shahabuddeen, Aguilar Mawdsley, Ranjeva;
    AGAINST: *Vice-President* Oda;

(d) *rejects*, by twelve votes to one, the preliminary objection based on the effect of the passage of time on the admissibility of Nauru's Application;

    IN FAVOUR: *President* Sir Robert Jennings; *Judges* Lachs, Ago, Schwebel, Bedjaoui,
        Ni, Evensen, Tarassov, Guillaume, Shahabuddeen, Aguilar Mawdsley, Ranjeva;
    AGAINST: *Vice-President* Oda;

(e) *rejects*, by twelve votes to one, the preliminary objection based on Nauru's alleged lack of good faith;

    IN FAVOUR: *President* Sir Robert Jennings; *Judges* Lachs, Ago, Schwebel, Bedjaoui,
        Ni, Evensen, Tarassov, Guillaume, Shahabuddeen, Aguilar Mawdsley, Ranjeva;
    AGAINST: *Vice-President* Oda;

(f) *rejects*, by nine votes to four, the preliminary objection based on the fact that New Zealand and the United Kingdom are not parties to the proceedings;

    IN FAVOUR: *Judges* Lachs, Bedjaoui, Ni, Evensen, Tarassov, Guillaume, Shahabuddeen, Aguilar Mawdsley, Ranjeva;
    AGAINST: *President* Sir Robert Jennings; *Vice-President* Oda; *Judges* Ago, Schwebel;

(g) *upholds,* unanimously, the preliminary objection based on the claim concerning the overseas assets of the British Phosphate Commissioners being a new one;

[**269**] (2) *finds,* by nine votes to four, that, on the basis of Article 36, paragraph 2, of the Statute of the Court, it has jurisdiction to entertain the Application filed by the Republic of Nauru on 19 May 1989 and that the said Application is admissible;

IN FAVOUR: *Judges* Lachs, Bedjaoui, Ni, Evensen, Tarassov, Guillaume, Shahabuddeen, Aguilar Mawdsley, Ranjeva;

AGAINST: *President* Sir Robert Jennings; *Vice-President* Oda; *Judges* Ago, Schwebel;

(3) *finds,* unanimously, that the claim concerning the overseas assets of the British Phosphate Commissioners, made by Nauru in its Memorial of 20 April 1990, is inadmissible.

[. . .]

SEPARATE OPINION OF JUDGE SHAHABUDDEEN (EXTRACT)

[. . .]

Part I. Whether the objection does not possess an exclusively preliminary character
[. . .]
[**276**] [. . .] Consequently, the question whether Australia had the obligation to ensure rehabilitation cannot be determined in this phase of the proceedings; it can only be determined at the merits stage. The existence of the obligation has simply to be assumed at this point. This being so, the only issues now open are the issues of law referred to above, that is to say, whether the obligation (if it existed) was joint, and, if it was, whether the propositions at (i) and (ii) above [not reproduced here] are well founded. These issues can be determined now and cannot justifiably be reserved for the merits. Nothing relating to the establishment at the merits stage of the existence of the alleged obligation to ensure rehabilitation can provide a reason for not dealing with those issues now.

[. . .]

Part II. Australia's position under the Trusteeship Agreement
[. . .]
[**282**] [. . .] Part of the problem concerns the correct appreciation of Nauru's case. There could be an impression that Nauru's claims directly concern Australia's part in the commercial operations of the phosphate industry. That impression would not be accurate. No doubt, Nauru's case has many branches; but the essence of the case – whether it is well founded or not being a matter for the merits – is that Australia, while having under the Trusteeship Agreement 'full powers of legislation, administration and jurisdiction in and over the Territory', failed to exercise these comprehensive governmental powers so as to regulate the phosphate industry in such a way as to secure the interests of the people of Nauru (CR 91/20, p. 83, and CR 91/22,

p. 45, Professor Crawford). In particular, says Nauru, there was failure to institute the necessary regulatory measures to ensure the rehabilitation of worked-out areas, not in the case of mining in any country, but in the case of large-scale open-cast mining in the minuscule area of this particular Trust Territory. The consequence, according to Nauru, was that the Territory became, or was in danger of becoming, incapable of serving as the national home of the people of Nauru, contrary to the fundamental objectives of the Trusteeship Agreement and of the Charter of the United Nations. In this respect, the question, as I understand it, is not simply whether rehabilitation was required by such environmental norms as were applicable at the time; the question is whether rehabilitation was required by an implied obligation of Australia under the Trusteeship Agreement not to allow the destruction of the small national homeland of the Nauruan people, or any substantial part of it, through an unregulated industrial process which went so far as to result at one stage in the making and consideration of serious proposals for resettlement of the Nauruan people altogether outside of Nauru. That, I think, is Nauru's case.

[...]

[300] [...] *Conclusion*

Australia's arguments are worthy of consideration, and there could be more than one view of their value. For the reasons given, I have not, however, been able to feel persuaded. In my opinion, the obligations of the three Governments under the Trusteeship Agreement were joint and several, and Australia could accordingly be sued alone. In the alternative, if the obligations were joint, this circumstance still did not prevent Nauru from suing Australia alone. Nor do I think that a possible judgment against Australia will amount to a determination of the responsibilities of New Zealand and the United Kingdom. Whether Australia in fact had an international obligation to ensure the rehabilitation of worked-out phosphate lands, whether, if so, it was in breach of that obligation, and what, if so, is the extent of responsibility which it thereby engaged, are different questions.

[303] DISSENTING OPINION OF VICE-PRESIDENT ODA (EXTRACT)

1. The main purpose of this opinion is to set forth my reasons for casting a negative vote on operative parts 1 *(b)*, *(c)*, *(d)* and *(e)* of the Judgment. The Application of Nauru was, to my mind, clearly inadmissible on those counts alone. My subsidiary purpose, which can be disposed of at once, is to state that my negative vote on operative part 1 *(f)* is motivated by my belief that it is premature to close the door on the objection concerned, which I find too closely connected with the merits for present decision; this particular vote on my part does not therefore signify that I necessarily accept this objection without further examination.

2. My vote against operative part 2 resulted as the logical conclusion of my belief that so many preliminary objections ought to have been upheld.

I. Re *operative parts 1* (b) *and* (c): *Concerning the existence of the claim in the present case*
[...]

[304] 4. I am unable to concur in these views of the Court. My view is different from that of the Judgment with regard to the significance of certain developments during the Trusteeship period. I have in particular some doubts whether there really existed, towards the end of that period, any Nauruan claim for land rehabilitation, and I feel unable to entertain what the Judgment refers to, without further elaboration, as the 'particular circumstances' (Judgment, paras. 23 and 30) prevailing at the termination of the Trusteeship. [...]

1. Negotiations between the Administering Authority and the Nauruan
authorities and their Agreement of November 1967
[...]

[311] [...] 12. I have thus followed the developments in which the demands of the Nauruan people for the rehabilitation of worked-out lands were presented in the talks between the Administering Authority and their representatives. It is extremely important to note that the Canberra Agreement reached by both parties (on the one hand, Australia, New Zealand and the United Kingdom; on the other, the Nauru Local Government Council) on 14 November 1967, just on the eve of the independence of Nauru, to arrange for the future operation, after independence, of the phosphate industry, did not make any mention of the issue of rehabilitation. Counsel for Nauru explained at the hearings that rehabilitation was not mentioned in the 1967 Agreement on the understanding that the issue would be dealt with separately. In fact that issue was not dealt with separately, and no suggestion seems to have been made by the Nauruan authorities to deal with this issue independently of that Agreement.

13. [...] The fact that the issue of rehabilitation was not mentioned at all cannot, therefore, be dismissed as irrelevant. Hence, while it is literally true that the *text* of the Agreement cannot be construed to imply a waiver, the *silence* of the Agreement remains, in my view, open to that conclusion.

[312] 2. Discussions within the United Nations system

14. The presentation by the Nauruan people of their demand for rehabilitation and the subsequent rejection of that demand by the Administering Authority, as well as the work of the Davey Committee to assess the feasibility of rehabilitation, were all problems which were dealt with within the United Nations Trusteeship System. The Trusteeship Council and the General Assembly paid due attention to those discussions between the Nauruan people and the Administering Authority, but were not in a position to intervene in order to take up the demands of the Nauruan people or to determine any violation by the Administering Authority of its obligation under the Trusteeship System.

[...]

[322] [...] 25. All claims arising from the implementation of the Trusteeship could have been settled only under the United Nations mechanism. No legal dispute within

the meaning of Article 36, paragraph 2, of the Statute could possibly have existed at that time with regard to the administration of Nauru under the United Nations Trusteeship on the eve of Nauru's independence, as no sovereign State was in a position to put forward a claim based on a purported breach of the obligations entered into by Australia, New Zealand and the United Kingdom, as the Administering Authority, during the Trusteeship period. A question, however, might have been raised if there was indeed any dispute outstanding between the independent State of Nauru and Australia, New Zealand and the United Kingdom at the time of Nauru's accession to independence. However, no claim to the rehabilitation of worked-out phosphate lands addressed to the Administering Authority of the Trusteeship by the people of Nauru was taken over by the State of Nauru at the time of independence in 1968. No United Nations document under which Nauru gained independence showed any evidence of a transfer of the claim or of the creation of a fresh claim for the independent State of Nauru.

[323] II. Re *operative parts 1 (d) and (e): Delay in the presentation of Nauru's claim and the question of Nauru's good faith*
[. . .]

27. [. . .] I hold the view that, by the time of the independence of Nauru, the claim of the Nauruan people to the rehabilitation of lands was no longer viable. I should add, in view of what the Court states, that it was well known at the time of independence that the claim of the Nauruan people had ceased to exist. [. . .]

[324] [. . .] 28. If, merely for the sake of argument, there did exist, at the time of independence, a claim of Nauru (as an independent State) against Australia, for the rehabilitation of the worked-out phosphate lands, then, according to the record, it was asserted at the very earliest during the talks which Nauru held with Australia in 1983. One cannot conceive that the claim which Nauru presented in its Application of 1989 or, even earlier, in its negotiations with Australia in 1983, could have been based on elements other than those which Nauru might have wished to have taken over in 1968. The fact that Nauru kept silent for more than 15 years on the subject of the alleged claim makes it inappropriate for the Court to entertain it and, if only on grounds of judicial propriety, the Court should therefore find that the Application is inadmissible.

29. In addition, the fact is that Nauru has been fully responsible for the mining of phosphate since its independence yet has not taken any steps towards the rehabilitation of the lands it has itself worked. To my mind, equity requires the conclusion that Nauru, by this conduct, combined with lack of due diligence, has disqualified itself from pursuing any allegation of Australian responsibility for the rehabilitation of lands which Australia worked during the Trusteeship period. For Nauru to bring a claim now can only lead one to doubt its good faith.

*

30. By saying that the Application of Nauru in the present case should be rejected as inadmissible, I am not denying the importance of the preservation [325] of an

environment from any damage that may be caused by the development or exploitation of resources, particularly in the developing regions of the world. In the light of the natural and social situation in which Nauru as a relatively new independent State is placed, and the particular relations between Australia and Nauru since the time of the League of Nations, I personally am second to none in hoping that some measures may well be considered by Australia for promoting the rehabilitation of the worked-out lands in parallel with the effort to be made by the State of Nauru itself in that direction.

[326] DISSENTING OPINION OF JUDGE AGO

[Translation]

1. I deeply regret being unable to associate myself with the Judges who have voted in favour of the present Judgment. I regret it all the more since I am certainly no less sensitive than my colleagues to the frustration felt by the Nauruans when they gaze upon the present state of their small island's territory. I also hope with all my heart that it will be possible for this people once again to find in its country of origin conditions of life favourable to its development.

But these perfectly justified emotional reactions should not blind us to the fact that the questions we have to consider in this preliminary phase are very specific questions of law and that it is by reference to the law, and only to the law, that they have to be answered.

2. My reason for taking the position I have indicated and for writing this opinion is that I am compelled to take note of an insurmountable contradiction between two facts. There is, on the one hand, the fact that the Government of Nauru has brought proceedings, against Australia alone, for the purpose of enforcing its claims with respect to the 'rehabilitation' of its territory. But it is, on the other hand, equally unquestionable that first the League of Nations and then the United Nations entrusted the task of administering Nauru jointly to three distinct sovereign entities, namely the United Kingdom, Australia and New Zealand. This authority was conferred on a basis of complete legal equality between the three Powers. To be sure, the participation of one of them, Australia, in the discharge of the tasks involved in administering the territory under the joint Trusteeship of three States might, in point of fact, be more substantial than that of the two others. But this could in no way affect the fundamental situation of equality of rights and obligations between the three partners, a situation which, in addition, was particularly guaranteed as regards the mining of phosphate deposits.

3. It is by reason of the contradiction referred to above that, in considering all the preliminary objections raised by Australia in the present case, I have felt unable to avoid ascribing decisive importance to one, namely the objection based on the fact that two of the three Powers to which Trusteeship over Nauru had been jointly assigned were not parties to the proceedings. I wish to make it perfectly clear that I

am referring to that objection alone, since, in the case of all the others, I fully concur with the majority of the Court in considering that they should be rejected.

4. I do not know for what reasons the newly independent State of Nauru elected to sue Australia alone. The Judgment to which the present [327] opinion is appended correctly points out, in paragraph 33,[5] that on the very day of the proclamation of the Republic, the Head Chief and future President of Nauru, Mr DeRoburt, told the press that:

> We hold it against Britain, Australia and New Zealand to recognize that it is their responsibility to rehabilitate one third of the island.

In the same context it should also be noted that in 1968 this same Mr DeRoburt had taken the initiative of proposing a meeting between the representatives of the three Governments that formerly had together made up the Administering Authority of the trust territory and representatives of the Nauruan Government

> to work out how best [an] airstrip could be constructed *as a rehabilitation project* and to determine the degree of financial and technical assistance the partner Governments would be able to offer (Memorial of Nauru, Vol. 4, Ann. 76; emphasis added).

5. There was therefore every reason to think that, if an application was to be submitted to the Court, it would be directed against the three States jointly. In my opinion the prerequisites for this were duly fulfilled. New Zealand and the United Kingdom had, like Australia, accepted the compulsory jurisdiction of the Court. The terms of New Zealand's acceptance were, in essence, the same as those of Australia's. As for the United Kingdom, its declaration did, it is true, diverge in certain respects from those of the two other States. But, had New Zealand as well as Australia been parties to the proceedings, it could fairly safely have been assumed that the United Kingdom would not have left its two former partners in the administration of Nauru and the exploitation of its mineral resources on their own. It is therefore most likely that it would not, by itself, have raised insurmountable obstacles. Particularly since the clause excluding from the acceptance of the compulsory jurisdiction of the International Court of Justice disputes with States Members of the Commonwealth – a clause originally inserted in the declaration in anticipation of the establishment of a special court for the Commonwealth – could easily have been regarded as obsolete, since that expectation has never been fulfilled. Furthermore, although Nauru had been admitted to the Commonwealth, the conditions of its admission did not make it a full member.

6. Nauru would therefore, at least, have had every reason to seek to bring an action before the Court against the three States affected by the claim it intended to put forward.

But, whatever may have been the reasons that led it to proceed otherwise, the fact remains that it did so. Its Government elected to bring proceedings [328] against Australia alone in respect of the obligation it claims to exist to 'rehabilitate' the part of

---

[5 Not reproduced in this volume.]

its territory worked out, prior to its independence, by the three States that had made up the 'Administering Authority'. Having taken this course, the Nauruan Government must face the consequences of that choice. It has thus placed the Court before a difficulty that is, in my opinion, insurmountable, namely that of determining the possible obligations of Australia in the area in question without at the same time *ipso facto* determining those of the other two States that are not parties to the proceedings. For otherwise the Court would manifestly overstep the limits of its jurisdiction.

The Judgment to which this opinion is appended expressly admits that:

> In the present case, a finding by the Court regarding the existence or the content of the responsibility attributed to Australia by Nauru might well have implications for the legal situation of the two other States concerned ... (Para. 55.)[6]

I welcome this admission. But surely, having made it, one cannot consider its consequences avoided by the mere assertion that

> no *finding in respect of that legal situation* will be needed as a basis for the Court's decision on Nauru's claims against Australia (*ibid.*; emphasis added).

In fact, it is precisely by ruling on these claims against Australia alone that the Court will, *inevitably*, affect the legal situation of the two other States, namely, their rights and their obligations. If, when dealing with the merits of the case, the Court were to recognize that responsibility and accordingly seek to determine the share of the responsibility falling upon Australia, it would thereby indirectly establish that the remainder of the responsibility would fall upon the two other States. Even if the Court were to decide – on what would, incidentally, be an extremely questionable basis – that Australia was to shoulder in full the responsibility in question, that decision would, equally inevitably and just as unacceptably, affect not only the 'interests' but also the legal situation of two States that are not parties to the proceedings. In either case, the exercise by the Court of its jurisdiction would be deprived of its indispensable consensual basis.

These are the reasons that have led me to conclude that the preliminary objection raised in this respect by Australia was well founded and should have been upheld by the Court.

[Reports: *ICJ Reports 1992*, p. 240; 97 *ILR* 1 at p. 8]

Agreement between Australia and the Republic of Nauru for the Settlement of the Case in the International Court of Justice Concerning Certain Phosphate Lands in Nauru (10 August 1993)[7]

The Republic of Nauru and Australia,

[6 Not reproduced in this volume.]

[7 The Agreement entered into force on 20 August 1993.]

Wishing to strengthen the existing friendly relations between the two countries, and

Wishing to settle amicably the application brought by the Republic of Nauru against Australia in the International Court of Justice,

Have agreed as follows:

Article 1

(1) Australia agrees that, in an effort to assist the Republic of Nauru in its preparations for its post-phosphate future, it shall pay the Republic of Nauru a cash settlement of one hundred and seven million dollars ($A107 million) as follows:

(a)   The sum of ten million dollars ($A10 million) on or before 31 August 1993.

(b)   The sum of thirty million dollars ($A30 million) as soon as it may lawfully be paid and not later than 31 December 1993.

(c)   The sum of seventeen million dollars ($A17 million) on 31 August 1994.

(d)   An amount of fifty million dollars ($A50 million) to be paid at an annual rate of $2.5 million dollars, maintained in real terms by reference to the Australian Bureau of Statistics' non-farm GDP deflator, for twenty years commencing in the financial year 1993–4.

The above payments are made without prejudice to Australia's long-standing position that it bears no responsibility for the rehabilitation of the phosphate lands worked out before 1 July 1967.

(2) At the end of the 20 year period referred to in paragraph (1)(d) the Republic of Nauru shall continue to receive development co-operation assistance from Australia at a mutually agreed level.

Article 2

In consequence of the undertakings by Australia in Article 1, the parties agree that they shall take the action necessary to discontinue the present proceedings brought by the Republic of Nauru against Australia in the International Court of Justice.

Article 3

The Republic of Nauru agrees that it shall make no claim whatsoever, whether in the International Court of Justice or otherwise, against all or any of Australia, the United Kingdom of Great Britain and Northern Ireland and New Zealand, their servants or agents arising out of or concerning the administration of Nauru during the period of the Mandate or Trusteeship or the termination of that administration, as well as any matter pertaining to phosphate mining, including matters pertaining to the British Phosphate Commissioners, their assets or the winding up thereof.

Article 4

This Agreement shall enter into force on the date on which the parties have notified each other that the constitutional requirements of each party for the entry into force of this Agreement have been complied with.

[*Sources*: Australian Treaty Series 1993 No. 26; 32 ILM 1474 (1993)]

Joint Declaration of Principles Guiding Relations between Australia and the Republic of Nauru (10 August 1993)

Australia and Nauru have a unique and historic relationship which both countries recognise and are determined to maintain and strengthen.

Australia and Nauru have close and historic ties between their peoples which both countries seek to continue and broaden.

Australia and Nauru have many common interests underlying their historic links and bonds of friendship which both Governments seek to advance with full regard for one another's distinct national characteristics.

Both Governments respect and seek to build on existing bilateral, regional and other mutually beneficial arrangements in accordance with their shared commitment to constructive co-operation.

Both Governments are strongly committed to regional co-operation in the South Pacific and to co-operation with other neighbours.

Both Governments are committed to promoting a stable regional environment in which the aspirations of the peoples of the region for security, peace, equity and development can best be realised.

The following principles are agreed:

Basic Principles

(1) The Governments and peoples of Australia and Nauru reaffirm their commitment to the maintenance and strengthening of close and friendly relations between their two countries.

(2) Relations between Nauru and Australia will be conducted in accordance with the principles of mutual respect for one another's independence, sovereignty and equality.

(3) Both Governments are committed to peaceful settlement of international disputes and to non-interference in the internal affairs of other countries.

(4) Citizens of either country will be accorded fair and just treatment in the other in accordance with law.

(5) The maintenance and strengthening of close and friendly relations between the two countries is an integral part of both Governments' independent foreign policies.

(6) Co-operation and exchanges between the two countries will be mutually beneficial and based on full participation by both countries, with due regard to the capacity, resources and development needs of both countries, and on mutual respect.

Promotion of Understanding

(7) Both Governments will seek to promote knowledge and understanding of the other country, and of the unique and historic relationship between their two countries.

Diplomatic Co-operation and Consular Representation

(8) The two Governments will seek to co-operate in pursuing shared national, regional and global interests through diplomacy and will assist one another in consular representation as far as practicable.

Trade, Investment and Private Sector Co-operation

(9) Both Governments desire to strengthen trade, investment and private sector co-operation between the two countries.

(10) Trade between the two countries will be on at least most-favoured nation terms and as free of both tariff and other restrictive regulations of commerce as may be consistent with both countries' domestic requirements and international commitments, recognising that Australia already offers free and unrestricted access into the Australian market for all Nauru products (except sugar) on a non-reciprocal basis under SPARTECA.

(11) Both Governments will seek to co-operate in ensuring Nauru receives the maximum economic benefits from the production and international marketing of its phosphate resources.

(12) The two Governments will accord to Nauruan and Australian companies and individuals resident in either country investment treatment no less favourable than that accorded to those of any third country.

(13) The two countries will encourage co-operation between the private sectors of their two countries in trade, investment and related areas.

Financial Services Co-operation

(14) Both Governments recognise the benefit of, and confirm, the unique arrangements which allow the Australian currency to be used by Nauru as its transactions currency.

(15) Australia particularly recognises the special needs of Nauru for investment in Australia and elsewhere through the Nauru Phosphate Royalties Trust which investment is designed to assist the post-phosphate economy and requirements of the Nauruan community.

Aviation Co-operation

(16) Having regard to the long-standing and friendly aviation relationship between Australia and Nauru, both Governments are committed to developing arrangements which would meet the requirements of the public for air travel between the two countries and to facilitate and promote their respective aviation interests. Both Governments will continue to encourage the development of air links on the Australia–Nauru route in accordance with the Air Services Agreement between the two Governments with an understanding of the role of Nauru in providing regular air links in and to the Central Pacific region.

Other Transport and Services Co-operation

(17) The two Governments will, in accordance with the laws and policies of both countries and having regard to Nauru's development needs, co-operate to encourage the efficient supply of transport and other services between the two countries.

Fisheries Surveillance Assistance

(18) Recognising the importance of fisheries resources to both countries assistance will be provided through airborne fisheries surveillance patrols of Nauru's exclusive economic zone by Australian Defence Force aircraft as resources permit and

as part of the regional co-operative framework already established under the Niue Treaty.

Health and Medical Co-operation

(19) Both Governments recognise the benefits Nauruans obtain from Australia's health and medical services and will work together to ensure maximum possible access to such services continues subject to both Governments' health, medical and welfare policies.

Rehabilitation and Environmental Co-operation

(20) Both Governments recognise both the challenge presented by rehabilitating the worked-out phosphate lands on Nauru, and the fragility of Nauru's ecosystems, and will work together to facilitate the progressive rehabilitation of Nauru and the protection of Nauru's environment.

Development Co-operation

(21) Development assistance will be provided as part of an agreed program of co-operation which contributes to development and self-reliance in Nauru, allows for forward planning and implementation in accordance with policies and priorities set by Nauru, and takes due account of both Governments' policies on development co-operation but with emphasis upon development assistance in accordance with a Nauruan rehabilitation program.

Communication and Travel

(22) The two Governments will seek to promote and facilitate communications and travel between the two countries, with due regard for one another's national interests and policies.

Legal Co-operation

(23) The two Governments will co-operate, in accordance with their international legal obligations and respective laws, in the area of law enforcement and seek to increase co-operation in other areas of the law.

Crime, Terrorism and Smuggling

(24) The two Governments will co-operate, in accordance with their respective laws and international obligations, to prevent, detect and prosecute crime, terrorism and smuggling.

Exchanges

(25) The two Governments will promote educational, scientific, cultural, sporting and other exchanges between individuals, groups and public office-holders with common interests.

(26) The two Governments will facilitate exchanges which contribute to the development of human resources, research capacity and technology in the public and private sectors.

Consultation

(27) The two Governments will endeavour to consult promptly and at an appropriate level of representation at the request of either.

(28) The two Governments will hold such other consultations as may be agreed.

Other Arrangements

(29) Commitments made under existing arrangements between the two countries will be respected, and developed in accordance with this Joint Declaration.

(30) The two Governments will endeavour to interpret and implement agreements and arrangements between them in the spirit of the principles and commitments contained in this Joint Declaration, without prejudice to commitments entered into under existing agreements between Nauru and Australia.

(31) The two Governments may give effect to this Joint Declaration in such further agreements and arrangements as may be agreed.

Review

(32) The two Governments will review the operation of this Joint Declaration at intervals of not more than five years.

[*Source*: 32 ILM 1476 (1993)]

Request for an Examination of the Situation in Accordance with Paragraph 63 of the Court's Judgment of 20 December 1974 in the *Nuclear Tests (New Zealand* v. *France) Case*[1]

International Court of Justice, The Hague

22 September 1995 (Bedjaoui, *President*; Schwebel, *Vice-President*; Oda, Guillaume, Shahabuddeen, Weeramantry, Ranjeva, Herczegh, Shi, Fleischhauer, Koroma, Vereshchetin, Ferrari Bravo and Higgins, *Judges*; Sir Geoffrey Palmer, *Judge* ad hoc)

Hazardous activities and substances – alleged radioactive contamination arising from French underground nuclear weapons tests in South Pacific – whether unlawful to undertake tests before conducting an environmental impact assessment – Court's ruling in 1974 that object of dispute had disappeared because of France's undertaking in 1974 to cease atmospheric tests – assumption in 1974 that no risk of contamination from underground testing – whether earlier proceedings and judgment limited to atmospheric nuclear testing or concerning all radioactive contamination caused by whatever means of testing – developments in scientific knowledge and international environmental law since 1974

Jurisdiction – request to International Court of Justice by New Zealand for resumption of proceedings begun in 1973 challenging legality of France's nuclear tests – whether Request was outside scope of paragraph 63 of 1974 Judgment – paragraph 63 related exclusively to atmospheric nuclear tests – whether jurisdiction for Court to consider underground testing or developments in international environmental law since 1974

SUMMARY   *The facts*   In 1973, New Zealand had made an application to the Court challenging the legality of French nuclear tests then taking place in the South Pacific. At that time France was conducting atmospheric

---

[1] The Hon. Paul East QC, Mr John McGrath QC, Mr Elihu Lauterpacht CBE, QC, Sir Kenneth Keith QC and Mr Don MacKay acted as Counsel for New Zealand. France was represented by Mr Marc Perrin de Brichambaut, Mr Pierre-Marie Dupuy, Mr Alain Pellet and Sir Arthur Watts KCMG, QC.

nuclear tests.[2] In 1974, France announced that it would cease conducting atmospheric nuclear tests and, on the basis of these undertakings by France, the Court ruled that it was no longer required to give a decision on the claim because the claim no longer had any object ('the 1974 Judgment'). In paragraph 63 of the 1974 Judgment the Court stated that:

> Once the Court has found that a State has entered into a commitment concerning its future conduct it is not the Court's function to contemplate that it will not comply with it. However, the Court observes that if the basis of this Judgment were to be affected, the Applicant could request an examination of the situation in accordance with the provisions of the Statute; the denunciation by France, by letter dated 2 January 1974, of the General Act for the Pacific Settlement of International Disputes, which is relied on as a basis of jurisdiction in the present case, cannot constitute by itself an obstacle to the presentation of such a request.[3]

Between 1974 and 1992, France conducted a number of underground nuclear tests at Mururoa and Fangataufa atolls in the South Pacific. Testing was halted by the French Government in 1992, but in June 1995 the French Government announced that it intended to conduct what it described as a final series of tests. New Zealand filed with the Court a Request for an Examination of the Situation pursuant to paragraph 63 of the 1974 Judgment. Australia submitted an application for permission to intervene in the case under Article 62 of the Statute of the Court. Applications for permission to intervene under Article 62 and declarations of intervention under Article 63 were submitted by Samoa, the Solomon Islands, the Marshall Islands and the Federated States of Micronesia.

New Zealand claimed that circumstances were such that the basis of the 1974 Judgment had been affected and that, under paragraph 63, it was entitled to request the resumption of the case begun in 1973. New Zealand argued (i) that the conduct of the proposed nuclear tests would violate New Zealand's rights under international law; and, further or in the alternative, (ii) that it was unlawful for France to conduct such tests before it had undertaken an environmental impact assessment ('EIA'). Unless an EIA established that the tests would not give rise to radioactive contamination, New Zealand maintained, its rights under international law would be violated. New Zealand also filed requests for the indication

---

[2] A summary and relevant extracts of the orders and judgments of the International Court of Justice in the *Nuclear Tests Case (New Zealand v. France)* are reproduced in this volume at p. 88 above.

[3] France had, after New Zealand filed its application in 1973 but before the Court had delivered its judgment in 1974, denounced the General Act for the Pacific Settlement of Disputes ('the General Act'), which had formed the basis for jurisdiction in the proceedings.

of provisional measures of protection requiring France to refrain from conducting underground nuclear tests and requiring it to conduct an EIA.

New Zealand maintained that paragraph 63 was activated because the concern of the 1973 application was with radioactive contamination arising from nuclear testing of whatever nature and the scope of the 1974 Judgment was not limited to atmospheric nuclear tests. New Zealand submitted that the Court had held that the dispute had become moot in 1974 by reason of France's undertakings, because atmospheric tests were the sole mode of testing used by France in the South Pacific at that time and because it was not then known that underground nuclear testing also involved risks of contamination. New Zealand submitted evidence indicating that underground nuclear tests in the South Pacific had already led to some contamination and that there was a risk of future contamination. New Zealand claimed, therefore, that the basis of the 1974 Judgment had been affected. New Zealand also submitted that France had failed to comply with the obligation to conduct an EIA under customary international law and under the Convention for the Protection of the Natural Resources and Environment of the South Pacific Region, 1986 ('the Noumea Convention'), to which France was a party.[4] New Zealand maintained that the Court had jurisdiction on the basis of France's adherence to the General Act for the Pacific Settlement of Disputes, 1928, at the time of the original application in 1973.

France contended that no basis existed which might found the Court's jurisdiction even *prima facie* and that the action by New Zealand was not within the framework of the earlier case, because that case related only to atmospheric tests, so that New Zealand's present request could not be linked to it. France asserted that, as the Court lacked jurisdiction in the absence of consent by France, neither the question of the designation of a judge *ad hoc* nor the indication of provisional measures arose, and that the action of New Zealand could not properly be entered in the Court's General List.

In view of the differences between France and New Zealand regarding the legal nature of the Request by New Zealand and its effect, both were invited to present to the Court informal *aide-mémoires* stating their positions on various issues which arose. In its *aide-mémoire*, New Zealand argued that the question of whether the present proceedings were the

---

[4] Article 12 of the Noumea Convention required Parties to the treaty to 'take all appropriate measures to prevent, reduce and control pollution in the Convention Area which might result from the testing of nuclear devices'. Article 16 of the Noumea Convention required the carrying out of an EIA before any major project 'which might affect the marine environment' was embarked upon.

continuation of the 1973–4 proceedings was itself a question of jurisdiction, or analogous to one. Accordingly, on an application for provisional measures of protection, New Zealand had only to establish a *prima facie* case for continuity of the proceedings commenced in 1973. New Zealand maintained that paragraph 63 of the 1974 Judgment demonstrated the Court's intention not to close the case and that the 'basis' of the 1974 Judgment which would permit resumption of the case extended to 'any developments that might reactivate New Zealand's concern that French testing could produce contamination of the Pacific marine environment by any artificial radioactive material'. New Zealand claimed that it had established a *prima facie* case for the continuity of proceedings and that it was, therefore, entitled to designate a Judge *ad hoc*.

France submitted an *aide-mémoire* but indicated that this was not an acceptance by France of the Court's jurisdiction and formed no part of proceedings governed by the Statute and Rules of the Court. In its *aide-mémoire,* France reiterated its assertion that the case of 1973–4 had been definitively closed by the 1974 Judgment. France maintained that it was the undertakings given in 1974 to cease atmospheric nuclear testing which constituted the basis for the Court's decision and that, therefore, underground tests were outside the scope of the 1974 Judgment and could not activate the mechanism under paragraph 63. France claimed that New Zealand's Request did not fall within any of the categories in the Statute under which an application could be brought, because it was neither a request for interpretation of an earlier judgment (Article 60 of the Statute) nor an application for revision (Article 61 of the Statute) and that, as the Court lacked jurisdiction in the matter, no procedural action could be taken, which also meant that New Zealand's request for provisional measures could not be examined.

On 8 September 1995, the Court informed the parties that a public sitting was to be held at which New Zealand and France were requested to address the Court on the question of whether the requests submitted by New Zealand fell within the provisions of paragraph 63. The Court also informed the parties that Sir Geoffrey Palmer would sit as judge *ad hoc* in the case.

In the ensuing oral proceedings, New Zealand claimed, *inter alia,* that the basis of the 1974 Judgment had been affected by changes in the factual situation because the assumption in the 1974 Judgment that the abandonment of atmospheric testing would end risks of contamination had since been shown to be incorrect. New Zealand also argued that changes in the law were capable of affecting the basis of the 1974 Judgment and sought to rely on changes in standards and procedures in international environmental law. New Zealand maintained that, in the 1974 Judgment, the Court was exercising its inherent right to determine its own procedure and that paragraph 63 was a mechanism enabling the resumption of the 1973–4 proceedings which had not been fully determined. It maintained that the reference in paragraph 63 to the provisions of the Statute referred only to provisions regulating the procedure applicable to the examination once the Request was made. France contended that the use of the phrase 'in accordance with the provisions of the Statute' in paragraph 63 meant that a request could be made only under the specific procedures in Articles 60 and 61 of the Statute. France maintained that New Zealand's Request was most closely related to Article 61 because New Zealand sought to rely on the existence of new facts but, because France's decision in 1995 to carry out underground tests had not existed at the time of the 1974 Judgment and the ten-year time-limit had expired, the criteria under Article 61 were not satisfied. New Zealand, France submitted, had not invoked any provision of the Statute to justify its procedure in law.

Held by the International Court of Justice (by twelve votes to three)   The Request was outside the scope of paragraph 63 of the 1974 Judgment and was dismissed. The request for interim measures and the applications to intervene were also dismissed.

(1)   The matter had to be entered in the General List even if for the sole purpose of the Court determining whether New Zealand's Request fulfilled the conditions under paragraph 63 of the 1974 Judgment.

(2)   In expressly laying down, in paragraph 63 of the 1974 Judgment, that New Zealand could request an examination of the situation, the Court could not have intended to limit New Zealand's access to the Court to those procedures provided under Articles 60 and 61 of the Statute or the filing of a new application under Article 40(1). The Court had thus not excluded a special procedure in the event of circumstances arising which affected the basis of the 1974 Judgment. That special procedure was inextricably linked with the existence of such circumstances and was not available in the absence of those circumstances.

(3)   Australia's application in the 1973–4 *Nuclear Tests (Australia v. France) Case* had related exclusively to atmospheric tests. In paragraph 63 of its Judgment in the New Zealand case, the Court had adopted the identical form of words used in paragraph 60 of the Judgment in the Australian case. In 1974, therefore, the Court had considered the

two cases to be identical as to their subject matter, relating exclusively to atmospheric tests. The Court's present examination was limited to an analysis of the 1974 Judgment and could not reopen the question of whether New Zealand had broader objectives in its 1973 application than the cessation of atmospheric tests. In addition, France's undertakings, upon which the 1974 Judgment was based, were specifically limited to the cessation of atmospheric testing. The 1974 Judgment dealt exclusively with atmospheric testing and it was not possible for the Court now to consider underground tests, developments in international environmental law and the conclusion of the Noumea Convention, all of which had occurred since 1974. The Request by New Zealand was not, therefore, within the scope of paragraph 63 and had to be dismissed. The Request was removed from the General List.

(4)   The order was made without prejudice to the obligations on States to respect and protect the natural environment.

(5)   The request for the indication of provisional measures and the applications to intervene were also dismissed.

Declaration of Vice-President Schwebel   France's claims in response to New Zealand's action were tantamount to an objection to the admissibility of New Zealand's Request and should have been so treated. In practice, that was what the Court had done.

Declaration of Judge Oda   While he supported the order of the Court dismissing the Request, it was to be hoped that no further tests of any kind of nuclear weapons would be carried out in the future.

Declaration of Judge Ranjeva   The Court should have dealt with the question of whether the 'basis' of the 1974 Judgment was 'affected' before considering whether procedural requirements were met. The approach adopted by the Court led to unnecessary consideration of procedural questions and emphasized procedural formalism over legal substance, contrary to the spirit of paragraph 63.

Separate Opinion of Judge Shahabuddeen   (1)   New Zealand claimed that the 1974 Judgment was based on the Court's assumption that underground tests were safe. It was not, however, certain whether the Court did, in fact, assume that underground tests were safe or whether it acted on the understanding that New Zealand was satisfied that such tests were safe.

(2)   New Zealand maintained that its action was a continuation of its 1973 application, and thus its Request hinged on the dispute presented in 1973 and could not expand on it. In the proceedings in 1973–4, however, the dispute was referred to by New Zealand and the Court as being a

dispute 'as to the legality of atmospheric nuclear tests'. The question of the legality of underground tests was, therefore, outside the limits of the dispute giving rise to the proceedings and as placed before the Court in 1973.

(3)   Where the Court had jurisdiction at the time an application was made, it could continue to exercise that jurisdiction in relation to the dispute presented in the application notwithstanding the termination of that jurisdiction in the course of the proceedings. The Court was not, however, entitled to exercise a terminated jurisdiction over new acts occurring after the termination of jurisdiction. The requests for a declaration as to the legality of underground tests and for measures restraining France from conducting such tests were new acts.

(4)   The Court's function was to determine disputes on the basis of international law. It could, especially where there was doubt, develop and advance the law on the basis of broad notions of justice. Where the law was clear, however, it had to prevail. The law was clear that the Court could not act unless there was a dispute before it and it could then act only within the limits of that dispute.

Dissenting Opinion of Judge Weeramantry   (1)   The Court had intended, by the inclusion of paragraph 63, to preserve its 1974 Judgment in its full integrity in case some event occurred which undermined the basis of that Judgment, although, at that time, it had believed that the threats to New Zealand's rights had been overcome by France's undertakings. The 1973–4 case was not *res judicata*. The Court had formulated a special procedure under paragraph 63 without any time limitation for New Zealand to reopen the proceedings in the case of certain eventualities. The phrase 'in accordance with the provisions of the Statute' merely indicated that New Zealand had to follow the usual procedural formalities required of any application made by any party to the Court but did not require New Zealand to satisfy the criteria under Article 60 or 61 of the Statute.

(2)   New Zealand had the right to ask the Court to examine the situation under paragraph 63 because the basis of the 1974 Judgment had been affected, the dispute had not disappeared, and New Zealand's claim in 1995 related to the same type of damage as that giving rise to the application in 1973. Although the Court's consideration in 1974 was limited to atmospheric tests because these were the only type of nuclear tests taking place at that time in the Pacific, the *ratio decidendi* of the 1974 Judgment was that New Zealand was entitled to protection against damage caused by radioactive contamination from the explosion of nuclear weapons in general. The means by which damage was brought about was

subsidiary to the main fact of damage and the prohibition of a specific means of testing formed part of the 1974 Judgment but was not the basis of the Judgment. Underground testing of nuclear weapons was regarded as safe in 1974 but it had since been shown to produce the type of damage complained of by New Zealand in its 1973 application. In considering the 1995 Request, the Court had a responsibility to have regard to the changes in scientific knowledge which underlay the assumptions behind its 1974 Judgment. Furthermore, to construe the 1974 Judgment as prohibiting radioactive fallout from atmospheric testing while permitting underground testing which might produce the same damage would go against the fundamental rule of interpretation that a legal document was not to be construed so as to lead to unreasonable or absurd results.

(3)   New Zealand was entitled to a consideration by the Court of its request for provisional measures. It had established a *prima facie* case that it was suffering, or likely to suffer, damage of the same nature of which it had complained in 1973.

(4) (a)   The intertemporal principle required the Court to consider the Request in the light of the scientific knowledge now available. If the basis of the 1974 Judgment was undermined by knowledge in 1995 and if the terms of that Judgment permitted reconsideration where its basis was undermined, the Court should apply the knowledge that it had today.

(b)   Under the principle of intergenerational equity, the Court was a trustee of the rights of the people of New Zealand in the future as well as today and it should thus have taken account of current scientific knowledge relating to the long-term effects of radioactive contamination.

(c)   The Court should have had regard to the precautionary principle, under which 'where there [were] threats of serious or irreversible damage, lack of full scientific certainty [c]ould not be used as a reason for postponing measures to prevent environmental degradation' (Bergen Economic Commission for Europe Ministerial Declaration on Sustainable Development, 1990). The precautionary principle had received widespread international acceptance and provided a basis for the Court to consider the Request and to prevent, on a provisional basis, the threatened environmental degradation, until such time as New Zealand's claims were proved unfounded by full scientific evidence.

(d)   An issue of such importance as that before the Court was one in which the principle of environmental impact assessment *prima facie* applied under contemporary international environmental law. The Court had a special place at the apex of international tribunals, enjoyed a special position of trust in relation to the principles of environmental law and was entitled to take into account the EIA principle when considering the present Request.

(e)   The illegality of introducing radioactive waste into the marine environment was well established and, as such, the Court was entitled to act upon the *prima facie* case made out by New Zealand.

(f)   The principle that no State was entitled to cause damage to other States was a long-established principle of international law and applied equally in modern environmental law and, specifically, in relation to damage caused to the environments of other States.

(5)   New Zealand had made out a *prima facie* case that the dangers which gave rise to its application in 1973 were present again as a consequence of the underground tests that France was conducting in the Pacific, thereby activating paragraph 63 and establishing a jurisdictional basis for the Request. The Court should have proceeded to consider whether a case had been made out for the grant of interim measures of protection and whether the intervenors should be allowed to intervene under Article 62 to protect their legal interests. It was inappropriate that matters of critical importance were not subjected to a preliminary examination simply by reason of a strict, inflexible, construction of paragraph 63.

Dissenting Opinion of Judge Koroma   (1)   The Court had applied the wrong standard of proof. Given the seriousness of the matter and the weight of legal and factual evidence presented, New Zealand had shown *prima facie* that the Request had a legal basis and that it fell within the provisions of paragraph 63. Whether the basis of the 1974 Judgment had been affected was a question of fact and any doubts arising in respect of this should have been resolved in favour of New Zealand given the gravity of the issues and the nature of the Request. New Zealand complained in 1973 about the radioactive effects of nuclear weapons testing. In 1973 there was an assumption that underground testing produced no radioactive effect. That assumption was no longer valid and this affected the basis of the 1974 Judgment, thus activating paragraph 63.

(2)   Duties were evolving under contemporary international law to refrain from causing serious damage which could reasonably be avoided and not to permit the escape of dangerous substances. Given such a trend, although nuclear testing *per se* was not prohibited, it could be considered illegal when it caused radioactive contamination. There was evidence before the Court to establish that there was a risk of contamination resulting from the proposed tests. The Court should have ruled that the Request was within paragraph 63 and indicated provisional measures. As the States which sought to intervene also faced the risk of radioactive

contamination, they should have been granted an opportunity to present their views to the Court.

Dissenting Opinion of Judge ad hoc *Sir Geoffrey Palmer* (1)   New Zealand had consistently opposed all nuclear weapons tests. The main contention of New Zealand in 1973 was that it was entitled to be free from the increased risk of nuclear contamination resulting from French testing in the South Pacific. In 1974 the Court did not find it necessary to consider the issue of the legal effect of France's undertaking to halt atmospheric testing and did not, therefore, resolve the dispute between the two States, as was evidenced by the other disputes which had arisen between France and New Zealand.[5]

(2)   The Court had, in 1974, established a mechanism by which New Zealand could return to the Court and the Court must have decided that this right provided an important and necessary safeguard. The Court did not decide the substantive issue before it but left open the opportunity to do so later. There was nothing in the language of paragraph 63 to restrict an examination by the Court to France's compliance with its undertaking not to resume atmospheric nuclear testing.

(3)   The jurisdictional basis for the Request rested upon the 1974 Judgment itself, which was delivered in accordance with the Statute. The phrase 'in accordance with the provisions of the Statute' simply meant that if paragraph 63 was activated, the Court would follow its usual procedures to deal with it. The Court was exercising its inherent power to regulate its own procedure.

(4)   New Zealand had shown that there was a *prima facie* case for examination of the situation. New Zealand had established that the gravity of radiation damage, if it occurred, was likely to be serious for the marine environment. In addition, developments in international environmental law were sufficient to meet the *prima facie* test that the legal circumstances had altered sufficiently to favour an examination of the situation under paragraph 63. The law to be applied in such circumstances was the law applicable at the date on which the Court sought to apply it, i.e. the law as it stood in 1995.

(5)   The Request gave rise to questions as to the proper scope of the judicial role. Public international law was traditionally concerned with relations between States. There had, however, been developments which had eroded the concept of State sovereignty on which the traditional concepts of international law rested. The Court had a responsibility to

---

[5] *Rainbow Warrior (New Zealand/France), Ruling of the UN Secretary-General of 1987*, 74 ILR 241; *Arbitration Award of 30 April 1990*, 82 ILR 499.

declare, develop and uphold international law while having regard to the limits of the law, particularly where political considerations arose. The Court had failed to take up the opportunity to develop environmental law and had failed to resolve the dispute before it.

There follows

Order of International Court of Justice, 22 September 1995 (extract)

[**302**] [. . .] 45. Whereas New Zealand bases its Request on paragraph 63 of the Judgment of 20 December 1974,[7] which provides:

> Once the Court has found that a State has entered into a commitment concerning its future conduct it is not the Court's function to contemplate that it will not comply with it. However, the Court observes that if the basis of this Judgment were to be affected, the Applicant could request an examination of the situation in accordance with the provisions of the Statute; the denunciation by France, by letter dated 2 January 1974, of the General Act for the Pacific Settlement of International Disputes, which is relied on as a basis of jurisdiction in the present case, cannot constitute by itself an obstacle to the presentation of such a request;

46. Whereas, in the present instance, the following question has to be answered *in limine*: 'Do the Requests submitted to the Court by the Government of New Zealand on 21 August 1995 fall within the provisions of paragraph 63 of the Judgment of the Court of 20 December 1974 in the case concerning *Nuclear Tests (New Zealand* v. *France)*?'; and whereas the Court has consequently limited the present proceedings to that question;

47. Whereas that question has two elements; whereas one concerns the courses of procedure envisaged by the Court in paragraph 63 of its 1974 Judgment, when it stated that 'the Applicant could request an examination of the situation *in accordance with the provisions of the Statute*'; and whereas the other concerns the question whether the 'basis' of that Judgment has been 'affected' within the meaning of paragraph 63 thereof;

[. . .]

---

[6] The declarations of Vice-President Schwebel and Judges Oda and Ranjeva are not reproduced in this volume but can be found at *ICJ Reports 1995*, pp. 309, 310 and 311 respectively. The dissenting opinion of Judge Koroma is also not reproduced in this volume but can be found at *ICJ Reports 1995*, p. 363.

[7] See p. 117 above.]

[304] [. . .] 55. Whereas the Court must now consider the second element of the question raised and determine whether *the basis of its Judgment of 20 December 1974 has been affected* by the facts to which New Zealand refers and whether the Court may consequently proceed to examine the situation as contemplated by paragraph 63 of that Judgment; and whereas, to that end, it must first define the basis of that Judgment by an analysis of its text;

56. Whereas the Court, in 1974, took as the point of departure of its reasoning the Application filed by New Zealand in 1973; whereas it affirmed in its Judgment of 20 December 1974 that it was its duty 'to isolate the real issue in the case and to identify the object of the claim'; whereas it subsequently added that 'it has never been contested that the Court is entitled to interpret the submissions of the parties, and in fact is bound to do so', this being 'one of the attributes of its judicial function' (*ICJ Reports 1974*, p. 466, para. 30); and whereas it continued as follows:

> In the circumstances of the present case, as already mentioned, the Court must ascertain the true subject of the dispute, the object and purpose of the claim . . . In doing so it must take into account not only the submission, but the Application as a whole, the arguments of the Applicant before the Court, and other documents referred to . . . (*ibid.*, p. 467, para. 31);[8]

57. Whereas, in the light of this, the Court referred, among other things, to a statement made by the Prime Minister of New Zealand that

> [t]he option of further atmospheric tests has been left open. Until we have an assurance that nuclear testing of this kind is finished for good, the dispute between New Zealand and France persists . . .;

and whereas it found that

> for purposes of the Application, the New Zealand claim is to be interpreted as applying only to atmospheric tests, not to any other form of testing, and as applying only to atmospheric tests so conducted as to give rise to radio-active fall-out on New Zealand territory (*ibid.*, p. 466, para. 29);[9]

[305] 58. Whereas on the same date, 20 December 1974, the Court furthermore delivered a Judgment in the *Nuclear Tests (Australia v. France)* case, in which Australia had asked, in express terms, that it 'adjudge and declare that . . . the carrying out of further atmospheric nuclear weapon tests . . . is not consistent with applicable rules of international law' (*ICJ Reports 1974*, p. 256, para. 11); whereas, having considered the Application of Australia, the Court employed in paragraph 60 of that Judgment a form of words identical to the one used in paragraph 63 of the Judgment in the *Nuclear Tests (New Zealand v. France)* case and adopted, in both Judgments, operative parts with the same content; and whereas for the Court the two cases appeared identical as to their subject-matter which concerned exclusively atmospheric tests;

[8 See p. 110 above.]
[9 See p. 110 above.]

59. Whereas the Court, in making these findings in 1974, had dealt with the question whether New Zealand, when filing its Application of 1973 instituting proceedings, might have had broader objectives than the cessation of atmospheric nuclear tests – the 'primary concern' of the Government of New Zealand, as it now puts it; and whereas, since the current task of the Court is limited to an analysis of the Judgment of 1974, it cannot now reopen this question;

60. Whereas, moreover, the Court, at that time, took note of the communiqué issued by the Office of the President of the French Republic on 8 June 1974, stating that

> in view of the stage reached in carrying out the French nuclear defence programme France will be in a position to pass on to the stage of underground explosions as soon as the series of tests planned for this summer is completed (*ibid.*, p. 469, para. 35);[10]

whereas it likewise referred to other official declarations of the French authorities on the same subject; and whereas it concluded, with reference to all those statements, that

> they must be held to constitute an engagement of the State, having regard to their intention and to the circumstances in which they were made (*ibid.*, p. 474, para. 51);[11]

61. Whereas the unilateral declarations of the French authorities were made publicly outside the Court and *erga omnes*, and expressed the French Government's intention to put an end to its atmospheric tests; whereas the Court, comparing the undertaking entered into by France with the claim asserted by New Zealand, found that it faced 'a situation in which the objective of the Applicant [had] in effect been accomplished' (*ibid.*, p. 475, para. 55);[12] and accordingly indicated that 'the object of the claim having clearly disappeared, there is nothing on which to give judgment' (*ibid.*, p. 477, para. 62);[13]

62. Whereas the basis of the Judgment delivered by the Court in the *Nuclear Tests (New Zealand v. France)* case was consequently France's [306] undertaking not to conduct any further atmospheric nuclear tests; whereas it was only, therefore, in the event of a resumption of nuclear tests in the atmosphere that that basis of the Judgment would have been affected; and whereas that hypothesis has not materialized;

63. Whereas, in analysing its Judgment of 1974, the Court has reached the conclusion that that Judgment dealt exclusively with atmospheric nuclear tests; whereas consequently it is not possible for the Court now to take into consideration questions relating to underground nuclear tests; and whereas the Court cannot, therefore, take account of the arguments derived by New Zealand, on the one hand from the conditions in which France has conducted underground nuclear tests since 1974, and on the other from the development of international law in recent decades – and particularly

[10] See p. 111 above.]
[11] See p. 114 above.]
[12] See p. 115 above.]
[13] See p. 117 above.]

the conclusion, on 25 November 1986, of the Noumea Convention – any more than of the arguments derived by France from the conduct of the New Zealand Government since 1974;

64. Whereas moreover the present Order is without prejudice to the obligations of States to respect and protect the natural environment, obligations to which both New Zealand and France have in the present instance reaffirmed their commitment;

65. Whereas the basis of the Judgment delivered on 20 December 1974 in the *Nuclear Tests (New Zealand v. France)* case has not been affected; whereas the 'Request for an Examination of the Situation' submitted by New Zealand on 21 August 1995 does not therefore fall within the provisions of paragraph 63 of that Judgment; and whereas that Request must consequently be dismissed;

66. Whereas, as indicated in paragraph 44 above, the 'Request for an Examination of the Situation' submitted by New Zealand in accordance with paragraph 63 of the 1974 Judgment has been entered in the General List for the sole purpose of allowing the Court to determine whether the conditions laid down in that text have been fulfilled in the present case; and whereas, following the present Order, the Court has instructed the Registrar, acting pursuant to Article 26, paragraph 1 *(b)*, of the Rules, to remove that Request from the General List as of 22 September 1995;

*

*   *

67. Whereas it follows from the conclusions reached by the Court in paragraph 65 above that it must likewise dismiss the 'Further Request for the Indication of Provisional Measures' submitted by New Zealand, as well as the 'Application for Permission to Intervene' submitted by Australia, and the 'Applications for Permission to Intervene' and 'Declarations of Intervention' submitted by Samoa, Solomon Islands, the Marshall Islands and the Federated States of Micronesia – all of which are proceedings incidental to the 'Request for an Examination of the [307] Situation' submitted by New Zealand; and whereas the Court has instructed the Registrar to so inform the States concerned in notifying them of the text of the present Order;

*

*   *

68. Accordingly,

THE COURT,

(1) By twelve votes to three,

Finds that the 'Request for an Examination of the Situation' in accordance with paragraph 63 of the Judgment of the Court of 20 December 1974 in the *Nuclear Tests (New Zealand v. France)* case, submitted by New Zealand on 21 August 1995, does not fall within the provisions of the said paragraph 63 and must consequently be dismissed;

> IN FAVOUR: *President* Bedjaoui; *Vice-President* Schwebel; *Judges* Oda, Guillaume, Shahabuddeen, Ranjeva, Herczegh, Shi, Fleischhauer, Vereshchetin, Ferrari Bravo, Higgins;

AGAINST: *Judges* Weeramantry, Koroma; *Judge* ad hoc Sir Geoffrey Palmer;

(2) By twelve votes to three,

Finds that the 'Further Request for the Indication of Provisional Measures' submitted by New Zealand on the same date must be dismissed;

> IN FAVOUR: *President* Bedjaoui; *Vice-President* Schwebel; *Judges* Oda, Guillaume, Shahabuddeen, Ranjeva, Herczegh, Shi, Fleischhauer, Vereshchetin, Ferrari Bravo, Higgins;
>
> AGAINST: *Judges* Weeramantry, Koroma; *Judge* ad hoc Sir Geoffrey Palmer;

(3) By twelve votes to three,

Finds that the 'Application for Permission to Intervene' submitted by Australia on 23 August 1995, and the 'Applications for Permission to Intervene' and 'Declarations of Intervention' submitted by Samoa and Solomon Islands on 24 August 1995, and by the Marshall Islands and the Federated States of Micronesia on 25 August 1995, must likewise be dismissed.

> IN FAVOUR: *President* Bedjaoui; *Vice-President* Schwebel; *Judges* Oda, Guillaume, Shahabuddeen, Ranjeva, Herczegh, Shi, Fleischhauer, Vereshchetin, Ferrari Bravo, Higgins;
>
> AGAINST: *Judges* Weeramantry, Koroma; *Judge* ad hoc Sir Geoffrey Palmer.

[. . .]

[312] SEPARATE OPINION OF JUDGE SHAHABUDDEEN (EXTRACT)

The growing recognition of the need to protect the natural environment is striking. Contemporary international law has been developing responsively. I understand New Zealand's concerns and agree with its case on several points. I agree that it was entitled to come to the Court, entitled to a hearing, entitled to a judge *ad hoc*, and that it was not shut out by the words in paragraph 63 of the 1974 Judgment, 'in accordance with the provisions of the Statute'. If I do not go the remainder of the way, the reason lies in what appears to me to be substantial legal obstacles, some of which I would like to explain.

I. The question of the basis of the Judgment

The central point in New Zealand's case is that the basis of the 1974 Judgment lay in an assumption by the Court that underground tests were safe, that more recent scientific evidence disproves that assumption, and that consequently the basis of the Judgment has been affected within the meaning of paragraph 63 of the Judgment.

A question could arise as to whether the true position was that the Court made an assumption that underground tests were safe, or whether it acted on an understanding that New Zealand was satisfied that such tests were safe, the Court itself being in no position to judge of a complex technical matter not put in issue and not examined. However, whether the distinction between these two possibilities can be made and, if so, with what significance are questions which need not be pursued for the reasons given in Sections II and III below.[14]

[...]

Conclusion

[316] [...] It does not follow from the fact that the Court may also be described as a court of law that it administers the law mechanically. Lacking the full measure of the judicial power available to some national courts, it has nevertheless found opportunity for enterprise and even occasional boldness. Especially where there is doubt, its forward course is helpfully illuminated by broad notions of justice. However, where the law is clear, the law prevails.

The law is clear that the Court cannot act unless there is a dispute before it, and then only within the limits of the dispute. The dispute which New Zealand referred to the Court in 1973 arose out of a claim by New Zealand which the Court found applied 'only to atmospheric tests, *not to any other form of testing*' (emphasis added). The Court would have been acting *ultra petita* in 1974 had it sought to adjudicate on the legality of underground tests (supposing it had been asked to do so), these being another form of testing. It is in respect of the legality of underground tests that New Zealand's present Request seeks relief. The matters sought to be so raised do not fall within the limits of the 1973 dispute by which the Court is still bound.

It is for these reasons that, although agreeing with New Zealand on some points, I have not found it possible to accept its main arguments.

DISSENTING OPINION OF JUDGE WEERAMANTRY

[319] This is a Request by which New Zealand seeks the continuation of the proceedings it filed in 1973. New Zealand is not entitled to commence fresh proceedings against France in view of the steps taken by France, since the institution of the case in 1973, to withdraw the bases of jurisdiction under which that case was filed. New Zealand's Request for an Examination of the Situation can only be entertained by the Court if it constitutes another phase of those earlier proceedings. The burden lies upon New Zealand to demonstrate this.

The fundamental question before the Court in this Request is whether the 'basis of this Judgment' of this Court in 1974 has been 'affected', for the Court in that Judgment left open to New Zealand the right to approach this Court again in that event. That question can only be decided by a two-fold process – an examination of the meaning of the term 'basis of this Judgment' and an examination of such factual material as New Zealand places before the Court to show that that 'basis' has been 'affected'.

I regret that the Court has chosen to determine the entire Request, involving, though it does, matters of profound moment to the entire global community, upon what seems to me to be an unduly limited construction of the phrase 'basis of this

[14 Not reproduced in this volume.]

Judgment', without a determination on the second question essential to its decision, namely, whether New Zealand has made out a prima facie case on the facts that such basis has been affected. It seems to me the two questions are integrally linked. As is so often the case with questions affecting the competence of the Court, a decision in this case can only be arrived at through an interaction of the legal and factual elements involved (see Ibrahim F. I. Shihata, *The Power of the International Court to Determine Its Own Jurisdiction*, 1965, p. 299).

The phrase 'basis of this Judgment' necessitates an enquiry into the grievance which brought New Zealand to the Court, the object of the proceedings, the remedies contained in the Judgment, the basis of facts and knowledge underlying the Judgment, the reasoning or *ratio decidendi* of the Judgment and, in short, the overall context in which the operative words are set. My conclusion, having regard to all these matters, is fundamentally different from that of the majority of my colleagues. The difference between the two approaches touches the fundamentals of the judicial process as I understand it, and this opinion contains some necessary observations in this regard.

The ensuing opinion is an attempt to describe what I conceive to be the correct approach to the momentous question which New Zealand's Request brings before the Court. In making these observations, I bear in mind of course that the scope of New Zealand's present Request is circumscribed within the limits of the initial pleadings on which that case commenced and that New Zealand can claim no more now than it claimed then. No grievances, no reliefs, no orders can be pleaded or [**320**] sought other than those which are strictly within the limits of that original Application.

Introduction

Unusual nature of New Zealand's Request

This Request for an Examination of the Situation is probably without precedent in the annals of the Court. It does not fit within any of the standard applications recognized by the Court's rules for the revision or interpretation of a judgment rendered by the Court. It is an unusual request generated by an unusual provision contained in the Court's Judgment of 1974.

Paragraph 63 of that Judgment reads as follows:

> Once the Court has found that a State has entered into a commitment concerning its future conduct it is not the Court's function to contemplate that it will not comply with it. However, the Court observes that if the basis of this Judgment were to be affected, the Applicant could request an examination of the situation in accordance with the provisions of the Statute; the denunciation by France, by letter dated 2 January 1974, of the General Act for the Pacific Settlement of International Disputes, which is relied on as a basis of jurisdiction in the present case, cannot constitute by itself an obstacle to the presentation of such a request. (*Nuclear Tests (New Zealand v. France), ICJ Reports 1974*, p. 477.)[15]

[15   See p. 117 above.]

Paragraph 63 was a precautionary provision which the Court included in its Judgment when it decided to act upon a unilateral declaration by France that it would discontinue atmospheric testing of nuclear weapons – a declaration which it considered to be legally binding. The Court used its undoubted powers of regulating its own procedure to devise a procedure *sui generis*.

This procedure went beyond the provision for interpretation of a judgment contained in Article 60 of the Court's Statute and the provision for revision contained in Article 61. The Court no doubt considered that in the circumstances before it, it needed to go beyond either of those provisions. It was seeking to meet a need different from the need for interpretation or for revision of the Judgment. It was also opening the door to New Zealand in a manner which reached beyond the period of limitation attached to applications for revision.

The rationale of the Court's action was totally different from the rationale underlying revision, for revision involves an alteration or modification of the Judgment, whereas the Court's action was aimed at preserving the Judgment in its full integrity, in the event that some event had occurred which undermined the basis of the Judgment. Moreover, had [**321**] revision been its intention, there was no necessity for the Court to make any special provision as the Statute would have operated automatically.

I therefore see no merit in the submission that an application under paragraph 63 is an application for revision under another guise. The two procedures are totally different in conception, nature and operation.

In devising a special provision dealing with a situation that could arise in the future and affect the *basis* of the Judgment, the Court was demonstrating its anxiety to preserve intact the basic assumptions on which the Judgment was constructed. We must conclude that the Court considered the matter too important to be left unprovided for.

The Court, well aware of the provisions in its established procedure relating to interpretation and revision, was not indulging in an exercise in tautology. It was devising an unprecedented procedure to meet an unprecedented situation.

Background to the Court's Judgment in 1974
The Court accepted the French declaration as reducing New Zealand's claim to one which no longer had any object. Indeed, in the Court's view, it had caused the dispute to disappear.

One can be in no doubt that the Court's understanding – and indeed New Zealand's – at the time was that the damage complained of by New Zealand would come to an end in view of the undertaking by France. Atmospheric tests were the only tests then being conducted by France in the Pacific. An unequivocal indication was given that they would be ended. To all appearances the dispute was therefore at an end.

Yet the Court was dealing with a matter of the utmost importance to the fundamental rights of the people of New Zealand. It did not leave open any possibilities for circumstances yet unseen to undermine the basis of its Judgment, nor did it leave

New Zealand defenceless in the protection of the very rights whose protection had brought it before the Court in the first instance. Though fully satisfied that the objective of New Zealand had been attained and the threats to its rights overcome, it still took the precaution of introducing into its Judgment this clause of its own devising.

It is under that clause that New Zealand requests the Court to consider the situation in the light of its assertion that the current underground nuclear tests produce the same kind of radioactive contamination of its environment as it complained of in 1973.

Questions of jurisdiction and admissibility

In the case instituted in 1973, the Court did not proceed to a finding on questions of jurisdiction and admissibility. The Order of 22 June 1973 [**322**] indicating certain provisional measures against the Parties was made on the basis that:

> it cannot be assumed *a priori* that such claims fall completely outside the purview of the Court's jurisdiction, or that the Government of New Zealand may not be able to establish a legal interest in respect of these claims entitling the Court to admit the Application (*Nuclear Tests (New Zealand v. France), Interim Protection, ICJ Reports 1973*, p. 140, para. 24).[16]

There was thus no determination on questions of admissibility or jurisdiction prior to that Order, nor was there a finding on these matters at any subsequent stage.

For the reasons set out above, this opinion does not in any way touch upon the merits of New Zealand's claim. It will confine itself initially to examining whether the basis of the 1974 Judgment has been in any way affected. It will be necessary for a determination of this question to refer to some matters of fact set out in New Zealand's Request and Application. But if these are referred to, they are only for an examination of the question whether there is prima facie a situation which reactivates the 1973 case through the key provided by paragraph 63 of the 1974 Judgment. It is impossible to determine whether the basis of that Judgment has been affected without some reference to such questions of fact.

Some preliminary questions

Is the 1974 Case dead?

One of the basic positions of France is that the Judgment of 1974 is *res judicata* and that the case instituted in 1973 is dead. In the picturesque language of its counsel, this was no legal Lazarus and no one could revive it.

France also calls in aid, in support of this view, the fact that no academic writing and no publication of the Court lists New Zealand's case against France as a case that is pending. Rather, it is listed even in official Court publications among cases that have been disposed of.

In addressing this question, certain incontrovertible propositions must first be noted:

[16 See p. 101 above.]

- the Court itself has stated in the Judgment that New Zealand may come back to the Court in certain eventualities, however one may define them;
- the Court specially fashioned this procedure to meet the particular needs of this case;
- this right is given without any limitation of time;
- no academic publications, nor indeed any official publications of the Court, can prevail against the express words of the Judgment itself;
- [323] the Court was within its undoubted inherent powers of regulating its own procedure in making this provision in the Judgment;
- the Court was concerned with possible future events which might undermine the basis of the Judgment;
- the Court deliberately chose a procedure other than revision or interpretation.

The argument that the case was dead is consequently one which seems to fly in the face of the Court's own words which kept it alive in certain eventualities. Far from being a revisionary procedure in another form, paragraph 63 is an independent procedure standing in its own right. Devised by the Court and carrying the full stamp of the Court's authority, its express words contradict the contention that the case is dead.

Paragraph 63 enables the case to be reopened by New Zealand if, but only if, the conditions it specifies be met – namely, that the basis of the Judgment has been affected. If that paragraph comes into operation, the case is revived, New Zealand's Request must be entertained by the Court and New Zealand's request for provisional measures must be considered. New Zealand would be approaching the Court under the very authority of the Court itself. New Zealand's right to approach the Court and the validity of New Zealand's Request to this effect cannot in these circumstances be in doubt. The Court would then also have to consider the interventions by Australia, Samoa, Solomon Islands, the Marshall Islands and the Federated States of Micronesia.

If, on the other hand, New Zealand does not have the key with which to open the door of paragraph 63, its Request must be dismissed and the occasion for taking the other steps specified above does not arise.

Whether New Zealand has that key – i.e., whether New Zealand is able to show that the basis of the Judgment is affected – is the crux of the matter before the Court.

Is paragraph 63 self-contradictory?
It was suggested in the course of the argument that the words 'in accordance with the provisions of the Statute' restrict New Zealand to the specific forms of approaching the Court which are provided in the Statute. I do not read these words so narrowly, for such a reading would negate the right which the Court was expressly giving to New Zealand by paragraph 63.

I read these words as meaning rather that the Court was ensuring that New Zealand must follow the usual procedural formalities required of any application made by any party to the Court.

I cannot subscribe to the view that the Court was giving New Zealand a right in the earlier part of that sentence which it was immediately taking [324] away by restricting New Zealand's application to existing Court procedure which did not indeed provide for any such application. The Court did not contradict itself in this manner, and to suggest as much is to do little credit to the remarkable foresight exhibited by the Court in providing New Zealand with the right which it did.

The Court's first task therefore is to examine whether New Zealand has brought before it circumstances which affect the basis of the 1974 Judgment. If it has, the Court must then proceed, in terms of its own Judgment, to examine those circumstances with the greatest of care in order to determine whether a situation has arisen which requires the Court to grant to New Zealand the relief it seeks.

Can New Zealand's Request be disposed of administratively?

It has been contended by France that this matter should be disposed of administratively. It is said in support of this position that New Zealand is bringing a fresh matter to the Court; that New Zealand is approaching the Court on the basis of a case that is dead; that there is no legally valid application before the Court; and that indeed the matter can be dealt with administratively on the basis of a manifest and patent lack of jurisdiction.

France submitted that the Court should take a decision *proprio motu* without any need for a public hearing. In support of its contention that the matter should be disposed of by means of an order without hearings, France relied upon the cases of *Treatment in Hungary of Aircraft and Crew of United States of America (ICJ Reports 1954,* pp. 101 and 105); *Aerial Incident of 4 September 1954 (ICJ Reports 1958,* pp. 160–1); *Aerial Incident of 7 November 1954 (ICJ Reports 1959,* p. 278).[17]

Those were cases of manifest and patent lack of jurisdiction where it was not possible for the Court to take any procedural steps, and are distinguishable from the present case, where New Zealand comes to the Court directly within the terms of an express provision of the Court's own Judgment. The Court needs to consider whether New Zealand is correct in its contention that the basis of the 1974 Judgment is affected by the current nuclear tests. If it is not, New Zealand would have no case, but if it is, there is a matter to be seriously considered. The decision [325] whether

---

[17] In 1973, likewise, the position of France, as stated in a letter to the Court delivered on 16 May 1973, was that the Court was 'manifestly not competent' to deal with the dispute, and that the Court should drop the matter from its docket. The grounds included the argument that the dispute concerned an activity connected with national defence and was thus excluded from the jurisdiction of the Court by the third French reservation to its declaration of acceptance of the compulsory jurisdiction of the Court. The Court rejected the French contention that the absence of jurisdiction was manifest (*Nuclear Tests (New Zealand v. France). Interim Protection, Order of 22 June 1973, ICJ Reports 1973,* p. 138 [not reproduced in this volume]).

there is or is not such a matter is obviously one which cannot be taken behind the closed doors of purely administrative orders, without a public hearing.

It would be contrary to the entire scheme of the administration of justice, as conceived in its Statute and practised by the Court, for the Court to dismiss such an application *in camera*, without a public hearing and even without the benefit of an *ad hoc* judge from the country in question – as France invited the Court to do. Such procedures, available in circumstances where there is a patent, complete and manifest lack of jurisdiction, are inapplicable to the present situation.

If, indeed, New Zealand makes out a prima facie case that the basis of the 1974 Judgment has been affected by supervening events, New Zealand has clearly the right to approach the Court, in terms of the Court's own Judgment, for a judicial determination of the situation arising from the resumption of nuclear testing. The Court will of course deny such relief if, upon a fuller examination of the matter, it is not satisfied that New Zealand's case has been substantiated. But it can only do so judicially.

The matter has, happily, been heard by the Court at a public hearing, at which both Parties have presented their submissions, and both Parties have been afforded the opportunity of a reply. In following this procedure, the Court has given due effect to such principles as *audi alteram partem* which are integral constituents of the rule of law and justice.

Moreover, under Article 79 (1) (Article 67 (1) at the time of the 1973 case) and Article 79 (7) (Article 67 (7) in 1973) of the Rules of Court, New Zealand was clearly entitled to a judicial determination of these preliminary objections to its application.

Correspondence between New Zealand's complaints in 1973 and 1995
New Zealand's complaints in 1973
To understand the basis of the Judgment, which New Zealand claims has been affected, it is necessary, preliminarily, to look at New Zealand's complaint to the Court in 1973.

New Zealand had come to the Court with a complaint that it was suffering damage of five specified descriptions from the radioactive fallout generated by French nuclear explosions in the Pacific. That damage was specified as follows:

> The rights to be protected are:
> (i) the rights of all members of the international community, including New Zealand, that no nuclear tests that give rise to radioactive fall-out be conducted;
> (ii) [326] the rights of all members of the international community, including New Zealand, to the preservation from unjustified, artificial radio-active contamination of the terrestrial, maritime and aerial environment and, in particular, of the environment of the region in which the tests are conducted and in which New Zealand, the Cook Islands, Niue and the Tokelau Islands are situated;
> (iii) the right of New Zealand that no radio-active material enter the territory of New Zealand, the Cook Islands, Niue or the Tokelau Islands, including their air space and territorial waters, as a result of nuclear testing;

(iv) the right of New Zealand that no radio-active material, having entered the terri-tory of New Zealand, the Cook Islands, Niue or the Tokelau Islands, including their airspace and territorial waters, as a result of nuclear testing, cause harm, including apprehension, anxiety and concern to the people and Government of New Zealand, and of the Cook Islands, Niue and the Tokelau Islands;

 (v) the right of New Zealand to freedom of the high seas, including freedom of navigation and overflight and the freedom to explore and exploit the resources of the sea and the sea-bed, without interference or detriment resulting from nuclear testing.

The fact that further nuclear tests at the French Pacific Test Centre will aggravate and extend the dispute between New Zealand and France is one of the grounds on which New Zealand seeks protection of the foregoing rights. In addition and independently, New Zealand has the right to the performance by France of its undertaking contained in Article 33 (3) of the General Act for the Pacific Settlement of International Disputes to abstain from any action whatsoever that may aggravate or extend the present dispute. *(ICJ Pleadings, Nuclear Tests*, Vol. II, Request for the Indication of Interim Measures of Protection, p. 49, para. 2.)

It will be noticed that in the entirety of this paragraph, there is no limitation to atmospheric tests, but that the reference throughout is in general terms to nuclear tests and nuclear testing.

Of particular significance, in the light of the present Request, were the identification of the dispute in paragraph 17 of the 1973 Application as including the effects of fallout on the '*natural resources of the sea*' (*ibid.*, p. 6), and the reference in paragraph 22 to the freedom to exploit the resources of the sea and the seabed, and the continued pollution of the maritime environment of New Zealand '*beyond the limits of national jurisdiction*' (*ibid.*, p. 7; emphasis added).

[327] The prayer of New Zealand was no less clear in its statement of the objective of the proceedings, for it said that New Zealand asks the Court to adjudge and declare:

> That the conduct by the French Government of *nuclear tests in the South Pacific region* that give rise to radioactive fallout constitutes a violation of New Zealand's rights under international law, and that these rights will be violated by any further such tests. (*ICJ Pleadings, Nuclear Tests*, Vol. II, Application, p. 9; emphasis added.)

So, also, paragraph 10 of New Zealand's Application:

> The New Zealand Government will seek a *declaration* that the conduct by the French Government of *nuclear tests in the South Pacific region* that give rise to radioactive fallout constitutes a violation of New Zealand's rights under international law, and that these rights will be violated by any further such tests. (*Ibid.*, p. 4; emphasis added.)

The Applicant's Memorial in paragraph 5 describes this request for a declaration as 'the principal issue before the Court' (*ibid.*, p. 146).

What was the gravamen of New Zealand's complaints? Was it the infringement of the various rights thus specified as resulting from nuclear tests, or was it atmospheric tests and atmospheric tests alone?

It seems reasonable to conclude that New Zealand's complaint to the Court was in relation to the alleged infringement of its rights under international law, which resulted from unjustified artificial radioactive contamination of its terrestrial, maritime and aerial environment. The means used at that stage to bring about this result was atmospheric tests and New Zealand naturally complained against these. The means was subsidiary to the central fact of injury. It was in the injury that the complaint was grounded. The injury was the larger context within which the specific act causing damage was set.

Nowhere in the pleadings, submissions or Judgment is there the slightest suggestion of any acceptance by New Zealand of the principle that the same damage would be tolerated without complaint, if caused by nuclear explosions in another medium. It seems unreasonable to suggest that New Zealand would have been quite content to endure damage by radioactive contamination so long as it did not occur from atmospheric tests.

Nor could the Court have endorsed the view that the dispute had disappeared, or that the claim by New Zealand no longer had any object if there was the suggestion of a possibility of radioactive contamination resulting from the underground tests. Nor could it have viewed France's undertaking as a reservation, even by remotest implication, of the right [328] to cause nuclear contamination of the environment provided it was not caused by atmospheric testing.

The state of knowledge in 1974

The state of knowledge at the time is relevant. The belief of the 1960s that underground testing was safe is reflected in the terms of the Partial Test Ban Treaty of 1963 (to which the United States of America, the United Kingdom and the Union of Soviet Socialist Republics were parties), which banned nuclear weapons tests in the atmosphere, in outer space and underwater. Tests in these media were thought to raise the environmental concerns uppermost in the minds of the contracting States, but underground testing was thought to have 'the potential for essentially total confinement of the radioactive products formed' (A. C. McEwan, 'Environmental Effects of Underground Nuclear Explosions', in Goldblat and Cox (eds.), *Nuclear Weapon Tests: Prohibition or Limitation?*, 1988, p. 83).

Even two years after the 1974 Judgment, a major treaty was entered into which displayed an international expectation that underground nuclear explosions were safe. The Peaceful Nuclear Explosions Treaty, signed on 28 May 1976 between the United States and the Soviet Union, provided for underground nuclear explosions for peaceful purposes, as this seemed to meet the need for 'safe' nuclear energy for major construction works. Goldblat and Cox, in the study already referred to, observe:

> For many years, peaceful nuclear explosions (PNEs) had been seen as potentially valuable activities for a variety of purposes. In the United States, the so-called Plowshare Programme set out to explore possible uses of PNEs for digging canals or for other industrial ends, such as gas stimulation or oil recovery from otherwise uneconomic deposits. However, progress was slow, given the necessity of systematic tests using both

conventional and nuclear explosives, because the need to minimize the risks required careful experimentation. By the mid-1970s, industrial interest in the use of underground nuclear explosions for non-military purposes had waned in the USA, *while public concern over possible environmental hazards had increased.* These hazards include – in addition to the release of radioactive material – shock wave effects which may occur close to the points of detonation. The programme was terminated in 1977, shortly after the signing of the PNET. (Jozef Goldblat and David Cox, 'Summary and Conclusions', *ibid.*, p. 13; emphasis added.)

[329] The expectations of the early 1970s that underground tests provided a safe alternative were obviously belied by later experience. As McEwan observes:

> Venting to the atmosphere has, however, occurred for a number of underground tests, other than those associated with Plowshare-type projects, and more minor sub-surface ventings may occur more commonly. (*Op. cit.*, p. 83.)

Here perhaps lies the key to understanding the readiness of the Court and the Parties in 1974 to welcome underground tests as a means of cessation of radioactive harm to New Zealand, and as eliminating its grievances.

Knowledge and experience not available in 1974 are available now, placing upon the Court the duty, in the interests not only of New Zealand but of the world community generally, to use the power it reserved to itself in 1974 to re-examine the situation if the basis of its Judgment has been affected. If what seemed safe in 1974 now reveals its hazards in a manner not known or expected then, there is a responsibility lying upon the Court to take note of this change in the fundamental assumptions underlying its Judgment of 1974.

If the Court had then the knowledge we have now of the possibility of leakage due to fissures, porosity, water seepage, subsidences and sheering off of parts of the atoll, it would be strange indeed if the Court committed New Zealand to this danger, and considered that, despite so exposing New Zealand, it was fully removing New Zealand's grievance of radioactive damage. That would be a total *non sequitur.* It would also lead to the apparent absurdity of the Court endorsing radioactive contamination so long as it was committed by means other than atmospheric testing.

Another strange result would be that, as New Zealand submitted, the Court would have been building into its Judgment a massive escape clause for France – a clause to the effect that France reserved the right to conduct unsafe testing. It was quite clear in all the circumstances that the assurance of underground testing which France was offering was understood as an assurance of a safe for an unsafe method of testing. Just as the atmospheric testing was known to be unsafe, the underground testing was thought to be safe. When France gave the assurance that it would stop the atmospheric testing and that it was ready to move to underground testing, it was a statement which in all the circumstances of the case was understood to be a shift to a procedure which obviated the dangers of which New Zealand complained.

[330] New Zealand's present grievances
New Zealand now tells the Court that the self-same type of damage it complained of in 1973, namely, radioactive contamination resulting from nuclear explosions by France in the Pacific, does now occur from underground testing. It says that these proposed underground tests will infringe the rights of New Zealand in the same way as the atmospheric tests did in 1973.

According to the material placed before the Court by New Zealand, underground tests produce all the five species of damage specified in paragraph 2 of its Request for the Indication of Interim Measures of Protection, dated 14 May 1973: namely, (i) violation of the right to be free of radioactive fallout;[18] (ii) violation of the right to the preservation from unjustified, artificial radioactive contamination of the terrestrial, maritime and aerial environment; (iii) violation of the right that New Zealand air space and territorial waters be free of the entry of radioactive material; (iv) the apprehension, anxiety and concern resulting from such entry; (v) violation of the right to exploitation of the resources of the sea without interference or detriment resulting from nuclear testing.

The gist of New Zealand's complaint in 1973 was that damage or harm from radioactivity in the five ways it specified was being caused by France. The only way in which it was then being caused was by atmospheric testing of nuclear weapons.

The gist of New Zealand's complaint today is that the same type of damage or harm from radioactivity is being caused by France. It is caused, as alleged before, by the detonation of nuclear weapons in the Pacific, but today the venue is underground, where formerly it was atmospheric. New Zealand's position, however, is that the damage is the same; the infringement of New Zealand's rights is the same; the agency of physical causation is the same, namely, the explosion of nuclear weapons. The only difference is that that agency of causation is detonated not above ground but underground. Hence the Request to the Court for protection against the same damage from which it sought protection in 1973.

Hence, also, appears the wisdom of the Court's precautionary provision in 1974 enabling New Zealand to come before the Court again.

[331] *Interpretation of paragraph 63*
The terms of paragraph 63
How does one ascertain the 'basis of a judgment'? The phrase seems to go to the heart of the judgment, the reasoning on which it proceeds, the foundation on which it rests. To search for the basis of a judgment, does one look only at what the judgment expressly decrees, or does one have regard also to such matters as the context in which the judgment was delivered, the harm or mischief complained of, the request of parties to which that judgment was an answer, and the object of the proceedings? It seems quite clear that a proper and legally sustainable approach to this

---

[18] 'Fallout' is not limited to atmospheric debris. The *Oxford English Dictionary* defines 'fallout' as 'Radioactive refuse of a nuclear bomb explosion' (2nd ed., Vol. V, 1989, p. 696).

question requires a consideration of the Court's order or decree, not in isolation but in context.

It is necessary now to look at the carefully drawn language used by the Court to confer this right on New Zealand.

How would the expression 'basis of the judgment' be understood according to the ordinary significance of language? And what does it mean in the special context of this case?

While the nature of a judgment's commands or prohibitions are important, so also is the basic object which it sought to achieve. It would strain both language and juridical principle to hold that the basis of a judgment can be found in its commands or prohibitions alone, considered apart from its reasons, or in its reasons alone, considered apart from its commands and prohibitions. As in all legal interpretation, it must be an interpretation in context.

Some insights may also be gained from discussions of the meaning of the expression *ratio decidendi*, which one examines in order to ascertain the basis of a judgment. The volumes written on what constitutes the *ratio decidendi* of a judgment (see, for example, Cross and Harris, *Precedent in English Law*, 4th ed., 1991) contain various formulations of its meaning, but all different versions go back to the central question of law or principle from which the eventual orders made in the case proceed. The orders, or in this case the means prohibited, are part of the judgment, but clearly not the *basis* of the judgment.

What is this central question of principle in the 1974 Judgment? It must surely be that New Zealand is entitled to protection against harm caused by radioactivity from the explosion of nuclear weapons. It surely cannot be that New Zealand is entitled to protection against harm caused by radioactivity so long as such radioactivity proceeds from atmospheric detonations, and that New Zealand is not entitled to such protection if the harm proceeds from underground explosions.

To make this point clearer still, suppose France had moved not to underground explosions but to underwater explosions alongside of Mururoa. Could anyone have claimed that this was a permissible activity within the terms of the 1974 Judgment? It would strain language and [**332**] credibility to argue that such was the intention of the Court. The conclusion appears patently clear that the basis of the Judgment was that harm must not be caused by nuclear tests and that New Zealand was entitled not to be exposed to radioactive contamination from French nuclear tests in the Pacific.

Another way of analysing the phrase is to observe that an order or directive statement contained in a judgment constitutes only a part of a judgment. The term 'judgment' goes beyond the merely operative portion of a judgment. The *basis* of a judgment goes deeper still into the area of the underlying principles on which it rests, rather than the external orders used to implement it.

As I read paragraph 63, it seems clear, in the Court's own language, that it was not contemplating a breach by France of its undertaking, or of the Court's Judgment, but that it still had some concerns that the 'substratum' of the Judgment might be affected in some way not then foreseeable. It is a tribute to the wisdom of the Court and to its foresight that it expressly provided for this possibility. The contrary contention, which necessarily implies that the Court was prepared to sanction similar damage so long as it did not occur from atmospheric testing, is clearly untenable and does little credit to the judgment and foresight of the Court of 1974.

The Court's formulation of the bases of the 1974 Judgment

These conclusions, based on ordinary rules of interpretation, are reinforced when one has regard to the Court's own observations in the Judgment itself.

The Court's recognition of this principle of contextual interpretation appears quite clearly from paragraph 59 of the Judgment, wherein the Court states: 'Thus the Court concludes that, the dispute having disappeared, the claim advanced by New Zealand no longer has any object.' These considerations, set out in one of the paragraphs immediately preceding the operative paragraph 63, show the context which the Court considered relevant. In fact, that paragraph posed two very definite and specifically formulated questions:

(a)   has the dispute disappeared?

(b)   has the claim of New Zealand no longer any object?

One is straight away led into the questions, 'What was the dispute?' and 'What was its claim?' The dispute comprised the grievances and the claim comprised the reliefs. The grievances appear, *inter alia*, from New Zealand's Application (para. 28) of 9 May 1973, New Zealand's Memorial (para. 190) of 29 October 1973, and in the Request for the Indication of Interim Measures of Protection (para. 2) of 14 May 1973, which spelt [333] out quite clearly the rights in respect of which it sought protection. The reliefs, read in the context of the grievances, can only mean the cessation of those grievances. The Court was satisfied according to its knowledge then that with France's undertaking the grievances came to an end and no further reliefs were necessary.

To be more specific, the Court's view therefore was that all the five heads of injury mentioned by New Zealand, which formed the subject of its dispute with France, had disappeared. If such injury had disappeared in all its five aspects, New Zealand's claim would surely no longer have any object. Such was the reasoning or the *ratio decidendi* which led the Court to its conclusions. Yet it considered the protection of New Zealand's rights to be so fundamental that it reinforced New Zealand's protections by inserting the precautionary provision that if the basis of the Judgment should be affected, New Zealand may approach the Court again.

The concentration in 1974 upon atmospheric tests

Much has been made in the proceedings before us of the concentration of New Zealand's presentation and the Court's Judgment upon atmospheric tests. From this the inference is sought to be drawn that this was New Zealand's only concern.

In the first place, as already pointed out, there is a liberal reference in the pleadings and the oral presentations to radioactive damage caused by France in explosions in the Pacific without limitation to atmospheric explosions.

In the second place, it must be remembered that atmospheric explosions were the only French explosions then taking place in the Pacific. It was not the province of New Zealand to speculate upon the unknown impact upon New Zealand of hypothetical underground explosions yet to take place in the future.

Court presentations take place upon the basis of practicalities and not upon guesses or speculations as to the likely effect of modalities of harm which are as yet hypothetical. The presentation of the matter in Court naturally concentrated on the practical and immediate aspect, and it would have been strange if it had not. The Court's attention likewise focused on this matter and it would have been strange if it had not.

Furthermore, if such speculation were inappropriate for the Parties, it was even more inappropriate for the Court to engage judicially in speculation upon this unknown field. It was not for New Zealand nor for the Court to engage in speculation as to the possible effects of underground testing which had never yet been used in a manner causing danger or damage to New Zealand, on which no material had been placed before the Court, and which was not the cause of the immediate damage of which New Zealand complained. Indeed, had counsel indulged in such a [**334**] speculative exercise, they may well have been asked to address the Court on practicalities rather than hypotheses.

Nor did New Zealand argue its case *solely* on the basis of atmospheric tests. As the Court itself observes in paragraph 29 of its Judgment, New Zealand's case was argued *mainly* in relation to atmospheric tests – nor could the case have been argued in the light of the information then available, except on the basis of atmospheric tests.

Dr Finlay, the Attorney-General for New Zealand, in opening New Zealand's case at the oral proceedings for the Request for Interim Measures of Protection on 24 May 1973, stated at the very outset of his submissions:

> The request relates to proceedings recently instituted by New Zealand against France asking the Court to adjudge and declare that the conduct by the French Government *in the South Pacific region of tests that give rise to radio-active fall-out* constitutes a violation of New Zealand's rights under international law, and that those rights will be violated by any further such tests. (*ICJ Pleadings, Nuclear Tests*, Vol. II, p. 100; emphasis added.)

The concentration on tests in the atmosphere, for the obvious reason that only such tests were then being conducted, did not mean a shift away from the central core of the case to the peripheries, or from the subject of the grievance to the particular means by which it was caused.

It is also of interest to note that both immediately before and after the hearings in Court in July 1974, the New Zealand Government officially indicated that its position was wider than the cessation of atmospheric testing.

The first statement, as recounted in paragraph 37 of the Judgment of 1974, was a Note of 17 June 1974 from the New Zealand Embassy in Paris categorically asserting that New Zealand's position was one of fundamental opposition to *all* nuclear testing:

> The announcement that France will proceed to underground tests in 1975, while presenting a new development, *does not affect New Zealand's fundamental opposition to*

all nuclear testing, nor does it in any way reduce New Zealand's opposition to the atmospheric tests set down for this year: the more so since the French Government is unable to give firm assurances that no atmospheric testing will be undertaken after 1974. (*ICJ Reports 1974,* p. 470;[19] emphasis added.)

The second statement was made on the day following the Judgment of the Court, on 21 December 1974, when the Prime Minister of New Zealand [335] made the observation that, 'The Court's finding achieves *in large measure* the immediate object for which these proceedings were brought' (emphasis added). The cessation of atmospheric tests was thus not the end-all of New Zealand's request.

The substance of the grievance and the means by which it is caused
In an examination of a matter such as this, there could well be a tendency for undue concentration on the means by which a wrong is committed, to the exclusion of the wrong itself. The means is often ancillary, for it is the wrong or injury sustained by a party that is the core of the complaint.

If harm to the person is threatened with a particular kind of weapon such as a sword, it is no justification to the offender if, upon the prohibition of the use of that weapon, he proceeds to cause the same harm by the use of another weapon, such as a club. A homely illustration could be used to test this proposition. If X should complain to the village elder that Y is threatening him with a sword in a manner causing reasonable apprehension of an intention to cause grievous harm, and the village elder orders Y to drop his sword, is that order to be construed as an order to refrain from causing bodily harm with a sword, or as an order to refrain from causing bodily harm, whatever the weapon used? If Y thereafter proceeds to harm X with a club, Y would surely not be able to contend that the order issued on him related to the use of a sword and that he did not violate it in any way by using a club. Clearly, a larger reason lies behind the order than the mere prohibition against inflicting harm with a sword. The unexpressed rationale lying behind the order, namely, the desire to protect X from bodily harm, lies at the very heart of the order, if it is to be construed in the light of common sense.

Another example of a slightly higher degree of sophistication is as follows. Suppose a person should complain to a court that his neighbour is seeking to burn his property by the act of throwing fire bombs at it. He asks the court for an injunction restraining such conduct. The court orders the respondent to desist from the act of throwing fire bombs and this undertaking is accepted by the complainant. Would there not be an undermining of the basis of this order if the neighbour, having desisted from throwing fire bombs, commences throwing firebrands instead? Would an objective observer, looking for the *basis* of the Court's order, confine it to fire bombs rather than look at the object of the order, the substance of the complaint, and the interest sought to be protected? In such a context, it would indeed be strange if an argument

[19 See p. 112 above.]

were set up that the complaint regarding firebrands must be the subject of a new case rather than a continuation of the existing one.

[336] In general terms, it would not harmonize with ordinary notions of justice that an order to protect the complainant by prohibiting the use of a given means of inflicting harm should be viewed as not comprising the causing of similar harm by the use of another means – least of all when that weapon is used to inflict the identical injury. In all matters of interpretation, the central object of any provision must be constantly borne in mind.

Some principles of interpretation

A fundamental rule of interpretation of any legal document is that it must not be so construed as to lead to results which are unreasonable or absurd. The interpretation that the Court was banning radioactive contamination by atmospheric tests but giving its tacit endorsement to radioactive contamination by underground tests seems to fall into this category. For reasons already discussed, the Court's order clearly did not contemplate that the shift to underground testing, in the state of knowledge at that time, would lead to these deleterious results. The Court could not, even by remotest implication, have reserved the right to France to cause similar kinds of nuclear contamination provided it was done by non-atmospheric testing.

Another way of looking at this matter is that it was a clear implication of the French declaration that the new procedures it was resorting to were to be free of the harm manifestly resulting from the old procedures.

To draw an analogy from another department of law, it is a well-known doctrine, universally recognized in the law, that there can be certain conditions not expressly specified in a document, which nevertheless are so clearly implied by its terms that a reasonable onlooker would say, 'Of course, that is understood.' The entire body of learning on the doctrine of the implied term in contract rests upon this rationale.

In regard to the underground tests which were announced by the French Government as replacing the atmospheric tests, it would surely be the view of an objective onlooker that the clear understanding, in regard to those tests, was that they would not affect such rights of New Zealand as it had sought to conserve by asking the Court for relief. The basis of the Judgment issued by the Court in answer to New Zealand's claim to protection was the implication that such protection ensued in consequence of France's declaration.

New Zealand's complaint related to the radioactive contamination of its terrestrial, maritime and aerial environment. That threat was now apparently at an end, for how else could the Court pronounce that New Zealand's claim had no longer any object?

Applying all the three tests formulated by the Court, the basis of the 1974 Judgment has been affected, the dispute has not disappeared, and [337] New Zealand's claim still has an object if the identical type of harm – namely, radioactive contamination – results from the new situation that has arisen. On all these three counts, all specifically part of the 1974 Judgment, New Zealand has the right to ask the Court to examine the situation in the light of paragraph 63.

Significance of opening sentence of paragraph 63

There is an important aspect of paragraph 63 which is deeply relevant to an understanding of the words 'if the basis of this Judgment were to be affected'. This aspect is reflected in the opening sentence of that paragraph, setting the context for the operative words that follow.

In the opening sentence, the Court makes it clear beyond any doubt that what it was contemplating was not any default by France in complying with its commitment. In the Court's own words, that was an aspect which 'it is not the Court's function to contemplate'.

This is in line with an entrenched body of principle contained both in its governing instruments and its settled practice, that once the Court has delivered judgment, it is *functus officio*. It has discharged the duty for which the parties approached it and resolved the dispute so far as a judgment according to law can resolve it. Enforcement is not and never has been the concern of the Court, either in terms of its Statute or in terms of its settled jurisprudence.

In formulating paragraph 63, the Court was making it clear beyond doubt that what it was contemplating was not a non-observance by France of its obligations. That was assumed. In short, the cessation of atmospheric tests was assumed.

But on the basis of compliance by France, there could still be considerations affecting the basis of the Judgment which parties could not contemplate at that time, but which might nevertheless entitle a party in all justice to ask the Court for an examination of the situation. The Court was providing for just such an eventuality as this – that while France complied with its undertaking, the basis of the Judgment could still in some way be affected.

Significance of the last sentence of paragraph 63

The Court provided in the same paragraph that the denunciation by France, by letter dated 2 January 1974, of the General Act for the Pacific Settlement of International Disputes, which was relied on as a basis of jurisdiction in the present case, cannot constitute by itself an obstacle to the presentation of a subsequent request by New Zealand. This sentence is a further indication by the Court that New Zealand was to have its [338] rights preserved on the basis of the existing Judgment, and that the existing case was not dead. The sentence is a clear anticipation of a possible return by New Zealand to the Court upon the basis of a Judgment which was still alive for this purpose.

It also demonstrates the considered and deliberate projection of the Court's mind into the problems of the future, without being content to close the book, so to speak, in 1974. Future jurisdiction had disappeared and New Zealand's right to implead France afresh had been destroyed, but this did not deter the Court from expressly empowering New Zealand to return to the Court on the basis of the original case if New Zealand was able to show the Court that the basis of the Judgment was affected.

The special need for a precautionary clause
In dealing with radioactive contamination, the Court was dealing for the first time with a force whose potential for causing damage to the human condition was as yet imperfectly understood. It was known to be capable of causing multiple deleterious effects to human health and environment. It was a force whose magnitude of destructive power had been awesomely demonstrated. The Court needed to be ultra-cautious.

The clause enabling New Zealand to approach the Court was a procedural innovation, reinforcing in a very special way the integrity of the Judgment which the Court was rendering. It was a provision ensuring that the Judgment would not be undermined by future acts or events which could not then be specified. It exhibited a concern for the realities rather than the forms of justice.

Against this background, it is significant that even in the case of *Nuclear Tests (Australia* v. *France)*, where the pleadings were more closely geared to atmospheric tests than in the case of *Nuclear Tests (New Zealand* v. *France)*, the Court still considered it necessary to give Australia the right to come back to the Court if circumstances should occur which affected the basis of the Judgment (*Nuclear Tests (Australia* v. *France)*, Judgment, *ICJ Reports 1974*, p. 272, para. 60). Even in the context of atmospheric tests, there could possibly be some unknown lingering after-effects which might affect the basis of the Judgment and need correction.

A fortiori, in the case of New Zealand, where there was a shortfall between the Judgment of the Court and the prayer of New Zealand, there was a greater need for the interests of New Zealand to be protected.

The Court's deep concern with the effects of French testing was indeed demonstrated not merely at this stage of the case, but from the stage of preliminary measures in 1973, when the Court manifested that concern by ordering interim measures of protection before any determination of jurisdiction and admissibility.

[339] *Interim measures*
The grant of interim measures
New Zealand has also requested interim measures now, as it did in 1973. In view of the Court's Order, this case does not proceed to the stage where such measures can be ordered. It is my view, however, that New Zealand has made out a prima facie case that it is suffering, or likely to suffer, damage of the nature which it complained of in 1973, and has thereby brought itself within the terms of paragraph 63. As a consequence, New Zealand would have reached the stage where it was entitled to a consideration by the Court of its request for interim measures.

New Zealand's Request on this occasion does not go so far as a request for an absolute declaration that nuclear tests violate the various enumerated rights of New Zealand, inasmuch as New Zealand is content, in the alternative, with a declaration that it is unlawful for France to conduct such tests *before* it has undertaken an Environmental Impact Assessment (EIA) according to accepted international standards. Such a procedure is within the power of France and if, as France has declared, the tests are environmentally safe, an EIA confirming this position would negate New Zealand's claim, and result in its dismissal.

The approach of the Court to preliminary measures in 1973
It is pertinent to this discussion to refer also to the approach of the Court in 1973 to the question of preliminary measures – an approach which reflected deep concern that damage of the sort complained of by New Zealand could cause irreparable prejudice to the rights which were the subject of dispute. The Court's approach displayed a willingness to act even before jurisdiction and admissibility were proved.

The Court of course made it clear that its decision in no way prejudiced the question of the jurisdiction of the Court to deal with the merits of the case (*ICJ Reports 1973*, p. 142, para. 34).[20]

It seems to me that the approach of the Court in the present case, when radioactive contamination by nuclear explosions is again complained of, might well have been on similar lines.

Some relevant legal principles
The inter-temporal principle
It is a truism that scientific knowledge increases exponentially. The knowledge of 1995 is not the knowledge of 1974. Nor was the knowledge [**340**] of 1974 the knowledge of the 1950s. There is perhaps as much of a differential between the knowledge relating to such matters between the 1970s and the 1950s as there is between the knowledge of the 1990s and the 1970s. The nature and effects of nuclear activity and radioactive contamination are matters of popular knowledge, having regard to such episodes as Chernobyl, which have demonstrated even to the layman how much more widespread the damaging effects of radioactive contamination are than was once believed. Elsewhere in this opinion reference has been made to the better understanding of the effects of underground nuclear explosions since 1974, when they were considered safe.

The Court is seised of the present Request at this point of time and must bring to bear upon it the scientific knowledge now available. A court, faced with a science-oriented problem of present and future damage in 1995, cannot resolve it by ignoring the knowledge acquired between 1974 and 1995, and by applying to the problem in hand the knowledge of 1974. That would be an exercise in unreality.

A similar question arose when New Zealand was asked at the time of the 1974 case why it did not protest against the larger and more dangerous nuclear explosions of the 1950s, just as today it is asked why it did not object to France's underground testing in the 1970s. The answer of Dr Finlay, the New Zealand Attorney-General, offers an interesting perspective on the inter-temporal principle. He observed:

> The plain answer is that an inter-temporal rule applies to fact as well as to law. In the world of the 1950s shoe shops in my country and in many others had X-ray machines

[20 See p. 103 above.]

through which the customer could see the bones of his feet in the shoes he was trying on. In the world of the 1970s we are appalled by, and forbid, these unnecessary exposures to the damaging effects of radiation. (*ICJ Pleadings, Nuclear Tests*, Vol. II, p. 255.)

So it is with the knowledge of the effects of underground explosions in the 1970s, as compared with the knowledge of the 1990s. That which was assumed then has been contradicted by later knowledge. The basic suppositions of fact on which public conduct was ordered have been undermined. If the basic assumption of the protection of a party's rights in 1974 is undermined by knowledge available in 1995, and if the terms of the protecting judgment make its reconsideration available to a party complaining that its basis has been undermined, this Court, when approached on the footing that the basis of the Judgment has been undermined, must apply to that question the knowledge it has today and not the knowledge of 1974. The question whether the basis of the Judgment has been affected is a question of practical reality and not of legal [**341**] abstractions viewed apart from their practical impact upon human life and the environment in the applicant State.

The concept of intergenerational rights
The case before the Court raises, as no case ever before the Court has done, the principle of intergenerational equity – an important and rapidly developing principle of contemporary environmental law.

Professor Lauterpacht, on behalf of New Zealand, adverted to this aspect when he submitted to the Court that if damage of the kind alleged had been inflicted on the environment by the people of the Stone Age, it would be with us today. Having regard to the information before us that the half-life of a radioactive by-product of nuclear tests can extend to over 20,000 years, this is an important aspect that an international tribunal cannot fail to notice. In a matter of which it is duly seised, this Court must regard itself as a trustee of those rights in the sense that a domestic court is a trustee of the interests of an infant unable to speak for itself. If this Court is charged with administering international law, and if this principle is building itself into the corpus of international law, or has already done so, this principle is one which must inevitably be a concern of this Court. The consideration involved is too serious to be dismissed as lacking in importance merely because there is no precedent on which it rests.

New Zealand's complaint that its rights are affected does not relate only to the rights of people presently in existence. The rights of the people of New Zealand include the rights of unborn posterity. Those are rights which a nation is entitled, and indeed obliged, to protect. In considering whether New Zealand has made out a prima facie case of damage to its interests sufficient to bring the processes of this Court into operation in terms of paragraph 63, this is therefore an important aspect not to be ignored.

In the words of an important recent work on this question:

> The starting proposition is that each generation is both a custodian and a user of our common natural and cultural patrimony. As custodians of this planet, we have certain

moral obligations to future generations which we can transform into legally enforceable norms. (See E. Brown Weiss, *In Fairness to Future Generations: International Law. Common Patrimony and Intergenerational Equity*, 1989, p. 21.)

The Stockholm Declaration on the Human Environment adopted by the United Nations Conference on the Environment at Stockholm, [342] 16 June 1972, formulated nearly a quarter century ago the principle of 'a solemn responsibility to protect and improve the environment for present and future generations' (Principle 1). This guideline sufficiently spells out the approach to this new principle which is relevant to the problem the Court faces of assessing the likely damage to the people of New Zealand. This Court has not thus far had occasion to make any pronouncement on this developing field. The present case presents it with a pre-eminent opportunity to do so, as it raises in pointed form the possibility of damage to generations yet unborn.

The precautionary principle
Where a party complains to the Court of possible environmental damage of an irreversible nature which another party is committing or threatening to commit, the proof or disproof of the matter alleged may present difficulty to the claimant as the necessary information may largely be in the hands of the party causing or threatening the damage.

The law cannot function in protection of the environment unless a legal principle is evolved to meet this evidentiary difficulty, and environmental law has responded with what has come to be described as the precautionary principle – a principle which is gaining increasing support as part of the international law of the environment (see Philippe Sands, *Principles of International Environmental Law*, Vol. I, pp. 208–10).

In 1990, the Ministers from 34 countries in the Economic Commission for Europe and the Commissioner for the Environment of the European Community, meeting at Bergen, Norway, issued the Bergen ECE Ministerial Declaration on Sustainable Development. Article 7 of this Declaration formulated the precautionary principle in these terms:

> In order to achieve sustainable development, policies must be based on the precautionary principle. Environmental measures must anticipate, prevent and attack the causes of environmental degradation. Where there are threats of serious or irreversible damage, lack of full scientific certainty should not be used as a reason for postponing measures to prevent environmental degradation. (Bergen ECE Ministerial Declaration on Sustainable Development, 15 May 1990, in Harald Hohmann (ed.), *Basic Documents of International Environmental Law*, Vol. 1, 1992, pp. 558–9.)

In paragraph 16 (*f*), the Declaration stressed the importance of optimizing democratic decision-making related to environment and development [343] issues, and it identified the following need as part of what it called the Bergen process:

> To undertake the prior assessment and public reporting of the environmental impact of projects which are likely to have a significant effect on human health and the environment and, so far as practicable, of the policies, programmes and plans which

underlie such projects and to ensure that East European and developing countries are assisted through bilateral and multilateral channels in evaluating the environmental impact and sustainability of their own development projects. To develop or expand procedures to assess the risks and potential environmental impacts of products. (*Op. cit.*, p. 565.)

The precautionary principle of course went further back in time than 1990. It is a principle of relevance to New Zealand in its application to this Court and one which inevitably calls for consideration in the context of this case.

New Zealand has placed materials before the Court to the best of its ability, but France is in possession of the actual information. The principle then springs into operation to give the Court the basic rationale for considering New Zealand's request and not postponing the application of such means as are available to the Court to prevent, on a provisional basis, the threatened environmental degradation, until such time as the full scientific evidence becomes available in refutation of the New Zealand contention.

Several environmental treaties have already accepted the precautionary principle (see Sands, *op. cit.*, pp. 210 *et seq.*). Among these are the 1992 Baltic Sea Convention and the 1992 Maastricht Treaty (Treaty on European Union, Title XVI, Art. 130r (2)), which states that Community policy on the environment '*shall* be based on the precautionary principle' (emphasis added). It is noteworthy that under the 1992 Convention for the Protection of the Marine Environment of the North-East Atlantic (OSPAR Convention), the parties (France and the United Kingdom), wishing to retain the option of dumping low and intermediate level radioactive wastes at sea, would be required to report to the OSPAR Commission on:

> the results of scientific studies which show that any potential dumping operations would not result in hazards to human health, harm to living resources or marine ecosystems, damage to amenities or interference with other legitimate uses of the sea (Ann. II, Art. 3 (3) *(c)*, cited from Sands, *op. cit.*, p. 212).

This last application of the precautionary principle, to which France is a party, has particular relevance to the matter presently before the Court.

[344] The provision in the Maastricht Treaty, incorporating the precautionary principle as the basis of European Community policy on the environment (Art. 130r (2)), would lead one to expect that the principle thus applicable to Europe would apply also to European activity in other global theatres.

Reference should be made finally to Principle 15 of the Rio Declaration on Environment and Development, 1992, which reads:

> In order to protect the environment, the precautionary approach shall be widely applied by States according to their capabilities. Where there are threats of serious or irreversible damage, lack of full scientific certainty shall not be used as a reason for postponing cost-effective measures to prevent environmental degradation. (*Report of the United Nations Conference on Environment and Development*, Rio de Janeiro, 3–14 June 1992, Vol. l, Ann. I, p. 6.)

Environmental Impact Assessment (EIA)

This principle is ancillary to the broader principle just discussed. As with the previous principle, this principle is gathering strength and international acceptance, and has reached the level of general recognition at which this Court should take notice of it.

The United Nations Environment Programme (UNEP) Guidelines of 1987 on 'Goals and Principles of Environmental Impact Assessment' states in Principle 1 that:

> States (including their competent authorities) should not undertake or authorize activities without prior consideration, at an early stage, of their environmental effects. Where the extent, nature or location of a proposed activity is such that it is likely to significantly affect the environment, a comprehensive environmental impact assessment should be undertaken in accordance with the following principles. (Hohmann, *op. cit.*, p. 187.)

A proper Environmental Impact Assessment should, according to Principle 4, include:

(a)   A description of the proposed activity;

(b)   A description of the potentially affected environment, including specific information necessary for identifying and assessing the environmental effects of the proposed activity;

(c)   A description of practical alternatives, as appropriate;

(d)   An assessment of the likely or potential environmental impacts of the proposed activity and alternatives, including the direct, indirect, cumulative, short-term and long-term effects;

(e)   [345] An identification and description of measures available to mitigate adverse environmental impacts of the proposed activity and alternatives, and an assessment of those measures;

(f)   An indication of gaps in knowledge and uncertainties which may be encountered in compiling the required information;

(g)   An indication of whether the environment of any other State or areas beyond national jurisdiction is likely to be affected by the proposed activity or alternatives;

(h)   A brief, non-technical summary of the information provided under the above headings. (Hohmann, *op. cit.*, p. 188.)

It is clear that on an issue of the magnitude of that which brings New Zealand before this Court the principle of Environmental Impact Assessment would prima facie be applicable in terms of the current state of international environmental law.

This Court, situated as it is at the apex of international tribunals, necessarily enjoys a position of special trust and responsibility in relation to the principles of environmental law, especially those relating to what is described in environmental law as the Global Commons. When a matter is brought before it which raises serious environmental issues of global importance, and a prima facie case is made out of the possibility of environmental damage, the Court is entitled to take into account the Environmental Impact Assessment principle in determining its preliminary approach.

Of course the situation may well be proved to be otherwise and fears currently expressed may prove to be groundless. But that stage is reached only after the Environmental Impact Assessment and not before.

The illegality of introducing radioactive waste into the marine environment
This principle is too well established to need discussion. The marine environment belongs to all, and any introduction of radioactive waste into one's territorial waters must necessarily raise the danger of its spread into the wider ocean spaces that belong to all.

If such danger can be shown prima facie to exist or be within the bounds of reasonable possibility, the burden shifts on those who claim such action is safe to establish that this is indeed so. As observed already, the 1992 OSPAR Convention between France and the United Kingdom requires a report that any proposed dumping of low and intermediate level radioactive wastes would not result in hazards to human health and marine resources. Such is the standard observed internationally. Until [**346**] such time, a judicial tribunal is entitled to act upon the prima facie case that New Zealand has made out.

The Report of the Rio Conference of 1992 deals in Chapter 22 of Agenda 21 with 'Safe and Environmentally Sound Management of Radioactive Wastes'. Paragraph 22.5 *(c)* deals specifically with this problem in terms that States should:

> Not promote or allow the storage or disposal of high-level, intermediate-level and low-level radioactive wastes near the marine environment unless they determine that scientific evidence, consistent with the applicable internationally agreed principles and guidelines, shows that such storage or disposal poses no unacceptable risk to people and the marine environment or does not interfere with other legitimate uses of the sea, making, in the process of consideration, appropriate use of the concept of the precautionary approach. (*Report of the United Nations Conference on Environment and Development* (A/CONF.151/26/Rev.1), Vol. I, Ann. II, pp. 371–2.)

France supported Agenda 21. Indeed, President Mitterrand gave it such strong support as to suggest that the Secretary-General of the United Nations should be entrusted with the task of taking stock of the implementation of Agenda 21 every year (*ibid.*, Vol. III, p. 195).

The President also observed:

> Secondly, it would be useful to determine more clearly the role, or the responsibility, of the countries of the North. I think that they have to preserve and restore their own domain (water, air, towns, countryside), a task which their Governments are tackling unevenly. *That they have to refrain from any action harmful to the environment of the countries of the South.* Such is the purpose of France's very strict laws on the export of wastes. (*Ibid.*, p. 194; emphasis added.)

It scarcely needs citation of authority to establish so self-evident a principle.

The principle that damage must not be caused to other nations
The conclusions just reached are reinforced by a fundamental principle of modern environmental law which must here be noted. It is well entrenched in international law and goes as far back as the *Trail Smelter* case (*Reports of International Arbitral Awards*, 1938, Vol. III, p. 1905) and perhaps beyond (see also *Corfu Channel, Merits, Judgment, ICJ Reports 1949*, p. 4).

[347] This basic principle, that no nation is entitled by its own activities to cause damage to the environment of any other nation, appears as Principle 2 of the Rio Declaration on the Environment, 1992:

> States have, in accordance with the Charter of the United Nations and the principles of international law, the sovereign right to exploit their own resources pursuant to their own environmental and developmental policies, and the responsibility to ensure that activities within their jurisdiction or control do not cause damage to the environment of other States or of areas beyond the limits of national jurisdiction. (*Report of the United Nations Conference on Environment and Development* (A/CONF.151/26/Rev.1), Vol. I, Ann. I, p. 3.)

Other international instruments that embody this principle are the Stockholm Declaration on the Human Environment (1972, Principle 21) and the 1986 Noumea Convention, Article 4 (6) of which states:

> Nothing in this Convention shall affect the sovereign right of States to exploit, develop and manage their own natural resources pursuant to their own policies, taking into account their duty to protect and preserve the environment. Each Party shall ensure that activities within its jurisdiction or control do not cause damage to the environment of other States or of areas beyond the limits of its national jurisdiction. (Hohmann, *Basic Documents of International Environmental Law*, 1992, Vol. 2, p. 1063.)

It is in the context of such a deeply entrenched principle, grounded in common sense, case law, international conventions, and customary international law that the Court must reach a determination as to whether a prima facie case of danger to its rights has been made out by New Zealand.

Has New Zealand made out a prima facie case?
The approach to the question of proof
As stressed in this opinion, it is essential, in order to activate the procedures of the Court, that New Zealand should make out at least a prima facie case that the dangers which brought it to Court in 1973 are now present again in consequence of the underground nuclear tests that France has commenced in the Pacific. There must therefore be an examination of the facts in order to decide whether the jurisdictional basis exists for New Zealand's present Request.

The ensuing examination is therefore undertaken as an integral part of the preliminary jurisdictional question and is not a part of any examination of the merits.

[348] There are two ways of approaching this question. The first is to place the burden of proof fairly and squarely upon New Zealand, and to ask whether a prima facie

case has been made out of the presence of such dangers as New Zealand complains of.

The second approach is to apply the principle of environmental law under which, where environmental damage of any sort is threatened, the burden of proving that it will not produce the damaging consequences complained of is placed upon the author of that damage. In this view of the matter, the Court would hold that the environmental damage New Zealand complains of is prima facie established in the absence of proof by France that the proposed nuclear tests are environmentally safe.

It will be noted in this connection that all the information bearing upon this matter is in the possession of the Respondent. The Applicant has only indirect or secondary information, but has endeavoured to place before the Court such information as it has been able, to the best of its ability, to marshal for the purposes of this application.

The second approach is sufficiently well established in international law for the Court to act upon it. Yet, it is sufficient for present purposes to act upon the first approach, throwing the burden of proof upon New Zealand.

What is the nature of the prima facie case that New Zealand has made out?

The scientific fact-finding missions

New Zealand has placed before the Court such scientific material as is available to it, and has referred, in particular, to three scientific reports in support of its submissions regarding the unreliability of Mururoa and Fangataufa atolls as repositories of nuclear wastes. It states that the French Government has not permitted a full scientific investigation of Mururoa atoll, but that three limited investigations are all that have been allowed on Mururoa, and none at all at Fangataufa where the larger explosions have occurred.

These are the investigations of Mr M. H. Tazieff, a noted French vulcanologist, in 1982; that of a team of scientists led by Mr Hugh Atkinson, a former Director of New Zealand's National Radiation Laboratory, in 1983; and that of a scientific and film team, led by Commander Cousteau, in 1987.

Mr Tazieff commented that a systematic study over a number of years was required of the most mobile radionuclides in ground water and in the sea, for an assessment of the effectiveness of the containment of radioactivity (Tazieff Report, p. 7, cited in New Zealand's Request, para. 38); while Commander Cousteau concluded that leakage could occur on a time scale of 100–300 years, a significantly shorter period than previous estimates (*ibid.*, para. 40, in reliance upon the Cousteau Mission Report). The conclusions of the Atkinson Report are dealt with later.

[349] France replies to New Zealand's contentions by asserting that the New Zealand descriptions envisaged 'disasters of Hollywoodian proportions', while the tests are, in fact, environmentally safe (CR 95/20, p. 62). Professor de Brichambaut, for France, stated, *inter alia*, that traces of radioactivity on Mururoa are infinitesimal; that the level of radioactivity is the same as on all the atolls in the South Pacific; that it is considerably lower than the levels found in Paris, Darwin, Chile or Colombia. He submitted that the level of radioactive elements (measured in micrograys per year) is

262 in Mururoa, 463 in Tahiti, 815 in Australia and 900 in New Zealand. He added that in Holland it is 280, just above the level in Mururoa. He also gave the Court various statistics in relation to doses of radioactivity measured in the Polynesian population (*ibid.*, p. 55).

However, the main question on which the Court would need to reach a prima facie conclusion is the question of the safety of Mururoa as a repository of radioactive waste, both over the long term, in consequence of natural impairment of the atoll, and in the short term in consequence of nuclear explosions.

These matters are dealt with in the ensuing paragraphs.

The danger of radioactive contamination resulting from France's underground tests could perhaps be considered under the following heads:

 (a)   the nature of the nuclear tests proposed;
 (b)   the structure of Mururoa and Fangataufa atolls;
 (c)   the impact upon the atolls of the previous explosions;
 (d)   the impact upon Mururoa of the proposed new series of explosions;
 (e)   the internationally accepted safety standards for the storage of radioactive wastes;
 (f)   the danger to marine life of the release of radioactive substances into the ocean; and
 (g)   the possibility of accident.

If, upon a review of these matters, it can reasonably be stated that a prima facie case has been made out of possible danger from radioactive contamination resulting from France's nuclear tests in the Pacific, New Zealand would be entitled to submit that it has discharged the burden lying upon it of showing that it comes within the terms of paragraph 63.

The possible dangers will now be outlined under the heads enumerated, bearing in mind that, in a case of this magnitude, even a prima facie finding of possible dangers is not to be lightly reached. The relevant material must be therefore examined with the greatest care. The ensuing discussion aims at ascertaining whether, upon an objective analysis, New Zealand has made out a prima facie case that the dangers it complained of in 1973 now exist in 1995, thereby activating paragraph 63 of the 1974 Judgment.

[350] *The nature of underground nuclear tests*

The information placed before the Court is to the effect that holes of a depth of around 1,000 metres are drilled into the ground surface of the atoll. New Zealand states that the details of location of the test shafts have not been released by France. The structure of the atoll consists of a coral crown over a volcanic base. Many tests have also been conducted in the lagoon area adjacent to the coral rim.

A cylinder containing the explosive device and a large amount of instrumentation is then dropped into the hole. The shaft is packed tight with material, including a special kind of concrete, to stop the escape through the shaft into the atmosphere of radioactive material from the explosion.

Upon detonation, everything at the bottom of the shaft is vaporized and a ball-shaped chamber forms in the structure of the surrounding rock. For the small 10-kiloton blasts, the chamber would be approximately 50 metres in diameter and for explosions of around 100 kilotons the chamber might be around 120 metres in diameter.

The immense heat of the explosion vitrifies the rock around it and much of the radioactive material released by the explosion is contained within this vitrified rock and within the explosion chamber.

New Zealand submits that another effect of the explosion is an earthquake shock which may measure between 4 and 6 on the Richter scale. This may fracture some of the upper limestone layers of the atoll and may generate landslides towards the outer flanks of the atoll.

I refer again to McEwan's technical study on 'Environmental effects of underground nuclear explosions':

> The greatest environmental impacts of underground tests result from seismic and local shock wave effects. The latter include ground movements, subsidence, collapse crater formation, cliff falls and submarine slides which may occur within a few kilometres of the detonation points. (*Op. cit.*, p. 89.)

The important question also arises of the possibility of venting, i.e., the escape of vapours, liquid and other by-products of the explosion from the confined space in which the explosions occur. The *Report of a New Zealand, Australian and Papua New Guinea Scientific Mission to Mururoa Atoll*, which was headed by Mr H. R. Atkinson, Retired Director of the National Radiation Laboratory, Christchurch (one of the three reports deposited along with the New Zealand Request), observes:

> [351] Venting of gaseous and volatile fission products from the underground test sites does occur at the time of detonation. The radio-nuclides vented include ones other than the noble gases (which are admitted by the French) and there is evidence that their magnitude is greater than would be expected simply through the back-packing of the placement bore being 'less than perfect'. (*Report of a New Zealand, Australian and Papua New Guinea Scientific Mission to Mururoa Atoll*, p. 132.)

The structure of Mururoa and Fangataufa atolls

The structure of the atoll is said to consist of a coral crown upon a volcanic base. Water percolates through the entire rock structure. Whether through prior explosions or otherwise, there is a network of fissures in the structure of the atoll.

The Atkinson Report contained the following descriptions of the atoll structure of Mururoa:

> Mururoa in common with other atolls is made up of two sequences; the upper limestones of 180–500 m thickness, overlying volcanics of several thousand metres thickness. (*Ibid.*, p. 7.)

The limestones, comprised of superimposed successions of reefs, are for the most part porous and permeable with many horizons of particularly high porosity and permeability. The flanks of the atoll however are protected by aprons of low permeability. (*Ibid.*, pp. 7–8.)

The French claim that any leakage from the volcanics to the limestones will be stopped by the impermeable transition zone is not borne out by the data inspected.

The transition zone which occurs between the volcanics and limestones is highly variable in thickness and rock type and this casts doubt on its ability to act as an impermeable barrier to potential radioactive leakage. The potential exists for leakage of water from detonation cavities to the biosphere in less than 1000 years. (*Ibid.*, p. 8.)

The claim that the transition zone acts as a barrier to long-term leakage can, on the basis of geological evidence, be discounted. The volcanics in their virgin state offer a poor to moderate geo-chemical barrier and a moderate to good hydrological barrier. The testing programme is reducing the effectiveness of both. (*Ibid.*, p. 9.)

The McEwan study, already referred to, observes that:

> Leakage of radioactive material from an underground testing site may occur if there is ground water present at the emplacement depth [352] at the time of explosion, or if fracturing of rock subsequently allows ground water access to the cavity. (*Op. cit.*, p. 85.)

Having regard to the saturation of the rock structure with water, this seems to be, prima facie, a factor to be taken into account.

The impact upon the atolls of previous explosions

The Atkinson Report concludes:

> The integrity of the carbonate part of the atoll has been impaired.
> – Fissures have formed in the limestones as a result of testing.
> – Surface subsidence to the order of 1 m has affected over 1 km² of the north-eastern region and 1.5 km² of the south-west margin. Such subsidence is the direct result of cumulative compaction in the limestones, and propagated by testing.
> – Submarine slides, particularly along the southern margin, have resulted from a number of tests at Mururoa. The effect of these slides is to strip the outer rim of the atoll of its protective impermeable limestone.
> Fissuring and removal of the apron limestone through sliding will both serve to increase lateral and vertical water transport in the carbonate body of the atoll. (*Op. cit.*, pp. 105–6.)

All three of these heads seem to be of great importance to the issue before the Court. Fissures can conceivably widen and afford an outlet to the sea. The subsidence to an extent of one metre of a square kilometre of the atoll's surface reflects a structural movement serious enough to cause concern. The stripping of the outer rim of the atoll must also be thought, in the absence of contrary evidence, to weaken the protective structure of the atoll.

The impact upon Mururoa of the proposed new series of explosions

It is of course impossible to state, on the available scientific material, how many more explosions the structure of the atoll can withstand without some major structural damage such as may release the pent-up radioactive debris of over 100 explosions contained within the atoll's structure. It may be that the structure could withstand one thousand more explosions, or it may be that the structure is nearing the end of its endurance of continuing explosions.

There is, according to New Zealand, an ever-present danger that the already fissured structure of the atoll cannot be guaranteed to remain intact and that even one more explosion could well be the force that can [353] trigger off a major structural collapse. The structure has already been buffeted by explosions equivalent to some 150 times the power of the Hiroshima bomb. There are over 126 shafts drilled into a segment of an atoll which is less than 28 km long. We do not have the benefit of an impact assessment survey of the ability of the atoll's structure to withstand these shocks.

In the words of New Zealand's counsel, Professor Lauterpacht, New Zealand could ask whether the world can be confident that the present series of tests may not place upon the camel of Mururoa the straw that breaks its back.

The internationally accepted safety standards for the storage of radioactive wastes

At the conclusion of the hearings, I addressed a question to both Parties as to whether there are internationally accepted criteria for the selection of geological repositories for radioactive wastes, requesting a brief list of such criteria, if there were any.

The French reply was:

> Il n'existe actuellement aucune norme officielle internationale concernant les critères géologiques de stockage des déchets radioactifs. Les études scientifiques menées quant à la nature des roches les plus appropriées aboutissent à un consensus sur la nécessité d'avoir un environnement géologique stable, une faible perméabilité des roches et un contexte propice à une rétention des radioéléments par les roches.[21]

New Zealand, however, referred to the International Atomic Energy Agency's Safety Standard, 'Safety Principles and Technical Criteria for the Underground Disposal of High Level Radioactive Wastes' (Safety Series No. 99, 1989),[22] a document

---

[21] Letter from France dated 15 September 1995, replies to the questions put by Judge Weeramantry, No. 2:

> There is currently no official international norm relating to the geological criteria for the storage of radioactive waste. The scientific investigations of the nature of the most appropriate rocks lead to a consensus on the need to have a geologically stable environment, rocks of a low permeability and a context favourable to a retention of radioelements by the rocks. *[Translation by the Registry.]*

[22] Letter from New Zealand dated 15 September 1995, replies to the questions put by Judge Weeramantry, No. 2.

which New Zealand states has been superseded by more detailed studies. The criteria set out in this document include the following:

> *Criterion No. 7: Site geology*
> The repository shall be located at sufficient depth to protect adequately the emplaced waste from external events and processes in [354] a host rock having properties that adequately restrict the deterioration of physical barriers and the transport of radionuclides from the repository to the environment.
>
> *Criterion No. 8: Consideration of natural resources*
> The repository site shall be selected, to the extent practicable, to avoid proximity to valuable natural resources or materials which are not readily available from other sources.

These criteria, when applied to Mururoa, raise prima facie concerns as to its safety for purposes of storage of radioactive waste.

The International Atomic Energy Agency Safety Guide, 'Safety of Geological Disposal Facilities' (Safety Series No. 111-G-4.1, 1994) also gives some useful indications of factors having a bearing on this question. Guidelines 412 and 413 are particularly significant:

> 412. The hydrogeological characteristics and setting of the geological environment should tend to restrict groundwater flow within the repository and should support safe waste isolation for the required times.
>
> 413. An evaluation of the mechanisms of groundwater movement, as well as an analysis of the direction and rate of flow will be an important input to the safety assessment of any site because the most likely mode of radionuclide release is by groundwater flow. Irrespective of the nature of the waste or the disposal option, a geological environment capable of restricting flow to, through and from the repository will contribute to preventing unacceptable radionuclide releases. Natural features such as aquifers or fracture zones are potential release pathways for radionuclides. Such paths should be limited in the repository host rock so that the protective functions of the geological and engineered barrier system remain compatible. The dilution capacity of the hydrogeological system may also be important and should be evaluated. Siting should be optimised in such a way as to favour long and slow moving groundwater pathways from the repository to the environment.

These are of course matters on which the Court in due course would have received fuller information had the matter proceeded to a hearing on the substantive question of New Zealand's request.

Alongside of these criteria and guidelines, it would be useful to look at some of the conclusions of the Atkinson Report. Conclusion 3 of the Atkinson Report states, in regard to underground testing at Mururoa, that:

> [355] The radioactive residues of underground testing can with some justification be equated to high-level radioactive waste. It is not expected that Mururoa would meet the generally accepted criteria on site selection for a geologic repository for high-level radioactive wastes. (Atkinson Report, p. 133.)

An index to altered world perceptions of the environmentally deleterious effects of radioactive waste, whether resulting from peaceful or military purposes, is the concern shown at the Rio Conference on Environment and Development in 1992. Chapter 22 of the Report of the Conference is devoted to 'Safe and Environmentally Sound Management of Radioactive Wastes'. Though the wastes there referred to are those generated from peaceful activities, the concerns expressed are relevant in the present context.

Paragraph 22.1 of the Report observed that:

> the activity concentration, especially in sealed radiation sources, might be high, thus justifying very stringent radiological protection measures (*Report of the United Nations Conference on Environment and Development*, Rio de Janeiro, 3–14 June 1992 (A/CONF.151/26/Rev. 1), Vol. I, Agenda 21, Ann. II, p. 370),

and paragraph 22.8 observed that:

> States, in cooperation with international organizations, where appropriate, should:
> (a) Promote research and development of methods for the safe and environmentally sound treatment, processing and disposal, including deep geological disposal, of high-level radioactive waste;
> (b) Conduct research and assessment programmes concerned with evaluating the health and environmental impact of radioactive waste disposal. (*Ibid.*, p. 372.)

It seems clear therefore that whatever the source of radioactive materials, the care with which they are stored underground is a matter of international concern. The porous nature of Mururoa is one which gives rise to special concern in the absence of an EIA relating to not merely the retentive properties of the soil of Mururoa, but also in regard to its ability to withstand repeated atomic blasts.

The danger to marine life of the release of radioactive substances into the ocean

In the light of these circumstances, it can scarcely be said that New Zealand has not made out at least a prima facie case that there is a danger of a rupture of the atoll's structure, with the possibility of release [356] into the ocean of a vast quantity of pent-up radioactive materials. Such a case can of course be rebutted by appropriate scientific evidence, but till such time affords a sufficient basis for New Zealand to maintain its claim that radioactive contamination from nuclear explosions affects its rights now, as it did in 1973.

A world that has known the effects upon the food chain several hundreds of miles away from Chernobyl may well wonder what the effects may be upon the marine food chain of such a release of radioactivity. Such questions may be raised even more pointedly in the absence of an EIA by France prior to the present series of tests.

Should a radioactive leak affect the food chain in the Pacific, the rights affected would be not only those of New Zealanders, but of all the Pacific peoples, many of whom are dependent on fishing for their livelihood. The danger of radioactive contamination affecting plankton and moving up the food chain to all forms of marine life is a factor to be reckoned with, even if it were in small quantities. Migratory species such as tuna could carry this contamination of the food chain much further afield. Should there be a release of pent-up radioactive waste of over a hundred explosions through a major crack or fissuring of the structure of the atoll, the consequences could well be catastrophic.

The half-life of radioactive by-products varies from 14,000 to 24,000 years. Plutonium 239 has a half-life of 24,000 years, and plutonium 240 a half-life of 6,570 years, according to the responses of both Parties to a question I asked at the oral hearings.

The question may well arise whether the French Government can indeed offer any sort of assurance that the by-products released from over 100 nuclear explosions would be safely contained within the fragile structure of Mururoa for several multiples of tens of thousands of years. The possibility of such contamination must therefore be viewed with concern. The atoll has already sustained fissure cracks in consequence of prior explosions totalling the fire power of over 150 Hiroshima-type explosions.[23] A Pacific islander could indeed have serious fears as to whether this brittle and porous island structure could withstand internally the force of even one Hiroshima-type explosion. By and large, the Pacific islanders live in total dependence upon the sea, and it is not to be wondered at that some of them are waiting at the door of this Court in [357] the hope that they will be heard, by way of intervention, in a matter of fundamental importance to their health, their way of life and their livelihood.

Having regard to the developments of international law embracing the principle of intergenerational rights and responsibilities, this is an environmental risk of which, in the absence of rebutting material from France, New Zealand and the islands covered by its Request are entitled, prima facie, to complain. It may be that France has material with which it can satisfy the Court on that issue, but no such material has been offered. Having regard to the course of geological events, a guarantee of stability of such an island formation for hundreds of thousands of years does not seem within the bounds of likelihood or possibility.

As for New Zealand, New Zealand has from the very commencement of this case couched its claim in terms, 'including apprehension, anxiety and concern, to the people and Government of New Zealand and of the Cook Islands, Niue and Tokelau Islands', and on the basis of the violation of its rights to the exploitation of the seas. Those were New Zealand's concerns in 1974 and those particular concerns are redoubled now by the current nuclear tests.

The possibility of accident

The best intentioned and regulated of human activities must always face the possibility of an accident resulting from some unforeseen circumstance. The history of underground testing at Mururoa has not been free of accident.

---

[23] See the list of French nuclear tests at Mururoa and Fangataufa in Annex 4 of the New Zealand Request for an Examination of the Situation, reproduced from J. Bouchez and R. Lecomte, *Les atolls de Mururoa et de Fangataufa*, 1995, Vol. II.

According to New Zealand, an official publication of the French Atomic Energy Commission acknowledged that a device which had become stuck in the detonation shaft was exploded at a depth of approximately 987 metres, 110 metres less than planned. The test generated a submarine landslide of about one million cubic metres of material off the mass of the atoll which set off a tsunami which washed over part of the atoll, seriously injuring two persons.

Other accidents cited by New Zealand are:

(a) In June 1987 officials on Mururoa admitted to Cousteau the accidental release of approximately 1.5 teraBecquerels of radioactive iodine plus other volatile material.

(b) In 1992 scientists of the Combined Radiological Safety Service on Mururoa acknowledged that 0.2 teraBecquerels of radioactive iodine had been accidentally released in 1990 in similar [**358**] circumstances. (New Zealand's Request for an Examination of the Situation, para. 54.)

Having regard to the information furnished to the Court by New Zealand as summarized above, and in the absence of specific scientific material or impact assessment studies by France, the possibility of accident is another ground which goes to make out the prima facie case that New Zealand would be obliged to present.

Among the important rights of New Zealand that are threatened are its maritime rights. The 1973 Application of New Zealand covered radioactive damage caused to New Zealand's rights by French nuclear explosions in the Pacific. The fear of such radioactive pollution which brought New Zealand to the Court in 1973 is now appearing again.

The reasonableness of that fear has been proved at least prima facie, thereby enabling New Zealand to claim that the basis of the 1974 Judgment which protected New Zealand against such radioactive contamination has been affected.

New Zealand's application should therefore, in my view, be proceeded with by the Court to the next stage, which is the stage of enquiring whether a case has been made out for the issue of interim measures of protection.

All this would be done as another phase of the 1973 application filed by New Zealand.

The position of the intervenors

It follows from the views expressed earlier that the Court could have proceeded to consider whether the intervenors, Australia, Samoa, Solomon Islands, the Marshall Islands and the Federated States of Micronesia, should be permitted to intervene in those proceedings. Their contention is that they have an interest of a legal nature in the present proceedings and that they are not seeking to introduce a new dispute before the Court, but are seeking permission to assert their legal interests in an existing dispute in accordance with Article 62 of the Statute. They have very real concerns in regard to their undoubted right to the preservation of their own environment from the danger of radioactive contamination resulting from the conduct of another State. They have quite clearly gone to great lengths to seek legal advice, prepare substantial materials and file carefully prepared pleadings in support of their application for intervention.

It would, in this area as well, have served the substantial interests of justice if, upon a different view of the preliminary question, the matter had proceeded to further enquiry. The intervenors would then have been heard on their right to intervene. If they were found, after a hearing, to have had no right to intervene, they would then have left this Court [359] satisfied that the Court had heard them on their right to intervention and that procedural rules relating to intervention did not permit the Court to grant them redress. As it is they leave the Court without even the benefit of a hearing.

Concluding remarks

The altogether unusual nature of this case prompts a few reflections on the nature of the judicial process. These observations have equal relevance to domestic and international judiciaries, for the judge, whether domestic or international, is equally the servant of the concept of justice.

I wish to cite preliminarily a statement by Justice Cardozo, one of the foremost thinkers on the judicial process. Substitute for the word 'cases' the words 'international conventions, international custom, general principles of law, judicial decisions and teachings of publicists', and the thought expressed by Cardozo holds good also for the international judge.

Cardozo observed that the judge's duty was not simply to match the colours of the case at hand with the colours of the many samples spread out upon the judicial desk:

> If that were all there was to our calling, there would be little of intellectual interest about it. The man who had the best card index of the cases would also be the wisest judge. It is when the colors do not match, when the references in the index fail, when there is no decisive precedent, that the serious business of the judge begins. (Benjamin N. Cardozo, *The Nature of the Judicial Process*, 1921, pp. 20–1.)

This is a case for which there is no matching sample – whether in international conventions, international custom, general principles of law, judicial decisions or teachings of publicists. It presents a challenge to the Court.

This is also a case in which the processes of logical reasoning can well lead to one conclusion or the other. The processes of reasoning set out in this dissenting opinion lead to the conclusion that the Court's 1974 Judgment left open the possibility that, in the event of similar damage occurring by a means other than atmospheric testing, New Zealand should be able to bring this before the Court. The Judgment of the Court upon this Application proceeds, also by a logical chain of reasoning, to arrive at the opposite conclusion, namely, that atmospheric testing and atmospheric testing alone was the subject of the Judgment. The late Professor Julius Stone, who, in addition to his considerable standing in the world of international law, was also one of the deepest researchers into judicial reasoning in our time, referred to such situations as 'leeways of judicial [**360**] choice' (*Legal System and Lawyers' Reasonings*, 1964; see, especially, Chapter 8 on 'Reasons and Reasoning in Judicial and Juristic Argument').

We here enter an area well traversed in legal philosophy for nearly a century. In 1897 the great Justice Holmes gave classic expression to this problem. He observed that the fallacy of:

> the logical method and form flatter that longing for certainty and for repose which is in every human mind. But certainty generally is illusion and repose is not the destiny of man. Behind the logical form lies a judgment as to the relative worth and importance of competing legislative grounds, often an inarticulate and unconscious judgment, it is true, and yet the very root and nerve of the whole proceeding. You can give any conclusion a logical form. ('The Path of the Law', *Harvard Law Review*, 1897, Vol. X, p. 466.)

Since then a deluge of writing has illuminated this subject. In this Court – perhaps even more so than in any domestic jurisdiction – these reflections regarding the judicial process are more than ever relevant, for the discipline of international law has deeper philosophical roots than most other legal disciplines. Names such as Llewellyn, Cardozo, Perelman, Julius Stone, not to mention numerous others, illuminate the pathway towards an understanding that the forms of logical reasoning do not inevitably lead to a one and only conclusion.

Black-letter law and legal logic do not assist us when we reach a fork in the road. The realist and sociological schools of jurisprudence shed much light on this problem, which is as pertinent to the judicial function before this Court as it is in the domestic courts.

The relevance of this approach to seminal cases like the *Nuclear Tests* cases has not passed unnoticed. Amidst the vast scholarly literature generated by the decisions of 1973 and 1974[24] are discussions examining the decisions in the light of the philosophical approaches of the Legal [**361**] Realist and Sociological Schools of Jurisprudence,[25] for they have a vital bearing upon the international judicial process. The limits of logic and black-letter legal analysis will no doubt be similarly examined in the light of the Court's determination of this case.

The issues brought before the Court are momentous. They can, according to New Zealand, affect the integrity of marine life in the Pacific for many multiples of

---

[24] See, for example, John Dugard, 'The Nuclear Tests Cases and the South West Africa Cases: Some Realism about the International Judicial Decision', *Virginia Journal of International Law*, 1975–6, Vol. 15, pp. 463–504; Jerome B. Elkind, 'Footnote to the Nuclear Test Cases: Abuse of Right – A Blind Alley for Environmentalists', *Vanderbilt Journal of Transnational Law*, 1976, Vol. 9, pp. 57–97; Thomas M. Franck, 'Word Made Law: The Decision of the ICJ in the Nuclear Test Cases', *American Journal of International Law*, 1975, Vol. 69, pp. 612–20; Dinesh Khosla, 'Nuclear Test Cases: Judicial Valour v. Judicial Discretion', *Indian Journal of International Law*, 1978, Vol. 18, pp. 322–44; Pierre Lellouche, 'The Nuclear Tests Cases: Judicial Silence v. Atomic Blasts', *Harvard International Law Journal*, 1975, Vol. 16, pp. 614–37.

[25] See Edward McWhinney, *The World Court and the Contemporary International Law-Making Process*, 1979, p. 34; see, also, Edward McWhinney, 'International Law-Making and the Judicial Process: The World Court and the French Nuclear Tests Case', *Syracuse Journal of International Law and Commerce*, 1975, Vol. 3, No. 1, p. 9.

24,000 years, the half-life of one of the by-products of nuclear explosions, should they reach to the sea. A prima facie case has been made out of the possibility of release into the ocean of the pent-up radioactive debris of around 127 nuclear explosions on Mururoa alone. That pent-up debris is currently confined in a medium whose stability gives rise to serious doubts. This is a major matter to be examined and it raises the fears of radioactive contamination that were entertained in 1973. Prima facie a case has been made out for a fuller examination of these matters.

The Court has refused to take this step on the basis that paragraph 63 of the 1974 Judgment relates only to atmospheric tests, although the claim was brought before the Court in general terms relating to nuclear explosions in the Pacific. This is a strict construction which is clearly not the only reasonable construction justifiable in logic. On the basis of this strict and inflexible construction, matters of critical importance to the global environment are passed by without the benefit of a preliminary examination. A less rigid construction, which is also possible, has been rejected. The latter course which, in my view, was not unavailable to the Court, should have been chosen in view of the momentous issues involved.

The views of two eminent judges on this Court may be of assistance in this regard. It was the view of Judge Lauterpacht, a view cited with evident approval by Judge Fitzmaurice, that:

> a tribunal such as the International Court has a duty, both to the parties and in the general interests of the law, that may go considerably beyond a bare decision, and may go beyond the issues the consideration of which will technically suffice to motivate the decision (Sir Gerald Fitzmaurice, *The Law and Procedure of the International Court of Justice*, 1986, Vol. II, p. 653).

Judge Fitzmaurice's own view, expressed in terms of comparing a minor tribunal with one standing at the apex of judicial organization, was as follows:

> [362] The sort of bare order or finding that may suit many of the purposes of the magistrate or county court judge will by no means do for the Court of Appeal, the House of Lords or the Judicial Committee of the Privy Council, and their equivalents in other countries. International tribunals at any rate have usually regarded it as an important part of their function, not only to decide, but, in deciding, to expound generally the law having a bearing on the matters decided. (*Op. cit.*, p. 648.)

New Zealand has placed a strong prima facie case before the Court. The Court is still far from the stage of reaching an affirmative finding of fact. All it needs to know at this stage is whether a prima facie case exists for giving the Court the ability to enquire into the grave matter brought before it.

If two views are possible on this matter, the Court should in my view lean towards that which does not shut out enquiry, but leaves the matter open for definitive determination after both Parties have marshalled their arguments and the Court is in a better position to decide. When, at this initial stage, the Court determines that even a prima facie case has not been made out, enabling it to view the matter in greater depth, it is in effect giving a definitive determination prematurely on a matter of the utmost importance, not merely to the Applicant who comes before it but to the entire international community.

I regret that the Court has not availed itself of the opportunity to enquire more fully into this matter and of making a contribution to some of the seminal principles of the evolving corpus of international environmental law.[26] The Court has too long been silent on these issues and, in the words of ancient wisdom, one may well ask 'If not now, when?'

DISSENTING OPINION OF JUDGE *AD HOC* SIR GEOFFREY PALMER (EXTRACT)

[400] *[. . .] The factual environmental argument*

55. Having concluded that the Court is not precluded by the terms of its 1974 Judgment from entering into an examination of it, I now come to a discussion of the arguments of whether it should in the circumstances exercise in 1995 the possibility left open in 1974. Such an analysis necessarily requires some reference to the facts.
[. . .]

[403] [. . .] The calculus of environmental risk

67. The Court is not in a position to make definitive conclusions on the scientific evidence on the basis of the material put before it. Listening to the submissions at the oral hearings did, however, convince me that there were real issues at large here. The true question related to the assessment of the level of risk. The two nations appeared to have very different approaches to that subject. It is, however, an issue which could be determined were the Court to give it a full hearing.

[404] 68. There are a number of factors to be weighed in deciding whether New Zealand satisfied the prima facie standard outlined above which would warrant a decision that the basis of the 1974 Judgment had altered and should be examined. These factors are:

- the ultrahazardous nature of nuclear explosions and the dangerous nature of the waste they produce;
- the length of time that some of the nuclear materials remain hazardous which is measured in tens of thousands of years or longer;
- the fragile nature of the atoll structure and the cumulative effect of a large number of nuclear explosions upon the structure;
- the fact that atolls cannot be distinguished from the marine environment and must be thought of as an inherent part of the ocean ecosystem;
- the high number of tests which have been concentrated within a small area;

---

[26] Apart from *Certain Phosphate Lands in Nauru (Nauru v. Australia) (ICJ Reports 1992)* [see p. 124 above], *Corfu Channel (ICJ Reports 1949)* and the *Nuclear Tests* cases, there is no assistance the Court has given in this most vital area of contemporary international law. The first was only peripherally related to environmental law as it was settled after the Court's judgment on preliminary objections. The *Corfu Channel* case laid down the environmentally important principle that, if a nation knows that harmful effects may occur to other nations from facts within its knowledge and fails to disclose them, it will be liable to the nation that suffers damage. In the *Nuclear Tests* cases of 1973, the Court did not decide the principal environmental issue brought before it.

- the proximity of the testing to the marine environment;
- the high quantities of dangerous nuclear wastes now accumulated on the test sites;
- the risks of radiation entering the food chain through plankton, tuna and other fish;
- the risks of further fissures and shearing off of part of the atoll structure occurring as the result of further testing.

69. It cannot be doubted that France has engaged in activities that have substantially altered the natural environment of the test sites in the Pacific. These actions have been intentional and they have been under scientific scrutiny, especially by French scientists. But the unintended repercussions of intentional human action are often the most important. The nature of the risks inherent in the activity itself would suggest caution to be appropriate. Some means of calculating those risks is necessary to arrive at a determination of whether New Zealand has satisfied the test. This calculus I suggest should contain a number of elements:

- the magnitude of the recognizable risk of harm by nuclear contamination in the circumstances;
- the probability of the risk coming to pass;
- the utility and benefits of the conduct being assessed – viz. nuclear testing by France;
- the cost of the measures needed to avert the risk.

70. In my opinion what is required under the test the Court should apply is a risk–benefit analysis. There must be a balancing of the risks of the activity, the probability of harm, the utility of the activity and the measures needed to eliminate the risk. This is similar to a calculus of the **[405]** risk analysis in the law of torts in some common law jurisdictions (see *Prosser and Keeton on the Law of Torts*, 5th ed., 1984, pp. 169–73; Richard A. Epstein, *Cases and Materials on Torts*, 5th ed., 1990, pp. 150–68; *Blyth* v. *Birmingham Water Works*, 11 Exchequer 781, 156 English Reports 1047 (1856); *United States* v. *Carroll Towing Co.*, 159 Federal Reports 2d 169 (2d Cir. 1947)). But it is submitted that it is an appropriate analytical construct with some modifications for measuring the issue here.

71. The gravity of the radiation harm if it occurs is likely to be serious for the marine environment. The magnitude of the risk that the harm will occur must be regarded as significant given the destructive force of nuclear explosions and the possibility of other disturbances or abnormal situations occurring in the course of the long life of the dangerous substances. The costs of averting the risk in this instance are low – they consist of France providing a fully scientifically verifiable environment impact assessment in accordance with modern environmental practice which demonstrates that the proposed tests will not result in nuclear contamination. No doubt France and New Zealand would differ greatly on the utility of nuclear testing but it can reasonably be said that the extra tests proposed cannot have great value given the number that have preceded them. They are of diminishing marginal value, if they have any value at all. If the calculus of the risk analysis were applied in

this way, then on these facts a prima facie case is made out by New Zealand in my opinion.

72. The test put forward here derives from [*sic*] support from the recent work of the International Law Commission where it laid down that for the purposes of draft Articles under its consideration 'risk of causing significant transboundary harm' an expression which refers 'to the combined effect of the probability of occurrence of an accident and the magnitude of its injurious impact' (Report of the International Law Commission on the work of its forty-sixth session, 2 May–22 July 1994, *Official Records of the General Assembly, Forty-ninth Session, Supplement No. 10* (A/49/10), p. 400).

73. The conclusion of this segment of the opinion is as follows: judged on the prima facie standard a case on the environmental facts has been made out to examine the Judgment.

The legal environmental issues

74. The second argument advanced by New Zealand as to why the Court should examine the 1974 Judgment revolved around the changes in the state of international law relating to the environment in general and nuclear testing in particular in the period between 1974 and the 1995 [**406**] hearings. In order to evaluate that submission it is necessary to briefly traverse those developments in the broad before becoming specific.

The development of international environmental law

75. When this case began in 1973 it was shortly after the international meeting at Stockholm which produced the Stockholm Declaration of the United Nations Conference on the Human Environment (adopted by the United Nations Conference on the Human Environment at Stockholm, 16 June 1972, 11 *ILM* 1416 (1972) (Stockholm Declaration)). It was that Conference that started the march of the new field of international environmental law toward international legal maturity. At that time only 25 countries possessed national environmental ministries. The Declaration advanced the development of the principles of international environmental law. It can confidently be stated that some of those principles stated in the Declaration have received such widespread support in State practice coupled with a sense on the part of States that they are legally binding that they have by now entered into the framework of customary international law. The impact of human activities on the environment in a comprehensive way was brought to the attention of the international community, in effect for the first time by Stockholm. Preambular paragraph 6 of the Stockholm Declaration said: 'A point has been reached in history when we must shape our actions throughout the world with a more prudent care for their environmental consequences.' It is important to recall that explicit reference was made by New Zealand in its 1973 Request (*ICJ Pleadings, Nuclear Tests*, Vol. II, pp. 55–6, paras. 33, 34 and 35 with explicit reliance being placed on Principles 6, 7, 21 and 26).

76. Principle 1 of the Stockholm Declaration established that the people bear 'a solemn responsibility to protect and improve the environment for present and future

generations'. Principle 2 talks of the need to safeguard natural resources including air, land and water. Principle 6 laid down that the discharge of toxic substances must be halted where they were in such quantities or concentrations 'to exceed the capacity of the environment to render them harmless...'. Principle 7 requires States to take all possible steps to prevent pollution to the seas by substances liable to create hazards for human health and marine life. Principle 18 asked for 'the identification, avoidance and control of environmental risks ...'. Principle 21 required States to

> ensure that activities within their jurisdiction or control do not cause damage to the environment of other States or of areas beyond the limits of national jurisdiction.

[**407**] Principle 26 dealt with the need to spare the environment and people 'the effects of nuclear weapons and all other means of mass destruction'.

77. In recent years the proliferation of international conventions and treaties on the global environment has been considerable. There are more than a hundred multilateral environmental instruments in force many of which have been negotiated since the 1972 Stockholm Declaration. The United Nations Environment Programme register listed 152 in 1991 before the significant outburst of activity at the Rio de Janeiro United Nations Conference on Environment and Development in 1992. For present purposes the important point about the development of international environmental law is that its most important flowering and expansion spans the period of this case – it started in earnest about the time this case began and reached a crescendo at Rio in 1992.

78. Indeed the consensus flowing from Rio is itself significant in the context of the arguments being advanced in the present case. The Rio Declaration refined, advanced, sharpened and developed some of the principles adopted at Stockholm (Rio Declaration on Environment and Development, adopted by the United Nations Conference on Environment and Development at Rio de Janeiro, 13 June 1992, 31 *ILM* 874 (1992) (Rio Declaration)). Many of the principles were repeated but some new ones make an appearance:

Principle 15:

> In order to protect the environment, the precautionary approach shall be widely applied by States according to their capabilities. Where there are threats of serious or irreversible damage, lack of full scientific certainty shall not be used as a reason for postponing cost-effective measures to prevent environmental degradation.

Principle 17:

> Environmental impact assessment, as a national instrument, shall be undertaken for proposed activities that are likely to have a significant adverse impact on the environment and are subject to a decision of a competent national authority.

79. Maurice Strong who was Secretary-General of both the Stockholm and the Rio Conferences has summed up his view of the need to develop the mechanisms of international environmental law still further. He said:

> To manage our common future on this planet, we will need a new global legal regime based essentially on the extension into international life of the rule of law, together with reliable mechanisms for accountability and enforcement that provide the basis for the effective [**408**] functioning of national societies. (Foreword by Maurice F. Strong to L. D. Guruswamy *et al., International Environmental Law and World Order,* 1994, p. vii.)

80. This Court in this very case in 1974 made a contribution to the growing field of international environmental law. The *Nuclear Tests* cases have come to be cited as one of a quartet of cases that offer some protection for the environment through the medium of customary international law. Others include the *Corfu Channel (United Kingdom v. Albania) (ICJ Reports 1949,* p. 4) establishing the principle of every State's obligation not to allow knowingly its territory to be used for acts contrary to the rights of other States. The *Trail Smelter (United States v. Canada)* (III *Reports of International Arbitral Awards (RIAA)* 1905 (1938 and 1941)) established that no State has the right to use or permit the use of its territory in such a way as to cause injury by fumes in the territory of another State. The *Lake Lanoux Arbitration* (XII *RIAA* 281 (1957)) turned on the interpretation of a particular treaty but it may establish the principle that a State has the duty to give notice when its actions may impair the environmental enjoyment of another State. To these should now be added the contribution of this Court if only because of the environmental degradation with which the case dealt (*Certain Phosphate Lands in Nauru (Nauru v. Australia), Preliminary Objections, Judgment, ICJ Reports 1992,* p. 240).[27] Significantly, by the Court deciding to hear the case, a result was produced by way of settlement. The principles established by these cases have been included in Principle 21 of the Stockholm Declaration and Principle 2 of the Rio Declaration.

81. But authoritative decisions in the area of international environment law are scarce enough. They certainly lag behind the plethora of conventional law that has sprung into existence in the more than 20 years spanning the life of this case. The nature of some of the issues is helpfully discussed in the Report of the International Law Commission on the work of its forty-sixth session, 2 May–22 July 1994, on 'International Liability for Injurious Consequences Arising out of Acts Not Prohibited by International Law' (*Official Records of the General Assembly, Forty-ninth Session, Supplement No. 10* (A/49/10), pp. 367 ff.), a subject with which the Commission has been grappling since 1978 without definitive result. The Commission is giving priority in its work to prevention of activities having a risk of causing transboundary harm.

82. Indeed, following Rio and perhaps because of it, this Court on 6 August 1993 exercising its powers under Article 26 of the Statute of the [**409**] International Court of Justice set up a Chamber of seven Judges to deal with environmental matters. The Court in an ICJ communiqué (93/20, 19 July 1993) announced:

> In view of the developments in the field of environmental law and protection which have taken place in the last few years, and considering that it should be prepared to the fullest possible extent to deal with any environmental case falling within its jurisdiction,

---

[27] See p. 124 above.]

the Court has now deemed it appropriate to establish a seven-member Chamber for Environmental Matters . . .

83. The forces that led the Court to establish a Chamber for consideration of environmental cases is reflected in the quantity of work being done by highly qualified publicists of the various nations upon the subject of international environmental law. Such works include A. Kiss and D. Shelton, *International Environmental Law*, 1991; P. Birnie and A. Boyle, *International Law and the Environment*, 1992; P. Sands *et al.*, *Principles of International Environmental Law – Documents in International Environmental Law*, 2 volumes, 1995; L. Guruswamy *et al.*, *International Environmental Law and World Order*, 1994; J. Carroll (ed.), *International Environmental Diplomacy*, 1988; E. B. Weiss, *In Fairness to Future Generations: International Law, Common Patrimony, and Intergenerational Equity*, 1989; E. B. Weiss (ed.), *Environmental Change and International Law*, 1992; C. Stone, *The Gnat is Older than Man: Global Environment and Human Agenda*, 1993; P. Sand, *Lessons Learned in Global Environmental Governance*, 1990; G. Handl (ed.), *Yearbook of International Environmental Law*, 1990, and annually. The periodical literature is so vast on the subject that it cannot be cited.

84. The obvious and overwhelming trend of these developments from Stockholm to Rio has been to establish a comprehensive set of norms to protect the global environment. There is a widespread recognition now that there are risks that threaten our common survival. We cannot permit the onward march of technology and development without giving attention to the environmental limits that must govern these issues. Otherwise the paradigm of sustainable development embraced by the world at the Rio Conference cannot be achieved (World Commission on Environment and Development, *Our Common Future*, 1987, p. 5; see also D. H. Meadows, D. L. Meadows and J. Randers, *Beyond the Limits*, 1992).

International law on radioactive hazards

85. It was against the background outlined above that Sir Kenneth Keith, QC, for New Zealand sought to establish four legal propositions:

   (i)   [410] States must ensure that activities within their jurisdiction or control do not cause damage to the environment of other States or of areas beyond the limits of their jurisdiction.

   (ii) Any addition of radioactive material to the environment or exposure of individuals to radiation must be justified. Such addition or exposure must be for good reason.

   (iii) Any disposal or introduction of artificially created radioactive material into the marine environment is heavily circumscribed. It is in general forbidden.

   (iv) Any introduction of radioactive material into the marine environment as a result of nuclear tests is forbidden. The world community no longer accepts that the testing of nuclear weapons can be used to justify marine contamination.

The law now sets higher standards in an 'increasingly interdependent world', Sir Kenneth told the Court (CR 95/20, p. 10).

86. New Zealand in support of its propositions relied upon the Stockholm and Rio Declarations and in particular on the 1986 Convention for the Protection of the Natural Resources and Environment of the South Pacific Region concluded at Noumea, 25 November 1986, entered into force 22 August 1990 (26 *ILM* 38 (1987)). New Zealand and France both are parties to the Convention. These legal materials and others cited to the Court established in the view of New Zealand an increasingly strict attitude to the addition of radioactive material to the general environment and the exposure of individuals to radiation. In relation to the marine environment it was even more exacting. Among the materials cited in support of these propositions were: Article 14 of the Draft Articles considered in the 1994 Annual Report of the International Law Commission mentioned above; the International Atomic Energy Agency, Safety Series No. 77, *Principles for Limiting Releases of Radioactive Effluents into the Environment*, 1986; Agenda 21, Chapter 22, of the Rio Declaration, 'Safe and Environmentally Sound Management of Radioactive Wastes', paragraph 5 (para. 100 of the New Zealand Request); Convention on the High Seas concluded at Geneva 29 April 1958, entered into force 30 September 1962 (450 *UNTS* 82, Art. 25); United Nations Convention on the Law of the Sea concluded at Montego Bay, 10 December 1982, entered into force 16 November 1994 (21 *ILM* 1261 (1982), Part XII, Art. 194); Convention on Biological Diversity, concluded at Rio de Janeiro 5 June 1992, entered into force 29 December 1993 (31 *ILM* 818 (1992), Arts. 3 and 14); Statute of the International Atomic Energy Agency, 26 October 1956 (276 *UNTS* 3, Art. 34); Convention for the Protection of the Marine Environment of the North-East Atlantic, concluded at Paris, September 1992 (32 *ILM* 1069 (1993), Ann. II, Art. 3 (3) *(a)* and *(b))*; Convention [411] on the Prevention of Marine Pollution by Dumping of Wastes and Other Matter, concluded at London, 19 December 1972 (11 *ILM* 1291 (1972)), Annex I; Resolution of Consultative Meeting LDC 21 (9) on Dumping Radioactive Wastes at Sea, 1985.

Environmental Impact Assessment

87. At this point, Mr D. J. MacKay for New Zealand went on to develop this segment of the argument by pointing to the application of the emerging international law on environmental impact assessment (EIA) and the precautionary principle in their application to the facts of this case. In both respects the law had changed dramatically, thus supporting the view that the basis of the Court's Judgment was affected. It was submitted that other parties likely to be affected by the risks have a right to know what the investigations for the EIA are, have a right to propose additional investigations and a right to verify for themselves the result of such investigations. As the law now stands it is a matter of legal duty to first establish before undertaking an activity that the activity does not involve any unacceptable risk to the environment. An EIA is simply a means of establishing a process to comply with that international legal duty. New Zealand pointed to a number of international instruments, including

Article 205 of the United Nations Law of the Sea Convention, that make explicit reference to EIA.

88. Under Article 12 that has been adopted by the International Law Commission in the course of its deliberations, the Commission has decided that before a State carries out activities which involve a risk of causing significant transboundary harm through their physical consequences

> a State shall ensure that an assessment is undertaken of the risk of such activity. Such an assessment shall include an evaluation of the possible impact of that activity on persons or property as well as in the environment of other States.

The Noumea Convention referred to earlier also contains an explicit obligation in Article 16 to conduct environmental impact assessments before embarking upon any major project which might affect the marine environment. A more explicit measure appears in Article 12 of that Convention producing a duty to prevent, reduce and control pollution in the Convention area which might result from the testing of nuclear devices.

[412] Precautionary principle

89. So far as the precautionary principle is concerned New Zealand submitted that in the circumstances it required two things. First, that the assessment must be carried out before and not after the activities are undertaken. Second, that it is for the State contemplating these activities to carry out the assessment and to demonstrate that there is no real risk. It is not for potentially affected States to demonstrate that there will be a risk.

90. I have set out these arguments in some detail because they exhibit the issues that would have been traversed had the case gone to the next stage. France did not address arguments on these points since it at all times regarded the issues before the Court as threshold issues that did not require it to meet the arguments put above. It would be wrong in these circumstances to reach substantive conclusions on the application of the arguments to the facts of the case. It is, however, appropriate to reach a conclusion on what the principles of law discussed establish from the point of view of meeting the test required to examine again the 1974 case.

Conclusion

91. What those principles of international law establish in my view are the following propositions:

(a) international environmental law has developed rapidly and is tending to develop in a way that provides comprehensive protection for the natural environment;

(b) international law has taken an increasingly restrictive approach to the regulation of nuclear radiation;

(c)   customary international law may have developed a norm of requiring environmental impact assessment where activities may have a significant effect on the environment;

(d)   the norm involved in the precautionary principle has developed rapidly and may now be a principle of customary international law relating to the environment;

(e)   there are obligations based on Conventions that may be applicable here requiring environmental impact assessment and the precautionary principle to be observed.

Taken together, in application to the present dispute, the legal developments are sufficient to meet a prima facie test that the legal circumstances have altered sufficiently to favour an examination of the 1974 case. Let me emphasize again, however, this is not to say what principles of law may apply here in the particular circumstances or indeed what their content might be. That is for the next stage.

92. It is necessary to say something about the application of principles of law at the stage they have reached in 1995 to a case that was pleaded [413] and first dealt with in the mid 1970s. The harm complained of – nuclear contamination – is a continuing one. It seems apparent to me that the applicable law must be determined, in a circumstance like the present one, at the date the Court is called on to apply it. The converse proposition cannot stand in my opinion.

93. In my view it would exert a salutary and needed influence on international environmental law for this Court to enter upon full hearings and a serious consideration of the issues of this case, whatever ultimate result was eventually reached. There is a pressing need to develop the law in the area. Given the possibility left open expressly in 1974 that in appropriate circumstances the Court could return to these issues, it would be possible to examine the 1974 decision in light of massive changes in the legal principles that have been developed in the period between the Court's two considerations of the issues. In the event, however, because a majority of the Court has taken another view New Zealand's effort to hold France accountable under the principles of international environmental law will fail.

[. . .]

[**419**] *Concluding observations*

111. The nature of the dispute between France and New Zealand has been apparent for the whole period spanned by this case in this Court, except between 1991 and 1995 when France observed a moratorium on testing. The dispute is palpably about nuclear testing in the Pacific in all its forms. The official citation for this case was and remains *Nuclear Tests (New Zealand v. France)* case. Despite that fact, the Court in its 1995 judgment has chosen to draw a fundamental distinction between atmospheric testing and underground testing.

112. It might have been thought by some that the present application was an appropriate occasion upon which to push out the boat from the shore a little towards

the incoming tide of international environmental jurisprudence. The Court failed to decide the issue in 1974 and it has failed again in 1995.

113. The 1974 Judgment created widespread controversy in the international legal literature, some learned commentators regarding it as imaginative and innovative, others called it a landmark of political caution, weak in law and logic. A third group thought the decision a lost opportunity for dealing with international environmental law. (D. P. Verma, 'The Nuclear Tests Cases: An Inquiry into the Judicial Response of the International Court of Justice', 8 *South African Yearbook of International Law* 20 (1982); Edward McWhinney, *The World Court and the Contemporary International Law-Making Process*, 1979; R. St J. Macdonald and Barbara Hough, 'The Nuclear Tests Case Revisited', 20 *German Yearbook of International Law* 337 (1977); Jerome B. Elkind, 'Footnote to the Nuclear Tests Cases: Abuse of Right – A Blind Alley for Environmentalists', 9 *Vanderbilt Journal of Transnational Law* 57 (1976); Thomas M. Franck, 'Word Made Law: The Decision of the ICJ in the Nuclear Test Cases', 69 *American Journal of International Law* 612 (1975).) A similar range of reaction to the Court's treatment of the present phase of the case is predictable.

114. In its essence this case has to be understood as an environmental case. New technology has given humankind massive ability to alter the natural environment. The consequences of these activities need to be carefully analysed and examined unless we are to imperil those who come after us. It is a concern well known to international law (see generally E. B. Weiss, *In Fairness to Future Generations*, 1989). As Professor Edith Brown Weiss points out:

> We, as a species, hold the natural and cultural environment of our planet in common, both with other members of the present generation and with other generations, past and future. At any given [420] time, each generation is both a custodian or trustee of the planet for future generations and a beneficiary of its fruits. This imposes obligations upon us to care for the planet and gives us certain rights to use it. (P. 17.)

Further, the special problems created for the law by nuclear energy and tests flow from the ultrahazardous nature of nuclear energy and nuclear explosions (A. Boyle, 'Nuclear Energy and International Law: An Environmental Perspective', 60 *British Year Book of International Law* 257 (1989); G. Handl, 'Transboundary Nuclear Accidents: The Post-Chernobyl Multilateral Legislative Agenda', 15 *Ecology Law Quarterly* 203 (1988).)

115. The issues generated for the environment by nuclear testing and nuclear accidents demonstrate that States have been unwilling to act as good stewards for or guardians of the environment. The experience suggests that environmental rights ought to be established at the international level and be enforceable there.

116. If in 1995 this Court had been prepared to enter into the next phase of the case, the dispute may at last have been put to rest. For far too long this issue has given rise to substantial, even painful difficulties in the relations between France and New Zealand. The two functions of this Court as I understand it are to act as an institution

to settle disputes and to clarify and develop the law. Regrettably the dispute has not been put to rest and the law has not been developed.

117. In this case the Court had an opportunity to make a contribution to one of the most critical environmental issues of our time. It has rejected the opportunity for technical legal reasons which could in my opinion have been decided the other way, fully consonant with proper legal reasoning. It is true that much of the jurisdiction of this Court rests upon the consent of States. It is true that France has withdrawn the consent that allowed the 1974 case to be heard. That is not an adequate reason to refrain from re-opening the case, a possibility that the Judgment in 1974 expressly contemplated. The case is one the Court had the power to decide then; it has the power to decide it now. But the Court refuses to decide it.

[. . .]

[**421**] [. . .] 119. Finally, let me add that I have had the opportunity of reading the elegant and persuasive dissenting opinion of my colleague Judge Weeramantry. I agree with it.

[Reports: *ICJ Reports 1995*, p. 288; 106 *ILR* 1 at p. 10]

Legality of the Use by a State of Nuclear Weapons in Armed Conflict (Request by the World Health Organization for an Advisory Opinion)[1]

International Court of Justice, The Hague

8 July 1996 (Bedjaoui, *President*; Schwebel, *Vice-President*; Oda, Guillaume, Shahabuddeen, Weeramantry, Ranjeva, Herczegh, Shi, Fleischhauer, Koroma, Vereshchetin, Ferrari Bravo and Higgins, *Judges*)

Hazardous activities and substances – nuclear weapons – whether use of nuclear weapons prohibited by international humanitarian law – protection of health and the environment in war and armed conflict

International organisations – specialised agencies of the United Nations – World Health Organization (WHO) – competence to request advisory opinion regarding legality of using nuclear weapons – whether question arising within the scope of the activities of WHO – constitution of WHO – interpretation – approach to interpretation of constituent treaties – nature of specialised agency – United Nations and specialised agencies as a coherent system – position of WHO within the United Nations system – principle of speciality

Jurisdiction – International Court of Justice – advisory jurisdiction – requests by specialised agencies of the United Nations – jurisdictional requirements – role of the Court in considering request for an advisory opinion – interpretation of question – Article 65 of the Statute of the International Court – Article 96(2) of the United Nations Charter – agreement between United Nations and WHO – WHO Constitution

---

[1] The Advisory Opinion given by the Court in response to a request by the United Nations General Assembly, which concerned the legality of the use and threat of use of nuclear weapons, is reported at p. 238 below.

The World Health Organization was represented by Mr Claude-Henri Vignes. The States that made written or oral statements at the proceedings and their representatives (where applicable) are listed at paragraphs 6 and 9 of the Advisory Opinion, which paragraphs are not reproduced in this volume but can be found at *ICJ Reports 1996*, pp. 68–9.

War and armed conflict – nuclear weapons – whether use of nuclear weapons prohibited in international humanitarian law – protection of health and the environment in war and armed conflict

SUMMARY   *The facts*   The World Health Organization ('WHO'), a specialised agency of the United Nations, requested an advisory opinion from the International Court of Justice on the following question:

In view of the health and environmental effects, would the use of nuclear weapons by a State in war or other armed conflict be a breach of its obligations under international law including the WHO Constitution?

The request was made pursuant to Resolution WHA 46.40 adopted by the World Health Assembly on 14 May 1993. In 1994, the United Nations General Assembly adopted Resolution 49/75 K, which welcomed the earlier WHO request and made a separate request for an advisory opinion regarding the legality of the use, or threat of use, of nuclear weapons. The Court invited written statements from the WHO and the Member States of WHO regarding the WHO request. Thirty-five States submitted written statements in response. In November 1995, the Court heard oral statements from the WHO, concerning the WHO request, and from twenty States, regarding both the WHO and General Assembly requests. A number of the States which made written and oral statements challenged the jurisdiction of the Court to give the advisory opinion requested on the ground that the question posed in Resolution 46.40 was a question which did not arise within the scope of the activities of the WHO and which was, in any event, of a political, rather than a legal, character.

Held by the International Court of Justice (by eleven votes to three)   The Court was not able to give the advisory opinion requested of it under World Health Assembly Resolution WHA 46.40.

(1)   In accordance with Article 65(1) of the Statute of the International Court of Justice and Article 96(2) of the United Nations Charter, three conditions had to be satisfied in order to found the jurisdiction of the Court when a request for an advisory opinion was submitted to it by a specialised agency. First, the agency requesting the opinion had to be duly authorised, under the Charter, to request opinions from the Court. Secondly, the opinion requested had to be on a legal question. Thirdly, the question had to be one arising within the scope of the activities of the requesting agency.

(2)   There was no doubt that the first requirement was satisfied. Article 76 of the WHO Constitution provided that, once authorised by the United Nations General Assembly, the WHO might request an opinion from the Court on 'any legal question arising within the competence of the Organization'. Article X(2) of the Agreement of 10 July 1948 between the United Nations and the WHO gave the required authorisation from the General Assembly.

(3)   The second requirement was also satisfied. The question posed required the Court to identify the obligations of States under the rules of law invoked and to assess whether the behaviour in question conformed to those obligations. It was therefore a legal question. The fact that the question also had political aspects did not deprive it of its character as a legal question. Moreover, in situations where political considerations were prominent, it might be particularly necessary for an international organisation to obtain an advisory opinion regarding the legal issues involved. The political motives which might have inspired the request and the political implications which an opinion might have were irrelevant in determining whether or not the Court possessed jurisdiction.

(4)   The WHO request did not, however, relate to a legal question which arose within the scope of the activities of the WHO.

(a)   The constituent instruments of international organisations were treaties whose object was to create new subjects of international law endowed with a certain autonomy, to which the parties entrusted the task of realising common goals. As such, they were subject to the well-established rules of treaty interpretation but could raise specific problems of interpretation, owing to their character. Of particular relevance in resolving such problems was the subsequent practice of the parties in the application of the treaty concerned.

(b)   The functions of the WHO were listed in Article 2 of its Constitution. Interpreted in accordance with their ordinary meaning, in their context, and in the light of the object and purpose of the WHO Constitution, as well as of the practice followed by the WHO, the terms of Article 2 could be read as authorising the WHO to deal with the effects on health of the use of nuclear weapons, or of any other hazardous activity, and to take preventive measures aimed at protecting the health of populations in the event of such weapons being used or such activities engaged in. The question posed, however, related not to the effects of the use of nuclear weapons on health, but to the legality of the use of such weapons in view of their health and environmental effects. The competence of the WHO to deal with those effects was not dependent on the legality of the acts which caused them. The question whether those acts were lawful was not, therefore, one arising within the scope of the activities of the WHO.

(c) International organisations were subjects of international law, which, unlike States, did not possess general competence but were governed by the principle of speciality. They were invested by the States which created them with powers, the limits of which were a function of the common interests whose promotion those States entrusted to them. Although organisations possessed certain implied powers, to ascribe to the WHO the competence to address the legality of the use of nuclear weapons would be tantamount to disregarding the principle of speciality, for such competence could not be deemed a necessary implication of the WHO Constitution in the light of the purposes assigned to the WHO by its Member States.

(d) Moreover, as a specialised agency, the WHO had to work within the framework of the United Nations. The Charter of the United Nations laid the basis of a system designed to organise international cooperation in a coherent fashion. The WHO Constitution had, therefore, to be interpreted in the light of the overall logic of the United Nations system, under which responsibility for questions concerning the use of force and regulation of armaments was allocated elsewhere.

(e) The practice of the WHO confirmed these conclusions. The WHO had not dealt with the legality of the use of nuclear weapons prior to the adoption of WHA Resolution 46.40. That the WHO at times referred to or applied rules of international law regarding the legality of using certain weapons did not mean that it had received a mandate itself to address the legality of the use of those weapons.

(5) The jurisdiction of the Court to give the opinion requested by Resolution 46.40 could not be made good simply by reference to the presumption that Resolution 46.40 had been validly adopted. The question whether a resolution had been validly adopted from the procedural point of view and the question whether that resolution was *intra vires* were two separate issues. Although it was for the WHO, in the first instance, to determine its own competence, it was for the Court to determine whether the conditions for the establishment of its own jurisdiction had been satisfied. Nor did the fact that the United Nations General Assembly, in Resolution 49/75 K, expressly welcomed Resolution WHA 46.40 enlarge the competence of the WHO to request an advisory opinion.

Declaration of Judge Ranjeva The structure of the question posed did not permit the Court to exercise the jurisdiction which it had.

Declaration of Judge Ferrari Bravo   The right of specialised agencies, as opposed to that of organs of the United Nations, to seise the Court with a request for an advisory opinion needed to be carefully restricted if a correct division between the competences of different bodies was to be maintained.

Separate Opinion of Judge Oda   The question whether the use of nuclear weapons was contrary to the WHO Constitution was separate from that of whether such use was contrary to general international law and had not been considered in the Advisory Opinion. The WHO lacked competence to request an advisory opinion on the question posed in Resolution WHA 46.40 and this lack of competence had been pointed out by the Legal Counsel to the WHO (as well as by several States) at the time that the resolution was adopted. The resolution had been initiated by some non-governmental organisations, not because an opinion was necessary for the work of the WHO.

Dissenting Opinion of Judge Shahabuddeen   The question posed by the WHO did not relate to the legality of the use of nuclear weapons under general international law but only under international law in connection with the obligations of States under the WHO Constitution. If the use of nuclear weapons constituted a breach of the obligations of States under the WHO Constitution, the WHO could take appropriate remedial action. The WHO was, therefore, competent to ask the question posed. The implication of the Court's Opinion was that States did not have an obligation under the WHO Constitution to refrain from the use of nuclear weapons. That was an answer, on the merits, to the question, not a reason for refusing to answer, and should have been identified as such.

Dissenting Opinion of Judge Weeramantry   (1) The question was concerned not with the legality or illegality of the use of nuclear weapons in general but with the obligations of States in relation to health, the environment and the WHO Constitution. It was therefore materially different from the question posed by the United Nations General Assembly. The Court should have examined these specific aspects of the WHO question. The WHO had clear responsibilities regarding health and the environment.

(2)   The effects on health of a use of nuclear weapons were well documented and would be catastrophic. Any institution concerned with public health needed to know whether the use of such weapons stood within the international legal system or not.

(3)   Only nine of the 189 Member States of WHO had questioned its competence to make the present request. That request sought the

Court's opinion on matters which were of direct concern to the WHO and thus arose within the scope of its activities.

(4)   The Court should have taken the opportunity presented by the request to consider the obligations of States regarding the environment. International environmental law had undergone extensive development and the obligations of States in that regard would be significantly affected by any use of nuclear weapons. Similarly, States had obligations in respect of health which would be violated by the use of nuclear weapons.

(5)   A literal interpretation was inappropriate in considering the obligations of States under the WHO Constitution, which had to be interpreted in the light of its object and purpose. The principle of speciality did not mean that there could be no overlap between the activities of the WHO and those of other organs and agencies of the United Nations.

(6)   The WHO's prior efforts in relation to peace, the use of weapons and the threat of nuclear war confirmed that the question posed by the WHO arose within the scope of its activities.

(7)   The objections raised by a minority of States to jurisdiction and admissibility should have been rejected. The Court had a duty to act as a judicial institution and as a principal organ of the United Nations.

(8)   The Court should have declared that the use of nuclear weapons would violate the obligations of States under international law in relation to health and the environment and the obligations of Member States under the WHO Constitution.

Dissenting Opinion of Judge Koroma   (1)   The decision that the Court lacked jurisdiction to respond to the request for an advisory opinion was unprecedented and contrary to the jurisprudence of the Court. The effects on health and the environment and the socio-economic effects of any use of nuclear weapons were matters of the utmost importance to the WHO, in view of the objects and purposes of that organisation. It was therefore unreal to say that the question posed by the WHO did not arise within the scope of its activities.

(2)   In the present case, the Court had taken an unduly narrow and restrictive view of its advisory jurisdiction. It should have paid far more attention to the broad objectives of the WHO. Seen in the light of those objectives, the question posed by the WHO clearly arose within the scope of its activities and thus fell within the jurisdiction of the Court. The previous case law of the Court had always indicated a liberal approach to jurisdictional questions in connection with requests for advisory opinions.

(3)   The WHO's question was not about the illegality of the use of nuclear weapons *per se* but about whether their use would be contrary to the obligations of States with regard to health and the environment and under the WHO Constitution. That Constitution, properly interpreted, and the practice of the WHO demonstrated the competence of the WHO in relation to this question and its concern with it.

(4)   International humanitarian law imposed specific obligations regarding the conduct of hostilities and the use of weapons which would be violated by the use of nuclear weapons. The use of nuclear weapons would also violate the obligations of States regarding the protection of the environment in time of war or armed conflict and the obligations of Member States under the WHO Constitution. Had the Court taken this opportunity to make that clear, its opinion could have assisted the WHO in preventive work.

There follows

Advisory Opinion of International Court of Justice on Legality of the Use by a State of Nuclear Weapons in Armed Conflict, 8 July 1996 (extract)

[66] 1. By a letter dated 27 August 1993, filed in the Registry on 3 September 1993, the Director-General of the World Health Organization (hereinafter called 'the WHO') officially communicated to the Registrar a decision taken by the World Health Assembly to submit a question to the Court for an advisory [67] opinion. The question is set forth in resolution WHA46.40 adopted by the Assembly on 14 May 1993. That resolution, certified copies of the English and French texts of which were enclosed with the said letter, reads as follows:

> The Forty-sixth World Health Assembly,
> Bearing in mind the principles laid down in the WHO Constitution;
> Noting the report of the Director-General on health and environmental effects of nuclear weapons;[3]
> Recalling resolutions WHA34.38, WHA36.28 and WHA40.24 on the effects of nuclear war on health and health services;

---

[2]   The declarations and opinions not reported in this volume are reproduced in *ICJ Reports* as follows: the declaration of Judge Ranjeva can be found at *ICJ Reports 1996*, p. 86; the declaration of Judge Ferrari Bravo can be found at *ICJ Reports 1996*, p. 87; the separate opinion of Judge Oda can be found at *ICJ Reports 1996*, p. 88; and the dissenting opinion of Judge Shahabuddeen can be found at *ICJ Reports 1996*, p. 97.

[3]   Document A46/30.

Recognizing that it has been established that no health service in the world can alleviate in any significant way a situation resulting from the use of even one single nuclear weapon;[4]

Recalling resolutions WHA42.26 on WHO's contribution to the international efforts towards sustainable development and WHA45.31 which draws attention to the effects on health of environmental degradation and recognizing the short- and long-term environmental consequences of the use of nuclear weapons that would affect human health for generations;

Recalling that primary prevention is the only appropriate means to deal with the health and environmental effects of the use of nuclear weapons;[5]

Noting the concern of the world health community about the continued threat to health and the environment from nuclear weapons;

Mindful of the role of WHO as defined in its Constitution to act as the directing and coordinating authority on international health work (Article 2 *(a)*); to propose conventions, agreements and regulations (Article 2 *(k)*); to report on administrative and social techniques affecting public health from preventive and curative points of view (Article 2 *(p)*); and to take all necessary action to attain the objectives of the Organization (Article 2 *(v)*);

Realizing that primary prevention of the health hazards of nuclear weapons requires clarity about the status in international law of their use, and that over the last 48 years marked differences of opinion have been expressed by Member States about the lawfulness of the use of nuclear weapons;

1. *Decides*, in accordance with Article 96 (2) of the Charter of the United Nations, Article 76 of the Constitution of the World Health Organization and Article X of the Agreement between the United Nations and the World Health Organization approved by the General Assembly of the United Nations on 15 November 1947 in its resolution 124 (II), to [**68**] request the International Court of Justice to give an advisory opinion on the following question:

> In view of the health and environmental effects, would the use of nuclear weapons by a State in war or other armed conflict be a breach of its obligations under international law including the WHO Constitution?

2. *Requests* the Director-General to transmit this resolution to the International Court of Justice, accompanied by all documents likely to throw light upon the question, in accordance with Article 65 of the Statute of the Court.

[. . .]

[**71**] [. . .] 10. The Court has the authority to give advisory opinions by virtue of Article 65 of its Statute, paragraph 1 of which reads as follows:

> The Court may give an advisory opinion on any legal question at the request of whatever body may be authorized by or in accordance with the Charter of the United Nations to make such a request.

It is also stated, in Article 96, paragraph 2, of the Charter that the

---

[4] See *Effects of Nuclear War on Health and Health Services* (2nd ed.), Geneva, WHO, 1987.
[5] [Ibid.]

specialized agencies, which may at any time be so authorized by the General Assembly, may also request advisory opinions of the Court on legal questions arising within the scope of their activities.

Consequently, three conditions must be satisfied in order to found the jurisdiction of the Court when a request for an advisory opinion is submitted to it by a specialized agency: the agency requesting the opinion must be duly authorized, under the Charter, to request opinions from the [72] Court; the opinion requested must be on a legal question; and this question must be one arising within the scope of the activities of the requesting agency (cf. *Application for Review of Judgement No. 273 of the United Nations Administrative Tribunal, Advisory Opinion, ICJ Reports 1982*, pp. 333–4).

[...]

12. There is thus no doubt that the WHO has been duly authorized, in accordance with Article 96, paragraph 2, of the Charter, to request advisory opinions of the Court. The first condition which must be met in order to found the competence of the Court in this case is thus fulfilled. Moreover, this point has not been disputed; and the Court has in the past agreed to deal with a request for an advisory opinion submitted by the WHO (see *Interpretation of the Agreement of 25 March 1951 between the WHO and Egypt, Advisory Opinion, ICJ Reports 1980*, pp. 73 *et seq.*).

[...]

[73] [...] 15. The Court must therefore first satisfy itself that the advisory opinion requested does indeed relate to a 'legal question' within the meaning of its Statute and the United Nations Charter.

The Court has already had occasion to indicate that questions

> framed in terms of law and rais[ing] problems of international law ... are by their very nature susceptible of a reply based on law ... [and] appear ... to be questions of a legal character (*Western Sahara, Advisory Opinion, ICJ Reports 1975*, p. 18, para. 15).

16. The question put to the Court by the World Health Assembly does in fact constitute a legal question, as the Court is requested to rule on whether,

> in view of the health and environmental effects, ... the use of nuclear weapons by a State in war or other armed conflict [would] be a breach of its obligations under international law including the WHO Constitution.

To do this, the Court must identify the obligations of States under the rules of law invoked, and assess whether the behaviour in question conforms to those obligations, thus giving an answer to the question posed based on law.

The fact that this question also has political aspects, as, in the nature of things, is the case with so many questions which arise in international life, does not suffice to deprive it of its character as a 'legal question' and to 'deprive the Court of a competence expressly conferred on it by its Statute' (*Application for Review of Judgement No. 158 of the United Nations Administrative Tribunal, Advisory Opinion, ICJ Reports 1973*, p. 172, para. 14). Whatever its political aspects, the Court cannot refuse to admit the legal character of a question which invites it to discharge an essentially judicial task, namely, an assessment of the legality of the possible conduct of States with regard to the obligations imposed upon them **[74]** by international law (cf. *Conditions of Admission of a State to Membership in the United Nations (Article 4 of Charter), Advisory Opinion, 1948, ICJ Reports 1947–1948*, pp. 61–2; *Competence of the General Assembly for the Admission of a State to the United Nations, Advisory Opinion, ICJ Reports 1950*, pp. 6–7; *Certain Expenses of the United Nations (Article 17, paragraph 2, of the Charter), Advisory Opinion, ICJ Reports 1962*, p. 155).

Furthermore, as the Court said in the Opinion it gave in 1980 concerning the *Interpretation of the Agreement of 25 March 1951 between the WHO and Egypt:*

> Indeed, in situations in which political considerations are prominent it may be particularly necessary for an international organization to obtain an advisory opinion from the Court as to the legal principles applicable with respect to the matter under debate, especially when these may include the interpretation of its constitution. (*ICJ Reports 1980*, p. 87, para. 33.)

17. The Court also finds that the political nature of the motives which may be said to have inspired the request and the political implications that the opinion given might have are of no relevance in the establishment of its jurisdiction to give such an opinion.

* *

18. The Court will now seek to determine whether the advisory opinion requested by the WHO relates to a question which arises 'within the scope of [the] activities' of that Organization, in accordance with Article 96, paragraph 2, of the Charter.

[...]

[76] [...] 21. Interpreted in accordance with their ordinary meaning, in their context and in the light of the object and purpose of the WHO Constitution, as well as of the practice followed by the Organization, the provisions of its Article 2 may be read as authorizing the Organization to deal with the effects on health of the use of nuclear weapons, or of any other hazardous activity, and to take preventive measures aimed at protecting the health of populations in the event of such weapons being used or such activities engaged in.

The question put to the Court in the present case relates, however, *not to the effects* of the use of nuclear weapons on health, but to the *legality* of the use of such weapons *in view of their health and environmental effects*. Whatever those effects might be, the competence of the WHO to deal with them is not dependent on the legality of the acts that caused them. Accordingly, it does not seem to the Court that the provisions of Article 2 of the WHO Constitution, interpreted in accordance with the criteria referred to above, can be understood as conferring upon the Organization a competence to address the legality of the use of nuclear weapons, and thus in turn a competence to ask the Court about that.

22. World Health Assembly resolution WHA46.40, by which the Court has been seised of this request for an opinion, expressly refers, in its Preamble, to the functions

indicated under subparagraphs *(a)*, *(k)*, *(p)* and *(v)* of Article 2 under consideration. These functions are defined as:

> *(a)*   to act as the directing and co-ordinating authority on international health work;
>
> . . .
>
> *(k)*   [77] to propose conventions, agreements and regulations, and make recommendations with respect to international health matters and to perform such duties as may be assigned thereby to the Organization and are consistent with its objective;
>
> . . .
>
> *(p)*   to study and report on, in co-operation with other specialized agencies where necessary, administrative and social techniques affecting public health and medical care from preventive and curative points of view, including hospital services and social security;
>
> . . .
>
> [and]
>
> *(v)*   generally to take all necessary action to attain the objective of the Organization.

In the view of the Court, none of these functions has a sufficient connection with the question before it for that question to be capable of being considered as arising 'within the scope of [the] activities' of the WHO. The causes of the deterioration of human health are numerous and varied; and the legal or illegal character of these causes is essentially immaterial to the measures which the WHO must in any case take in an attempt to remedy their effects. In particular, the legality or illegality of the use of nuclear weapons in no way determines the specific measures, regarding health or otherwise (studies, plans, procedures, etc.), which could be necessary in order to seek to prevent or cure some of their effects. Whether nuclear weapons are used legally or illegally, their effects on health would be the same. Similarly, while it is probable that the use of nuclear weapons might seriously prejudice the WHO's material capability to deliver all the necessary services in such an eventuality, for example, by making the affected areas inaccessible, this does not raise an issue falling within the scope of the Organization's activities within the meaning of Article 96, paragraph 2, of the Charter. The reference in the question put to the Court to the health and environmental effects, which according to the WHO the use of a nuclear weapon will always occasion, does not make the question one that falls within the WHO's functions.

23. However, in its Preamble, resolution WHA46.40 refers to 'primary prevention' in the following terms:

> Recalling that primary prevention is the only appropriate means to deal with the health and environmental effects of the use of nuclear weapons;[6]
>
> . . .
>
> [78] Realizing that primary prevention of the health hazards of nuclear weapons requires clarity about the status in international law of their use, and that over the last

---

[6] See *Effects of Nuclear War on Health and Health Services* (2nd ed.), Geneva, WHO, 1987.

48 years marked differences of opinion have been expressed by Member States about
the lawfulness of the use of nuclear weapons;

...

The document entitled *Effects of Nuclear War on Health and Health Services*, to which the
Preamble refers, is a report prepared in 1987 by the Management Group created by
the Director-General of the WHO in pursuance of World Health Assembly resolution
WHA36.28; this report updates another report on the same topic, which had been
prepared in 1983 by an international committee of experts in medical sciences and
public health, and whose conclusions had been approved by the Assembly in its above-
mentioned resolution. As several States have observed during the present proceedings,
the Management Group does indeed emphasize in its 1987 report that 'the only
approach to the treatment of health effects of nuclear warfare is primary prevention,
that is, the prevention of nuclear war' (Summary, p. 5, para. 7). However, the Group
states that 'it is not for [it] to outline the political steps by which this threat can
be removed or the preventive measures to be implemented' (*ibid.*, para. 8); and the
Group concludes:

> However, WHO can make important contributions to this process by systemati-
> cally distributing information on the health consequences of nuclear warfare and by
> expanding and intensifying international cooperation in the field of health. (*Ibid.*, para.
> 9.)

24. The WHO could only be competent to take those actions of 'primary prevention' which fall within the functions of the Organization as defined in Article 2 of
its Constitution. In consequence, the references to this type of prevention which are
made in the Preamble to resolution WHA46.40 and the link there suggested with the
question of the legality of the use of nuclear weapons do not affect the conclusions
reached by the Court in paragraph 22 above.

25. The Court need hardly point out that international organizations are subjects
of international law which do not, unlike States, possess a general competence.
International organizations are governed by the 'principle of speciality', that is to say,
they are invested by the States which create them with powers, the limits of which are
a function of the common interests whose promotion those States entrust to them.
[...]

[79] [...] In the opinion of the Court, to ascribe to the WHO the competence
to address the legality of the use of nuclear weapons – even in view of their health
and environmental effects – would be tantamount to disregarding the principle of
speciality; for such competence could not be deemed a necessary implication of the
Constitution of the Organization in the light of the purposes assigned to it by its
member States.

26. The World Health Organization is, moreover, an international organization
of a particular kind. As indicated in the Preamble and confirmed by Article 69 of
its Constitution, 'the Organization shall be brought into relation with the United

Nations as one of the specialized agencies referred to in Article 57 of the Charter of the United Nations'. Article 57 of the Charter defines 'specialized agencies' as follows:

> 1. The various specialized agencies, established by intergovernmental agreement and having wide international responsibilities, as defined in their basic instruments, in economic, social, cultural, educational, health, and related fields, shall be brought into relationship with the United Nations in accordance with the provisions of Article 63.
>
> [80] 2. Such agencies thus brought into relationship with the United Nations are hereinafter referred to as 'specialized agencies'.

Article 58 of the Charter reads:

> The Organization shall make recommendations for the co-ordination of the policies and activities of the specialized agencies.

Article 63 of the Charter then provides:

> 1. The Economic and Social Council may enter into agreements with any of the agencies referred to in Article 57, defining the terms on which the agency concerned shall be brought into relationship with the United Nations. Such agreements shall be subject to approval by the General Assembly.
>
> 2. It may co-ordinate the activities of the specialized agencies through consultation with and recommendations to such agencies and through recommendations to the General Assembly and to the Members of the United Nations.

As these provisions demonstrate, the Charter of the United Nations laid the basis of a 'system' designed to organize international co-operation in a coherent fashion by bringing the United Nations, invested with powers of general scope, into relationship with various autonomous and complementary organizations, invested with sectorial powers. The exercise of these powers by the organizations belonging to the 'United Nations system' is co-ordinated, notably, by the relationship agreements concluded between the United Nations and each of the specialized agencies. In the case of the WHO, the agreement of 10 July 1948 between the United Nations and that Organization actually refers to the WHO Constitution in the following terms in Article I:

> The United Nations recognizes the World Health Organization as the specialized agency responsible for taking such action as may be appropriate under its Constitution for the accomplishment of the objectives set forth therein.

It follows from the various instruments mentioned above that the WHO Constitution can only be interpreted, as far as the powers conferred upon that Organization are concerned, by taking due account not only of the general principle of speciality, but also of the logic of the overall system contemplated by the Charter. If, according to the rules on which that system is based, the WHO has, by virtue of Article 57 of the Charter, 'wide international responsibilities', those responsibilities are necessarily restricted to the sphere of public 'health' and cannot encroach on the responsibilities of other parts of the United Nations system. And there is no doubt that questions concerning the use of force, the regulation of armaments and disarmament are within the competence of the United Nations and lie outside that of the specialized agencies. Besides, any other conclusion would render virtually meaningless the notion of a specialized agency; it is difficult to imagine what other meaning that [81] notion could have if such an organization need only show that the use of certain weapons could affect its objectives in order to be empowered to concern itself with the legality of such use. It is therefore difficult to maintain that, by authorizing various specialized agencies to request opinions from the Court under Article 96, paragraph 2, of the Charter, the General Assembly intended to allow them to seise the Court of questions belonging within the competence of the United Nations.

For all these reasons, the Court considers that the question raised in the request for an advisory opinion submitted to it by the WHO does not arise 'within the scope of [the] activities' of that Organization as defined by its Constitution.

27. A consideration of the practice of the WHO bears out these conclusions. None of the reports and resolutions referred to in the Preamble to World Health Assembly resolution WHA46.40 is in the nature of a practice of the WHO in regard to the legality of the threat or use of nuclear weapons. The Report of the Director-General (doc. A46/30), referred to in the third paragraph of the Preamble, the aforementioned resolutions WHA34.38 and WHA36.28, as well as resolution WHA40.24, all of which are referred to in the fourth paragraph, as well as the above-mentioned report of the Management Group of 1987 to which reference is made in the fifth and seventh paragraphs, deal exclusively, in the case of the first, with the health and environmental *effects* of nuclear weapons, and in the case of the remainder, with the *effects* of nuclear weapons on health and health services. As regards resolutions WHA42.26 and WHA45.31, referred to in the sixth paragraph of the Preamble to resolution WHA46.40, the first concerns the WHO's contribution to international efforts towards sustainable development and the second deals with the effects on health of environmental degradation. None of these reports and resolutions deals with the legality of the use of nuclear weapons.

Resolution WHA46.40 itself, adopted, not without opposition, as soon as the question of the legality of the use of nuclear weapons was raised at the WHO, could not be taken to express or to amount on its own to a practice establishing an agreement between the members of the Organization to interpret its Constitution as empowering it to address the question of the legality of the use of nuclear weapons.

Nowhere else does the Court find any practice of this kind. In particular, such a practice cannot be inferred from isolated passages of certain resolutions of the World Health Assembly cited during the present proceedings, such as resolution WHA15.51 on the role of the physician in the preservation and development of peace, resolution WHA22.58 concerning co-operation between the WHO and the United Nations in regard to chemical and bacteriological weapons and the effects of their [82] possible use, and resolution WHA42.24 concerning the embargo placed on medical supplies for political reasons and restrictions on their movement. The Court has also noted that the WHO regularly takes account of various rules of international law in the exercise of its functions; that it participates in certain activities undertaken in the legal sphere at the international level – for example, for the purpose of drawing up an international code of practice on transboundary movements of radioactive waste; and that it participates in certain international conferences for the progressive development and codification of international law. That the WHO, as a subject of international law, should be led to apply the rules of international law or concern itself with their development is in no way surprising; but it does not follow that it has received a mandate, beyond the terms of its Constitution, itself to address the legality or illegality of the use of weaponry in hostilities.

[. . .]

[84] [. . .] 31. Having arrived at the view that the request for an advisory opinion submitted by the WHO does not relate to a question which arises 'within the scope of [the] activities' of that Organization in accordance with Article 96, paragraph 2, of the Charter, the Court finds that an essential condition of founding its jurisdiction in the present case is absent and that it cannot, accordingly, give the opinion requested. Consequently, the Court is not called upon to examine the arguments which were laid before it with regard to the exercise of its discretionary power to give an opinion.

*

*   *

32. For these reasons,

THE COURT,

By eleven votes to three,

Finds that it is not able to give the advisory opinion which was requested of it under World Health Assembly resolution WHA46.40 dated 14 May 1993.

IN FAVOUR: *President* Bedjaoui; *Vice-President* Schwebel; *Judges* Oda, Guillaume, Ranjeva, Herczegh, Shi, Fleischhauer, Vereshchetin, Ferrari Bravo, Higgins; AGAINST: *Judges* Shahabuddeen, Weeramantry, Koroma.

[. . .]

DISSENTING OPINION OF JUDGE WEERAMANTRY (EXTRACT)

[. . .]

[104] *I. Preliminary*

It has been argued that the question asked by the World Health Organization (WHO) travels outside its legitimate concerns. The Court has accepted that argument. I respectfully dissent.

The question on which WHO seeks the Court's opinion is as follows:

> In view of the health and environmental effects, would the use of nuclear weapons by a State in war or other armed conflict be a breach of its obligations under international law including the WHO Constitution?

I read this question as containing an enquiry in relation to State obligations in three particular areas:

(a)　State obligations in regard to health;

(b)　State obligations in regard to the environment; and

(c)　State obligations under the WHO Constitution.

This opinion will endeavour to show that the question asked is directly within WHO's legitimate and mandated area of concern. It relates to an issue fundamental to global health. It relates to the integrity of the human environment which is fundamental to global health. It relates to the fundamental constitutional objective of WHO, which is the attainment by all peoples of the highest possible level of health.

[...]

[139] [...] *IV. State obligations*

1. State obligations in regard to the environment

The Court is asked whether the use of nuclear weapons is a breach of State obligations in relation to the environment. The Court has not considered this question. The Court's Opinion (para. 16) states that

> **[140]** the Court must identify the obligations of States under the rules of law invoked, and assess whether the behaviour in question conforms to those obligations, thus giving an answer to the question posed based on law,

but does not proceed to identify and examine those obligations in order to answer the question. I consider that it needs more attention. It is moreover an area very much within the legitimate concerns of WHO.

The question asked by WHO affords the Court an opportunity for contributing to an important aspect of this development, for it focuses attention on the vital question of the duties of States in regard to the environment. I regret this opportunity has not been taken by the Court.

(a) The progress of environmental law

From rather hesitant and tentative beginnings, environmental law has progressed rapidly under the combined stimulus of ever more powerful means of inflicting irreversible environmental damage and an ever increasing awareness of the fragility of the global environment. Together these have brought about a universal concern with activities that may damage the global environment, which is the common inheritance of all nations, great and small. To use the words of a well-known text on international environmental law:

> The global environment constitutes a huge, intricate, delicate and interconnected web in which a touch here or palpitation there sends tremors throughout the whole system. Obligations *erga omnes*, rules *jus cogens*, and international crimes respond to this state of affairs by permitting environmental wrongs to be guarded against by all nations.[7]

---

[7] *International Environmental Law and World Order*, Guruswamy, Palmer and Weston, 1994, p. 344.

Such compelling facts do not admit of any exceptions, however powerful the actor or compelling the purpose, for it is increasingly clear that what is at stake can well be the very survival of humanity. Nuclear weapons bring us to such a limit situation, and therefore attract the principles of environmental law. As was observed in the preamble of the Treaty of Tlatelolco:

> nuclear weapons, whose terrible effects are suffered, indiscriminately and inexorably, by military forces and civilian population alike, constitute, through the persistence of the radioactivity they release, an attack on the integrity of the human species and ultimately may even render the whole earth uninhabitable.

[141] *(b) The growth of the notion of State obligations*

The Declaration of the United Nations Conference on the Human Environment (Stockholm), adopted on 16 June 1972, was designed to 'inspire and guide the peoples of the world in the preservation and enhancement of the human environment'. Principle 1 of that Declaration states that:

> Man has the fundamental right to freedom, equality and adequate conditions of life, in an environment of a quality that permits a life of dignity and well-being, and he bears a solemn responsibility to protect and improve the environment for present and future generations . . .

Principle 21 has a direct relevance to WHO's enquiry, for it deals specifically with the *obligation of States* not to damage or endanger significantly the environment beyond their jurisdiction. Principle 2 of the Rio Declaration gives expression to the same principle. Both may be said to be articulations, in the context of the environment, of general principles of customary law. In the words of *Corfu Channel*, there is a 'general and well-recognized' principle that every State is under an 'obligation not to allow knowingly its territory to be used for acts contrary to the rights of other States' (*ICJ Reports 1949*, p. 22).

Principle 24 of the Rio Declaration on Environment and Development (1992), whereby States are called upon to 'respect international law providing protection for the environment in times of armed conflict and cooperate in its further development, as necessary', is a further expression of this general principle. It cannot therefore be gainsaid that the concept of State responsibility in regard to the environment is today an established part of international law.

(c) Active and passive State obligations

There is a State obligation lying upon every member State of the community of nations to protect the environment, not merely in the negative sense of refraining from causing harm, but in the positive sense of contributing affirmatively to the improvement of the environment. A wide recognition of this principle was evidenced when, in 1971, the General Assembly affirmed 'the responsibility of the international community to *take action* to preserve and enhance the environment' (General Assembly resolution 2849 (XXVI); emphasis added).

For the purposes of the present case, however, it is not necessary to enter the area of *active* State responsibility to conserve the environment – an aspect now receiving increasing attention. The *passive* responsibility not to damage the environment is sufficient for the purposes of this [142] case, for it is patently clear that any State action which damages the environment in the way that nuclear weapons do is a violation of the obligation of environmental protection which modern international law places upon States. A contrary view would negative the basic logic of environmental law and send a tremor through the foundations of this vital subdiscipline of modern international law.

(d) The juristic nature of State obligations

In relation to environmental obligations, the notion is evolving of duties owed *erga omnes* and of rights assertible *erga omnes*, irrespective of the compartmentalization of the planetary population into nation States.

The concept of an *erga omnes* right is not new. In 1915, the eminent American jurist, Elihu Root, who later became a member of the Committee which drafted the Statute of the Permanent Court, stated, in a paper on 'The Outlook for International Law':

> Wherever in the world the laws which should protect the independence of nations, the inviolability of their territory, the lives and property of their citizens, are violated, all other nations have a right to protest against the breaking down of the law.[8]

Such thinking is the background against which the damage caused to the environment must be considered, for the purpose of ascertaining whether the use of a nuclear weapon by a State is in conflict with State obligations under international law.

The concept of obligations *erga omnes* has, of course, received recognition in the Court's jurisprudence, though in a different context, in *Barcelona Traction, Light and Power Company, Limited, Second Phase (ICJ Reports 1970,* p. 3).

Indeed, in some areas, modern discussions of State responsibility take the matter even further, to elevate serious breach of State duty in regard to the environment to the level of an international crime when they state that:

> a serious breach of an international obligation of essential importance for the safeguarding and preservation of the human environment, such as those prohibiting massive pollution of the atmosphere or of the seas

may result in an international crime.[9]

---

[8] *Proceedings of the American Society of International Law*, 1915, Vol. 2, pp. 7–9, cited in Guruswamy, Palmer and Weston, *op. cit.*, p. 345.

[9] International Law Commission, Draft Article 19 (3) (*d*) on State Responsibility, *Yearbook of the International Law Commission*, 1976, Vol. II, Part II, p. 96.

It is not necessary for present purposes to examine the various levels of State obligations in respect of the environment, which may range from **[143]** obligations *erga omnes*, through obligations which are in the nature of *jus cogens*, all the way up to the level of international crime.

(e) Multilateral treaty obligations

There have been, since the Stockholm Declaration of the United Nations Conference on the Human Environment (1972), over one hundred multilateral environmental instruments which are in force. A United Nations Environment Programme is in force, major instruments have been signed regarding the law of the sea, transboundary pollution, hazardous waste, nuclear accidents, the ozone layer, endangered species – to name but a few. The United Nations Environment Programme register of multilateral treaties affecting the environment revealed as many as 152 treaties in May 1991.[10]

The multifarious international instruments relating to the environment, to which reference has been made, build up the rising tide of international acceptance which creates in its totality a universal acceptance of State obligation which in turn translates itself into law. All of the areas they deal with are areas affected by the nuclear weapon to an extent which is impermissible under these instruments, had the damage been caused by any other agency.

The areas named are a small sample of the areas of State obligations under international law which are affected by the nuclear weapon. What WHO wants to know, in view of the close linkage of a pure environment with human health, is whether there is a breach of such State obligations when a State uses a nuclear weapon. It cannot, in my view, be denied this information, which lies at the very heart of its constitutional mandate of safeguarding global health.

[. . .]

[169] [. . .] *VIII. Conclusion*

For the reasons set out above, it seems clear that
1. WHO has an interest in matters of global health, even though they also concern questions of peace and security.
2. WHO has an interest in environmental matters, even though they also concern questions of peace and security.
3. The fact that other organs in the United Nations system are expressly charged with responsibilities in the area of peace and security does not preclude WHO from concerning itself with matters of peace and security to the extent that they affect global health and the global environment.
4. There are compelling medical and environmental reasons which require WHO to take an interest in the matter on which it seeks an opinion.

---

[10] See Geoffrey Palmer, 'New Ways to Make International Environmental Law'. *American Journal of International Law*, 1992, Vol. 86, p. 262.

5. There are several constitutional provisions rendering the requested opinion relevant to WHO.
6. The impossibility of curative steps forces WHO into the area of prevention.
7. WHO has a legitimate interest in knowing whether the use of nuclear weapons constitutes a violation of State obligations in relation to health.
8. WHO has a legitimate interest in knowing whether the use of nuclear weapons constitutes a violation of State obligations in relation to the environment.
9. WHO has a legitimate interest in knowing whether State obligations under its own Constitution are violated by the use of nuclear weapons.
10. *There are State obligations under international law in regard to health which would be violated by the use of nuclear weapons.*
11. *There are State obligations under international law in regard to the environment which would be violated by the use of nuclear weapons.*
12. *There are State obligations under international law in regard to the WHO Constitution which would be violated by the use of nuclear weapons.*

DISSENTING OPINION OF JUDGE KOROMA (EXTRACT)

[. . .]

[**175**] [. . .] *Health-related environmental effects of the use of nuclear weapons*
Effects of actual use
Furthermore and according to the material, within the extensive destruction of the built environment, a nuclear explosion would destroy public health and sanitary facilities, thus opening the way for the spread of disease. Water supplies would be contaminated not only by radioactivity but also by pathogenic bacteria and viruses; sewage treatment and waste disposal facilities would almost completely disappear.

Great numbers of putrefying human bodies and animal carcasses as well as untreated waste and sewage would provide an easy breeding ground for flies and other insects. Diseases like salmonellosis (food [**176**] poisoning), shigellosis (dysentery), infectious hepatitis, amoebic dysentery, malaria, typhus, streptococcal and staphylococcal infections (pus-producing), respiratory infections and tuberculosis would occur in epidemic form over vast areas.

In addition to the acquired health risk for survivors from high-dose external radiation, the report points out that longer-lived radioisotopes would lead to a risk for the population over a large area and over long periods. An impaired immune system would contribute later to an increased incidence of cancer.

With regard to environmental effects, the report states that if a number of powerful nuclear weapons were used at the same time, global environmental disturbance and climatic changes would take place. As regards trees, evergreens would be especially vulnerable to radiation, coniferous forests would be liable to suffer most, whereas weeds which are more resistant would proliferate. Radiation, the report continued, would be harmful to crops and the food chain; livestock would be harmed and milk and meat products contaminated. Plant pests which are particularly resistant would abound. The marine ecosystem would become contaminated and suffer similarly. For all practical intents, the report points out, there would be a severe shortage of edible and sustaining substances, at a time when the victims' needs were greatest.

Thus, in a conflict involving the use of nuclear weapons, climatic and environmental changes would occur with extensive health implications.

The socio-economic effects of the use of nuclear weapons
While noting the socio-economic impact of the use of nuclear weapons, the report finds that this would be devastating. After a nuclear war, besides the extensive breakdown of health facilities, attendant social structures, the economic system, communication lines and the very fabric of society would be severely disrupted.
   [...]
   [**180**] [...] In the light of the foregoing, to hold as the Court has done, that these matters do not lie within the competence or scope of activities of the WHO borders on the unreal and smacks of cynicism, and the law is not cynical.
   [...]

[**185**] [...] *Environmental obligations*
The environmental obligations assumed by States, it is also argued, would be violated by the use of nuclear weapons. Such obligations are said to be found in various international legal instruments, among which is the 1907 Hague Convention IV Respecting the Laws and Customs of War on Land, Article 55 of which states that:

> The occupying State shall be regarded only as administrator and usufructuary of public buildings, real estate, forests, and agricultural estates belonging to the hostile State, and situated in the occupied country. It must safeguard the capital of these properties, and administer them in accordance with the rules of usufruct.

This principle is said to be further reflected in the 1949 Geneva Convention IV relative to the Protection of Civilian Persons in Time of War, Article 53 of which provides as follows:

> Any destruction by the Occupying Power of real or personal property belonging individually or collectively to private persons, or to the State, or to other public authorities, or to social or cooperative organizations, is prohibited, except where such destruction is rendered absolutely necessary by military operations.

The 1977 Additional Protocol I to the 1949 Geneva Conventions was also invoked as having imposed obligations on environmental protection against military activities. The provisions of the Protocol in this regard [**186**] were said to represent the development of the relevant principles embodied in the 1899 and 1907 Hague Conventions. Article 35 of Protocol I – Basic Rules – stipulates that

> 1. In any armed conflict, the right of the Parties to the conflict to choose methods or means of warfare is not unlimited.
>
> . . .
>
> 3. It is prohibited to employ methods or means of warfare which are intended, or may be expected, to cause widespread, long-term and severe damage to the natural environment.

Article 53 declares that

> Without prejudice to the provisions of the Hague Convention for the Protection of Cultural Property in the Event of Armed Conflict of 14 May 1954, and of other relevant international instruments, it is prohibited:
>
> . . .
>
> (c) to make such objects the object of reprisals.

According to Article 54,

> 1. Starvation of civilians as a method of warfare is prohibited.
> 2. It is prohibited to attack, destroy, remove or render useless objects indispensable to the survival of the civilian population, such as foodstuffs, agricultural areas for the production of foodstuffs, crops, livestock, drinking water installations and supplies and irrigation works, for the specific purpose of denying them for their sustenance value to the civilian population or to the adverse Party, whatever the motive, whether in order to starve out civilians, to cause them to move away, or for any other motive.
>
> . . .
>
> 4. These objects shall not be made the object of reprisals.

Article 55 obliges States to observe the following during military conflict in relation to the natural environment

> 1. Care shall be taken in warfare to protect the natural environment against widespread, long-term and severe damage. This protection includes a prohibition of the use of methods or means of warfare which are intended or may be expected to cause such damage to the natural environment and thereby to prejudice the health or survival of the population.
> 2. Attacks against the natural environment by way of reprisals are prohibited.

The general prohibition of Article 55 of the Protocol is said to be made more specific in Article 56, which provides that 'dams, dykes and nuclear electrical generating stations' shall not be made the object of attack [187] 'even where these objects are military objectives'. Article 56, paragraph 1, forbids attack upon military objectives located at or in the vicinity of these works or installations

> if such attack may cause the release of dangerous forces and consequent severe losses among the civilian population. Other military objectives located at or in the vicinity of these works or installations shall not be made the object of attack if such attack may cause the release of dangerous forces from the works or installations and consequent severe losses among the civilian population.

Also considered relevant is the Rio Declaration on Environment and Development, which was adopted during the Rio Conference in 1992 and which stipulates that

> Warfare is inherently destructive of sustainable development. States shall therefore respect international law providing protection for the environment in times of armed conflict and co-operate in its further development, as necessary. (Principle 24.)

It was submitted that States would be in breach of their legal obligations were nuclear weapons, given their established characteristics, to be used in war or other armed conflict, as such use would violate the obligations undertaken by States in relation to the protection of the natural environment.

[. . .]

[215] [. . .] *Environmental obligations*
As far as the environmental obligations assumed by States are concerned, these are to be found both in customary international law and in the provisions of treaties as well. Taken together, they impose legal restraints against environmental warfare *per se* or the means of waging it. Article 25 of the Hague Convention IV of 1907 prohibits, as we have seen, '*attack* or bombardment by *whatever* means of towns, villages, dwellings or buildings which are undefended' (emphasis added). Belligerent parties are prohibited, directly or indirectly, from inflicting unnecessary damage on the environment.

The Geneva Protocol of 1925 is also relevant in this connection as it prohibits the use in war of chemical or biological agents, and the Bacteriological and Toxin Weapons Convention of 1972 prohibits the possession of biological agents.

Articles 53 and 147 of the 1949 Fourth Geneva Convention also provide a degree of indirect protection for the environment, in the context of protecting property rights in occupied territories. Thus, an occupying Power which destroys, for example, industrial installations in an occupied territory, causing consequent damage to the environment, would be in breach of its obligations under the Convention, provided that such destruction was not justified by military necessity. If such destruction is extensive, it would constitute a grave breach of the Convention, or even a war crime, in accordance with Article 147.

Article 35 of Additional Protocol I of 1977 also prohibits the employment of methods or means of warfare which are intended or may be expected to cause widespread, long-term and severe damage to the natural environment; Article 55, as we have seen, imposes an obligation upon States Parties to take care in warfare to protect the natural environment against such damage; Article 54 protects objects indispensable to the survival of the civilian population; while Article 56 protects certain installations containing dangerous forces, namely dams, dykes and nuclear electrical generating stations which are not to be made the object of [216] attack, even where those objects are military objectives, if such attack might cause the release of dangerous forces and consequent severe losses among the civilian population. Other military objectives located at or in the vicinity of these works or installations are not to be made the object of attack if such attack may cause the release of dangerous forces from the works or installations and consequent severe losses among the civilian population.

Also considered applicable to the question under consideration is the 1977 Convention on the Modification of the Environment. The Convention prohibits the hostile use of environmental modification techniques having 'widespread, long-lasting or severe effects "as the means of damage"'. An environmental modification technique is defined as any technique for changing – through the 'deliberate manipulation' of natural processes – the dynamics, composition or structure of space or of the earth, including its atmosphere, lithosphere, hydrosphere and biota.

Also relevant, in this connection, is the principle of environmental security intended to secure the environment and given expression in Principle 24 of the Rio Declaration on Environment and Development to the effect that

> Warfare is inherently destructive of sustainable development. States shall therefore respect international law providing protection for the environment in times of armed conflict and co-operate in its future development, as necessary.

It is thus in terms of these obligations that the health and environmental effects produced by the use of nuclear weapons are to be judged. According to the available material, nuclear weapons when used did, in an instant, take a tremendous toll of human lives. Estimates of the number of people who had died by the end of 1945 following the atomic bombing of Hiroshima and Nagasaki amounted to approximately 140,000 in Hiroshima and 74,000 in Nagasaki. Of the people who were exposed to thermal radiation, 90 to 100 per cent died within a week. In addition to direct injury from the bomb blasts, death was said to have been caused by several interrelated factors such as being crushed under buildings, injuries caused by splinters of glass, radiation damage, food shortages or shortages of doctors and medical personnel. Over 320,000 people who survived but were affected by radiation still suffer from various malignant tumours caused by radiation, including leukaemia, thyroid cancer, breast cancer, lung cancer, gastric cancer, cataracts and a variety of other after-effects.

[217] From another source that had experienced the effects of the use of nuclear weapons, the Court learned that the explosion that took place on the island had caused what looked like a snowfall for the first time in its people's history. Such 'snow', it was later discovered, was in fact radioactive fallout from the nuclear explosion. As a result of the contamination to which their bodies were exposed, the islanders experienced blisters and other sores over the weeks that followed. Their serious internal and external exposure to radioactivity caused them long-term health problems that have affected four generations of the island's inhabitants. Such effects are said to be indistinguishable from poison, a 'substance which when introduced into the body can kill or cause injury to health'. Uranium, a central component of nuclear weapons, is regarded as one of the most toxic substances. Accordingly, when used, nuclear weapons would expose human beings to effects indistinguishable from those of poison. Such use would be in breach of the obligations prohibiting the use of poison

or poisonous weapons. The effects could also be both long-term, intergenerational and affect a wide area as well.

Yet, the detonations which took place in Hiroshima and Nagasaki, as well as the nuclear explosions in the Marshall Islands, have been considered relatively minor when compared to the destructive power of today's nuclear weapons. As we have seen, a massive nuclear attack on modern cities like Boston or London would result in the death of millions of people. The use of such weapons would produce delayed radioactive fallout across potentially great distances and over extended periods of time. The radiation effects, it is said, are not unlike effects produced by chemical and biological weapons. As opposed to conventional weapons, nuclear weapons, even those with fairly low yields, are capable of causing harm to non-combatants – including civilians – and neutral parties alike.

On the basis of the material before the Court, and in view of their health and environmental consequences, it is undeniable that nuclear weapons when used would be in breach of the obligations assumed by States under international law. These obligations include:

(i) a limitation on the choice of methods and means of warfare;

(ii) the prohibition from using poison or poisonous weapons intended to cause unnecessary suffering;

(iii) the prohibition from causing unnecessary and superfluous suffering;

(iv) the requirement that belligerent parties respect the distinction between military objectives and non-military objects, as well as between persons participating in the hostilities and members of the civilian population;

(v) the prohibition of armed attacks against the civilian population;

(vi) [218] the prohibition of wanton destruction of cities, towns or villages, or devastation not justified by military necessity;

(vii) the requirement not to attack, or bombard, by whatever means undefended towns, villages, dwellings or buildings;

(viii) the requirement not to employ methods or means of warfare which are intended or may be expected to cause widespread, long-term and severe damage to the natural environment.

It is also clear that, because of their health and environmental effects, the use of nuclear weapons would be in breach of the provisions of the WHO Constitution, whose objective is the attainment by all peoples of the highest possible level of health. Health, it will be recalled, is defined as a state of complete physical, mental and social well-being, and the WHO is enjoined to promote and protect the health of all peoples, by, among other activities, directing and co-ordinating international health, assisting Governments upon request to strengthen health services, promoting material and child health and welfare and fostering the ability to live harmoniously in a changing environment.

Given the health and environmental effects of nuclear weapons, a State that is a party to the Constitution of the WHO and which uses nuclear weapons will be in breach of both the letter and spirit of that Constitution which, *inter alia*, calls for the co-operation of individuals and States for the attainment of health and peace by all peoples as well as the objective of the Organization itself.

The Court, in its Opinion, has stated that having found that it lacked jurisdiction in the present case, it could not examine the arguments which were expounded before it with regard to the propriety of giving such an Opinion. This position notwithstanding, it is my view that if the Court had allowed itself to consider the abundance of material at its disposal, it could have reached a different conclusion other than the one arrived at.

[. . .]

[**223**] [. . .] On the basis of the aforesaid, I find that the Court's Opinion is inadequately reasoned, has failed to address the crucial issues raised and is inconsistent with its jurisprudence. I, therefore, find myself unable to concur with it. On the other hand, and on the basis of the material before the Court, applying the law to that material, I am of the firm conviction that a State would be in breach of its obligations under international law, including the WHO Constitution, were it to use nuclear weapons in war [**224**] or other armed conflict in view of the health and environmental consequences. To put a question of this kind to the Court is indeed within the competence and scope of the activities of the WHO.

[Reports: *ICJ Reports 1996*, p. 66; 110 *ILR* 1 at p. 6]

Legality of the Threat or Use of Nuclear Weapons (Request by the United Nations General Assembly for an Advisory Opinion)[1]

International Court of Justice, The Hague

8 July 1996 (Bedjaoui, *President*; Schwebel, *Vice-President*; Oda, Guillaume, Shahabuddeen, Weeramantry, Ranjeva, Herczegh, Shi, Fleischhauer, Koroma, Vereshchetin, Ferrari Bravo and Higgins, *Judges*)

Hazardous activities and substances – nuclear weapons – effect of use of nuclear weapons upon the environment

Human rights – war – nuclear weapons – whether human rights treaties applicable to military operations in time of armed conflict – right to life – International Covenant on Civil and Political Rights, 1966 – relationship between the law of human rights and international humanitarian law

International humanitarian law – relationship between international environmental law and international humanitarian law – Principle 24, Rio Declaration – United Nations Environmental Modification Treaty, 1977 – Additional Protocol I, 1977, Article 35(3)

International organisations – United Nations – General Assembly – competence – security issues – nuclear weapons – role of the Assembly in view of involvement of the Security Council – whether Assembly competent to request advisory opinion from the International Court of Justice – resolutions of the General Assembly – whether a source of law – normative significance of resolutions in the light of the practice of States

Jurisdiction – International Court of Justice – advisory jurisdiction – request by United Nations General Assembly – request for advisory opinion concerning whether the use or threat of use of nuclear weapons permitted under international law – whether within the jurisdiction of the Court – United

---

[1] The Advisory Opinion given by the Court in response to a request by the World Health Organization, which also concerned the legality of using nuclear weapons, is reported at p. 212 above.

Nations Charter, Article 96(1) – discretion of Court not to reply to question – Statute of the Court, Article 65(1) – whether question posed a legal question – whether motives for asking the question relevant – role of the Court in advisory proceedings

Sources of international law – custom – requirements of custom – importance of actual State practice – persistent objector principle – opinio juris – United Nations General Assembly resolutions – normative significance – resolutions on the use of nuclear weapons

Treaties – treaties for the protection of the environment – whether applicable to military operations in time of armed conflict

War and armed conflict – nuclear weapons – whether use or threat of use of nuclear weapons lawful – applicable law – relevance of law on the environment and human rights

SUMMARY   *The facts*   In 1994, the United Nations General Assembly adopted Resolution 49/75 K, which requested that the International Court of Justice urgently render an advisory opinion on the following question:

Is the threat or use of nuclear weapons in any circumstance permitted under international law?

Resolution 49/75 K was adopted by seventy-eight votes to forty-three, with thirty-eight abstentions. At the time that it was adopted, the International Court already had before it a request for an advisory opinion on a question regarding the legality of the use of nuclear weapons, submitted by the World Health Organization ('WHO'). In the preamble of Resolution 49/75 K, the General Assembly expressly welcomed the request by the WHO. Twenty-eight States submitted written statements to the Court regarding the General Assembly's request. In November 1995, the Court held hearings which dealt with both the General Assembly and WHO requests. Twenty-two States participated.

Held by the International Court of Justice

Dispositif
    (by thirteen votes to one)   (1)   The Court decided to comply with the request for an advisory opinion.
    (unanimously)   (2)(A)   There was in neither customary nor conventional international law any specific authorisation of the threat or use of nuclear weapons;

(by eleven votes to three)   (B)   In neither customary nor conventional international law was there any comprehensive and universal prohibition of the threat or use of nuclear weapons as such;

(unanimously)   (C)   A threat or use of force by means of nuclear weapons that was contrary to Article 2, paragraph 4, of the United Nations Charter and that failed to meet all the requirements of Article 51 was unlawful;

(unanimously)   (D)   A threat or use of nuclear weapons should also be compatible with the requirements of the international law applicable in armed conflict, particularly those of the principles and rules of international humanitarian law, as well as with specific obligations under treaties and other undertakings which expressly deal with nuclear weapons;

(by seven votes to seven, by the President's casting vote)   (E)   It followed from the above-mentioned requirements that the threat or use of nuclear weapons would generally be contrary to the rules of international law applicable in armed conflict, and in particular the principles and rules of humanitarian law. However, in view of the current state of international law, and of the elements of fact at its disposal, the Court could not conclude definitively whether the threat or use of nuclear weapons would be lawful or unlawful in an extreme circumstance of self-defence, in which the very survival of a State would be at stake;

(unanimously)   (F)   There existed an obligation to pursue in good faith and bring to a conclusion negotiations leading to nuclear disarmament in all its aspects under strict and effective international control.

Jurisdiction to respond to the question posed by the General Assembly   (1) The Court had jurisdiction to respond to the question posed by the General Assembly.

(a)   Article 96(1) of the United Nations Charter provided that the General Assembly was competent to request an advisory opinion on any legal question. Even if there was an implied limitation that the question had to be one which arose within the scope of the Assembly's activities, that requirement was satisfied. The competence of the Assembly and the Security Council to request advisory opinions under Article 96(1) was not confined to those circumstances in which the organ in question was empowered to take binding decisions.

(b)   The question posed by the General Assembly required the Court to identify the obligations of States under the rules of law invoked and to assess whether the behaviour in question conformed to those obligations. It was therefore a legal question. The fact that the question also had political aspects did not deprive it of its character as a legal question. Moreover, in situations where political considerations were prominent, it might be particularly necessary for an international organisation to obtain an advisory opinion regarding the legal issues involved. The political motives which might have inspired the request and the political implications which an opinion might have were irrelevant in determining whether or not the Court possessed jurisdiction.

(2) Once it was established that the Court had jurisdiction, Article 65(1) of the Statute of the Court nevertheless gave the Court a discretion as to whether or not to give an advisory opinion. Only compelling reasons, however, should lead the Court to decline to give an opinion in a case in which it had jurisdiction. No such compelling reasons existed in the present case.

(a) The criticism of some States that the question posed was 'vague and abstract' was misplaced. The fact that the question posed did not relate to a specific dispute was not a reason for declining to give an opinion. The advisory jurisdiction was not intended to resolve disputes between States. Nor did the nature of the question mean that the Court would be required to construct hypothetical scenarios regarding possible uses of nuclear weapons.

(b) So far as the effect and utility of the opinion were concerned, the Assembly had the right to determine for itself the usefulness of an opinion in the light of its own needs. The political factors which might have prompted the request for an opinion and the distribution of votes on Resolution 49/75 K were not matters for the Court to consider. Nor should the Court decline to give an opinion merely on account of contested submissions about the possible effect on disarmament negotiations.

(c) In answering the question, the Court would not be adopting a legislative function, something which it was clearly not entitled to do. Its task was to engage in the normal judicial function of ascertaining the existence or otherwise of legal principles.

The formulation of the question posed by the General Assembly It was unnecessary to pronounce upon possible divergences between the English and French texts of the question, since the purpose was clearly to determine the legality or illegality of the threat or use of nuclear weapons. Since the nuclear-weapon States appearing before the Court accepted that their independence to act was restricted by international law, the argument about the legal consequences to be drawn from the fact that the question asked whether the threat or use of nuclear weapons was 'permitted' by international law, rather than whether it was 'prohibited', and the questions of burden of proof to which this choice of words was said to give rise, were without particular significance for the disposition of the issues before the Court.

Applicable law   (1)   The protection of the International Covenant on Civil and Political Rights did not cease in time of war, except as provided by Article 4 of the Covenant, and the right not to be arbitrarily deprived of life applied in hostilities. Whether the deprivation of life in the course of hostilities was arbitrary, however, had to be determined by reference to the *lex specialis*, namely the law of armed conflict.

(2)   The prohibition on genocide would be relevant to a use of nuclear weapons if the recourse to nuclear weapons entailed the element of intent to destroy a particular group in whole or in part required by Article II of the Genocide Convention, but it would only be possible to arrive at the conclusion that such intent existed after having taken due account of the circumstances of each case.

(3)   While existing international law relating to the protection of the environment did not specifically prohibit the use of nuclear weapons, it indicated important factors which had to be taken into account in the context of the implementation of the principles and rules of the law applicable in armed conflict. Respect for the environment was one of the factors which was relevant in assessing whether a particular military action met the requirements of necessity and proportionality.

(4)   The most directly relevant law governing the question before the Court was that relating to the use of force, enshrined in the United Nations Charter, and the law applicable in armed conflict, which regulated the conduct of hostilities, together with any treaties specifically concerned with nuclear weapons which the Court considered applicable. For the Court correctly to apply that law, it had to bear in mind the unique characteristics of nuclear weapons and, in particular, their destructive capability.

The legality or illegality of the use of nuclear weapons   (1)   The prohibition of the use of force in Article 2(4) of the Charter and the exception for the right of self-defence under Article 51 were applicable to the use of any type of weapon. The right of self-defence was subject to certain limitations, including those of proportionality and necessity. While the unique characteristics of nuclear weapons and the risks associated with their use were factors to be taken into account, the proportionality principle might not, in itself, exclude the use of nuclear weapons in all circumstances. The principles of self-defence, however, had to be applied in conjunction with the law on the conduct of hostilities; the use of a weapon which was unlawful *per se*, whether under customary law or treaty, did not become lawful merely because it was used for a purpose which was legitimate under the Charter. The Court also took account of Security Council Resolution 984 (1995), in which the Council welcomed the guarantees given by the nuclear-weapon States. It was not necessary to consider the use of nuclear weapons by way of reprisal, beyond noting that armed reprisals in peacetime were considered unlawful and that belligerent reprisals were subject to the principle of proportionality. Whether a signalled intention to use force in certain circumstances amounted to a threat to use force, contrary to Article 2(4) of the Charter, depended on various factors, in particular whether the use of force which was envisaged would be lawful.

(2) Neither customary international law nor treaty law applicable in armed conflict contained any specific authorisation of the use of nuclear weapons, or any other weapon. However, there was no rule or principle of international law which made the legality of using a particular weapon dependent upon such authorisation. The illegality of the use of certain weapons did not result from the absence of authorisation but was formulated in terms of prohibition.

(3) There was no prohibition of recourse to nuclear weapons as such.

(a) The prohibitions in various treaties of the use of poison and poisoned weapons covered weapons whose primary or exclusive effect was to poison or asphyxiate, and State practice had not treated those prohibitions as applicable to nuclear weapons.

(b) The many international negotiations specifically concerned with nuclear weapons had not produced a treaty laying down a general prohibition similar to the prohibitions of chemical and biological weapons. The various treaties which had been adopted limiting the manufacture, possession and testing of nuclear weapons as well as their deployment in certain parts of the world pointed to an increasing concern in the international community with nuclear weapons but did not, by themselves, constitute a prohibition of their use. The declarations made by certain States in connection with the Non-Proliferation Treaty and the Treaties of Tlatelolco and Raratonga were also significant in this regard.

(c) No specific prohibition of the use of nuclear weapons had evolved in customary law, the substance of which had to be looked for primarily in the practice and *opinio juris* of States. The fact that nuclear weapons had not been used since 1945 and the practice of a policy of deterrence by a number of States did not permit the finding that there was an *opinio juris* that the use of nuclear weapons was necessarily unlawful. Resolutions of the United Nations General Assembly, though not legally binding, might nevertheless have normative value if they pointed to the emergence of a rule or an *opinio juris*. The existence of a number of resolutions of the General Assembly regarding nuclear weapons was evidence of international concern but fell short of establishing that a specific prohibition of such weapons had already emerged as part of the *lex lata*.

(4) (a)   The laws of armed conflict regulated the conduct of hostilities between States and included limitations upon the methods and means of warfare; in particular, those laws prohibited the targeting of civilians and civilian objects and the use of weapons which were likely to cause unnecessary suffering. Those laws were clearly established as part of the corpus of international law and it was unnecessary for the purposes of the proceedings for the Court to determine whether they had acquired the character of *jus cogens*.

(b)   The laws of armed conflict, and in particular those relating to the methods and means of warfare, were applicable to the use of nuclear weapons, just as they were applicable to the use of conventional weapons. The fact that nuclear weapons were developed after the emergence of many of the rules in question did not affect this conclusion. It was unnecessary for the Court to elaborate on the applicability to nuclear weapons of Additional Protocol I to the Geneva Conventions.

(5)   The principle of neutrality, whatever the content of that principle, was applicable to the use of nuclear weapons.

(6)   In view of the unique characteristics of nuclear weapons, the use of such weapons seemed scarcely reconcilable with respect for the requirements of the laws of armed conflict and neutrality. Nevertheless, the Court did not have before it sufficient elements to enable it to conclude with certainty that the use of nuclear weapons would necessarily be at variance with those requirements in any circumstance. Moreover, the Court had also to consider the fact that a policy of deterrence had been pursued by an appreciable section of the international community for many years and had to take account of the fundamental right of every State to resort to self-defence when its survival was at stake.

(7)   The obligation in Article VI of the Nuclear Non-Proliferation Treaty required States to negotiate in good faith on effective measures for nuclear disarmament. This goal remained of vital importance to the international community.

(8)   The Court's Opinion had to be read as a whole and its reply to the question posed should be read in the light of the entirety of the reasoning in paragraphs 20–103 of the Opinion.

Declaration of President Bedjaoui   The Court had been obliged to acknowledge that the question posed concerned an area in which there was no clear and immediate answer in the existing law. That fact had been recognised in operative paragraph 2E. That paragraph should not, however, be interpreted as leaving the door ajar to recognition of the legality of the threat or use of nuclear weapons. The Court took note of the existence of an advanced process of change in the relevant international law, in which the old rule of international law was already defunct but the new rule had not yet come into existence. There was an apparent conflict between intransgressible principles of humanitarian law on the one hand and the right to self-defence where survival was at issue on the other. In the context of nuclear weapons, it would be foolhardy to set the survival of a State above all other considerations. With regard to nuclear disarmament, there was now a general obligation, opposable *erga omnes*, to negotiate in good faith and to achieve a specified result.

Declaration of Judge Herczegh   The fundamental principles of international humanitarian law categorically and unequivocally prohibited the use of weapons of mass destruction and did not recognise any exceptions to those principles. There was an inconsistency between the wording of operative paragraphs 2C and 2E which the Court should have addressed.

Declaration of Judge Shi   The practice of nuclear deterrence fell within the realm of international politics, not international law, and the Court should not have placed reliance upon it, especially since the groups of States concerned were not a large proportion of the membership of the international community.

Declaration of Judge Vereshchetin   The Court had been entitled to recognise the uncertain state of the law relating to the threat or use of nuclear weapons. It had stated that the use of such weapons would generally be incompatible with the rules of international law applicable in armed conflict. To have gone further would have been wrong in view of the fact that the Court's judicial function was limited to stating the law as it is. Moreover, the Court had to take account of the fact that complete prohibitions of categories of weapons had always been established by treaty.

Declaration of Judge Ferrari Bravo   There was, as yet, no precise and specific rule prohibiting nuclear weapons and drawing the fullest conclusions from that prohibition. Nevertheless, the rules produced over the last fifty years with regard to the humanitarian law of armed conflict were incompatible with the development of nuclear weapons. Moreover, the earliest resolutions of the General Assembly had articulated a prohibition of nuclear weapons, even if the subsequent 'cold war' meant that the implementation of that prohibition became impossible. This was something which the Opinion should have stated with greater clarity.

Separate Opinion of Judge Guillaume   (1)   The statement, in operative paragraph 2A, that there was no rule of international law authorising the use of nuclear weapons was unnecessary, since the Court had made clear that the illegality of the use of a weapon stemmed not from the absence of authorisation but from the presence of a prohibition.

(2)   Since nuclear weapons were not incapable of distinguishing between military and civilian targets, any assessment of the legality of their use required a comparison of the military advantages anticipated from a particular attack with the likely collateral damage and degree of suffering. Similarly, the law of neutrality required a balancing of the military advantages with the effect upon neutral States. The Court should, therefore, have held that the use of nuclear weapons was compatible with the law in extreme cases and the first part of operative paragraph 2E should be read in that way. The second part of operative paragraph 2E was deficient because it did not explicitly recognise the legality of nuclear deterrence.

(3)   If there was no definite prohibition of the use of nuclear weapons, then such conduct would be lawful, since the sovereignty of States meant that what was not prohibited was lawful.

Separate Opinion of Judge Ranjeva   (1)   The first part of operative paragraph 2E was the essential part of the Advisory Opinion and was to be read as a statement that there existed in international law a general prohibition of the threat or use of nuclear weapons.

(2)   The second clause of operative paragraph 2E, however, lacked certain judicial clarity. The nature of the question posed by the General Assembly, which the Court had been right to answer, called for a reply of a different kind.

(3)   The law of armed conflict could not be interpreted as containing lacunae, especially on so important a subject. Moreover, the duty of a belligerent to observe that law existed irrespective of who was the aggressor and who was acting in self-defence.

Separate Opinion of Judge Fleischhauer   The use of nuclear weapons was subject to both the laws of armed conflict and the law on self-defence but there was a tension between those two bodies of law which was reflected in the Court's Opinion. Nuclear weapons were in many ways the negation of the humanitarian principles which lay behind the laws of armed conflict, for they caused immeasurable suffering, could not distinguish between civilian and military targets and could not respect the territorial integrity of neutral States. That law could not, however, be given automatic precedence over the law of self-defence, which was why the statement in the first clause of operative paragraph 2E was qualified by that contained in the second clause. The Court should, however, have gone further and stated that the law of armed conflict and the law of self-defence were of equal standing and international law had not yet evolved a rule by which the two could be reconciled in the case of nuclear weapons. The use of nuclear weapons therefore remained a legal possibility in an extreme case of self-defence.

Dissenting Opinion of Vice-President Schwebel (1) The practice of a significant number of States – the nuclear-weapon States and their allies – suggested that the use of nuclear weapons was regarded as lawful in certain circumstances or, at least, was not wholly outlawed. That practice was confirmed by the Nuclear Non-Proliferation Treaty, the negative security assurances and the position taken by the Security Council, as well as by inference from the other treaties which regulated nuclear issues without providing for the illegality of any use of nuclear weapons.

(2) The resolutions of the United Nations General Assembly did not begin to establish an *opinio juris* to the effect that the use of nuclear weapons was illegal. The Assembly had no authority to enact international law. Its resolutions could be regarded as stating rules of international law only if they were declaratory of existing customary law, which was clearly not the case here.

(3) While the principles of international humanitarian law applicable in armed conflicts applied to the use of nuclear weapons, their application to a particular case was far from easy. The use of nuclear weapons against a city was unlawful under these principles, while the use of a tactical nuclear weapon against a target such as a submarine was not. Between these extremes lay a wide range of cases in which it could not be presumed that a use of nuclear weapons would necessarily be disproportionate. Whether the use of a nuclear weapon was lawful in a particular case would thus depend upon the facts of that case.

(4) The second clause of Article 2E was an unjustifiable pronouncement of *non liquet*. Far from justifying the inconclusive answer in this clause, recent practice, including that in the 1990–1 Gulf War, demonstrated that the use of nuclear weapons in an extreme case of self-defence was lawful. There was a formidable body of evidence from the Gulf War that an aggressor was deterred from using chemical and biological weapons by the prospect of a nuclear response.

(5) Operative paragraph 2F did not respond to the question posed by the General Assembly and was not based upon the arguments put before the Court.

Dissenting Opinion of Judge Oda   (1)   The Court should have exercised its judicial discretion not to respond to the request from the General Assembly. The question put by the General Assembly was inadequate and the request was made not so much in order to ascertain the opinion of the Court as to seek the Court's endorsement of an alleged legal axiom. The reference in the question to a 'threat of nuclear weapons' was not properly explained. There was also a lack of any meaningful consensus amongst the Member States of the United Nations with regard to the request and no indication as to why the *lex lata* regarding nuclear weapons was in need of clarification or exposition by the Court.

(2)   Part of the immediate background to the request to the Court was the history of unsuccessful attempts to bring about a convention prohibiting the use, or threat of use, of nuclear weapons. The negotiation of such a convention had been the subject of discussion and of a number of initiatives for over thirty years but these attempts had come to nothing. The Court was then requested to endorse the proposition that the use, or threat of use, of nuclear weapons was not permitted. That was not the role of the Court under the advisory jurisdiction.

(3)   The extension of the Nuclear Non-Proliferation Treaty regime, together with the regimes of certain regional treaties, presupposed that the possession of nuclear weapons by five States was lawful and meant that the use of such weapons, though prohibited in certain circumstances, could not be wholly excluded.

(4)   The Court had an undoubted discretion, in the exercise of its advisory function, to decline to give an opinion and it should have exercised that discretion in the present case for reasons of judicial propriety. While it was highly desirable that nuclear weapons be eliminated, a decision on that matter was a function of political negotiations. The Court was confined to stating the existing law and should do so only in response to a genuine need.

Dissenting Opinion of Judge Shahabuddeen   (1)   State practice was not determinative in the present case. If there had been no rule prohibiting the use of nuclear weapons at the start of the nuclear age, the practice of the nuclear-weapon States and their supporters would have prevented the evolution of such a rule, while if such a rule had existed, the opposition of other States would have prevented the evolution of a new rule reversing it and permitting the use of nuclear weapons. The question was therefore whether a prohibitory rule existed at the time of the development of nuclear weapons.

(2)   The Charter assumed that mankind would continue to exist. The use of nuclear weapons would call this assumption into question. The use of nuclear weapons was unacceptable to the international community. Nuclear weapons were unique in their destructive capacity and scientific characteristics and the international community had shown by a series of treaties and other actions that it would not accept them.

(3)   The effects of use of nuclear weapons were wholly incompatible with the principles of the law of neutrality. Only nuclear weapons posed a substantial threat of collateral damage to neutral territory from belligerent acts outside that territory.

(4)   There was no *non liquet* in the law applicable to nuclear weapons, irrespective of whether one started from the proposition that the use of a weapon was lawful unless it was prohibited or from the proposition that such use was unlawful unless authorised.

(5)   The fact that the General Assembly called for the conclusion of a convention prohibiting the use of nuclear weapons did not justify the conclusion that the Assembly was not pronouncing the existing illegality of nuclear weapons. The question was whether the Assembly had been justified in concluding that the use of nuclear weapons was illegal under existing international law.

(6)   However far-reaching the rights conferred by sovereignty might be, they nevertheless existed within a framework and could not involve the violation of that framework. Even if there was no prohibition of the use of nuclear weapons, there was nothing in the sovereignty of States that would entitle them to embark upon a course of conduct which could effectively destroy the world. International law had developed since the decision in the *Lotus* case and the Court could not now avoid the conclusion that international law did not authorise a State to embark on a course of action which could result in the destruction of civilisation and mankind itself.

(7)   The Court could, and should, have held that the use of nuclear weapons was prohibited by the principles of international humanitarian law. States did not have an unlimited right to choose the methods and means of warfare which they would employ. Their choice was circumscribed by the prohibition of weapons which were indiscriminate or caused unnecessary suffering. These were principles against which the legality of each weapon could be judged irrespective of whether there was an international *opinio juris* determining that that weapon contravened the principle in question. The material before the Court was sufficient

to justify a finding that the use of nuclear weapons would violate both the unnecessary suffering principle and the underlying principles of the Martens Clause.

(8)   While there was (and could have been), at the start of the nuclear age, no rule which prohibited the use of nuclear weapons as such, there were rules which prohibited the use of any weapons which produced the effects which nuclear weapons produced. Those rules had not been modified or displaced by the emergence of a subsequent rule by which the use of nuclear weapons might be justified, since the objections of the non-nuclear-weapon States prevented the emergence of any such rule.

(9)   The Non-Proliferation Treaty and the regional nuclear treaties did not justify the inference that the use of nuclear weapons might be lawful in certain circumstances. On the contrary, they showed that the opponents of nuclear weapons, the majority of States, did not accept the legality of the use of such weapons.

Dissenting Opinion of Judge Weeramantry   (1)   The Court should have given an opinion to the effect that the use of nuclear weapons was un-lawful in all circumstances. It was the failure explicitly to make such a statement and the qualifications which the Court had introduced which made operative paragraphs 2B and 2E unacceptable. The request by the General Assembly concerned a topic of the utmost importance, as had been demonstrated by the interest shown in the proceedings not only by States but also by members of the public. While the Court's function was to state the law as it was, not to suggest how it might change, the Court had had an unprecedented opportunity to make a contribution to the furtherance of peace by clarifying the existing law relating to weaponry in its application to nuclear weapons. Although it was regrettable that the Court had missed that opportunity, the Opinion nevertheless had a number of positive aspects and, in particular, its logic pointed clearly towards the conclusion that there could never be a lawful use of nuclear weapons.

(2)   Nuclear weapons were unique both in their nature and in their effects. The destructive effects of nuclear weapons on the lives and health of humans and animals and on the natural environment were now so well documented as to be beyond debate. Terrible as was the evidence of the effects of the Hiroshima and Nagasaki bombings, the nuclear weapons available fifty years later were capable of far greater destruction. Even among weapons of mass destruction, many of which were already banned under international law, nuclear weapons stood alone, unmatched for

their potential to damage all that humanity had built over centuries and all that humanity relied upon for its continued existence. The best scientific testimony was that nuclear weapons could not be used without causing unnecessary suffering, having indiscriminate effects upon civilians and causing disproportionate damage to the territories of neutral States.

(3)   Any use of any type of nuclear weapon was incompatible with the principles and rules of international humanitarian law.

(a)   International humanitarian law reflected elementary considerations with which the use of a nuclear weapon was wholly at odds. Moreover, those humanitarian concerns were firmly based in a wide range of cultures.

(b)   International humanitarian law included not only specific provisions but also general principles derived from the dictates of the public conscience and reflected in the Martens Clause. The application of those principles by the international community in the numerous General Assembly resolutions on nuclear weapons and the various international agreements demonstrated that the use of nuclear weapons could not be reconciled with fundamental principles of humanity. The illegality of nuclear weapons thus existed independently of any specific prohibition.

(c)   The relevant provisions of international humanitarian law were the prohibition of weapons calculated to cause unnecessary suffering, the principle of proportionality, the principle of discrimination, the duty of respect for the territory of non-belligerent States and the prohibition of genocide. In addition, nuclear weapons were properly regarded as contravening the prohibition on poison and poisoned weapons. The prohibition against environmental damage and the relevant principles of the law of human rights were also important. The use of nuclear weapons would clearly be contrary to all of these provisions.

(4)   There was no scope for an exception to the illegality of nuclear weapons merely because the weapons were used in self-defence or under the authorisation of the Security Council. Neither self-defence nor the mandate of the Security Council entitled a State to disregard fundamental principles of humanitarian law applicable to any use of force.

(5)   The illegality of the use of nuclear weapons was not dependent upon any particular school of juristic thought. It followed from both positivist and other legal premises. It was also incompatible with the aims of war as rationally conceived. The nature of nuclear decision-making was such that the Court should have given a far clearer answer than it had done.

(6)   The international community had repeatedly made clear its opposition to nuclear weapons. The Nuclear Non-Proliferation Treaty and other agreements might tolerate the possession of nuclear weapons but could not be read as an acceptance that their use might ever be lawful.

(7)   The philosophy of nuclear deterrence did not justify the threat or use of nuclear weapons. Nor could the doctrine of belligerent reprisals or the concept of necessity furnish a justification for their use. While different categories of nuclear weapons existed, the differences between them were not sufficient to affect the application of the law and the use of any nuclear weapons would be unlawful.

(8)   The Court had been right to give an Opinion. The arguments that it should not have done so were unconvincing.

Dissenting Opinion of Judge Koroma   (1)   The use of nuclear weapons would, in any circumstance, be contrary to international law and the Court should have said so. The prevention of war by nuclear weapons was a matter for international law and one with which the Court had jurisdiction to deal if called upon to do so, as it had been in the present case.

(2)   The Court had found that the principles and rules of humanitarian law were applicable to the use of nuclear weapons. There was therefore no basis for holding that the Court could not definitively determine the legality or illegality of the use of such weapons. Even if such a determination was difficult, it was one which the Court, within the judicial function, was nonetheless entitled to make. By failing to do so, the Court had missed an opportunity to contribute to the prevention of nuclear war and had made serious inroads into the present restraints relating to the use of nuclear weapons.

(3)   The proposition that a State might be entitled to resist a threat to its own survival by destroying humanity as a whole was unsustainable. The right of self-defence was a legal right subject to restraints of law. Nor did the right of self-defence permit conduct which would otherwise be incompatible with the law governing the conduct of hostilities.

(4)   The use of nuclear weapons would, in any circumstances, violate the principles of humanitarian law, in particular the Martens Clause, the use of indiscriminate weapons and the prohibition of weapons calculated to cause unnecessary suffering. The unique destructive effects of nuclear weapons had been sufficiently established and demonstrated that the use of such weapons could never be compatible with the principles of humanitarian law.

(5)   Advisory opinions of the Court made an important contribution to crystallising and developing the law. The Court could, and should, have performed that function in the present case but had retreated from doing so. In addition, the Court's comments on the relevance of the law of human rights and genocide failed to recognise the importance of those areas of the law to the question before the Court. The law on the environment had an effect which went beyond merely imposing a general duty of respect. The Court had also given insufficient weight to the resolutions of the General Assembly and should not have given legal recognition to the doctrine of deterrence.

(6)   The Court could also have found that there was a specific prohibition of nuclear weapons in the Geneva Conventions and Additional Protocol I, which contained provisions with which the use of such weapons could not be reconciled.

Dissenting Opinion of Judge Higgins   (1)   The Court's decision that the question before it was a legal question and sufficiently precise for the Court not to decline to answer was inconsistent with the *non liquet* which the Court pronounced on the central issue.

(2)   The principle of proportionality in self-defence limited the use of force which might be justified to that which was necessary to reply to an attack; it was not a requirement of symmetry between the mode of attack and the mode of response.

(3)   The finding in the first clause of operative paragraph 2E had not been sufficiently justified by the reasoning of the Court in its Opinion. The Court should have demonstrated how the principles which it considered applicable led to the conclusion in that paragraph. While the Court had rightly identified certain principles of the law of armed conflict which applied to nuclear weapons, it had failed to explain their application. The Court had not shown that the use of nuclear weapons would necessarily cause unnecessary suffering or disproportionate civilian casualties. Both tests involved a balancing act which the Court had not performed. If a nuclear weapon could not be used in a way which would permit a distinction between civilians and the military, then its use was unlawful, but it could not be presumed that all uses of all nuclear weapons fell into that category.

(4)   The first clause of operative paragraph 2E was not juridically meaningful and its relationship with the second clause had not been properly explained. The result was the pronouncement of a *non liquet*, a concept which formed no part of the Court's jurisprudence.

Advisory Opinion of International Court of Justice on Legality of the Threat or Use of Nuclear Weapons, 8 July 1996 (extract)

[**227**] 1. The question upon which the advisory opinion of the Court has been requested is set forth in resolution 49/75 K adopted by the General Assembly of the United Nations (hereinafter called the 'General Assembly') on 15 December 1994. By a letter dated 19 December 1994, received in the Registry by facsimile on 20 December 1994 and filed in the original on 6 January 1995, the Secretary-General of the United Nations officially communicated to the Registrar the decision taken by the General Assembly to submit the question to the Court for an advisory opinion. Resolution 49/75 K, the English text of which was enclosed with the letter, reads as follows:

The General Assembly,

Conscious that the continuing existence and development of nuclear weapons pose serious risks to humanity,

Mindful that States have an obligation under the Charter of the United [**228**] Nations to refrain from the threat or use of force against the territorial integrity or political independence of any State,

Recalling its resolutions 1653 (XVI) of 24 November 1961, 33/71 B of 14 December 1978, 34/83 G of 11 December 1979. 35/152 D of 12 December 1980, 36/92 I of 9 December 1981, 45/59 B of 4 December 1990 and 46/37 D of 6 December 1991, in which it declared that the use of nuclear weapons would be a violation of the Charter and a crime against humanity,

Welcoming the progress made on the prohibition and elimination of weapons of mass destruction, including the Convention on the Prohibition of the Development, Production and Stockpiling of Bacteriological (Biological) and Toxin Weapons and on Their Destruction[3] and the Convention on the Prohibition of the Development, Production, Stockpiling and Use of Chemical Weapons and on Their Destruction,[4]

---

[2] The individual declarations and opinions not reproduced in this volume can be found as follows: the declaration of President Bedjaoui at *ICJ Reports 1996*, p. 268; the declaration of Judge Herczegh at *ICJ Reports 1996*, p. 275; the declaration of Judge Shi at *ICJ Reports 1996*, p. 277; the declaration of Judge Vereshchetin at *ICJ Reports 1996*, p. 279; the declaration of Judge Ferrari Bravo at *ICJ Reports 1996*, p. 282; the separate opinion of Judge Guillaume at *ICJ Reports 1996*, p. 287; the separate opinion of Judge Ranjeva at *ICJ Reports 1996*, p. 294; the separate opinion of Judge Fleischhauer at *ICJ Reports 1996*, p. 305; the dissenting opinion of Vice-President Schwebel at *ICJ Reports 1996*, p. 311; the dissenting opinion of Judge Oda at *ICJ Reports 1996*, p. 330; the dissenting opinion of Judge Shahabuddeen at *ICJ Reports 1996*, p. 375; and the dissenting opinion of Judge Higgins at *ICJ Reports 1996*, p. 583.

[3] Resolution 2826 (XXVI), annex.

[4] See *Official Records of the General Assembly, Forty-seventh Session, Supplement No. 27* (A/47/27), appendix I.

Convinced that the complete elimination of nuclear weapons is the only guarantee against the threat of nuclear war,

Noting the concerns expressed in the Fourth Review Conference of the Parties to the Treaty on the Non-Proliferation of Nuclear Weapons that insufficient progress had been made towards the complete elimination of nuclear weapons at the earliest possible time,

Recalling that, convinced of the need to strengthen the rule of law in international relations, it has declared the period 1990–1999 the United Nations Decade of International Law,[5]

Noting that Article 96, paragraph 1, of the Charter empowers the General Assembly to request the International Court of Justice to give an advisory opinion on any legal question,

Recalling the recommendation of the Secretary-General, made in his report entitled 'An Agenda for Peace',[6] that United Nations organs that are authorized to take advantage of the advisory competence of the International Court of Justice turn to the Court more frequently for such opinions,

Welcoming resolution 46/40 of 14 May 1993 of the Assembly of the World Health Organization, in which the organization requested the International Court of Justice to give an advisory opinion on whether the use of nuclear weapons by a State in war or other armed conflict would be a breach of its obligations under international law, including the Constitution of the World Health Organization,

Decides, pursuant to Article 96, paragraph 1, of the Charter of the United Nations, to request the International Court of Justice urgently to render its advisory opinion on the following question: 'Is the threat or use of nuclear weapons in any circumstance permitted under international law?'

[. . .]

[241] 27. In both their written and oral statements, some States furthermore argued that any use of nuclear weapons would be unlawful by reference to existing norms relating to the safeguarding and protection of the environment, in view of their essential importance.

Specific references were made to various existing international treaties and instruments. These included Additional Protocol I of 1977 to the Geneva Conventions of 1949, Article 35, paragraph 3, of which prohibits the employment of 'methods or means of warfare which are intended, or may be expected, to cause widespread, long-term and severe damage to the natural environment'; and the Convention of 18 May 1977 on the Prohibition of Military or Any Other Hostile Use of Environmental Modification Techniques, which prohibits the use of weapons which have 'widespread, long-lasting or severe effects' on the environment (Art. 1). Also cited were Principle 21 of the Stockholm Declaration of 1972 and Principle 2 of the Rio Declaration of 1992 which express the common conviction of the States concerned that they have a duty

> to ensure that activities within their jurisdiction or control do not cause damage to the environment of other States or of areas beyond the limits of national jurisdiction.

---

[5] Resolution 44/23.
[6] A/47/277–S/24111.

These instruments and other provisions relating to the protection and safeguarding of the environment were said to apply at all times, in war as well as in peace, and it was contended that they would be violated by the use of nuclear weapons whose consequences would be widespread and would have transboundary effects.

28. Other States questioned the binding legal quality of these precepts of environmental law; or, in the context of the Convention on the Prohibition of Military or Any Other Hostile Use of Environmental Modification Techniques, denied that it was concerned at all with the use of nuclear weapons in hostilities; or, in the case of Additional Protocol 1, denied that they were generally bound by its terms, or recalled that they had reserved their position in respect of Article 35, paragraph 3, thereof.

It was also argued by some States that the principal purpose of environmental treaties and norms was the protection of the environment in time of peace. It was said that those treaties made no mention of nuclear weapons. It was also pointed out that warfare in general, and nuclear warfare in particular, were not mentioned in their texts and that it would be destabilizing to the rule of law and to confidence in international negotiations if those treaties were now interpreted in such a way as to prohibit the use of nuclear weapons.

29. The Court recognizes that the environment is under daily threat and that the use of nuclear weapons could constitute a catastrophe for the environment. The Court also recognizes that the environment is not an abstraction but represents the living space, the quality of life and the very health of human beings, including generations unborn. The [242] existence of the general obligation of States to ensure that activities within their jurisdiction and control respect the environment of other States or of areas beyond national control is now part of the corpus of international law relating to the environment.

30. However, the Court is of the view that the issue is not whether the treaties relating to the protection of the environment are or are not applicable during an armed conflict, but rather whether the obligations stemming from these treaties were intended to be obligations of total restraint during military conflict.

The Court does not consider that the treaties in question could have intended to deprive a State of the exercise of its right of self-defence under international law because of its obligations to protect the environment. Nonetheless, States must take environmental considerations into account when assessing what is necessary and proportionate in the pursuit of legitimate military objectives. Respect for the environment is one of the elements that go to assessing whether an action is in conformity with the principles of necessity and proportionality.

This approach is supported, indeed, by the terms of Principle 24 of the Rio Declaration, which provides that:

> Warfare is inherently destructive of sustainable development. States shall therefore respect international law providing protection for the environment in times of armed conflict and cooperate in its further development, as necessary.

31. The Court notes furthermore that Articles 35, paragraph 3, and 55 of Additional Protocol I provide additional protection for the environment. Taken together, these provisions embody a general obligation to protect the natural environment against widespread, long-term and severe environmental damage; the prohibition of methods and means of warfare which are intended, or may be expected, to cause such damage; and the prohibition of attacks against the natural environment by way of reprisals.

These are powerful constraints for all the States having subscribed to these provisions.

32. General Assembly resolution 47/37 of 25 November 1992 on the 'Protection of the Environment in Times of Armed Conflict' is also of interest in this context. It affirms the general view according to which environmental considerations constitute one of the elements to be taken into account in the implementation of the principles of the law applicable in armed conflict: it states that 'destruction of the environment, not justified by military necessity and carried out wantonly, is clearly contrary to existing international law'. Addressing the reality that certain instruments are not yet binding on all States, the General Assembly in this resolution '[a]ppeals to all States that have not yet done so to consider becoming parties to the relevant international conventions'.

[243] In its recent Order in the *Request for an Examination of the Situation in Accordance with Paragraph 63 of the Court's Judgment of 20 December 1974 in the* Nuclear Tests (New Zealand v. France) Case,[7] the Court stated that its conclusion was 'without prejudice to the obligations of States to respect and protect the natural environment' (*Order of 22 September 1995, ICJ Reports 1995*, p. 306, para. 64).[8] Although that statement was made in the context of nuclear testing, it naturally also applies to the actual use of nuclear weapons in armed conflict.

33. The Court thus finds that while the existing international law relating to the protection and safeguarding of the environment does not specifically prohibit the use of nuclear weapons, it indicates important environmental factors that are properly to be taken into account in the context of the implementation of the principles and rules of the law applicable in armed conflict.

*

34. In the light of the foregoing the Court concludes that the most directly relevant applicable law governing the question of which it was seised, is that relating to the use of force enshrined in the United Nations Charter and the law applicable in armed conflict which regulates the conduct of hostilities, together with any specific treaties on nuclear weapons that the Court might determine to be relevant.

* *

35. In applying this law to the present case, the Court cannot however fail to take into account certain unique characteristics of nuclear weapons.

[7] See p. 149 above.]
[8] See p. 162 above.]

The Court has noted the definitions of nuclear weapons contained in various treaties and accords. It also notes that nuclear weapons are explosive devices whose energy results from the fusion or fission of the atom. By its very nature, that process, in nuclear weapons as they exist today, releases not only immense quantities of heat and energy, but also powerful and prolonged radiation. According to the material before the Court, the first two causes of damage are vastly more powerful than the damage caused by other weapons, while the phenomenon of radiation is said to be peculiar to nuclear weapons. These characteristics render the nuclear weapon potentially catastrophic. The destructive power of nuclear weapons cannot be contained in either space or time. They have the potential to destroy all civilization and the entire ecosystem of the planet.

The radiation released by a nuclear explosion would affect health, agriculture, natural resources and demography over a very wide area. [244] Further, the use of nuclear weapons would be a serious danger to future generations. Ionizing radiation has the potential to damage the future environment, food and marine ecosystem, and to cause genetic defects and illness in future generations.

36. In consequence, in order correctly to apply to the present case the Charter law on the use of force and the law applicable in armed conflict, in particular humanitarian law, it is imperative for the Court to take account of the unique characteristics of nuclear weapons, and in particular their destructive capacity, their capacity to cause untold human suffering, and their ability to cause damage to generations to come.

[...]

[256] 74. The Court not having found a conventional rule of general scope, nor a customary rule specifically proscribing the threat or use of nuclear weapons *per se*, it will now deal with the question whether recourse to nuclear weapons must be considered as illegal in the light of the principles and rules of international humanitarian law applicable in armed conflict and of the law of neutrality.

[...]

[259] [...] 85. Turning now to the applicability of the principles and rules of humanitarian law to a possible threat or use of nuclear weapons, the Court notes that doubts in this respect have sometimes been voiced on the ground that these principles and rules had evolved prior to the invention of nuclear weapons and that the Conferences of Geneva of 1949 and 1974–7 which respectively adopted the four Geneva Conventions of 1949 and the two Additional Protocols thereto did not deal with nuclear weapons specifically. Such views, however, are only held by a small minority. In the view of the vast majority of States as well as writers there can be no doubt as to the applicability of humanitarian law to nuclear weapons.

86. The Court shares that view. Indeed, nuclear weapons were invented after most of the principles and rules of humanitarian law applicable in armed conflict had already come into existence; the Conferences of 1949 and 1974–7 left these weapons aside, and there is a qualitative as well as quantitative difference between nuclear weapons and all conventional arms. However, it cannot be concluded from this that the established principles and rules of humanitarian law applicable in armed conflict

did not apply to nuclear weapons. Such a conclusion would be incompatible with the intrinsically humanitarian character of the legal principles in question which permeates the entire law of armed conflict and applies to all forms of warfare and to all kinds of weapons, those of the past, those of the present and those of the future. In this respect it seems significant that the thesis that the rules of humanitarian law do not apply to the new weaponry, because of the newness of the latter, has not been advocated in the present proceedings. On the contrary, the newness of nuclear weapons has been expressly rejected as an argument against the application to them of international humanitarian law.

[...]

[260] [...] 87. Finally, the Court points to the Martens Clause, whose continuing existence and applicability is not to be doubted, as an affirmation that the principles and rules of humanitarian law apply to nuclear weapons.

[...]

[261][...] 89. The Court finds that as in the case of the principles of humanitarian law applicable in armed conflict, international law leaves no doubt that the principle of neutrality, whatever its content, which is of a fundamental character similar to that of the humanitarian principles and rules, is applicable (subject to the relevant provisions of the United Nations Charter), to all international armed conflict, whatever type of weapons might be used.

*

90. Although the applicability of the principles and rules of humanitarian law and of the principle of neutrality to nuclear weapons is hardly disputed, the conclusions to be drawn from this applicability are, on the other hand, controversial.

[...]

[263] 97. Accordingly, in view of the present state of international law viewed as a whole, as examined above by the Court, and of the elements of fact at its disposal, the Court is led to observe that it cannot reach a definitive conclusion as to the legality or illegality of the use of nuclear weapons by a State in an extreme circumstance of self-defence, in which its very survival would be at stake.

*
*   *

98. Given the eminently difficult issues that arise in applying the law on the use of force and above all the law applicable in armed conflict to nuclear weapons, the Court considers that it now needs to examine one further aspect of the question before it, seen in a broader context.

In the long run, international law, and with it the stability of the international order which it is intended to govern, are bound to suffer from the continuing difference of views with regard to the legal status of weapons as deadly as nuclear weapons. It is consequently important to put an end to this state of affairs: the long promised complete nuclear disarmament appears to be the most appropriate means of achieving that result.

99. In these circumstances, the Court appreciates the full importance of the recognition by Article VI of the Treaty on the Non-Proliferation of Nuclear Weapons of an obligation to negotiate in good faith a nuclear disarmament. This provision is worded as follows:

> Each of the Parties to the Treaty undertakes to pursue negotiations in good faith on effective measures relating to cessation of the nuclear arms race at an early date and to nuclear disarmament, and on a treaty on general and complete disarmament under strict and effective international control.

[264] The legal import of that obligation goes beyond that of a mere obligation of conduct; the obligation involved here is an obligation to achieve a precise result – nuclear disarmament in all its aspects – by adopting a particular course of conduct, namely, the pursuit of negotiations on the matter in good faith.

[...]

[265] [...] The importance of fulfilling the obligation expressed in Article VI of the Treaty on the Non-Proliferation of Nuclear Weapons was also reaffirmed in the final document of the Review and Extension Conference of the parties to the Treaty on the Non-Proliferation of Nuclear Weapons, held from 17 April to 12 May 1995.

In the view of the Court, it remains without any doubt an objective of vital importance to the whole of the international community today.

[...]

105. For these reasons,

THE COURT,

(1) By thirteen votes to one,

Decides to comply with the request for an advisory opinion;

IN FAVOUR: *President* Bedjaoui; *Vice-President* Schwebel; *Judges* Guillaume, Shahabuddeen, Weeramantry, Ranjeva, Herczegh, Shi, Fleischhauer, Koroma, Vereshchetin, Ferrari Bravo, Higgins;

AGAINST: *Judge* Oda;

(2) [266] *Replies* in the following manner to the question put by the General Assembly:

A. Unanimously,

There is in neither customary nor conventional international law any specific authorization of the threat or use of nuclear weapons;

B. By eleven votes to three,

There is in neither customary nor conventional international law any comprehensive and universal prohibition of the threat or use of nuclear weapons as such;

IN FAVOUR: *President* Bedjaoui; *Vice-President* Schwebel; *Judges* Oda, Guillaume, Ranjeva, Herczegh, Shi, Fleischhauer, Vereshchetin, Ferrari Bravo, Higgins;

AGAINST: *Judges* Shahabuddeen, Weeramantry, Koroma;

C. Unanimously,

A threat or use of force by means of nuclear weapons that is contrary to Article 2, paragraph 4, of the United Nations Charter and that fails to meet all the requirements of Article 51, is unlawful;

D. Unanimously,

A threat or use of nuclear weapons should also be compatible with the requirements of the international law applicable in armed conflict, particularly those of the principles and rules of international humanitarian law, as well as with specific obligations under treaties and other undertakings which expressly deal with nuclear weapons;

E. By seven votes to seven, by the President's casting vote,

It follows from the above-mentioned requirements that the threat or use of nuclear weapons would generally be contrary to the rules of international law applicable in armed conflict, and in particular the principles and rules of humanitarian law;

However, in view of the current state of international law, and of the elements of fact at its disposal, the Court cannot conclude definitively whether the threat or use of nuclear weapons would be lawful or unlawful in an extreme circumstance of self-defence, in which the very survival of a State would be at stake;

> IN FAVOUR: *President* Bedjaoui; *Judges* Ranjeva, Herczegh, Shi, Fleischhauer, Vereshchetin, Ferrari Bravo;
>
> AGAINST: *Vice-President* Schwebel; *Judges* Oda, Guillaume, Shahabuddeen, Weeramantry, Koroma, Higgins;

F. **[267]** Unanimously,

There exists an obligation to pursue in good faith and bring to a conclusion negotiations leading to nuclear disarmament in all its aspects under strict and effective international control.

DISSENTING OPINION OF JUDGE WEERAMANTRY (EXTRACT)

[. . .] *II. Nature and effects of nuclear weapons*

3. The effects of the nuclear weapons

[. . .]

[454] [. . .]*(a) Damage to the environment and the ecosystem*[9]

The extent of damage to the environment, which no other weapon is capable of causing, has been summarized in 1987 by the World Commission on the Environment and Development in the following terms:

---

[9] On environmental law, see further Section III.10 *(f)* below.

The likely consequences of nuclear war make other threats to the environment pale into insignificance. Nuclear weapons represent a qualitatively new step in the development of warfare. One thermonuclear bomb can have an explosive power greater than all the explosives used in wars since the invention of gunpowder. In addition to the destructive effects of blast and heat, immensely magnified by these weapons, they introduce a new lethal agent – ionising radiation – that extends lethal effects over both space and time.[10]

Nuclear weapons have the potential to destroy the entire ecosystem of the planet. Those already in the world's arsenals have the potential of destroying life on the planet several times over.

Another special feature of the nuclear weapon, referred to at the hearings, is the damage caused by ionizing radiation to coniferous forests, crops, the food chain, livestock and the marine ecosystem.

(b) Damage to future generations

[. . .]

[**455**] [. . .] It is to be noted in this context that the rights of future generations have passed the stage when they were merely an embryonic right struggling for recognition. They have woven themselves into international law through major treaties, through juristic opinion and through general principles of law recognized by civilized nations.

Among treaties may be mentioned, the 1979 London Ocean Dumping Convention, the 1973 Convention on International Trade in Endangered Species, and the 1972 Convention Concerning the Protection of the World Cultural and Natural Heritage. All of these expressly incorporate the principle of protecting the natural environment for future generations, and elevate the concept to the level of binding State obligation.

Juristic opinion is now abundant, with several major treatises appearing upon the subject and with such concepts as intergenerational equity and the common heritage of mankind being academically well established.[11] Moreover, there is a growing awareness of the ways in which a multiplicity of traditional legal systems across the globe protect the environment for future generations. To these must be added a series of major [**456**] international declarations commencing with the 1972 Stockholm Declaration on the Human Environment.

When incontrovertible scientific evidence speaks of pollution of the environment on a scale that spans hundreds of generations, this Court would fail in its trust if it did not take serious note of the ways in which the distant future is protected by present law. The ideals of the United Nations Charter do not limit themselves to the present, for they look forward to the promotion of social progress and better standards of life and they fix their vision, not only on the present, but on 'succeeding generations'.

---

[10] World Commission on Environment and Development ('the Brundtland Commission'), *Our Common Future*, 1987, p. 295, cited in CR 95/22, p. 55.

[11] For further references, see Edith Brown Weiss, *In Fairness to Future Generations: International Law, Common Patrimony and Intergenerational Equity*, 1989.

This one factor of impairment of the environment over such a seemingly infinite time span would by itself be sufficient to call into operation the protective principles of international law which the Court, as the pre-eminent authority empowered to state them, must necessarily apply.

[. . .]

(d) The nuclear winter

One of the possible after-effects of an exchange of nuclear weapons is the nuclear winter, a condition caused by the accumulation of hundreds of millions of tons of soot in the atmosphere, in consequence of fires in cities, in forests and the countryside, caused by nuclear weapons. The smoke cloud and the debris from multiple explosions blots out sunlight, resulting in crop failures throughout the world and global starvation. Starting with the paper by Turco, Toon, Ackerman, Pollack and Sagan (known as the TTAPS study after the names of its authors) on 'Nuclear [457] Winter: Global Consequences of Multiple Nuclear Explosions',[12] an enormous volume of detailed scientific work has been done on the effect of the dust and smoke clouds generated in nuclear war. The TTAPS study showed that smoke clouds in one hemisphere could within weeks move into the other hemisphere.[13] TTAPS and other studies show that a small temperature drop of a few degrees during the ripening season, caused by the nuclear winter, can result in extensive crop failure even on a hemispherical scale. Such consequences are therefore ominous for noncombatant countries also.

---

[12] *Science*, 23 December 1983, Vol. 222, p. 1283.

[13] The movement of a cloud of dust particles from one hemisphere to another, with the resultant effects resembling those of a nuclear winter, are not futuristic scenarios unrelated to past experience. In 1815, the eruption of the Indonesian volcano, Tambora, injected dust and smoke into the atmosphere on a scale so great as to result in worldwide crop failure and darkness in 1816. The *Scientific American*, March 1984, p. 58, reproduced a poem, 'Darkness', written by Lord Byron, thought to have been inspired by this year without a summer. At a hearing of the United States Senate on the effects of nuclear war, in December 1983, the Russian physicist, Kapitza, drew attention to this poem, in the context of the effects of nuclear war, referring to it as one well known to Russians through its translation by the novelist Ivan Turgenev. Here are some extracts, capturing with poetic vision the human despair and the environmental desolation of the post-nuclear scene:

> A fearful hope was all the world contain'd;
> Forests were set on fire – but hour by hour
> They fell and faded – and the crackling trunks
> Extinguish'd with a crash – and all was black.
> The brows of men by the despairing light
> Wore an unearthly aspect, as by fits
> The flashes fell upon them; some lay down
> And hid their eyes and wept;. . .
>
> . . . The world was void,
> The populous and the powerful was a lump,
> Seasonless, herbless, treeless, manless, lifeless
> A lump of death – a chaos of hard clay
> The rivers, lakes, and ocean all stood still,
> And nothing stirr'd within their silent depths;
> Ships sailorless lay rotting on the sea. . .

There is now a consensus that the climatic effects of a nuclear winter and the resulting lack of food aggravated by the destroyed [**458**] infrastructure could have a greater overall impact on the global population than the immediate effects of the nuclear explosions. The evidence is growing that in a post-war nuclear world Homo Sapiens will not have an ecological niche to which he could flee. It is apparent that life everywhere on this planet would be threatened.[14]

[. . .]

[**463**] [. . .] *(i) Transnational damage*

Once a nuclear explosion takes place, the fallout from even a single local detonation cannot be confined within national boundaries.[15] According to WHO studies, it would extend hundreds of kilometres downwind and the gamma ray exposure from the fallout could reach the human body, even outside national boundaries, through radioactivity deposited in the ground, through inhalation from the air, through consumption of contaminated food, and through inhalation of suspended radioactivity. The diagram [not reproduced here] appended to this opinion, extracted from the WHO Study, comparing the areas affected by conventional bombs and nuclear weapons, demonstrates this convincingly. Such is the danger to which neutral populations would be exposed.

All nations, including those carrying out underground tests, are in agreement that extremely elaborate protections are necessary in the case of underground nuclear explosions in order to prevent contamination of the environment. Such precautions are manifestly quite impossible in the [**464**] case of the use of nuclear weapons in war – when they will necessarily be exploded in the atmosphere or on the ground. The explosion of nuclear weapons in the atmosphere creates such acknowledgedly deleterious effects that it has already been banned by the Partial Nuclear Test Ban Treaty, and considerable progress has already been made towards a Total Test Ban Treaty. If the nuclear powers now accept that explosions below ground, in the carefully controlled conditions of a test, are so deleterious to health and the environment that they should be banned, this ill accords with the position that above ground explosions in uncontrolled conditions are acceptable.

The transboundary effects of radiation are illustrated by the nuclear meltdown in Chernobyl which had devastating effects over a vast area, as the by-products of that nuclear reaction could not be contained. Human health, agricultural and dairy produce and the demography of thousands of square miles were affected in a manner never known before. On 30 November 1995, the United Nation's Under-Secretary-General for Humanitarian Affairs announced that thyroid cancers, many of them being diagnosed in children, are 285 times more prevalent in Belarus than before the accident, that about 375,000 people in Belarus, Russia and Ukraine remain displaced

---

[14] Wilfrid Bach, 'Climatic Consequences of Nuclear War', in Proceedings of the Sixth World Congress of the International Physicians for the Prevention of Nuclear War (IPPNW), Cologne, 1986, published as *Maintain Life on Earth!*, 1987, p. 154.

[15] See diagram appended from *Effects of Nuclear War on Health and Health Services*, World Health Organization, 2nd ed., 1987, p. 16.

and often homeless – equivalent to numbers displaced in Rwanda by the fighting there – and that about 9 million people have been affected in some way.[16] Ten years after Chernobyl, the tragedy still reverberates over large areas of territory, not merely in Russia alone, but also in other countries such as Sweden. Such results, stemming from a mere accident rather than a deliberate attempt to cause damage by nuclear weapons, followed without the heat or the blast injuries attendant on a nuclear weapon. They represented radiation damage alone – only one of the three lethal aspects of nuclear weapons. They stemmed from an event considerably smaller in size than the explosions of Hiroshima and Nagasaki.

[. . .]

[469] [. . .] *(m) Damage to food productivity*

Unlike other weapons, whose direct impact is the most devastating part of the damage they cause, nuclear weapons can cause far greater damage by their delayed after-effects than by their direct effects. The detailed technical study, *Environmental Consequences of Nuclear War*, while referring to some uncertainties regarding the indirect effects of nuclear war, states:

> What can be said with assurance, however, is that the Earth's human population has a much greater vulnerability to the indirect effects of nuclear war, especially mediated through impacts on food productivity and food availability, than to the direct effects of nuclear war itself.[17]

The nuclear winter, should it occur in consequence of multiple nuclear exchanges, could disrupt all global food supplies.

After the United States tests in the Pacific in 1954, fish caught in various parts of the Pacific, as long as eight months after the explosions, were contaminated and unfit for human consumption, while crops in various parts of Japan were affected by radioactive rain. These were among the findings of an international Commission of medical specialists appointed by the Japanese Association of Doctors against A- and H-bombs.[18] Further:

> The use of nuclear weapons contaminates water and food, as well as the soil and the plants that may grow on it. This is not only in the area covered by immediate nuclear radiation, but also a much larger unpredictable zone which is affected by the radio-active fallout.[19]

[472] [. . .] 5. The differences in scientific knowledge between the present time and 1945

On 17 July 1945, United States Secretary of War, Stimson, informed Prime Minister Churchill of the successful detonation of the experimental [473] nuclear bomb in

---

[16] *New York Times Service*, reported in *International Herald Tribune*, 30 November 1995.

[17] SCOPE publication 28, released at the Royal Society, London, on 6 January 1986, Vol. I, p. 481.

[18] As referred to in N. Singh and E. McWhinney, *Nuclear Weapons and Contemporary International Law*, 1989, p. 124.

[19] *Ibid.*, p. 122.

the New Mexican desert, with the cryptic message 'Babies satisfactorily born.'[20] A universe of knowledge has grown up regarding the effects of the bomb since that fateful day when the advent of this unknown weapon could, even cryptically, be so described.

True, much knowledge regarding the power of the bomb was available then, but the volume of knowledge now available on the effects of nuclear weapons is exponentially greater. In addition to numerous military studies, there have been detailed studies by WHO and other concerned organizations such as International Physicians for the Prevention of Nuclear War (IPPNW); the TTAPS studies on the nuclear winter; the studies of the Scientific Committee on Problems of the Environment (SCOPE); the International Council of Scientific Unions (ICSU); the United Nations Institute of Disarmament Research (UNIDIR); and literally hundreds of others. Much of this material has been placed before the Court or deposited in the library by WHO and various States that have appeared before the Court in this matter.

Questions of knowledge, morality and legality in the use of nuclear weapons, considered in the context of 1995, are thus vastly different from those questions considered in the context of 1945, and need a totally fresh approach in the light of this immense quantity of information. This additional information has a deep impact upon the question of the legality now before the Court.

Action with full knowledge of the consequences of one's act is totally different in law from the same action taken in ignorance of its consequences. Any nation using the nuclear weapon today cannot be heard to say that it does not know its consequences. It is only in the context of this knowledge that the question of legality of the use of nuclear weapons can be considered in 1996.

[...]

III. Humanitarian law

10. Specific rules of the humanitarian law of war

[...]

[497] As noted at the commencement of Part III, most of the States which support the view that the use of nuclear weapons is lawful acknowledge that international humanitarian law applies to their use, and that such use must conform to its principles. Among the more important of the relevant principles of international law are:

- (*a*)   the prohibition against causing unnecessary suffering;
- (*b*)   the principle of proportionality;
- (*c*)   the principle of discrimination between combatants and non-combatants;
- (*d*)   the obligation to respect the territorial sovereignty of non-belligerent States;
- (*e*)   the prohibition against genocide and crimes against humanity;
- (*f*)   the prohibition against causing lasting and severe damage to the environment;
- (*g*)   human rights law.

[...]

---

[20] Winston Churchill, *The Second World War*, Vol. 6, 'Triumph and Tragedy', 1953, p. 63.

[**502**] [...] (f) *The prohibition against environmental damage*

The environment, the common habitat of all Member States of the United Nations, cannot be damaged by any one or more members to the detriment of all others. Reference has already been made, in the context of dictates of public conscience (Section III.6 above), to the fact that the principles of environmental protection have become 'so deeply rooted in the conscience of mankind that they have become particularly essential rules of general international law'.[21] The International Law Commission has indeed classified massive pollution of the atmosphere or of the seas as an international crime.[22] These aspects have been referred to earlier.

Environmental law incorporates a number of principles which are violated by nuclear weapons. The principle of intergenerational equity and the common heritage principle have already been discussed. Other principles of environmental law, which this request enables the Court to recognize and use in reaching its conclusions, are the precautionary principle, the principle of trusteeship of earth resources, the principle that the [**503**] burden of proving safety lies upon the author of the act complained of, and the 'polluter pays principle', placing on the author of environmental damage the burden of making adequate reparation to those affected.[23] There have been juristic efforts in recent times to formulate what have been described as 'principles of ecological security' – a process of norm creation and codification of environmental law which has developed under the stress of the need to protect human civilization from the threat of self-destruction.

One writer,[24] in listing eleven such principles, includes among them the 'Prohibition of Ecological Aggression', deriving this principle *inter alia* from such documents as the 1977 Convention on the Prohibition of Military or Any Other Hostile Use of Environmental Modification Techniques which entered into force on 5 October 1978 (1108 *UNTS*, p. 151), and the United Nations General Assembly resolution 'Historical responsibility of States for the preservation of nature for present and future generations' (General Assembly resolution 35/8 of 30 October 1980).

The same writer points out that,

> Under Soviet [now Russian] legal doctrine, the deliberate and hostile modification of the environment – ecocide – is unlawful and considered an international crime.[25]

Another writer, drawing attention to the need for a co-ordinated, collective response to the global environmental crisis and the difficulty of envisioning such a response, observes:

---

[21] Report of the International Law Commission on the work of its twenty-eighth session, *Yearbook of the International Law Commission*, 1976, Vol. II, Part II, p. 109, para. 33.

[22] Draft Article 19 (3) (d) on 'State Responsibility' of the International Law Commission, *ibid.*, p. 96.

[23] See the references to these principles in my dissenting opinion in *Request for an Examination of the Situation in Accordance with Paragraph 63 of the Court's Judgment of 20 December 1974 in the Nuclear Tests (New Zealand v. France) Case, ICJ Reports 1995*, pp. 339–47.

[24] A. Timoshenko, 'Ecological Security: Global Change Paradigm', *Columbia Journal of International Environmental Law and Policy*, 1990, Vol. 1, p. 127.

[25] Timoshenko, *op. cit.*

> But circumstances are forcing just such a response; if we cannot embrace the preservation of the earth as our new organizing principle, the very survival of our civilization will be in doubt.[26]

Here, forcefully stated, is the driving force behind today's environmental law – the 'new organizing principle' of preservation of the earth, without which all civilization is in jeopardy.

A means already at work for achieving such a co-ordinated collective response is international environmental law, and it is not to be wondered [504] at that these basic principles ensuring the survival of civilization, and indeed of the human species, are already an integral part of that law.

The same matter is put in another perspective in an outstanding study, already referred to:

> The self-extinction of our species is not an act that anyone describes as sane or sensible; nevertheless, it is an act that, without quite admitting it to ourselves, we plan in certain circumstances to commit. Being impossible as a fully intentional act, unless the perpetrator has lost his mind, it can come about only through a kind of inadvertence – as a 'side effect' of some action that we do intend, such as the defense of our nation, or the defense of liberty, or the defense of socialism, or the defense of whatever else we happen to believe in. To that extent, our failure to acknowledge the magnitude and significance of the peril is a necessary condition for doing the deed. We can do it only if we don't quite know what we're doing. If we did acknowledge the full dimensions of the peril, admitting clearly and without reservation that any use of nuclear arms is likely to touch off a holocaust in which the continuance of all human life would be put at risk, extinction would at that moment become not only 'unthinkable' but also undoable.[27]

These principles of environmental law thus do not depend for their validity on treaty provisions. They are part of customary international law. They are part of the *sine qua non* for human survival.

Practical recognitions of the principle that they are an integral part of customary international law are not difficult to find in the international arena. Thus, for example, the Security Council, in resolution 687 of 1991, referred to Iraq's liability 'under international law . . . for environmental damage' resulting from the unlawful invasion of Kuwait. This was not a liability arising under treaty, for Iraq was not a party to either the 1977 ENMOD Convention, nor the 1977 Protocols, nor any other specific treaty dealing expressly with the matter. Iraq's liability to which the Security Council referred in such unequivocal terms was clearly a liability arising under customary international law.[28]

---

[26] A. Gore, *Earth in the Balance: Ecology and the Human Spirit*, 1992, p. 295, cited in Guruswamy, Palmer and Weston, *International Environmental Law and World Order*, 1994, p. 264.

[27] Jonathan Schell, *The Fate of the Earth*, 1982, p. 186.

[28] A submission to this effect was made by the Solomon Islands in the hearings before the Court (CR 95 / 32, Sands, p. 71).

Nor are these principles confined to either peace or war, but cover both situations, for they proceed from general duties, applicable alike in peace and war.[29]

[505] The basic principle in this regard is spelt out by Article 35 (3) of the 1977 Additional Protocol I to the Geneva Convention in terms prohibiting

> methods or means of warfare which are intended, or may be expected, to cause widespread, long-term and severe damage to the natural environment.

Article 55 prohibits

> the use of methods or means of warfare which are intended or may be expected to cause such damage to the natural environment and thereby to prejudice the health or survival of the population.

The question is not whether nuclear weapons were or were not intended to be covered by these formulations. It is sufficient to read them as stating undisputed principles of customary international law. To consider that these general principles are not explicit enough to cover nuclear weapons, or that nuclear weapons were designedly left unmentioned and are therefore not covered, or even that there was a clear understanding that these provisions were not intended to cover nuclear weapons, is to emphasize the incongruity of prohibiting lesser weapons of environmental damage, while leaving intact the infinitely greater agency of causing the very damage which it was the rationale of the treaty to prevent.

If there are general duties arising under customary international law, it clearly matters not that the various environmental agreements do not specifically refer to damage by nuclear weapons. The same principles apply whether we deal with belching furnaces, leaking reactors or explosive weapons. The mere circumstance that coal furnaces or reactors are not specifically mentioned in environmental treaties cannot lead to the conclusion that they are exempt from the incontrovertible and well-established standards and principles laid down therein.

Another approach to the applicability of environmental law to the matter before the Court is through the principle of good neighbourliness, which is both impliedly and expressly written into the United Nations Charter. This principle is one of the bases of modern international law, which has seen the demise of the principle that sovereign States could pursue their own interests in splendid isolation from each other. A world order in which every sovereign State depends on the same global environment generates a mutual interdependence which can only be implemented by co-operation and good neighbourliness.

The United Nations Charter spells this out as 'the general principle of good-neighbourliness, due account being taken of the interests and well-being of the rest of the world, in social, economic, and commercial matters' (Art. 74). A course of action that can destroy the global environment will take to its destruction not only

---

[29] See, for example, the phraseology of Principle 21 of the Stockholm Declaration and Principle 2 of the Rio Declaration, referring to the duties of States to prevent damage to the environment of other States.

the environment, but the social, [**506**] economic and commercial interests that cannot exist apart from that environment. The Charter's express recognition of such a general duty of good neighbourliness makes this an essential part of international law.

This Court, from the very commencement of its jurisprudence, has supported this principle by spelling out the duty of every State not to 'allow knowingly its territory to be used for acts contrary to the rights of other States' (*Corfu Channel, ICJ, Reports 1949*, p. 22).

The question of State responsibility in regard to the environment is dealt with more specifically in my dissenting opinion on the WHO request (*ICJ, Reports 1996*, pp. 139–43),[30] and that discussion must be regarded as supplementary to the discussion of environmental considerations in this opinion. As therein pointed out, damage to the environment caused by nuclear weapons is a breach of State obligation, and this adds another dimension to the illegality of the use or threat of use of nuclear weapons.

[. . .]

IV. Self-defence
[. . .]

[**517**] [. . .] 6. Environmental damage

Similar considerations exist here, as in regard to genocide. The widespread contamination of the environment may even lead to a nuclear winter and to the destruction of the ecosystem. These results will ensue equally, whether the nuclear weapons causing them are used in aggression or in self-defence.

International law relating to the environment, in so far as it concerns nuclear weapons, is dealt with at greater length in my dissenting opinion on the World Health Organization request (*ICJ Reports 1996*, pp. 139–43),[31] and the discussion in that opinion should be considered as supplementary to the above discussion.

[. . .]

DISSENTING OPINION OF JUDGE KOROMA (EXTRACT)

[. . .]

[**578**] [. . .] With regard to the protection and safeguarding of the natural environment, the Court reached the conclusion that existing international law does not prohibit the use of nuclear weapons, but that important environmental factors are to be taken into account in the context of the implementation of the principles and rules of law applicable in armed conflict. The Court also found that relevant treaties in relation to the protection of the natural environment could not have intended to deprive a State of the exercise of its right to self-defence under international law.

In my view, what is at issue is not whether a State might be denied its right to self-defence under the relevant treaties intended for the protection of the natural

[30] See pp. 227–30 above.]
[31] *Ibid.*]

environment, but rather that, given the known qualities of nuclear weapons when exploded as well as their radioactive effects which not only contaminate human beings but the natural environment as well including agriculture, food, drinking water and the marine ecosystem over a wide area, it follows that the use of such weapons would not only cause severe and widespread damage to the natural environment, but would deprive human beings of drinking water and other resources needed for survival. In recognition of this, the First Additional Protocol of 1977 makes provision for the preservation of objects indispensable to the survival of the civilian population, such as foodstuffs, agricultural produce, drinking water installations, etc. The Advisory Opinion should have considered the question posed in relation to the protection of the natural environment from this perspective, rather than giving the impression that the argument advanced was about denying a State its legitimate right of self-defence.

[. . .]

[Reports: *ICJ Reports 1996*, p. 22; 110 *ILR* 163 at p. 177]

Case Concerning the Gabčíkovo–Nagymaros Project (Hungary/Slovakia)[1]

International Court of Justice, The Hague

5 February 1997 (Bedjaoui, *President*; Schwebel, *Vice-President*; Oda, Guillaume, Weeramantry, Ranjeva, Herczegh, Shi, Fleischhauer, Koroma, Vereshchetin and Parra-Aranguren, *Judges*; Skubiszewski, *Judge* ad hoc)

25 September 1997 (Schwebel, *President*; Weeramantry, *Vice-President*; Oda, Bedjaoui, Guillaume, Ranjeva, Herczegh, Shi, Fleischhauer, Koroma, Vereshchetin, Parra-Aranguren, Kooijmans and Rezek, *Judges*; Skubiszewski, *Judge* ad hoc)

Waters – rivers – joint investment project for the production of hydroelectricity, improvement of navigation and flood protection – effects on the environment – emergence of new norms of environmental law – sustainable development – equitable and reasonable share of the resources of an international watercourse

Responsibility and liability – state of necessity as a ground for precluding wrongfulness – Article 33 of the Draft Articles on State Responsibility[2] – essential interest – circumstances constituting an essential interest – whether safeguarding the ecological balance an essential interest of all States – grave and imminent peril – act having to constitute the only means of safeguarding the interest threatened – party having contributed to the occurrence of the state of necessity

Treaties – treaty between Hungary and Czechoslovakia, 16 September 1977 – termination – fundamental change of circumstances – progress of environmental

---

[1] Hungary was represented by HE Mr György Szénási, HE Mr Dénes Tomaj, Mr James Crawford, Mr Pierre-Marie Dupuy, Mr Alexandre Kiss, Mr László Valki, Mr Boldizsár Nagy and Mr Philippe Sands. The Slovak Republic was represented by HE Dr Peter Tomka, Dr Václav Mikulka, Mr Derek W. Bowett, Mr Stephen C. McCaffrey, Mr Alain Pellet, Mr Walter D. Sohier, Sir Arthur Watts, KCMG, QC, Mr Samuel S. Wordsworth, Mr Igor Mucha, Mr Karra Venkateswara Rao and Mr Jens Christian Refsgaard.

[2] This article was adopted by the International Law Commission in substantially the same terms in Article 25 of the Articles on Responsibility of States for Internationally Wrongful Acts.

knowledge – development of new norms of international environmental law – changes not unforeseen – treaty allowing Parties to take account of and apply new developments – whether radical transformation of Treaty obligations

Compliance – international environmental law norms – Treaty-based obligation to apply evolving environmental standards to protect water quality, nature and fishing interests

Damage and compensation – ex injuria jus non oritur *– objectives of Treaty – whether purpose and intention of parties in concluding Treaty prevail over literal interpretation – Treaty obligations overtaken by events – recognition of positions adopted by the parties after conclusion of Treaty – good faith negotiations – joint regime – reparation for acts committed by both Parties – intersecting wrongs – settlement of accounts for the construction*

SUMMARY   *The facts*   On 16 September 1977, Hungary and Czechoslovakia entered into a treaty ('the Treaty') concerning the construction and operation of the Gabčíkovo–Nagymaros System of Locks ('the Project'). The Project was an integrated joint investment aimed at the production of hydroelectricity, the improvement of navigation and flood protection. The Parties were to share the financing, construction and operation of the works, and to benefit in equal measure from the power generated.

The Treaty provided for the building of two series of locks, one upstream at Gabčíkovo in Czechoslovak territory, and the other downstream at Nagymaros in Hungarian territory, designed to constitute a 'single and indivisible system of works'. The upstream section principally comprised a reservoir above the weir at Dunakiliti (on Hungarian territory) and a bypass canal leading to the Gabčíkovo hydroelectric power plant. Downstream at Nagymaros, a further series of locks and a smaller hydroelectric plant were planned. The technical specifications of the system and the preliminary operating and maintenance rules were set out in a related instrument known as the 'Joint Contractual Plan'. Articles 15, 19 and 20 of the Treaty obliged the Parties to take appropriate measures in connection with the construction and operation of the locks to ensure the protection of water quality, nature and fishing interests.

Work on the Project began in 1978. By early 1989, the Gabčíkovo sector was well advanced, but the construction of the Nagymaros sector was only in a preliminary phase. The profound political and economic changes which occurred at this time throughout Central Europe engendered in public opinion and scientific circles a growing apprehension as to the economic and environmental viability of the Project. On 13 May 1989, the Hungarian Government decided to suspend works at Nagymaros pending completion of various studies. On 21 July 1989, the Hungarian Government extended the suspension of the works at Nagymaros, and suspended the works at Dunakiliti. On 27 October 1989, Hungary decided to abandon works at Nagymaros altogether and to maintain the status quo at Dunakiliti.

Czechoslovakia protested against this action, and the Parties began negotiations towards an agreed modification of the Project. Hungary proposed a draft treaty to exclude peak power operation (the mode of maximum power generation, but with greater potential ecological impact) of the Gabčíkovo power plant and the abandonment of the Nagymaros dam. Czechoslovakia expressed a willingness to consider new technical, operational and ecological guarantees for the Project if Hungary was prepared to commence work at Dunakiliti with a view to putting the Gabčíkovo sector into operation on a modified timetable. Czechoslovakia informed Hungary that it would otherwise be compelled to take unilateral measures to put the Gabčíkovo sector into operation without Hungarian cooperation. No agreement was reached.

In November 1991, Czechoslovakia commenced construction of what it termed the 'provisional solution'. 'Variant C', as this unilateral option was known, involved the construction of a new dam upstream of Dunakiliti exclusively on Czechoslovak territory at Čunovo. Discussions between the Parties continued to no avail: Hungary made clear its view that Variant C was a contravention of the 1977 Treaty; Czechoslovakia insisted on the implementation of Variant C as a condition for further negotiation. On 19 May 1992, the Hungarian Government transmitted to the Czechoslovak Government a *Note Verbale* terminating the 1977 Treaty and its related instruments with effect from 25 May 1992. Work on Variant C was largely completed on 27 October 1992, with the diversion of 80 to 90 per cent of the waters of the Danube into the Gabčíkovo bypass canal.

On 1 January 1993, Slovakia became an independent State as a successor State to Czechoslovakia. On 7 April 1993, Hungary and Slovakia concluded the 'Special Agreement for Submission to the International Court of Justice of the Differences between the Republic of Hungary and the Slovak Republic concerning the Gabčíkovo–Nagymaros Project'.[3] Article 2 of the Special Agreement provided that:

---

[3] The text of the Special Agreement (extracted) can be found at pp. 290–2.

1. The Court is requested to decide on the basis of the Treaty and rules and principles of general international law, as well as such other treaties as the Court may find applicable,

(a)   whether the Republic of Hungary was entitled to suspend and subsequently abandon, in 1989, the works on the Nagymaros Project and on the part of the Gabčíkovo Project for which the Treaty attributed responsibility to the Republic of Hungary;

(b)   whether the Czech and Slovak Federal Republic was entitled to proceed, in November 1991, to the 'provisional solution' and to put into operation from October 1992 this system, described in the Report of the Working Group of Independent Experts of the Commission of the European Communities, the Republic of Hungary and the Czech and Slovak Federal Republic dated 23 November 1992 (damming up of the Danube at river kilometre 1851.7 on Czechoslovak territory and resulting consequences on water and navigation course);

(c)   what are the legal effects of the notification, on 19 May 1992, of the termination of the Treaty by the Republic of Hungary.

2. The Court is also requested to determine the legal consequences, including the rights and obligations for the Parties, arising from its Judgment on the questions in paragraph 1 of this Article.

Order of 5 February 1997

The Court decided to hold a visit to a number of locations along the Danube. The visit took place between 1 and 4 April 1997 in accordance with arrangements agreed between the Parties.

Judgment of 25 September 1997

Held by the International Court of Justice

(1)   With regard to Article 2, paragraph 1, of the Special Agreement

(by fourteen votes to one) (A)   That Hungary was not entitled to suspend and subsequently abandon, in 1989, the works on the Nagymaros Project and on the part of the Gabčíkovo Project for which the Treaty and related instruments attributed responsibility to it;

(by nine votes to six) (B)   That Czechoslovakia was entitled to proceed, in November 1991, to the 'provisional solution' as described in the terms of the Special Agreement;

(by ten votes to five) (C)   That Czechoslovakia was not entitled to put into operation, from October 1992, this 'provisional solution';

(by eleven votes to four) (D)   That the notification, on 19 May 1992, of the termination of the Treaty and related instruments by Hungary did not have the legal effect of terminating them.

(2)   With regard to Article 2, paragraph 2, of the Special Agreement

(by twelve votes to three) (A)   That Slovakia, as successor to Czechoslovakia, became party to the Treaty as from 1 January 1993;

(*by thirteen votes to two*) (B)   That Hungary and Slovakia must negotiate in good faith in the light of the prevailing situation, and must take all necessary measures to ensure the achievement of the objectives of the Treaty, in accordance with such modalities as they might agree upon;

(*by thirteen votes to two*) (C)   That, unless the Parties otherwise agreed, a joint operational regime must be established in accordance with the Treaty;

(*by twelve votes to three*) (D)   That, unless the Parties otherwise agreed, Hungary should compensate Slovakia for the damage sustained by Czechoslovakia and by Slovakia on account of the suspension and abandonment by Hungary of works for which it was responsible; and that Slovakia should compensate Hungary for the damage it had sustained on account of the operation of the 'provisional solution' by Czechoslovakia and its maintenance in service by Slovakia;

(*by thirteen votes to two*) (E)   That the settlement of accounts for the construction and operation of the works must be effected in accordance with the relevant provisions of the Treaty and related instruments, taking due account of measures taken by the Parties in application of points 2(B) and (C) of the Judgment.

I. Article 2, paragraph 1, of the Special Agreement

(1)   The Parties both accepted that the 1977 Treaty and related instruments were validly concluded and duly in force throughout the operative period. The texts did not envisage the possibility of unilateral suspension or abandonment of the work provided for.

(2)   The Vienna Convention on the Law of Treaties was not directly applicable as both States ratified the Convention only after the conclusion of the 1977 Treaty. Nonetheless, the provisions of the Convention concerning the termination and the suspension of the operation of treaties set forth in Articles 60 to 62 were a codification of existing customary law.

(3)   The effect of Hungary's conduct was to render impossible the accomplishment of the system of works that the Treaty expressly described as 'single and indivisible'. By invoking a 'state of necessity' to justify its conduct, Hungary had placed itself within the ambit of the law of State responsibility, implying that, in the absence of necessity, its conduct would be unlawful. Hungary had also acknowledged that a state of necessity would not exempt it from a duty to compensate.

(4)   Necessity, however, could only be invoked on an exceptional basis. All of the strict conditions set forth in Article 33 of the Draft Articles on

State Responsibility had to be satisfied. The State concerned was not the sole judge of whether those conditions had been met.

(5)   The characterisation of an 'essential interest' was to be assessed in the light of each particular case, and was not restricted to matters affecting the 'existence' of the State. Safeguarding the ecological balance had come to be considered an essential interest of all States. Thus the concerns expressed by Hungary for its natural environment in the region affected by the Gabčíkovo–Nagymaros Project did relate to an essential interest of the State.

(6)   On several occasions in 1989, Hungary had expressed 'uncertainties' as to the ecological impact of the Gabčíkovo–Nagymaros Project and called for new scientific studies. However, a state of necessity could not exist without a 'peril' duly established at the relevant time period. Such a requirement had to be imminent, not merely possible. It would have been difficult to determine in light of the scientific record in 1989 that the alleged peril was sufficiently certain and therefore 'imminent'.

(7)   Hungary could also have resorted to other means to respond to the dangers it apprehended. Within the framework of the original Project, Hungary was in a position to control, at least partially, the distribution of water within the system, and could construct the works needed to regulate flows along the old bed of the Danube and the side-arms. Moreover, the Treaty provided for the possibility that each of the Parties might withdraw quantities of water exceeding those specified in the Joint Contractual Plan in exchange for a corresponding reduction of the share of electric power.

(8)   Hungary was thus not entitled to suspend, and subsequently to abandon, the works on the Nagymaros Project and on the part of the Gabčíkovo Project for which the 1977 Treaty and related instruments attributed responsibility to it.

(9)   In reaction to Hungary's suspension and abandonment of works and its refusal to resume performance of its obligations under the Treaty, Czechoslovakia had decided to put the Gabčíkovo system into operation unilaterally, under its exclusive control and for its own benefit. To justify those actions, Slovakia had invoked what it described as the 'principle of approximate application'. It was not necessary to determine the existence of such a principle because, even if such a principle existed, it could only be employed within the limits of the treaty in question. Despite having a certain external physical similarity to the original Project, Variant C differed sharply from it in its legal characteristics.

(10)   The 1977 Treaty provided for the construction of the Gabčíkovo–Nagymaros Barrage System Project as a joint investment consisting of a single and indivisible operational system of works, jointly owned and operated. By definition, this could not be carried out by unilateral action. In practice, the operation of Variant C had led Czechoslovakia to appropriate between 80 and 90 per cent of the waters of a shared international watercourse and international boundary river. Hungary, by the violation of its legal obligations under the Treaty, had not forfeited its basic right to an equitable and reasonable share of the resource. In putting Variant C into operation, Czechoslovakia had committed an internationally wrongful act.

(11)   However, a wrongful act or offence was frequently preceded by preparatory actions which were not to be confused with the act or offence itself. In so far as Czechoslovakia had confined itself to the execution on its own territory of the works necessary for the implementation of Variant C, which could have been abandoned if an agreement had been reached between the parties and had not therefore predetermined the final decision to be taken, it had not committed a wrongful act.

(12)   As the putting into operation of Variant C constituted an internationally wrongful act, it was not necessary to examine the issue of the duty to mitigate invoked by Slovakia.

(13)   Slovakia had argued that 'Variant C could be presented as a justified countermeasure to Hungary's illegal acts.' The diversion of the Danube carried out by Czechoslovakia was not a lawful countermeasure because it was not proportionate.

(14)   On 19 May 1992, the Hungarian Government transmitted to the Czechoslovak Government a Declaration notifying it of the termination by Hungary of the 1977 Treaty as of 25 May 1992. In its pleadings, Hungary presented five arguments in support of the lawfulness of its notification of termination. These were: (i) the existence of a state of necessity; (ii) the impossibility of performance of the Treaty; (iii) the occurrence of a fundamental change of circumstances; (iv) the material breach of the Treaty by Czechoslovakia; and (v) the development of new norms of international environmental law.

(15)   The 1977 Treaty did not contain any provision regarding its termination or the possibility of denunciation or withdrawal. On the contrary, the Treaty established a long-standing and durable regime of joint investment and joint operation. Consequently, the Treaty could be terminated only on the limited grounds enumerated in Articles 60

to 62 of the Vienna Convention which were declaratory of customary international law.

(16)   Necessity was not a ground for the termination of a treaty. It might only be invoked to negate the responsibility of a State that had failed to implement a treaty. The treaty might be ineffective as long as the condition of necessity continued to exist. The treaty nevertheless continued to exist, even if dormant, unless the parties agreed to terminate it. In the absence of such agreement, as soon as the state of necessity ceased to exist, the duty to comply with treaty obligations revived.

(17)   Article 61, paragraph 1, of the Vienna Convention required 'the permanent disappearance or destruction of an object indispensable for the execution' of the treaty to justify the termination of a treaty on grounds of impossibility of performance. Hungary contended that the essential object of the Treaty – a single and indivisible operational system of works, jointly owned and operated – had permanently disappeared and that the Treaty had become impossible to perform. The 1977 Treaty, however, provided a means to make required readjustments between economic and ecological imperatives. Thus the 'object', even if understood to embrace a legal regime, had not definitively ceased to exist. If the joint exploitation of the investment was no longer possible, Hungary was itself responsible. Article 61, paragraph 2, of the Vienna Convention precluded the invocation of impossibility by a party when the impossibility of performance resulted from that party's own breach.

(18)   Hungary further invoked a fundamental change of circumstances brought about by profound political and economic changes, and the progress of environmental knowledge and the development of new norms and prescriptions of international environmental law. The Treaty provided for a joint investment programme for the production of energy, the control of floods and the improvement of navigation on the Danube. The prevalent political conditions were not so closely linked to the object and purpose of the Treaty, nor the estimated profitability so fixed, that changes in these matters had radically altered the extent of the obligations to be performed. New developments in the state of environmental knowledge and of environmental law could not have been completely unforeseen. Articles 15, 19 and 20 of the Treaty allowed the Parties to take account of such developments and apply them when implementing those provisions.

(19)   The changed circumstances were not of such a nature that their effect would be radically to transform the extent of the obligations still

to be performed to accomplish the Project. Moreover, a fundamental change of circumstances must have been unforeseen, and the existence of the circumstances at the time of the Treaty's conclusion must have constituted an essential basis of the consent of the Parties to be bound by the Treaty. The stability of treaty relations required that the plea of fundamental change of circumstances be applied only in exceptional cases.

(20)   Articles 15, 19 and 20 of the Treaty obliged the Parties jointly and on a continuous basis to take appropriate measures necessary for the protection of water quality, nature and fishing interests. Hungary contended that Czechoslovakia had violated these articles by refusing to enter into negotiations in order to adapt the Project to new scientific and legal developments regarding the environment. In this case, both Parties could be said to have contributed to the creation of a situation which was not conducive to the conduct of fruitful negotiations. Only a material breach of a treaty by a State party might be relied upon by another party as a ground for termination. The violation of other rules of general international law might justify the taking of certain measures, including countermeasures, by the injured State, but did not constitute a ground for termination under the law of treaties.

(21)   Hungary's principal argument for invoking a material breach of the Treaty was the construction and putting into operation of Variant C. Czechoslovakia had violated the Treaty only when it had diverted the waters of the Danube in October 1992. The notification of termination by Hungary on 19 May 1992 had predated that diversion. Hungary had not yet suffered injury, and consequently was not entitled to invoke any such breach as a ground for termination. Moreover, Czechoslovakia had committed the internationally wrongful act as a result of Hungary's own prior wrongful conduct. Hungary had thus prejudiced its right to terminate the Treaty.

(22)   Hungary claimed that it was entitled to terminate the Treaty, because of new requirements of international law for the protection of the environment which precluded performance of the Treaty. Neither of the Parties contended that new peremptory norms of environmental law had emerged since the conclusion of the 1977 Treaty. The obligations in Articles 15, 19 and 20 entailed a joint responsibility to adapt the Treaty to emerging norms through a process of good faith consultation and negotiation.

(23)   Hungary maintained that by their conduct both Parties had repudiated the Treaty and that a bilateral treaty repudiated by both parties

could not survive. The reciprocal wrongful conduct of Hungary and Czechoslovakia did not justify the termination of the Treaty. The Court would set a precedent with disturbing implications for treaty relations and the integrity of the rule *pacta sunt servanda* if it were to conclude that a treaty in force between States, which the parties had implemented in considerable measure and at great cost over a period of years, might be unilaterally set aside on grounds of reciprocal non-compliance.

II. Article 2, paragraph 2, of the Special Agreement

(1)   The content of the 1977 Treaty indicated that it must be regarded as establishing a territorial regime within the meaning of Article 12 of the 1978 Vienna Convention on the Succession of States. It created rights and obligations 'attaching to' the parts of the Danube to which it related; thus the Treaty could not be affected by a succession of States. The Treaty became binding upon Slovakia on 1 January 1993.

(2)   The 1977 Treaty was still in force and consequently governed the relationship between the Parties. That relationship was also determined by the rules of other relevant conventions to which the two States were party, by the rules of general international law and, in this particular case, by the rules of State responsibility; but it was governed, above all, by the applicable rules of the 1977 Treaty as a *lex specialis*.

(3)   At the same time, it was essential that the factual situation as it had developed since 1989 be placed within the context of the preserved and developing treaty relationship in order to achieve the object and purpose in so far as that was feasible. What might have been a correct application of the law in 1989 or 1992 could be a miscarriage of justice if prescribed in 1997. Variant C had been in operation for nearly five years in a run-of-the-river mode. The weir at Nagymaros had not been built, and with the effective discarding by both Parties of peak power operation, there was no longer any point in building it.

(4)   The other objectives of the Treaty – navigability, flood control, ice control and protection of the environment – could adequately be served by the existing structures. The 1977 Treaty did not lay down a rigid system. In practice, the Parties, in adopting their subsequent positions, had acknowledged that the explicit terms of the Treaty were negotiable.

(5)   The Parties were under a legal obligation, during the negotiations to be held by virtue of Article 5 of the Special Agreement, to consider in what way the multiple objectives of the 1977 Treaty could best be served. The Parties were obliged by Articles 15 and 19 of the Treaty to assess

the impact of the Gabčíkovo power plant on the environment by current standards of evaluating environmental risks.

(6)   The purpose of the Treaty and the intentions of the Parties in concluding it should prevail over its literal interpretation. When bilateral negotiations without preconditions were held to give effect to the Judgment, a readiness to accept the assistance and expertise of a third party would evidence the good faith of the Parties.

(7)   The joint regime provided for in the Treaty should be restored. The works at Čunovo should become jointly operated in view of their pivotal role in the operation of what remained of the Project and for the water-management regime. Variant C, which operated in a manner incompatible with the Treaty, should be made to conform to it so as to accommodate both the economic operation of the system of electricity generation and the satisfaction of essential environmental concerns. By associating Hungary, on an equal footing, in its operation, management and benefits, Variant C would be transformed from a *de facto* status into a treaty-based regime reflecting in an optimal way the concept of common utilisation of shared water resources.

(8)   Reparation must, as far as possible, wipe out all the consequences of the illegal act (*Factory at Chorzów*, PCIJ, Series A, No. 17, p. 47).[4] In the present case, this would be achieved if the Parties resumed their cooperation in the utilisation of the shared water resources. Both Parties had committed internationally wrongful acts giving rise to damage. Consequently Hungary and Slovakia were each under an obligation to pay compensation and each entitled to obtain compensation. Given the intersecting wrongs of both Parties, the issue of compensation could satisfactorily be resolved if each of the Parties were to renounce or cancel all financial claims and counter-claims.

Declaration of President Schwebel   The construction of Variant C was inseparable from its being put into operation. Hungary's position as the Party initially in breach did not deprive it of the right to terminate the Treaty in response to Czechoslovakia's material breach.

Declaration of Judge Rezek   The 1977 Treaty was no longer in force as the Hungarian notification of 19 May 1992 constituted the formal act of termination of a treaty both Parties had already repudiated. The consequences were similar to those inferred by the majority.

Separate Opinion of Vice-President Weeramantry (1)   The Court had to strike a balance between environmental and developmental

---

[4] 4 *Ann Dig* 268.

considerations in light of the emerging concept of sustainable development. From the early 1970s, there had been widespread recognition of the
concept in a broad range of international and regional instruments, and
in State practice. This case presented an opportunity to strengthen the
concept, taking a multi-disciplinary approach to draw upon the world's
diversity of cultures and traditional legal systems. Sustainable development could be seen as one of the most ancient of ideas of human heritage,
and not merely a principle of modern international law.

(2)   A recognition of the principle of contemporaneity in the application of environmental norms applied to the joint supervisory regime
envisaged in the Court's Judgment, requiring the Parties to take into
consideration the emergence of new environmental standards in the application of the Treaty.

(3)   In entering into the 1977 Treaty, Hungary had taken a considered
decision, despite warnings of the possible environmental dangers, and
had continued to treat the Treaty as valid for nearly twelve years. In
reliance, Czechoslovakia had devoted substantial resources to the Project.
Present in this sequence of events were the ingredients of a legally binding
estoppel. However, in cases involving potential environmental damage
of a far-reaching and irreversible nature, the limitations of *inter partes*
adversarial procedure might not be appropriate to determine obligations
of an *erga omnes* character.

Separate Opinion of Judge Bedjaoui   (1)   The essential basis for the
interpretation of a treaty remained the 'fixed reference' to contemporary
international law at the time of its conclusion. The 'mobile reference' to
the law which subsequently developed was only applicable in exceptional
cases. The definition of 'environment' was essentially static, unlike the
evolutionary concept of the 'sacred trust' interpreted in the *Namibia*
case.[5]

(2)   An interpretation of a treaty which would amount to substituting
a completely different law to the one governing at the time of its conclusion would be a distorted revision. A State incurred specific obligations
contained in a body of law as it existed on the conclusion of the treaty
and in no wise incurred evolutionary and indeterminate duties.

(3)   In the present case, subsequent law relating to the environment
and international watercourses might be applied advisedly on the basis
of Articles 15, 19 and 20 for an 'evolutionary interpretation' of the 1977
Treaty.

---

[5]   49 *ILR* 2.

(4)   The 1977 Treaty had the threefold characteristic of being (i) a territorial treaty; (ii) a treaty to which Slovakia had succeeded; and (iii) a treaty which was still in force.

(5)   There was no theory of 'approximate application' in international law. If accepted, it would be a detriment to legal certainty and would signal the end of the cardinal principle *pacta sunt servanda*. The theory provided no reliable criterion for measuring a tolerable degree of 'approximation', and lacked the basic condition of the consent of the other State.

(6)   Variant C substantially differed in concept and design from the initial Project. It fell into one of the categories of breaches termed 'continuing', 'composite' or 'complex', each phase of which was unlawful. The unlawful nature of Variant C, from the commencement of its construction to the diversion of the river, could only be divisible if it had been shown that no phase of its implementation, apart from the diversion, prejudiced Hungary's rights and interests. It did not qualify as a countermeasure. It was a definitive, irreversible breach of the Treaty.

(7)   The intersecting violations committed by both Parties gave rise to two *effectivités*. The first was that Variant C was nearly complete, and represented a partial application of the Treaty. The second was that Hungary had abandoned work on all fronts and decided not to build the Nagymaros dam. These *effectivités* had been mutually recognised by the Parties, and provided signals in the attempt to find appropriate solutions.

(8)   The 1977 Treaty had largely been stripped of its material content, but remained a formal instrument, ready to accommodate new commitments by the Parties. In taking into consideration the *effectivités*, the Court had no intention to legitimise the unlawful facts established for which the Parties must assume responsibility. This made it possible to salvage Articles 15, 19 and 20, which would provide a basis for renegotiation. This would also make possible the conservation of the general philosophy and major principles of the Treaty.

(9)   The Parties must negotiate again in good faith conditions to restore Hungary to its status as a partner in the use of the water and co-owner of the works.

Separate Opinion of Judge Koroma   (1)   Variant C was a genuine application of the Treaty inasmuch as it constituted the minimum modification of the original Project necessary to realise its aims and objectives. Czechoslovakia would otherwise have been stranded with a largely finished but inoperative system.

(2)   Hungary had agreed within the context of the Project to the diversion of the Danube, modifying its entitlement to an equitable and reasonable share of the water of the Danube.

(3)   The finding of an intersection of wrongs and a reciprocal obligation of reparation suggested that the Court found the wrongful conduct of the Parties to be equivalent. The operation of Variant C was a genuine attempt by an injured party to secure the achievement of the agreed objectives of the Treaty in ways consistent with the Treaty, international law and equity.

Dissenting Opinion of Judge Oda   (1)   Hungary's claim of ecological necessity was ill-founded as the Project was prepared and designed with full consideration of its potential environmental impact. Any subsequent impact assessment could not justify its total abandonment.

(2)   Czechoslovakia was entitled to proceed with Variant C, both its construction and the diversion of the Danube, as an alternative means of implementing the Project in the face of Hungary's wrongful act. The cost of its construction should be borne in part by Hungary, in exchange for co-ownership. However, if the operation of Variant C had led to tangible damage to Hungary, Slovakia bore responsibility.

(3)   Negotiations between the Parties should be based on the understanding that Czechoslovakia was entitled to proceed to the implementation of Variant C and that it would in future form part of the Joint Contractual Plan. Its mode of operation should be defined to avoid peak mode and ensure an equitable share of the waters. The Parties should continue the environmental assessment of the region and search out technical remedies to prevent environmental damage.

Dissenting Opinion of Judge Ranjeva   (1)   The intersecting nature of the wrongs had a bearing both on the declaratory part and on the prescriptive part of the Judgment. The Court should have considered whether the Hungarian wrong caused a sufficiently proven risk which forced the construction and putting into operation of Variant C.

(2)   The distinction between 'proceeding to the provisional solution' and its 'putting into operation' was artificial as the two elements were part of a single, continuing act. The fact of substituting a national project in place of a joint international project was a serious breach of the Treaty. Limiting the sanction to the factual consequences of the breach itself represented a precedent with disturbing implications for treaty relations and the integrity of the rule *pacta sunt servanda*.

Dissenting Opinion of Judge Herczegh   (1)   The Project was an audacious scheme in scale, design and mode of operation, criticised not only by the Hungarian party but also by the Czechoslovak leaders as obsolete and contrary to nature. It was regrettable that the Court acknowledged the need to apply developing environmental norms and standards to new and continuing activities only in the prescriptive part of its Judgment.

(2) There was an obvious contradiction between a project designed for peak mode operation and the absence of an agreement between the parties as to this mode of operation. There was no legal obstacle to prevent the Project from being adapted to a less dangerous mode of operation.

(3) In suspending the construction of the Nagymaros dam, Hungary had acted under a state of necessity to safeguard an essential interest – the provision of drinking water for the 2 million inhabitants of the Hungarian capital – against a grave and imminent peril.

(4) The unilateral diversion of the Danube and its exclusive utilisation by Slovakia were a breach of a provision essential to the accomplishment of the object and purpose of the Treaty, whereas the conduct of Hungary simply delayed but did not preclude the commissioning of the power plant. Czechoslovakia had acted unlawfully when it embarked on the construction of the works necessary for the diversion.

(5) Since Variant C, from its commencement, constituted a grave breach of the Treaty, Hungary was entitled to terminate the Treaty. The Treaty did not survive the joint effect of the diversion of the Danube and Hungary's notification of its termination.

(6) The termination of the Treaty would not have left the Parties in a legal vacuum. The relationship was determined by rules of general international law and other treaties and conventions in force between the Parties. These were sufficient to ensure an equitable and reasonable sharing of the Danube waters.

Dissenting Opinion of Judge Fleischhauer (1)   Hungary validly terminated the 1977 Treaty by its notification of termination of 19 May 1992. The putting into operation of Variant C constituted a continuing wrongful act which extended from the passing from mere studies and planning to construction in November 1991 and lasted to the actual damming of the Danube in October 1992. Recourse to Variant C was neither automatic nor the only possible reaction to Hungary's violations of the Treaty. The fact that Hungary violated the Treaty first did not deprive it of the right to terminate the same Treaty in reaction to its later violation by Czechoslovakia.

(2)   After the valid termination of the Treaty, the Parties were released from any further obligation to perform, and the situation was governed by general international law and by those treaties that remain in force between the Parties. There was no legal obligation for Slovakia to provide for joint operation of Variant C or for sharing of profits. By reason of its past behaviour, Hungary was not entitled to restoration of the full flow of the Danube, but a water-management regime must be established that took account of Hungary's ecological needs. Each Party owed the other compensation: Hungary for damages arising out of the delays in construction caused by its suspension and subsequent abandonment of the Project; and Slovakia for losses and damages sustained out of the unilateral diversion of the Danube.

Dissenting Opinion of Judge Vereshchetin   Variant C met all of the conditions for the lawfulness of a countermeasure: it was a necessary, reversible and proportionate response to Hungary's violation of its Treaty obligations. The Court would impose the requirement of Variant C that it be the only means available to Czechoslovakia of asserting its rights and inducing Hungary's compliance. This over-reached the requirements established by the ILC Draft Articles on State Responsibility. Even accepting this requirement, there was no effective alternative option available to Czechoslovakia.

Dissenting Opinion of Judge Parra-Aranguren   Czechoslovakia was legally justified in adopting Variant C to guarantee the achievement of the object and purpose of the Treaty as a reaction to Hungary's violation of its obligations. Even assuming Variant C could be characterised as an internationally wrongful act, its wrongfulness was precluded because it was a legitimate countermeasure, meeting all the conditions required by Article 30 of the Draft Articles on State Responsibility.

Dissenting Opinion of Judge ad hoc *Skubiszewski*   (1)   Hungary, alone, followed a policy of freeing itself from the bonds of the Treaty. For its part, Czechoslovakia insisted on the implementation of the Treaty, though it was ready to adopt a flexible attitude with regard to the operation of the system. When the Treaty was negotiated, the state of knowledge was sufficient to assess the impact of the Project. Progress in science and knowledge was constant, and required adaptation and negotiation.

(2)   By its unilateral rejection of the Project, Hungary had precluded itself from asserting that the utilisation of the hydraulic force of the Danube was dependent on the condition of a prior agreement between it and Czechoslovakia. Czechoslovakia had the right to put Variant C

into operation, but it also had the duty to respect Hungary's right to an equitable and reasonable share of the waters of the Danube. To find the operation of Variant C unlawful overlooked the considerations of equity.

(3)   Pecuniary compensation could not wipe out all of the consequences of the abandonment of the Project by Hungary. The attainment of the objectives of the Treaty was legitimate under the Treaty, general law and equity. The question was not simply one of damages for loss sustained, but the creation of a new system of utilisation of the water. Negotiations between the Parties should not focus on the enforcement of responsibility and compensation, but on seeking a common solution.

There follows

Order of International Court of Justice, 5 February 1997 (extract)

[3] Having regard to the Special Agreement between the Republic of Hungary and the Slovak Republic, signed in Brussels on 7 April 1993 and notified jointly to the Court on 2 July 1993, whereby the Parties submitted to the Court the differences between them concerning the Gabčíkovo–Nagymaros Project,

Having regard to the Memorials, Counter-Memorials and Replies [4] which were filed by the Parties within the time-limits fixed to that end by the Orders dated 14 July 1993 and 20 December 1994;

Whereas, by a letter dated 16 June 1995, the Agent of Slovakia asked the Court 'to be so good as to implement its powers under Article 66 of the Rules of Court and to decide to visit the locality to which the case concerning the *Gabčíkovo–Nagymaros Project* relates, and there to exercise its functions with regard to the obtaining of

---

[6]   The declarations of President Schwebel and Judge Rezek are not reproduced in this volume but can be found at *ICJ Reports 1997*, pp. 85 and 86 respectively. The dissenting opinions of Judges Ranjeva, Fleischhauer, Vereshchetin and Parra-Aranguren are not reproduced in this volume but can be found at *ICJ Reports 1997*, pp. 170, 204, 219 and 227 respectively.

evidence'; and whereas a copy of that letter was duly transmitted to the Agent of Hungary;

Whereas, by a letter dated 28 June 1995, the Agent of Hungary informed the Court that if it 'should decide that a visit to the various areas affected by the Project (or, more precisely, affected by variant C) would be useful, Hungary would be pleased to co-operate in organizing such a visit';

Whereas, further to certain exchanges of views between the President of the Court and the Agents of the Parties on 30 June 1995, the Agents, by a letter dated 14 November 1995, jointly notified the Court of the text of a 'Protocol of Agreement between the Republic of Hungary and the Slovak Republic with a view to proposing to the International Court of Justice the arrangements for a visit *in situ* in the case concerning the *Gabčíkovo–Nagymaros Project*', done in Budapest and New York on 14 November 1995, and signed by them;

Whereas by the terms of that Protocol the Parties 'propose[d] by mutual agreement to the Court that it should effect a visit' *in situ* under the conditions set forth therein; and whereas those conditions included the outline of a programme, the precise dates and details of which were to be defined at a later time by the Court, after ascertaining the view of the Parties;

Whereas, during a meeting held by the President of the Court with the Agents of the Parties on 5 December 1996, the Agents agreed on dates at which the proposed visit might take place; and whereas the Registrar confirmed to them, by letters dated 6 December 1996, that those dates were agreeable to the Court;

Whereas the Agents of the Parties jointly notified to the Court, by letter dated 3 February 1997, the text of Agreed Minutes done at Budapest and at New York on 3 February 1997, and signed by them; and whereas those Agreed Minutes supplemented the Protocol of Agreement of 14 November 1995 and contained detailed proposals for the conduct of the visit *in situ*;

Whereas it appears to the Court that to exercise its functions with regard to the obtaining of evidence at a place or locality to which the case relates may facilitate its task in the instant case, and whereas the proposals made by the Parties to that end may be accepted,

[5] THE COURT,

Unanimously,

(1) *Decides* to exercise its functions with regard to the obtaining of evidence by visiting a place or locality to which the case relates;

(2) *Decides* to adopt to that end the arrangements proposed by the Parties in the Protocol of Agreement dated 14 November 1995, as subsequently specified, in accordance with the provisions of that Protocol, in the Agreed Minutes dated 3 February 1997.

[. . .]

[Reports: *ICJ Reports 1997*, p. 3; 116 *ILR* 1 at p. 15]

Judgment of International Court of Justice, 25 September 1997 (extract)

[10] 1. By a letter dated 2 July 1993, filed in the Registry of the Court on the same day, the Ambassador of the Republic of Hungary (hereinafter called 'Hungary') to the Netherlands and the Chargé d'affaires *ad interim* of the Slovak Republic (hereinafter called 'Slovakia') to the Netherlands jointly notified to the Court a Special Agreement in English that had been signed at Brussels on 7 April 1993 and had entered into force on 28 June 1993, on the date of the exchange of instruments of ratification.

2. The text of the Special Agreement reads as follows:

[11] *The Republic of Hungary and the Slovak Republic,*

Considering that differences have arisen between the Czech and Slovak Federal Republic and the Republic of Hungary regarding the implementation and the termination of the Treaty on the Construction and Operation of the Gabčíkovo–Nagymaros Barrage System signed in Budapest on 16 September 1977 and related instruments (hereinafter referred to as 'the Treaty'), and on the construction and operation of the 'provisional solution';

Bearing in mind that the Slovak Republic is one of the two successor States of the Czech and Slovak Federal Republic and the sole successor State in respect of rights and obligations relating to the Gabčíkovo–Nagymaros Project;

Recognizing that the Parties concerned have been unable to settle these differences by negotiations;

Having in mind that both the Czechoslovak and Hungarian delegations expressed their commitment to submit the differences connected with the Gabčíkovo–Nagymaros Project in all its aspects to binding international arbitration or to the International Court of Justice;

Desiring that these differences should be settled by the International Court of Justice;

Recalling their commitment to apply, pending the Judgment of the International Court of Justice, such a temporary water management régime of the Danube as shall be agreed between the Parties;

Desiring further to define the issues to be submitted to the International Court of Justice,

Have agreed as follows:

Article 1

The Parties submit the questions contained in Article 2 to the International Court of Justice pursuant to Article 40, paragraph 1, of the Statute of the Court.

Article 2

(1) The Court is requested to decide on the basis of the Treaty and rules and principles of general international law, as well as such other treaties as the Court may find applicable,

(*a*)   whether the Republic of Hungary was entitled to suspend and subsequently abandon, in 1989, the works on the Nagymaros Project and on the part of the Gabčíkovo Project for which the Treaty attributed responsibility to the Republic of Hungary;

(*b*)   whether the Czech and Slovak Federal Republic was entitled to proceed, in November 1991, to the 'provisional solution' and to put into operation from October 1992 this system, described in the Report of the Working Group of Independent Experts of the Commission of the European Communities, the Republic of Hungary and the Czech and Slovak Federal Republic dated 23 November 1992 (damming up of the Danube at river kilometre 1851.7 on Czechoslovak territory and resulting consequences on water and navigation course);

(c) [12] what are the legal effects of the notification, on 19 May 1992, of the termination of the Treaty by the Republic of Hungary.

(2) The Court is also requested to determine the legal consequences, including the rights and obligations for the Parties, arising from its Judgment on the questions in paragraph 1 of this Article.

Article 3

(1) All questions of procedure and evidence shall be regulated in accordance with the provisions of the Statute and the Rules of Court.

(2) However, the Parties request the Court to order that the written proceedings should consist of:

(a) a Memorial presented by each of the Parties not later than ten months after the date of notification of this Special Agreement to the Registrar of the International Court of Justice;

(b) a Counter-Memorial presented by each of the Parties not later than seven months after the date on which each has received the certified copy of the Memorial of the other Party;

(c) a Reply presented by each of the Parties within such time-limits as the Court may order.

(d) The Court may request additional written pleadings by the Parties if it so determines.

(3) The above-mentioned parts of the written proceedings and their annexes presented to the Registrar will not be transmitted to the other Party until the Registrar has received the corresponding part of the proceedings from the said Party.

Article 4

(1) The Parties agree that, pending the final Judgment of the Court, they will establish and implement a temporary water management régime for the Danube.

(2) They further agree that, in the period before such a régime is established or implemented, if either Party believes its rights are endangered by the conduct of the other, it may request immediate consultation and reference, if necessary, to experts, including the Commission of the European Communities, with a view to protecting those rights; and that protection shall not be sought through a request to the Court under Article 41 of the Statute.

(3) This commitment is accepted by both Parties as fundamental to the conclusion and continuing validity of the Special Agreement.

Article 5

(1) The Parties shall accept the Judgment of the Court as final and binding upon them and shall execute it in its entirety and in good faith.

(2) Immediately after the transmission of the Judgment the Parties shall enter into negotiations on the modalities for its execution.

(3) If they are unable to reach agreement within six months, either Party may request the Court to render an additional Judgment to determine the modalities for executing its Judgment.

Article 6

(1) The present Special Agreement shall be subject to ratification.

(2) **[13]** The instruments of ratification shall be exchanged as soon as possible in Brussels.

(3) The present Special Agreement shall enter into force on the date of exchange of instruments of ratification. Thereafter it will be notified jointly to the Registrar of the Court.

In witness whereof the undersigned being duly authorized thereto, have signed the present Special Agreement and have affixed thereto their seals.

[. . .]

[17] [. . .] 15. The present case arose out of the signature, on 16 September 1977, by the Hungarian People's Republic and the Czechoslovak People's Republic, of a treaty 'concerning the construction and operation of the Gabčíkovo–Nagymaros System of Locks' (hereinafter called the '1977 Treaty'). The names of the two contracting States have varied over the years; hereinafter they will be referred to as Hungary and Czechoslovakia. The 1977 Treaty entered into force on 30 June 1978.

It provides for the construction and operation of a System of Locks by the parties as a 'joint investment'. According to its Preamble, the barrage system was designed to attain

> the broad utilization of the natural resources of the Bratislava–Budapest section of the Danube river for the development of water **[18]** resources, energy, transport, agriculture and other sectors of the national economy of the Contracting Parties.

The joint investment was thus essentially aimed at the production of hydroelectricity, the improvement of navigation on the relevant section of the Danube and the protection of the areas along the banks against flooding. At the same time, by the terms of the Treaty, the contracting parties undertook to ensure that the quality of water in the Danube was not impaired as a result of the Project, and that compliance with the obligations for the protection of nature arising in connection with the construction and operation of the System of Locks would be observed.

16. The Danube is the second longest river in Europe, flowing along or across the borders of nine countries in its 2,860-kilometre course from the Black Forest eastwards to the Black Sea. For 142 kilometres, it forms the boundary between Slovakia and Hungary. The sector with which this case is concerned is a stretch of approximately 200 kilometres, between Bratislava in Slovakia and Budapest in Hungary. Below Bratislava, the river gradient decreases markedly, creating an alluvial plain of gravel and sand sediment. This plain is delimited to the north-east, in Slovak territory, by the Malý Danube and to the south-west, in Hungarian territory, by the Mosoni Danube. The boundary between the two States is constituted, in the major part of that region,

by the main channel of the river. The area lying between the Malý Danube and that channel, in Slovak territory, constitutes the Žitný Ostrov; the area between the main channel and the Mosoni Danube, in Hungarian territory, constitutes the Szigetköz. Čunovo and, further downstream, Gabčíkovo, are situated in this sector of the river on Slovak territory, Čunovo on the right bank and Gabčíkovo on the left. Further downstream, after the confluence of the various branches, the river enters Hungarian territory and the topography becomes hillier. Nagymaros lies in a narrow valley at a bend in the Danube just before it turns south, enclosing the large river island of Szentendre before reaching Budapest (see sketch-map No. 1, p. 19 below).[7]

17. The Danube has always played a vital part in the commercial and economic development of its riparian States, and has underlined and reinforced their interdependence, making international co-operation essential. Improvements to the navigation channel have enabled the Danube, now linked by canal to the Main and thence to the Rhine, to become an important navigational artery connecting the North Sea to the Black Sea. In the stretch of river to which the case relates, flood protection measures have been constructed over the centuries, farming and forestry practised, and, more recently, there has been an increase in population and industrial activity in the area. The cumulative effects on the river and on the environment of various human activities over the years have not all been favourable, particularly for the water régime.

[20] Only by international co-operation could action be taken to alleviate these problems. Water management projects along the Danube have frequently sought to combine navigational improvements and flood protection with the production of electricity through hydroelectric power plants. The potential of the Danube for the production of hydroelectric power has been extensively exploited by some riparian States. The history of attempts to harness the potential of the particular stretch of the river at issue in these proceedings extends over a 25-year period culminating in the signature of the 1977 Treaty.

[. . .]

[29] 27. The Court will now turn to a consideration of the questions submitted by the Parties. In terms of Article 2, paragraph 1 (*a*), of the Special Agreement, the Court is requested to decide first

> whether the Republic of Hungary was entitled to suspend and subsequently abandon, in 1989, the works on the Nagymaros Project and on the part of the Gabčíkovo Project for which the Treaty attributed responsibility to the Republic of Hungary.

[. . .]

[35] [. . .] 40. Throughout the proceedings, Hungary contended that, although it did suspend or abandon certain works, on the contrary, it never suspended the application of the 1977 Treaty itself. To justify its conduct, it relied essentially on a 'state of ecological necessity'.

[7 Not reproduced in this volume.]

Hungary contended that the various installations in the Gabčíkovo–Nagymaros System of Locks had been designed to enable the Gabčíkovo power plant to operate in peak mode. Water would only have come through the plant twice each day, at times of peak power demand. Operation in peak mode required the vast expanse (60 km^2) of the planned reservoir at Dunakiliti, as well as the Nagymaros dam, which was to alleviate the tidal effects and reduce the variation in the water level downstream of Gabčíkovo. Such a system, considered to be more economically profitable than using run-of-the-river plants, carried ecological risks which it found unacceptable.

According to Hungary, the principal ecological dangers which would have been caused by this system were as follows. At Gabčíkovo/Dunakiliti, under the original Project, as specified in the Joint Contractual Plan, the residual discharge into the old bed of the Danube was limited to 50 m^3/s, in addition to the water provided to the system of side-arms. That volume could be increased to 200 m^3/s during the growing season. Additional discharges, and in particular a number of artificial floods, could also be effected, at an unspecified rate. In these circumstances, the groundwater level would have fallen in most of the Szigetköz. Furthermore, the groundwater would then no longer have been supplied by the Danube – which, on the contrary, would have acted as a drain – but by the reservoir of stagnant water at Dunakiliti and the side-arms which would have become silted up. In the long term, the quality of water would have been seriously impaired. As for the surface water, risks of eutrophication would have arisen, particularly in the reservoir; instead of the old Danube there would have been a river choked with sand, where only a relative trickle of water would have flowed. The network of arms would have been for the most part cut off from the principal bed. The fluvial fauna and flora, like those in the alluvial plains, would have been condemned to extinction.

As for Nagymaros, Hungary argued that, if that dam had been built, [36] the bed of the Danube upstream would have silted up and, consequently, the quality of the water collected in the bank-filtered wells would have deteriorated in this sector. What is more, the operation of the Gabčíkovo power plant in peak mode would have occasioned significant daily variations in the water level in the reservoir upstream, which would have constituted a threat to aquatic habitats in particular. Furthermore, the construction and operation of the Nagymaros dam would have caused the erosion of the riverbed downstream, along Szentendre Island. The water level of the river would therefore have fallen in this section and the yield of the bank-filtered wells providing two-thirds of the water supply of the city of Budapest would have appreciably diminished. The filter layer would also have shrunk or perhaps even disappeared, and fine sediments would have been deposited in certain pockets in the river. For this twofold reason, the quality of the infiltrating water would have been severely jeopardized.

From all these predictions, in support of which it quoted a variety of scientific studies, Hungary concluded that a 'state of ecological necessity' did indeed exist in 1989.

41. In its written pleadings, Hungary also accused Czechoslovakia of having violated various provisions of the 1977 Treaty from before 1989 – in particular Articles 15 and 19 relating, respectively, to water quality and nature protection – in refusing to take account of the now evident ecological dangers and insisting that the works be continued, notably at Nagymaros. In this context Hungary contended that, in accordance with the terms of Article 3, paragraph 2, of the Agreement of 6 May 1976 concerning the Joint Contractual Plan, Czechoslovakia bore responsibility for research into the Project's impact on the environment; Hungary stressed that the research carried out by Czechoslovakia had not been conducted adequately, the potential effects of the Project on the environment of the construction having been assessed by Czechoslovakia only from September 1990. However, in the final stage of its argument, Hungary does not appear to have sought to formulate this complaint as an independent ground formally justifying the suspension and abandonment of the works for which it was responsible under the 1977 Treaty. Rather, it presented the violations of the Treaty prior to 1989, which it imputes to Czechoslovakia, as one of the elements contributing to the emergence of a state of necessity.

[. . .]

[**37**] [. . .] 44. In the course of the proceedings, Slovakia argued at length that the state of necessity upon which Hungary relied did not constitute a reason for the suspension of a treaty obligation recognized by the law of treaties. At the same time, it cast doubt upon whether 'ecological necessity' or 'ecological risk' could, in relation to the law of State responsibility, constitute a circumstance precluding the wrongfulness of an act.

In any event, Slovakia denied that there had been any kind of 'ecological state of necessity' in this case either in 1989 or subsequently. It invoked the authority of various scientific studies when it claimed that Hungary had given an exaggeratedly pessimistic description of the situation. Slovakia did not, of course, deny that ecological problems could have arisen. However, it asserted that they could to a large extent have been remedied. It accordingly stressed that no agreement had been reached with respect to the modalities of operation of the Gabčíkovo power plant in peak mode, and claimed that the apprehensions of Hungary related only to operating conditions of an extreme kind. In the same way, it contended that the original Project had undergone various modifications since 1977 and that it would have been possible to modify it even further, for example with respect to the discharge of water reserved for the old bed of the Danube, or the supply of water to the side-arms by means of underwater weirs.

45. Slovakia moreover denied that it in any way breached the 1977 Treaty – particularly its Articles 15 and 19 – and maintained, *inter alia*, that according to the terms of Article 3, paragraph 2, of the Agreement of 6 May 1976 relating to the Joint Contractual Plan, research into the impact of the Project on the environment was not the exclusive responsibility of Czechoslovakia but of either one of the parties, depending on the location of the works.

Lastly, in its turn, it reproached Hungary with having adopted its unilateral measures of suspension and abandonment of the works in violation [**38**] of the provisions of Article 27 of the 1977 Treaty (see paragraph 18 above),[8] which it submits required prior recourse to the machinery for dispute settlement provided for in that Article. [. . .]

[39] [. . .] 48. The Court cannot accept Hungary's argument to the effect that, in 1989, in suspending and subsequently abandoning the works for which it was still responsible at Nagymaros and at Dunakiliti, it did not, for all that, suspend the application of the 1977 Treaty itself or then reject that Treaty. The conduct of Hungary at that time can only be interpreted as an expression of its unwillingness to comply with at least some of the provisions of the Treaty and the Protocol of 6 February 1989, as specified in the Joint Contractual Plan. The effect of Hungary's conduct was to render impossible the accomplishment of the system of works that the Treaty expressly described as 'single and indivisible'.

The Court moreover observes that, when it invoked the state of necessity in an effort to justify that conduct, Hungary chose to place itself from the outset within the ambit of the law of State responsibility, thereby implying that, in the absence of such a circumstance, its conduct would have been unlawful. The state of necessity claimed by Hungary – supposing it to have been established – thus could not permit of the conclusion that, in 1989, it had acted in accordance with its obligations under the 1977 Treaty or that those obligations had ceased to be binding upon it. It would only permit the affirmation that, under the circumstances, Hungary would not incur international responsibility by acting as it did. Lastly, the Court points out that Hungary expressly acknowledged that, in any event, such a state of necessity would not exempt it from its duty to compensate its partner.

*

49. The Court will now consider the question of whether there was, in 1989, a state of necessity which would have permitted Hungary, without incurring international responsibility, to suspend and abandon works that it was committed to perform in accordance with the 1977 Treaty and related instruments.

50. In the present case, the Parties are in agreement in considering that the existence of a state of necessity must be evaluated in the light of the criteria laid down by the International Law Commission in Article 33 of the Draft Articles on the International Responsibility of States that it adopted on first reading. That provision is worded as follows:

> *Article 33. State of Necessity*
>
> (1) A state of necessity may not be invoked by a State as a ground for precluding the wrongfulness of an act of that State not in conformity with an international obligation of the State unless:
>
> (*a*)   the act was the only means of safeguarding an essential interest of the State against a grave and imminent peril; and

---

[8 Not reproduced in this volume.]

(b) [**40**] the act did not seriously impair an essential interest of the State towards which the obligation existed.

(2) In any case, a state of necessity may not be invoked by a State as a ground for precluding wrongfulness:

(a) if the international obligation with which the act of the State is not in conformity arises out of a peremptory norm of general international law; or

(b) if the international obligation with which the act of the State is not in conformity is laid down by a treaty which, explicitly or implicitly, excludes the possibility of invoking the state of necessity with respect to that obligation; or

(c) if the State in question has contributed to the occurrence of the state of necessity. (*Yearbook of the International Law Commission*, 1980, Vol. II, Part 2, p. 34.)

[. . .]

51. The Court considers, first of all, that the state of necessity is a ground recognized by customary international law for precluding the wrongfulness of an act not in conformity with an international obligation. It observes moreover that such ground for precluding wrongfulness can only be accepted on an exceptional basis. The International Law Commission was of the same opinion when it explained that it had opted for a negative form of words in Article 33 of its Draft

> in order to show, by this formal means also, that the case of invocation of a state of necessity as a justification must be considered as really constituting an exception – and one even more rarely admissible than is the case with the other circumstances precluding wrongfulness . . . (*ibid.*, p. 51, para. 40).

Thus, according to the Commission, the state of necessity can only be invoked under certain strictly defined conditions which must be cumulatively satisfied; and the State concerned is not the sole judge of whether those conditions have been met.

52. In the present case, the following basic conditions set forth in Draft Article 33 are relevant: it must have been occasioned by an 'essential interest' of the State which is the author of the act conflicting with one of its international obligations; that interest must have been threatened by a 'grave and imminent peril'; the act being challenged must [**41**] have been the 'only means' of safeguarding that interest; that act must not have 'seriously impair[ed] an essential interest' of the State towards which the obligation existed; and the State which is the author of that act must not have 'contributed to the occurrence of the state of necessity'. Those conditions reflect customary international law.

The Court will now endeavour to ascertain whether those conditions had been met at the time of the suspension and abandonment, by Hungary, of the works that it was to carry out in accordance with the 1977 Treaty.

53. The Court has no difficulty in acknowledging that the concerns expressed by Hungary for its natural environment in the region affected by the Gabčíkovo–Nagymaros Project related to an 'essential interest' of that State, within the meaning given to that expression in Article 33 of the Draft of the International Law Commission.

The Commission, in its Commentary, indicated that one should not, in that context, reduce an 'essential interest' to a matter only of the 'existence' of the State, and that the whole question was, ultimately, to be judged in the light of the particular case (see *Yearbook of the International Law Commission*, 1980, Vol. II, Part 2, p. 49, para. 32); at the same time, it included among the situations that could occasion a state of necessity, 'a grave danger to . . . the ecological preservation of all or some of [the] territory [of a State]' (*ibid.*, p. 35, para. 3); and specified, with reference to State practice, that 'It is primarily in the last two decades that safeguarding the ecological balance has come to be considered an "essential interest" of all States.' (*Ibid.*, p. 39, para. 14.)

The Court recalls that it has recently had occasion to stress, in the following terms, the great significance that it attaches to respect for the environment, not only for States but also for the whole of mankind:

> the environment is not an abstraction but represents the living space, the quality of life and the very health of human beings, including generations unborn. The existence of the general obligation of States to ensure that activities within their jurisdiction and control respect the environment of other States or of areas beyond national control is now part of the corpus of international law relating to the environment. (*Legality of the Threat or Use of Nuclear Weapons, Advisory Opinion, ICJ Reports 1996*, pp. 241–2, para. 29.)[9]

54. The verification of the existence, in 1989, of the 'peril' invoked by Hungary, of its 'grave and imminent' nature, as well as of the absence of any 'means' to respond to it, other than the measures taken by Hungary to suspend and abandon the works, are all complex processes.

[42] As the Court has already indicated (see paragraphs 33 *et seq.*),[10] Hungary on several occasions expressed, in 1989, its 'uncertainties' as to the ecological impact of putting in place the Gabčíkovo–Nagymaros barrage system, which is why it asked insistently for new scientific studies to be carried out.

The Court considers, however, that, serious though these uncertainties might have been they could not, alone, establish the objective existence of a 'peril' in the sense of a component element of a state of necessity.

[. . .]

The Hungarian argument on the state of necessity could not convince the Court unless it was at least proven that a real, 'grave' and 'imminent' 'peril' existed in 1989 and that the measures taken by Hungary were the only possible response to it.

Both Parties have placed on record an impressive amount of scientific material aimed at reinforcing their respective arguments. The Court has given most careful attention to this material, in which the Parties have developed their opposing views as to the ecological consequences of the Project. It concludes, however, that, as will be shown below, it is not necessary in order to respond to the questions put to it in the Special Agreement for it to determine which of those points of view is scientifically better founded.

[9 See p. 256 above.]
[10 Not reproduced in this volume.]

55. The Court will begin by considering the situation at Nagymaros. As has already been mentioned (see paragraph 40), Hungary maintained that, if the works at Nagymaros had been carried out as planned, the environment – and in particular the drinking water resources – in the area would have been exposed to serious dangers on account of problems linked to the upstream reservoir on the one hand and, on the other, the risks of erosion of the riverbed downstream.

The Court notes that the dangers ascribed to the upstream reservoir were mostly of a long-term nature and, above all, that they remained uncertain. Even though the Joint Contractual Plan envisaged that the Gabčíkovo [43] power plant would 'mainly operate in peak-load time and continuously during high water', the final rules of operation had not yet been determined (see paragraph 19 above);[11] however, any dangers associated with the putting into service of the Nagymaros portion of the Project would have been closely linked to the extent to which it was operated in peak mode and to the modalities of such operation. It follows that, even if it could have been established – which, in the Court's appreciation of the evidence before it, was not the case – that the reservoir would ultimately have constituted a 'grave peril' for the environment in the area, one would be bound to conclude that the peril was not 'imminent' at the time at which Hungary suspended and then abandoned the works relating to the dam.

With regard to the lowering of the riverbed downstream of the Nagymaros dam, the danger could have appeared at once more serious and more pressing, in so far as it was the supply of drinking water to the city of Budapest which would have been affected. The Court would however point out that the bed of the Danube in the vicinity of Szentendre had already been deepened prior to 1980 in order to extract building materials, and that the river had from that time attained, in that sector, the depth required by the 1977 Treaty. The peril invoked by Hungary had thus already materialized to a large extent for a number of years, so that it could not, in 1989, represent a peril arising entirely out of the project. The Court would stress, however, that, even supposing, as Hungary maintained, that the construction and operation of the dam would have created serious risks, Hungary had means available to it, other than the suspension and abandonment of the works, of responding to that situation. It could for example have proceeded regularly to discharge gravel into the river downstream of the dam. It could likewise, if necessary, have supplied Budapest with drinking water by processing the river water in an appropriate manner. The two Parties expressly recognized that that possibility remained open even though – and this is not determinative of the state of necessity – the purification of the river water, like the other measures envisaged, clearly would have been a more costly technique.

56. The Court now comes to the Gabčíkovo sector. It will recall that Hungary's concerns in this sector related on the one hand to the quality of the surface water in the Dunakiliti reservoir, with its effects on the quality of the groundwater in the region, and on the other hand, more generally, to the level, movement and quality

[11 Not reproduced in this volume.]

of both the surface water and the groundwater in the whole of the Szigetköz, with their effects on the fauna and flora in the alluvial plain of the Danube (see paragraph 40 above).

Whether in relation to the Dunakiliti site or to the whole of the Szigetköz, the Court finds here again, that the peril claimed by Hungary was to be considered in the long term, and, more importantly, remained uncertain. As Hungary itself acknowledges, the damage that it apprehended [44] had primarily to be the result of some relatively slow natural processes, the effects of which could not easily be assessed.

Even if the works were more advanced in this sector than at Nagymaros, they had not been completed in July 1989 and, as the Court explained in paragraph 34 above,[12] Hungary expressly undertook to carry on with them, early in June 1989. The report dated 23 June 1989 by the *ad hoc* Committee of the Hungarian Academy of Sciences, which was also referred to in paragraph 35[13] of the present Judgment, does not express any awareness of an authenticated peril – even in the form of a definite peril, whose realization would have been inevitable in the long term – when it states that:

> The measuring results of an at least five-year monitoring period following the completion of the Gabčíkovo construction are indispensable to the trustworthy prognosis of the ecological impacts of the barrage system. There is undoubtedly a need for the establishment and regular operation of a comprehensive monitoring system, which must be more developed than at present. The examination of biological indicator objects that can sensitively indicate the changes happening in the environment, neglected till today, have to be included.

The report concludes as follows:

> It can be stated, that the environmental, ecological and water quality impacts were not taken into account properly during the design and construction period until today. Because of the complexity of the ecological processes and lack of the measured data and the relevant calculations the environmental impacts cannot be evaluated.
>
> The data of the monitoring system newly operating on a very limited area are not enough to forecast the impacts probably occurring over a longer term. In order to widen and to make the data more frequent a further multi-year examination is necessary to decrease the further degradation of the water quality playing a dominant role in this question. The expected water quality influences equally the aquatic ecosystems, the soils and the recreational and tourist land-use.

The Court also notes that, in these proceedings, Hungary acknowledged that, as a general rule, the quality of the Danube waters had improved over the past 20 years, even if those waters remained subject to hypertrophic conditions.

However 'grave' it might have been, it would accordingly have been difficult, in the light of what is said above, to see the alleged peril as sufficiently certain and therefore 'imminent' in 1989.

[12 Not reproduced in this volume.]
[13 Not reproduced in this volume.]

The Court moreover considers that Hungary could, in this context [45] also, have resorted to other means in order to respond to the dangers that it apprehended. In particular, within the framework of the original Project, Hungary seemed to be in a position to control at least partially the distribution of the water between the bypass canal, the old bed of the Danube and the side-arms. It should not be overlooked that the Dunakiliti dam was located in Hungarian territory and that Hungary could construct the works needed to regulate flows along the old bed of the Danube and the side-arms. Moreover, it should be borne in mind that Article 14 of the 1977 Treaty provided for the possibility that each of the parties might withdraw quantities of water exceeding those specified in the Joint Contractual Plan, while making it clear that, in such an event, 'the share of electric power of the Contracting Party benefiting from the excess withdrawal shall be correspondingly reduced'.

57. The Court concludes from the foregoing that, with respect to both Nagymaros and Gabčíkovo, the perils invoked by Hungary, without prejudging their possible gravity, were not sufficiently established in 1989, nor were they 'imminent'; and that Hungary had available to it at that time means of responding to these perceived perils other than the suspension and abandonment of works with which it had been entrusted. What is more, negotiations were under way which might have led to a review of the Project and the extension of some of its time-limits, without there being need to abandon it. The Court infers from this that the respect by Hungary, in 1989, of its obligations under the terms of the 1977 Treaty would not have resulted in a situation 'characterized so aptly by the maxim *summum jus summa injuria*' (*Yearbook of the International Law Commission*, 1980, Vol. II, Part 2, p. 49, para. 31).

Moreover, the Court notes that Hungary decided to conclude the 1977 Treaty, a Treaty which – whatever the political circumstances prevailing at the time of its conclusion – was treated by Hungary as valid and in force until the date declared for its termination in May 1992. As can be seen from the material before the Court, a great many studies of a scientific and technical nature had been conducted at an earlier time, both by Hungary and by Czechoslovakia. Hungary was, then, presumably aware of the situation as then known, when it assumed its obligations under the Treaty. Hungary contended before the Court that those studies had been inadequate and that the state of knowledge at that time was not such as to make possible a complete evaluation of the ecological implications of the Gabčíkovo–Nagymaros Project. It is nonetheless the case that although the principal object of the 1977 Treaty was the construction of a System of Locks for the production of electricity, improvement of navigation on the Danube and protection against flooding, the need to ensure the protection of the environment had not escaped the parties, as can be seen from Articles 15, 19 and 20 of the Treaty.

What is more, the Court cannot fail to note the positions taken by Hungary after the entry into force of the 1977 Treaty. In 1983, Hungary asked that the works under the Treaty should go forward more slowly, [46] for reasons that were essentially economic but also, subsidiarily, related to ecological concerns. In 1989, when, according to Hungary itself, the state of scientific knowledge had undergone a significant development, it asked for the works to be speeded up, and then decided, three months later, to suspend them and subsequently to abandon them. The Court is not however unaware that profound changes were taking place in Hungary in 1989, and that, during that transitory phase, it might have been more than usually difficult to co-ordinate the different points of view prevailing from time to time.

The Court infers from all these elements that, in the present case, even if it had been established that there was, in 1989, a state of necessity linked to the performance of the 1977 Treaty, Hungary would not have been permitted to rely upon that state of necessity in order to justify its failure to comply with its treaty obligations, as it had helped, by act or omission, to bring it about.

58. It follows that the Court has no need to consider whether Hungary, by proceeding as it did in 1989, 'seriously impair[ed] an essential interest' of Czechoslovakia, within the meaning of the aforementioned Article 33 of the Draft of the International Law Commission – a finding which does not in any way prejudice the damage Czechoslovakia claims to have suffered on account of the position taken by Hungary.

Nor does the Court need to examine the argument put forward by Hungary, according to which certain breaches of Articles 15 and 19 of the 1977 Treaty, committed by Czechoslovakia even before 1989, contributed to the purported state of necessity; and neither does it have to reach a decision on the argument advanced by Slovakia, according to which Hungary breached the provisions of Article 27 of the Treaty, in 1989, by taking unilateral measures without having previously had recourse to the machinery of dispute settlement for which that Article provides.

*   *

59. In the light of the conclusions reached above, the Court, in reply to the question put to it in Article 2, paragraph 1 *(a)*, of the Special Agreement (see paragraph 27 above), finds that Hungary was not entitled to suspend and subsequently abandon, in 1989, the works on the Nagymaros Project and on the part of the Gabčíkovo Project for which the 1977 Treaty and related instruments attributed responsibility to it.

*

*   *

60. By the terms of Article 2, paragraph 1 *(b)*, of the Special Agreement, the Court is asked in the second place to decide

> *(b)*   whether the Czech and Slovak Federal Republic was entitled to proceed, in November 1991, to the 'provisional solution' [47] and to put into operation from October 1992 this system, described in the Report of the Working Group of Independent Experts of the Commission of the European Communities, the Republic of Hungary and the Czech and Slovak Federal Republic dated 23 November 1992 (damming up of the Danube at river kilometre 1851.7 on Czechoslovak territory and resulting consequences on water and navigation course).

[...]

[52] [...] 72. [...] the Court wishes to make clear that it is aware of the serious problems with which Czechoslovakia was confronted as a result of Hungary's decision to relinquish most of the construction of the System of Locks for which it was responsible by virtue of the 1977 Treaty. Vast investments had been made, the construction at Gabčíkovo was all but finished, the bypass canal was completed, and Hungary itself, in 1991, had duly fulfilled its obligations under the Treaty in this respect in completing work on the tailrace canal. It emerges from the report, dated 31 October 1992, of the tripartite fact-finding mission the Court has referred to in paragraph 24[14] of the present Judgment, that not using the system would have **[53]** led to considerable financial losses, and that it could have given rise to serious problems for the environment.

[...]

76. It is not necessary for the Court to determine whether there is a principle of international law or a general principle of law of 'approximate application' because, even if such a principle existed, it could by definition only be employed within the limits of the treaty in question. In the view of the Court, Variant C does not meet that cardinal condition with regard to the 1977 Treaty.

77. As the Court has already observed, the basic characteristic of the 1977 Treaty is, according to Article 1, to provide for the construction of the Gabčíkovo–Nagymaros System of Locks as a joint investment constituting a single and indivisible operational system of works. This element is equally reflected in Articles 8 and 10 of the Treaty providing for joint ownership of the most important works of the Gabčíkovo–Nagymaros Project and for the operation of this joint property as a co-ordinated single unit. By definition all this could not be carried **[54]** out by unilateral action. In spite of having a certain external physical similarity with the original Project, Variant C thus differed sharply from it in its legal characteristics.

78. Moreover, in practice, the operation of Variant C led Czechoslovakia to appropriate, essentially for its use and benefit, between 80 and 90 per cent of the waters of the Danube before returning them to the main bed of the river, despite the fact that the Danube is not only a shared international watercourse but also an international boundary river.

Czechoslovakia submitted that Variant C was essentially no more than what Hungary had already agreed to and that the only modifications made were those which had become necessary by virtue of Hungary's decision not to implement its treaty obligations. It is true that Hungary, in concluding the 1977 Treaty, had agreed to the damming of the Danube and the diversion of its waters into the bypass canal. But it was only in the context of a joint operation and a sharing of its benefits that Hungary had given its consent. The suspension and withdrawal of that consent constituted a violation of Hungary's legal obligations, demonstrating, as it did, the refusal by Hungary of joint operation; but that cannot mean that Hungary forfeited its basic

---

[14 Not reproduced in this volume.]

right to an equitable and reasonable sharing of the resources of an international watercourse.

The Court accordingly concludes that Czechoslovakia, in putting Variant C into operation, was not applying the 1977 Treaty but, on the contrary, violated certain of its express provisions, and, in so doing, committed an internationally wrongful act. [...]

[**56**] [...] The Court considers that Czechoslovakia, by unilaterally assuming control of a shared resource, and thereby depriving Hungary of its right to an equitable and reasonable share of the natural resources of the Danube – with the continuing effects of the diversion of these waters on the ecology of the riparian area of the Szigetköz – failed to respect the proportionality which is required by international law.

86. Moreover, as the Court has already pointed out (see paragraph 78), the fact that Hungary had agreed in the context of the original Project to the diversion of the Danube (and, in the Joint Contractual Plan, to a provisional measure of withdrawal of water from the Danube) cannot be understood as having authorized Czechoslovakia to proceed with a unilateral diversion of this magnitude without Hungary's consent.

87. The Court thus considers that the diversion of the Danube carried out by Czechoslovakia was not a lawful countermeasure because it was not proportionate. It is therefore not required to pass upon one other condition for the lawfulness of a countermeasure, namely that its purpose must be to induce the wrongdoing State to comply with its obligations [**57**] under international law, and that the measure must therefore be reversible.

*   *

88. In the light of the conclusions reached above, the Court, in reply to the question put to it in Article 2, paragraph 1 *(b)*, of the Special Agreement (see paragraph 60), finds that Czechoslovakia was entitled to proceed, in November 1991, to Variant C in so far as it then confined itself to undertaking works which did not predetermine the final decision to be taken by it. On the other hand, Czechoslovakia was not entitled to put that Variant into operation from October 1992.

*
*   *

89. By the terms of Article 2, paragraph 1 *(c)*, of the Special Agreement, the Court is asked, thirdly, to determine 'what are the legal effects of the notification, on 19 May 1992, of the termination of the Treaty by the Republic of Hungary'. [...]

[**58**] [...] 91. On 19 May 1992, the Hungarian Government transmitted to the Czechoslovak Government a Declaration notifying it of the termination by Hungary of the 1977 Treaty as of 25 May 1992. In a letter of the same date from the Hungarian Prime Minister to the Czechoslovak Prime Minister, the immediate cause for termination was specified to be Czechoslovakia's refusal, expressed in its letter of 23 April 1992, to suspend the work on Variant C during mediation efforts of the

Commission of the European Communities. In its Declaration, Hungary stated that it could not accept the deleterious effects for the environment and the conservation of nature of the implementation of Variant C which would be practically equivalent to the dangers caused by the realization of the original Project. It added that Variant C infringed numerous international agreements and violated the territorial integrity of the Hungarian State by diverting the natural course of the Danube.

* *

92. During the proceedings, Hungary presented five arguments in support of the lawfulness, and thus the effectiveness, of its notification of termination. These were the existence of a state of necessity; the impossibility of performance of the Treaty; the occurrence of a fundamental change of circumstances; the material breach of the Treaty by Czechoslovakia; and, finally, the development of new norms of international environmental law. Slovakia contested each of these grounds.

[...]

[**62**] [...] 97. Finally, Hungary argued that subsequently imposed requirements of international law in relation to the protection of the environment precluded performance of the Treaty. The previously existing obligation not to cause substantive damage to the territory of another State had, Hungary claimed, evolved into an *erga omnes* obligation of prevention of damage pursuant to the 'precautionary principle'. On this basis, Hungary argued, its termination was 'forced by the other party's refusal to suspend work on Variant C'.

Slovakia argued, in reply, that none of the intervening developments in environmental law gave rise to norms of *jus cogens* that would override the Treaty. Further, it contended that the claim by Hungary to be entitled to take action could not in any event serve as legal justification for termination of the Treaty under the law of treaties, but belonged rather 'to the language of self-help or reprisals'.

* *

98. The question, as formulated in Article 2, paragraph 1 *(c)*, of the Special Agreement, deals with treaty law since the Court is asked to determine what the legal effects are of the notification of termination of the Treaty.

[...]

100. The 1977 Treaty does not contain any provision regarding its termination. Nor is there any indication that the parties intended to admit the possibility of denunciation or withdrawal. On the contrary, the Treaty establishes a long-standing and durable régime of joint investment [**63**] and joint operation. Consequently, the parties not having agreed otherwise, the Treaty could be terminated only on the limited grounds enumerated in the Vienna Convention.

[...]

102. Hungary also relied on the principle of the impossibility of performance as reflected in Article 61 of the Vienna Convention on the Law of Treaties.

[...]

103. Hungary contended that the essential object of the Treaty – an economic joint investment which was consistent with environmental protection and which was operated by the two contracting parties jointly – had permanently disappeared and that the Treaty had thus become impossible to perform. It is not necessary for the Court to determine whether the term 'object' in Article 61 can also be understood to embrace a legal régime as in any event, even if that were the case, it **[64]** would have to conclude that in this instance that régime had not definitively ceased to exist. The 1977 Treaty – and in particular its Articles 15, 19 and 20 – actually made available to the parties the necessary means to proceed at any time, by negotiation, to the required readjustments between economic imperatives and ecological imperatives. The Court would add that, if the joint exploitation of the investment was no longer possible, this was originally because Hungary did not carry out most of the works for which it was responsible under the 1977 Treaty; Article 61, paragraph 2, of the Vienna Convention expressly provides that impossibility of performance may not be invoked for the termination of a treaty by a party to that treaty when it results from that party's own breach of an obligation flowing from that treaty.

*

104. Hungary further argued that it was entitled to invoke a number of events which, cumulatively, would have constituted a fundamental change of circumstances. In this respect it specified profound changes of a political nature, the Project's diminishing economic viability, the progress of environmental knowledge and the development of new norms and prescriptions of international environmental law (see paragraph 95 above).[15]

The Court recalls that, in the *Fisheries Jurisdiction* case, it stated that

> Article 62 of the Vienna Convention on the Law of Treaties, . . . may in many respects be considered as a codification of existing customary law on the subject of the termination of a treaty relationship on account of change of circumstances (*ICJ Reports 1973*, p. [18], para. 36).[16]

The prevailing political situation was certainly relevant for the conclusion of the 1977 Treaty. But the Court will recall that the Treaty provided for a joint investment programme for the production of energy, the control of floods and the improvement of navigation on the Danube. In the Court's view, the prevalent political conditions were thus not so closely linked to the object and purpose of the Treaty that they constituted an essential basis of the consent of the parties and, in changing, radically altered the extent of the obligations still to be performed. The same holds good for the economic system in force at the time of the conclusion of the 1977 Treaty. Besides, even though the estimated profitability of the Project might have appeared less in 1992 than in 1977, it does not appear from the record before the Court that it was

[15] Not reproduced in this volume.]
[16] See p. 23 above.]

bound to diminish to such an extent that the treaty obligations of the parties would have been radically transformed as a result.

The Court does not consider that new developments in the state of [65] environmental knowledge and of environmental law can be said to have been completely unforeseen. What is more, the formulation of Articles 15, 19 and 20, designed to accommodate change, made it possible for the parties to take account of such developments and to apply them when implementing those treaty provisions.

The changed circumstances advanced by Hungary are, in the Court's view, not of such a nature, either individually or collectively, that their effect would radically transform the extent of the obligations still to be performed in order to accomplish the Project. A fundamental change of circumstances must have been unforeseen; the existence of the circumstances at the time of the Treaty's conclusion must have constituted an essential basis of the consent of the parties to be bound by the Treaty. The negative and conditional wording of Article 62 of the Vienna Convention on the Law of Treaties is a clear indication moreover that the stability of treaty relations requires that the plea of fundamental change of circumstances be applied only in exceptional cases.

[. . .]

[67] [. . .] 111. Finally, the Court will address Hungary's claim that it was entitled to terminate the 1977 Treaty because new requirements of international law for the protection of the environment precluded performance of the Treaty.

112. Neither of the Parties contended that new peremptory norms of environmental law had emerged since the conclusion of the 1977 Treaty, and the Court will consequently not be required to examine the scope of Article 64 of the Vienna Convention on the Law of Treaties. On the other hand, the Court wishes to point out that newly developed norms of environmental law are relevant for the implementation of the Treaty and that the parties could, by agreement, incorporate them through the application of Articles 15, 19 and 20 of the Treaty. These articles do not contain specific obligations of performance but require the parties, in carrying out their obligations to ensure that the quality of water in the Danube is not impaired and that nature is protected, to take new environmental norms into consideration when agreeing upon the means to be specified in the Joint Contractual Plan.

By inserting these evolving provisions in the Treaty, the parties recognized the potential necessity to adapt the Project. Consequently, the [68] Treaty is not static, and is open to adapt to emerging norms of international law. By means of Articles 15 and 19, new environmental norms can be incorporated in the Joint Contractual Plan.

The responsibility to do this was a joint responsibility. The obligations contained in Articles 15, 19 and 20 are, by definition, general and have to be transformed into specific obligations of performance through a process of consultation and negotiation. Their implementation thus requires a mutual willingness to discuss in good faith actual and potential environmental risks.

It is all the more important to do this because as the Court recalled in its Advisory Opinion on the *Legality of the Threat or Use of Nuclear Weapons*, 'the environment is not an abstraction but represents the living space, the quality of life and the very health of human beings, including generations unborn' (*ICJ Reports 1996*, p. 241, para. 29;[17] see also paragraph 53 above).

The awareness of the vulnerability of the environment and the recognition that environmental risks have to be assessed on a continuous basis have become much stronger in the years since the Treaty's conclusion. These new concerns have enhanced the relevance of Articles 15, 19 and 20.

113. The Court recognizes that both Parties agree on the need to take environmental concerns seriously and to take the required precautionary measures, but they fundamentally disagree on the consequences this has for the joint Project. In such a case, third-party involvement may be helpful and instrumental in finding a solution, provided each of the Parties is flexible in its position.

[...]

[69] 115. In the light of the conclusions it has reached above, the Court, in reply to the question put to it in Article 2, paragraph 1 *(c)*, of the Special Agreement (see paragraph 89), finds that the notification of termination by Hungary of 19 May 1992 did not have the legal effect of terminating the 1977 Treaty and related instruments.

*

*   *

116. In Article 2, paragraph 2, of the Special Agreement, the Court is requested to determine the legal consequences, including the rights and obligations for the Parties, arising from its Judgment on the questions formulated in paragraph 1. In Article 5 of the Special Agreement the Parties agreed to enter into negotiations on the modalities for the execution of the Judgment immediately after the Court has rendered it.

[...]

[72] [...] 123. [...] Taking all these factors into account, the Court finds that the content of the 1977 Treaty indicates that it must be regarded as establishing a territorial régime within the meaning of Article 12 of the 1978 Vienna Convention. It created rights and obligations 'attaching to' the parts of the Danube to which it relates; thus the Treaty itself cannot be affected by a succession of States. The Court therefore concludes that the 1977 Treaty became binding upon Slovakia on 1 January 1993.

[...]

[73] [...] 125. The Court now turns to the other legal consequences arising from its Judgment.

[...]

[75] [...] 130. The Court observes that the part of its Judgment which answers the questions in Article 2, paragraph 1, of the Special Agreement has a declaratory character. It deals with the *past* conduct of the Parties and determines the lawfulness or unlawfulness of that conduct between 1989 and 1992 as well as its effects on the existence of the Treaty.

[17 See p. 256 above.]

131. Now the Court has, on the basis of the foregoing findings, to [76] determine what the *future* conduct of the Parties should be. This part of the Judgment is prescriptive rather than declaratory because it determines what the rights and obligations of the Parties are. The Parties will have to seek agreement on the modalities of the execution of the Judgment in the light of this determination, as they agreed to do in Article 5 of the Special Agreement.

*   *

132. In this regard it is of cardinal importance that the Court has found that the 1977 Treaty is still in force and consequently governs the relationship between the Parties. That relationship is also determined by the rules of other relevant conventions to which the two States are party, by the rules of general international law and, in this particular case, by the rules of State responsibility; but it is governed, above all, by the applicable rules of the 1977 Treaty as a *lex specialis*.

133. The Court, however, cannot disregard the fact that the Treaty has not been fully implemented by either party for years, and indeed that their acts of commission and omission have contributed to creating the factual situation that now exists. Nor can it overlook that factual situation – or the practical possibilities and impossibilities to which it gives rise – when deciding on the legal requirements for the future conduct of the Parties.

This does not mean that facts – in this case facts which flow from wrongful conduct – determine the law. The principle *ex injuria jus non oritur* is sustained by the Court's finding that the legal relationship created by the 1977 Treaty is preserved and cannot in this case be treated as voided by unlawful conduct.

What is essential, therefore, is that the factual situation as it has developed since 1989 shall be placed within the context of the preserved and developing treaty relationship, in order to achieve its object and purpose in so far as that is feasible. For it is only then that the irregular state of affairs which exists as the result of the failure of both Parties to comply with their treaty obligations can be remedied.

134. What might have been a correct application of the law in 1989 or 1992, if the case had been before the Court then, could be a miscarriage of justice if prescribed in 1997. The Court cannot ignore the fact that the Gabčíkovo power plant has been in operation for nearly five years, that the bypass canal which feeds the plant receives its water from a significantly smaller reservoir formed by a dam which is built not at Dunakiliti but at Čunovo, and that the plant is operated in a run-of-the-river mode and not in a peak hour mode as originally foreseen. Equally, the Court cannot ignore the fact that, not only has Nagymaros not been built, but that, with the effective discarding by both Parties of peak power operation, there is no longer any point in building it.

135. As the Court has already had occasion to point out, the 1977 Treaty was not only a joint investment project for the production of [77] energy, but it was designed to serve other objectives as well: the improvement of the navigability of the Danube, flood control and regulation of ice-discharge, and the protection of the natural environment. None of these objectives has been given absolute priority over

the other, in spite of the emphasis which is given in the Treaty to the construction of a System of Locks for the production of energy. None of them has lost its importance. In order to achieve these objectives the parties accepted obligations of conduct, obligations of performance, and obligations of result.

136. It could be said that that part of the obligations of performance which related to the construction of the System of Locks – in so far as they were not yet implemented before 1992 – have been overtaken by events. It would be an administration of the law altogether out of touch with reality if the Court were to order those obligations to be fully reinstated and the works at Čunovo to be demolished when the objectives of the Treaty can be adequately served by the existing structures.

137. Whether this is indeed the case is, first and foremost, for the Parties to decide. Under the 1977 Treaty its several objectives must be attained in an integrated and consolidated programme, to be developed in the Joint Contractual Plan. The Joint Contractual Plan was, until 1989, adapted and amended frequently to better fit the wishes of the parties. This Plan was also expressly described as the means to achieve the objectives of maintenance of water quality and protection of the environment.

138. The 1977 Treaty never laid down a rigid system, albeit that the construction of a system of locks at Gabčíkovo and Nagymaros was prescribed by the Treaty itself. In this respect, however, the subsequent positions adopted by the parties should be taken into consideration. Not only did Hungary insist on terminating construction at Nagymaros, but Czechoslovakia stated, on various occasions in the course of negotiations, that it was willing to consider a limitation or even exclusion of operation in peak hour mode. In the latter case the construction of the Nagymaros dam would have become pointless. The explicit terms of the Treaty itself were therefore in practice acknowledged by the parties to be negotiable.

139. The Court is of the opinion that the Parties are under a legal obligation, during the negotiations to be held by virtue of Article 5 of the Special Agreement, to consider, within the context of the 1977 Treaty, in what way the multiple objectives of the Treaty can best be served, keeping in mind that all of them should be fulfilled.

140. It is clear that the Project's impact upon, and its implications for, the environment are of necessity a key issue. The numerous scientific reports which have been presented to the Court by the Parties – even if their conclusions are often contradictory – provide abundant evidence that this impact and these implications are considerable.

In order to evaluate the environmental risks, current standards must be taken into consideration. This is not only allowed by the wording of [78] Articles 15 and 19, but even prescribed, to the extent that these articles impose a continuing – and thus necessarily evolving – obligation on the parties to maintain the quality of the water of the Danube and to protect nature.

The Court is mindful that, in the field of environmental protection, vigilance and prevention are required on account of the often irreversible character of damage to the environment and of the limitations inherent in the very mechanism of reparation of this type of damage.

Throughout the ages, mankind has, for economic and other reasons, constantly interfered with nature. In the past, this was often done without consideration of the effects upon the environment. Owing to new scientific insights and to a growing awareness of the risks for mankind – for present and future generations – of pursuit of such interventions at an unconsidered and unabated pace, new norms and standards have been developed, set forth in a great number of instruments during the last two decades. Such new norms have to be taken into consideration, and such new standards given proper weight, not only when States contemplate new activities but also when continuing with activities begun in the past. This need to reconcile economic development with protection of the environment is aptly expressed in the concept of sustainable development.

For the purposes of the present case, this means that the Parties together should look afresh at the effects on the environment of the operation of the Gabčíkovo power plant. In particular they must find a satisfactory solution for the volume of water to be released into the old bed of the Danube and into the side-arms on both sides of the river.

141. It is not for the Court to determine what shall be the final result of these negotiations to be conducted by the Parties. It is for the Parties themselves to find an agreed solution that takes account of the objectives of the Treaty, which must be pursued in a joint and integrated way, as well as the norms of international environmental law and the principles of the law of international watercourses. The Court will recall in this context that, as it said in the *North Sea Continental Shelf* cases:

> [the Parties] are under an obligation so to conduct themselves that the negotiations are meaningful, which will not be the case when either of them insists upon its own position without contemplating any modification of it (*ICJ Reports 1969*, p. 47, para. 85).

142. What is required in the present case by the rule *pacta sunt servanda*, as reflected in Article 26 of the Vienna Convention of 1969 on the Law of Treaties, is that the Parties find an agreed solution within the co-operative context of the Treaty.

Article 26 combines two elements, which are of equal importance. It provides that 'Every treaty in force is binding upon the parties to it and [**79**] must be performed by them in good faith.' This latter element, in the Court's view, implies that, in this case, it is the purpose of the Treaty, and the intentions of the parties in concluding it, which should prevail over its literal application. The principle of good faith obliges the Parties to apply it in a reasonable way and in such a manner that its purpose can be realized.

143. During this dispute both Parties have called upon the assistance of the Commission of the European Communities. Because of the diametrically opposed positions the Parties took with regard to the required outcome of the trilateral talks which were envisaged, those talks did not succeed. When, after the present Judgment is given, bilateral negotiations without pre-conditions are held, both Parties can profit from the assistance and expertise of a third party. The readiness of the Parties to accept such assistance would be evidence of the good faith with which they conduct bilateral negotiations in order to give effect to the Judgment of the Court.

144. The 1977 Treaty not only contains a joint investment programme, it also establishes a régime. According to the Treaty, the main structures of the System of Locks are the joint property of the Parties; their operation will take the form of a co-ordinated single unit; and the benefits of the project shall be equally shared.

Since the Court has found that the Treaty is still in force and that, under its terms, the joint régime is a basic element, it considers that, unless the Parties agree otherwise, such a régime should be restored.

145. Article 10, paragraph 1, of the Treaty states that works of the System of Locks constituting the joint property of the contracting parties shall be operated, as a co-ordinated single unit and in accordance with jointly agreed operating and operational procedures, by the authorized operating agency of the contracting party in whose territory the works are built. Paragraph 2 of that Article states that works on the System of Locks owned by one of the contracting parties shall be independently operated or maintained by the agencies of that contracting party in the jointly prescribed manner.

The Court is of the opinion that the works at Čunovo should become a jointly operated unit within the meaning of Article 10, paragraph 1, in view of their pivotal role in the operation of what remains of the Project and for the water-management régime. The dam at Čunovo has taken over the role which was originally destined for the works at Dunakiliti, and therefore should have a similar status.

146. The Court also concludes that Variant C, which it considers operates in a manner incompatible with the Treaty, should be made to conform to it. By associating Hungary, on an equal footing, in its operation, management and benefits, Variant C will be transformed from a *de facto* status into a treaty-based régime.

It appears from various parts of the record that, given the current state [80] of information before the Court, Variant C could be made to function in such a way as to accommodate both the economic operation of the system of electricity generation and the satisfaction of essential environmental concerns.

Regularization of Variant C by making it part of a single and indivisible operational system of works also appears necessary to ensure that Article 9 of the Treaty, which provides that the contracting parties shall participate in the use and in the benefits of the System of Locks in equal measure, will again become effective.

147. Re-establishment of the joint regime will also reflect in an optimal way the concept of common utilization of shared water resources for the achievement of the several objectives mentioned in the Treaty, in concordance with Article 5, paragraph 2, of the Convention on the Law of the Non-Navigational Uses of International Watercourses, according to which:

> Watercourse States shall participate in the use, development and protection of an international watercourse in an equitable and reasonable manner. Such participation includes both the right to utilize the watercourse and the duty to cooperate in the protection and development thereof, as provided in the present Convention. (General Assembly doc. A/51/869 of 11 April 1997.)

*   *

148. Thus far the Court has indicated what in its view should be the effects of its finding that the 1977 Treaty is still in force. Now the Court will turn to the legal consequences of the internationally wrongful acts committed by the Parties.

149. The Permanent Court of International Justice stated in its Judgment of 13 September 1928 in the case concerning the *Factory at Chorzów*:

> reparation must, as far as possible, wipe out all the consequences of the illegal act and reestablish the situation which would, in all probability, have existed if that act had not been committed (*PCIJ, Series A, No. 17*, p. 47).

150. Reparation must, 'as far as possible', wipe out all the consequences of the illegal act. In this case, the consequences of the wrongful acts of both Parties will be wiped out 'as far as possible' if they resume their co-operation in the utilization of the shared water resources of the Danube, and if the multi-purpose programme, in the form of a co-ordinated single unit, for the use, development and protection of the watercourse is implemented in an equitable and reasonable manner. What it is possible for the Parties to do is to re-establish co-operative administration of what remains of the Project. To that end, it is open to them to agree to maintain the works at Čunovo, with changes in the mode of operation in respect of the allocation of water and electricity, and not to build works at Nagymaros.

[81] 151. The Court has been asked by both Parties to determine the consequences of the Judgment as they bear upon payment of damages. According to the Preamble to the Special Agreement, the Parties agreed that Slovakia is the sole successor State of Czechoslovakia in respect of rights and obligations relating to the Gabčíkovo–Nagymaros Project. Slovakia thus may be liable to pay compensation not only for its own wrongful conduct but also for that of Czechoslovakia, and it is entitled to be compensated for the damage sustained by Czechoslovakia as well as by itself as a result of the wrongful conduct of Hungary.

152. The Court has not been asked at this stage to determine the quantum of damages due, but to indicate on what basis they should be paid. Both Parties claimed to have suffered considerable financial losses and both claim pecuniary compensation for them.

It is a well-established rule of international law that an injured State is entitled to obtain compensation from the State which has committed an internationally wrongful act for the damage caused by it. In the present Judgment, the Court has concluded that both Parties committed internationally wrongful acts, and it has noted that those acts gave rise to the damage sustained by the Parties; consequently, Hungary and Slovakia are both under an obligation to pay compensation and are both entitled to obtain compensation.

Slovakia is accordingly entitled to compensation for the damage suffered by Czechoslovakia as well as by itself as a result of Hungary's decision to suspend and subsequently abandon the works at Nagymaros and Dunakiliti, as those actions caused the postponement of the putting into operation of the Gabčíkovo power plant, and changes in its mode of operation once in service.

Hungary is entitled to compensation for the damage sustained as a result of the diversion of the Danube, since Czechoslovakia, by putting into operation Variant C, and Slovakia, in maintaining it in service, deprived Hungary of its rightful part in the shared water resources, and exploited those resources essentially for their own benefit.

153. Given the fact, however, that there have been intersecting wrongs by both Parties, the Court wishes to observe that the issue of compensation could satisfactorily be resolved in the framework of an overall settlement if each of the Parties were to renounce or cancel all financial claims and counter-claims.

154. At the same time, the Court wishes to point out that the settlement of accounts for the construction of the works is different from the issue of compensation, and must be resolved in accordance with the 1977 Treaty and related instruments. If Hungary is to share in the operation and benefits of the Čunovo complex, it must pay a proportionate share of the building and running costs.

*

*   *

[82] 155. For these reasons,

THE COURT,

   (1)   Having regard to Article 2, paragraph 1, of the Special Agreement,

A. By fourteen votes to one,

Finds that Hungary was not entitled to suspend and subsequently abandon, in 1989, the works on the Nagymaros Project and on the part of the Gabčíkovo Project for which the Treaty of 16 September 1977 and related instruments attributed responsibility to it;

> IN FAVOUR: *President* Schwebel; *Vice-President* Weeramantry; *Judges* Oda, Bedjaoui, Guillaume, Ranjeva, Shi, Fleischhauer, Koroma, Vereshchetin, Parra-Aranguren, Kooijmans, Rezek; *Judge* ad hoc Skubiszewski;
>
> AGAINST: *Judge Herczegh;*

B. By nine votes to six,

Finds that Czechoslovakia was entitled to proceed, in November 1991, to the 'provisional solution' as described in the terms of the Special Agreement;

> IN FAVOUR: *Vice-President* Weeramantry; *Judges* Oda, Guillaume, Shi, Koroma, Vereshchetin, Parra-Aranguren, Kooijmans; *Judge* ad hoc Skubiszewski;
>
> AGAINST: *President* Schwebel; *Judges* Bedjaoui, Ranjeva, Herczegh, Fleischhauer, Rezek;

C. By ten votes to five,

Finds that Czechoslovakia was not entitled to put into operation, from October 1992, this 'provisional solution';

IN FAVOUR: *President* Schwebel; *Vice-President* Weeramantry; *Judges* Bedjaoui, Guillaume, Ranjeva, Herczegh, Shi, Fleischhauer, Kooijmans, Rezek;

AGAINST: *Judges* Oda, Koroma, Vereshchetin, Parra-Aranguren; *Judge* ad hoc Skubiszewski;

D. By eleven votes to four,

Finds that the notification, on 19 May 1992, of the termination of the Treaty of 16 September 1977 and related instruments by Hungary did not have the legal effect of terminating them;

IN FAVOUR: *Vice-President* Weeramantry; *Judges* Oda, Bedjaoui, Guillaume, Ranjeva, Shi, Koroma, Vereshchetin, Parra-Aranguren, Kooijmans; *Judge* ad hoc Skubiszewski;

AGAINST: *President* Schwebel; *Judges* Herczegh, Fleischhauer, Rezek;

[83] (2) Having regard to Article 2, paragraph 2, and Article 5 of the Special Agreement,

A. By twelve votes to three,

Finds that Slovakia, as successor to Czechoslovakia, became a party to the Treaty of 16 September 1977 as from 1 January 1993;

IN FAVOUR: *President* Schwebel; *Vice-President* Weeramantry; *Judges* Oda, Bedjaoui, Guillaume, Ranjeva, Shi, Koroma, Vereshchetin, Parra-Aranguren, Kooijmans; *Judge* ad hoc Skubiszewski;

AGAINST: *Judges* Herczegh, Fleischhauer, Rezek;

B. By thirteen votes to two,

Finds that Hungary and Slovakia must negotiate in good faith in the light of the prevailing situation, and must take all necessary measures to ensure the achievement of the objectives of the Treaty of 16 September 1977, in accordance with such modalities as they may agree upon;

IN FAVOUR: *President* Schwebel; *Vice-President* Weeramantry; *Judges* Oda, Bedjaoui, Guillaume, Ranjeva, Shi, Koroma, Vereshchetin, Parra-Aranguren, Kooijmans, Rezek; *Judge* ad hoc Skubiszewski;

AGAINST: *Judges* Herczegh, Fleischhauer;

C. By thirteen votes to two,

Finds that, unless the Parties otherwise agree, a joint operational régime must be established in accordance with the Treaty of 16 September 1977;

IN FAVOUR: *President* Schwebel; *Vice-President* Weeramantry; *Judges* Oda, Bedjaoui, Guillaume, Ranjeva, Shi, Koroma, Vereshchetin, Parra-Aranguren, Kooijmans, Rezek; *Judge* ad hoc Skubiszewski;

AGAINST: *Judges* Herczegh, Fleischhauer;

D. By twelve votes to three,

Finds that, unless the Parties otherwise agree, Hungary shall compensate Slovakia for the damage sustained by Czechoslovakia and by Slovakia on account of the suspension and abandonment by Hungary of works for which it was responsible; and Slovakia shall compensate Hungary for the damage it has sustained on account of the putting into operation of the 'provisional solution' by Czechoslovakia and its maintenance in service by Slovakia;

IN FAVOUR: *President* Schwebel; *Vice-President* Weeramantry; *Judges* Bedjaoui, Guillaume, Ranjeva, Herczegh, Shi, Fleischhauer, Parra-Aranguren, Kooijmans, Rezek; *Judge* ad hoc Skubiszewski;

AGAINST: *Judges* Oda, Koroma, Vereshchetin;

[84] E. By thirteen votes to two,

Finds that the settlement of accounts for the construction and operation of the works must be effected in accordance with the relevant provisions of the Treaty of 16 September 1977 and related instruments, taking due account of such measures as will have been taken by the Parties in application of points 2 B and 2 C of the present operative paragraph.

IN FAVOUR: *President* Schwebel; *Vice-President* Weeramantry; *Judges* Oda, Bedjaoui, Guillaume, Ranjeva, Shi, Koroma, Vereshchetin, Parra-Aranguren, Kooijmans, Rezek; *Judge* ad hoc Skubiszewski;

AGAINST: *Judges* Herczegh, Fleischhauer.

[...]

[88] SEPARATE OPINION OF VICE-PRESIDENT WEERAMANTRY

Introduction

This case raises a rich array of environmentally related legal issues. A discussion of some of them is essential to explain my reasons for voting as I have in this very difficult decision. Three issues on which I wish to make some observations, supplementary to those of the Court, are the role played by the principle of sustainable development in balancing the competing demands of development and environmental protection; the protection given to Hungary by what I would describe as the principle of continuing environmental impact assessment; and the appropriateness of the use of *inter partes* legal principles, such as estoppel, for the resolution of problems with an *erga omnes* connotation such as environmental damage.

A. The concept of sustainable development

Had the possibility of environmental harm been the only consideration to be taken into account in this regard, the contentions of Hungary could well have proved conclusive.

Yet there are other factors to be taken into account – not the least important of which is the developmental aspect, for the Gabčíkovo scheme is important to Slovakia from the point of view of development. The Court must hold the balance even between the environmental considerations and the developmental considerations raised by the respective Parties. The principle that enables the Court to do so is the principle of sustainable development.

The Court has referred to it as a concept in paragraph 140 of its Judgment. However, I consider it to be more than a mere concept, but as a principle with normative value which is crucial to the determination of this case. Without the benefits of its insights, the issues involved in this case would have been difficult to resolve.

Since sustainable development is a principle fundamental to the determination of the competing considerations in this case, and since, although it has attracted attention only recently in the literature of international law, it is likely to play a major role in determining important environmental disputes of the future, it calls for consideration in some detail. Moreover, this is the first occasion on which it has received attention in the jurisprudence of this Court.

[89] When a major scheme, such as that under consideration in the present case, is planned and implemented, there is always the need to weigh considerations of development against environmental considerations, as their underlying juristic bases – the right to development and the right to environmental protection – are important principles of current international law.

In the present case we have, on the one hand, a scheme which, even in the attenuated form in which it now remains, is important to the welfare of Slovakia and its people, who have already strained their own resources and those of their predecessor State to the extent of over two billion dollars to achieve these benefits. Slovakia, in fact, argues that the environment would be improved through the operation of the Project as it would help to stop erosion of the river bed, and that the scheme would be an effective protection against floods. Further, Slovakia has traditionally been short of electricity, and the power generated would be important to its economic development. Moreover, if the Project is halted in its tracks, vast structural works constructed at great expense, even prior to the repudiation of the Treaty, would be idle and unproductive, and would pose an economic and environmental problem in themselves.

On the other hand, Hungary alleges that the Project produces, or is likely to produce, ecological damage of many varieties, including harm to river bank fauna and flora, damage to fish breeding, damage to surface water quality, eutrophication, damage to the groundwater régime, agriculture, forestry and soil, deterioration of the quality of drinking water reserves, and sedimentation. Hungary alleges that many of these dangers have already occurred and more will manifest themselves, if the scheme continues in operation. In the material placed before the Court, each of these dangers is examined and explained in considerable detail.

How does one handle these considerations? Does one abandon the Project altogether for fear that the latter consequences might emerge? Does one proceed with the scheme because of the national benefits it brings, regardless of the suggested environmental damage? Or does one steer a course between, with due regard to both considerations, but ensuring always a continuing vigilance in respect of environmental harm?

It is clear that a principle must be followed which pays due regard to both considerations. Is there such a principle, and does it command recognition in international law? I believe the answer to both questions is in the affirmative. The principle is the principle of sustainable development and, in my view, it is an integral part of modern international law. It is clearly of the utmost importance, both in this case and more generally.

I would observe, moreover, that both Parties in this case agree on the **[90]** applicability to this dispute of the principle of sustainable development. Thus, Hungary states in its pleadings that:

> Hungary and Slovakia agree that the principle of sustainable development, as formulated in the Brundtland Report, the Rio Declaration and Agenda 21 is applicable to this dispute . . .
>
> International law in the field of sustainable development is now sufficiently well established, and both Parties appear to accept this. (Reply of Hungary, paras. 1.45 and 1.47.)

Slovakia states that 'inherent in the concept of sustainable development is the principle that developmental needs are to be taken into account in interpreting and applying environmental obligations' (Counter-Memorial of Slovakia, para. 9.53; see also paras. 9.54–9.59).

Their disagreement seems to be not as to the existence of the principle but, rather, as to the way in which it is to be applied to the facts of this case (Reply of Hungary, para. 1.45).

The problem of steering a course between the needs of development and the necessity to protect the environment is a problem alike of the law of development and of the law of the environment. Both these vital and developing areas of law require, and indeed assume, the existence of a principle which harmonizes both needs.

To hold that no such principle exists in the law is to hold that current law recognizes the juxtaposition of two principles which could operate in collision with each other, without providing the necessary basis of principle for their reconciliation. The untenability of the supposition that the law sanctions such a state of normative anarchy suffices to condemn a hypothesis that leads to so unsatisfactory a result.

Each principle cannot be given free rein, regardless of the other. The law necessarily contains within itself the principle of reconciliation. That principle is the principle of sustainable development.

This case offers a unique opportunity for the application of that principle, for it arises from a Treaty which had development as its objective, and has been brought to a standstill over arguments concerning environmental considerations.

The people of both Hungary and Slovakia are entitled to development for the furtherance of their happiness and welfare. They are likewise entitled to the preservation of their human right to the protection of their environment. Other cases raising environmental questions have been considered by this Court in the context of environmental pollution arising from such sources as nuclear explosions, which are far removed from development projects. The present case thus focuses attention, as no other case has done in the jurisprudence of this Court, on the question of the harmonization of developmental and environmental concepts.

[91] (a) Development as a principle of international law

Article 1 of the Declaration on the Right to Development, 1986, asserted that 'The right to development is an inalienable human right.' This Declaration had the overwhelming support of the international community[1] and has been gathering strength since then.[2] Principle 3 of the Rio Declaration, 1992, reaffirmed the need for the right to development to be fulfilled.

'Development' means, of course, development not merely for the sake of development and the economic gain it produces, but for its value in increasing the sum total of human happiness and welfare.[3] That could perhaps be called the first principle of the law relating to development.

To the end of improving the sum total of human happiness and welfare, it is important and inevitable that development projects of various descriptions, both minor and major, will be launched from time to time in all parts of the world.

(b) Environmental protection as a principle of international law

The protection of the environment is likewise a vital part of contemporary human rights doctrine, for it is a *sine qua non* for numerous human rights such as the right to

---

[1] 146 votes in favour, with one vote against.

[2] Many years prior to the Declaration of 1986, this right had received strong support in the field of human rights. As early as 1972, at the Third Session of the Institut international de droits de l'homme, Judge Kéba Mbaye, President of the Supreme Court of Senegal and later to be a Vice-President of this Court, argued strongly that such a right existed. He adduced detailed argument in support of his contention from economic, political and moral standpoints. (See K. Mbaye, 'Le droit au développement comme un droit de l'homme', *Revue des droits de l'homme*, 1972, Vol. 5, p. 503.)

Nor was the principle without influential voices in its support from the developed world as well. Indeed, the genealogy of the idea can be traced much further back even to the conceptual stages of the Universal Declaration of Human Rights, 1948.

Mrs Eleanor Roosevelt, who from 1946 to 1952 served as the Chief United States representative to Committee III, Humanitarian, Social and Cultural Affairs, and was the first Chairperson, from 1946 to 1951, of the United Nations Human Rights Commission, had observed in 1947, 'We will have to bear in mind that we are writing a bill of rights for the world and that one of the most important rights is the opportunity for development.' (M. Glen Johnson, 'The Contribution of Eleanor and Franklin Roosevelt to the Development of the International Protection for Human Rights', *Human Rights Quarterly*, 1987, Vol. 9, p. 19, quoting Mrs Roosevelt's column, 'My Day', 6 February 1947.)

General Assembly resolution 642 (VII) of 1952, likewise, referred expressly to 'integrated economic and social development'.

[3] The Preamble to the Declaration on the Right to Development (1986) recites that development is a comprehensive, economic, social and cultural process which aims at the constant improvement and well-being of the entire population and of all individuals on the basis of their active, free and meaningful participation in development and in the fair distribution of the benefits resulting therefrom.

health and the right to life itself. It is [92] scarcely necessary to elaborate on this, as damage to the environment can impair and undermine all the human rights spoken of in the Universal Declaration and other human rights instruments.

While, therefore, all peoples have the right to initiate development projects and enjoy their benefits, there is likewise a duty to ensure that those projects do not significantly damage the environment.

(c) Sustainable development as a principle of international law

After the early formulations of the concept of development, it has been recognized that development cannot be pursued to such a point as to result in substantial damage to the environment within which it is to occur. Therefore development can only be prosecuted in harmony with the reasonable demands of environmental protection. Whether development is sustainable by reason of its impact on the environment will, of course, be a question to be answered in the context of the particular situation involved.

It is thus the correct formulation of the right to development that that right does not exist in the absolute sense, but is relative always to its tolerance by the environment. The right to development as thus refined is clearly part of modern international law. It is compendiously referred to as sustainable development.

The concept of sustainable development can be traced back, beyond the Stockholm Conference of 1972, to such events as the Founex meeting of experts in Switzerland in June 1971;[4] the conference on environment and development in Canberra in 1971; and United Nations General Assembly resolution 2849 (XXVI). It received a powerful impetus from the Stockholm Declaration which, by Principle 11, stressed the essentiality of development as well as the essentiality of bearing environmental considerations in mind in the developmental process. Moreover, many other Principles of that Declaration[5] provided a setting for the development of the concept of sustainable development[6] and more than one-third of the Stockholm Declaration related to the harmonization of environment and development.[7] The Stockholm Conference also produced an Action Plan for the Human Environment.[8]

[93] The international community had thus been sensitized to this issue even as early as the early 1970s, and it is therefore no cause for surprise that the 1977 Treaty, in Articles 15 and 19, made special reference to environmental considerations. Both Parties to the Treaty recognized the need for the developmental process to be in harmony with the environment and introduced a dynamic element into the Treaty which enabled the Joint Project to be kept in harmony with developing principles of international law.

---

[4] See *Sustainable Development and International Law*, Winfried Lang (ed.), 1995, p. 143.
[5] For example, Principles 2, 3, 4, 5, 8, 9, 12, 13 and 14.
[6] These principles are thought to be based to a large extent on the Founex Report – see *Sustainable Development and International Law*, Winfried Lang (ed.), *supra*, p. 144.
[7] *Ibid.*
[8] Action Plan for the Human Environment, United Nations doc. A/CONF.48/14/Rev.1. See especially Chapter II which devoted its final section to development and the environment.

Since then, it has received considerable endorsement from all sections of the international community, and at all levels.

Whether in the field of multilateral treaties,[9] international declarations;[10] the foundation documents of international organizations;[11] the practices of international financial institutions;[12] regional declarations and planning documents;[13] or State practice,[14] there is a wide and general recognition of the concept. The Bergen ECE Ministerial Declaration on Sustainable Development of 15 May 1990, resulting from a meeting of [94] Ministers from 34 countries in the ECE region, and the Commissioner for the Environment of the European Community, addressed 'The challenge of sustainable development of humanity' (para. 6), and prepared a Bergen Agenda for Action which included a consideration of the Economics of Sustainability, Sustainable Energy Use, Sustainable Industrial Activities, and Awareness Raising and Public

[9] For example, the United Nations Convention to Combat Desertification (The United Nations Convention to Combat Desertification in those Countries Experiencing Serious Droughts and/or Desertification, Particularly in Africa), 1994, Preamble, Art. 9 (1); the United Nations Framework Convention on Climate Change, 1992 (*ILM*, 1992, Vol. XXXI, p. 849, Arts. 2 and 3); and the Convention on Biological Diversity (*ILM*, 1992, Vol. XXXI, p. 818, Preamble, Arts. 1 and 10 – 'sustainable use of biodiversity').

[10] For example, the Rio Declaration on Environment and Development, 1992, emphasizes sustainable development in several of its Principles (e.g., Principles 4, 5, 7, 8, 9, 20, 21, 22, 24 and 27 refer expressly to 'sustainable development' which can be described as the central concept of the entire document); and the Copenhagen Declaration, 1995 (paras. 6 and 8), following on the Copenhagen World Summit for Social Development, 1995.

[11] For example, the North American Free Trade Agreement (Canada, Mexico, United States) (NAFTA, Preamble, *ILM*, 1993, Vol. XXXII, p. 289); the World Trade Organization (WTO) (paragraph 1 of the Preamble of the Marrakesh Agreement of 15 April 1994, establishing the World Trade Organization, speaks of the 'optimal use of the world's resources in accordance with the objective of sustainable development' – *ILM*, 1994, Vol. XXXIII, pp. 1143–4); and the European Union (Art. 2 of the ECT).

[12] For example, the World Bank Group, the Asian Development Bank, the African Development Bank, the Inter-American Development Bank, and the European Bank for Reconstruction and Development all subscribe to the principle of sustainable development. Indeed, since 1993, the World Bank has convened an annual conference related to advancing environmentally and socially sustainable development (ESSD).

[13] For example, the Langkawi Declaration on the Environment, 1989, adopted by the 'Heads of Government of the Commonwealth representing a quarter of the world's population' which adopted 'sustainable development' as its central theme; Ministerial Declaration on Environmentally Sound and Sustainable Development in Asia and the Pacific, Bangkok, 1990 (doc. 38a, p. 567); and Action Plan for the Protection and Management of the Marine and Coastal Environment of the South Asian Seas Region, 1983 (para. 10: 'sustainable, environmentally sound development').

[14] For example, in 1990, the Dublin Declaration by the European Council on the Environmental Imperative stated that there must be an acceleration of effort to ensure that economic development in the Community is 'sustainable and environmentally sound' (*Bulletin of the European Communities*, 6, 1990, Ann. II, p. 18). It urged the Community and Member States to play a major role to assist developing countries in their efforts to achieve 'long-term sustainable development' (*ibid.*, p. 19). It said, in regard to countries of Central and Eastern Europe, that remedial measures must be taken 'to ensure that their future economic development is sustainable' (*ibid.*). It also expressly recited that:

> As Heads of State or Government of the European Community, . . . [w]e intend that action by the Community and its Member States will be developed . . . on the principles of sustainable development and preventive and precautionary action. (*Ibid.*, Conclusions of the Presidency, Point 1.36, pp. 17–18.)

Participation. It sought to develop 'sound national indicators for sustainable development' (para. 13 *(b)*) and sought to encourage investors to apply environmental standards required in their home country to investments abroad. It also sought to encourage UNEP, UNIDO, UNDP, IBRD, ILO, and appropriate international organizations to support member countries in ensuring environmentally sound industrial investment, observing that industry and government should co-operate for this purpose (para. 15 *(f)*).[15] A Resolution of the Council of Europe, 1990, propounded a European Conservation Strategy to meet, *inter alia*, the legitimate needs and aspirations of all Europeans by seeking to base economic, social and cultural development on a rational and sustainable use of natural resources, and to suggest how sustainable development can be achieved.[16]

The concept of sustainable development is thus a principle accepted not merely by the developing countries, but one which rests on a basis of worldwide acceptance.

In 1987, the Brundtland Report brought the concept of sustainable development to the forefront of international attention. In 1992, the Rio Conference made it a central feature of its Declaration, and it has been a focus of attention in all questions relating to development in the developing countries.

[95] The principle of sustainable development is thus a part of modern international law by reason not only of its inescapable logical necessity, but also by reason of its wide and general acceptance by the global community.

The concept has a significant role to play in the resolution of environmentally related disputes. The components of the principle come from well-established areas of international law – human rights, State responsibility, environmental law, economic and industrial law, equity, territorial sovereignty, abuse of rights, good neighbourliness – to mention a few. It has also been expressly incorporated into a number of binding and far-reaching international agreements, thus giving it binding force in the context of those agreements. It offers an important principle for the resolution of tensions between two established rights. It reaffirms in the arena of international law that there must be both development and environmental protection, and that neither of these rights can be neglected.

The general support of the international community does not of course mean that each and every member of the community of nations has given its express and specific support to the principle – nor is this a requirement for the establishment of a principle of customary international law.

As Brierly observes:

> It would hardly ever be practicable, and all but the strictest of positivists admit that it is not necessary, to show that every state has recognized a certain practice, just as in English law the existence of a valid local custom or custom of trade can be established without proof that every individual in the locality, or engaged in the trade, has practised the custom. This test of *general* recognition is necessarily a vague one; but it is of the nature of customary law, whether national or international . . . [17]

---

[15] *Basic Documents of International Environmental Law*, Harald Hohmann (ed.), Vol. 1, 1992, p. 558.
[16] *Ibid.*, p. 598.
[17] J. Brierly, *The Law of Nations*, 6th ed., 1963, p. 61; emphasis added.

Evidence appearing in international instruments and State practice (as in development assistance and the practice of international financial institutions) likewise amply supports a contemporary general acceptance of the concept.

Recognition of the concept could thus, fairly, be said to be worldwide.[18]

[96] (d) The need for international law to draw upon the world's diversity of cultures in harmonizing development and environmental protection

This case, which deals with a major hydraulic project, is an opportunity to tap the wisdom of the past and draw from it some principles which can strengthen the concept of sustainable development, for every development project clearly produces an effect upon the environment, and humanity has lived with this problem for generations.

This is a legitimate source for the enrichment of international law, which source is perhaps not used to the extent which its importance warrants.

In drawing into international law the benefits of the insights available from other cultures, and in looking to the past for inspiration, international environmental law would not be departing from the traditional methods of international law, but would, in fact, be following in the path charted out by Grotius. Rather than laying down a set of principles *a priori* for the new discipline of international law, he sought them also *a posteriori* from the experience of the past, searching through the whole range of cultures available to him for this purpose.[19] From them, he drew the durable principles which had weathered the ages, on which to build the new international order of the future. Environmental law is now in a formative stage, not unlike international law in its early stages. A wealth of past experience from a variety of cultures is available to it. It would be pity indeed if it were left untapped merely because of attitudes of formalism which see such approaches as not being entirely *de rigueur*.

I cite in this connection an observation of Sir Robert Jennings that, in taking note of different legal traditions and cultures, the International Court (as it did in the *Western Sahara* case):

> was asserting, not negating, the Grotian subjection of the totality of international relations to international law. It seems to the writer, indeed, that at the present juncture in the development of the international legal system it may be more important to stress the imperative need to develop international law to comprehend within itself the rich diversity of cultures, civilizations and legal traditions . . .[20]

Moreover, especially at the frontiers of the discipline of international [97] law, it needs to be multi-disciplinary, drawing from other disciplines such as history, sociology, anthropology, and psychology such wisdom as may be relevant for its purpose. On the need for the international law of the future to be interdisciplinary, I refer to

---

[18] See, further, L. Krämer, *EC Treaty and Environmental Law*, 2nd ed., 1995, p. 63, analysing the environmental connotation in the word 'sustainable' and tracing it to the Brundtland Report.

[19] Julius Stone, *Human Law and Human Justice*, 1965, p. 66: 'It was for this reason that Grotius added to his theoretical deductions such a mass of concrete examples from history.'

[20] Sir Robert Y. Jennings, 'Universal International Law in a Multicultural World', in *International Law and the Grotian Heritage: A Commemorative Colloquium on the Occasion of the Fourth Centenary of the Birth of Hugo Grotius*, edited and published by the TMC Asser Institute, The Hague, 1985, p. 195.

another recent extra-judicial observation of that distinguished former President of the Court that:

> there should be a much greater, and a practical, recognition by international lawyers that the rule of law in international affairs, and the establishment of international justice, are inter-disciplinary subjects.[21]

Especially where this Court is concerned, 'the essence of true universality'[22] of the institution is captured in the language of Article 9 of the Statute of the International Court of Justice which requires the 'representation of the *main forms of civilization* and of the principal legal systems of the world' (emphasis added). The struggle for the insertion of the italicized words in the Court's Statute was a hard one, led by the Japanese representative, Mr Adatci,[23] and, since this concept has thus been integrated into the structure and the Statute of the Court, I see the Court as being charged with a duty to draw upon the wisdom of the world's several civilizations, where such a course can enrich its insights into the matter before it. The Court cannot afford to be monocultural, especially where it is entering newly developing areas of law.

This case touches an area where many such insights can be drawn to the enrichment of the developing principles of environmental law and to a clarification of the principles the Court should apply.

It is in this spirit that I approach a principle which, for the first time in its jurisprudence, the Court is called upon to apply – a principle which will assist in the delicate task of balancing two considerations of enormous importance to the contemporary international scene and, potentially, of even greater importance to the future.

(e) Some wisdom from the past relating to sustainable development

There are some principles of traditional legal systems that can be woven into the fabric of modern environmental law. They are specially pertinent to the concept of sustainable development which was well [98] recognized in those systems. Moreover, several of these systems have particular relevance to this case, in that they relate to the harnessing of streams and rivers and show a concern that these acts of human interference with the course of nature should always be conducted with due regard to the protection of the environment. In the context of environmental wisdom generally, there is much to be derived from ancient civilizations and traditional legal systems in Asia, the Middle East, Africa, Europe, the Americas, the Pacific, and Australia – in fact, the whole world. This is a rich source which modern environmental law has left largely untapped.

As the Court has observed, 'Throughout the ages mankind has, for economic and other reasons, constantly interfered with nature.' (Judgment, para. 140.)

---

[21] 'International Lawyers and the Progressive Development of International Law', *Theory of International Law at the Threshold of the 21st Century*, Jerzy Makarczyk (ed.), 1996, p. 423.

[22] Jennings, 'Universal International Law in a Multicultural World', *op. cit.*, p. 189.

[23] On this subject of contention, see *Procès-Verbaux of the Proceedings of the Committee, 16 June–24 July 1920*, esp. p. 136.

The concept of reconciling the needs of development with the protection of the environment is thus not new. Millennia ago these concerns were noted and their twin demands well reconciled in a manner so meaningful as to carry a message to our age.

I shall start with a system with which I am specially familiar, which also happens to have specifically articulated these two needs – development and environmental protection – in its ancient literature. I refer to the ancient irrigation-based civilization of Sri Lanka.[24] It is a system which, while recognizing the need for development and vigorously implementing schemes to this end, at the same time specifically articulated the need for environmental protection and ensured that the technology it employed paid due regard to environmental considerations. This concern for the environment was reflected not only in its literature and its technology, but also in its legal system, for the felling of certain forests was prohibited, game sanctuaries were established, and royal edicts decreed that the natural resource of water was to be used to the last drop without any wastage.

This system, some details of which I shall touch on,[25] is described by [99] Arnold Toynbee in his panoramic survey of civilizations. Referring to it as an 'amazing system of waterworks',[26] Toynbee describes[27] how hill streams were tapped and their water guided into giant storage tanks, some of them four thousand acres in extent,[28] from which channels ran on to other larger tanks.[29] Below each great tank and each great channel were hundreds of little tanks, each the nucleus of a village.

The concern for the environment shown by this ancient irrigation system has attracted study in a recent survey of the Social and Environmental Effects of Large Dams,[30] which observes that among the environmentally related aspects of its

---

[24] This was not an isolated civilization, but one which maintained international relations with China, on the one hand, and with Rome (1st c.) and Byzantium (4th c.), on the other. The presence of its ambassadors at the Court of Rome is recorded by Pliny (lib. vi c. 24), and is noted by Grotius – *De Jure Praedae Commentarius*, G. L. Williams and W. H. Zeydol (eds.), *Classics of International Law*, James B. Scott (ed.), 1950, pp. 240–1. This diplomatic representation also receives mention in world literature (e.g., Milton, *Paradise Regained*, Book IV). See also Grotius' reference to the detailed knowledge of Ceylon possessed by the Romans – Grotius, *Mare Liberum* (Freedom of the Seas), trans. R. van Deman Magoffin, p. 12. The island was known as Taprobane to the Greeks, Serendib to the Arabs, Lanka to the Indians, Ceilao to the Portuguese, and Zeylan to the Dutch. Its trade with the Roman Empire and the Far East was noted by Gibbon.

[25] It is an aid to the recapitulation of the matters mentioned that the edicts and works I shall refer to have been the subject of written records, maintained contemporaneously and over the centuries. See footnote 38 below.

[26] Arnold J. Toynbee, *A Study of History*, Somervell's Abridgment, 1960, Vol. 1, p. 257.

[27] *Ibid.*, p. 81, citing John Still, *The Jungle Tide*.

[28] Several of these are still in use, e.g., the *Tissawewa* (3rd c. BC); the *Nuwarawewa* (3rd c. BC); the *Minneriya tank* (275 AD); the *Kalawewa* (5th c. AD); and the *Parakrama Samudra* (Sea of Parakrama, 11th c. AD).

[29] The technical sophistication of this irrigation system has been noted also in Joseph Needham's monumental work on *Science and Civilization in China*. Needham, in describing the ancient irrigation works of China, makes numerous references to the contemporary irrigation works of Ceylon, which he discusses at some length. See especially, Vol. 4, *Physics and Physical Technology*, 1971, pp. 368 *et seq.* Also p. 215: 'We shall see how skilled the ancient Ceylonese were in this art.'

[30] Edward Goldsmith and Nicholas Hildyard, *The Social and Environmental Effects of Large Dams*, 1985, pp. 291–304.

irrigation systems were the 'erosion control tank' which dealt with the problem of silting by being so designed as to collect deposits of silt before they entered the main water storage tanks. Several erosion control tanks were associated with each village irrigation system. The significance of this can well be appreciated in the context of the present case, where the problem of silting has assumed so much importance.

Another such environmentally related measure consisted of the 'forest tanks' which were built in the jungle above the village, not for the purpose of irrigating land, but to provide water to wild animals.[31]

[100] This system of tanks and channels, some of them two thousand years old, constitute in their totality several multiples of the irrigation works involved in the present scheme. They constituted development as it was understood at the time, for they achieved in Toynbee's words, 'the arduous feat of conquering the parched plains of Ceylon for agriculture'.[32] Yet they were executed with meticulous regard for environmental concerns, and showed that the concept of sustainable development was consciously practised over two millennia ago with much success.

Under this irrigation system, major rivers were dammed and reservoirs created, on a scale and in a manner reminiscent of the damming which the Court saw on its inspection of the dams in this case.

This ancient concept of development was carried out on such a large scale that, apart from the major reservoirs,[33] of which there were several [101] dozen, between

---

[31] For these details, see Goldsmith and Hildyard, *ibid.*, pp. 291 and 296. The same authors observe:

> Sri Lanka is covered with a network of thousands of man-made lakes and ponds, known locally as *tanks* (after *tanque*, the Portuguese word for reservoir). Some are truly massive, many are thousands of years old, and almost all show a high degree of sophistication in their construction and design. Sir James Emerson Tennent, the nineteenth century historian, marvelled in particular at the numerous channels that were dug underneath the bed of each lake in order to ensure that the flow of water was 'constant and equal as long as any water remained in the tank'.

[32] Toynbee, *op. cit.*, p. 81. Andrew Carnegie, the donor of the Peace Palace, the seat of this Court, has described this ancient work of development in the following terms:

> The position held by Ceylon in ancient days as the great granary of Southern Asia explains the precedence accorded to agricultural pursuits. Under native rule the whole island was brought under irrigation by means of artificial lakes, constructed by dams across ravines, many of them of great extent – one still existing is twenty miles in circumference – but the system has been allowed to fall into decay. (Andrew Carnegie, *Round the World*, 1879 (1933 ed.), pp. 155–60.)

[33] The first of these major tanks was thought to have been constructed in 504 BC (Sir James Emerson Tennent, *Ceylon*, 1859, Vol. I, p. 367). A few examples, straddling 15 centuries, were:
  - the *Vavunik-kulam* (3rd c. BC) (1,975 acres water surface, 596 million cubic feet water capacity); the *Pavatkulam* (3rd or 2nd c. BC) (2,029 acres water surface, 770 million cubic feet water capacity) – Parker, *Ancient Ceylon*, 1909, pp. 363, 373;
  - the *Tissawewa* (3rd c. BC); and the *Nuwarawewa* (3rd c. BC), both still in service and still supplying water to the ancient capital Anuradhapura, which is now a provincial capital;
  - the *Minneriya tank* (275 AD) ('The reservoir upwards of twenty miles in circumference . . . the great embankment remains nearly perfect') (Tennent, *op. cit.*, Vol. II, p. 600);
  - the *Topawewa* (4th c. AD), area considerably in excess of 1,000 acres;

25,000 and 30,000 minor reservoirs were fed from these reservoirs through an intricate network of canals.[34]

The philosophy underlying this gigantic system,[35] which for upwards of two thousand years served the needs of man and nature alike, was articulated in a famous principle laid down by an outstanding monarch[36] that 'not even a little water that comes from the rain is to flow into the ocean without being made useful to man'.[37] According to the ancient chronicles,[38] these works were undertaken 'for the benefit of the country', and 'out of compassion for all living creatures'.[39] This complex of irrigation works was aimed at making the entire country a granary. They embodied the concept of development *par excellence*.

- the *Kalawewa* (5th c. AD) – embankment 3.25 miles long, rising to a height of 40 feet, tapping the river Kala Oya and supplying water to the capital Anuradhapura through a canal 50 miles in length;
- the *Yodawewa* (5th c. AD). Needham describes this as 'A most grandiose conception ... the culmination of Ceylonese hydraulics ... an artificial lake with a six-and-a-half mile embankment on three sides of a square, sited on a sloping plain and not in a river valley at all.' It was fed by a 50-mile canal from the river Malvatu-Oya;
- the *Parakrama Samudra* (Sea of Parakrama) (11th c. AD), embankment 9 miles long, up to 40 feet high, enclosing 6,000 acres of water area. (Brohier, *Ancient Irrigation Works in Ceylon*, 1934, p. 9.)

[34] On the irrigation systems, generally, see H. Parker, *Ancient Ceylon, op. cit.*; R. L. Brohier, *Ancient Irrigation Works in Ceylon*, 1934; Edward Goldsmith and Nicholas Hildyard, *op. cit.*, pp. 291–304. Needham, describing the ancient canal system of China, observes that 'it was comparable only with the irrigation contour canals of Ceylon, not with any work in Europe' (*op. cit.*, Vol. 4, p. 359).

[35] 'so vast were the dimensions of some of these gigantic tanks that many still in existence cover an area from fifteen to twenty miles in circumference' (Tennent, *op. cit.*, Vol. I, p. 364).

[36] King Parakrama Bahu (1153–86 AD). This monarch constructed or restored 163 major tanks, 2,376 minor tanks, 3,910 canals, and 165 dams. His masterpiece was the Sea of Parakrama, referred to in footnote 33. All of this was conceived within the environmental philosophy of avoiding any wastage of natural resources.

[37] See Toynbee's reference to this:

> The idea underlying the system was very great. It was intended by the tank-building kings that none of the rain which fell in such abundance in the mountains should reach the sea without paying tribute to man on the way. (*Op. cit.*, p. 81.)

[38] *The Mahavamsa*, Turnour's translation, Chap. XXXVII, p. 242. The *Mahavamsa* was the ancient historical chronicle of Sri Lanka, maintained contemporaneously by Buddhist monks, and an important source of dating for South Asian history. Commencing at the close of the 4th century AD, and incorporating earlier chronicles and oral traditions dating back a further eight centuries, this constitutes a continuous record for over 15 centuries – see *The Mahavamsa or The Great Chronicle of Ceylon*, translated into English by Wilhelm Geiger, 1912, Introduction, pp. ix–xii. The King's statement, earlier referred to, is recorded in the *Mahavamsa* as follows:

> In the realm that is subject to me are ... but few fields which are dependent on rivers with permanent flow ... Also by many mountains, thick jungles and by widespread swamps my kingdom is much straitened. Truly, in such a country not even a little water that comes from the rain must flow into the ocean without being made useful to man. (*Ibid.*, Chap. LXVIII, verses 8–12.)

[39] See also, on this matter, Emerson Tennent, *op. cit..* Vol. I, p. 311.

Just as development was the aim of this system, it was accompanied by a systematic philosophy of conservation dating back to at least the third century BC. The ancient chronicles record that when the King (Devanampiya Tissa, 247–207 BC) was on a hunting trip (around 223 BC), the Arahat[40] Mahinda, son of the Emperor Asoka of India, preached to him [102] a sermon on Buddhism which converted the king. Here are excerpts from that sermon:

> O great King, the birds of the air and the beasts have as equal a right to live and move about in any part of the land as thou. The land belongs to the people and all living beings; thou art only the guardian of it.[41]

This sermon, which indeed contained the first principle of modern environmental law – the principle of trusteeship of earth resources – caused the king to start sanctuaries for wild animals – a concept which continued to be respected for over twenty centuries. The traditional legal system's protection of fauna and flora, based on this Buddhist teaching, extended well into the eighteenth century.[42]

The sermon also pointed out that even birds and beasts have a right to freedom from fear.[43]

The notion of not causing harm to others and hence *sic utere tuo ut alienum non laedas* was a central notion of Buddhism. It translated well into environmental attitudes. '*Alienum*' in this context would be extended by Buddhism to future generations as well, and to other component elements of the natural order beyond man himself, for the Buddhist concept of duty had an enormously long reach.

This marked concern with environmental needs was reflected also in royal edicts, dating back to the third century BC, which ordained that certain primeval forests should on no account be felled. This was because adequate forest cover in the highlands was known to be crucial to the irrigation system as the mountain jungles intercepted and stored the monsoon rains.[44] They attracted the rain which fed the river and irrigation systems of the country, and were therefore considered vital.

Environmental considerations were reflected also in the actual work of construction and engineering. The ancient engineers devised an answer to the problem of silting (which has assumed much importance in the present case), and they invented a device (the *bisokotuwa* or valve pit), the counterpart of the sluice, for dealing with this environmental problem,[45] [103] by controlling the pressure and the quantity of

---

[40] A person who has attained a very high state of enlightenment. For its more technical meaning, see Walpola Rahula, *History of Buddhism in Ceylon*, 1956, pp. 217–21.

[41] This sermon is recorded in *The Mahavamsa*, Chap. XIV.

[42] See K. N. Jayatilleke, 'The Principles of International Law in Buddhist Doctrine', *Recueil des cours de l'Académie de droit international*, Vol. 120, 1967, p. 558.

[43] For this idea in the scriptures of Buddhism, see *Digha Nikaya*, III, Pali Text Society, p. 850.

[44] Goldsmith and Hildyard, *op. cit.*, p. 299. See, also, R. L. Brohier, 'The Interrelation of Groups of Ancient Reservoirs and Channels in Ceylon', *Journal of the Royal Asiatic Society (Ceylon)*, 1937, Vol. 34, No. 90, p. 65. Brohier's study is one of the foremost authorities on the subject.

[45] H. Parker, *Ancient Ceylon, op. cit.*, p. 379:

the outflow of water when it was released from the reservoir.[46] Weirs were also built, as in the case of the construction involved in this case, for raising the levels of river water and regulating its flow.[47]

This juxtaposition in this ancient heritage of the concepts of development and environmental protection invites comment immediately from those familiar with it. Anyone interested in the human future would perceive the connection between the two concepts and the manner of their reconciliation.

Not merely from the legal perspective does this become apparent, but even from the approaches of other disciplines.

Thus Arthur C. Clarke, the noted futurist, with that vision which has enabled him to bring high science to the service of humanity, put his finger on the precise legal problem we are considering when he observed: 'the small Indian Ocean island ... provides textbook examples of many modern dilemmas: *development* versus *environment*',[48] and proceeds immediately to recapitulate the famous sermon, already referred to, relating to the trusteeship of land, observing, 'For as King Devanampiya Tissa was told three centuries before the birth of Christ, we are its guardians – *not* its owners.'[49]

The task of the law is to convert such wisdom into practical terms – [104] and the law has often lagged behind other disciplines in so doing. Happily for international law, there are plentiful indications, as recited earlier in this opinion, of that degree of 'general recognition among states of a certain practice as obligatory'[50] to give the principle of sustainable development the nature of customary law.

> Since about the middle of the last century, open wells, called 'valve towers' when they stand clear of the embankment or 'valve pits' when they are in it, have been built in numerous reservoirs in Europe. Their duty is to hold the valves, and the lifting-gear for working them, by means of which the outward flow of water is regulated or totally stopped. Such also was the function of the *bisokotuwa* of the Sinhalese engineers; they were the first inventors of the valve-pit more than 2,100 years ago.

[46] H. Parker, *op. cit.* Needham observes:

> Already in the first century AD they [the Sinhalese engineers] understood the principle of the oblique weir ... But perhaps the most striking invention was the intake-towers or valve towers *(Bisokotuwa)* which were fitted in the reservoirs perhaps from the 2nd Century BC onwards, certainly from the 2nd Century AD ... In this way silt and scum-free water could be obtained and at the same time the pressure-head was so reduced as to make the outflow controllable. (Joseph Needham, *Science and Civilization in China, op. cit.*, Vol. 4, p. 372.)

[47] K. M. de Silva, *A History of Sri Lanka*, 1981, p. 30.

[48] Arthur C. Clarke, 'Sri Lanka's Wildlife Heritage', *National Geographic*, August 1983, No. 2, p. 254; emphasis added.

[49] Arthur C. Clarke has also written:

> Of all Ceylon's architectural wonders, however, the most remarkable – and certainly the most useful – is the enormous irrigation system which, for over two thousand years, has brought prosperity to the rice farmers in regions where it may not rain for six months at a time. Frequently ruined, abandoned and rebuilt, this legacy of the ancient engineers is one of the island's most precious possessions. Some of its artificial lakes are ten or twenty kilometres in circumference, and abound with birds and wildlife. (*The View from Serendip*, 1977, p. 121.)

[50] J. Brierly, *The Law of Nations, op. cit.*, p. 61.

This reference to the practice and philosophy of a major irrigation civilization of the pre-modern world[51] illustrates that when technology on this scale was attempted it was accompanied by a due concern for the environment. Moreover, when so attempted, the necessary response from the traditional legal system, as indicated above, was one of affirmative steps for environmental protection, often taking the form of royal decrees, apart from the practices of a sophisticated system of customary law which regulated the manner in which the irrigation facilities were to be used and protected by individual members of the public.

The foregoing is but one illustrative example of the concern felt by prior legal systems for the preservation and protection of the environment. There are other examples of complex irrigation systems that have sustained themselves for centuries, if not millennia.

My next illustration comes from two ancient cultures of sub-Saharan Africa – those of the Sonjo and the Chagga, both Tanzanian tribes.[52] Their complicated networks of irrigation furrows, collecting water from the mountain streams and transporting it over long distances to the fields below, have aroused the admiration of modern observers not merely for their technical sophistication, but also for the durability of the complex irrigation systems they fashioned. Among the Sonjo, it was considered to be the sacred duty of each generation to ensure that the system was kept in good repair and all able-bodied men in the villages were expected to take part.[53] The system comprised a fine network of small canals, reinforced by a superimposed network of larger channels. The water did [105] not enter the irrigation area unless it was strictly required, and was not allowed to pass through the plots in the rainy season. There was thus no over-irrigation, salinity was reduced, and water-borne diseases avoided.[54]

Sir Charles Dundas, who visited the Chagga in the first quarter of this century, was much impressed by the manner in which, throughout the long course of the furrows, society was so organized that law and order prevailed.[55] Care of the furrows was a prime social duty, and if a furrow was damaged, even accidentally, one of the elders would sound a horn in the evening (which was known as the call to the furrows), and

---

[51] It is possible that in no other part of the world are there to be found within the same space the remains of so many works for irrigation, which are at the same time of such great antiquity and of such vast magnitude as in Ceylon ... (Bailey, *Report on Irrigation in Uva*, 1859; see also R. L. Brohier, *Ancient Irrigation Works in Ceylon, op. cit.*, p. 1);

No people in any age or country had so great practice and experience in the construction of works for irrigation. (Sir James Emerson Tennent, *op. cit.*, Vol. I, p. 468);

The stupendous ruins of their reservoirs are the proudest monuments which remain of the former greatness of their country ... Excepting the exaggerated dimensions of Lake Moeris in Central Egypt, and the mysterious 'Basin of Al Aram' ... no similar constructions formed by any race, whether ancient or modern, exceed in colossal magnitude the stupendous tanks of Ceylon. (Sir James Emerson Tennent, quoted in Brohier, *supra*, p. 1.)

[52] Goldsmith and Hildyard, *op. cit.*, pp. 282–91.

[53] *Ibid.*, pp. 284–5.

[54] Goldsmith and Hildyard, *op. cit.*, p. 284.

[55] Sir Charles Dundas, *Kilimanjaro and Its Peoples*, 1924, p. 262.

next morning everyone would leave their normal work and set about the business of repair.[56] The furrow was a social asset owned by the clan.[57]

Another example is that of the *qanats*[58] of Iran, of which there were around 22,000, comprising more than 170,000 miles[59] of underground irrigation channels built thousands of years ago, and many of them still functioning.[60] Not only is the extent of this system remarkable, but also the fact that it has functioned for thousands of years and, until recently, supplied Iran with around 75 per cent of the water used for both irrigation and domestic purposes.

By way of contrast, where the needs of the land were neglected, and massive schemes launched for urban supply rather than irrigation, there was disaster. The immense works in the Euphrates Valley in the third millennium BC aimed not at improving the irrigation system of the local tribesmen, but at supplying the requirements of a rapidly growing urban society (e.g., a vast canal built around 2400 BC by King Entemenak) led to seepage, flooding and over-irrigation.[61] Traditional farming methods and later irrigation systems helped to overcome the resulting problems of waterlogging and salinization.

China was another site of great irrigation works, some of which are still in use over two millennia after their construction. For example, the ravages of the Mo river were overcome by an excavation through a [106] mountain and the construction of two great canals. Needham describes this as 'one of the greatest of Chinese engineering operations which, now 2,200 years old, is still in use today'.[62] An ancient stone inscription teaching the art of river control says that its teaching 'holds good for a thousand autumns'.[63] Such action was often inspired by the philosophy recorded in the *Tao Te Ching* which 'with its usual gemlike brevity says "Let there be no action [contrary to Nature] and there will be nothing that will not be well regulated"'.[64] Here, from another ancient irrigation civilization, is yet another expression of the idea of the rights of future generations being served through the harmonization of human developmental work with respect for the natural environment.

Regarding the Inca civilization at its height, it has been observed that it continually brought new lands under cultivation by swamp drainage, expansion of irrigation works, terracing of hillsides and construction of irrigation works in dry zones, the goal being always the same – better utilization of all resources so as to maintain

---

[56] Goldsmith and Hildyard, *op. cit.*, p. 289.

[57] See further Fidelio T. Masao, 'The Irrigation System in Uchagga: An Ethno-Historical Approach', *Tanzania Notes and Records*, No. 75, 1974.

[58] *Qanats* comprise a series of vertical shafts dug down to the aquifer and joined by a horizontal canal – see Goldsmith and Hildyard, *op. cit.*, p. 277.

[59] Some idea of the immensity of this work can be gathered from the fact that it would cost around one million dollars to build an eight kilometres *qanat* with an average tunnel depth of 15 metres (*ibid.*, p. 280).

[60] *Ibid.*, p. 277.

[61] Goldsmith and Hildyard, *op. cit.*, p. 308.

[62] *Op. cit.*, Vol. 4, p. 288.

[63] *Ibid.*, p. 295.

[64] Needham, *Science and Civilization in China*, Vol. 2, *History of Scientific Thought*, 1969, p. 69.

an equilibrium between production and consumption.[65] In the words of a noted writer on this civilization, 'in this respect we can consider the Inca civilization triumphant, since it conquered the eternal problem of *maximum use* and *conservation of soil*'.[66] Here, too, we note the harmonization of developmental and environmental considerations.

Many more instances can be cited of irrigation cultures which accorded due importance to environmental considerations and reconciled the rights of present and future generations. I have referred to some of the more outstanding. Among them, I have examined one at greater length, partly because it combined vast hydraulic development projects with a meticulous regard for environmental considerations, and partly because both development and environmental protection are mentioned in its ancient records. That is sustainable development *par excellence*; and the principles on which it was based must surely have a message for modern law.

Traditional wisdom which inspired these ancient legal systems was able to handle such problems. Modern legal systems can do no less, achieving a blend of the concepts of development and of conservation of the environment, which alone does justice to humanity's obligations to itself and [107] to the planet which is its home. Another way of viewing the problem is to look upon it as involving the imperative of balancing the needs of the present generation with those of posterity.

In relation to concern for the environment generally, examples may be cited from nearly every traditional system, ranging from Australasia and the Pacific Islands, through Amerindian and African cultures to those of ancient Europe. When Native American wisdom, with its deep love of nature, ordained that no activity affecting the land should be undertaken without giving thought to its impact on the land for seven generations to come;[67] when African tradition viewed the human community as three-fold – past, present and future – and refused to adopt a one-eyed vision of concentration on the present; when Pacific tradition despised the view of land as merchandise that could be bought and sold like a common article of commerce,[68] and viewed land as a living entity which lived and grew with the people and upon whose sickness and death the people likewise sickened and died; when Chinese and Japanese culture stressed the need for harmony with nature; and when Aboriginal custom, while maximizing the use of all species of plant and animal life, yet decreed that no

---

[65] Jorge E. Hardoy, *Pre-Columbian Cities*, 1973, p. 415.

[66] John Collier, *Los indios de las Americas*, 1960, cited in Hardoy, *op. cit.*, p. 415. See also Donald Collier, 'Development of Civilization on the Coast of Peru', in *Irrigation Civilizations: A Comparative Study*, Julian H. Steward (ed.), 1955.

[67] On Native American attitudes to land, see Guruswamy, Palmer and Weston (eds.), *International Environmental Law and World Order*, 1994, pp. 298–9. On American Indian attitudes, see further J. Callicott, 'The Traditional American Indian and Western European Attitudes towards Nature: An Overview', *Environmental Ethics*, 1982, Vol. 4, p. 293; A. Wiggins, 'Indian Rights and the Environment', *Yale J. Int'l Law*, 1993, Vol. 18, p. 345; J. Hughes, *American Indian Ecology*, 1983.

[68] A Pacific Islander, giving evidence before the first Land Commission in the British Solomons (1919– 24), poured scorn on the concept that land could be treated 'as if it were a thing like a box' which could be bought and sold, pointing out that land was treated in his society with respect and with due regard for the rights of future generations. (Peter G. Sack, *Land between Two Laws*, 1993, p. 33.)

land should be used by man to the point where it could not replenish itself,[69] these varied cultures were reflecting the ancient wisdom of the human family which the legal systems of the time and the tribe absorbed, reflected and turned into principles whose legal validity cannot be denied. Ancient Indian teaching so respected the environment that it was illegal [108] to cause wanton damage, even to an enemy's territory in the course of military conflict.[70]

Europe, likewise, had a deep-seated tradition of love for the environment, a prominent feature of European culture, until the industrial revolution pushed these concerns into the background. Wordsworth in England, Thoreau in the United States, Rousseau in France, Tolstoy and Chekhov in Russia, Goethe in Germany spoke not only for themselves, but represented a deep-seated love of nature that was instinct in the ancient traditions of Europe – traditions whose gradual disappearance these writers lamented in their various ways.[71]

Indeed, European concern with the environment can be traced back through the millennia to such writers as Virgil, whose *Georgics*, composed between 37 and 30 BC, extols the beauty of the Italian countryside and pleads for the restoration of the traditional agricultural life of Italy, which was being damaged by the drift to the cities.[72]

This survey would not be complete without a reference also to the principles of Islamic law that inasmuch as all land belongs to God, land is never the subject of human ownership, but is only held in trust, with all the connotations that follow of due care, wise management, and custody for future generations. The first principle of modern environmental law – the principle of trusteeship of earth resources – is thus categorically formulated in this system.

The ingrained values of any civilization are the source from which its legal concepts derive, and the ultimate yardstick and touchstone of their validity. This is so in international and domestic legal systems alike, save that international law would

---

[69] On Aboriginal attitudes to land, see E. M. Eggleston, *Fear, Favour and Affection*, 1976. For all their concern with the environment, the Aboriginal people were not without their own development projects:

> There were remarkable Aboriginal water control schemes at Lake Condah, Toolondo and Mount William in south-western Victoria. These were major engineering feats, each involving several kilometres of stone channels connecting swamp and watercourses.
> At Lake Condah, thousands of years before Leonardo da Vinci studied the hydrology of the northern Italian lakes, the original inhabitants of Australia perfectly understood the hydrology of the site. A sophisticated network of traps, weirs and sluices were designed . . . (Stephen Johnson *et al.*, *Engineering and Society: An Australian Perspective*, 1995, p. 35.)

[70] Nagendra Singh, *Human Rights and the Future of Mankind*, 1981, p. 93.

[71] Commenting on the rise of naturalism in all the arts in Europe in the later Middle Ages, one of this century's outstanding philosophers of science has observed:

> The whole atmosphere of every art exhibited direct joy in the apprehension of the things around us. The craftsmen who executed the later mediaeval decorative sculpture, Giotto, Chaucer, Wordsworth, Walt Whitman, and at the present day the New England poet Robert Frost, are all akin to each other in this respect. (Alfred North Whitehead, *Science and the Modern World*, 1926, p. 17.)

[72] See the *Georgics*, Book II, l. 36 ff.; l. 458 ff. Also *Encyclopaedia Britannica*, 1992, Vol. 29, pp. 499–500.

require a worldwide recognition of those values. It would not be wrong to state that the love of nature, the desire for its preservation, and the need for human activity to respect the [109] requisites for its maintenance and continuance are among those pristine and universal values which command international recognition.

The formalism of modern legal systems may cause us to lose sight of such principles, but the time has come when they must once more be integrated into the corpus of the living law. As stated in the exhaustive study of *The Social and Environmental Effects of Large Dams*, already cited, 'We should examine not only what has caused modern irrigation systems to *fail*; it is much more important to understand what has made traditional irrigation societies to *succeed*.'[73]

Observing that various societies have practised sustainable irrigation agriculture over thousands of years, and that modern irrigation systems rarely last more than a few decades, the authors pose the question whether it was due to the achievement of a 'congruence of fit' between their methods and 'the nature of land, water and climate'.[74] Modern environmental law needs to take note of the experience of the past in pursuing this 'congruence of fit' between development and environmental imperatives.

By virtue of its representation of the main forms of civilization, this Court constitutes a unique forum for the reflection and the revitalization of those global legal traditions. There were principles ingrained in these civilizations as well as embodied in their *legal systems*, for legal systems include not merely written legal systems but traditional legal systems as well, which modern researchers have shown to be no less legal systems than their written cousins, and in some respects even more sophisticated and finely tuned than the latter.[75]

Living law which is daily observed by members of the community, and compliance with which is so axiomatic that it is taken for granted, is not deprived of the character of law by the extraneous test and standard of reduction to writing. Writing is of course useful for establishing certainty, but when a duty such as the duty to protect the environment is so well accepted that all citizens act upon it, that duty is part of the legal system in question.[76]

Moreover, when the Statute of the Court described the sources of international law as including the 'general principles of law recognized [110] by civilized nations', it expressly opened a door to the entry of such principles into modern international law.

(f) Traditional principles that can assist in the development of modern environmental law

As modern environmental law develops, it can, with profit to itself, take account of the perspectives and principles of traditional systems, not merely in a general way, but with reference to specific principles, concepts, and aspirational standards.

---

[73] Goldsmith and Hildyard, *op. cit.*, p. 316.

[74] *Ibid.*

[75] See, for example, M. Gluckman, *African Traditional Law in Historical Perspective*, 1974, *The Ideas in Barotse Jurisprudence*, 2nd ed., 1972, and *The Judicial Process among the Barotse*, 1955; A. L. Epstein, *Juridical Techniques and the Judicial Process: A Study in African Customary Law*, 1954.

[76] On the precision with which these systems assigned duties to their members, see Malinowski, *Crime and Custom in Savage Society*, 1926.

Among those which may be extracted from the systems already referred to are such far-reaching principles as the principle of trusteeship of earth resources, the principle of intergenerational rights, and the principle that development and environmental conservation must go hand in hand. Land is to be respected as having a vitality of its own and being integrally linked to the welfare of the community. When it is used by humans, every opportunity should be afforded to it to replenish itself. Since flora and fauna have a niche in the ecological system, they must be expressly protected. There is a duty lying upon all members of the community to preserve the integrity and purity of the environment.

Natural resources are not individually, but collectively, owned, and a principle of their use is that they should be used for the maximum service of people. There should be no waste, and there should be a maximization of the use of plant and animal species, while preserving their regenerative powers. The purpose of development is the betterment of the condition of the people.

Most of them have relevance to the present case, and all of them can greatly enhance the ability of international environmental law to cope with problems such as these if and when they arise in the future. There are many routes of entry by which they can be assimilated into the international legal system, and modern international law would only diminish itself were it to lose sight of them – embodying as they do the wisdom which enabled the works of man to function for centuries and millennia in a stable relationship with the principles of the environment. This approach assumes increasing importance at a time when such a harmony between humanity and its planetary inheritance is a prerequisite for human survival.

Sustainable development is thus not merely a principle of modern international law. It is one of the most ancient of ideas in the human heritage. Fortified by the rich insights that can be gained from millennia [111] of human experience, it has an important part to play in the service of international law.

B. The principle of continuing Environmental Impact Assessment
(a) The principle of continuing Environmental Impact Assessment

Environmental Impact Assessment (EIA) has assumed an important role in this case.

In a previous opinion[77] I have had occasion to observe that this principle was gathering strength and international acceptance, and had reached the level of general recognition at which this Court should take notice of it.[78]

---

[77] *Request for an Examination of the Situation in Accordance with Paragraph 63 of the Court's Judgment of 20 December 1974 in the Nuclear Tests (New Zealand v. France) Case, ICJ Reports 1995,* p. 344 [see p. 186 above]. See, also, *Legality of the Use by a State of Nuclear Weapons in Armed Conflict, ICJ Reports 1996,* p. 140 [see p. 227 above].

[78] Major international documents recognizing this principle (first established in domestic law under the 1972 National Environmental Protection Act of the United States) are the 1992 Rio Declaration (Principle 17); United Nations General Assembly resolution 2995 (XXVII), 1972; the 1978 UNEP Draft Principles of Conduct (Principle 5); Agenda 21 (paras. 7.41 *(b)* and 8.4); the 1974 Nordic

I wish in this opinion to clarify further the scope and extent of the environmental impact principle in the sense that environmental impact assessment means not merely an assessment prior to the commencement of the project, but a continuing assessment and evaluation as long as the project is in operation. This follows from the fact that EIA is a dynamic principle and is not confined to a pre-project evaluation of possible environmental consequences. As long as a project of some magnitude is in operation, EIA must continue, for every such project can have unexpected consequences; and considerations of prudence would point to the need for continuous monitoring.[79]

The greater the size and scope of the project, the greater is the need for a continuous monitoring of its effects, for EIA before the scheme can never be expected, in a matter so complex as the environment, to anticipate every possible environmental danger.

In the present case, the incorporation of environmental considerations into the Treaty by Articles 15 and 19 meant that the principle of EIA was also built into the Treaty. These provisions were clearly not restricted to EIA before the project commenced, but also included the concept of [112] monitoring during the continuance of the project. Article 15 speaks expressly of monitoring of the water quality during the *operation* of the System of Locks, and Article 19 speaks of compliance with obligations for the protection of nature arising in connection with the construction and *operation* of the System of Locks.

Environmental law in its current state of development would read into treaties which may reasonably be considered to have a significant impact upon the environment, a duty of environmental impact assessment and this means also, whether the treaty expressly so provides or not, a duty of monitoring the environmental impacts of any substantial project during the operation of the scheme.

Over half a century ago the *Trail Smelter Arbitration*[80] recognized the importance of continuous monitoring when, in a series of elaborate provisions, it required the parties to monitor subsequent performance under the decision.[81] It directed the Trail Smelter to install observation stations, equipment necessary to give information of gas conditions and sulphur dioxide recorders, and to render regular reports which the Tribunal would consider at a future meeting. In the present case, the Judgment of the Court imposes a requirement of joint supervision which must be similarly understood and applied.

The concept of monitoring and exchange of information has gathered much recognition in international practice. Examples are the Co-operative Programme for the Monitoring and Evaluation of the Long-Range Transmission of Air Pollutants in Europe, under the ECE Convention, the Vienna Convention for the Protection of the

Environmental Protection Convention (Art. 6); the 1985 EC Environmental Assessment Directive (Art. 3); and the 1991 Espoo Convention. The status of the principle in actual practice is indicated also by the fact that multilateral development banks have adopted it as an essential precaution (World Bank Operational Directive 4.00).

[79] *Trail Smelter Arbitration* (United Nations, *Reports of International Arbitral Awards (RIAA)*, 1941, Vol. III, p. 1907).

[80] *RIAA*, 1941, Vol. III, p. 1907.

[81] See *ibid.*, pp. 1934–7.

Ozone Layer, 1985 (Arts. 3 and 4), and the Convention on Long-Range Transboundary Air Pollution, 1979 (Art. 9).[82] There has thus been growing international recognition of the concept of continuing monitoring as part of EIA.

The Court has indicated in its Judgment (para. 155 (2) (C)) that a joint operational régime must be established in accordance with the Treaty of 16 September 1977. A continuous monitoring of the scheme for its environmental impacts will accord with the principles outlined, and be a part of that operational régime. Indeed, the 1977 Treaty, with its contemplated régime of joint operation and joint supervision, had itself a built-in régime of continuous joint environmental monitoring. This principle of environmental law, as reinforced by the terms of the Treaty and as now incorporated into the Judgment of the Court (para. 140), would require the Parties to take upon themselves an obligation to set up the machinery for continuous watchfulness, anticipation and evaluation [113] at every stage of the project's progress, throughout its period of active operation.

Domestic legal systems have shown an intense awareness of this need and have even devised procedural structures to this end. In India, for example, the concept has evolved of the 'continuous mandamus' – a court order which specifies certain environmental safeguards in relation to a given project, and does not leave the matter there, but orders a continuous monitoring of the project to ensure compliance with the standards which the court has ordained.[83]

EIA, being a specific application of the larger general principle of caution, embodies the obligation of continuing watchfulness and anticipation.

(b) The principle of contemporaneity in the application of environmental norms
This is a principle which supplements the observations just made regarding continuing assessment. It provides the standard by which the continuing assessment is to be made.

This case concerns a treaty that was entered into in 1977. Environmental standards and the relevant scientific knowledge of 1997 are far in advance of those of 1977. As the Court has observed, new scientific insights and a growing awareness of the risks for mankind have led to the development of new norms and standards:

> Such new norms have to be taken into consideration, and such new standards given proper weight, not only when States contemplate new activities but also when continuing with activities begun in the past. (Para. 140.)

This assumes great practical importance in view of the continued joint monitoring that will be required in terms of the Court's Judgment.

Both Parties envisaged that the project they had agreed upon was not one which would be operative for just a few years. It was to reach far into the long-term future, and be operative for decades, improving in a permanent way the natural features

---

[82] *ILM*, 1979, Vol. XVIII, p. 1442.

[83] For a reference to environmentally related judicial initiatives of the courts of the SAARC Region, see the Proceedings of the Regional Symposium on the Role of the Judiciary in Promoting the Rule of Law in the Area of Sustainable Development, held in Colombo, Sri Lanka, 4–6 July 1997, shortly to be published.

that it dealt with, and forming a lasting contribution to the economic welfare of both participants.

If the Treaty was to operate for decades into the future, it could not [114] operate on the basis of environmental norms as though they were frozen in time when the Treaty was entered into.

This inter-temporal aspect of the present case is of importance to all treaties dealing with projects impacting on the environment. Unfortunately, the Vienna Convention offers very little guidance regarding this matter which is of such importance in the environmental field. The provision in Article 31, paragraph 3 *(c)*, providing that 'any relevant rules of international law applicable in the relations between the parties' shall be taken into account, scarcely covers this aspect with the degree of clarity requisite to so important a matter.

Environmental concerns are live and continuing concerns whenever the project under which they arise may have been inaugurated. It matters little that an undertaking has been commenced under a treaty of 1950, if in fact that undertaking continues in operation in the year 2000. The relevant environmental standards that will be applicable will be those of the year 2000.

As this Court observed in the *Namibia* case, 'an international instrument has to be interpreted and applied within the framework of the entire legal system prevailing at the time of the interpretation' (*Legal Consequences for States of the Continued Presence of South Africa in Namibia (South West Africa) notwithstanding Security Council Resolution 276 (1970), Advisory Opinion, ICJ Reports 1971*, p. 31, para. 53), and these principles are 'not limited to the rules of international law applicable at the time the treaty was concluded'.[84]

Environmental rights are human rights. Treaties that affect human rights cannot be applied in such a manner as to constitute a denial of human rights as understood at the time of their application. A Court cannot endorse actions which are a violation of human rights by the standards of their time merely because they are taken under a treaty which dates back to a period when such action was not a violation of human rights.

Support for this proposition can be sought from the opinion of Judge Tanaka in *South West Africa*, when he observed that a new customary law could be applied to the interpretation of an instrument entered into more than 40 years previously (*ICJ Reports 1966*, pp. 293–4). The ethical and human rights related aspects of environmental law bring it within the category of law so essential to human welfare that we cannot apply to today's problems in this field the standards of yesterday. Judge Tanaka reasoned that a party to a humanitarian instrument has no right to act in a manner which is today considered inhuman, even though the action be taken under an instrument of 40 years ago. Likewise, no action should be permissible which is today considered environmentally [115] unsound, even though it is taken under an instrument of more than 20 years ago.

---

[84] *Oppenheim's International Law*, R. Y. Jennings and A. Watts (eds.), 1992, p. 1275, note 21.

Mention may also be made in this context of the observation of the European Court of Human Rights in the *Tyrer* case that the Convention is a 'living instrument' which must be interpreted 'in the light of present-day conditions'.[85]

It may also be observed that we are not here dealing with questions of the *validity* of the Treaty which fall to be determined by the principles applicable at the time of the Treaty, but with the *application* of the Treaty.[86] In the application of an environmental treaty, it is vitally important that the standards in force *at the time of application* would be the governing standards.

A recognition of the principle of contemporaneity in the application of environmental norms applies to the joint supervisory régime envisaged in the Court's Judgment, and will be an additional safeguard for protecting the environmental interests of Hungary.

C. The handling of erga omnes *obligations in* inter partes *judicial procedure*
(a) The factual background: the presence of the elements of estoppel
It is necessary to bear in mind that the Treaty of 1977 was not one that suddenly materialized and was hastily entered into, but that it was the result of years of negotiation and study following the first formulations of the idea in the 1960s. During the period of negotiation and implementation of the Treaty, numerous detailed studies were conducted by many experts and organizations, including the Hungarian Academy of Sciences.

The first observation to be made on this matter is that Hungary went into the 1977 Treaty, despite very clear warnings during the preparatory studies that the Project might involve the possibility of environmental damage. Hungary, with a vast amount of material before it, both for and against, thus took a considered decision, despite warnings of possible danger to its ecology on almost all the grounds which are advanced today.

Secondly, Hungary, having entered into the Treaty, continued to treat it as valid and binding for around 12 years. As early as 1981, the Government [116] of Hungary had ordered a reconsideration of the Project and researchers had then suggested a postponement of the construction, pending more detailed ecological studies. Yet Hungary went ahead with the implementation of the Treaty.

Thirdly, not only did Hungary devote its own effort and resources to the implementation of the Treaty but, by its attitude, it left Czechoslovakia with the impression that the binding force of the Treaty was not in doubt. Under this impression, and in pursuance of the Treaty which bound both Parties, Czechoslovakia committed enormous resources to the Project. Hungary looked on without comment or protest and, indeed, urged Czechoslovakia to more expeditious action. It was clear to Hungary that Czechoslovakia was spending vast funds on the Project – resources clearly so large as to strain the economy of a State whose economy was not particularly strong.

---

[85] Judgment of the Court, *Tyrer* case, 25 April 1978, para. 31, publ. Court A, Vol. 26, at 15, 16.
[86] See further Rosalyn Higgins, 'Some Observations on the Inter-Temporal Rule in International Law', in *Theory of International Law at the Threshold of the 21st Century, op. cit.*, p. 173.

Fourthly, Hungary's action in so entering into the Treaty in 1977 was confirmed by it as late as October 1988 when the Hungarian Parliament approved of the Project, despite all the additional material available to it in the intervening space of 12 years. A further reaffirmation of this Hungarian position is to be found in the signing of a Protocol by the Deputy Chairman of the Hungarian Council of Ministers on 6 February 1989, reaffirming Hungary's commitment to the 1977 Project. Hungary was in fact interested in setting back the date of completion from 1995 to 1994.

Ninety-six days after the 1989 Protocol took effect, i.e., on 13 May 1989, the Hungarian Government announced the immediate suspension for two months of work at the Nagymaros site. It abandoned performance on 20 July 1989, and thereafter suspended work on all parts of the Project. Formal termination of the 1977 Treaty by Hungary took place in May 1992.

It seems to me that all the ingredients of a legally binding estoppel are here present.[87]

The other Treaty partner was left with a vast amount of useless project construction on its hands and enormous incurred expenditure which it had fruitlessly undertaken.

(b) The context of Hungary's actions

In making these observations, one must be deeply sensitive to the fact that Hungary was passing through a very difficult phase, having regard [117] to the epochal events that had recently taken place in Eastern Europe. Such historic events necessarily leave their aftermath of internal tension. This may well manifest itself in shifts of official policy as different emergent groups exercise power and influence in the new order that was in the course of replacing that under which the country had functioned for close on half a century. One cannot but take note of these realities in understanding the drastic official changes of policy exhibited by Hungary.

Yet the Court is placed in the position of an objective observer, seeking to determine the effects of one State's changing official attitudes upon a neighbouring State. This is particularly so where the latter was obliged, in determining its course of action, to take into account the representations emanating from the official repositories of power in the first State.

Whatever be the reason for the internal changes of policy, and whatever be the internal pressures that might have produced this, the Court can only assess the respective rights of the two States on the basis of their official attitudes and pronouncements. Viewing the matter from the standpoint of an external observer, there can be little doubt that there was indeed a marked change of official attitude towards the Treaty, involving a sharp shift from full official acceptance to full official rejection. It is on this basis that the legal consequence of estoppel would follow.

---

[87] On the application of principles of estoppel in the jurisprudence of this Court and its predecessor, see *Legal Status of Eastern Greenland, PCIJ, Series A/B, No. 53*, p. 22; *Fisheries (United Kingdom v. Norway), ICJ Reports 1951*, p. 116; *Temple of Preah Vihear, ICJ Reports 1962*, p. 151. For an analysis of this jurisprudence, see the separate opinion of Judge Ajibola in *Territorial Dispute (Libyan Arab Jamahiriya/Chad), ICJ Reports 1994*, pp. 77–83.

(c) Is it appropriate to use the rules of *inter partes* litigation to determine *erga omnes* obligations?

This recapitulation of the facts brings me to the point where I believe a distinction must be made between litigation involving issues *inter partes* and litigation which involves issues with an *erga omnes* connotation.

An important conceptual problem arises when, in such a dispute *inter partes*, an issue arises regarding an alleged violation of rights or duties in relation to the rest of the world. The Court, in the discharge of its traditional duty of deciding *between the parties*, makes the decision which is in accordance with justice and fairness *between the parties*. The procedure it follows is largely adversarial. Yet this scarcely does justice to rights and obligations of an *erga omnes* character – least of all in cases involving environmental damage of a far-reaching and irreversible nature. I draw attention to this problem as it will present itself sooner or later in the field of environmental law, and because (though not essential to the decision actually reached) the facts of this case draw attention to it in a particularly pointed form.

There has been conduct on the part of Hungary which, in ordinary [**118**] *inter partes* litigation, would prevent it from taking up wholly contradictory positions. But can momentous environmental issues be decided on the basis of such *inter partes* conduct? In cases where the *erga omnes* issues are of sufficient importance, I would think not.

This is a suitable opportunity, both to draw attention to the problem and to indicate concern at the inadequacies of such *inter partes* rules as determining factors in major environmental disputes.

I stress this for the reason that *inter partes* adversarial procedures, eminently fair and reasonable in a purely *inter partes* issue, may need reconsideration in the future, if ever a case should arise of the imminence of serious or catastrophic environmental danger, especially to parties other than the immediate litigants.

Indeed, the inadequacies of technical judicial rules of procedure for the decision of scientific matters has for long been the subject of scholarly comment.[88]

We have entered an era of international law in which international law subserves not only the interests of individual States, but looks beyond them and their parochial concerns to the greater interests of humanity and planetary welfare. In addressing such problems, which transcend the individual rights and obligations of the litigating States, international law will need to look beyond procedural rules fashioned for purely *inter partes* litigation.

When we enter the arena of obligations which operate *erga omnes* rather than *inter partes*, rules based on individual fairness and procedural compliance may be inadequate. The great ecological questions now surfacing will call for thought upon this matter. International environmental law will need to proceed beyond weighing

---

[88] See, for example, Peter Brett, 'Implications of Science for the Law', *McGill Law Journal*, 1972, Vol. 18, p. 170, at p. 191. For a well-known comment from the perspective of sociology, see Jacques Ellul, *The Technological Society*, trans. John Wilkinson, 1964, pp. 251, 291–300.

the rights and obligations of parties within a closed compartment of individual State self-interest, unrelated to the global concerns of humanity as a whole.

The present case offers an opportunity for such reflection.

*

*   *

Environmental law is one of the most rapidly developing areas of international law and I have thought it fit to make these observations on a few aspects which have presented themselves for consideration in this case. [119] As this vital branch of law proceeds to develop, it will need all the insights available from the human experience, crossing cultural and disciplinary boundaries which have traditionally hemmed in the discipline of international law.

[120] SEPARATE OPINION OF JUDGE BEDJAOUI (EXTRACT)

[Translation]

1. In my view, the majority of the Court has not sufficiently clarified two questions, i.e., the *applicable law* and the *nature* of the 1977 Treaty. In no way do I disagree with the analysis of the majority of the Court on these two points which will necessitate just a little finer shading and clarification from me at a later stage.

[...]

3. I agree with the majority of the Court on its general approach to the question of the *applicable law*. I shall refer to only one aspect of this question that I consider to be fundamental and that touches upon the applicability in this case of the conventions and other instruments *subsequent* to the 1977 Treaty, and concerning the environment and the law of international watercourses.

4. Hungary asks the Court to interpret the 1977 Treaty in the light of the new, more developed and more exacting law of the environment, and of the law of international watercourses. In support of its argument, it principally relies upon the Advisory Opinion rendered by the Court in 1971 in the *Namibia* case (*Legal Consequences for States of the Continued Presence of South Africa in Namibia (South West Africa) notwithstanding Security Council Resolution 276 (1970), Advisory Opinion, ICJ Reports 1971*, p. 16). In that case, the Court stated that a treaty should be interpreted 'within the framework of the entire legal system prevailing at the time of the interpretation' (*ibid.*, p. 31).

[121] 5. Taken literally and in isolation, there is no telling where this statement may lead. The following precautions must be taken:
   - an *'evolutionary interpretation'* can only apply *in the observation of the general rule of interpretation* laid down in Article 31 of the Vienna Convention on the Law of Treaties;
   - the *'definition'* of a concept must not be confused with the *'law'* applicable to that concept;
   - the *'interpretation'* of a treaty must not be confused with its *'revision'*.

A. *The 'evolutionary interpretation' can only be applied if the general rule of interpretation in Article 31 of the Vienna Convention on the Law of Treaties is respected*
(a) Respect for the principle *pacta sunt servanda* unless there is incompatibility with a peremptory norm appertaining to *jus cogens*

6. (i) It may be useful first to restate the obvious: *pacta sunt servanda.* Inasmuch as the 1997 Treaty is regarded as being in force for the purposes of a judicial interpretation, it is necessarily binding upon the parties. They are under an obligation to perform it in *good faith* (Article 26 of the 1969 Vienna Convention).

(ii) Moreover the parties cannot, in principle, evade a traditional interpretation based on Article 31 of the Vienna Convention unless the Treaty which they concluded in the past has become incompatible with a norm of *jus cogens.* Both Hungary and Slovakia appear to agree that this is not the case of the 1977 Treaty.

(b) The interpretation of the Treaty must comply with the intentions of the parties expressed at the time of its conclusion

7. (i) The Court's dictum, seized upon by Hungary in order to justify its *'evolutionary interpretation'*, needs to be put back into its proper context. Before settling on this dictum, the Court had been at pains, in the same 1971 Opinion and on the same page, to emphasize *'the primary necessity* of interpreting an instrument in accordance with the intentions of the parties at the time of its conclusion' (*ICJ Reports 1971*, p. 31; emphasis added).

(ii) The intentions of the parties are presumed to have been influenced by *the law in force at the time the Treaty was concluded*, the law which they were supposed to know, and not by future law, as yet unknown. As Ambassador Mustapha Kamil Yasseen, quoted by Hungary (Counter-Memorial of Hungary, para. 6.13), put it, only international law existing [122] when the Treaty was concluded 'could influence the intention of the Contracting States . . . , as the law which did not yet exist at that time could not logically have any influence on this intention'.[89]

(iii) Moreover, Hungary espouses this very classical approach by stating: 'the 1977 Treaty must *in the first place* be interpreted in the light of the international law prevailing at the time of its conclusion' (Counter-Memorial of Hungary, para. 6.28; emphasis added).

(c) Primacy of the principle of the *'fixed reference'* (*renvoi fixe*) over the principle of the *'mobile reference'* (*renvoi mobile*)

8. Hence, the essential basis for the interpretation of a treaty remains the *'fixed reference'* to contemporary international law at the time of its conclusion. The *'mobile reference'* to the law which will subsequently have developed can be recommended only in exceptional cases of the sort we shall be looking at.

---

[89] M. K. Yasseen, 'L'interprétation des traités d'aprés la Convention de Vienne sur le droit des traités', *Recueil des cours de l'Académie de droit international de La Haye*, Vol. 151 (1976), p. 64.

B.   'Definition' *of a concept not to be confused with the* 'law' *applicable to that concept*

9. In the *Namibia* case, the Court had to interpret a very special situation. Among the obligations of the Mandatory Power, the treaty instituting a 'C' Mandate over South West Africa referred to that of a *'sacred trust'*. It was then for the Court to interpret that phrase. It could only do so by observing the reality, which shows that this notion of a *'sacred trust'*, fashioned in 1920 in the era of colonization, was not comparable to the idea people had of it half a century later in the period of successive decolonizations. The Court thus considered that the matters to be interpreted, such as the 'sacred trust', 'were not static, but were by definition evolutionary' (*ICJ Reports 1971*, p. 31). This being so, *the method of the mobile reference*, in other words the reference to new contemporary law, was wholly suitable for an interpretation seeking to avoid archaic elements, was in tune with modern times and was useful as regards the action of the Applicant, which in this case was the Security Council.

10. But the Court patently knew that it was pursuing this approach because the situation was special. Nowhere did it state that its method of the mobile reference was subsequently to become mandatory and extend to all cases of interpretation. The *definition* of the *'sacred trust'* is evolutionary. It is *the law* corresponding to the period when this concept is [123] being interpreted which must be applied to the concept. On the other hand, the *environment* remains the environment. It is water, air, earth, vegetation, etc. As a basic *definition*, the environment is not evolutionary. Its components remain the same. On the other hand, its *'status'* may change, deteriorate or improve, but this is different from a definition by its components.

11. I would add that what evolved in the case of the Mandate was the *object of the treaty* which created it. This *object* was the sacred trust. Yet this object has not evolved at all in the *Gabčíkovo–Nagymaros* case. The point here was to consent to a joint investment and to build a number of structures. This object, or objective, remains, even if the actual *means* of achieving it may evolve or become more streamlined.

C.   'Interpretation' *of a treaty not to be confused with its* 'revision'

12. An interpretation of a treaty which would amount to substituting a completely different law to the one governing it at the time of its conclusion would be a *distorted revision*. The *'interpretation'* is not the same as the *'substitution'*, for a negotiated and approved text, of a completely different text, which has neither been negotiated nor agreed. Although there is no need to abandon the *'evolutionary interpretation'*, which may be useful, not to say necessary in very limited situations, it must be said that it cannot automatically be applied to any case.

13. In general, it is noteworthy that the classical rules of interpretation do not require a treaty to be interpreted *in all circumstances* in the context of the entire legal system prevailing at the time of the interpretation, in other words, in the present case, that the 1977 Treaty should be interpreted *'in the context'* and in the light of the new contemporary law of the environment or of international watercourses. Indeed, it is quite the opposite that these rules of interpretation prescribe, seeking as they do

to recommend an interpretation consonant with the intentions of the parties at the time the Treaty was concluded.

14. In general, in a treaty, a State incurs specific obligations contained in a body of law as it existed on the conclusion of the treaty and *in no wise incurs evolutionary and indeterminate duties.* A State cannot incur unknown obligations whether for the future or even the present.

15. In this case, the new law of the environment or of international watercourses could have been incorporated into the 1977 Treaty with the consent of the parties and by means of the *'procedural mechanisms'* laid down in the Treaty. That would be a *'revision'* of the Treaty accepted within the limits of that Treaty. Similarly, the new law might have played a role in the context of a *'reinterpretation'* of the Treaty but provided it did so *with the consent* of the other party.

[124] *D. Cautiously take subsequent law into account as an element of interpretation or modification in very special situations*

16. It is true that one cannot be excessively rigid without failing to allow for the movement of life. The new law might, in principle, be relevant in two ways: as an element of the *interpretation* of the content of the 1977 Treaty and as an element of the *modification* of that content.

17. *The former case,* that of interpretation, is the simpler of the two. *In general,* there is certainly good reason to protect the autonomy of the will. But *in our case,* Articles 15, 19, and 20 of the 1977 Treaty are fortunately drafted in extremely vague terms (in them, reference is made to *'protection'* – without any further qualification – of water, nature or fishing). In the absence of any other specification, respecting the autonomy of the will implies precisely that provisions of this kind are interpreted in an evolutionary manner, in other words, taking account of the criteria adopted by *the general law* prevailing in each period considered. If this is the case, should it not be acknowledged that these criteria have evolved appreciably over the past 20 years? The new law, both the law of the environment and the law of international watercourses, may therefore advisedly be applied on the basis of Articles 15, 19 and 20 of the 1977 Treaty, for an 'evolutionary interpretation' of the Treaty.

18. This is the first major case brought before the Court in which there is such a sensitive ecological background that it has moved to centre stage, threatening to divert attention from treaty law. International public opinion would not have understood had the Court disregarded the new law, whose application was called for by Hungary. Fortunately the Court has been able to graft the new law onto the stock of Articles 15, 19 and 20 of the 1977 Treaty. And Slovakia, it must be said, was not opposed to taking this law into consideration. However in applying the so-called principle of *the evolutionary interpretation* of a treaty in the present case, the Court should have clarified the issue more and should have recalled that the general rule governing the interpretation of a treaty remains that set out in Article 31 of the 1969 Vienna Convention.

19. Concluding this consideration of the issue of the applicable law, let me say that considerable progress has been made over the last 20 or 30 years in mankind's knowledge of the environment. What has actually progressed however, all that could progress, is on the one hand the scientific explanation of ecological damage and on the other the technical means for limiting or eliminating such damage. The phenomenon of damage, as such, has existed since the dawn of time, each time that mankind has opposed the forces of nature. This means that damage was a known factor, before and after the 1977 Treaty, and this was the meaning behind my question to the Parties.

*

*   *

[125] 20. It seems to me that the issue of the *nature* of the 1977 Treaty and its related instruments warranted more attention from the majority of the Court. Actually, it is a crucial question. The nature of the Treaty largely conditions the succession of Slovakia to this instrument, which constitutes the substance of the applicable law, and which remains in force despite *intersecting violations* by both Parties.

21. The 1977 Treaty (including its related instruments) has the three-fold characteristic

   – of being a *territorial treaty*;
   – of being a treaty to which Slovakia validly *succeeded*; and
   – of being a treaty which is still *in force today*.

22. The Treaty in question is a *territorial* treaty:
   – *because it 'marries' the territories of two States*; it creates obligations between the States relating either to the use of a part of the territory of each of the two States or to restrictions as to its use. It creates a sort of *territorial 'dependency'* of one State in relation to the other; it institutes a *'territorial link'* between them in respecting the established frontiers. The operation of the Gabčíkovo hydroelectric power plant on Slovak territory is conditioned by the Dunakiliti dam on Hungarian territory. And the operation of that plant in 'peak power' mode is subordinate to the creation of the dam at Nagymaros on Hungarian territory;
   – *because it creates a specific regional area between two neighbouring countries*; it concerns the joint construction and use of major structures, all constructed on the Danube, itself a frontier river, or around and for the river. Such regulation by treaty of a watercourse in a frontier zone affects navigation on this stretch of the river as well as the use and apportionment of the frontier waters and makes the two States partners in the benefits of an industrial activity producing energy. All this creates a *specific regional area and frontier régime*, undeniably giving the Treaty instituting this space and this régime the character of a 'territorial treaty';
   – *lastly because it has a dual function, both confirming and slightly modifying the frontier between the two States*; the frontier had already been determined by

other, previous instruments. However the 1977 Treaty concerns the regulation of a river which determines the State frontier between the two parties as the median line of its main channel. Moreover, the Treaty nonetheless contains a provision on the demarcation of the State boundary line, making it a boundary Treaty confirming the frontier. In addition it provides for a minor modification of the boundary line once the construction of the system of dams is completed. For this purpose it announces a limited exchange of territory on the basis of a separate treaty. Lastly, the 1977 Treaty thus affects not only the boundary *line*, but even its nature, since the frontier is no longer constituted *de facto* by the actual thalweg.

[**126**] 23. The Treaty is an instrument to which undeniably *Slovakia succeeded*:
  – because it is a territorial treaty, the principle in such cases being automatic succession;
  – because the type of succession concerned here (the dissolution of a State) is governed by the rule of continuity of succession;
  – because Slovakia itself, prior to the dissolution of Czechoslovakia, participated in the conclusion of the Treaty; and lastly
  – because, on its emergence, Slovakia declared that it was bound by all treaties concluded by the predecessor State, without ever excluding the 1977 Treaty.

24. The Special Agreement concluded by the Parties in 1993 cannot have been easy to draw up. The text appears to have been *inspired* by the desire to reconcile elements which remain contradictory. One of the Parties – Hungary – acknowledges that the 1977 Treaty applies to itself, Hungary, until its termination on 19 May 1992, but does not apply to the other Party. According to Hungary, that Party – Slovakia – did not inherit *the formal instrument* itself, but *its material content* made up of 'the rights and obligations' which Slovakia allegedly derived from this – according to Hungary – now defunct Treaty.

25. With this convoluted structure as backdrop, the Court apparently has to judge not two States on the basis of one and the same treaty but to judge
  (i)   on the basis of one and the same treaty, one party to the dispute, Hungary, and a State now dissolved, Czechoslovakia, which is not a party to the dispute, and
  (ii) at the same time, on another basis which is not *directly* the Treaty, two States, Hungary and Slovakia, the latter of which is not recognized to have the status of successor State to the Treaty concerned.

26. Slovakia did indeed succeed to the 1977 Treaty, which *is still in force* today between the two Parties in contention, despite the intersecting violations of it by the Parties. I concur with the reasoning and conclusions of the majority of the Court in adjudging and declaring on the one hand that both Hungary and Slovakia violated the Treaty, and on the other that the Treaty remains in force. However, I shall shortly go a little further than the majority of the Court on this question of the infringements

of the Treaty, which I hold to be *intersecting violations*, resulting in *effectivités* which must be reconciled with the *survival* of the Treaty.

[...]

[142] SEPARATE OPINION OF JUDGE KOROMA (EXTRACT)

[...]

Prior to the adoption of the Treaty and the commencement of the Project itself, both Czechoslovakia and Hungary had recognized that whatever measures were taken to modify the flow of the river, such as those contemplated by the Project, they would have environmental effects, some adverse. Experience had shown that activities carried on upstream tended to produce effects downstream, thus making international co-operation all the more essential. With a view to preventing, avoiding and mitigating such impacts, extensive studies on the environment were undertaken by the Parties prior to the conclusion of the Treaty. The Treaty itself, in its Articles 15, 19 and 20, imposed strict obligations regarding [143] the protection of the environment which were to be met and complied with by the contracting parties in the construction and operation of the Project.

When in 1989 Hungary, concerned about the effects of the Project on its natural environment, suspended and later abandoned works for which it was responsible under the 1977 Treaty this was tantamount to a violation not only of the Treaty itself but of the principle of *pacta sunt servanda.*

Hungary invoked the principle of necessity as a legal justification for its termination of the Treaty. It stated, *inter alia,* that the construction of the Project would have significantly changed that historic part of the Danube with which the Project was concerned; that as a result of operation in peak mode and the resulting changes in water level, the flora and fauna on the banks of the river would have been damaged and water quality impaired. It was also Hungary's contention that the completion of the Project would have had a number of other adverse effects, in that the living conditions for the biota of the banks would have been drastically changed by peak-mode operation, the soil structure ruined and its yield diminished. It further stated that the construction might have resulted in the waterlogging of several thousand hectares of soil and that the groundwater in the area might have become over-salinized. As far as the drinking water of Budapest was concerned, Hungary contended that the Project would have necessitated further dredging; this would have damaged the existing filter layer allowing pollutants to enter nearby water supplies.

On the other hand, the PHARE Report on the construction of the reservoir at Čunovo and the effect this would have on the water quality offered a different view. The Report was commissioned by the European Communities with the co-operation of, first, the Government of the Czech and Slovak Federal Republic and, later, the Slovak Republic. It was described as presenting a reliable integrated modelling system for analysing the environmental impact of alternative management régimes in the Danubian lowland area and for predicting changes in water quality as well as conditions in the river, the reservoir, the soil and agriculture.

As to the effects of the construction of the dam on the ecology of the area, the Report reached the conclusion that whether the post-dam scenarios represented an improvement or otherwise would depend on the ecological objectives in the area, as most fundamental changes in ecosystems depended on the discharge system and occurred slowly over many years or decades, and, no matter what effects might have been felt in the ecosystem thus far, they could not be considered as irreversible.

With regard to water quality, the Report stated that groundwater quality in many places changed slowly over a number of years. With this in mind, comprehensive modelling, some of which entailed modelling impacts for periods of up to 100 years, was undertaken and the conclusion [144] reached that no problems were predicted in relation to groundwater quality.

The Court in its Judgment, quite rightly in my view, acknowledges Hungary's genuine concerns about the effect of the Project on its natural environment. However, after careful consideration of the conflicting evidence, it reached the conclusion that it was not necessary to determine which of these points of view was scientifically better founded in order to answer the question put to it in the Special Agreement. Hungary had not established to the satisfaction of the Court that the construction of the Project would have led to the consequences it alleged. Further, even though such damages might occur, they did not appear imminent in terms of the law, and could otherwise have been prevented or redressed. The Court, moreover, stated that such uncertainties as might have existed and had raised environmental concerns in Hungary could otherwise have been addressed without having to resort to unilateral suspension and termination of the Treaty. In effect, the evidence was not of such a nature as to entitle Hungary to unilaterally suspend and later terminate the Treaty on grounds of ecological necessity. In the Court's view, to allow that would not only destabilize the security of treaty relations but would also severely undermine the principle of *pacta sunt servanda*.

Thus it is not as if the Court did not take into consideration the scientific evidence presented by Hungary in particular regarding the effects on its environment of the Project, but the Court reached the conclusion that such evidence was not sufficient to allow Hungary unilaterally to suspend or terminate the Treaty. This finding, in my view, is not only of significance to Slovakia and Hungary – the Parties to the dispute – but it also represents a significant statement by the Court rejecting the argument that obligations assumed under a validly concluded treaty can no longer be observed because they have proved inconvenient or as a result of the emergence of a new wave of legal norms, irrespective of their legal character or quality. Accordingly, not for the first time and in spite of numerous breaches over the years, the Court has in this case upheld and reaffirmed the principle that every treaty in force is binding upon the parties and must be performed in good faith (Article 26 of the Vienna Convention on the Law of Treaties).

Nor can this finding of the Court be regarded as a mechanical application of the principle of *pacta sunt servanda* or the invocation of the maxim *summum jus summa injuria* but it ought rather to be seen as a re-affirmation of the principle that a validly concluded treaty can be suspended or terminated only with the consent of all the parties concerned. Moreover, the Parties to this dispute can also draw comfort from the Court's finding in upholding the continued validity of the Treaty and enjoining them to fulfil their obligations under the Treaty so as to achieve its aims and objectives.

[145] I also concur with the Court's findings that Czechoslovakia was entitled to proceed, in November 1991, to Variant C in so far as it then confined itself to undertaking works which did not predetermine its final decision. On the other hand, I cannot concur with the Court's finding that Czechoslovakia was not entitled to put Variant C into operation from October 1992. The Court reached this latter conclusion after holding that Hungary's suspension and abandonment of the works for which it was responsible under the 1977 Treaty was unlawful, and after acknowledging the serious problems with which Czechoslovakia was confronted as a result of Hungary's decision to abandon the greater part of the construction of the System of Locks for which it was responsible under the Treaty. The Court likewise recognized that huge investments had been made, that the construction at Gabčíkovo was all but finished, the bypass canal completed, and that Hungary itself, in 1991, had duly fulfilled its obligations under the Treaty in this respect by completing work on the tailrace canal. The Court also recognized that not using the system would not only have led to considerable financial losses of some $2.5 billion but would have resulted in serious consequences for the natural environment.

[. . .]

[148] [. . .] the Court concluded that Czechoslovakia, by putting into operation Variant C, did not apply the Treaty, but, on the contrary, violated certain of its express provisions and in so doing committed an internationally wrongful act. In its reasoning, the Court stated that it had placed emphasis on the 'putting into operation' of Variant C, the unlawfulness residing in the damming of the Danube.

[. . .]

[149] [. . .] In my view Variant C was therefore a genuine application of the Treaty and it was indispensable for the realization of its object and purpose. If it had not proceeded to its construction, according to the material before the Court, Czechoslovakia would have been stranded with a largely finished but inoperative system, which had been very expensive both in terms of cost of construction and in terms of acquiring the necessary land. The environmental benefits in terms of flood control, which was a primary object and purpose of the Treaty, would not have been attained. Additionally, the unfinished state of the constructions would have exposed them to further deterioration through continued inoperation.

Variant C was also held to be unlawful by the Court because, in its opinion, Czechoslovakia, by diverting the waters of the Danube to operate Variant C, unilaterally assumed control of a shared resource and thereby deprived Hungary of its right to an equitable share of the natural resources of the river – with the continuing effects of the diversion of these waters upon the ecology of the riparian area of the Szigetköz – and failed to respect the degree of proportionality required by international law.

The implication of the Court's finding that the principle of equitable utilization was violated by the diversion of the river is not free from doubt. That principle, which is now set out in the Convention on the Non-Navigational Uses of International Watercourses, is not new.

While it is acknowledged that the waters of rivers must not be used in such a way as to cause injury to other States and in the absence of any settled rules an equitable solution must be sought (case of the *Diversion of Water from the Meuse, Judgment, 1937, PCIJ, Series A/B, No. 70*) this rule applies where a treaty is absent. In the case under consideration Article 14, paragraph 2, of the 1977 Treaty provides that the contracting parties may, without giving prior notice, both withdraw from the Hungarian–Czechoslovak section of the Danube, and subsequently make use of the quantities of water specified in the water balance of the approved Joint Contractual Plan. Thus, the withdrawal of excess quantities of water from the Hungarian–Czechoslovak section of the Danube to operate the Gabčíkovo section of the system was contemplated with compensation to the other party in the form of an increased share of electric power. In other words, Hungary had agreed within the context of the Project to the diversion of the Danube (and, in the Joint Contractual Plan, to a provisional measure of withdrawal of water from the Danube). Accordingly, it would appear that the normal entitlement of the Parties [150] to an equitable and reasonable share of the water of the Danube under general international law was duly modified by the 1977 Treaty which considered the Project as a *lex specialis*. Slovakia was thus entitled to divert enough water to operate Variant C, and more especially so if, without such diversion, Variant C could not have been put into productive use. It is difficult to appreciate the Court's finding that this action was unlawful in the absence of an explanation as to how Variant C should have been put into operation. On the contrary, the Court would appear to be saying by implication that, if Variant C had been operated on the basis of a 50–50 sharing of the waters of the Danube, it would have been lawful. However, the Court has not established that a 50–50 ratio of use would have been sufficient to operate Variant C optimally. Nor could the Court say that the obligations of the Parties under the Treaty had been infringed or that the achievement of the objectives of the Treaty had been defeated by the diversion. In the case concerning the *Diversion of Water from the Meuse*, the Court found that, in the absence of a provision requiring the consent of Belgium, 'the Netherlands are entitled . . . to dispose of the waters of the Meuse at Maestricht' provided that the treaty obligations incumbent on it were not ignored (*Judgment, 1937, PCIJ, Series A/B, No. 70*, p. 30). Applying this test in the circumstances which arose, Variant C can be said to have been permitted by the 1977 Treaty as a reasonable method of implementing it. Consequently Variant C did not violate the rights of Hungary and was consonant with the objectives of the Treaty régime.

Moreover the principle of equitable and reasonable utilization has to be applied with all the relevant factors and circumstances pertaining to the international watercourse in question as well as to the needs and uses of the watercourse States concerned. Whether the use of the waters of a watercourse by a watercourse State is reasonable or equitable and therefore lawful must be determined in the light of all the circumstances. To the extent that the 1977 Treaty was designed to provide for the operation of the Project, Variant C is to be regarded as a genuine attempt to achieve that objective.

[. . .]

[**151**] [. . .] The Judgment also alluded to 'the continuing effects of the diversion of these waters on the ecology of the riparian area of the Szigetköz'. It is not clear whether by this the Court had reached the conclusion that significant harm had been caused to the ecology of the area by the operation of Variant C.

In the light of the foregoing considerations, I take the view that the operation of Variant C should have been considered as a genuine attempt by an injured party to secure the achievement of the agreed objectives of the 1977 Treaty, in ways not only consistent with that Treaty but with international law and equity.

[. . .]

[**152**] [. . .] It is my view that this case, because of the circumstances surrounding it, is one which calls for the application of the principles of equity.

The importance of the River Danube for both Hungary and Slovakia cannot be overstated. Both countries, by means of the 1977 Treaty, had agreed to co-operate in the exploitation of its resources for their mutual benefit. That Treaty, in spite of the period in which it was concluded, would seem to have incorporated most of the environmental imperatives of today, including the precautionary principle, the principle of equitable and reasonable utilization and the no-harm rule. None of these principles was proved to have been violated to an extent sufficient to have warranted the unilateral termination of the Treaty. The Court has gone a long way, rightly in my view, in upholding the principle of the sanctity of treaties. Justice would have been enhanced had the Court taken account of special circumstances as mentioned above.

DISSENTING OPINION OF JUDGE ODA (EXTRACT)

II. The suspension and subsequent abandonment of the works by Hungary in 1989 (Special Agreement, Art. 2, para 1 (a); Art. 2, para. 2)

1. Special Agreement, Article 2, Paragraph 1 (a)

8. Under the terms of the Special Agreement, the Court is requested to answer the question

> whether [Hungary] was entitled to suspend and subsequently abandon, in 1989, the works on the Nagymaros Project and on the part of the Gabčíkovo Project for which the Treaty attributed responsibility to [Hungary] (Art. 2, para. 1 *(a)*).

[. . .]

[**159**] [. . .] Let me examine the situation in more detail. Hungary relies, in connection with the Dunakiliti dam and the diversion of waters into the bypass canal at Dunakiliti, upon the deterioration of the environment in the Szigetköz region owing to the reduced quantity of available water in the old Danube river bed. In my view,

however, the decrease in the amount of water flowing into the old bed of the Danube as a result of the operation of the bypass canal would have been an inevitable outcome of the whole Project as provided for in the 1977 Treaty.

11. (*Hungary's ill-founded claim of ecological necessity.*) Certain effects upon the environment of the Szigetköz region were clearly anticipated by and known to Hungary at the initial stage of the planning of the whole Project. Furthermore, there was no reason for Hungary to believe that an environmental assessment made in the 1980s would give quite different results from those obtained in 1977, and require the total abandonment of the whole Project.

I have no doubt that the Gabčíkovo–Nagymaros System of Locks was, in the 1970s, prepared and designed with full consideration of its potential impact on the environment of the region, as clearly indicated by the fact that the 1977 Treaty itself incorporated this concept as its Article 19 (entitled Protection of Nature), and I cannot believe that this assessment made in the 1970s would have been significantly different from an ecological assessment 10 years later, in other words, in the late 1980s. It is a fact that the ecological assessment made in the 1980s did not convince scientists in Czechoslovakia.

I particularly endorse the view taken by the Court when rejecting the argument of Hungary, that ecological necessity cannot be deemed to justify its failure to complete the construction of the Nagymaros dam, and that Hungary cannot show adequate grounds for that failure by claiming that the Nagymaros dam would have adversely affected the downstream water which is drawn to the bank-filtered wells constructed on Szentendre Island and used as drinking water for Budapest (Judgment, para. 40).

12. (*Environment of the river Danube.*) The 1977 Treaty itself spoke of the importance of the protection of water quality, maintenance of the bed of the Danube and the protection of nature (Arts. 15, 16, 19), and the whole structure of the Gabčíkovo–Nagymaros System of Locks was certainly founded on an awareness of the importance of environmental protection. It cannot be said that the drafters of either the Treaty itself or of [160] the JCP failed to take due account of the environment. There were, in addition, no particular circumstances in 1989 that required any of the research or studies which Hungary claimed to be necessary, and which would have required several years to be implemented. If no campaign had been launched by environmentalist groups, then it is my firm conviction that the Project would have gone ahead as planned.

What is more, Hungary had, at least in the 1980s, no intention of withdrawing from the work on the Gabčíkovo power plant. One is at a loss to understand how Hungary could have thought that the operation of the bypass canal and of the Gabčíkovo power plant, to which Hungary had not objected at the time, would have been possible without the completion of the works at Dunakiliti dam.

13. (*Ecological necessity and State responsibility.*) I would like to make one more point relating to the matter of environmental protection under the 1977 Treaty. The performance of the obligations under that Treaty was certainly the joint responsibility of both Hungary and Czechoslovakia. If the principles which were taken as the basis of the 1977 Treaty or of the JCP had been contrary to the general rules of international law – environmental law in particular – the two States, which had reached agreement

on their joint investment in the whole Project, would have been held *jointly* responsible for that state of affairs and *jointly* responsible to the international community. This fact does not imply that the *one party* (Czechoslovakia, and later Slovakia) bears responsibility *towards the other* (Hungary).

What is more, if a somewhat more rigorous consideration of environmental protection had been needed, this could certainly have been given by means of remedies of a technical nature to those parts of the JCP – not the 1977 Treaty itself – that concern the concrete planning or operation of the whole System of Locks. In this respect, I do not see how any of the grounds advanced by Hungary for its failure to perform its Treaty obligations (and hence for its violation of the Treaty by abandoning the construction of the Dunakiliti dam) could have been upheld as relating to a state of 'ecological necessity'.

14. (*General comments on the preservation of the environment.*) If I may give my views on the environment, I am fully aware that concern for the preservation of the environment has rapidly entered the realm of international law and that a number of treaties and conventions have been concluded on either a multilateral or bilateral basis, particularly since the Declaration on the Human Environment was adopted in 1972 at Stockholm and reinforced by the Rio de Janeiro Declaration in 1992, drafted 20 years after the Stockholm Declaration.

It is a great problem for the whole of mankind to strike a satisfactory balance between more or less contradictory issues of economic development [**161**] on the one hand and preservation of the environment on the other, with a view to maintaining sustainable development. Any construction work relating to economic development would be bound to affect the existing environment to some extent but modern technology would, I am sure, be able to provide some acceptable ways of balancing the two conflicting interests.

[. . .]

[**167**] [. . .]   *V. The final settlement (Special Agreement, Article 5)*

30. Hungary and Slovakia have agreed under Article 5 of the Special Agreement, that: 'Immediately after the transmission of the Judgment the Parties shall enter into negotiations on the modalities for its execution.'

[. . .]

The way in which the waters are divided at Čunovo should be negotiated in order to maintain the original plan, that is, an equitable share of the waters – and this should be spelt out in any revision or amendment of the JCP. The equitable sharing of the water must both meet Hungary's concern for the environment in the Szigetköz region and allow satisfactory operation of the Gabčíkovo power plant by Slovakia, as well as the [**168**] maintenance of the bypass canal for flood prevention and the improvement of navigation facilities. I would suggest that the JCP should be revised or some new version drafted during the negotiations under Article 5 of the Special Agreement in order to comply with the modalities which I have set out above.

33. (*Reassessment of the environmental effect*). Whilst the whole Project of the Gabčíkovo–Nagymaros System of Locks is now in operation, in its modified form

(that is, with the Čunovo dam instead of the Dunakiliti dam diverting the water to the bypass canal and with the abandonment of the work on the Nagymaros dam/power plant), the Parties are under an obligation in their mutual relations, under Articles 15, 16 and 19 of the 1977 Treaty, and, perhaps in relations with third parties, under an obligation in general law concerning environmental protection, to preserve the environment in the region of the river Danube.

The Parties should continue the environmental assessment of the whole region and search out remedies of a technical nature that could prevent the environmental damage which might be caused by the new Project.

[. . .]

[176] DISSENTING OPINION OF JUDGE HERCZEGH (EXTRACT)

[Translation]

I am most regretfully unable to share the position of the majority of Members of the Court as expressed in this Judgment, and I find myself obliged to draft a dissenting opinion to set out the facts and reasons which explain the different conclusions I have reached.

The subject of the dispute between Hungary and Czechoslovakia, and later Hungary and Slovakia, was the construction of a system of locks on the Danube (hereinafter called 'the G/N Project') intended to enhance 'the broad utilization of the natural resources of the Bratislava–Budapest section of the Danube . . .'. According to the Treaty concluded in Budapest on 16 September 1977,

> the joint utilization of the Hungarian–Czechoslovak section of the Danube will . . . significantly contribute to bringing about the socialist integration of the States members of the Council for Mutual Economic Co-operation . . .

The Project seemed in other respects likely to have a considerable impact on the environment. The Court, called upon by the Parties to resolve the dispute, was thus confronted with not only the implementation of the law of treaties, but also the problems raised by protection of the environment, and with questions concerning the international responsibility of States.

In its Advisory Opinion given to the General Assembly on 8 July 1996 on the *Legality of the Threat or Use of Nuclear Weapons*, the Court declared that it recognized

> that the environment is not an abstraction but represents the living space, the quality of life and the very health of human beings, including generations unborn. The existence of the general obligation of States to ensure that activities within their jurisdiction and control respect the environment of other States or of areas beyond national control is now part of the corpus of international law relating to the environment. (*ICJ Reports 1996*, pp. 241–2, para. 29.)[90]

[90 See p. 256 above.]

This Judgment of the Court cites that passage and stresses the importance of respecting the environment, but then does not take due account of the application of that principle to the construction and operation of the G/N Project.

The Court only grants a very modest place to ecological considerations [177] in the 'declaratory' part of its Judgment. As a judicial organ, the Court was admittedly not empowered to decide scientific questions touching on biology, hydrology, and so on, or questions of a technical type which arose out of the G/N Project; but it could – and even should – have ruled on the legal consequences of certain facts alleged by one Party and either admitted or not addressed by the other, in order to assess their respective conduct in this case.

Before determining the facts which could thus be pertinent, I must make a few preliminary observations on the characteristics of the G/N Project. The Project was an audacious scheme, in a class of its own and the first to be designed as a system of locks for the exploitation in peak mode of the hydroelectric resources of the Danube. The locks built on the German and Austrian sections of the Danube do not operate in peak mode; moreover, the dams on the Rhine operating in that mode are much more modest works.

That mode of operation involved and involves risks which were not altogether unknown to those responsible for drawing up the plans for the G/N Project, but its designers reasoned within the confines of what was known in the 1960s and 1970s – and that way of thinking is today considered outmoded, and rightly so. They accordingly minimized the risks, whilst at the same time having an imperfect understanding of the damage they could cause, and therefore of the possible solutions.

[. . .]

Given the declarations of the Czechoslovak leaders, it is somewhat surprising that the Court adopted the approach that the ecological risks listed by Hungary in 1989 were already known when the Treaty was concluded but remained uncertain, and the provisions of Articles 15, 19 and 20 covered the protection of the natural environment, water quality, and [178] so forth, whereas it could and should have concerned itself with the problems which the interpretation and implementation of these provisions might raise in the field. However, the Judgment merely mentions the aims of the Project and the advantages it was presumed to offer.

Unfortunately, that picture is a far cry from reality. It is difficult to see otherwise why the Minister, Mr Vavroušek, would have considered the G/N Project contained in the 1977 Treaty to be 'old', of an 'obsolete' character, and needing to be 'changed' or 'modified', and so on. Moreover, the key question is not whether the Treaty contained certain provisions protecting the environment, but whether those provisions had been effectively implemented during the construction of the G/N Project.

Since the negotiations which led to the conclusion of the 1977 Treaty, ecological knowledge has become considerably broader and deeper whilst international environmental law has also progressed. In its Advisory Opinion on the *Legal Consequences for States of the Continued Presence of South Africa in Namibia (South West Africa) notwithstanding Security Council Resolution 276 (1970)*, the Court found that:

Moreover, an international instrument has to be interpreted and applied within the framework of the entire legal system prevailing at the time of the interpretation. In the domain to which the present proceedings relate, the last fifty years ... have brought important developments ... In this domain, as elsewhere, the *corpus juris gentium* has been considerably enriched, and this the Court, if it is faithfully to discharge its functions, may not ignore. (*ICJ Reports 1971*, pp. 31–2, para. 53.)

What held good for the Mandate system of the League of Nations also holds good for the duty to safeguard the natural environment, the only difference being that instead of a 50-year period, we have to look at a 20-year period in this case. Under Article 19 of the 1977 Treaty,

The Contracting Parties shall, through the means specified in the joint contractual plan, ensure compliance with the obligations for the protection of nature arising in connection with the construction and operation of the System of Locks.

The original Hungarian wording uses, instead of the word 'obligations', the word 'requirements', but that does not in any way affect its essential scope: the protection of nature was to be ensured in a manner commensurate with the requirements of the day, that is to say, in 1989, in accordance with the requirements of 1989, and not those that might have prevailed in 1977. Likewise, and in so far as it is accepted, as it is by the majority of the Members of the Court, that the Treaty still applies as it stands, the same would hold good for 1997, and it is in accordance with [179] present-day requirements that the scope of the Parties' treaty obligations with regard to protection of the environment should be defined.

The Court, in the 'prescriptive' part of its Judgment, states:

Owing to new scientific insights and to a growing awareness of the risks for mankind – for present and future generations – of pursuit of such interventions at an unconsidered and unabated pace, new norms and standards have been developed, set forth in a great number of instruments during the last two decades. Such new norms have to be taken into consideration, and such new standards given proper weight, not only when States contemplate new activities but also when continuing with activities begun in the past. (Para. 140.)

It is regrettable that the Court did not follow this principle even in the reasoning which led to its reply to the first question put to it in the Special Agreement.

To have perceived the shortcomings of a project – to avoid using the word 'error' – and to recognize that one is the source of those shortcomings are two very different things which may sometimes be very far apart. The principal argument put forward, in 1991, by the Czechoslovak party in favour of the G/N Project, was based on the fact that the Project was almost completed. By the acceleration of the works laid down in the Protocol of 6 February 1989, certain Hungarian leaders wanted to do the same thing – to claim that a point of no return had been reached – in order to deal with increasing opposition and resistance. Political changes during that year prevented them from achieving that aim.

The crucial problem posed by the G/N Project was that of peak mode operation, for which the 1977 Treaty makes no provision. Slovakia confirmed repeatedly that there was no agreement between the contracting parties with regard to the peak mode operation of the system of locks.

[...]

[180] [...] Between 1977 and 1989 Hungarian experts became aware of the ecological dangers potentially caused not only by the peak mode operation of the system of locks, but also by the construction of certain works of the system which had been designed with a view to such a mode of operation: more particularly the Nagymaros dam and the storage reservoir at [181] Dunakiliti as initially designed, that is, with an enormous surface area of 60 square kilometres, neither construction being indispensable or even of use if the Gabčíkovo power plant were to be operated in run-of-the-river mode. [...]

It is therefore difficult to understand why Czechoslovakia insisted with some vigour that Hungary had to continue with the construction of the Nagymaros dam – when its primary purpose was to allow peak mode operation of the Gabčíkovo power station – if the mode of operation, as Slovakia expressly concedes, was never the subject of an agreement between the Parties. There was therefore no legal obstacle to prevent the G/N Project from being modified for adaptation to a less dangerous mode of operation.

[...]

[182] [...] In order to justify its conduct, Hungary put forward various grounds and these included, *inter alia*, a state of necessity, the main and decisive reason. A state of necessity does not have the effect of extinguishing or suspending a treaty, but it is a circumstance exonerating the State from the responsibility it incurs in committing an act not in conformity with its international obligations.

[...]

[188] [...] The Court held that the state of necessity, as a ground for precluding the wrongfulness of an act not in conformity with an international obligation, can only be accepted on an exceptional basis and, referring to the relevant International Law Commission Report, added that

> the state of necessity can only be invoked under certain strictly defined conditions which must be cumulatively satisfied; and the State concerned is not the sole judge of whether those conditions have been met (para. 51).

I entirely concur with that approach, but I cannot accept the conclusions drawn in this case by the Court. It has concluded that, with respect to both Nagymaros and Gabčíkovo,

> the perils invoked by Hungary, without prejudging their possible gravity, were not sufficiently established in 1989, nor were they 'imminent'; and ... Hungary had available to it at that time means of responding to these perceived perils other than the suspension and abandonment of works with which it had been entrusted (para. 57).

This is absolutely not the case. As far as Hungary was concerned, what was at stake was the safeguarding of an essential interest against a peril which was grave and imminent, that is to say certain and inevitable, and any measures taken to counteract that peril would have radically transformed the scope of the obligations to be performed under the Treaty. By suspending and abandoning the works at Nagymaros, Hungary has not impaired an essential interest of Czechoslovakia, and it is precisely by constructing the dam at Nagymaros that it would have contributed to an unequalled state of necessity and to a situation catastrophic for its capital. The existence of the peril alleged by Hungary was recognized – at least in part – by the other Party, and Hungary therefore did not act in an arbitrary manner.

[...]

[**189**] [...] Moreover, it must be acknowledged that the ecological considerations that now weigh against the dam are the same as those holding in 1989. If it has finally been concluded that the dam should not have been built in 1997, this is because in reality it should not have been built in 1989, either.

The dispute between the two Parties is very much the result of their geographical situations. The harmonization of the interests of the countries upstream and downstream is the crucial problem of the law governing international watercourses. During the work done by the United Nations on the Draft Convention on the Law of the Non-Navigational Uses of International Watercourses, the upstream countries complained that the provisions of the draft limited their right to use and develop the resources of those watercourses, whereas the downstream countries criticized the provisions of the draft by maintaining that they failed to protect their interests adequately and even allowed significant damage to be inflicted upon them. As far as the course of the Danube is concerned, Slovakia is an upstream country and Hungary a downstream country. In this Judgment the Court should have maintained a balance, admittedly hard to achieve, between the interests of the upstream and the downstream countries, and have ensured that harmonious progress in enhancement of the natural resources would be carefully organized to prevent the long-term disadvantages from outweighing the immediate advantages. Unfortunately, in the present case, it has not succeeded in doing so.

I have found it necessary to stress this question since the position to be taken, in particular, on whether Hungary was entitled to suspend and subsequently abandon the works at Nagymaros, and to suspend those at Dunakiliti, to a large extent determines the replies, or at least the reasoning, for the questions which follow.

[...]

[232] DISSENTING OPINION OF JUDGE SKUBISZEWSKI (EXTRACT)

1. While agreeing with the Court in all its other holdings, I am unable to concur in the broad finding that Czechoslovakia was not entitled to put Variant C into operation from October 1992 (Judgment, para. 155, point 1 C). The finding is too general. In my view the Court should have distinguished between, on the one hand, Czechoslovakia's

right to take steps to execute and operate certain works on its territory and, on the other, its responsibility towards Hungary resulting from the diversion of most of the waters of the Danube into Czechoslovak territory, especially in the period preceding the conclusion of the 1995 Agreement (Judgment, para. 25.)[91]

I

[...]

[233][...] 5. When Czechoslovakia and Hungary were negotiating and concluding their Treaty, they knew very well what they were doing. They made a conscious choice. A joint investment of such proportions inevitably entails some changes in the territories of the countries involved, including an impact on the environment. In particular, the two States were facing the dichotomy of socio-economic development and preservation of nature. Articles 15, 19 and 20 show that the two States paid attention to environmental risks and were willing to meet them. In the 1970s, when the Treaty was being negotiated, the state of knowledge was sufficient to permit the two partners to assess the impact their Project would have on the various areas of life, one of them being the environment. The number of studies was impressive indeed. The progress of science and knowledge is constant; thus, with regard to such a project, that progress becomes a reason for adaptation and, consequently, for entering into negotiations, no matter how long and difficult.

6. By its unilateral rejection of the Project, Hungary has precluded itself from asserting that the utilization of the hydraulic force of the Danube was dependent on the condition of a prior agreement between it and Czechoslovakia (and subsequently Slovakia). For this is what the Treaty was and is about: mutual regulation of the national competence of each riparian State, in particular, to use the hydraulic force of the river. Mutual rights and obligations have been created under the Treaty, but [234] during the period 1989 to 1992 Hungary progressively repudiated them. It thus created an estoppel situation for itself.

II

[...]

[236] [...] 11. In the *Lake Lanoux* case the Tribunal expressed its position on the right of each riparian State to act unilaterally in the following terms:

> In fact, States are today perfectly conscious of the importance of the conflicting interests brought into play by the industrial use of international rivers, and of the necessity to reconcile them by mutual concessions. The only way to arrive at such compromises of interests is to conclude agreements on an increasingly comprehensive basis. International practice reflects the conviction that States ought to strive to conclude such agreements: there would thus appear to be an obligation to accept in good faith all communications and contracts which could, by a broad comparison of interests and by reciprocal good will, provide States with the best conditions for concluding agreements. ...

[91 Not reproduced in this volume.]

> But international practice does not so far permit more than the following conclusion: the rule that States may utilize the hydraulic power of international watercourses only on condition of a *prior* agreement between the interested States cannot be established as a custom, even less as a general principle of law. The history of the formulation of the multilateral Convention signed at Geneva on December 9, 1923, relative to the Development of Hydraulic Power Affecting More than One State, is very characteristic in this connection. The initial project was based on the obligatory and paramount character of agreements whose purpose was to harness the hydraulic forces of international watercourses. But this formulation was rejected, and the Convention, in its final form, provides (Article I) that '[it] in no way alters the freedom of each State, within the framework of international law, to carry out on its territory all operations for the development of hydraulic power which it desires'; there is provided only an obligation upon the interested signatory States to join in a common study of a development programme; the execution of this programme is obligatory only for those States which have formally subscribed to it. (*RIAA*, Vol. XII, p. 308, para. 13; *ILR*, Vol. 24, 1957, p. 129, para. 13; footnote omitted)

[**237**] I think that the Court would agree that this is an exact statement of general law. That law is applicable in the present case. Czechoslovakia had the right to put the Gabčíkovo complex into operation. It also had the duty to respect Hungary's right to an equitable and reasonable share of the waters of the Danube.

[. . .]

III

[**239**] [. . .] 21. The degree to which Czechoslovakia has implemented the Treaty has reached such proportions that it would be both unreasonable and harmful to stop the completion of certain works and to postpone indefinitely the operation of the bypass canal, the Gabčíkovo hydroelectric power plant, navigation locks and appurtenances thereto, in so far as that operation was possible without Hungarian co-operation or participation. To find, as the Court does, that such operation is unlawful overlooks the considerations of equity. At the same time Hungary's right under general international law to an equitable and reasonable sharing of the waters of the Danube had to be preserved notwithstanding its repudiation of the Project and the Treaty.

IV

22. A State that concluded a treaty with another State providing for the execution of a project like Gabčíkovo–Nagymaros cannot, when that project is near completion, simply say that all should be cancelled and the [**240**] only remaining problem is compensation. This is a situation where, especially under equitable principles, the solution must go beyond mere pecuniary compensation. The Court has found that the refusal by Hungary to implement the Treaty was unlawful. By breaching the Treaty, Hungary could not deprive Czechoslovakia and subsequently Slovakia of all the benefits of the Treaty and reduce their rights to that of compensation. The advanced stage of the work on the Project made some performance imperative in

order to avoid harm: Czechoslovakia and Slovakia had the right to expect that certain parts of the Project would become operational.

23. Thus, pecuniary compensation could not, in the present case, wipe out even some, not to speak of all, of the consequences of the abandonment of the Project by Hungary. How could an indemnity compensate for the absence of flood protection, improvement of navigation and production of electricity? The attainment of these objectives of the 1977 Treaty was legitimate not only under the Treaty but also under general law and equity. The benefits could in no way be replaced and compensated by the payment of a sum of money. Certain works had to be established and it was vital that they be made operational. For the question here is not one of damages for loss sustained, but the creation of a new system of use and utilization of the water.

24. Once a court, whether international or municipal, has found that a duty established by a rule of international law has been breached, the subject to which the act is imputable must make adequate reparation. The finding in point 2 D of the operative paragraph is the consequence of the holdings in point 1. Absence of congruence between the vote on one or more of the findings in point 1 and the vote on point 2 D should be explained in order that any implication of an uncertainty regarding the foregoing principle on reparation may be eliminated.

25. The formulation of the finding in point 1 C of the operative paragraph does not correspond to the possibility of different evaluations concerning the various elements of the 'provisional solution'. There is equally no reflection of that possibility in the formulation of the finding in point 2 D. Indeed, the terms of that point made the position of those judges who voted against point 1 C quite difficult. The same applies to point 2 D when a judge does not agree with *all* the findings in point 1, though I think that there is a way out of this difficulty.

26. It is on the basis of the position taken in this dissenting opinion that I have voted in favour of the finding in point 2 D. However, there is a further reason which made it possible for me to accept that finding. That reason is linked to the task of the Court under Article 2, paragraph 2, of the Special Agreement and the ensuing negotiations of the [241] Parties on the modalities of the execution of the Judgment (Art. 5, para. 2). My understanding of point 2 D of the operative paragraph is that the enforcement of responsibility and the obligation to compensate, though elaborated upon by the Court in the part of the Judgment devoted to Article 2, paragraph 2, of the Special Agreement (paras. 148–51) need not be a primary factor in the negotiations on the future of the Gabčíkovo–Nagymaros Project. It should be noted that the said finding refers to the issue of compensation in rather general terms. At the same time the Court gives its support to what I would describe as the 'zero option' (para. 153 of the Judgment). In my view the underlying message of point 2 D to the negotiating Governments is that, notwithstanding their legal claims and counterclaims for compensation, they should seek – and find – a common solution.

[Reports: *ICJ Reports 1997*, p. 7; 116 *ILR* 1 at p. 17]

Fisheries Jurisdiction Case
(Spain *v.* Canada)[1]

International Court of Justice, The Hague

4 December 1998 (Schwebel, *President*; Weeramantry, *Vice-President*; Oda,
Bedjaoui, Guillaume, Ranjeva, Herczegh, Shi, Fleischhauer, Koroma,
Vereshchetin, Higgins, Parra-Aranguren, Kooijmans and Rezek, *Judges*;
Lalonde[2] and Torres Bernárdez,[3] *Judges* ad hoc)

*Jurisdiction – International Court of Justice – optional clause – Statute of
the Court, Article 36(2) – declaration accepting jurisdiction of the Court –
reservations – right of State making declaration to define scope of acceptance
of jurisdiction – Whether reservations to be construed restrictively –
distinction between substantive law and rules governing jurisdiction of the
Court – principles to be applied in interpretation of declaration and reservations – intention of State making declaration – principle of good faith*

*Powers and procedures of tribunals – procedure – International Court of
Justice – preliminary objections – whether objection possessing an exclusively
preliminary character – duty of the Court in dealing with preliminary objections*

*Waters – sea – high seas – jurisdiction – fisheries – conservation measures –
arrest of Spanish vessel by Canada outside Canadian waters – legality – whether
dispute falling within jurisdiction of International Court of Justice*

*Waters – maritime environment – fisheries conservation – limit of conservation
measures – compatibility with regime of the high seas*

---

[1] Spain was represented by Mr José Antonio Pastor Ridruejo, Mr Aurelio Pérez Giralda, Mr Pierre-
Marie Dupuy, Mr Keith Highet, Mr Antonio Remiro Brotóns and Mr Luis Ignacio Sánchez
Rodríguez. Canada was represented by HE Mr Philippe Kirsch QC, Mr Blair Hankey, Mr L. Alan
Willis QC, Mr Prosper Weil, Ms Louise de La Fayette, Mr Paul Fauteux, Mr John F. G. Hannaford,
Ms Ruth Ozols Barr, Ms Isabelle Poupart and Ms Laurie Wright.
[2] Judge *ad hoc* nominated by Canada.
[3] Judge *ad hoc* nominated by Spain.

SUMMARY   *The facts*   On 9 March 1995, Canadian Government vessels
intercepted and boarded the *Estai*, a vessel flying the Spanish flag, approximately 245 miles from the Canadian coast. The vessel was seized and
her master arrested on charges of violating the Coastal Fisheries Protection Act and implementing regulations. The master was later released on
payment of bail and the vessel on the posting of a bond. Spain objected
that Canada had exceeded its jurisdiction and violated international law.
Spain commenced proceedings by application in the International Court
of Justice.

In its application, Spain requested: (a) that the Court declare that the
legislation of Canada, in so far as it claimed to exercise jurisdiction over
ships flying a foreign flag on the high seas, outside the exclusive economic
zone of Canada, was not opposable to Spain; (b) that the Court adjudge
and declare that Canada was bound to refrain from any repetition of the
acts complained of, and to offer reparation in the form of an indemnity
to cover all the damages and injuries occasioned; and (c) that the Court
declare that the boarding of the *Estai*, the measures of coercion applied
and the exercise of jurisdiction over the vessel and its master constituted a
violation of international law. The application invoked as the basis of the
jurisdiction of the Court the declarations whereby Canada and Spain had
accepted the compulsory jurisdiction of the Court in accordance with
Article 36(2) of its Statute.

Canada maintained that the Court lacked jurisdiction by reason of paragraph 2(d) of the Canadian Declaration under Article 36(2) of the Statute.
That paragraph excluded from the jurisdiction of the Court 'disputes
arising out of or concerning conservation and management measures
taken by Canada with respect to vessels fishing in the NAFO Regulatory
Area, as defined in the Convention on Future Multilateral Co-operation
in the Northwest Atlantic Fisheries, 1978, and the enforcement of such
measures'. It was agreed by the Parties that the question of jurisdiction
should be determined before any proceedings on the merits. In their written and oral submissions, the Spanish Government requested the Court
to adjudge and declare that its application was admissible and that the
Court had jurisdiction. Spain argued that the nature of the dispute between the Parties was related to Canada's lack of entitlement to exercise
jurisdiction on the high seas, and the non-opposability of its amended
coastal fisheries protection legislation and regulations to third States,
including Spain. In their written and oral submissions, the Canadian
Government asked the Court to adjudge and declare that the Court had
no jurisdiction to adjudicate upon the Application filed by Spain on 28

March 1995. Canada maintained that the dispute arose out of and concerned conservation and management measures taken by Canada with respect to Spanish fishing vessels fishing in the NAFO Regulatory Area and thus fell within the reservation to the Canadian acceptance of the Court's compulsory jurisdiction.

Held by the International Court of Justice (by twelve votes to five) The Court lacked jurisdiction.

(1) It was for the Court itself, while giving particular attention to the formulation of the dispute chosen by the Applicant, to determine, on an objective basis and by examining the position of both Parties, the nature of the dispute. The Court would not confine itself to the formulation adopted by the Applicant and would base its decision not only on the Application and final submissions, but on diplomatic exchanges, public statements and other pertinent evidence. The specific acts which gave rise to the dispute were the Canadian activities on the high seas in relation to the pursuit of the *Estai*, the means used to accomplish the arrest and the fact of the arrest and the detention of the vessel and the arrest of its master. That conduct arose out of Canada's amended Coastal Fisheries Protection Act and implementing regulations. The essence of the dispute between the Parties was whether these acts violated Spain's rights under international law and required reparation.

(2) The Court had to decide whether the Parties had conferred upon it jurisdiction in respect of that dispute. The matter of jurisdiction was a question of law to be resolved in the light of the relevant facts. There was no burden of proof to be discharged in the matter of jurisdiction. The Court had to determine from all the facts and taking into account all the arguments advanced by the Parties whether the arguments militating in favour of jurisdiction were preponderant, and to ascertain whether the Parties had intended to confer jurisdiction upon the Court in respect of the dispute.

(3) It was for each State, in formulating its declaration under Article 36(2) of the Statute, to decide the limits it placed upon its acceptance of the jurisdiction of the Court. Conditions or reservations did not derogate from a wider acceptance already given but operated to define the parameters of the State's acceptance of the compulsory jurisdiction of the Court. There was no requirement that such conditions or reservations be given a restrictive interpretation. An additional reservation contained in a new declaration of acceptance of the Court's jurisdiction was not to be interpreted as a derogation from a more comprehensive acceptance given in an

earlier declaration. It was the declaration in existence that alone had to be interpreted. A declaration of acceptance of the compulsory jurisdiction of the Court was a unilateral act of State sovereignty. The regime relating to the interpretation of declarations made under Article 36 of the Statute was not identical to that established for the interpretation of treaties by the Vienna Convention on the Law of Treaties, 1969. The Court would interpret the relevant words of a declaration including a reservation in a natural and reasonable way, having due regard to the intention of the State concerned at the time when it accepted the compulsory jurisdiction of the Court.

(4)   Subparagraph (d) of paragraph 2 of Canada's declaration of 10 May 1994 was not only an integral part of the current declaration but an essential component of it and, therefore, of the acceptance by Canada of the Court's compulsory jurisdiction. There were close links between Canada's new declaration and its new coastal fisheries protection legislation. It was evident from the parliamentary debates and the various statements by the Canadian authorities that the purpose of the new declaration was to prevent the Court from exercising its compulsory jurisdiction over matters which might arise with regard to the international legality of the amended legislation and its implementation.

(5)(a)   The term 'disputes arising out of or concerning' excluded from the jurisdiction of the Court not only disputes whose immediate 'subject-matter' was the measures in question and their enforcement but also those 'concerning' such measures and, more generally, those having their 'origin' in those measures. In examining the term 'conservation and management measures' the Court concluded that the 'measures' taken by Canada in amending its coastal fisheries protection legislation and regulations constituted 'conservation and management measures' in the sense in which that expression was commonly understood in international law and practice and had been used in the Canadian reservation.

(b)   The reference in the Canadian reservation to 'vessels fishing . . .' included all vessels fishing in the area in question.

(c)   The use of force authorised by Canadian legislation and regulations fell within the ambit of what was commonly understood as enforcement of conservation and management measures and thus fell under the provisions of paragraph 2(d) of Canada's declaration. This was so notwithstanding that the reservation did not mention the use of force. Boarding, inspection, arrest and minimum use of force for those purposes were all contained within the concept of enforcement of conservation

and management measures according to a 'natural and reasonable' interpretation of this concept.

(6)   The dispute had its origin in the amendment made by Canada
to its coastal fisheries protection legislation and regulations and in the
pursuit, boarding and seizure of the *Estai* which resulted. It was therefore
a dispute 'arising out of' and 'concerning' 'conservation and management
measures taken by Canada with respect to vessels fishing in the NAFO
Regulatory Area' and 'the enforcement of such measures'. It followed
that this dispute came within the terms of the reservation contained in
paragraph 2(d) of the Canadian declaration of 10 May 1994.

Separate Opinion of President Schwebel   A reservation to a declaration
under the optional clause could not be regarded as ineffective because it
excluded the jurisdiction of the Court in respect of actions which were
illegal under international law. One of the purposes of States in making
reservations might be to debar the Court from passing upon actions of the
declarant State that might be or were legally questionable. The Canadian
reservation was an essential element of the declaration, but for which the
declaration would not have been made. The Court was not free to hold
the reservation invalid or ineffective while holding the remainder of the
declaration to be in force.

Separate Opinion of Judge Oda   The only issue in dispute was whether
Canada had violated the rule of international law by claiming and exercising fisheries jurisdiction on the high seas on the ground of its hon-
estly held belief that the conservation of certain fish stocks was urgently
required as a result of the fishery conservation crisis in the North-West
Atlantic. A declaration to accept the compulsory jurisdiction of the Court
under Article 36(2) of the Statute, and any reservation attached thereto,
must, because of the declaration's unilateral character, be interpreted not
only in a natural way and in context, but also with particular regard for
the intention of the State which had made it. It was clear that Canada
had intended to reserve from the jurisdiction of the Court any dispute
which might arise following the enactment and enforcement of legislation concerning fishing in its offshore areas, whether within its exclusive
economic zone or outside it.

Separate Opinion of Judge Koroma   Once it was established that a dispute
fell within the category excluded in a reservation, then the Court was
precluded from exercising jurisdiction in respect of that dispute, whatever
the scope of the rules which had purportedly been violated. The Court's
jurisdiction to adjudicate derived from the Statute and the consent of a
State as expressed in its declaration, not from the applicable substantive

law. Compulsory jurisdiction was based on the previous consent of the State concerned and subject to the limits of that consent.

Separate Opinion of Judge Kooijmans   The judgment bore testimony to the inherent weakness of the Optional Clause system. The making of reservations by a State to its declaration of acceptance had never been controversial. Canada had submitted a new declaration in order to prevent the Court from scrutinising the legality of an action it intended to undertake. It would not have been beyond the Court's mandate to draw attention to the risks to which the Optional Clause system was exposed, since this system was an integral and essential element of the Statute.

Dissenting Opinion of Vice-President Weeramantry   The reservation was valid but it was for the Court to interpret it and the Court enjoyed a measure of discretion in this regard. The dispute fell within the general grant of jurisdiction, rather than within the reservation, where violations were of basic principles of international law. While a State had unfettered autonomy to decide whether to enter the Optional Clause system, once it did so it was bound by its rules and by the basic principles of international law. It was not possible to contract out of the applicability of the latter once a State had opted to enter the system. The objection raised by Canada was not of an exclusively preliminary character as, if some of the circumstances alleged by Spain were established, they would give jurisdiction to the Court under the general part of the declaration.

Dissenting Opinion of Judge Bedjaoui   (1)   Similar reservations formulated by Canada on two separate occasions appeared to reflect its reluctance to submit to the jurisdiction of the Court on issues which Canada regarded as vital. The purpose of the reservation was to protect Canada's claims to special jurisdiction over the high seas in conservation matters. The terms of the reservation disclosed, *prima facie*, a violation of a basic principle of international law. It was Spain, as the Applicant, which had a clear procedural right to seek, and to obtain, from the Court a ruling on the subject of the dispute which it had submitted and on that alone, to the exclusion of all others. Spain complained of a very serious infringement of a right of exclusive jurisdiction over vessels flying its flag on the high seas. Canada invoked issues of fishing and of the conservation and management of fisheries within the NAFO Regulatory Area which was excluded from the jurisdiction of the Court. Although there was a connection between the issues identified by Canada and the subject-matter of the dispute, it in no way justified the substitution by the Court of the second subject for the first one as defined by the Applicant.

(2)   A State's freedom to attach reservations to its declaration of acceptance of the Court's jurisdiction must be exercised in conformity with the Statute and Rules of the Court, with the Charter of the United Nations and with international law. Canada had failed to recognise that recourse to a reservation, in circumstances where a State wished to undertake specific acts of doubtful international legality, risked having a seriously damaging effect on the credibility of the Optional Clause system. This was a case where Article 79(7) of the Rules of Court should have been applied, with the result that examination of the definition and precise content of 'conservation and management measures' would have been postponed to the merits phase, these being matters not having an exclusively preliminary character. The Court was bound to declare itself competent at this stage to undertake an examination of the merits in order to determine whether the measures taken against the Spanish vessels were in fact conservation and protection measures.

Dissenting Opinion of Judge Ranjeva   In place of the subject of the dispute as it was defined by the Applicant, the judgment had substituted a different subject, without the support of relevant case law. The Court was necessarily bound by the terms of the claim as formulated in the application. A reservation to jurisdiction, while unilateral in origin, was international in its effects, since it became part of the network made up of all the declarations under Article 36(2). It was difficult to see how the Canadian reservation could be interpreted without recourse to the rules, principles and methods of interpretation of international agreements and outside the framework of the Law of the Sea Convention, 1982.

Dissenting Opinion of Judge Vereshchetin   The scope of the dispute between the Parties was much broader than the pursuit and arrest of the *Estai*. The dispute involved the different perceptions by the Parties of the rights and obligations which a coastal State might have in certain areas of the high seas. The Court had no good reason for redefining and narrowing the subject-matter of the dispute presented by the Applicant. While a State was free to join, or not to join, the Optional Clause system, its freedom to make reservations and conditions to its declaration was not absolute. The Court could not accord to a document the legal effect sought by the State from which it emanated, without having regard to the compatibility of the document with the basic requirements of international law. The scope of the Canadian reservation, as well as its implication for the Court's jurisdiction, could not be established with certainty by the Court. Therefore, the correct course of action would have been to find that the objections of Canada did not have an exclusively preliminary character.

Dissenting Opinion of Judge ad hoc *Torres Bernárdez*   The Court had jurisdiction to adjudicate on the dispute before it. Three principles had to be considered. First, there was the principle of good faith, which had a fundamental role both in the *modus operandi* of the Optional Clause system and in the interpretation and application by the Court of declarations made by States under Article 36(2) of its Statute. Secondly, there was the distinction between, on the one hand, the principle of consent by the States concerned to the jurisdiction of the Court and, on the other, an interpretation, in accordance with the rules of interpretation laid down by international law, of the consent objectively demonstrated in declarations at the time of their deposit with the Secretariat-General of the United Nations. Finally, there was the fundamental requirement of international procedure that the sovereign right of the Applicant State to define the subject-matter of the dispute must be respected as much as the sovereign right of the Respondent State to oppose the Court's jurisdiction by presenting preliminary or other objections, or by filing a counter-claim of its own.

There follows

Judgment of International Court of Justice on Jurisdiction, 4 December 1998 (extract)

[. . .]

[446][. . .] 23. Neither of the Parties denies that there exists a dispute between them. Each Party, however, characterizes the dispute differently. Spain has characterized the dispute as one relating to Canada's lack of entitlement to exercise jurisdiction on the high seas, and the non-opposability of its amended Coastal Fisheries Protection legislation and regulations to third States, including Spain. Spain further maintains that Canada, by its conduct, has violated Spain's rights under international law and that such violation entitles it to reparation. Canada states that the dispute concerns

---

[4] The separate opinions of President Schwebel and Judges Koroma and Kooijmans are not reproduced in this volume but can be found at *ICJ Reports 1998*, pp. 470, 486 and 489 respectively. The dissenting opinions of Vice-President Weeramantry, Judges Bedjaoui and Ranjeva and Judge *ad hoc* Torres Bernárdez are not reproduced in this volume but can be found at *ICJ Reports 1998*, pp. 496, 516, 553 and 582 respectively.

the adoption of measures for the conservation and management of fisheries stocks with respect to vessels fishing in the NAFO Regulatory Area and their enforcement.

24. Spain contends that the purpose of its Application is not to seise the Court of a dispute concerning fishing on the high seas or the management and conservation of biological resources in the NAFO Regulatory Area. Claiming that its exclusive jurisdiction over ships flying its flag on the high seas has been disregarded and swept aside, it argues that

> the object of the Spanish Application relates essentially to Canada's entitlement in general, and in particular in relation to Spain, to exercise its jurisdiction on the high seas against ships flying the Spanish flag and their crews, and to enforce that right by a resort to armed force.

25. Spain maintains that the Agreement of 20 April 1995 between the European Community and Canada on fisheries in the context of the NAFO Convention (see paragraph 21 above)[5] settled as between Canada [447] and the Community certain aspects of a dispute provoked by the unilateral actions of Canada within the area of the high seas subject to regulation by NAFO (an organization of which both the Community and Canada are members). Spain also stresses that it co-operated in the conclusion of this Agreement as a member State of the Community, to which, it states, competence in respect of fisheries conservation and management has been transferred. However, according to Spain, its Application is based on a right exclusive to itself and concerns a dispute whose subject-matter differs from that covered by the Agreement; this dispute, therefore, is not merely a matter of fisheries conservation and management.

26. For its part, Canada is of the view that:

> this case arose out of and concerns conservation and management measures taken by Canada with respect to Spanish vessels fishing in the NAFO Regulatory Area and the enforcement of such measures.

Canada contended at the hearing that Spain's Application constitutes

> a claim in State responsibility on account of Canada's alleged violation of the international obligations incumbent upon it under the rules and principles of general international law,

and maintained that a dispute consists of an indivisible whole comprising facts and rules of law. In its view the Court cannot have jurisdiction with regard to one of these elements and not have jurisdiction with regard to the other.

27. Canada, referring to the notes of protest addressed to it by the European Community and by Spain (see paragraph 20 above,[6] points out that they contain no trace of any distinction between a dispute with the European Community and a dispute with Spain, and that both the protests of the Community and those by the

---

[5 Not reproduced in this volume.]
[6 not reproduced in this volume.]

Spanish authorities 'are founded on the dual, inextricably linked grounds of the fisheries protection legislation and general principles of international law'. Canada argues that this conclusion is confirmed by the Agreement of 20 April 1995 between the European Community and Canada, inasmuch as 'here, too, those questions relating to fisheries and those relating to State jurisdiction, legal entitlement and respect for the rights of the flag State are closely interlinked'.

28. Spain insists that it is free, as the Applicant in this case, to characterize the dispute that it wishes the Court to resolve.

[. . .]

[**457**][. . .]61. The Court recalls that subparagraph 2 (*d*) of the Canadian declaration excludes the Court's jurisdiction in the following terms:

> disputes arising out of or concerning conservation and management measures taken by Canada with respect to vessels fishing in the NAFO Regulatory Area, as defined in the Convention on Future Multilateral Co-operation in the Northwest Atlantic Fisheries, 1978, and the enforcement of such measures (see paragraph 14 above).[7]

Canada contends that the dispute submitted to the Court is precisely of the kind envisaged by the cited text; it falls entirely within the terms of the subparagraph and the Court accordingly has no jurisdiction to entertain it.

[**458**] For Spain, on the other hand, whatever Canada's intentions, they were not achieved by the words of the reservation, which does not cover the dispute; thus the Court has jurisdiction. In support of this view Spain relies on four main arguments: first, the dispute which it has brought before the Court falls outside the terms of the Canadian reservation by reason of its subject-matter; secondly, the amended Coastal Fisheries Protection Act and its implementing regulations cannot, in international law, constitute 'conservation and management measures'; thirdly, the reservation covers only 'vessels' which are stateless or flying a flag of convenience; and fourthly, the pursuit, boarding and seizure of the *Estai* cannot be regarded in international law as 'the enforcement of . . .' conservation and management 'measures'. The Court will examine each of these arguments in turn.

*

62. The Court will begin by pointing out that, in excluding from its jurisdiction '*disputes arising out of or concerning*' the conservation and management measures in question and their enforcement, the reservation does not reduce the criterion for exclusion to the 'subject-matter' of the dispute. The language used in the English version – '*disputes arising out of or concerning*' – brings out more clearly the broad and comprehensive character of the formula employed. The words of the reservation exclude not only disputes whose immediate 'subject-matter' is the measures in question and their enforcement, but also those '*concerning*' such measures and, more generally, those having their 'origin' in those measures ('*arising out of*') – that is to

[⁷ Not reproduced in this volume.]

say, those disputes which, in the absence of such measures, would not have come into being. Thus the scope of the Canadian reservation appears even broader than that of the reservation which Greece attached to its accession to the General Act of 1928 ('disputes relating to the territorial status of Greece'), which the Court was called upon to interpret in the case concerning the *Aegean Sea Continental Shelf (ICJ Reports 1978*, p. 34, para. 81, and p. 36, para. 86).

63. The Court has already found, in the present case, that a dispute does exist between the Parties, and it has identified that dispute (see paragraph 35 above).[8] It must now determine whether that dispute has as its subject-matter the measures mentioned in the reservation or their enforcement, or both, or concerns those measures, or arises out of them. In order to do this, the fundamental question which the Court must now decide is the meaning to be given to the expression '*conservation and management measures . . .*' and '*enforcement of such measures*' in the context of the reservation.

*

64. Spain recognizes that the term '*measure*' is 'an abstract word signifying an act or provision, a démarche or the course of an action, conceived [**459**] with a precise aim in view' and that in consequence, in its most general sense, the expression '*conservation and management measure*' must be understood as referring to an act, step or proceeding designed for the purpose of the 'conservation and management of fish'.

However, in Spain's view this expression, in the particular context of the Canadian reservation, must be interpreted more restrictively.

Initially, Spain contended that the reservation did not apply to the Canadian legislation, which merely represented 'the legal title which [was] the origin and basis of the prohibition of fishing on the high seas', or 'frame of reference'. The reservation covered only 'the consequences of that Act for the conservation and management of resources', that is to say 'the actual procedures for enforcement or implementation of the Act'. However, in oral argument, it no longer pursued this point.

Spain's main argument, on which it relied throughout the proceedings, is that the term 'conservation and management measures' must be interpreted here in accordance with international law and that in consequence it must, in particular, exclude any unilateral 'measure' by a State which adversely affected the rights of other States outside that State's own area of jurisdiction. Hence, in international law only two types of measures taken by a coastal State could, in practice, be regarded as 'conservation and management measures': those relating to the State's exclusive economic zone; and those relating to areas outside that zone, in so far as these came within the framework of an international agreement or were directed at stateless vessels. Measures not satisfying these conditions were not conservation and management measures but unlawful acts pure and simple. In the course of this argument, Spain referred

---

[8 Not reproduced in this volume.]

to Article 1 (1) *(b)* of the 'Agreement for the Implementation of the Provisions of the United Nations Convention on the Law of the Sea of 10 December 1982 Relating to the Conservation and Management of Straddling Fish Stocks and Highly Migratory Fish Stocks' (hereinafter referred to as the 'United Nations Agreement on Straddling Stocks of 1995'), which reads as follows

> 1. For the purposes of this Agreement:
>
> ...
>
> *(b)* 'Conservation and management measures' means measures to conserve and manage one or more species of living marine resources that are adopted and applied consistent with the relevant rules of international law as reflected in the Convention and this Agreement.

65. Canada, by contrast, stresses the very wide meaning of the word 'measure'. It takes the view that this is a 'generic term', which is used in international conventions to encompass statutes, regulations and administrative action.

[**460**] Canada further argues that the expression 'conservation and management measures' is 'descriptive' and not 'normative'; it covers 'the whole range of measures taken by States with respect to the living resources of the sea'. Canada further states that 'a generic category is never limited to the known examples it contains'. Finally, Canada contends that the United Nations Agreement on Straddling Stocks of 1995 is not relevant for the purpose of determining the general meaning of the expression in question and its possible scope in other legal instruments.

66. The Court need not linger over the question whether a 'measure' may be of a 'legislative' nature. As the Parties have themselves agreed, in its ordinary sense the word is wide enough to cover any act, step or proceeding, and imposes no particular limit on their material content or on the aim pursued thereby. Numerous international conventions include 'laws' among the 'measures' to which they refer (see for example, as regards 'conservation and management measures', Articles 61 and 62 of the 1982 United Nations Convention on the Law of the Sea). There is no reason to suppose that any different treatment should be applied to the Canadian reservation, the text of which itself refers not to measures adopted by the executive but simply to 'Canada', that is to say the State as a whole, of which the legislature is one constituent part. Moreover, as the Court has already pointed out (see paragraph 60),[9] the purpose of the reservation was specifically to protect 'the integrity' of the Canadian coastal fisheries protection legislation. Thus to take the contrary view would be to disregard the evident intention of the declarant and to deprive the reservation of its effectiveness.

67. The Court would further point out that, in the Canadian legislative system as in that of many other countries, a statute and its implementing regulations cannot be dissociated. The statute establishes the general legal framework and the regulations permit the application of the statute to meet the variable and changing circumstances through a period of time. The regulations implementing the statute can have no legal

[9 Not reproduced in this volume.]

existence independently of that statute, while conversely the statute may require implementing regulations to give it effect.

68. The Court shares with Spain the view that an international instrument must be interpreted by reference to international law. However, in arguing that the expression 'conservation and management measures' as used in the Canadian reservation can apply only to measures 'in conformity with international law', Spain would appear to mix two issues. It is one thing to seek to determine whether a concept is known to a system of law, in this case international law, whether it falls within the categories proper to that system and whether, within that system, a particular meaning attaches to it: the question of the existence and content of the concept within the system is a matter of definition. It is quite another matter to seek to determine whether a specific act falling within the scope of a concept known to a system of law violates the normative rules of that system: the question of the conformity of the act with the system is a question of legality.

[**461**] 69. At this stage of the proceedings, the task of the Court is simply to determine whether it has jurisdiction to entertain the dispute. To this end it must interpret the terms of the Canadian reservation, and in particular the meaning attaching in the light of international law to the expression 'conservation and management measures' as used in that reservation.

70. According to international law, in order for a measure to be characterized as a 'conservation and management measure', it is sufficient that its purpose is to conserve and manage living resources and that, to this end, it satisfies various technical requirements.

It is in this sense that the terms 'conservation and management measures' have long been understood by States in the treaties which they conclude. Notably, this is the sense in which 'conservation and management measures' is used in paragraph 4 of Article 62 of the 1982 United Nations Convention on the Law of the Sea (see also 1923 Convention between the United States of America and Canada for the Preservation of the Halibut Fisheries of the Northern Pacific Ocean, especially Articles 1 and 2; 1930 Convention between the United States of America and Canada for the Preservation of the Halibut Fisheries of the Northern Pacific Ocean and Bering Sea, Arts. 1, 2 and 3; 1949 International Convention for the Northwest Atlantic Fisheries, Art. IV (2) and especially Art. VIII; 1959 North-East Atlantic Fisheries Convention, Art. 7; 1973 Convention on Fishing and Conservation of the Living Resources in the Baltic Sea and the Belts, Art. I and especially Art. X. Cf. 1958 Geneva Convention on Fishing and Conservation of the Living Resources of the High Seas, Art. 2). The same usage is to be found in the practice of States. Typically, in their enactments and administrative acts, States describe such measures by reference to such criteria as: the limitation of catches through quotas; the regulation of catches by prescribing periods and zones in which fishing is permitted; and the setting of limits on the size of fish which may be caught or the types of fishing gear which may be used (see, among very many examples, Algerian Legislative Decree No. 94-13 of 28 May 1994, establishing the general rules relating to fisheries; Argentine Law No. 24922 of

6 January 1998, establishing the Federal Fishing Régime; Malagasy Ordinance No. 93-022 of 1993 regulating fishing and aquaculture; New Zealand Fisheries Act 1996; as well as, for the European Union, the basic texts formed by Regulation (EEC) No. 3760/92 of 20 December 1992, establishing a Community system for fisheries and aquaculture, and Regulation (EC) No. 894/97 of 29 April 1997, laying down certain technical measures for the conservation of fisheries resources. For NAFO practice, see its document entitled Conservation and Enforcement Measures (NAFO/FC/Doc. 96/1). International law thus characterizes 'conservation and management measures' by reference to factual and scientific criteria.

In certain international agreements (for example the United Nations [462] Agreement on Straddling Stocks of 1995 and the 'Agreement to Promote Compliance with International Conservation and Management Measures by Fishing Vessels on the High Seas' (FAO, 1993), neither of which has entered into force) the parties have expressly stipulated, 'for purposes of th[e] Agreement', that what is generally understood by 'conservation and management measures' must comply with the obligations of international law that they have undertaken pursuant to these agreements, such as, compatibility with maximum sustainable yield, concern for the needs of developing States, the duty to exchange scientific data, effective flag State control of its vessels, and the maintenance of detailed records of fishing vessels.

The question of who may take conservation and management measures, and the areas to which they may relate, is neither in international law generally nor in these agreements treated as an element of the definition of conservation and management measures. The authority from which such measures derive, the area affected by them, and the way in which they are to be enforced do not belong to the essential attributes intrinsic to the very concept of conservation and management measures; they are, in contrast, elements to be taken into consideration for the purpose of determining the legality of such measures under international law.

71. Reading the words of the reservation in a 'natural and reasonable' manner, there is nothing which permits the Court to conclude that Canada intended to use the expression 'conservation and management measures' in a sense different from that generally accepted in international law and practice. Moreover, any other interpretation of that expression would deprive the reservation of its intended effect.

72. The Court has already given a brief description of the amendments made by Canada on 12 May 1994 to the Coastal Fisheries Protection Act and on 25 May 1994 and 3 March 1995 to the Coastal Fisheries Protection Regulations (see paragraphs 15, 17 and 18).[10]

It is clear on reading Section 5.2 of the amended Act that its sole purpose is to prohibit certain sorts of fishing, while Sections 7, 7.1 and 8.1 prescribe the means for giving effect to that prohibition. The same applies to the corresponding provisions of the amended Regulations. In its version of 25 May 1994, subsection 2 of Section 21 of the Regulations, which implements Section 5.2 of the Act, defines the protected

[10 Not reproduced in this volume.]

straddling stocks and 'the prescribed classes' of vessels, and states that for such vessels 'a prohibition against fishing for straddling stocks, preparing to fish for straddling stocks or catching and retaining straddling stocks is a prescribed conservation and management measure'. Table V to Section 21 of the Regulations as amended on 3 March 1995 lists seven types of 'conservation and management measures' applicable to ships flying the Spanish or Portuguese flag; the first two of these specify the species of fish in respect of which fishing is prohibited in certain areas and during [**463**] certain periods; the next two specify the types of fishing gear which are prohibited; the fifth lays down size limits; while the last two lay down certain rules with which ships must comply in connection with inspection by protection officers.

73. The Court concludes from the foregoing that the 'measures' taken by Canada in amending its coastal fisheries protection legislation and regulations constitute 'conservation and management measures' in the sense in which that expression is commonly understood in international law and practice and has been used in the Canadian reservation.

*

74. The conservation and management measures to which this reservation refers are measures '*taken by Canada with respect to vessels fishing in the NAFO Regulatory Area, as defined in the Convention on Future Multilateral Co-operation in the Northwest Atlantic Fisheries, 1978*'.

Article I, paragraph 2, of that Convention defines the NAFO 'Regulatory Area' as 'that part of the Convention Area which lies beyond the areas in which coastal States exercise fisheries jurisdiction'; paragraph 1 of this same Article states that the 'Convention Area' is 'the area to which this Convention applies' and defines that area by reference to geographical co-ordinates.

The NAFO 'Regulatory Area' is therefore indisputably part of the high seas. The Court need not return to the doubts which this part of the reservation may have raised on the Spanish side, in view of the construction placed by the latter on the expression 'conservation and management measures'. For its part the Court has determined that this expression must be construed in a general and customary sense, without any special connotations with regard to place.

75. Thus the only remaining issue posed by this part of the reservation is the meaning to be attributed to the word 'vessels'. Spain argues that it is clear from the parliamentary debates which preceded the adoption of Bill C-29 that the latter was intended to apply only to stateless vessels or to vessels flying a flag of convenience. It followed, according to Spain – in view of the close links between the Act and the reservation – that the latter also covered only measures taken against such vessels.

Canada accepts that, when Bill C-29 was being debated, there were a number of references to stateless vessels and to vessels flying flags of convenience, for at the time such vessels posed the most immediate threat to the conservation of the stocks that it sought to protect. However, Canada denies that its intention was to restrict the scope of the Act and the reservation to these categories of vessels.

76. The Court will begin by once again pointing out that declarations [**464**] of acceptance of its jurisdiction must be interpreted in a manner which is in harmony with the 'natural and reasonable' way of reading the text, having due regard to the intention of the declarant. The Canadian reservation refers to 'vessels fishing . . .', that is to say all vessels fishing in the area in question, without exception. It would clearly have been simple enough for Canada, if this had been its real intention, to qualify the word 'vessels' so as to restrict its meaning in the context of the reservation. In the opinion of the Court the interpretation proposed by Spain cannot be accepted, for it runs contrary to a clear text, which, moreover, appears to express the intention of its author.

77. Furthermore, the Court cannot share the conclusions drawn by Spain from the parliamentary debates cited by it. It is, indeed, evident from the replies given by the Canadian Ministers of Fisheries and Oceans and for Foreign Affairs to the questions put to them in the House of Commons and in the Senate that at that time the principal target of the Bill was stateless vessels and those flying flags of convenience; however, these were not the only vessels covered. Thus the Minister of Fisheries and Oceans expressed himself as follows before the House of Commons:

> as to what is meant by 'vessels of a prescribed class', it is simply a reference that allows the government to prescribe or designate a class, a type or kind of vessel we have determined is fishing in a manner inconsistent with conservation rules and therefore against which conservation measures could be taken.
>
> *For example*, we could prescribe stateless vessels. Another example is that we could prescribe flags of convenience. That is all that is meant. (Emphasis added.)

Similarly, the Minister for Foreign Affairs stated in the Senate:

> We have said from the outset, and Canada's representatives abroad in our various embassies have explained to our European partners and other parties, that this measure is directed *first of all* toward vessels that are unflagged or that operate under so-called flags of convenience. (Emphasis added.)

Furthermore, the following statement by the Minister of Fisheries and Oceans to the Speaker of the House of Commons leaves no doubt as to the scope of the proposed Act:

> The legislation gives Parliament of Canada the authority to designate any class of vessel for enforcement of conservation measures. The legislation does not categorize whom we would enforce against. The legislation makes clear that any vessel fishing in a manner inconsistent with good, widely acknowledged conservation rules could be subject to action by Canada. We cite as an example the [**465**] NAFO conservation rules. Any vessel from any nation fishing at variance with good conservation rules could under the authority granted in the legislation be subject to action by Canada. There are no exceptions.

This is confirmed by the inclusion in the 'prescribed classes of foreign fishing vessels', as a result of the amendment of 3 March 1995, of vessels flying the Spanish and Portuguese flags (see paragraph 18 above).[11] Indeed, it should not be forgotten that, through the enactment of the legislation by means of regulations as well as statute, from the outset the potential was deliberately left open to add prescribed classes of vessels, the term 'class' referring not only to types of vessels but also to the flags the vessels were flying.

*

78. The Court must now examine the phrase *'and the enforcement of such measures'*, on the meaning and scope of which the Parties disagree. Spain contends that an exercise of jurisdiction by Canada over a Spanish vessel on the high seas entailing the use of force falls outside of Canada's reservation to the Court's jurisdiction. Spain advances several related arguments in support of this thesis. First, Spain says that the use of force by one State against a fishing vessel of another State on the high seas is necessarily contrary to international law; and as Canada's reservation must be interpreted consistently with legality, it may not be interpreted to subsume such use of force within the phrase 'the enforcement of such measures'. Spain further asserts that the particular use of force directed against the *Estai* was in any event unlawful and amounted to a violation of Article 2, paragraph 4, of the Charter, giving rise to a separate cause of action not caught by the reservation.

79. The Court has already indicated that there is no rule of interpretation which requires that reservations be interpreted so as to cover only acts compatible with international law. As explained above, this is to confuse the legality of the acts with consent to jurisdiction (see paragraphs 55 and 56 above).[12] Thus the Court has no need to consider further these aspects of Spain's argument.

80. By Section 18.1 of the 1994 Act, the enforcement of its provisions in the NAFO Regulatory Area was made subject to the application of criminal law. In turn, Section 25 of the Criminal Code was amended following the adoption of Bill C-8 (see paragraph 16 above).[13] Spain contends in this context that Canada has thus provided for penal measures related to the criminal law and not enforcement of conservation and management measures. Spain also contends that the expression 'enforcement of such measures' in paragraph 2 *(d)* of Canada's declaration contained no mention of the use of force and that the expression should not be interpreted to include it – not least because the relevant provisions of the [466] 1982 United Nations Law of the Sea Convention relating to enforcement measures also make no mention of the use of force.

81. The Court notes that, following the adoption of Bill C-29, the Coastal Fisheries Protection Act authorized protection officers to board and inspect any fishing vessel in the NAFO Regulatory Area and 'in the manner and to the extent prescribed by the regulations, use force that is intended or is likely to disable a foreign fishing vessel', if the officer 'believes on reasonable grounds that the force is necessary for the purpose

[11] Not reproduced in this volume.]
[12] Not reproduced in this volume.]
[13] Not reproduced in this volume.]

of arresting' the master or crew (Section 8.1). Such provisions are of a character and type to be found in legislation of various nations dealing with fisheries conservation and management, as well as in Article 22 (1) *(f)* of the United Nations Agreement on Straddling Stocks of 1995.

82. The Coastal Fisheries Protection Regulations Amendment of May 1994 specifies in further detail that force may be used by a protection officer under Section 8.1 of the Act only when he is satisfied that boarding cannot be achieved by 'less violent means reasonable in the circumstances' and if one or more warning shots have been fired at a safe distance (Sections 19.4 and 19.5). These limitations also bring the authorized use of force within the category familiar in connection with enforcement of conservation measures.

83. As to Spain's contention that Section 18.1 of the 1994 Act and the amendment of Section 25 of the Criminal Code constitute measures of penal law other than enforcement of fisheries conservation measures, and thus fall outside of the reservation, the Court notes that the purpose of these enactments appears to have been to control and limit any authorized use of force, thus bringing it within the general category of measures in enforcement of fisheries conservation.

84. For all of these reasons the Court finds that the use of force authorized by the Canadian legislation and regulations falls within the ambit of what is commonly understood as enforcement of conservation and management measures and thus falls under the provisions of paragraph 2 *(d)* of Canada's declaration. This is so notwithstanding that the reservation does not in terms mention the use of force. Boarding, inspection, arrest and minimum use of force for those purposes are all contained within the concept of enforcement of conservation and management measures according to a 'natural and reasonable' interpretation of this concept.

*   *

[467] 85. In this Judgment, the Court has had to interpret the words of the Canadian reservation in order to determine whether or not the acts of Canada, of which Spain complains, fall within the terms of that reservation, and hence whether or not it has jurisdiction. For this purpose the Court has not had to scrutinize or prejudge the legality of the acts referred to in paragraph 2 *(d)* of Canada's declaration.

Because the lawfulness of the acts which the reservation to the Canadian declaration seeks to exclude from the jurisdiction of the Court has no relevance for the interpretation of the terms of that reservation, the Court has no reason to apply Article 79, paragraph 7, of its Rules in order to declare that Canada's objection to the jurisdiction of the Court does not possess, in the circumstances of the case, an exclusively preliminary character.

*   *

86. In the course of the proceedings Spain argued that the reservation contained in paragraph 2 *(d)* of Canada's declaration might be thought to have the characteristics of an 'automatic reservation' and thus be in breach of Article 36, paragraph 6,

of the Statute. It is clear from the Court's interpretation of the reservation as set out above that it cannot be regarded as having been drafted in terms such that its application would depend upon the will of its author. The Court has had full freedom to interpret the text of the reservation, and its reply to the question whether or not it has jurisdiction to entertain the dispute submitted to it depends solely on that interpretation.

*

*   *

87. In the Court's view, the dispute between the Parties, as it has been identified in paragraph 35 of this Judgment, had its origin in the amendments made by Canada to its coastal fisheries protection legislation and regulations and in the pursuit, boarding and seizure of the *Estai* which resulted therefrom. Equally, the Court has no doubt that the said dispute is very largely concerned with these facts. Having regard to the legal characterization placed by the Court upon those facts, it concludes that the dispute submitted to it by Spain constitutes a dispute 'arising out of' and 'concerning' 'conservation and management measures taken by Canada with respect to vessels fishing in the NAFO Regulatory Area' and 'the enforcement of such measures'. It follows that this dispute comes within the terms of the reservation contained in paragraph 2 *(d)* of the Canadian declaration of 10 May 1994. The Court consequently has no jurisdiction to adjudicate upon the present dispute.

*

*   *

88. Finally, the Court notes that, in its Counter-Memorial of February 1996, Canada maintained that any dispute with Spain had been settled, [**468**] since the filing of the Application, by the agreement concluded on 20 April 1995 between the European Community and Canada, and that the Spanish submissions were now without object. However, at the beginning of Canada's oral argument, its Agent informed the Court that his Government intended to challenge the Court's jurisdiction solely on the basis of its reservation: 'It is on this problem, and no other, that the Court is called upon to rule.' This position was confirmed at the end of the oral proceedings. Spain nonetheless draws attention to the 'Court's statutory duty to verify the existence of a dispute between States in order to exercise its function'.

It is true that it is for the Court to satisfy itself, whether at the instance of a party or *proprio motu*, that a dispute has not become devoid of purpose since the filing of the Application and that there remains reason to adjudicate that dispute (see *Northern Cameroons (Cameroon v. United Kingdom), Preliminary Objections, Judgment, ICJ Reports 1963*, p. 38; *Nuclear Tests (Australia v. France), Judgment, ICJ Reports 1974*, p. 271, para. 58). The Court has, however, reached the conclusion in the present case that it has no jurisdiction to adjudicate the dispute submitted to it by Spain (see paragraph 87 above). That being so, in the view of the Court it is not required to determine *proprio motu* whether or not that dispute is distinct from the dispute which was the subject of the Agreement of 20 April 1995 between the European Community and Canada, and whether or not the Court would have to find it moot.

*

*   *

89. For these reasons,

THE COURT,

By twelve votes to five,

Finds that it has no jurisdiction to adjudicate upon the dispute brought before it by the Application filed by the Kingdom of Spain on 28 March 1995.

> IN FAVOUR: *President* Schwebel; *Judges* Oda, Guillaume, Herczegh, Shi, Fleischhauer, Koroma, Higgins, Parra-Aranguren, Kooijmans, Rezek; *Judge* ad hoc Lalonde;
>
> AGAINST: *Vice-President* Weeramantry; *Judges* Bedjaoui, Ranjeva, Vereshchetin; *Judge* ad hoc Torres Bernárdez.

[...]

SEPARATE OPINION OF JUDGE ODA (EXTRACT)

[...]

III. Exclusion from the Court's jurisdiction of 'disputes arising out of or concerning conservation and management measures taken by Canada'

[...]

[**479**] [...] 10. It is clear, given the basic principle that the Court's jurisdiction is based on the consent of sovereign States, that a declaration to accept the compulsory jurisdiction of the Court under Article 36, paragraph 2, of the Statute, and any reservations attached thereto, must, because of the declaration's unilateral character, be interpreted not only in a natural way and in context, *but also* with particular regard for the intention of the declarant State. Any interpretation of a *respondent* State's declaration against the intention of that State will contradict the very nature of the Court's jurisdiction, because the declaration is an instrument drafted unilaterally.

There may well be occasions when a *respondent* State seeks to interpret restrictively the scope of an *applicant* State's acceptance of the Court's jurisdiction, especially if one considers that a *respondent* State's obligation to comply with the Court's jurisdiction greatly depends on the scope of the *applicant* State's acceptance of the Court's jurisdiction (cf. Article 36, paragraph 2, of the Statute), but this is, of course, not the situation in the present case.

11. Once Canada had excluded from the Court's jurisdiction certain disputes – namely, 'disputes arising out of and concerning conservation and management measures' – the meaning of the reservation should, as I have explained above, be interpreted according to the intention of Canada. I am at a loss to understand why the

Court should have felt it [480] necessary to devote so much time to its interpretation of the wording of that reservation.

In particular, I do not understand why the Court should have wished to consider whether the expression 'conservation and management measures' in Canada's reservation 2 *(d)* ought to be interpreted according to an allegedly established and normative concept of 'conservation and management measures'. I feel particularly that paragraph 70 of the Judgment has been drafted under a misunderstanding of the subject, namely the law of the sea.

The first sentence of paragraph 70 makes no sense to me and I have no idea whether there is such a rule or concept in international law. I assume that this paragraph was included in the Court's Judgment in order to pay lip-service to some of my colleagues who dissent from the Judgment and who hold the view that the exercise of jurisdiction on the high seas does not fall within the bounds of 'conservation and management measures'. Their view is perfectly correct, but the matter is quite irrelevant and does not need to be mentioned in the Judgment. In my view, the references in the Judgment to certain international treaties or national legislation are quite meaningless and may even be misleading.

12. 'Conservation' of marine living resources is a general concept of marine science which has been widely used since the time that the depletion of certain resources in certain areas began to be noticed due to the over-exploitation of those resources. In fact, as the need for international co-operation for 'conservation' has long been recognized, certain international agreements were concluded even in the earlier part of this century (for example, the 1911 Convention for the Protection and Preservation of Fur Seals and Sea Otters in the North Pacific Ocean; the 1923 International Convention for the Preservation of the Halibut Fisheries of the Northern Pacific Ocean; the 1930 Convention for Protection of Sockeye Salmon Fisheries, etc.).

The Proclamation on 'Policy of the United States with respect to Coastal Fisheries in Certain Areas of the High Seas' made by President Truman of the United States of America in September 1945, immediately after the end of the war, is regarded as far-sighted, in that it drew the world's attention to the pressing need for the conservation and protection of fishery resources, particularly in offshore areas (see S. Oda, *The International Law of the Ocean Development*, Vol. I, p. 342). Over the following years, a number of international conventions – both multilateral and bilateral – covering the conservation of certain marine living resources were concluded (I itemize, just as examples, some of the treaties made at that time: the 1946 Convention for the Regulation of Whaling; the 1949 International Convention for the Northwest Atlantic Fisheries (the predecessor of the NAFO Convention); the 1949 Convention for the Establishment of an Inter-American Tropical Tuna Commission; the 1952 International Convention for the High Seas Fisheries of the North Pacific [481] Ocean; the 1957 Interim Convention on Conservation of North Pacific Fur Seals; the 1959 North-East Atlantic Fisheries Convention; and, the 1966 International Convention for the Conservation of Atlantic Tunas). The measures for conservation adopted in each case vary according to the treaty in which they appear and were enforced through the national legislation of the individual States parties to each treaty.

The International Technical Conference on the Conservation of the Living Resources of the Sea was convened by the United Nations in Rome in 1955, and that was the first worldwide conference to produce a report dealing with the issues of conservation of marine resources. That Conference did not provide for any particular measures for any particular stocks or in any particular region (see S. Oda, *The International Law of the Ocean Development*, Vol. I, p. 356).

13. The 'conservation' of marine living resources was thus not a new concept and the object of conserving those resources had already been implemented in various measures and regulations at international and national levels according to the particular situation – namely, fish stocks and regions. Once measures for conserving marine resources were agreed upon internationally, they were then implemented through the national legislation applicable to the nationals of each individual State.

Another point should be noted, namely that fisheries regulations were adopted not only for the purpose of 'conservation' but were also taken as part of the chain of 'management' measures adopted by each State in pursuance of their respective national economic or social policies. Particularly when 'conservation' could no longer be effected only through regulations limiting the mesh-size of fishing nets and the fixing of fishing seasons or fishing areas (which regulations were imposed in equal manner upon the nationals of the States parties), it became necessary to fix the total allowable catch of specific stocks in particular regions. Thus, 'conservation' issues turned to the more political question of the 'management' – namely, allocation and distribution – of marine resources.

In addition, the number of States who attempted – under the pretext of conservation of resources – to secure marine resources in their offshore areas and to exclude foreign fishing vessels from those areas increased. In this respect, it is important to take note of the concept of maritime sovereignty strongly advanced in the 1950s by some Latin American States (see, for example, the 1952 Santiago Declaration adopted at the Conference on the Exploration and Conservation of the Marine Resources of the South Pacific, in S. Oda, *The International Law of the Ocean Development*, Vol. I, p. 345). In this process there occurred, on a [482] number of occasions, incidents involving the arrest of foreign fishing vessels on the high seas, namely, beyond the area that falls under the national jurisdiction of coastal States (see S. Oda, 'New Trends in the Regime of the Sea – A Consideration of the Problems of Conservation and Distribution of Marine Resources, I and II', *Zeitschrift für Ausländisches Öffentliches Recht und Völkerrecht*, Bd. 18 (1957–8); and, S. Oda, *International Control of Sea Resources*, Leiden, 1962).

14. In these circumstances, marine living resources had become a matter of great concern to the international community and to the United Nations. At the First United Nations Conference on the Law of the Sea convened in Geneva in 1958, the Convention on Fishing and Conservation of the Living Resources of the High Seas was adopted to provide for 'the right [of all States] to engage in fishing on the high

seas, subject ... to the provisions ... concerning conservation of the living resources of the high seas' and 'the duty [of all States] to adopt, or to co-operate with other States in adopting, such measures for their respective nationals as may be necessary for the conservation of the living resources of the high seas' (Art. 1).

In the 1970s, by which time the monopoly of coastal fisheries far beyond the limit of the territorial sea had become more or less a general practice, the concept of the exclusive economic zone, to justify the exclusive control of coastal fisheries, was emerging. Bearing in mind that the fisheries regulations in offshore areas could no longer be a matter of exclusive concern to each coastal State, the Third United Nations Conference on the Law of the Sea, convened over the period 1973 to 1982, produced in 1982 at Montego Bay the United Nations Convention on the Law of the Sea. That Convention provides, on the one hand, for the duty of each coastal State to 'determine the allowable catch of the living resources in its exclusive economic zone' (Art. 61, para. 1) and for the obligation of each coastal State to 'promote the objective of optimum utilization of the living resources in the exclusive economic zone' (Art. 62, para. 1), and, on the other hand with regard to high seas fishing, contains certain provisions concerning 'conservation and management of the living resources of the high seas' (Part VII, Sec. 2). However, that Convention certainly does not seek to define 'conservation and management measures'.

In 1995 at United Nations Headquarters in New York, the so-called Straddling Fish Stocks Convention was agreed upon to implement the provisions of the 1982 Law of the Sea Convention relating to the conservation and management of straddling fish stocks and highly migratory fish stocks in order to ensure the long-term conservation and sustainable use of these stocks – which stocks, of course, have no awareness of the artificial boundary of the exclusive economic zone.

15. It is important to note that the 1958, 1982 and 1995 United [483] Nations Conventions covering marine living resources do not directly impose any concrete 'measures' for conservation of any particular stocks or 'management' of any particular fishing activities. Rather, each State party is obliged to adopt through its own national legislation various appropriate measures for the 'conservation' of resources, designed to apply to fishing vessels, whether national or foreign, in its own area of the exclusive economic zone, and is also obliged to reach agreement with other States for joint measures of conservation on the high seas. It should be noted that there exists no fixed or concrete concept of 'conservation and management *measures*'.

16. It appears to me from the manner in which the Court referred in paragraph 70 of the Judgment to certain international treaties or national legislation, selected at random, that it has misunderstood the true nature of these instruments and has not dealt with the development of the law of the sea in a proper manner.

It is clear to me that Canada, having reserved from the Court's jurisdiction any 'disputes arising out of or concerning conservation and management measures', had in mind – in a very broad sense and without restriction and showing great common sense – any dispute which might arise following the enactment and enforcement of legislation concerning fishing, either for the purpose of conservation of stocks or for management of fisheries (allocation of the catch), in its offshore areas, whether within its exclusive economic zone or outside it.

[. . .]

DISSENTING OPINION OF JUDGE VERESHCHETIN (EXTRACT)

[. . .]

II. The effects of the Canadian reservation on the Court's jurisdiction in this case
[. . .]

[576] [. . .] 12. In our case the legal situation is different. The Canadian reservation admits of more than one interpretation. It is not the reservation itself, but rather its current interpretation by Canada that is challenged by Spain. Nor has the Court any reason to find that the content of the Canadian reservation makes it *ab initio* manifestly inconsistent with the basic principles of international law and therefore inapplicable. The task of the Court in the present case is to find which of the possible interpretations of the reservation is correct and, depending on this finding, to resolve the dispute over its jurisdiction in the case.

According to the well-established rules for the interpretation of declarations and reservations thereto, the Court must read them as a whole and accord the natural and ordinary meaning to the words used in the text. At the same time, the Court has specifically emphasized in the past that:

> the Court cannot base itself on a purely grammatical interpretation of the text. It must seek the interpretation which is in harmony with a natural and reasonable way of reading the text, having due regard to the intention of [the declarant State] at the time when it accepted the compulsory jurisdiction of the Court. (*Anglo-Iranian Oil Co., Preliminary Objection, ICJ Reports 1952*, p. 104.)

13. For the Court, the question of legality cannot be totally irrelevant to 'a natural and reasonable way of reading the text'. Since the function of the Court is to decide disputes in accordance with international law (Article 38, paragraph 1, of the Statute), every international document must be construed by the Court in the light of international law. The language of the Court is the language of international law. A term of a declaration or of a reservation may have a wider or narrower meaning in common parlance or in some other discipline, but for the Court 'the natural and ordinary' meaning of the term is that attributed to it in international [577] law. For natural scientists, for the fisheries industry, conservation and management of fisheries resources remain conservation and management irrespective of the location and legality of this activity. This does not mean, however, that from the position of international law we can characterize as conservation and management, for example, measures for the protection of straddling fish stocks taken by one State in the territorial waters of a neighbouring State without the consent of the latter. International law recognizes the importance and encourages the development of transborder co-operation for

the protection of natural resources, including straddling fish stocks, but it does not admit the possibility of providing this protection by way of violation of fundamental principles of international law. The terms of the art for the Court are the terms used in the context of international law, even though they may have a somewhat different meaning in other disciplines.

14. It follows that the expression 'conservation and management measures', as used in the Canadian reservation, must be read by the Court as referring only to measures accepted within the system of modern international law. A natural source in which to seek definitions of terms and concepts used in the context of the new international law of the sea is the relevant multilateral agreements, particularly those drawn up recently. The meaning of the concept 'conservation and management measures' in the international law of the sea is defined in the Agreement for the Implementation of the Provisions of the United Nations Convention on the Law of the Sea of 10 December 1982 Relating to the Conservation and Management of Straddling Fish Stocks and Highly Migratory Fish Stocks (hereinafter referred to as the 'United Nations Agreement on Straddling Stocks of 1995').[14]

15. This Agreement and the terms used therein are eminently relevant for the issue under consideration. Indeed, the Agreement is contemporaneous with the emergence of the dispute. Its objective ('to ensure the long-term conservation and sustainable use of straddling fish stocks and highly migratory fish stocks' – Article 2) coincides with the proclaimed objective of the Canadian measures. Both the measures under the Agreement and the Canadian measures are designed for application beyond areas under national jurisdiction. The Agreement was drawn up 'for the implementation of the provisions of the United Nations Convention on the Law of the Sea of 10 December 1982', that is, it is intimately linked [578] to the *'Magna Carta'* of the modern law of the sea.[15] Moreover, both Canada and Spain have signed (but not yet ratified) this Agreement.

Article 1, paragraph 1 *(b)*, of the Agreement provides that:

> 'Conservation and management measures' means measures to conserve and manage one or more species of living marine resources *that are adopted and applied consistent with the relevant rules of international law* as reflected in the Convention and this Agreement. (Emphasis added.)

Even more specific in this regard is another recent international legal instrument directly related to the problems of conservation and management on the high seas,

---

[14] Adopted without a vote on 4 August 1995 at the United Nations Conference on Straddling Fish Stocks and Highly Migratory Fish Stocks. One hundred and thirty-eight States and many international organizations participated in the Conference. As of now, the Agreement has been signed by more than 60 States, but has not yet come into force.

[15] According to the mandate of the Conference which adopted the agreement, '[t]he work and results of the conference should be fully consistent with the provisions of the United Nations Convention on the Law of the Sea, in particular the rights and obligations of coastal States and States fishing on the high seas'. See Report of the United Nations Conference on Environment and Development, Rio de Janeiro, 3–14 June 1992, Vol. I: Resolutions adopted by the Conference, Res. I, Ann. II, para. 17.40.

namely: the Agreement to Promote Compliance with International Conservation and Management Measures by Fishing Vessels on the High Seas. This so-called 'Compliance Agreement' was adopted in 1993 by the Twenty-seventh Session of the FAO Conference and forms an integral part of the Code of Conduct for Responsible Fisheries.[16] Article I of this Agreement, entitled 'definitions', contains a definition of 'international conservation and management measures' which, among other elements – identical to those in the above-cited definition – also includes the element of legality, which is formulated in the following way: '[measures] that are adopted and applied in accordance with the relevant rules of international law as reflected in the 1982 United Nations Convention on the Law of the Sea'.

16. It follows from the texts just cited that, contrary to what is said in the Judgment, in international law, in order for a measure to be characterized as a 'conservation and management measure' or an 'international conservation and management measure', *it is not sufficient that* 'its purpose is to conserve and manage living resources and that, to this end, it satisfies various technical requirements' (paragraph 70 of the Judgment). Another essential requirement – indeed a *sine qua non* – is that the adoption and application of such a measure be 'consistent' or 'in accordance' with the relevant rules of **[579]** international law and, more specifically and primarily, with the Law of the Sea Convention.

Moreover, as the legislative history of the United Nations Agreement on Straddling Stocks of 1995 shows, Canada was among the States which formally proposed to include in Article 1 of the Agreement the definition of 'international conservation and management measures', which definition embraced the requirement of the adoption and application of such measures 'in accordance with the principles of international law as reflected in the United Nations Convention on the Law of the Sea . . .'.[17]

17. The argument in the Judgment that 'the practice of States' supports the view that the exigencies of international law are irrelevant for the definition of the concept 'conservation and management measures' does not accord with a number of facts. None of the instruments of national legislation and regulations, cited in the Judgment as evidence of 'typical' practice of States (para. 70), contain any definition whatsoever of 'conservation and management measures', but all of them do contain special clauses providing for the application of those laws and regulations in the waters under national jurisdiction (that is, in harmony with international law). Some of these instruments specifically stipulate that their interpretation and application must be in a manner

---

[16] FAO Fisheries Department. Agreement to Promote Compliance with International Conservation and Management Measures by Fishing Vessels on the High Seas. Twenty-five acceptances are required for the Agreement to come into force. As of now, ten acceptances have been received, including that of Canada. Significantly, Canada accepted the Agreement on 20 May 1994, that is, only 10 days after the filing of its declaration of acceptance of the compulsory jurisdiction of the Court, which declaration contained the reservation discussed.

[17] Draft Convention on the Conservation and Management of Straddling Fish Stocks and Highly Migratory Fish Stocks on the High Seas (submitted by the delegations of Argentina, Canada, Chile, Iceland and New Zealand), doc. A/CONF.164/L.11 of 14 July 1993.

consistent with international obligations (see, for example, New Zealand Fisheries Act 1996, Art. 5).

18. I agree with the statement in the Judgment that:

> [r]eading the words of the reservation [of Canada] in a 'natural and reasonable' manner, there is nothing which permits the Court to conclude that Canada intended to use the expression 'conservation and management measures' in a sense different from that generally accepted in international law (para. 71).

But I fundamentally disagree that the meaning given by the Judgment to the concept of 'conservation and management measure' accords with the meaning of this concept accepted in modern international law, as evidenced by the two above-cited recent multilateral agreements and their legislative history.

19. In the process of interpretation, following the jurisprudence of the Court, 'due regard' should also be given to the intention of the State author of the declaration/reservation at the time when such declaration/reservation was made. 'Due regard' does not mean that this factor should be controlling and definitive for the outcome of the interpretation by the Court, but it must certainly play an important role in ascertaining [580] the purpose of the legal instrument. The purpose intended by the State author must be primarily sought in the wording of the document itself. In some cases, the Court has found 'a decisive confirmation of the intention' of the declarant State in the text itself of the examined declaration/reservation. (See case concerning *Anglo-Iranian Oil Co., Preliminary Objection, Judgment, ICJ Reports 1952*, p. 107.)

20. As a general premise, the Court should proceed from the presumption that the intent was to remain within the orbit of international law. The purpose of the declaration/reservation must be presumed as legal. The Permanent Court of International Justice stressed that the Court cannot presume an abuse of rights (*Certain German Interests in Polish Upper Silesia, Merits, Judgment No. 7, 1926, PCIJ, Series A, No. 7*, p. 30). The present Court in the *Right of Passage* case stated that:

> It is a rule of interpretation that a text emanating from a Government must, in principle, be interpreted as producing and as intended to produce effects in accordance with existing law and not in violation of it. (*Right of Passage over Indian Territory, Preliminary Objections, Judgment, ICJ Reports 1957*, p. 142.)

The Court cannot impute to a State bad faith, an intent by way of a reservation to cover a violation of international law.

21. Basing itself on the presumed lawfulness of Canada's intent, the Court cannot read into the text of the reservation of Canada an intention to violate the fundamental principle of the freedom of the high seas and at the same time to avoid review of this conduct by the Court. Rather, it should seek to interpret the reservation as consistent with international law and, therefore, to construe the words 'conservation and management measures' in the sense accepted in recent multilateral agreements (see *supra*, para. 16) or, at the very least in a sense having some justification in international law.

22. The purpose intended to be served by the declaration/reservation may also be sought by the Court in any available evidence pertaining to the adoption of the instrument. The evidence furnished by Canada to this effect is ambivalent. Parliamentary statements, made at the time when the declaration and the reservation thereto had just been deposited, would appear to limit the application of the envisaged measures to 'pirate vessels' (which would be consistent with international law). Both the Minister for Foreign Affairs and the Minister for Fisheries and Oceans principally spoke of stateless or 'pirate vessels' as the target of the proposed legislation (Bill C-29), whose 'integrity' the reservation was intended to protect. In light of the link between that legislation and the reservation, the above statements could be viewed as the official interpretation of the reservation by Canada at the time of its deposit.

Only some one year later did Canada introduce the regulations by which Act C-29 was applied to Spanish and Portuguese vessels. [**581**] Arguably, those regulations are not relevant to the interpretation of the reservation at the time of its deposit. It follows that the parliamentary debate and other evidence submitted by Canada cannot be relied on in order to draw conclusions as to '*the evident* intention of the declarant' (paragraph 66 of the Judgment; emphasis added) at the time material for the interpretation of the reservation.

*

*   *

23. In view of the above considerations, the scope (*ratione materiae* and *ratione personae*) of the Canadian reservation, as well as its implications for the Court's jurisdiction in this case, appear much less clear than it may seem on the face of the matter. The clarification of these issues requires further analyses of facts and law and the conclusive establishment whether the measures taken by Canada, including their enforcement, fall within the terms of the reservation. This can be done only at the merits stage.

24. On the other hand, already at the present stage, it is amply clear that legal uncertainties surrounding the Canadian reservation make it impossible for the Court, relying on this reservation, to arrive with confidence at the conclusion that it has no jurisdiction to entertain the broad legal dispute over the title under international law for a coastal State to act on the high seas with the use of force against vessels of other States. In my view, the correct course of action for the Court would have been to find that in the circumstances of the case the objections of Canada did not have an exclusively preliminary character.

[Reports: *ICJ Reports 1998*, p. 432; 123 *ILR* 189 at p. 195]

II

DECISIONS OF THE INTERNATIONAL
TRIBUNAL FOR THE LAW OF THE SEA

Southern Bluefin Tuna Cases
(New Zealand *v.* Japan)
(Australia *v.* Japan)[1]

International Tribunal for the Law of the Sea, Hamburg

27 August 1999 (Mensah, *President*; Wolfrum, *Vice-President*; Zhao, Caminos, Marotta Rangel, Yankov, Yamamoto, Kolodkin, Park, Bamela Engo, Nelson, Chandrasekhara Rao, Akl, Anderson, Vukas, Warioba, Laing, Treves, Marsit, Eiriksson and Ndiaye, *Judges*; Shearer, *Judge* ad hoc)

Powers and procedures of tribunals – International Tribunal for the Law of the Sea – provisional measures of protection – binding character – purpose – jurisdiction – Law of the Sea Convention, 1982, Articles 290 and 297 – requirement of urgency – whether power of the Tribunal to order provisional measures different from that of the International Court of Justice

Conservation – management of fish stocks – marine environment – precautionary principle – whether part of customary international law – whether different from a precautionary approach – Convention for the Conservation of Southern Bluefin Tuna, 1993 – Straddling Stocks Agreement, 1995 – relevance for application of the Law of the Sea Convention

SUMMARY   *The facts*   New Zealand and Australia each requested that an arbitral tribunal be constituted, in accordance with Annex VII of the United Nations Convention on the Law of the Sea, 1982 ('the Law of the Sea Convention'), to adjudge and declare that Japan had violated its obligations under Articles 64 and 116 to 119 of the Law of the Sea Convention with regard to the conservation and management of the southern bluefin tuna stock,

---

[1] The Award of the Arbitral Tribunal of 4 August 2000 is reproduced in this volume at p. 495 below.
    Australia and New Zealand were represented by: Timothy Caughley, Agent and Counsel for New Zealand; William Campbell, Agent and Counsel for Australia; Daryl Williams, Attorney-General of the Commonwealth of Australia, Counsel for Australia; Bill Mansfield, Counsel and Advocate for New Zealand; James Crawford SC, Counsel for Australia; Mr Henry Burmester QC, Counsel for Australia. Japan was represented by Mr Kazuhiko Togo, Agent; Mr Robert T. Greig, Counsel; and Mr Nisuke Ando, Counsel.

thereby violating the rights of the two Applicant States.[2] New Zealand and Australia requested that the International Tribunal for the Law of the Sea prescribe provisional measures of protection pending the constitution of the arbitral tribunal.[3] The measures requested would have placed limits on the amount of southern bluefin tuna to be caught by Japanese nationals and would have required Japan to cease experimental fishing and observe the precautionary principle. Japan opposed the requests and contended, *inter alia*, that there was no basis for the proposed arbitral tribunal to exercise jurisdiction, since any disputes between the Parties were of a scientific, rather than a legal, character. Japan also contended that if there were legal disputes between the Parties they concerned the application of the Convention for the Conservation of Southern Bluefin Tuna, 1993 ('the 1993 Convention'), not the provisions of the Law of the Sea Convention.[4]

Held by the International Tribunal for the Law of the Sea   (1)   Before prescribing provisional measures, the Tribunal had to satisfy itself that there was a *prima facie* basis for the jurisdiction of the arbitral tribunal. That requirement was satisfied in the present case.

(a)   The differences between the Parties included differences on points of law which constituted disputes regarding the interpretation or application of the Law of the Sea Convention. The conduct of the Parties within the Commission established by the 1993 Convention and in their relations with non-parties to that Convention was relevant to an evaluation of the extent to which the Parties were in compliance with their obligations under the Law of the Sea Convention.

(b)   The procedures under the 1993 Convention did not preclude the Parties from invoking the dispute settlement provisions of the Law of the Sea Convention.

(c)   Australia and New Zealand had engaged in negotiations and consultations with Japan. A State Party was not obliged to continue with such negotiations under Part XV, section 1, of the Law of the Sea Convention when it had concluded that the possibilities of settlement had been exhausted.

(2)   The stocks of bluefin tuna had become seriously depleted, giving rise to concern. While the Tribunal was not in a position conclusively to assess the scientific evidence, measures were needed as a matter of urgency to preserve the rights of the Parties, to conserve the remaining stocks and to protect the marine environment. Catches, including those

---

[2] The relevant provisions of the two Statements of Claim are set out at pp. 397–9 below.
[3] The measures requested are set out at pp. 399–400 below.
[4] Japan's submissions are set out at pp. 400–1 below.

in experimental fishing, should not exceed the total catches set by the Parties for the previous year except under agreed criteria.

Accordingly, the Tribunal ordered

(by twenty votes to two)   (a)   That the three Parties should each ensure that no action was taken which might aggravate or extend the disputes submitted to the arbitral tribunal;

(by twenty votes to two)   (b)   That the three Parties should each ensure that no action was taken which might prejudice the carrying out of any decision on the merits which the arbitral tribunal might render;

(by eighteen votes to four)   (c)   That the three Parties should each ensure that, unless they agreed otherwise, their annual catches should not exceed the annual national allocations last agreed by them and that, in calculating the annual catches for 1999 and 2000, and without prejudice to any decision of the arbitral tribunal, account should be taken of any catch taken during 1999 as part of an experimental fishing programme;

(by twenty votes to two)   (d)   That the three Parties should each refrain from conducting an experimental fishing programme except with the consent of the other Parties or unless the experimental catch was accounted for against its national allocation;

(by twenty-one votes to one)   (e)   that the three Parties should resume negotiations without delay with a view to reaching agreement on measures for the conservation and management of southern bluefin tuna;

(by twenty votes to two)   (f)   That the three Parties should make further efforts to reach agreement with other States and fishing entities engaged in fishing for southern bluefin tuna, with a view to ensuring the conservation and promoting the objective of optimum utilisation of the stock.

Joint Declaration of Vice-President Wolfrum and Judges Caminos, Marotta Rangel, Yankov, Anderson and Eiriksson   A reduction in catches would assist the stock to recover. Article 64 of the Convention laid down a duty to cooperate to that end.

Declaration of Judge Warioba   The Tribunal had gone beyond what was permitted in a decision on provisional measures and entered into certain matters which should have been reserved to the merits. Reference to the protection of the marine environment was permissible only when expressly requested by a party or when absolutely necessary and urgent.

Separate Opinion of Judge Laing   (1)   The criterion of 'irreparability' was not appropriate in every case. The requirement of procedural urgency was designed to ensure that the Tribunal did not trespass on the province of the arbitral tribunal in a case such as the present.

(2)   It was not possible to determine on this application whether the precautionary principle formed part of customary international law.

However the Convention recognised a precautionary approach, which the Tribunal had adopted without express reference.

Separate Opinion of Judge Treves   The requirement of temporal and qualitative urgency was an essential feature of the provisional measures jurisdiction. By resorting to the precautionary approach in order to assess the urgency of the measures requested, the Tribunal was not taking a decision on whether the precautionary principle was part of customary international law, nor was it necessary for it to do so.

Separate Opinion of Judges Yamamoto and Park   If the experimental fishing programme commenced by Japan was to be suspended, the retaliatory measures taken by Australia should likewise be suspended.

Separate Opinion of Judge ad hoc Shearer (1) It was necessary only for the Tribunal to find that there was a *prima facie* basis for the jurisdiction of the arbitral tribunal. However, in the present case, the demonstration of the arbitral tribunal's jurisdiction went beyond being merely *prima facie*. It was clear that the present dispute related to the interpretation or application of the Convention and the dispute resolution procedure of the Convention was therefore applicable.

(2)   The Tribunal had behaved less as a court of law than as an agency of diplomacy. It could and should have ordered provisional measures in stronger terms. Japan had been exceeding its annual quota by conducting an experimental fishing programme without the consent of the other parties to the 1993 Convention.

(3)   The Straddling Stocks Agreement of 1995, though not yet in force, referred to the precautionary approach and was an appropriate point of reference.

(4)   The power of the Tribunal to prescribe provisional measures was in some respects broader than that of the International Court of Justice but in other respects narrower. The Tribunal had no power to order measures without a request from a party and without giving the parties the opportunity to be heard. If Article 89(5) of the Rules of the Tribunal purported to give a power to act beyond the bounds of what had been requested, it was *ultra vires*.

Dissenting Opinion of Judge Vukas   The requirement of urgency, which was a precondition for the grant of provisional measures, was not satisfied in the present case. Experimental fishing by Japan in the next few months did not pose a sufficient threat to the survival of the southern bluefin tuna. The matter should have been left to be dealt with by the arbitral tribunal.

Dissenting Opinion of Judge Eiriksson   The Tribunal should have confined itself to prescribing measures which had clear and specific objectives and not included a requirement not to aggravate or extend the dispute or a requirement not to take action which might prejudice the carrying out of any decision of the arbitral tribunal. It was wrong to enact such broadly worded measures in binding form.

There follows

Order of International Tribunal for the Law of the Sea on Request for Provisional Measures, 27 August 1999 (extract)

[. . .]

[**155**] [. . .] 28. *Whereas*, in the Notification of 15 July 1999 and the attached Statement of Claim, New Zealand alleged that Japan had failed to comply with its obligation to cooperate in the conservation of the southern bluefin tuna stock by, *inter alia*, undertaking unilateral experimental fishing for southern bluefin tuna in 1998 and 1999 and, accordingly, had requested the arbitral tribunal to be constituted under Annex VII (hereinafter 'the arbitral tribunal') to adjudge and declare:

> 1. That Japan has breached its obligations under Articles 64 and 116 to 119 of UNCLOS [United Nations Convention on the Law of the Sea] in relation to the conservation and management of the SBT [southern bluefin tuna] stock, including by:
> (a) failing to adopt necessary conservation measures for its nationals fishing on the high seas so as to maintain or restore the SBT stock to levels which can produce the maximum sustainable yield, as required by Article 119 and contrary to the obligation in Article 117 to take necessary conservation measures for its nationals;
> (b) carrying out unilateral experimental fishing in 1998 and 1999 which has or will result in SBT being taken by Japan over and above previously agreed Commission [Commission for the Conservation of Southern Bluefin Tuna] national allocations;
> [**156**](c) taking unilateral action contrary to the rights and interests of New Zealand as a coastal State as recognised in Article 116(b) and allowing its nationals to catch additional SBT in the course of experimental fishing in a way which discriminates against New Zealand fishermen contrary to Article 119 (3);

---

[5] The joint separate opinion of Judges Yamamoto and Park is not reproduced in this volume but can be found at 117 *ILR* 180; the dissenting opinion of Judge Eiriksson is also not reproduced in this volume but can be found at 117 *ILR* 194.

(d)   failing in good faith to co-operate with New Zealand with a view to ensuring the conservation of SBT, as required by Article 64 of UNCLOS;

(e)   otherwise failing in its obligations under UNCLOS in respect of the conservation and management of SBT, having regard to the requirements of the precautionary principle.

  2. That, as a consequence of the aforesaid breaches of UNCLOS, Japan shall:

(a)   refrain from authorising or conducting any further experimental fishing for SBT without the agreement of New Zealand and Australia;

(b)   negotiate and co-operate in good faith with New Zealand, including through the Commission, with a view to agreeing future conservation measures and TAC [total allowable catch] for SBT necessary for maintaining and restoring the SBT stock to levels which can produce the maximum sustainable yield;

(c)   ensure that its nationals and persons subject to its jurisdiction do not take any SBT which would lead to a total annual catch of SBT above the amount of the previous national allocations agreed with New Zealand and Australia until such time as agreement is reached with those States on an alternative level of catch; and

(d)   restrict its catch in any given fishing year to its national allocation as last agreed in the Commission subject to the reduction of such catch by the amount of SBT taken by Japan in the course of its unilateral experimental fishing in 1998 and 1999.

  3. That Japan pay New Zealand's costs of the proceedings;

29. *Whereas*, in the Notification of 15 July 1999 and the attached Statement of Claim, Australia alleged that Japan had failed to comply with its obligation to cooperate in the conservation of the southern bluefin tuna stock by, *inter alia*, undertaking unilateral experimental fishing for southern bluefin tuna in 1998 and 1999 and, accordingly, had requested the arbitral tribunal to adjudge and declare:

  (1) That Japan has breached its obligations under Articles 64 and 116 to 119 of UNCLOS in relation to the conservation and management of the SBT stock, including by:

(a)   failing to adopt necessary conservation measures for its nationals fishing on the high seas so as to maintain or restore the SBT stock to levels which can produce the maximum sustainable yield, as required by Article 119 of UNCLOS and contrary to the obligation in Article 117 to take necessary conservation measures for its nationals;

(b)   carrying out unilateral experimental fishing in 1998 and 1999 which has or will result in SBT being taken by Japan over and above previously agreed Commission national allocations;

[157](c)   taking unilateral action contrary to the rights and interests of Australia as a coastal state as recognised in Article 116(b) and allowing its nationals to catch additional SBT in the course of experimental fishing in a way which discriminates against Australian fishermen contrary to Article 119 (3);

(d)   failing in good faith to co-operate with Australia with a view to ensuring the conservation of SBT, as required by Article 64 of UNCLOS; and

(e)   otherwise failing in its obligations under UNCLOS in respect of the conservation and management of SBT, having regard to the requirements of the precautionary principle.

  (2) That, as a consequence of the aforesaid breaches of UNCLOS, Japan shall:

(a) refrain from authorising or conducting any further experimental fishing for SBT without the agreement of Australia and New Zealand;

(b) negotiate and co-operate in good faith with Australia, including through the Commission, with a view to agreeing future conservation measures and TAC for SBT necessary for maintaining and restoring the SBT stock to levels which can produce the maximum sustainable yield;

(c) ensure that its nationals and persons subject to its jurisdiction do not take any SBT which would lead to a total annual catch of SBT by Japan above the amount of the previous national allocation for Japan agreed with Australia and New Zealand until such time as agreement is reached with those States on an alternative level of catch; and

(d) restrict its catch in any given fishing year to its national allocation as last agreed in the Commission, subject to the reduction of such catch for the current year by the amount of SBT taken by Japan in the course of its unilateral experimental fishing in 1998 and 1999.

(3) That Japan pay Australia's costs of the proceedings;

30. *Whereas*, in their Notifications of 15 July 1999, Australia and New Zealand requested that Japan agree to certain provisional measures with respect to the disputes pending the constitution of the arbitral tribunal or agree that the question of provisional measures be forthwith submitted to the Tribunal and furthermore reserved the right, if Japan did not so agree within two weeks, immediately on the expiry of the two-week period and without further notice to request the Tribunal to prescribe the provisional measures;

31. *Whereas* the provisional measures requested by New Zealand in the Request to the Tribunal dated 30 July 1999 are as follows:

(1) that Japan immediately cease unilateral experimental fishing for SBT;

(2) that Japan restrict its catch in any given fishing year to its national allocation as last agreed in the Commission for the Conservation of Southern Bluefin Tuna ('the Commission'), subject to the reduction of such catch by the amount of SBT taken by Japan in the course of its unilateral experimental fishing in 1998 and 1999;

(3) that the parties act consistently with the precautionary principle in fishing for SBT pending a final settlement of the dispute;

[158] (4) that the parties ensure that no action of any kind is taken which might aggravate, extend or render more difficult of solution the dispute submitted to the Annex VII Arbitral Tribunal; and

(5) that the parties ensure that no action is taken which might prejudice their respective rights in respect of the carrying out of any decision on the merits that the Annex VII Arbitral Tribunal may render;

32. *Whearas* the provisional measures requested by Australia in the Request to the Tribunal dated 30 July 1999 are as follows:

(1) that Japan immediately cease unilateral experimental fishing for SBT;

(2) that Japan restrict its catch in any given fishing year to its national allocation as last agreed in the Commission for the Conservation of Southern Bluefin Tuna ('the

Commission'), subject to the reduction of such catch by the amount of SBT taken by Japan in the course of its unilateral experimental fishing in 1998 and 1999;

(3) that the parties act consistently with the precautionary principle in fishing for SBT pending a final settlement of the dispute;

(4) that the parties ensure that no action of any kind is taken which might aggravate, extend or render more difficult of solution the dispute submitted to the Annex VII Arbitral Tribunal; and

(5) that the parties ensure that no action is taken which might prejudice their respective rights in respect of the carrying out of any decision on the merits that the Annex VII Arbitral Tribunal may render;

33. *Whereas* submissions and arguments presented by Japan in its Statement in Response include the following:

Australia and New Zealand must satisfy two conditions before a tribunal constituted pursuant to Annex VII would have jurisdiction over this dispute such that this Tribunal may entertain a request for provisional measures pursuant to Article 290(5) of UNCLOS pending constitution of such an Annex VII tribunal. First, the Annex VII tribunal must have prima facie jurisdiction. This means among other things that the dispute must concern the interpretation or application of UNCLOS and not some other international agreement. Second, Australia and New Zealand must have attempted in good faith to reach a settlement in accordance with the provisions of UNCLOS Part XV, Section 1. Since Australia and New Zealand have satisfied neither condition, an Annex VII tribunal would not have prima facie jurisdiction and accordingly this Tribunal is without authority to prescribe any provisional measures.

. . .

In the event that the Tribunal determines that this matter is properly before it and an Annex VII tribunal would have prima facie jurisdiction, then, pursuant to ITLOS [International Tribunal for the Law of the Sea] Rules Article 89(5), Japan respectfully requests that the Tribunal grant Japan provisional relief in the form of prescribing that Australia and New Zealand urgently and in good faith recommence negotiations with Japan for a period of six months to reach a consensus on the outstanding issues between them, including a protocol for a continued EFP [experimental fishing programme] and the determination of a [159] TAC and national allocations for the year 2000. Should the parties not reach a consensus within six months following the resumption of these negotiations, the Tribunal should prescribe that any remaining disagreements would be, consistent with Parties' December 1998 agreement and subsequent Terms of Reference to the EFPWG [experimental fishing programme working group] . . ., referred to the panel of independent scientists for their resolution.

The . . . Statement of Facts and the history of negotiations between Australia, New Zealand and Japan concerning conservation of SBT, chronicles the bad faith exhibited by Australia and New Zealand in terminating consultations and negotiations over the terms of a joint experimental fishing program and their rash resort to proceedings under UNCLOS despite the absence of any controversy thereunder and the failure to exhaust the amicable provisions for dispute resolution that Part XV mandates be fully utilized. Accordingly, this Tribunal should require Australia and New Zealand to fulfil their obligations to continue negotiations over this scientific dispute.

... Submissions

Upon the foregoing Response and the Annexes hereto, the Government of Japan submits that the Request for provisional measures by Australia and New Zealand should be denied and Japan's counter-request for provisional measures should be granted;

34. *Whereas* Australia and New Zealand, in their final submissions at the public sitting held on 20 August 1999, requested the prescription by the Tribunal of the following provisional measures:

(1) that Japan immediately cease unilateral experimental fishing for SBT;

(2) that Japan restrict its catch in any given fishing year to its national allocation as last agreed in the Commission for the Conservation of Southern Bluefin Tuna ('the Commission'), subject to the reduction of such catch by the amount of SBT taken by Japan in the course of its unilateral experimental fishing in 1998 and 1999;

(3) that the parties act consistently with the precautionary principle in fishing for SBT pending a final settlement of the dispute;

(4) that the parties ensure that no action of any kind is taken which might aggravate, extend or render more difficult of solution the dispute submitted to the Annex VII Arbitral Tribunal; and

(5) that the parties ensure that no action is taken which might prejudice their respective rights in respect of the carrying out of any decision on the merits that the Annex VII Arbitral Tribunal may render;

35. *Whereas*, at the public sitting held on 20 August 1999, Japan presented its final submissions as follows:

First, the request of Australia and New Zealand for the prescription of provisional measures should be denied.

Second, despite all the submissions made by Japan, in the event that the Tribunal were to determine that this matter is properly before it and an Annex VII tribunal would have prima facie jurisdiction and that the Tribunal were to determine that it could and should prescribe provisional measures, then, [**160**] pursuant to ITLOS Rules Article 89(5), the International Tribunal should grant provisional measures in the form of prescribing that Australia and New Zealand urgently and in good faith recommence negotiations with Japan for a period of six months to reach a consensus on the outstanding isssues between them, including a protocol for a continued EFP and the determination of a TAC and national allocations for the year 2000. The Tribunal should prescribe that any remaining disagreements would be, consistent with the Parties' December 1998 agreement and subsequent Terms of Reference to the EFP Working Group, referred to the panel of independent scientists for their resolution, should the parties not reach consensus within six months following the resumption of these negotiations;

36. *Considering* that, pursuant to Articles 286 and 287 of the Convention, Australia and New Zealand have both instituted proceedings before the arbitral tribunal against Japan in their disputes concerning southern bluefin tuna;

37. *Considering* that Australia and New Zealand on 15 July 1999 notified Japan of the submission of the disputes to the arbitral tribunal and of the Requests for provisional measures;

38. *Considering* that on 30 July 1999, after the expiry of the time-limit of two weeks provided for in Article 290, paragraph 5, of the Convention, Australia and New Zealand submitted to the Tribunal Requests for provisional measures;

39. *Considering* that Article 290, paragraph 5, of the Convention provides in the relevant part that:

> Pending the constitution of an arbitral tribunal to which a dispute is being submitted under this section, any court or tribunal agreed upon by the parties or, failing such agreement within two weeks from the date of the request for provisional measures, the International Tribunal for the Law of the Sea ... may prescribe, modify or revoke provisional measures in accordance with this article if it considers that prima facie the tribunal which is to be constituted would have jurisdiction and that the urgency of the situation so requires;

40. *Considering* that, before prescribing provisional measures under Article 290, paragraph 5, of the Convention, the Tribunal must satisfy itself that prima facie the arbitral tribunal would have jurisdiction;

41. *Considering* that Australia and New Zealand have invoked as the basis of jurisdiction of the arbitral tribunal Article 288, paragraph 1, of the Convention which reads as follows:

> A court or tribunal referred to in article 287 shall have jurisdiction over any dispute concerning the interpretation or application of this Convention which is submitted to it in accordance with this Part;

42. *Considering* that Japan maintains that the disputes are scientific rather than legal;

43. *Considering* that, in the view of the Tribunal, the differences between the parties also concern points of law;

[161] 44. *Considering* that, in the view of the Tribunal, a dispute is a 'disagreement on a point of law or fact, a conflict of legal views or of interests' (*Mavrommatis Palestine Concessions, Judgment No. 2*, 1924, PCIJ, Series A, No. 2, p. 11), and '[i]t must be shown that the claim of one party is positively opposed by the other' (*South West Africa*, Preliminary Objections, Judgment, *ICJ Reports 1962*, p. 328);

45. *Considering* that Australia and New Zealand allege that Japan, by unilaterally designing and undertaking an experimental fishing programme, has failed to comply with obligations under Articles 64 and 116 to 119 of the Convention on the Law of the Sea, with provisions of the Convention for the Conservation of Southern Bluefin Tuna of 1993 (hereinafter 'the Convention of 1993') and with rules of customary international law;

46. *Considering* that Japan maintains that the dispute concerns the interpretation or implementation of the Convention of 1993 and does not concern the interpretation or application of the Convention on the Law of the Sea;

47. *Considering* that Japan denies that it has failed to comply with any of the provisions of the Convention on the Law of the Sea referred to by Australia and New Zealand;

48. *Considering* that, under Article 64, read together with Articles 116 to 119, of the Convention, States Parties to the Convention have the duty to cooperate directly or through appropriate international organizations with a view to ensuring conservation and promoting the objective of optimum utilization of highly migratory species;

49. *Considering* that the list of highly migratory species contained in Annex I to the Convention includes southern bluefin tuna: *thunnus maccoyii;*

50. *Considering* that the conduct of the parties within the Commission for the Conservation of Southern Bluefin Tuna established in accordance with the Convention of 1993, and in their relations with non-parties to that Convention, is relevant to an evaluation of the extent to which the parties are in compliance with their obligations under the Convention on the Law of the Sea;

51. *Considering* that the fact that the Convention of 1993 applies between the parties does not exclude their right to invoke the provisions of the Convention on the Law of the Sea in regard to the conservation and management of southern bluefin tuna;

52. *Considering* that, in the view of the Tribunal, the provisions of the Convention on the Law of the Sea invoked by Australia and New Zealand appear to afford a basis on which the jurisdiction of the arbitral tribunal might be founded;

[**162**] 53. *Considering* that Japan argues that recourse to the arbitral tribunal is excluded because the Convention of 1993 provides for a dispute settlement procedure;

54. *Considering* that Australia and New Zealand maintain that they are not precluded from having recourse to the arbitral tribunal since the Convention of 1993 does not provide for a compulsory dispute settlement procedure entailing a binding decision as required under Article 282 of the Convention on the Law of the Sea;

55. *Considering* that, in the view of the Tribunal, the fact that the Convention of 1993 applies between the parties does not preclude recourse to the procedures in Part XV, section 2, of the Convention on the Law of the Sea;

56. *Considering* that Japan contends that Australia and New Zealand have not exhausted the procedures for amicable dispute settlement under Part XV, section 1, of the Convention, in particular Article 281, through negotiations or other agreed peaceful means, before submitting the disputes to a procedure under Part XV, section 2, of the Convention;

57. *Considering* that negotiations and consultations have taken place between the parties and that the records show that these negotiations were considered by Australia and New Zealand as being under the Convention of 1993 and also under the Convention on the Law of the Sea;

58. *Considering* that Australia and New Zealand have invoked the provisions of the Convention in diplomatic notes addressed to Japan in respect of those negotiations;

59. *Considering* that Australia and New Zealand have stated that the negotiations had terminated;

60. *Considering* that, in the view of the Tribunal, a State Party is not obliged to pursue procedures under Part XV, section 1, of the Convention when it concludes that the possibilities of settlement have been exhausted;

61. *Considering* that, in the view of the Tribunal, the requirements for invoking the procedures under Part XV, section 2, of the Convention have been fulfilled;

62. *Considering* that, for the above reasons, the Tribunal finds that the arbitral tribunal would prima facie have jurisdiction over the disputes;

63. *Considering* that, according to Article 290, paragraph 5, of the Convention, provisional measures may be prescribed pending the constitution of the arbitral tribunal if the Tribunal considers that the urgency of the situation so requires;

64. *Considering*, therefore, that the Tribunal must decide whether provisional measures are required pending the constitution of the arbitral tribunal;

65. *Considering* that, in accordance with Article 290, paragraph 5, of [163] the Convention, the arbitral tribunal, once constituted, may modify, revoke or affirm any provisional measures prescribed by the Tribunal;

66. *Considering* that Japan contends that there is no urgency for the prescription of provisional measures in the circumstances of this case;

67. *Considering* that, in accordance with Article 290 of the Convention, the Tribunal may prescribe provisional measures to preserve the respective rights of the parties to the dispute or to prevent serious harm to the marine environment;

68. *Considering* that Australia and New Zealand contend that by unilaterally implementing an experimental fishing programme Japan has violated the rights of Australia and New Zealand under Articles 64 and 116 to 119 of the Convention;

69. *Considering* that Australia and New Zealand contend that further catches of southern bluefin tuna, pending the hearing of the matter by an arbitral tribunal, would cause immediate harm to their rights;

70. *Considering* that the conservation of the living resources of the sea is an element in the protection and preservation of the marine environment;

71. *Considering* that there is no disagreement between the parties that the stock of southern bluefin tuna is severely depleted and is at its historically lowest levels and that this is a cause for serious biological concern;

72. *Considering* that Australia and New Zealand contend that, by unilaterally implementing an experimental fishing programme, Japan has failed to comply with its obligations under Articles 64 and 118 of the Convention, which require the parties to cooperate in the conservation and management of the southern bluefin tuna stock, and that the actions of Japan have resulted in a threat to the stock;

73. *Considering* that Japan contends that the scientific evidence available shows that the implementation of its experimental fishing programme will cause no further threat to the southern bluefin tuna stock and that the experimental fishing programme remains necessary to reach a more reliable assessment of the potential of the stock to recover;

74. *Considering* that Australia and New Zealand maintain that the scientific evidence available shows that the amount of southern bluefin tuna taken under the experimental fishing programme could endanger the existence of the stock;

75. *Considering* that the Tribunal has been informed by the parties that commercial fishing for southern bluefin tuna is expected to continue throughout the remainder of 1999 and beyond;

76. *Considering* that the catches of non-parties to the Convention of 1993 have increased considerably since 1996;

77. *Considering* that, in the view of the Tribunal, the parties should in the circumstances act with prudence and caution to ensure that [**164**] effective conservation measures are taken to prevent serious harm to the stock of southern bluefin tuna;

78. *Considering* that the parties should intensify their efforts to cooperate with other participants in the fishery for southern bluefin tuna with a view to ensuring conservation and promoting the objective of optimum utilization of the stock;

79. *Considering* that there is scientific uncertainty regarding measures to be taken to conserve the stock of southern bluefin tuna and that there is no agreement among the parties as to whether the conservation measures taken so far have led to the improvement in the stock of southern bluefin tuna;

80. *Considering* that, although the Tribunal cannot conclusively assess the scientific evidence presented by the parties, it finds that measures should be taken as a matter of urgency to preserve the rights of the parties and to avert further deterioration of the southern bluefin tuna stock;

81. *Considering* that, in the view of the Tribunal, catches taken within the framework of any experimental fishing programme should not result in total catches which exceed the levels last set by the parties for each of them, except under agreed criteria;

82. *Considering* that, following the pilot programme which took place in 1998, Japan's experimental fishing as currently designed consists of three annual programmes in 1999, 2000 and 2001;

83. *Considering* that the Tribunal has taken note that, by the statement of its Agent before the Tribunal on 20 August 1999, Japan made a 'clear commitment that the 1999 experimental fishing programme will end by 31 August';

84. *Considering*, however, that Japan has made no commitment regarding any experimental fishing programmes after 1999;

85. *Considering* that, for the above reasons, in the view of the Tribunal, provisional measures are appropriate under the circumstances;

86. *Considering* that, in accordance with article 89, paragraph 5, of the Rules, the Tribunal may prescribe measures different in whole or in part from those requested;

87. *Considering* the binding force of the measures prescribed and the requirement under Article 290, paragraph 6, of the Convention that compliance with such measures be prompt;

88. *Considering* that, pursuant to Article 95, paragraph 1, of the Rules, each party is required to submit to the Tribunal a report and information on compliance with any provisional measures prescribed;

89. *Considering* that it may be necessary for the Tribunal to request further information from the parties on the implementation of provisional measures and that it is appropriate that the President be authorized to request such information in accordance with Article 95, paragraph 2, of the Rules;

[165] 90. *For these reasons,*

THE TRIBUNAL,

1. *Prescribes,* pending a decision of the arbitral tribunal, the following measures:

By 20 votes to 2,

(a) Australia, Japan and New Zealand shall each ensure that no action is taken which might aggravate or extend the disputes submitted to the arbitral tribunal;

IN FAVOUR: President Mensah; Vice-President Wolfrum; Judges Zhao, Caminos, Marotta Rangel, Yankov, Yamamoto, Kolodkin, Park, Bamela Engo, Nelson, Chandrasekhara Rao, Akl, Anderson, Warioba, Laing, Treves, Marsit, Ndiaye; Judge *ad hoc* Shearer;

AGAINST: Judges Vukas, Eiriksson.

By 20 votes to 2,

(b) Australia, Japan and New Zealand shall each ensure that no action is taken which might prejudice the carrying out of any decision on the merits which the arbitral tribunal may render;

IN FAVOUR: President Mensah; Vice-President Wolfrum; Judges Zhao, Caminos, Marotta Rangel, Yankov, Yamamoto, Kolodkin, Park, Bamela Engo, Nelson, Chandrasekhara Rao, Akl, Anderson, Warioba, Laing, Treves, Marsit, Ndiaye; Judge *ad hoc* Shearer;

AGAINST: Judges Vukas, Eiriksson.

By 18 votes to 4,

(c) Australia, Japan and New Zealand shall ensure, unless they agree otherwise, that their annual catches do not exceed the annual national allocations at the levels last agreed by the parties of 5,265 tonnes, 6,065 tonnes and 420 tonnes, respectively; in calculating the annual catches for 1999 and 2000, and without prejudice to any decision of the arbitral tribunal, account shall be taken of the catch during 1999 as part of an experimental fishing programme;

IN FAVOUR: President Mensah; Vice-President Wolfrum; Judges Caminos, Marotta Rangel, Yankov, Kolodkin, Park, Bamela Engo, [166] Nelson, Chandrasekhara Rao, Akl, Anderson, Laing, Treves, Marsit, Eiriksson, Ndiaye; Judge *ad hoc* Shearer;

AGAINST: Judges Zhao, Yamamoto, Vukas, Warioba.

By 20 votes to 2,

(d) Australia, Japan and New Zealand shall each refrain from conducting an experimental fishing programme involving the taking of a catch of southern bluefin tuna, except with the agreement of the other parties or unless the experimental catch is counted against its annual national allocation as prescribed in subparagraph (c);

IN FAVOUR: President Mensah; Vice-President Wolfrum; Judges Zhao, Caminos, Marotta Rangel, Yankov, Kolodkin, Park, Bamela Engo, Nelson, Chandrasekhara Rao, Akl, Anderson, Warioba, Laing, Treves, Marsit, Eiriksson, Ndiaye; Judge *ad hoc* Shearer;

AGAINST: Judges Yamamoto, Vukas.

By 21 votes to 1,

(e) Australia, Japan and New Zealand should resume negotiations without delay with a view to reaching agreement on measures for the conservation and management of southern bluefin tuna;

IN FAVOUR: President Mensah; Vice-President Wolfrum; Judges Zhao, Caminos, Marotta Rangel, Yankov, Yamamoto, Kolodkin, Park, Bamela Engo, Nelson, Chandrasekhara Rao, Akl, Anderson, Warioba, Laing, Treves, Marsit, Eiriksson, Ndiaye; Judge *ad hoc* Shearer,

AGAINST: Judge Vukas.

By 20 votes to 2,

(f) Australia, Japan and New Zealand should make further efforts to reach agreement with other States and fishing entities engaged in fishing for southern bluefin tuna, with a view to ensuring conservation and promoting the objective of optimum utilization of the stock;

IN FAVOUR: President Mensah; Vice-President Wolfrum; Judges Zhao, Caminos, Marotta Rangel, Yankov, Yamamoto, Kolodkin, Park, Bamela Engo, Nelson, Chandrasekhara Rao, Akl, Anderson, Laing, Treves, Marsit, Eiriksson, Ndiaye; Judge *ad hoc* Shearer;

[167] AGAINST: Judges Vukas, Warioba.

By 21 votes to 1,

2. Decides that each party shall submit the initial report referred to in Article 95, paragraph 1, of the Rules not later than 6 October 1999, and authorizes the President of the Tribunal to request such further reports and information as he may consider appropriate after that date;

IN FAVOUR: President Mensah; Vice-President Wolfrum; Judges Zhao, Caminos, Marotta Rangel, Yankov, Yamamoto, Kolodkin, Park, Bamela Engo, Nelson, Chandrasekhara Rao, Akl, Anderson, Warioba, Laing, Treves, Marsit, Eiriksson, Ndiaye; Judge *ad hoc* Shearer;

AGAINST: Judge Vukas.

By 21 votes to 1,

3. Decides, in accordance with Article 290, paragraph 4, of the Convention and article 94 of the Rules, that the provisional measures prescribed in this Order shall

forthwith be notified by the Registrar through appropriate means to all States Parties to the Convention participating in the fishery for southern bluefin tuna.

IN FAVOUR: President Mensah; Vice-President Wolfrum; Judges Zhao, Caminos, Marotta Rangel, Yankov, Yamamoto, Kolodkin, Park, Bamela Engo, Nelson, Chandrasekhara Rao, Akl, Anderson, Warioba, Laing, Treves, Marsit, Eiriksson, Ndiaye; Judge *ad hoc* Shearer;

AGAINST: Judge Vukas.

[. . .]

[**168**] JOINT DECLARATION BY VICE-PRESIDENT WOLFRUM, JUDGES CAMINOS, MAROTTA RANGEL, YANKOV, ANDERSON AND EIRIKSSON

As regards the state of the stock of southern bluefin tuna, we fully share the views of the Tribunal set out in paragraphs 71, 77 and 80 of the Order. The scientific evidence presented to the Tribunal indicates that the stock has been severely depleted and is presently in a poor state. There remain uncertainties over the life cycle of the stock, as well as differences of opinion among scientists concerning the prospects for its future recovery. Cooperation among the members of the Commission for the Conservation of Southern Bluefin Tuna, at both the scientific and governmental levels, has not been effective in recent years; and during this same period catches by non-members of the Commission and new entrants to the fishery have risen significantly.

In the circumstances, a reduction in the catches of all those concerned in the fishery in the immediate short term would assist the stock to recover over the medium to long term. Article 64 of the Convention lays down, as stated in the Order, a duty to cooperate to that end.

DECLARATION BY JUDGE WARIOBA

I have voted against the operative paragraphs 1(c) and (f) not because I disagree with the substance but because I believe they are issues which belong properly to the merits.

Australia, Japan and New Zealand agreed on a total allowable catch (TAC) of 11,750 tonnes in 1989 and subsequently decided each year to maintain the same, up to 1997. The disagreement arose because Japan wanted the TAC to be increased while Australia and New Zealand held a contrary view. The respective positions were based on the appreciation of scientific evidence. Since the Tribunal has admitted in paragraph 80 that it cannot conclusively assess the scientific evidence presented by the parties, it has no basis of prescribing an order that sets a TAC. That issue should be left to the arbitral tribunal to determine.

[**169**] Australia, Japan and New Zealand should of course continue negotiations with other fishing States and entities with a view to ensuring the conservation and promoting the objective of optimum utilization. I am sure they will continue to do so in addition to continuing cooperation in matters on which they do not have a

dispute. The order of the Tribunal should be confined to issues that are the subject matter of dispute placed before it. The relationship of the parties to this dispute does not include non-parties to the 1993 Agreement.

I further disagree with references to the protection of the marine environment in paragraphs 67 and 68 of the Order. What is stated in those paragraphs is true but has no relevance here. Every activity in the oceans will of necessity affect the environment. It is not necessary for the Tribunal to include consideration of marine environment in every case. The Tribunal can do so only when it has been requested by a party or parties or when it considers it absolutely necessary and urgent. It was not so in this case.

SEPARATE OPINION BY JUDGE LAING (EXTRACT)

Introduction

1. I agree with the Agent for Japan that this is an 'historic proceeding'. Three outstanding global citizens are before this Tribunal in a case involving regional cooperation in which significant natural and economic resources are involved. The case presents the issue of how scientific uncertainty[6] can be handled in a judicial context. It involves questions relating to the interpretation of the 1982 United Nations Convention on the Law of the Sea (UNCLOS) and its interaction with cognate conventions. Above all, in this case the Tribunal makes decisions of fundamental importance to the institution of provisional measures and potentially of critical relevance to an aspect of international environmental law.

[. . .]

[172] [. . .] Precautionary approach

12. One such possible set of policies relates to special devices designed for the protection of the environment. The Applicants based their requests for provisional measures on Articles 64, 116–19 and 300 of UNCLOS; the 1993 Convention, the parties' practice thereunder, 'as well as their obligations under general international law', in particular the 'precautionary principle' which, according to the Statement

---

[6] In this case, eminent scientists have expressed diametrically opposed opinions on several critical issues relating to the Applicants' assertion on and scientific reports that the stock of Southern Bluefin Tuna is under serious threat. *Inter alia*, these have been on: predictions of the future level of parental biomass; changes in size composition; projections on the level of recovery; the appropriate approaches to necessary scientific investigation; the rate of recruitment of young fish to the stock; the increase in mortality rates of juvenile fish; whether an Experimental Fishing Programme (EFP) can or should be conducted unilaterally; the nature and scope of an appropriate EFP; the impact of fishing by non-parties to a fisheries management Convention; the actual structure and impact of EFPs designed by Japan (critiques about hypotheses; testing modalities; number of on-board monitors; whether additional catch of 2,000 fish per annum would be very significant if combined with the Total Allowable Catch; if the stock effectively decreases after the survey and general quota reductions occur, whether it may be impossible to prove that these were not provoked by the survey; method of data review and analysis; access to data by non-survey States; independence of reviewers; constraints on vessel location). Miscellaneous documents annexed to Response.

of Claim in the arbitral proceedings, annexed to the [173] Request for provisional measures, 'must direct any party in the application and implementation of those articles'.

They argued that the principle

> must be applied by States in taking decisions about actions which entail threats of serious or irreversible damage to the environment while there is scientific uncertainty about the effect of such actions. The principle requires caution and vigilance in decision-making in the face of such uncertainty.

13. The Tribunal's Order does not refer to the 'precautionary principle'. Instead, in the recitals it chronicles the opposing views of the Applicants and Respondents about the condition of the stock in view of the allegations about the impact thereon of utilization. It also recites that 'the parties should in the circumstances act with "prudence and caution" to ensure that effective conservation measures are taken to prevent serious harm to the stock'. It further notes the scientific disagreement about appropriate measures to conserve the stock and the non-agreement of the parties about whether the measures actually taken have led to improvement. This aspect of the recitals states the Tribunal's conclusion about the need for Article 290-type of measures despite the Tribunal's inability conclusively to assess the scientific evidence. In my view, these statements are pregnant with meaning. In order to clarify and critique what I understand that the Tribunal has stated, I must first explore the background of the so-called precautionary principle of international environmental relations and law.

Background on environmental precaution

14. The notion of environmental precaution largely stems from diplomatic practice and treaty-making in the spheres, originally, of international marine pollution and, now, of biodiversity, climate change, pollution generally and, broadly, the environment. Its main thesis is that, in the face of serious risk to or grounds (as appropriately qualified) for concern about the environment, scientific uncertainty or the absence of complete proof should not stand in the way of positive action to minimize risks or take actions of a conservatory, preventative or curative nature. In addition to scientific uncertainty, the most frequently articulated conditions or circumstances are concerns of an intergenerational nature and forensic or proof difficulties, generally in the context of rapid change and perceived high risks. The thrust of the notion is vesting a broad dispensation to policy makers, seeking to provide guidance to administrative and other decision-makers and shifting the burden of proof to the State in control of the territory from which the harm might emanate or to the responsible actor. The notion [174] has been rapidly adopted in most recent instruments and policy documents on the protection and preservation of the environment.[7]

---

[7] Of note is para. 17.21 of Agenda 21, adopted at the 1992 Rio Conference on the Environment and Development. Paragraph 17.1 also calls for 'new approaches to the marine and coastal area management and development, at the national, regional and global levels, approaches that are integrated in context and are precautionary and anticipatory in ambit. . .'. Paragraph 15 of the Rio

15. Even as questioning of the acceptability of the precautionary notion diminishes, challenges increase regarding such specifics as: the wide potential ambit of its coverage; the clarity of operational criteria; the monetary costs of environmental regulation; possible public health risks associated with the very remedies improvised to avoid risk; diversity and vagueness of articulations of the notion; uncertainties about attendant obligations, and the imprecision and subjectivity of such a value-laden notion.[8] Nevertheless, the notion has been 'broadly accepted for international action, even if the consequence of its application in a given situation remains open to interpretation' (A. D'Amato and K. Engel, *International Environmental Law Anthology* (1966) 22).

16. Nevertheless, it is not possible, on the basis of the materials available and arguments presented on this application for provisional measures, to determine whether, as the Applicants contend, customary international law recognizes a precautionary principle.[9]

Precaution in marine living resource management

17. However, it cannot be denied that UNCLOS adopts a precautionary approach. This may be gleaned, *inter alia*, from preambular paragraph 4, identifying as an aspect of the 'legal order for the seas and oceans' 'the conservation of their living resources . . .'. Several provisions in Part V of the Convention, e.g. Articles 63–6, on [175] conservation and utilization of a number of species in the exclusive economic zone, identify conservation as a crucial value. So do Article 61, specifically dealing with conservation in general, and Article 64, dealing with conservation and optimum utilization of highly migratory species (such as tuna). Article 116, on the right to fish on the high seas, *inter alia* reiterates the conservation obligation on nationals of non-coastal/distant fishing States while fishing in the exclusive economic zone of other States. Article 117 explicitly articulates the duty of all States 'to take, or to cooperate with other States in taking, measures for their respective nationals as

Declaration, adopted at the same Conference, provides that 'In order to protect the environment, the precautionary approach shall be widely applied by States according to their capabilities. Where there are threats of serious or irreversible damage, lack of full scientific certainty shall not be used as a reason for postponing cost-effective measures to prevent environmental degradation.' See generally *Request for Examination of the Situation in Accordance with Paragraph 63 of the Court's Judgment of 20 December 1974 in the Nuclear Tests (New Zealand v France)* case, Separate Opinion by Judge Weeramantry, *ICJ Reports 1995*, 288, 341–4 [see pp. 183–5 above]; *The Precautionary Principle and International Law: The Challenge of Implementation* (D. Freestone and E. Hey, eds., 1996); D. Freestone and E. Hey in Freestone and Hey 1996, 19–28, 258; A. Kiss in Freestone and Hey 1996, 3–16, 258; *The Global Environment: Institutions, Law and Policy* (K. Vig and R. Axlerod, eds., 1999); A. D'Amato and K. Engel, *International Environmental Law Anthology* (1996); J. Cameron and J. Abouchar, in Freestone and Hey 1996, 29–52; C. Burton, 22 *Harv. Env. LR* 509–58 (1998); M. Kamminga in Freestone and Hey 1996, 171–86; O. McIntyre and T. Mosedale, 9 *Jo. Env. L* 221–41 (1997); W. Gullett, 14 *Env. & Pl. LJ* 52–69 (1997).

[8] P. Sands in Freestone and Hey 1996, 134; F. Cross, 53 *Wash. & Lee LR* 851–925 (1996); J. Hickey and V. Walker, 14 *Va. Env. LJ* 423–54 (1995); J. Macdonald, 26 *ODIL* 255–86 (1995).

[9] It might be noted that treaties and formal instruments use different language of obligation; the notion is stated variously (as a principle, approach, concept, measures, action); no authoritative judicial decision unequivocally supports the notion; doctrine is indecisive, and domestic juridical materials uncertain or evolving.

may be necessary for' conservation of living resources in the high seas. Article 118 requires inter-State cooperation in the conservation and management of high seas living resources. Such cooperation is to extend to negotiations leading to the establishment of subregional or regional fisheries organizations. And Article 119, entitled 'conservation of the living resources of the high seas', deals with the allocation of allowable catches and 'establishing other conservation measures'. Although paragraph 1(a) refers to measures, based on the best scientific evidence, for production of the maximum sustainable yield, the conservatory thrust of this Article is vigorously reaffirmed by the treatment, in paragraph (b), of the effects of management measures on associated or dependent species the populations of which should be maintained or restored 'above levels at which their reproduction may become seriously threatened'. Article 116, in association with the Part V Articles mentioned above, has been stated to point to the precautionary 'principle' of fisheries management, while Article 119 has been said to reflect a precautionary 'approach' 'when scientific data is not available or is inadequate to enable comprehensive decision-making' (*Virginia Commentary*, vol. IV, 288, 310). Most of these are the very provisions before this Tribunal today. Strikingly, also, Article 290(1)'s reference to serious harm to the marine environment as a basis for provisional measures also underscores the salience of the approach.

18. I have drawn the reader's attention to several recitals in the Order that are of particular interest in the connection. The Tribunal also recites the apparently key importance in this case of serious harm to the marine environment as a crucial, perhaps *the* crucial criterion or condition for provisional measures and it prescribes as provisional measures a prohibition of experimental programmes except by agreement of all three parties and annual catch limits (quotas), which include the concept of payback for catch taken over quota in 1999. The Tribunal's apparent willingness to base an edifice of provisional measures for possible harm to marine living resources on the language of Article 290 dealing with serious harm to the environment must be approached with some prudence since scientific views might differ about the underlying question. Besides, Article 194(5) of the [176] Convention,[10] which partly deals with the matter, is not unequivocal and the precautionary approach remains very general. I therefore hold that reliance on the preservation of rights formula of Article 290(1) must continue to be the main engine of this aspect of provisional measures.

19. In view of my earlier discussion, it becomes evident that the Tribunal has adopted the precautionary approach for the purposes of provisional measures in such a case as the present. In my view, adopting an *approach*, rather than a principle, appropriately imports a certain degree of flexibility and tends, though not dispositively,

---

[10] Article 194(5) of UNCLOS states that measures taken in accordance with Part XII, on protection and preservation of the marine environment, shall include those necessary to protect and preserve rare and fragile ecosystems as well as the habitat of depleted, threatened or endangered species and other forms of marine life. Impliedly, the ingredients of the marine environment include living resources. However it is evident that this does not dispose of the question posed in the text.

to underscore reticence about making premature pronouncements about desirable normative structures.

20. My conclusions so far are bolstered by such recent precedents as paragraph 17.21 of Agenda 21. It is also reinforced by various provisions in Articles 6 and 7 of the Code of Conduct for Responsible Fisheries of the Food and Agriculture Organization and Articles 5(c) and 6 of the Straddling Stocks Agreement, with detailed requirements for the application of the precautionary approach. In the present context, it matters little that the former is a voluntary Code and the latter is not yet in force.[11] With some cogency, these developments were judicially presaged by the International Court of Justice in 1974:

> [E]ven if the Court holds that Iceland's extension of its fishery limits is not opposable to the Applicant, this does not mean that the Applicant is under no obligation to Iceland with respect to fishing in disputed waters in the 12-mile to 50-mile zone. On the contrary, both States have an obligation to take full account of each other's rights and of any fishery waters. It is one of the advances in maritime international law, resulting from the intensification of fishing, that the former *laissez-faire* treatment of the living resources of the sea in the high seas has been replaced by a recognition of a duty to have due regard to the rights of other States and the needs of conservation for the benefit of all. Consequently, both Parties have the obligation to keep under review the fishery resources in the disputed waters and to examine together, in the light of scientific and other available information, the measures required for the conservation and development, and equitable exploitation, of those resources, taking into account any international agreement in force between them... (*Fisheries Jurisdiction* case, 1974 *ICJ Reports*, 3, 31, para. 72).[12]

[177] 21. The Tribunal has not followed the suggestion that has been made in this case that potential damage to fish stocks should not be treated as, e.g., damage by a dam. However, in my view, while the Tribunal has drawn its conclusions and based its prescriptions in the face of scientific uncertainty, it has not, *per se*, engaged in an explicit reversal of the burden of proof. I believe that, where possible, such matters are best reserved for the stage of the merits, i.e. for the arbitral tribunal.[13] The cautiousness of the Tribunal's Order thus becomes apparent. This is commendable, since this entire area is fraught with difficulty.

---

[11] These developments were foreshadowed by the 1982 resolution of the International Whaling Commission, imposing a ban on commercial whaling, and by the 1989 United Nations General Assembly resolution recommending modalities for introducing a ban on fishing with driftnets. However, I am not quite certain whether these two precedents are more consistent with the pretension of establishing a more comprehensive normative framework than I believe the approach connotes.

[12] See pp. 40–1 above.]

[13] In fact, in the area of fisheries management, such a decision should be made with great care, because of its possible impact on fishermen which, prima facie, could be unfair and unrealistic, unless the level of scientific certainty about probable damages increases.

Conclusion

22. It is ironic that these disagreements about science and natural resources should result in judicial proceedings when the Respondent consumes the overwhelming majority of the harvest of southern bluefin tuna and is therefore the ultimate financial resource. It might also appear to be regrettable that Japan has been made a party in its first international adjudication in over 90 years. However, this is not surprising, since the judicial resolution of disputes is now one of the most pervasive phenomena of contemporary international life. In fact, this is one of the most notable features of UNCLOS, which devotes three of its nine annexes to compulsory dispute resolution. It might be predicted that this trend will continue, and that devices like provisional measures and the precautionary notion will be frequently featured. It is nevertheless hoped that the parties will be able to craft an expeditious resolution of their problem.

SEPARATE OPINION BY JUDGE TULLIO TREVES (EXTRACT)

1. I concur with the Order of the Tribunal. The reasons set out in it in support of the urgency of the measures prescribed require, however, a few developments and clarifications.

[. . .]

[**178**] [. . .] 6. The fact that in Article 290, paragraph 1, of the UN Convention on the Law of the Sea provisional measures may be prescribed 'to prevent serious harm to the marine environment' and not only to preserve the respective rights of the parties, noted in paragraph 67 of the Order, is relevant for establishing the criterion for determining whether there is urgency in the qualitative sense whenever the measures, even though requested for the preservation of the rights of a party, concern rights whose preservation is necessary to prevent serious damage to the environment. The statement in paragraph 70 of the Order that 'the conservation of the living resources of the sea is an element in the protection and preservation of the marine environment' [**179**] must be seen in this light. On the basis of that statement, it seems reasonable to hold that the prevention of serious harm to the southern bluefish tuna stock is the appropriate standard for prescribing measures in the present case. This standard can apply to measures for the preservation of the rights of the parties because these rights concern the conservation of that very stock. This point is not entirely clear in the Order. Prevention of serious harm to the stock of southern bluefin tuna is mentioned, in paragraph 77, as the purpose of action to be taken by the parties, and not as the standard for prescribing provisional measures.

7. But are the requirements for temporal and qualitative urgency satisfied in the case submitted to the Tribunal?

8. The urgency needed in the present case does not, in my opinion, concern the danger of a collapse of the stock in the months which will elapse between the reading of the Order and the time when the arbitral tribunal will be in a position to prescribe provisional measures. This event, in light of scientific evidence, is uncertain and unlikely. The urgency concerns the stopping of a trend towards such collapse.

The measures prescribed by the Tribunal aim at stopping the deterioration in the southern bluefin tuna stock. Each step in such deterioration can be seen as 'serious harm' because of its cumulative effect towards the collapse of the stock. There is no controversy that such deterioration has been going on for years. However, as there is scientific uncertainty as to whether the situation of the stock has recently improved, the Tribunal must assess the urgency of the prescription of its measures in the light of prudence and caution. This approach, which may be called precautionary, is hinted at in the Order, in particular in paragraph 77. However, that paragraph refers it to the future conduct of the parties. While, of course, a precautionary approach by the parties in their future conduct is necessary, such precautionary approach, in my opinion, is necessary also in the assessment by the Tribunal of the urgency of the measures it might take. In the present case, it would seem to me that the requirement of urgency is satisfied only in the light of such precautionary approach. I regret that this is not stated explicitly in the Order.

9. I fully understand the reluctance of the Tribunal in taking a position as to whether the precautionary approach is a binding principle of customary international law. Other courts and tribunals, recently confronted with this question, have avoided to give [*sic*] an answer. In my opinion, in order to resort to the precautionary approach for assessing the urgency of the measures to be prescribed in the present case, it is not necessary to hold the view that this approach is dictated by a rule of customary international law. The precautionary approach can be seen as a logical consequence of the need to ensure that, when the arbitral tribunal decides on the merits, the factual situation has not [**180**] changed. In other words, a precautionary approach seems to me inherent in the very notion of provisional measures. It is not by chance that in some languages the very concept of 'caution' can be found in the terms used to designate provisional measures: for instance, in Italian, *misure cautelari*, in Portuguese, *medidas cautelares*, in Spanish, *medidas cautelares* or *medidas precautorias*.

10. It may be added that the Agreement for the Implementation of the Provisions of the United Nations Convention on the Law of the Sea of 10 December 1982 Relating to the Conservation and Management of Straddling Fish Stocks and Highly Migratory Fish Stocks, opened to signature on 5 December 1995, which envisages the very situations considered in the present case, brings support to some of the points made above. The agreement has not yet come into force and has been signed, but not ratified, by Australia, Japan and New Zealand. It seems, nonetheless, significant for evaluating the trends followed by international law. Even though this Agreement is independent from the United Nations Law of the Sea Convention, it has remarkable links with it. Article 4 provides that the Agreement 'shall be interpreted in the context and in a manner consistent with the [United Nations Law of the Sea] Convention', and Article 30 adopts *mutatis mutandis*, for the settlement of disputes concerning the interpretation and application of the Agreement, the provisions set out in Part XV of the United Nations Convention on the Law of the Sea.

11. Article 32, paragraph 2, of the Agreement of 5 December 1995 (a provision meant to apply *mutatis mutandis* [to] the dispute settlement provisions of the UN-CLOS and applicable 'without prejudice to article 290'), provides that the power of

prescribing provisional measures shall include that of prescribing them 'to prevent damage to the stocks in question'. Thus the standard set by the Straddling Stocks Agreement is even lower that that of 'serious harm' set out in Article 290, paragraph 1 of the Law of the Sea Convention. Moreover, the Agreement adopts and develops in detail the precautionary approach. In particular, Article 7 states, *inter alia*, that: 'The absence of adequate scientific information shall not be used as a reason for postponing or failing to take conservation and management measures' (paragraph 2).

SEPARATE OPINION BY JUDGE *AD HOC* SHEARER (EXTRACT)

[. . .]

Jurisdiction
[. . .]

[183] [. . .] The argument that the present dispute does not relate to the interpretation or application of the United Nations Convention on the Law of the Sea is, to my mind, highly artificial and without substance. The purpose of the CCSBT, which was signed by the three parties on 10 May 1993 and entered into force on 20 May 1994, is set in context by the preambular recitals, which include 'Paying due regard to the rights and obligations of the Parties under relevant principles of international law', and 'Noting the adoption of the United Nations Convention on the Law of the Sea in 1982'. The objective of the parties is more particularly declared to be 'to ensure, through appropriate management, the conservation and optimum utilisation of southern bluefin tuna' (Article 1). That the intention of the CCSBT was to give effect to the prospective obligations of the parties under the United Nations Convention on the Law of the Sea with respect to tuna as a highly migratory species is clear when the wording of Article 1 is compared with that of Article 64 of the United Nations Convention on the Law of the Sea. That Article provides:

> 1. The coastal State and other States whose nationals fish in the region for the highly migratory species listed in Annex I shall co-operate directly or through appropriate international organizations with a view to ensuring conservation and promoting the objective of optimum utilization of such species throughout the region, both within and beyond the exclusive economic zone . . .

Southern bluefin tuna is listed as a highly migratory species in Annex I to the Convention. The Commission for the Conservation of Southern Bluefin Tuna is an 'appropriate organization' for the purposes of Article 64, and also for the purposes of Articles 118 and 119, which relate to high seas fisheries in general. Although only Australia, Japan, and New Zealand are presently parties to the CCSBT, that convention is open to accession by other States. It has been remarked by at least two jurists of note that the CCSBT was 'the first agreement signed since the adoption of the Law of the Sea Convention to give effect to the principles of article 64'. (R. R. Churchill and A. V. Lowe, *The Law of the Sea* (3rd edn, 1999), 313–14.) It is to be noted that Australia,

Japan [**184**] and New Zealand ratified the United Nations Convention on the Law of the Sea shortly after the conclusion of the CCSBT (on 4 October 1994, 20 June 1996, and 19 July 1996, respectively).

It thus seems clear that a dispute between the parties regarding their duty to co-operate (other than, perhaps, a technical dispute regarding the powers and procedures of the Commission established under the CCSBT) is a dispute arising under the United Nations Convention on the Law of the Sea.

Once this conclusion has been reached, the separate dispute resolution procedures provided for by Article 16 of the CCSBT can be regarded as establishing a parallel but not exclusive dispute resolution procedure. The provisions of Section 1 of Part XV of the United Nations Convention on the Law of the Sea (Articles 279–85) do not give primacy to provisions such as Article 16 of the CCSBT. Even if they could be so regarded, as a dispute resolution procedure chosen by the parties under Article 280, there is no exclusion of any further procedure under Part XV of the Convention (Article 281). Nor does Article 282 constitute a bar. Under that Article dispute resolution procedures adopted by parties to a general, regional, or bilateral agreement shall be applied in lieu of procedures under Part XV, but only if such a procedure 'entails a binding decision'. As has already been noted, the provisions of Article 16 of the CCSBT are circular and do not entail a binding decision.[14]

[. . .]

[**185**] [. . .] *Provisional measures*
On the issue of provisional measures I wish to make three further remarks.

In the first place, I would have supported the prescription of provisional measures in stronger terms than those adopted. In particular I would have supported an order finding that Japan was prima facie in breach of its international obligations, under the CCSBT, the United Nations Convention on the Law of the Sea, and under customary international law, in conducting unilaterally experimental fishing programmes in 1998 and 1999 outside the catch limitations previously agreed between the parties. A direct order to Japan alone to suspend this programme would have been justified.

It seems to me, with respect, that the Tribunal, in its prescription of measures in this case, has behaved less as a court of law and more as an agency of diplomacy. While diplomacy, and a disposition to assist the parties in resolving their dispute amicably, have their proper place in the judicial settlement of international disputes, the Tribunal should not shrink from the consequences of proven facts.

The ineluctable fact proved before the Tribunal is that Japan, for the past two years, has been conducting an experimental fishing programme without the consent of the other two parties to the CCSBT in excess of its annual quota as last agreed by the Commission. 'Experimental fishing' is not a concept recognized, as such, either

---

[14] The word 'entail' means 'necessitate', or 'involve unavoidably'. The word used in the French text of Article 282 is 'aboutissant'. The verb 'aboutir' means 'avoir pour résultat' or 'arriver finalement'.

by the CCSBT or by the United Nations Convention on the Law of the Sea. The expression is not a term of art. It can be characterized, in theory, as one of a number of means of testing the recovery of fish stocks in various places and at various stages of their growth. To that extent it was within the powers of the Commission established under the CCSBT to approve an experimental fishing programme as part of its scientific studies aimed at obtaining more accurate data concerning southern bluefin tuna stocks. But agreement on experimental fishing in 1998 and 1999 was not forthcoming in view of the failure of the parties to agree upon a change to the previously agreed total annual catch (TAC) and the catches for experimental fishing that would be allowed in addition to the annual national allocations of the TAC.

Australia and New Zealand argued before the Tribunal that, in conducting a unilateral experimental fishing programme in 1998 and 1999 without the consent of Australia and New Zealand, Japan was in breach of its obligations, not only under the CCSBT, but also under [186] Articles 64, and 117–19 of the United Nations Convention on the Law of the Sea. These Articles, which relate to highly migratory species both within and beyond exclusive economic zones, and to fishing generally on the high seas, impose a duty to co-operate with a view to conservation and optimum utilization. In addition, Australia and New Zealand invoked the precautionary principle, arguing that that principle, in the face of scientific uncertainty regarding the southern bluefin tuna stocks, should be applied in limiting the catches of the parties to those last agreed when the Commission established under the CCSBT was still functioning effectively. Japan rejected the status of the precautionary principle as one of general international law, although it stated that it was as fully committed, in its own long-term interest, as Australia and New Zealand to the sustainable exploitation of the southern bluefin tuna fishery.

Japan described the present dispute as one of science, not of law. All three parties were agreed that the southern bluefin tuna stocks were at historically low levels. However, they differed markedly on whether the scientific data available showed an upward trend from that level. In Japan's view the scientific evidence showed a recovery of stocks and thus supported a higher TAC. In the view of Australia and New Zealand the scientific evidence did not show any such recovery and thus would not support any increase in the TAC for the present. It followed from that position that any experimental fishing programme that took significant quantities of fish above the agreed TAC constituted a threat to the stocks requiring urgent removal.

It is to be noted that the parties agreed on a TAC of 11,750 tonnes, with annual national catch allocations of 6,065, 5,265, and 420 tonnes to Japan, Australia, and New Zealand respectively, in 1989. This was at a time when the parties were co-operating without the benefit of a formal written agreement. After the three parties entered into the CCSBT in 1993 the annual TAC, and national allocations thereunder, set in 1989, were reaffirmed. No other TAC or national allocations have since been agreed. References in the Tribunal's order to these allocations 'as last agreed' by the parties are to be understood as references to the figures first set in 1989. Since the Commission under the CCSBT was established in 1994, Australia and New Zealand have taken a precautionary approach and have been unwilling to increase the TAC, despite Japan's arguments that the scientific evidence supported the sustainability of an increase. Because the Commission operates on the unanimity principle, no change in the TAC or national allocations could be effected. There is thus stalemate in the Commission on this issue.

The precautionary principle / approach
The difficulties of applying the precautionary principle to fisheries management have been well explained in a recent work of persuasive [187] authority. (Francisco Orrego Vicuña, *The Changing International Law of High Seas Fisheries* (1999).) There is a considerable literature devoted to the emergence of the precautionary principle in international law generally (see, for example, David Freestone and Ellen Hay (eds.), *The Precautionary Principle and International Law: The Challenge of Implementation* (1996)), but whether that principle can of itself be a mandate for action, or provide definitive answers to all questions of environmental policy, must be doubted. (See Philippe Sands, *Principles of Environmental Law* (1995), vol. I, 211–13.) As Professor Orrego Vicuña has remarked, 'Scientific uncertainty is normally the rule in fisheries management and a straightforward application of the precautionary principle would have resulted in the impossibility of proceeding with any activity relating to marine fisheries' (at p. 157). Hence, there is a preference by some to use the word 'approach' rather than 'principle'. That this is so, particularly in the case of fisheries management, is confirmed by the wording of Article 6 of the Agreement for the Implementation of the Provisions of the United Nations Convention on the Law of the Sea Relating to the Conservation and Management of Straddling Fish Stocks and Highly Migratory Fish Stocks, 4 December 1995, which obliges States Parties to apply 'the precautionary approach'. Annex II to the Agreement lays down 'guidelines' for the application of the precautionary approach. This Agreement, which has not yet entered into force, was signed by all three parties to the present dispute. It is thus an instrument of important reference to the parties in view of its probable future application to them, and in the meantime, at least, as a set of standards and approaches commanding broad international acceptance.

The Tribunal has not found it necessary to enter into a discussion of the precautionary principle / approach. However, I believe that the measures ordered by the Tribunal are rightly based upon considerations deriving from a precautionary approach.
[. . .]

DISSENTING OPINION OF JUDGE VUKAS (EXTRACT)

[. . .]
[**193**][. . .] 6. In conclusion, I would like to restate my main reasons for not agreeing to the provisional measures requested by Australia and New Zealand as being urgent:
(a) With or without a measure prescribed by the Tribunal, the experimental fishing programme of Japan in 1999 ends in a few days.

(b) The evidence submitted by the Applicants has failed to convince me that the forthcoming months are decisive for the survival of the southern bluefin tuna. However, it is not only the evidence submitted by the parties that brought me to that conclusion. Even more convincing is the attitude of all those who fish for southern bluefin tuna. They do not convince me that they are concerned with the situation of the stock. Notwithstanding their pretended concern about the future of the stock, none of them intends to reduce the pace of its regular catch. Not only Japan, but Australia and New Zealand have also not expressed their intention to reduce their regular catch in the remaining months of 1999. The same is the situation with the States which are not parties to the 1993 Convention.

(c) Japan's request[s] for the prescription of two provisional measures are only counter-requests in case prima facie jurisdiction is found to exist. Japan denies the existence of [the] Tribunal's jurisdiction, and it does not claim that the measures it proposes are urgent.

On the basis of the above-mentioned, I have to conclude that no 'urgency of the situation' in respect of the southern bluefin tuna stock has been confirmed, and that, consequentially, there are no 'rights of the parties to the dispute' (Article 290, paragraph 1) which should be preserved by the provisional measures requested from the Tribunal by New Zealand and Australia. Any request for the prescription of provisional measures the parties may have at a later stage, can be addressed to the arbitral tribunal to be constituted in the forthcoming months in accordance with Annex VII.

[Report: 117 *ILR* 148]

The MOX Plant Case
(Ireland *v.* United Kingdom)[1]

International Tribunal for the Law of the Sea, Hamburg

3 December 2001 (Chandrasekhara Rao, *President*; Nelson, *Vice-President*;
Caminos, Marotta Rangel, Yankov, Yamamoto, Kolodkin, Park, Bamela Engo,
Mensah, Akl, Anderson, Vukas, Wolfrum, Treves, Marsit, Eiriksson, Ndiaye,
Jesus and Xu, *Judges*; Székely, *Judge* ad hoc)

*Waters – Irish Sea – protection of the marine environment – United Nations
Convention on the Law of the Sea, 1982 – environmental effects of the MOX plant
and of international movements of radioactive materials – obligation to cooperate in taking measures to protect and preserve the Irish Sea – precautionary
principle*

*Powers and procedures of tribunals – provisional measures – Article 290(5)
of Convention – conditions to be satisfied for granting provisional measures under Article 290(5) – whether* prima facie *basis for the jurisdiction of the Annex VII arbitral tribunal – whether urgent necessity for prescription of provisional measures pending the constitution of Annex VII arbitral tribunal – irreparable prejudice – serious harm to the marine environment – requirement of urgency not satisfied – power of International*

---

[1] Ireland initiated two separate arbitrations against the United Kingdom in relation to the approval
of the MOX Plant. The first arbitration, commenced on 15 June 2001, resulted in a Final Award
of the OSPAR Tribunal of 2 July 2003 and is reported at p. 552 below. The second arbitration,
commenced on 25 October 2001, resulted in the Arbitral Tribunal's Order No. 3 of 24 June 2003
and Order No. 4 of 14 November 2003, and is reported at p. 521 below. On 14 November 2003, the
Arbitral Tribunal suspended proceedings until judgment had been given by the European Court of
Justice in proceedings instituted by the European Community against Ireland or until the Tribunal
otherwise determined (see p. 539 below). This Order of the International Tribunal for the Law
of the Sea resulted from Ireland's request for provisional measures filed on 9 November 2001 in
connection with the second arbitration.

Ireland was represented in these proceedings by David J. O'Hagan, Chief State Solicitor, as Agent;
Michael McDowell SC, Attorney-General; Eoghan Fitzsimons SC, Philippe Sands and Vaughan
Lowe, as Counsel and Advocates. The United Kingdom was represented by Michael Wood CMG,
as Agent; Lord Goldsmith QC, Attorney-General; Richard Plender QC, Daniel Bethlehem and
Samuel Wordsworth, as Counsel.

Tribunal to prescribe provisional measures different in whole or in part from those requested

Jurisdiction – Article 282 of Convention – whether Ireland's submission of dispute under Article 32 of OSPAR Convention, 1992, precludes recourse to Annex VII arbitral tribunal – whether Ireland's public intention to initiate separate proceedings under the EC Treaty and the Euratom Treaty precludes recourse to Annex VII arbitral tribunal – Article 282 concerned with general, regional or bilateral agreements providing for the settlement of disputes concerning the interpretation and application of Convention – Article 282 not applicable to the dispute submitted to the Annex VII arbitral tribunal

SUMMARY   *The facts*   On 25 October 2001, Ireland requested that an arbitral tribunal be constituted in accordance with Annex VII of the United Nations Convention on the Law of the Sea, 1982 ('the Convention'). Ireland claimed that the United Kingdom had violated obligations under the Convention by granting approval for the operation of the Mixed Oxide Plant ('the MOX plant') at the Sellafield site on the north-west coast of England. The MOX plant made mixed oxide fuel from plutonium and uranium oxides. The United Kingdom had decided on 3 October 2001 that the manufacture of MOX fuel was justified in accordance with the requirements of Article 6(1) of Directive 96/29/Euratom.

Ireland claimed that the United Kingdom had violated three sets of obligations under both the Convention and principles of general international law on the interpretation of the Convention:

(a)   obligations to cooperate with Ireland in taking measures to protect and preserve the Irish Sea (Articles 123 and 197 of the Convention);

(b)   obligations to carry out a prior environmental assessment of the effects on the environment of the MOX plant and of international movements of radioactive materials associated with the operation of the plant (Article 206 of the Convention); and

(c)   obligations to protect the marine environment of the Irish Sea, including by taking all necessary measures to prevent, reduce and control further radioactive pollution of the Irish Sea, including releases of radioactive materials and/or wastes from the MOX plant and/or international movements associated with the MOX plant resulting from terrorist acts (Articles 192 and 193, 194, 207, 211, 212 and 213 of the Convention).[2]

---

[2]   The relevant provisions of the Statement of Claim are set out at paragraph 26 of the Order of the International Tribunal for the Law of the Sea made on 3 December 2001 ('Order') (see p. 427–8 below).

On 9 November 2001, Ireland requested that the International Tribunal for the Law of the Sea ('the Tribunal') prescribe provisional measures of protection[3] pending the constitution of the arbitral tribunal under Article 290(5) of the Convention.[4]

The United Kingdom opposed the requests and contended, *inter alia*, that Ireland had failed to make out a *prima facie* case that the action that the United Kingdom proposed to take would, even in the long term, infringe the rights of Ireland under the Convention or cause serious harm to the marine environment. The United Kingdom contended also that there was no urgent necessity for the Tribunal to prescribe provisional measures pending the constitution of the Annex VII arbitral tribunal since there were no steps to be taken or authorised by the United Kingdom in the intervening period which might arguably prejudice Ireland's rights under the Convention

In addition, the United Kingdom contended that there was no basis for the proposed Annex VII arbitral tribunal to exercise jurisdiction in view of Article 282 of the Convention,[5] since the main elements of the dispute were governed by the compulsory dispute settlement procedures contained in the Convention for the Protection of the Marine Environment of the North-East Atlantic ('OSPAR Convention') or the 1957 Treaty Establishing the European Atomic Energy Community ('Euratom Treaty') or the Treaty Establishing the European Community ('EC Treaty'). In this respect, the United Kingdom referred to the decision by Ireland to commence arbitration proceedings under the OSPAR Convention in June 2001, in order to gain access to reports on the economic and environmental aspects of the MOX plant commissioned by the United Kingdom.[6] Ireland maintained that the arbitral proceedings under the OSPAR Convention concerned Article 9 of that Convention only, and

---

[3] The measures requested are set out in paragraph 27 of the Order (see pp. 428–9 below).

[4] Article 290(5) of the Convention provided in relevant part that: 'Pending the constitution of an arbitral tribunal to which a dispute is being submitted under this section, any court or tribunal agreed upon by the parties or, failing such agreement within two weeks from the date of the request for provisional measures, the International Tribunal for the Law of the Sea . . . may prescribe, modify or revoke provisional measures in accordance with this article if it considers that *prima facie* the tribunal which is to be constituted would have jurisdiction and that the urgency of the situation so requires . . . '

[5] Article 282 of the Convention provided that: 'If the States Parties which are parties to a dispute concerning the interpretation or application of this Convention have agreed, through a general, regional or bilateral agreement or otherwise, that such dispute shall, at the request of any party to the dispute, be submitted to a procedure that entails a binding decision, that procedure shall apply in lieu of the procedures provided for in this Part, unless the parties to the dispute otherwise agree . . . '

[6] A summary of these proceedings and the Final Award of the OSPAR Tribunal are published in this volume at p. 552 below.

that the substantive issues of legality of the United Kingdom's conduct in relation to the MOX plant were not in issue in the OSPAR arbitration.

Held by the International Tribunal for the Law of the Sea   (1)   Before prescribing provisional measures, the Tribunal had to satisfy itself that there was a *prima facie* basis for the jurisdiction of the arbitral tribunal to be constituted under Annex VII of the Convention. That requirement was satisfied in the present case.

(a)   The dispute concerned the interpretation and application of the provisions of the Convention. Only the dispute settlement provisions under the Convention were relevant to the dispute between the Parties. Article 282 of the Convention was not applicable to the dispute.

(b)   The dispute settlement procedures under the OSPAR Convention, the EC Treaty and the Euratom Treaty dealt with disputes concerning the interpretation or application of those agreements only, and did not preclude the Parties from invoking the dispute settlement provisions of the Convention.

(c)   Ireland and the United Kingdom had engaged in an exchange of views up to the submission of the dispute to the Annex VII arbitral tribunal. Ireland had submitted the dispute to the Annex VII arbitral tribunal only after the United Kingdom had indicated that it would not immediately suspend the authorisation of the MOX plant. A State Party was not obliged to continue with an exchange of views when it had concluded that the possibilities of reaching agreement had been exhausted.

(2)   The evidence before the Tribunal did not show either that irreparable prejudice would occur to any rights of Ireland or that serious harm to the marine environment would occur solely as a result of the commissioning of the MOX plant before the constitution of the Annex VII arbitral tribunal.

(3)   In the circumstances of the case, the provisional measures requested by Ireland were not required as a matter of urgency in the short period before the constitution of the Annex VII arbitral tribunal.

(4)   Prudence and caution required that Ireland and the United Kingdom cooperate in exchanging information concerning risks or effects of the operation of the MOX plant and in devising ways to deal with those risks or effects.

(5)   Under Article 89(5) of the Rules, the Tribunal could prescribe measures different in whole or in part from those requested.

Accordingly, the Tribunal ordered (unanimously)   That Ireland and the United Kingdom cooperate and enter into consultations forthwith in order to:

(a)   exchange further information with regard to possible consequences
       for the Irish Sea arising out of the commissioning of the MOX plant;
(b)   monitor risks or effects of the operation of the MOX plant for the
       Irish Sea;
(c)   devise, as appropriate, measures to prevent pollution of the marine
       environment which might result from the operation of the MOX
       plant.

*Joint Declaration of Judges Caminos, Yamamoto, Park, Akl, Marsit, Eiriksson
and Jesus*   The present case was characterised by an almost complete
lack of cooperation between Ireland and the United Kingdom with
respect to the environmental impact of the planned operations, and a
lack of agreement on the scientific evidence on the environmental consequences of the operation of the MOX plant. In these circumstances, the
most effective measure that the Tribunal could have adopted would have
been to require the Parties to cooperate forthwith in accordance with
fundamental principles of the Convention and general international law.

Separate Opinion of Vice-President Nelson   Articles 281 and 282 of the
Convention contained the crucial test as to whether there could be any
resort to the compulsory procedures set out in section 2 of Part XV of the
Convention. The Tribunal was correct to conclude that Article 282 was
not applicable to the dispute submitted to the Annex VII arbitral tribunal.

Separate Opinion of Judge Mensah   The Tribunal was correct to pay
little attention to the evidence on the existence or nature of long-term
potential risks of damage to Ireland or harm to the marine environment
as a result of the commissioning of the MOX plant. The Tribunal could
not act unless satisfied that there might be irreparable prejudice before
the constitution of the Annex VII arbitral tribunal. This requirement
applied to both procedural rights and the substantive rights under the
Convention to which Ireland referred in its claims.

Separate Opinion of Judge Anderson   The Tribunal should have disposed
of the case by declining the request for provisional measures and encouraging, rather than prescribing, further contacts between the Parties on
matters of immediate concern to Ireland.

Separate Opinion of Judge Wolfrum   (1)   An agreement for the purposes of Article 282 to submit a dispute concerning the interpretation
or application of the Convention to other institutions could not be presumed. Such an intention had to be expressed explicitly in the relevant
agreement.

(2)   There was no room for the application of the precautionary principle for the prescription of provisional measures in the present case
even if it were accepted that it formed part of customary international

law. The reasoning of the Order in the *Southern Bluefin Tuna Cases*[7] was not applicable as the situation there was different from that in the present case.

Separate Opinion of Judge Treves   (1)   The interpretation of Article 282 adopted by the Tribunal was justifiable in light of the function of this provision in the context of Part XV of the Convention. It would be incompatible with the purpose of Article 282 seen in the context of the Convention to allow a dispute concerning the interpretation of the Convention to be left to be dealt with in separate parts by different courts or tribunals and taken away from the only tribunal competent to deal with it in its entirety.

(2)   In deciding not to prescribe the provisional measures requested by Ireland, it appeared that the Tribunal drew a distinction between the substantive rights invoked by Ireland not to be polluted or exposed to the risk of pollution, and the procedural rights relating to cooperation and information. While the Tribunal did not find the requirement of urgency to be satisfied as far as the former rights were concerned, it implicitly considered it as satisfied in regard to the latter.

Separate Opinion of Judge Jesus   The interpretation of Article 282 adopted by the Tribunal was too narrow since it would eliminate some cases whereby the choice of procedure under that article might be applicable. The OSPAR Convention did not apply in the present case since the issues covered by that convention were different from and narrower than those brought by Ireland before the Annex VII arbitral tribunal.

Separate Opinion of Judge ad hoc *Székely*   (1)   The Tribunal had behaved less as a court of law than as an agency of diplomacy. The Tribunal should have ordered the provisional measures sought by Ireland.

(2)   The Tribunal never fully appreciated the evidence adduced by Ireland in support of its request for provisional measures. The Tribunal should have applied the precautionary principle in the face of scientific uncertainty regarding the effects of the operation of the MOX plant. Had it done so, the application of that principle would have led the Tribunal to grant the provisional measures requested by Ireland regarding the suspension of the commissioning of the MOX plant.

There follows

Order of International Tribunal for the Law of the Sea on Request for Provisional Measures, 3 December 2001[8] (extract)   427

---

[7] The *Southern Bluefin Tuna Cases* are reproduced in this volume at p. 393 above.

[8] Although not reproduced in this volume, the separate opinion of Vice-President Nelson can be found at 126 *ILR* 279 and the separate opinion of Judge Jesus can be found at 126 *ILR* 301.

Order of International Tribunal for the Law of the Sea on Request for Provisional Measures, 3 December 2001 (extract)

[. . .]

[**265**] [. . .] 1. *Whereas* Ireland and the United Kingdom are States Parties to the Convention;

2. *Whereas*, on 9 November 2001, Ireland filed with the Registry of the Tribunal by facsimile a Request for the prescription of provisional measures under article 290, paragraph 5, of the Convention 'in the dispute concerning the MOX plant, international movements of radioactive materials, and the protection of the marine environment of the Irish Sea' between Ireland and the United Kingdom;

[. . .]

[**268**] [. . .] 26. *Whereas*, in the Notification and Statement of Claim of 25 October 2001, Ireland requested the arbitral tribunal to be constituted under Annex VII (hereinafter 'the Annex VII arbitral tribunal') to adjudge and declare:

1) That the United Kingdom has breached its obligations under Articles 192 and 193 and/or Article 194 and/or Article 207 and/or Articles 211 and 213 of UNCLOS in relation to the authorisation of the MOX plant, including by failing to take the necessary measures to prevent, reduce and control pollution of the marine environment of the Irish Sea from (1) intended discharges of radioactive materials and/or wastes from the MOX plant, and/or (2) accidental releases of radioactive materials and/or wastes from the MOX plant and/or international movements associated [with] the MOX plant, and/or (3) releases of radioactive materials and/or wastes from the MOX plant and/or international movements associated [with] the MOX plant [. . .] resulting from terrorist act;

2) That the United Kingdom has breached its obligations under Articles 192 and 193 and/or Article 194 and/or Article 207 and/or Articles 211 and 213 of UNCLOS in relation to the authorisation of the MOX plant by failing (1) properly or at all to assess the risk of terrorist attack on the MOX plant and international movements of radioactive material associated with the plant, and/or (2) properly or at all to prepare a comprehensive response strategy or plan to prevent, contain and respond to terrorist attack on the MOX plant and international movements of radioactive waste associated with the plant;

3) That the United Kingdom has breached its obligations under Articles 123 and 197 of UNCLOS in relation to the authorisation of the MOX plant, [**269**] and has failed to cooperate with Ireland in the protection of the marine environment of the Irish Sea *inter alia* by refusing to share information with Ireland and/or refusing to carry out a proper environmental assessment of the impacts on the marine environment of the MOX plant and associated activities and/or proceeding to authorise the operation of the MOX plant whilst proceedings relating to the settlement of a dispute on access to information were still pending;

4) That the United Kingdom has breached its obligations under Article 206 of UNCLOS in relation to the authorisation of the MOX plant, including by

   (a) failing, by its 1993 Environmental Statement, properly and fully to assess the potential effects of the operation of the MOX plant on the marine environment of the Irish Sea; and/or

   (b) failing, since the publication of its 1993 Environmental Statement, to assess the potential effects of the operation of the MOX plant on the marine environment by reference to the factual and legal developments which have arisen since 1993, and in particular since 1998; and/or

   (c) failing to assess the potential effects on the marine environment of the Irish Sea of international movements of radioactive materials to be transported to and from the MOX plant; and/or

   (d) failing to assess the risk of potential effects on the marine environment of the Irish Sea arising from terrorist act or acts on the MOX plant and/or on international movements of radioactive material to and from the MOX plant.

5) That the United Kingdom shall refrain from authorizing or failing to prevent (a) the operation of the MOX plant and/or (b) international movements of radioactive materials into and out of the United Kingdom related to the operation of the MOX plant or any preparatory or other activities associated with the operation of the MOX until such time as (1) there has been carried out a proper assessment of the environmental impact of the operation of the MOX plant as well as related international movements of radioactive materials, and (2) it is demonstrated that the operation of the MOX plant and related international movements of radioactive materials will result in the deliberate discharge of no radioactive materials, including wastes, directly or indirectly into the marine environment of the Irish Sea, and (3) there has been agreed and adopted jointly with Ireland a comprehensive strategy or plan to prevent, contain and respond to terrorist attack on the MOX plant and international movements of radioactive waste associated with the plant;

6) That the United Kingdom pays Ireland's costs of the proceedings;

27. *Whereas* the provisional measures requested by Ireland in the Request to the Tribunal dated 9 November 2001 were as follows:

[**270**] (1) that the United Kingdom immediately suspend the authorisation of the MOX plant dated 3 October 2001, alternatively take such other measures as are necessary to prevent with immediate effect the operation of the MOX plant;

(2) that the United Kingdom immediately ensure that there are no movements into or out of the waters over which it has sovereignty or exercises sovereign rights of any radioactive substances or materials or wastes which are associated with the operation of, or activities preparatory to the operation of, the MOX plant;

(3) that the United Kingdom ensure that no action of any kind is taken which might aggravate, extend or render more difficult of solution the dispute submitted to the Annex VII tribunal (Ireland hereby agreeing itself to act so as not to aggravate, extend or render more difficult of solution that dispute); and

(4) that the United Kingdom ensure that no action is taken which might prejudice the rights of Ireland in respect of the carrying out of any decision on the merits that the Annex VII tribunal may render (Ireland likewise will take no action of that kind in relation to the United Kingdom);

[. . .]

[**271**] [. . .] 30. *Whereas*, at the public sitting held on 20 November 2001, the United Kingdom presented its final submissions as follows:

The United Kingdom requests the International Tribunal for the Law of the Sea to:

(1) reject Ireland's request for provisional measures;

(2) order Ireland to bear the United Kingdom's costs in these proceedings;

31. *Considering* that, in accordance with article 287 of the Convention, Ireland has, on 25 October 2001, instituted proceedings before the Annex VII arbitral tribunal against the United Kingdom 'in the dispute concerning the MOX plant, international movements of radioactive materials, and the protection of the marine environment of the Irish Sea';

32. *Considering* that Ireland on 25 October 2001 notified the United Kingdom of the submission of the dispute to the Annex VII arbitral tribunal and of the Request for provisional measures;

33. *Considering* that, on 9 November 2001, after the expiry of the time-limit of two weeks provided for in article 290, paragraph 5, of the Convention, and pending the constitution of the Annex VII arbitral tribunal, Ireland submitted to the Tribunal a Request for provisional measures;

[. . .]

[**275**] [. . .] 63. *Considering* that, in accordance with article 290, paragraph 1, of the Convention, the Tribunal may prescribe provisional measures to preserve the respective rights of the parties to the dispute or to prevent serious harm to the marine environment;

64. *Considering* that, according to article 290, paragraph 5, of the Convention, provisional measures may be prescribed pending the constitution of the Annex VII arbitral tribunal if the Tribunal considers that the urgency of the situation so requires in the sense that action prejudicial to the rights of either party or causing serious harm to the marine environment is likely to be taken before the constitution of the Annex VII arbitral tribunal;

65. *Considering* that the Tribunal must, therefore, decide whether provisional measures are required pending the constitution of the Annex VII arbitral tribunal;

66. *Considering* that, in accordance with article 290, paragraph 5, of the Convention, the Annex VII arbitral tribunal, once constituted, may modify, revoke or affirm any provisional measures prescribed by the Tribunal;

67. *Considering* that Ireland contends that its rights under certain provisions of the Convention, in particular articles 123, 192 to 194, 197, 206, 207, 211, 212 and 213 thereof, will be irrevocably violated if the MOX plant commences its operations before the United Kingdom fulfils its duties under the Convention;

68. *Considering* that Ireland contends further that once plutonium is introduced into the MOX plant and it commences operations some discharges into the marine environment will occur with irreversible consequences;

69. *Considering* that Ireland contends further that, if the plant becomes operational, the danger of radioactive leaks and emissions, whether arising from the operation of the plant, or resulting from industrial accidents, terrorist attacks, or other causes, would be greatly magnified;

[276] 70. *Considering* that Ireland argues that the commissioning of the plant is, in practical terms, itself a near-irreversible step and it is not possible to return to the position that existed before the commissioning of the MOX plant simply by ceasing to feed plutonium into the system;

71. *Considering* that Ireland argues that the precautionary principle places the burden on the United Kingdom to demonstrate that no harm would arise from discharges and other consequences of the operation of the MOX plant, should it proceed, and that this principle might usefully inform the assessment by the Tribunal of the urgency of the measures it is required to take in respect of the operation of the MOX plant;

72. *Considering* that the United Kingdom contends that it has adduced evidence to establish that the risk of pollution, if any, from the operation of the MOX plant would be infinitesimally small;

73. *Considering* that the United Kingdom maintains that the commissioning of the MOX plant on or around 20 December 2001 will not, even arguably, cause serious harm to the marine environment or irreparable prejudice to the rights of Ireland, in the period prior to the constitution of the Annex VII arbitral tribunal or at all;

74. *Considering* that the United Kingdom contends that neither the commissioning of the MOX plant nor the introduction of plutonium into the system is irreversible, although decommissioning would present the operator of the plant with technical

and financial difficulties, if Ireland were to be successful in its claim before the Annex VII arbitral tribunal;

75. *Considering* that the United Kingdom argues that Ireland has failed to supply proof that there will be either irreparable damage to the rights of Ireland or serious harm to the marine environment resulting from the operation of the MOX plant and that, on the facts of this case, the precautionary principle has no application;

76. *Considering* that the United Kingdom states that the manufacture of MOX fuel presents negligible security risks and it has in place very extensive security precautions in terms of the protection of the Sellafield site;

77. *Considering* that the United Kingdom states that it hopes to reach agreement with Ireland on the constitution of the Annex VII arbitral tribunal within a short space of time;

78. *Considering* that, at the public sitting held on 20 November 2001, the United Kingdom has stated that 'there will be no additional [277] marine transports of radioactive material either to or from Sellafield as a result of the commissioning of the MOX plant';

79. *Considering* that at the same sitting the United Kingdom stated further that 'there will be no export of MOX fuel from the plant until summer 2002' and that 'there is to be no import to the THORP plant of spent nuclear fuel pursuant to contracts for conversion to the MOX plant within that period either' and clarified that the word 'summer' should be read as 'October';

80. *Considering* that the Tribunal places on record the assurances given by the United Kingdom as specified in paragraphs 78 and 79;

81. *Considering* that, in the circumstances of this case, the Tribunal does not find that the urgency of the situation requires the prescription of the provisional measures requested by Ireland, in the short period before the constitution of the Annex VII arbitral tribunal;

82. *Considering,* however, that the duty to cooperate is a fundamental principle in the prevention of pollution of the marine environment under Part XII of the Convention and general international law and that rights arise therefrom which the Tribunal may consider appropriate to preserve under article 290 of the Convention;

83. *Considering* that, in accordance with article 89, paragraph 5, of the Rules, the Tribunal may prescribe measures different in whole or in part from those requested;

84. *Considering* that, in the view of the Tribunal, prudence and caution require that Ireland and the United Kingdom cooperate in exchanging information concerning risks or effects of the operation of the MOX plant and in devising ways to deal with them, as appropriate;

85. *Considering* that Ireland and the United Kingdom should each ensure that no action is taken which might aggravate or extend the dispute submitted to the Annex VII arbitral tribunal;

86. *Considering* that, pursuant to article 95, paragraph 1, of the Rules, each party is required to submit to the Tribunal a report and information on compliance with any provisional measures prescribed;

87. *Considering* that it may be necessary for the Tribunal to request further information from the parties on the implementation of provisional measures and that it is appropriate that the President be authorized to request such information in accordance with article 95, paragraph 2, of the Rules;

88. *Considering* that, in the present case, the Tribunal sees no need to depart from the general rule, as set out in article 34 of its Statute, that each party shall bear its own costs;

[278] 89. *For these reasons,*

THE TRIBUNAL,

1. Unanimously,

Prescribes, pending a decision by the Annex VII arbitral tribunal, the following provisional measure under article 290, paragraph 5, of the Convention:

> Ireland and the United Kingdom shall cooperate and shall, for this purpose, enter into consultations forthwith in order to:
> (a)   exchange further information with regard to possible consequences for the Irish Sea arising out of the commissioning of the MOX plant;
> (b)   monitor risks or the effects of the operation of the MOX plant for the Irish Sea;
> (c)   devise, as appropriate, measures to prevent pollution of the marine environment which might result from the operation of the MOX plant.

2. Unanimously,

Decides that Ireland and the United Kingdom shall each submit the initial report referred to in article 95, paragraph 1, of the Rules not later than 17 December 2001, and *authorizes* the President of the Tribunal to request such further reports and information as he may consider appropriate after that date.

3. Unanimously,

Decides that each party shall bear its own costs.

[. . .]

JOINT DECLARATION OF JUDGES CAMINOS, YAMAMOTO, PARK, AKL, MARSIT, EIRIKSSON AND JESUS

The dispute between Ireland and the United Kingdom as it appears before the Tribunal is characterized by an almost total lack of agreement on the scientific evidence with respect to the possible consequences of the operation of the MOX plant on the marine environment of the Irish Sea.

[279] Under these circumstances of scientific uncertainty, the Tribunal might have been expected to have followed the path it took in the *Southern Bluefin Tuna Cases* to prescribe a measure preserving the existing situation. In its wisdom, it did not do so. It decided, in the circumstances of the case, that, in the short period before the

constitution of an arbitral tribunal under Annex VII to the United Nations Convention on the Law of the Sea, the urgency of the situation did not require it to lay down, as binding legal obligations, the measures requested by Ireland.

We have supported this decision. The circumstances of the case which have influenced us in this regard include, first, as for Ireland's request that marine transport associated with the plant cease, that the United Kingdom has made assurances that there would be no such transport in the relevant period. Second, with respect to Ireland's request to prevent the commissioning of the plant, we are influenced by the United Kingdom statement that the commissioning of the plant and the introduction of plutonium into the system is not irreversible.

More importantly, our position is a response to another characteristic of the dispute as presented to the Tribunal, that is, the almost complete lack of cooperation between the Governments of Ireland and the United Kingdom with respect to the environmental impact of the planned operations. It is clear that this state of affairs has its origin in a long-standing dispute with respect to other activities at the Sellafield site, but those activities are not before the Tribunal.

The Tribunal has identified the duty to cooperate as a fundamental principle in the regime of the prevention of pollution of the marine environment under Part XII of the Convention and general international law. Against the background of that duty, we regard the most effective measure that the Tribunal could have adopted was to require the parties to cooperate forthwith. It is not, we trust, an idle hope that the results of the consultations prescribed will include a common understanding of the scientific evidence and a common appreciation of the measures which must be taken with respect to the plant to prevent harm to the marine environment.

SEPARATE OPINION OF JUDGE MENSAH (EXTRACT)

[285] [. . .] These considerations lead me to the view that the Tribunal acted correctly in not concentrating too much attention on the existence or nature of 'long-term' potential risks of damage to Ireland or harm to the marine environment as a result of the commissioning of the MOX plant. On that issue, there is a clear and palpable difference of opinion between the parties, and the evidence or lack of evidence is such that reasonable minds can and will probably differ as to the conclusions to be drawn. But, in my view, it was not necessary or even appropriate for this Tribunal to decide on that issue. The Annex VII arbitral tribunal will have ample opportunity (and hopefully fuller and more relevant information) to consider and take a view on the matter; as it is its exclusive competence to do. And, in any case, it is important to note that whatever conclusion the Tribunal might have reached on the matter could be modified or rejected by that arbitral tribunal. In the present case, all that was required of the Tribunal was to consider whether any rights of Ireland or the United Kingdom or any threat of serious harm to the marine environment needed protection in the period prior to the composition of the Annex VII arbitral tribunal.

On that point, I agree with the conclusion that the evidence before the Tribunal does not suffice to show either that irreversible prejudice might occur to any rights of Ireland or that serious harm to the marine environment might occur, solely as a result of the commissioning of the MOX plant, *in the period between now and the constitution of the Annex VII arbitral tribunal*. In coming to this conclusion I have taken into account the information that the constitution of the Annex VII arbitral tribunal is expected to be completed before the beginning of the spring of 2002, as well as the commitment made by the United Kingdom that there will be no maritime transport of radioactive material before the summer of 2002 (paragraphs 78 and 79 of the Order).

[286] [. . .] As far as the substantive right of Ireland not to have its marine environment polluted as a result of the commissioning and operation of the MOX plant is concerned, the evidence presented is, in my view, not sufficient to show that the commissioning of the MOX plant on 20 December would, in itself, result in irreparable damage to Ireland before the constitution of the Annex VII arbitral tribunal. Both parties appear to agree in their submissions, that neither the authorization of the MOX plant nor its commissioning is technically irreversible. Indeed, the evidence suggests that it is the United Kingdom that runs a greater risk if it goes ahead with commissioning and is later ordered by the Annex VII arbitral tribunal to take other action in connection with the commissioning or operation of the plant.

But, while I share the Tribunal's conclusion that, in the circumstances of this case, the urgency of the situation does not require the prescription of the provisional measures requested by Ireland, I would have felt more comfortable if the Tribunal had indicated in clear and specific terms the reason for this conclusion. As I see it, the reason is that it is not reasonable to believe that any pollution of Ireland's marine environment might occur in the period between the issue of the Order of this Tribunal and the constitution of the Annex VII arbitral tribunal, sometime before the spring of 2002.

With regard to the 'procedural rights' (co-operation and consultation) which Ireland claims have been violated by the United Kingdom, I agree with the Tribunal that some at least of these are 'rights' that may 'be appropriate for protection' by provisional measures under article 290 of the Convention (paragraph 82 of the Order). However, I do not find that any irreparable prejudice to Ireland has occurred or might occur before the constitution of the arbitral tribunal. In my view none of the violations of the procedural rights arising from the duty to co-operate or to consult or to undertake appropriate environmental assessments are [287] 'irreversible' in the sense that they cannot effectively be enforced against the United Kingdom by decision of the Annex VII arbitral tribunal, if the arbitral tribunal were to conclude that any such violations have in fact occurred. For example, it would be within the competence of the Annex VII arbitral tribunal to order the United Kingdom either to decommission the MOX plant altogether or to go back to the drawing board and take action to comply with any applicable procedural requirements that the arbitral tribunal finds should have been followed before giving final authorization for the MOX plant. Thus, in my view, the violations of the 'procedural rights' about which Ireland complains are capable of being made good by reparations that the arbitral tribunal may consider appropriate. I regret that the Tribunal did not consider it necessary to deal explicitly and directly with this aspect of the matter.

SEPARATE OPINION OF JUDGE ANDERSON (EXTRACT)

I have voted in favour of the Order because I concur fully with the reasoning of the Tribunal on the main substantive issues. In particular, I endorse the clear conclusion in paragraph 81 of the Order that

> in the circumstances of this case, the Tribunal does not find that the urgency of the situation requires the prescription of the provisional measures requested by Ireland in the short time before the constitution of the arbitral tribunal.

However, I consider that the Order goes too far in two respects (namely, jurisdiction and the dispositif), and not far enough in its findings regarding two other issues (namely, the preservation of rights and the prevention of serious harm to the marine environment). In accordance with article 8, paragraph 6, of the Resolution on the Internal Judicial Practice of the Tribunal, this separate opinion concentrates on these four points of difference with the Order.

[...]

[289] [...] *3. The first request of the Applicant (paragraphs 65 to 74 of the Order)*
In its principal submission, the Applicant sought the equivalent of an injunction restraining *pendente lite* the respondent from allowing the MOX plant to commence operations and production on 20 December [290] 2001 – a request which the Tribunal clearly did not accept. It is common ground that the plant is situated on the territory of the United Kingdom and thus under the sovereignty of the United Kingdom. In the terms of the draft articles on Prevention of Transboundary Harm from Hazardous Activities recently adopted by the International Law Commission, the plant will conduct 'activities not prohibited by international law'.[9] In the terms of the Convention on the Law of the Sea, the plant falls to be considered in the context of article 193, which reads:

> States have the sovereign right to exploit their natural resources pursuant to their environmental policies and in accordance with their duty to protect and preserve the marine environment.

The operation of the plant involves a dry process, but, as an indirect result of normal cleaning work, it is expected to result in the introduction of some very small amounts of liquid and gaseous substances and energy into the marine environment

---

[9] Draft article 1, in Report of the ILC (2001), paragraph 93. According to draft article 3, 'The State of origin shall take all appropriate measures to prevent transboundary harm or at any event to minimize the risk thereof.'

of the Irish Sea by two pathways: first, via an outfall structure, within the meaning of article 207, and secondly via the atmosphere, to which article 212 applies.

The question before the Tribunal was whether there would be irreparable harm to any of the rights claimed by the Applicant under articles 123, 192 to 194, 197, 206, 207, 211, 212 and 213 arising from alleged breaches of its duties under those articles by the Respondent. These rights were categorised, in broad terms, as the right to ensure that the Irish Sea will not be subject to additional radioactive pollution; procedural rights to have the respondent prepare proper environmental impact statements; and the right to cooperation and coordination over the protection of the Irish Sea as a semi-enclosed sea.[10] As regards the first category, in view of the small scale of the introductions from the MOX plant and its distance of over 100 miles from Ireland, it is not clear to me that there will be irreparable prejudice to any rights of the Applicant or 'serious harm to the marine environment' for the purposes of article 290, paragraph 5, especially recalling the short period of time before the constitution of the arbitral tribunal. Turning to the second category, in view of the existence not only of a national environmental impact statement and a study prepared for the EC Commission, but also the positive formal opinion issued by the EC Commission after a review by independent experts (on which both parties relied, albeit in different ways), it is not clear to me that any procedural rights claimed by the Applicant suffered irreparable prejudice.

[291] As regards the third category, cooperation and consultation, in regard to which the Applicant relied upon article 123, I would add the following. It is common ground that the Irish Sea satisfies the definition of a 'semi-enclosed sea' contained in article 122 of the Convention. Article 123 calls for the coordination, by States bordering a semi-enclosed sea, of the implementation of rights and duties with respect to the protection and preservation of the marine environment.

As regards the condition of the Irish Sea, the Applicant contended that 'as a result of radioactive pollution from Sellafield, the Irish Sea is amongst the most radioactively polluted seas in the world'.[11] The current status of the Irish Sea was described in a recently published study, undertaken by a member of a marine laboratory in the Isle of Man in the centre of the Irish Sea, in the following terms:

> There are several anthropogenic inputs which are of concern and require monitoring – sewage, heavy metals, organic compounds and radionuclides. None currently have widespread severe impact, and most inputs are being reduced. The overall prognosis for the Irish Sea is one of cautious optimism.[12]

The Tribunal was not called upon to make findings on these issues, having regard to the urgent and limited nature of these proceedings.

---

[10] ITLOS/PV.01/06, p. 28.

[11] Request for provisional measures, paragraph 10, citing the 'STOA Report'.

[12] R. G. Hartnold, 'The Irish Sea', in C. R. C. Sheppard (ed.) *Seas at the Millennium: An Environmental Evaluation* (2000), Vol. I, Preface to Chapter 6.

Turning to the content of article 123, it can be viewed in many ways as a particular application to the law of the sea of the general duty of States to cooperate, as laid down in article 2 of the Charter of the UN, as well as wider duties of *voisinage*. Article 123 was cast in weak terms ('should'/'shall endeavour') in order to safeguard the world-wide application of the Convention's provisions and its unified character.[13] Article 123 provides a choice: States bordering a semi-enclosed sea are to endeavour to coordinate their actions in certain matters (in simple terms, fisheries management, environmental protection and marine scientific research) either 'directly or through an appropriate regional organization'. In other words, article 123 does not require cooperation to be at the bilateral level so long as there is cooperation through an appropriate regional body. (One of the seas in mind during the Law of the Sea Conference was the Mediterranean Sea where some coastal States did not enjoy mutual recognition or maintain diplomatic relations.) In other words, there does not have to be a bilateral 'Irish Sea Conference' along the lines of the North Sea Conferences[14] in order to secure [292] compliance with article 123. Provided appropriate regional bodies exist, the necessary coordination can be achieved through them. In the case of the Irish Sea, the management of living resources is coordinated by means of the common fisheries policy of the EC; environmental protection, including the monitoring of the level of nuclear radiation, is coordinated through Euratom, the EC and OSPAR; and research into the scientific qualities of the waters and the status of the living resources is coordinated through the International Council for the Exploration of the Sea,[15] as well as through EC programmes. In my opinion, since the appropriate bodies do exist in regard to the Irish Sea and there is extensive, if not full, coordination through such bodies and since, moreover, there clearly have been some bilateral contacts between the parties at ministerial level in regard to the Irish Sea, there is little to be examined in the Applicant's claims under article 123.

On these points, therefore, the Order could have gone further, in my opinion, and reached conclusions upon the questions of preserving rights claimed by the Applicant and of 'serious harm to the marine environment', within the meaning of article 290. In particular, I would have been prepared to support findings that it had not been shown that any irreparable prejudice would be caused to the rights claimed by the Applicant, nor that serious harm to the marine environment would occur, before the constitution of the arbitral tribunal under Annex VII.

4. The second request of the Applicant (paragraphs 78 to 80 of the Order)
In view of paragraph 80 of the Order, the Tribunal was not called upon to examine the implications of the Applicant's second request. The request, had it been granted in the wide terms proposed, would appear to have required the Respondent to prohibit

---

[13] An account of the discussions on what became article 123 is to be found in the Virginia Commentary: see Nandan and Rosenne (eds.), *UN Convention on the Law of the Sea, A Commentary*, Volume III, at pp. 356 ff.

[14] Information is posted on http://www.dep.no/md/nsc/.

[15] The Irish Sea is ICES Statistical Area VIIa.

every vessel flying its flag and carrying radioactive substances, materials or wastes associated with the MOX plant from sailing in the internal and territorial waters of the United Kingdom, as well as in the waters beyond the territorial sea over which it exercises jurisdiction in accordance with Part XII of the Convention towards the maritime boundary with Ireland in the centre of the Irish Sea.[16] The request would also appear to have required the Respondent to prohibit foreign-flagged vessels[17] carrying such substances, [293] etc., from exercising rights of passage and navigation through waters under the sovereignty or jurisdiction of the United Kingdom. Such rights of third states are clearly provided for in the Convention: in particular, articles 17, 22, paragraph 2, 23 and 58 are relevant. Had it been necessary for the Tribunal to examine this very broad request, some much wider issues would have been raised.

SEPARATE OPINION OF JUDGE WOLFRUM (EXTRACT)

I concur fully with paragraph 89 as well as with the reasoning of the Order in general. The following observations are meant to add to the reasoning or to emphasise certain elements therein.

[. . .]

[294] [. . .] *Article 290 of the Convention*
Under article 290, paragraph 5, of the Convention the Tribunal was called upon to establish whether the urgency of the situation required [295] the prescription of provisional measures. This provision has to be read in conjunction with article 290, paragraph 1, of the Convention. According to the latter provisional measures may serve two different purposes namely either 'to preserve the respective rights of parties' or 'to prevent serious harm to the environment'. When interpreting the notion 'to preserve the respective rights of parties' account has to be taken of the fact that two different types of provisional measures have to be distinguished: one dealing with a future event and its consequences and the one where the event in question has already occurred. In the former case it is necessary to assess future developments. Such future developments do not have to be certain; probability is sufficient. The Tribunal was faced with the first alternative. Accordingly article 290, paragraph 1, of the Convention made it possible, in principle, to establish, whether the commissioning of the MOX plant could jeopardise the rights of Ireland to an extent that provisional measures were necessary.

Ireland has invoked the violation of several obligations under the Convention on the Law of the Sea by the United Kingdom. It has referred to two different rights, which allegedly have been violated by the United Kingdom. First the rights that the waters under the jurisdiction of Ireland must not be polluted by the introduction of

---

[16] As to which, see Report 9-5 in Charney and Alexander (eds.), *International Maritime Boundaries* (1993), Vol. II, p. 1767.

[17] Including, seemingly, even vessels which complied fully with internationally agreed standards applicable to such vessels, notably the INF Code under the SOLAS Convention.

radioactive material. These rights have been referred to as substantive ones. Second, Ireland claims its right to be informed on the possible impact of the MOX plant has been violated as well as its rights concerning a co-operation with the United Kingdom on the protection of the marine environment of the Irish Sea.

The Order, however, satisfies itself by stating in paragraph 81 that the urgency of the situation does not require the prescription of provisional measures requested by Ireland. This is justified by a reference to the short period before the Annex VII arbitral tribunal will be constituted. I agree that there was no urgency in this sense and therefore the request of Ireland had to be declined. Nevertheless, I would have found it preferable if the Order had indicated that, given the circumstance of the case, it would not have been within the mandate of the Tribunal concerning the prescription of provisional measures either for the protection of substantive rights invoked by Ireland or for the prevention of serious harm to the marine environment.

Ireland, amongst others, invokes article 194, paragraph 2, of the Convention. According to this provision, which also reflects customary international law, States are under an obligation to ensure that activities under their jurisdiction or control are conducted so as not to cause damage by pollution to other States and their environment. The notion of pollution is defined in article 1, paragraph 1(4), of the Convention. [296] Such definition contains two elements, namely the introduction of substances or energy – and radioactivity in [the] form of dust or otherwise qualifies as such – and that such introduction is likely to result in such deleterious effects as harm to living resources and marine life, etc. Both parties disagree on the potential impact of the MOX plant for the marine environment of the Irish Sea and on its present radioactive pollution.

It is still a matter of discussion whether the precautionary principle or the precautionary approach in international environmental law has become part of international customary law. The Tribunal did not speak of the precautionary principle or approach in its Order in the *Southern Bluefin Tuna Cases*.[18] Note should be taken of the fact, though, that the precautionary principle is part of the OSPAR Convention.

This principle or approach applied in international environmental law reflects the necessity of making environment-related decisions in the face of scientific uncertainty about the potential future harm of a particular activity. There is no general agreement as to the consequences which flow from the implementation of this principle other than [that] the burden of proof concerning the possible impact of a given activity is reversed. A State interested in undertaking or continuing a particular activity has to prove that it will result in no harm, rather than the other side having to prove that it will result in harm.

Nevertheless, Ireland could not, for several reasons, rely on the precautionary principle or approach in this case even it were to be accepted that it is part of international customary law. If the Tribunal would have prescribed provisional measures for the preservation of the marine environment under the jurisdiction of Ireland it could have

[18] See p. 393 above.

done so only after a summary assessment of the radioactivity of the Irish Sea, the potential impact the MOX plant might have and whether such impact prejudices the rights of Ireland. This, however, is an issue to be dealt with under the merits by the Annex VII arbitral tribunal. It should not be forgotten that provisional measures should not anticipate a judgment on the merits. This basic limitation for the prescription of provisional measures – emphasised by the International Court of Justice – finds its justification in the exceptional nature of provisional measures. Such limitation cannot be overruled by invoking the precautionary principle. Apart from that, the approach advanced by Ireland would have for result that the granting of provisional measures becomes automatic when an applicant argues with some plausibility that its rights may be prejudiced or that there was serious risk to the marine environment. This cannot be the function of provisional measures in particular since their prescription has to take into consideration the rights of all parties to the dispute. For the same reason it would have been not in conformity with [**297**] the limited jurisdiction the Tribunal has in prescribing provisional measures if it would have evaluated the documentary evidence submitted by both parties.

Ireland cannot rely on the reasoning of the Order in the *Southern Bluefin Tuna Cases*. The situation there was quite different. The parties had agreed that the tuna stock was at its '. . . historically lowest level . . .'. The Tribunal only stated that the parties should '. . . act with prudence and caution . . .' to ensure that effective conservation measures are taken to prevent serious harm. Here the Tribunal was in fact asked to qualify the possible introduction of radioactivity as 'deleterious' without being able to assess evidence about the situation prevailing in the Irish Sea. In my view there was, under the present circumstances, no room for applying the precautionary principle for the prescription of provisional measures for the preservation of the substantive rights of Ireland or the protection of the marine environment.

Ireland argues, as already indicated, that its procedural rights (rights concerning information and co-operation) have been violated and will be prejudiced if the MOX plant is commissioned. The obligation to co-operate with other States whose interests may be affected is a *Grundnorm* of Part XII of the Convention as of international customary law for the protection of the environment.

In general it has to be taken into consideration, though, that the provisions of the Convention on the Law of the Sea formulate obligations rather than rights. Is it possible to argue that obligations of States Parties under a multilateral treaty create, as a corollary, rights for each single other State Party? This is correct in bilateral relations. It would, however, be a simplification to say so in multilateral relations, such as the ones established by the Convention on the Law of the Sea. Some guidance may be drawn in this respect from the most recent draft of the International Law Commission on state responsibility. This draft distinguishes between obligations vis-à-vis another State in bilateral relations and obligations towards States Parties of a multilateral agreement. However, one may assume that Ireland at least has a legally protected interest that the United Kingdom lives up to its obligations to co-operate in the protection of the marine environment of the Irish Sea.

Nothing has been invoked by Ireland that suggests before the establishment of the Annex VII arbitral tribunal the suspension of the authorisation of the MOX plant or the prevention of its operation except the risks the United Kingdom encounters by commissioning the plant as scheduled. However, it is for the United Kingdom to decide whether it will face such risk.

[298] I fully endorse, however, paragraphs 82 to 84 of the Order considering that the obligation to co-operate is the overriding principle of international environmental law in particular when the interests of neighbouring States are at stake. The duty to co-operate denotes an important shift in the general orientation of the international legal order. It balances the principle of sovereignty of States and thus ensures that community interests are taken into account *vis-à-vis* individualistic States' interests. It is a matter of prudence and caution as well as in keeping with the overriding nature of the obligation to co-operate that the parties engage therein as prescribed in paragraph 89 of the Order.

SEPARATE OPINION OF JUDGE TREVES (EXTRACT)

1. While I agree with the decision and with its reasons, I wish to clarify certain aspects which, in my opinion, require to be seen in broader perspective.

[. . .]

[300] [. . .] 8. Resort to precautionary considerations is not mentioned in the Order as regards the preservation of substantive rights. In underlining, however, the lack of urgency in the short time before the constitution [301] of the Annex VII arbitral tribunal, the Order may be read, although it could be wished that it had been more explicit, as indicating that the scientific arguments brought by the parties did not focus precisely enough on whether the commissioning of the MOX plant could produce a significant increment, or the risk of a significant increment, of the radioactivity in the Irish sea during the few months before the Annex VII arbitral tribunal could be seized of a request concerning provisional measures. Scientific evidence linking risks to the marine environment specifically to the commissioning of the MOX plant within the relevant time-frame was not substantial and focussed enough to permit discussing whether such evidence was, or was not, conclusive as to the causal relationship between the activity envisaged and the risk to the marine environment.

9. Prudence and caution were nonetheless mentioned in paragraph 84 as requiring the cooperation and exchange of information which are the content of the measure prescribed by the Tribunal. It may be discussed whether a precautionary approach is appropriate as regards the preservation of procedural rights. It may be argued that compliance with procedural rights, relating to cooperation, exchange of information etc., is relevant for complying with the general obligation of due diligence in engaging in activities which might have an impact on the environment.

10. The process of cooperation in which the parties are to engage in implementing the Order should have the further result of avoiding the aggravation or the extension of the dispute and to bring what divides the parties into sharper focus before the Annex VII arbitral tribunal meets.

SEPARATE OPINION OF JUDGE *AD HOC* SZÉKELY (EXTRACT)

[**305**] [. . .] 8. In my view, the Tribunal never really appreciated, neither fully nor adequately, Ireland's reiterated central argument, against the commissioning and operation of the MOX plant as an addition to the Sellafield complex, which demanded appreciating its effects together with those of the added complex.

9. Instead, the Tribunal sought to decide on the requested provisional measures by looking at the MOX plant in isolation of the rest of the industrial complex to which it is meant to be integrated.

10. In paragraph 5 of Part 1 of its Request for provisional measures (p. 4), Ireland advanced the key concept that the MOX plant 'will further intensify nuclear activities in the coast of the Irish Sea', an [**306**] argument shared, for instance, by Norway while expressing its regret on the decision to authorize the plant (see paragraph 13 of the Request, p. 6). Ireland repeatedly reiterated this concept in the oral hearings.

11. This argument, in turn, necessarily brought into the forefront of the case the lamentable record of past performance of the Sellafield complex, plagued as it has been by several accidents (as stated in paragraph 15 of the Request, in p. 9, or the documented lack of a 'proper safety culture' alluded [to] in the Report of the United Kingdom Nuclear Installations Inspectorate, quoted in paragraph 16 of the Request, pp. 9–10), a matter which was equally disregarded by the Tribunal, even when it was an important indication of the risks involved not only in the potential commissioning and operation of the new integrated plant, but also of not granting the requested provisional measures.

12. I was particularly concerned that the Tribunal refused, despite the evidence, to properly apply the law when it came to article 206 of the Convention, a provision crucial for determining the viability of the requested provisional measures.

13. A mere reading of the surprisingly empty and superficial contents of the 1993 Environmental Impact Statement, is sufficient to fully support the Irish allegations, in the sense that the Statement is totally inadequate by any standard.

14. This Irish argument alone should have been sufficient for the Tribunal to take a positive stand toward the requested provisional measures, since the environmental impact assessment is a central tool of the international law of prevention.

15. Regrettably, the Tribunal failed to realize and accept that the 1993 Statement contains exclusively the unilateral assertions of, precisely, the proponent of the projected plant; that such assertions (invariably limited to simply allege that there would be no environmental impacts whatsoever), failed to be backed by the most elementary and appropriate scientific or technical support; that none of those assertions were independently validated (since the BNFL is a public limited company whose shares are all held by the United Kingdom Secretary of State for Trade and Industry and by the Treasury Solicitor); that the EIS was totally partial and incomplete in all respects (since it did not include a specific assessment of impacts in the marine environment, of impacts resulting from discharges or from the transport and international movements of radioactive materials, that is, the very activities that were the matter of the

requested provisional measures) and, above all, that since no potential impacts were admitted or identified in the Statement, it did not include, nor did the authorization to go ahead with the plant, any measures to prevent, mitigate, reduce or control any [**307**] potential environmental impacts (see paragraphs 22, 55 and 82–94 of its Request in pp. 12, 27 and 37–43).

16. The Tribunal did not lend any weight to the consequences of such dramatic failures, which meant that the United Kingdom did not comply with its obligations under article 206 of the Law of the Sea Convention, a compliance to which Ireland had a specific substantial right (which is additional to the fact that, by failing to provide Ireland with all the necessary reports and documentation surrounding the EIS, the United Kingdom equally failed to comply with its obligations under articles 204 and 205).

17. Consequently, the United Kingdom did not comply either with its obligations of prevention under articles 102, 103, 194 and 207 of the Convention, a compliance, again, to which Ireland was entitled as a substantial and not merely correlative, procedural right. This failure of the Tribunal explains in large measure why it decided not to grant Ireland the provisional measures it requested. The Tribunal resisted admitting that the above contraventions involve irreparable prejudice to Ireland's rights if the plant is commissioned without a previous adequate environmental impact assessment.

18. As surprisingly as the above, is the conclusion reached by the Tribunal, without any basis in law or in science, to give the United Kingdom, and not Ireland, the benefit of the doubt about the risk of harm alleged by Ireland. The Tribunal in the end acted on the United Kingdom allegation 'that the risk of pollution, if any, from the operation of the MOX plant would be infinitesimally small' (paragraph 72 of the Order's *Considerata*), even when the United Kingdom did not afford any sort of evidence to substantiate and support such radical allegation.

19. The Tribunal did the same regarding the allegations of the United Kingdom in the sense that 'the commissioning of the plant on or around 20 December 2001 will not, even arguably, cause serious harm to the environment or irreparable prejudice to the rights of Ireland' (see paragraph 73), that 'neither the commissioning of the MOX plant nor the introduction of plutonium into the system is irreversible' (see paragraph 74), and that 'the manufacture of MOX fuel presents negligible security risks' (see paragraph 76).

[. . .]

[**308**] [. . .] 22. In any case, since the Tribunal was not provided with legal and scientific support for the allegations of the United Kingdom and, since it was obviously not impressed by the evidence provided by Ireland to support its own allegations, it should have been responsive, in the face of such uncertainty, to the Irish demands regarding the application of the precautionary principle (see paragraphs 96 to 101 of the Request, pp. 43–6). It is regrettable that it did not do so, since acting otherwise would have led to granting the provisional measure requested by Ireland regarding the suspension of the commissioning of the plant.

23. Still, despite such reluctance of the Tribunal (and to add further to the already identified contradictions inherent to the Order), the Tribunal turns around in the

provisional measure it did decide to prescribe (in paragraph 2(c) of the operative part of the Order), and orders Ireland and the United Kingdom to enter into consultations forthwith in order to 'devise, as appropriate, measures to prevent pollution of the marine environment which might result from the operation of the MOX plant', an order which is truly striking after the Tribunal had chosen to believe that no such pollution was forthcoming. Or was it referring to measures to prevent the negligible and infinitesimally small pollution admitted by the United Kingdom? The Tribunal arrived late to the implementation of the Convention's prevention obligations but, at least in part, it finally did and, contradictory as it was with its denial of the requested provisional measures, such arrival had to be endorsed.

[309] 24. It does not appear that such contradiction was a new situation for the Tribunal. Again, in his Separate Opinion to the Tribunal's Order in the *Southern Bluefin Tuna Cases*, Judge *ad hoc* Shearer wrote: 'The Tribunal has not found it necessary to enter into a discussion of the precautionary principle / approach. However, I believe that the measures ordered by the Tribunal are rightly based upon considerations deriving from a precautionary approach'.[19] I fully share the same opinion regarding the Tribunal's alternative provisional measures that it ordered in this case.

25. In the end Ireland, by bringing the case to this Tribunal, got Britain to yield on the question of the transport of radioactive materials (by assuming at least a temporal commitment with the Tribunal, that was placed on record). Additionally, the Tribunal issued an Order that implies a good number of obligations mostly for the United Kingdom which, if faithfully executed, could still provide an opportunity for the preservation of Irish rights protected by the Convention, with the positive effect for both parties in the dispute, that sufficient room would be left for the arbitral tribunal to work efficiently on the merits.

[Report: 126 *ILR* 264]

[19 See p. 419 above.]

The '*Volga*' Case
(Russian Federation *v.* Australia)[1]

International Tribunal for the Law of the Sea, Hamburg

23 December 2002 (Nelson, *President*; Vukas, *Vice-President*; Caminos, Marotta
Rangel, Yankov, Yamamoto, Kolodkin, Park, Bamela Engo, Mensah,
Chandrasekhara Rao, Akl, Anderson, Wolfrum, Treves, Marsit, Ndiaye, Jesus,
Ballah and Cot, *Judges*; Shearer, *Judge* ad hoc)

*Waters – vessel illegally fishing Patagonian toothfish in exclusive economic zone
('EEZ') of Australia – arrest of vessel outside EEZ – United Nations Convention on the Law of the Sea, 1982 – Article 292 and Article 73 of Convention –
interpretation and application – 'reasonable bond or other financial security' –
whether bond set by Australia for release of vessel reasonable – whether circumstances of seizure of vessel relevant to assessment of bond – whether a 'good
behaviour bond' requiring use of vessel-monitoring system reasonable – whether
additional non-financial conditions of bond reasonable – assessment of gravity
of alleged offences – whether international concern over illegal fishing relevant
in assessment of reasonableness – bond sought by Australia not reasonable*

*Conservation – Patagonian toothfish – vessel illegally fishing Patagonian tooth-
fish in EEZ of Australia – international concern over illegal, unregulated and
unreported fishing in the Southern Ocean – Commission for the Conservation
of Antarctic Marine Living Resources ('CCAMLR')*

---

[1] The following judgments of the International Tribunal for the Law of the Sea on applications
for prompt release, which are not reported in this volume, can be found in the *International Law
Reports*: *M/V Saiga (No. 1)* (*Saint Vincent and the Grenadines* v. *Guinea*) 110 ILR 736, *The Camouco*
(*Panama* v. *France*) 125 ILR 164, *The Monte Confurco* (*Seychelles* v. *France*) 125 ILR 220, *The Grand Prince*
(*Belize* v. *France*) 125 ILR 272 and *The Juno Trader* (*Saint Vincent and the Grenadines* v. *Guinea-Bissau*)
128 ILR 267.

The Russian Federation was represented by Mr Pavel Grigorevich Dzubenko, as Agent; Mr
Valery Sergeevich Knyazev and Mr Kamil Abdulovich Bekiashev as Co-Agents; and Mr Andrew Tet-
ley and Mr Paul David, as Counsel. Australia was represented by Mr William McFadyen Campbell,
as Agent and Counsel; Mr John Langtry, as Co-Agent; and Mr David Bennett AO, QC, Mr James
Crawford SC and Mr Henry Burmester QC, as Counsel.

Powers and procedures of tribunals – International Tribunal for the Law of the Sea – jurisdiction – United Nations Convention on the Law of the Sea, 1982 – Article 292 of Convention – whether Russian Federation and Australia both State Parties to the Convention – whether jurisdiction established under Article 292 of Convention

SUMMARY   *The facts*   The *Volga*, a long-line fishing vessel flying the flag of the Russian Federation, was encountered by an Australian fisheries surveillance vessel outside the exclusive economic zone ('the EEZ') around the Australian Territory of Heard Island and McDonald Island. It was at that time warned not to enter the EEZ. On 6 February 2002, the *Volga* was detected within the EEZ. The *Volga* was arrested by the Royal Australian Navy on 7 February 2002 using a helicopter launched from the Naval vessel *HMAS Canberra*. The arrest occurred a few hundred metres outside the EEZ. Prior to the arrest, officers aboard the *HMAS Canberra* had plotted the position of the *Volga* to be within the EEZ. At the time of the arrest, a notice of seizure was served on the Master of the vessel, which specified that the *Volga* had been apprehended for illegal fishing inside the EEZ.

Following the arrest, the *Volga* was escorted to the Port of Fremantle, Western Australia, where it arrived on 19 February 2002. On 20 February 2002, a notice of seizure was issued under the Australian Fisheries Management Act 1991 ('the FMA'), providing for the seizure of the vessel, nets, equipment and catch, which consisted of 131 tonnes of Patagonian toothfish (*Dissostichus eleganiodes*).[2] On 6 March 2002, three members of the crew[3] (all of Spanish nationality) were charged with offences under the FMA[4] connected with illegal fishing in the EEZ and were admitted to bail. On 23 March 2002, the three crew members were released from custody following the payment of a bail bond by the owner of the *Volga*. They were subsequently permitted to return to Spain, under certain conditions, pending the hearing of the criminal charges against them.

---

[2] The harvest of Patagonian toothfish is subject to strict international conservation and management measures determined by the Commission for the Conservation of Antarctic Marine Living Resources ('CCAMLR'), established by the 1983 Convention on the Conservation of Antarctic Marine Living Resources. The Russian Federation and Australia are both State Parties to the Convention and Members of CCAMLR. The EEZ around the Territory of Heard Island and McDonald Island falls within the area subject to management by CCAMLR.

[3] The Master of the *Volga* was admitted to a Western Australian hospital on 25 February 2002 and later died.

[4] The crew were charged with an offence against section 100A of the FMA. Section 100A establishes an offence of strict liability where a person uses a foreign boat for commercial fishing in the EEZ without valid authorisation (a 'foreign fishing licence' under the Act).

On 20 May 2002, the catch seized from the *Volga* was sold by tender,[5] and the proceeds (AU $1,957,532) placed in trust pending the completion of the criminal proceedings against the crew. On 21 May 2002, the owner of the *Volga* instituted proceedings in the Federal Court of Australia to prevent the forfeiture of the vessel, fish, nets and equipment. The Federal Court proceedings were pending at the time of the Judgment of the International Tribunal for the Law of the Sea.

On 26 July 2002, Australia informed the owners of the *Volga* of the amount of the bond for the release of the vessel. The bond set by Australia (AU $3,332,500), consisted of three components: (i) the assessed value of the vessel, fuel, lubricants and fishing equipment (AU $1,920,000); (ii) an amount to secure payment of potential fines imposed in the criminal proceedings pending against members of the crew (AU $412,500); and (iii) an amount for the carriage by the *Volga* of a vessel-monitoring system ('VMS') – a satellite-based system that enables the position of a vessel to be located at any time (AU $1,000,000).

On 2 December 2002, solicitors acting for the Russian Federation filed an Application with the International Tribunal for the Law of the Sea under Article 292 of the United Nations Convention on the Law of the Sea, 1982.[6] The Russian Federation contended that Australia had contravened the articles of the Convention concerning the prompt release of vessels and crew, relying in particular on Article 73, paragraph 2, of the Convention, and sought an order that the *Volga* be released by Australia upon the payment of a bond or financial security not exceeding AU $500,000, or such other figure as determined by the Tribunal. Australia challenged the allegation of non-compliance with Article 73, paragraph 2, and maintained that the bond set by it for the release of the vessel and its crew was reasonable in light of the circumstances of the case.

Held by the International Tribunal for the Law of the Sea

(unanimously)   (1)   The Tribunal had jurisdiction under Article 292 of the Convention to hear the Application made by the Russian Federation. Both the Russian Federation and Australia were State Parties to the Convention. Australia did not contest jurisdiction. The status of the

---

[5] Section 106A of the FMA provides for the forfeiture to the Commonwealth of fish found on a boat that has been used in an offence against section 100A of the FMA.

[6] Article 292 of the Convention provides that an application for the release of a vessel may be made to the International Tribunal for the Law of the Sea by, or on behalf of, the flag State of the vessel, where the vessel has been detained by the authorities of a State Party to the Convention and it is alleged that the detaining State has not complied with the provisions of the Convention for the prompt release of the vessel or its crew upon the posting of a reasonable bond or other financial security.

Russian Federation as the flag State of the *Volga* was not contested. The Application by the Russian Federation was duly submitted in accordance with Article 292, paragraph 2, of the Convention, and satisfied the requirements of Articles 110 and 111 of the Rules of the Tribunal.

(unanimously) (2)   The Application with respect to the allegation of non-compliance with Article 73, paragraph 2, of the Convention was admissible.

(by nineteen votes to two) (3)   The allegation made by the Russian Federation that Australia had not complied with the provisions of the Convention for the prompt release of the vessel or its crew upon the posting of a reasonable bond or other financial security was well founded.

(by nineteen votes to two) (4)   The bond as sought by Australia was not reasonable within the meaning of Article 292 of the Convention.

(a)   The argument by the Russian Federation that the Tribunal should take into account the circumstances of the seizure of the *Volga* in assessing the reasonableness of the bond was rejected. Matters relating to the seizure of the vessel were not relevant to the proceedings under Article 292.

(b)   The argument by Australia that the problem of illegal fishing and the international concern it raised provided justification for the high level of the bond was rejected. International concerns over illegal, unregulated and unreported fishing were noted and understood. Notwithstanding those concerns, the Tribunal was required in Article 292 proceedings to assess whether the bond was reasonable in terms of Article 292 of the Convention. Among the factors under consideration were the penalties that might be imposed for the alleged offences under the laws of Australia. It was by reference to these penalties that the Tribunal made an assessment of the gravity of the alleged offence.

(c)   The argument by Australia that it could require, as part of the bond, the payment of an amount to guarantee carriage of a VMS as a form of 'good behaviour bond' to prevent possible future violations of Australian laws and international conservation measures was rejected. Article 73 was concerned with violations of coastal State laws alleged to have been committed. It was not concerned with possible future violations of the laws of coastal States. A 'good behaviour bond' to prevent future violations of the laws of a coastal State could not be considered as a bond or security within the meaning of Article 73, paragraph 2, read in conjunction with Article 292 of the Convention.

(d)   The argument by Australia that it could make the release of the *Volga* conditional upon the supply of information regarding the beneficial owner, financiers and insurers of the vessel was rejected. The expression 'bond or other security' in Article 73, paragraph 2, of the Convention must be seen in its context and in light of its object and purpose. The relevant context included the provisions of the Convention concerning the prompt release of vessels and crews upon the posting of a bond or security. As such, the expression 'bond or other security' in Article 73, paragraph 2 should be interpreted as referring to a bond or security of a financial nature. The object and purpose of Article 73, paragraph 2, read in conjunction with Article 292 of the Convention, were to provide the flag State with a mechanism for obtaining the prompt release of a vessel and crew arrested for alleged fisheries violations by posting a security of a financial nature whose reasonableness could be assessed in financial terms. The inclusion of non-financial conditions in such a security would defeat this object and purpose.

(e)   The argument by the Russian Federation that the proceeds of the sale of the catch seized from the *Volga* should be treated as security for the release of the vessel was rejected. A bond for the purposes of Article 292 was needed only to ensure the full protection of Australia's potential rights in the vessel and possible fines against the crew. As such, the proceeds of sale of the catch had no relevance to the bond to be set for the release of the vessel and the members of the crew. However, the proceeds of the sale of the catch were included in the overall amount to be retained by Australia or returned to the Russian Federation, as the case might be, depending on the final decisions on the merits of any case before the appropriate domestic forum against the vessel, its owner or its crew.

(f)   The amount of AU $1,920,000 sought by Australia for the release of the *Volga*, which represented the full value of the vessel, fuel, lubricants and fishing equipment, was reasonable in terms of Article 292 of the Convention.

(g)   The claim by the Russian Federation that the conditions set by the Australian courts for the release of the three crew members of the *Volga* were not reasonable was rejected. In light of the departure of the crew from Australia under conditions of bail, it was not necessary to deal with the issues raised by the Russian Federation. Setting a bond in respect of the three members of the crew would serve no practical purpose.

(by nineteen votes to two)   (5)   Australia was to release the *Volga* promptly upon the posting of a bond or other security determined by the Tribunal.

(by nineteen votes to two)   (6)   The bond or other security to be posted with Australia was set at AU $1,920,000.

(unanimously)   (7)   The bond was to be in the form of a bank guarantee from a bank present in Australia or having corresponding arrangements with an Australian bank or, if agreed to by the Parties, in any other form.

Declaration of Vice-President Vukas   The findings of the Tribunal with regard to the release of the *Volga* were endorsed. The appropriateness of the establishment of the EEZ around the Territory of Heard Island and McDonald Island under international law was questionable, having regard to the size, remote location and uninhabited status of those islands.

Declaration of Judge Marsit   It would have been desirable for the Tribunal to pronounce clearly and explicitly on the meaning and significance of the expression 'reasonable bond'. The meaning given to this expression must take into account not only the interests of the parties involved in a case but also the impact or effect of the jurisprudence of the Tribunal on any future cases that might affect one or more developing countries. This meant that a reasonable sum had to be reasonable for all parties concerned, irrespective of whether they were developed or developing countries.

Separate Opinion of Judge Cot   (1)   The Tribunal had a duty to respect the implementation by coastal States of their sovereign rights with regard to the conservation of living resources, particularly as those measures should be seen within the context of a concerted effort within the Food and Agriculture Organization and the CCAMLR. While the coastal State did not have the right to take measures that were arbitrary or would contravene an obligation under international law, it had a considerable margin of appreciation within that framework.

(2)   The margin of appreciation applied both to the measures taken by the coastal State under Article 73, paragraph 1, of the Convention and to the amount of the bond referred to in paragraph 2 of that Article. The Tribunal did not have to substitute its discretion for that of the coastal State unless the bond was not 'reasonable'. The Tribunal was not an appellate forum against a national court, nor was it the hierarchical superior of an administrative or government authority.

(3)   The Tribunal's control over what constituted a 'reasonable bond' came under what might be referred to as 'minimum control' in certain legal systems, this control of legality being exercised in particular with regard to errors in law. In deciding to combine release of the vessel with a bond imbued with a penal overtone, intended to ensure the

good behaviour of the vessel during the period pending the decision of the Australian courts, the Australian authorities had committed an error of law with regard to the lawful nature of the reasonable bond.

(4)   The bond or financial security provided for in Article 73, paragraph 2, and Article 292 was a provision of a purely financial nature. It could not be converted into a measure of court supervision. This interpretation was borne out by the context, object and purpose of the Convention, and also by the *travaux préparatoires*. It could not be combined with other conditions without having the effect of extending the coercive power of the coastal State to the detriment of the power of the flag State in the exclusive economic zone. Attaching conditions to the bond would have transformed the very nature of the procedure established by Article 292 of the Convention. This provided for *prompt* release of the vessel and *prompt* release of the crew, not the conditional release of them. Attaching conditions to the bond or financial security would have had the effect of complicating and slowing down the procedure, which would have lost its *prompt* character. This would be inconsistent with the meaning and purpose of Article 292.

Dissenting Opinion of Judge Anderson   (1)   The conclusion in paragraph 73 of the Judgment of the Tribunal that the full value of the vessel, including its gear and stores, represented reasonable financial security for the release of the vessel was supported.

(2)   The conclusion reached in paragraphs 81 to 83[7] of the Judgment that the circumstances surrounding the arrest of the *Volga* were not relevant in assessing the reasonableness of the security sought by Australia for the vessel's release was approved.

(3)   The duty of the coastal State to ensure the conservation of the living resources of the EEZ contained in Article 61 of the Convention, as well as the obligations of Contracting Parties to CCAMLR to protect the Antarctic ecosystem, were relevant factors in determining whether or not the amount of the bail money demanded for the release of a vessel such as the *Volga* was 'reasonable'.

(4)   The conclusion reached by the Tribunal that the proceeds of the sale of the catch had no relevance to the bond set for the release of the vessel and that the question of including those proceeds did not arise, whilst emphasising the consideration that the final destination of the

---

[7] Not reproduced in this volume but reported at 126 *ILR* 457.

proceeds depended upon the outcome of domestic legal proceedings, was endorsed.

(5)   Interpreted in its context and in the light of its object and purpose, Article 73 contained no explicit restriction upon the imposition of non-financial conditions for release of arrested vessels. Where the Convention limited the rights of coastal States in the matter of enforcement, it did so in express terms. For example, Article 73, paragraph 3, prohibited imprisonment and corporal punishment. Further limitations upon the rights of State Parties in what were important matters of domestic criminal procedure were not to be easily implied. The implication had to be a necessary one.

(6)   A 'good behaviour bond' represented a type of 'bond' within the meaning of Article 73, paragraph 2. It was financial, and the non-financial condition about good behaviour served the legitimate purpose of deterring further poaching in the EEZ pending the determination of the legal proceedings. A good behaviour bond would not necessarily be justified in all cases. The reasonableness of the demand had to be assessed against the facts of each case.

(7)   The good behaviour bond and the conditions sought by the Respondent were not unreasonable within the terms of Article 73, paragraph 2. The amount of the good behaviour bond might have been on the high side, but it did not exceed the 'margin of appreciation' to be accorded to domestic courts and domestic authorities.

(8)   The argument by the Russian Federation that non-pecuniary conditions could not count for the purposes of Article 73, paragraph 2, and were thus 'unlawful' was not well founded. It was based on an overly narrow, even legalistic interpretation of Article 73, paragraph 2, which took insufficient account of the context of domestic criminal law and procedure in many State Parties, the overall balance between the interests of the owners of the vessel and the coastal State, and the 'without prejudice' clause in Article 292, paragraph 3. In the light of the uncontested factual material before the Tribunal, the non-financial conditions were not unreasonable. For these reasons, the Application should have been dismissed as not 'well founded' (Article 113 of the Rules).

Dissenting Opinion of Judge ad hoc *Shearer*   (1)   The Tribunal should have been more willing to state or enter into an evaluation of the facts of the case. The present case related to grave allegations of illegal fishing in the context of the protection of endangered fish stocks in a remote and inhospitable part of the seas. In such a case, reasonableness could not be assessed in isolation from those circumstances.

(2)   Illegal fishing had to be punished with a high and deterrent level of monetary penalty. The necessity of deterrence as an element of the penalty was specifically recognised in the Agreement for the Implementation of the United Nations Convention on the Law of the Sea, 1982, relating to the Conservation and Management of Straddling and Highly Migratory Species, 1995, Article 19, paragraph 2. If deterrence was to be achieved, national courts had to take into account the gravity not only of the particular offence but also of the effects of offences generally on the conservation efforts of the international community. Penalties set by national courts should be set to deter further illegal activity. The Tribunal, and other international courts and tribunals, should be fully aware, and supportive, of these aims. In the present case, if highly deterrent penalties were required by the circumstances of the illegal, unreported and unregulated fishing in areas where fish stocks were endangered, such as in the Southern Ocean, the bond for the release of the vessel and the crew (or at least the leading crew members) must reflect the gravity of the offences.

(3)   The Tribunal should not have rejected that part of the bond imposed by Australia which required that the owner of the *Volga* agree to the carriage of a vessel-monitoring device and observance of CCAMLR conservation measures until the conclusion of legal proceedings. This requirement was quantified in monetary terms. It should not have been regarded by the Tribunal as a non-financial security. Such a narrow interpretation of the provisions of Article 73, paragraph 2, and Article 292 could not be supported. The words 'bond' and 'financial security' should be given a liberal and purposive interpretation in order to enable the Tribunal to take full account of the measures – including those made possible by modern technology – found necessary by many coastal States (and mandated by regional and sub-regional fisheries organisations) to deter, by way of judicial and administrative orders, the plundering of the living resources of the sea.

There follows

Judgment of International Tribunal for the Law of the Sea on Application for Prompt Release, 23 December 2002 (extract)
[. . .]

INTRODUCTION

[**443**][. . .] 29. In accordance with article 75, paragraph 2, of the Rules, the following final submissions were presented by the parties at the end of the hearing:

On behalf of the Russian Federation,

> The Russian Federation asks that the Tribunal make the following orders and declarations:

(a) A declaration that the Tribunal has jurisdiction under Article 292 of the United Nations Convention for the Law of the Sea 1982 ('UNCLOS') to hear the application.

(b) A declaration that the application is admissible.

(c) A declaration that the Respondent has contravened article 73(2) of UNCLOS in that the conditions set by the Respondent for the release of the *Volga* and three of its officers are not permitted under article 73(2) or are not reasonable in terms of article 73(2).

(d) An order that the Respondent release the *Volga* and the officers and its crew if a bond or security is provided by the owner of the vessel in an amount not exceeding AU $500,000 or in such other amount as the Tribunal in all the circumstances considers reasonable.

(e) An order as to the form of the bond or security referred to in paragraph 1(d).

(f) [**444**] An order that the Respondent pay the costs of the Applicant in connection with the application.

On behalf of Australia,

For the reasons set out in the Respondent's written and oral submissions, the Respondent requests that the Tribunal reject the application made by the Applicant.

[. . .]

[**452**] [. . .] NON-COMPLIANCE WITH ARTICLE 73, PARAGRAPH 2, OF THE CONVENTION

60. The Applicant alleges that the Respondent has not complied with article 73, paragraph 2, of the Convention concerning the prompt release of the three members of the crew and vessel, upon the posting of a reasonable bond or security. In support of the allegation it submits that the Respondent has set conditions for the release of the vessel and three members of the crew which are not permissible under article 73, paragraph 2, or are unreasonable in terms of article 73, paragraph 2, of the Convention.

61. The Respondent maintains that the bond it has set for the release of the *Volga* is reasonable, having regard to the value of the *Volga*, its fuel, lubricants and fishing equipment; the gravity of the offences and potential penalties; the level of international concern over illegal fishing; and the need to secure compliance with Australian laws and [453] international obligations pending the completion of domestic proceedings. The Respondent also contends that the bond set by Australia for the release of the crew members is reasonable.

62. When the Tribunal is called upon, under article 292 of the Convention, to assess whether the bond set by a party is reasonable, it must apply the Convention and other rules of international law not incompatible with the Convention.

63. In its previous judgments, the Tribunal indicated some of the factors that should be taken into account in assessing a reasonable bond for the release of a vessel or its crew under article 292 of the Convention. [. . .]

65. The Tribunal is required to determine whether or not the bond set by the Respondent is reasonable in terms of the Convention. [. . .] In assessing the reasonableness of the bond or other security, due account must be taken of the terms of the bond or security set by the detaining State, having regard to all the circumstances of the particular case.

66. The Tribunal will now deal with the application of the various factors in the present case.

[454] 67. Turning first to the gravity of the offences alleged to have been committed in the present case, it is noted that the offences relate to the conservation of the fishery resources in the exclusive economic zone. The Respondent has submitted that the potential penalties under Australian law indicate the grave nature of the offence and support its contention that the bond set for the release of the vessel and members of its crew is reasonable. The Respondent has pointed out that continuing illegal fishing in the area covered by the Convention for the Conservation of Antarctic Marine Living Resources ('CCAMLR') has resulted in a serious depletion of the stocks of Patagonian toothfish and is a matter of international concern. It has invited the Tribunal to take into account 'the serious problem of continuing illegal fishing in the Southern Ocean' and the dangers this poses to the conservation of fisheries resources and the maintenance of the ecological balance of the environment. According to the Respondent, this problem and the international concern that it raises provide ample justification for the measures it has taken, including the penalties provided in its legislation and the high level of bond that it has set for the release of ships and their crews when charged with violation of its laws.

68. The Tribunal takes note of the submissions of the Respondent. The Tribunal understands the international concerns about illegal, unregulated and unreported fishing and appreciates the objectives behind the measures taken by States, including the States Parties to CCAMLR, to deal with the problem.

69. The Tribunal must, however, emphasize that, in the present proceedings, it is called upon to assess whether the bond set by the Respondent is reasonable in terms of article 292 of the Convention. The purpose of the procedure provided for in article

292 of the Convention is to secure the prompt release of the vessel and crew upon the posting of a reasonable bond, pending completion of the judicial procedures before the courts of the detaining State. Among the factors to be considered in making the assessment are the penalties that may be imposed for the alleged offences under the laws of the Respondent. It is by reference to these penalties that the Tribunal may evaluate the gravity of the alleged offences. The Respondent has pointed out that the penalties provided for under its law in respect of the offences with which the members of the crew are charged indicate that these offences are grave. The Applicant does not deny that the alleged offences are considered to be grave under Australian law.

[...]

[**455**] [...] 73. In the view of the Tribunal, the amount of AU $1,920,000 sought by the Respondent for the release of the vessel, which represents the full value of the vessel, fuel, lubricants and fishing equipment and is not in dispute between the parties, is reasonable in terms of article 292 of the Convention.

74. Following the upholding of the appeal of the three members of the crew by the Supreme Court of Western Australia and their departure from Australia, the Tribunal considers that setting a bond in respect of the three members of the crew would serve no practical purpose. The Tribunal has noted the comments of the Applicant regarding the bail conditions set by the Supreme Court of Western Australia for permitting the three members of the crew to leave Australia. The Tribunal does not consider it necessary, in the present circumstances, to deal with the issues raised by the Applicant.

75. Besides requiring a bond, the Respondent has made the release of the vessel conditional upon the fulfilment of two conditions: that the vessel carry a VMS, and that information concerning particulars about the owner and ultimate beneficial owners of the ship be submitted to its authorities. The Respondent contends that the carrying of the VMS is necessary in order to prevent further illicit fishing once the ship is released. It further states that because the payment of a bond is a significant transaction it is entitled to know with whom the arrangements are to be made. The Applicant argues that such conditions find no basis in article 73, paragraph 2, and in the Convention in general, because only conditions that relate to the provision of a bond or security in the pecuniary sense can be imposed.

76. In the view of the Tribunal, it is not appropriate in the present proceedings to consider whether a coastal State is entitled to impose such [**456**] conditions in the exercise of its sovereign rights under the Convention. In these proceedings, the question to be decided is whether the 'bond or other security' mentioned in article 73, paragraph 2, of the Convention may include such conditions.

77. In interpreting the expression 'bond or other security' set out in article 73, paragraph 2, of the Convention, the Tribunal considers that this expression must be seen in its context and in light of its object and purpose. The relevant context includes the provisions of the Convention concerning the prompt release of vessels and crews upon the posting of a bond or security. These provisions are: article 292; article 220, paragraph 7; and article 226, paragraph 1(b). They use the expressions 'bond or other

financial security' and 'bonding or other appropriate financial security'. Seen in this context, the expression 'bond or other security' in article 73, paragraph 2, should, in the view of the Tribunal, be interpreted as referring to a bond or security of a financial nature. The Tribunal also observes, in this context, that where the Convention envisages the imposition of conditions additional to a bond or other financial security, it expressly states so. Thus article 226, paragraph 1(c), of the Convention provides that 'the release of a vessel may, whenever it would present an unreasonable threat of damage to the marine environment, be refused or made conditional upon proceeding to the nearest appropriate repair yard'. It follows from the above that the non-financial conditions cannot be considered components of a bond or other financial security for the purpose of applying article 292 of the Convention in respect of an alleged violation of article 73, paragraph 2, of the Convention. The object and purpose of article 73, paragraph 2, read in conjunction with article 292 of the Convention, is to provide the flag State with a mechanism for obtaining the prompt release of a vessel and crew arrested for alleged fisheries violations by posting a security of a financial nature whose reasonableness can be assessed in financial terms. The inclusion of additional non-financial conditions in such a security would defeat this object and purpose.

[...]

[457][...] 79. The Tribunal cannot, in the framework of proceedings under article 292 of the Convention, take a position as to whether the imposition of a condition such as what the Respondent referred to as a 'good behaviour bond' is a legitimate exercise of the coastal State's sovereign rights in its exclusive economic zone. The point to be determined is whether a 'good behaviour bond' is a bond or security within the meaning of these terms in articles 73, paragraph 2, and 292 of the Convention.

80. The Tribunal notes that article 73, paragraph 2, of the Convention concerns a bond or a security for the release of an 'arrested' vessel which is alleged to have violated the laws of the detaining State. A perusal of article 73 as a whole indicates that it envisages enforcement measures in respect of violations of the coastal State's laws and regulations alleged to have been committed. In the view of the Tribunal, a 'good behaviour bond' to prevent future violations of the laws of a coastal State cannot be considered as a bond or security within the meaning of article 73, paragraph 2, of the Convention read in conjunction with article 292 of the Convention.

[...]

[459] [...] OPERATIVE PROVISIONS

95. For these reasons,

THE TRIBUNAL,

(1) Unanimously,

Finds that the Tribunal has jurisdiction under article 292 of the Convention to entertain the Application made by the Russian Federation on 2 December 2002.

(2) Unanimously,

Finds that the Application with respect to the allegation of non-compliance with article 73, paragraph 2, of the Convention is admissible.

(3) By 19 votes to 2,

Finds that the allegation made by the Applicant that the Respondent has not complied with the provisions of the Convention for the prompt release of the vessel or its crew upon the posting of a reasonable bond or other financial security is well-founded;

FOR: *President* Nelson; *Vice-President* Vukas; *Judges* Caminos, Marotta Rangel, Yankov, Yamamoto, Kolodkin, Park, Bamela Engo, Mensah, Chandrasekhara Rao, Akl, Wolfrum, Treves, Marsit, Ndiaye, Jesus, Ballah, Cot;

AGAINST: *Judge* Anderson; *Judge* ad hoc Shearer.

[460] (4) By 19 votes to 2,

Decides that Australia shall promptly release the *Volga* upon the posting of a bond or other security to be determined by the Tribunal;

FOR: *President* Nelson; *Vice-President* Vukas; *Judges* Caminos, Marotta Rangel, Yankov, Yamamoto, Kolodkin, Park, Bamela Engo, Mensah, Chandrasekhara Rao, Akl, Wolfrum, Treves, Marsit, Ndiaye, Jesus, Ballah, Cot;

AGAINST: *Judge* Anderson; *Judge* ad hoc Shearer.

(5) By 19 votes to 2,

Determines that the bond or other security shall be AU $1,920,000, to be posted with Australia;

FOR: *President* Nelson; *Vice-President* Vukas; *Judges* Caminos, Marotta Rangel, Yankov, Yamamoto, Kolodkin, Park, Bamela Engo, Mensah, Chandrasekhara Rao, Akl, Wolfrum, Treves, Marsit, Ndiaye, Jesus, Ballah, Cot;

AGAINST: *Judge* Anderson; *Judge* ad hoc Shearer.

(6) Unanimously,

Determines that the bond shall be in the form of a bank guarantee from a bank present in Australia or having corresponding arrangements with an Australian bank or, if agreed to by the parties, in any other form.

(7) Unanimously,

Decides that each party shall bear its own costs.

DECLARATION OF VICE-PRESIDENT VUKAS (EXTRACT)

1. I voted in favour of the Tribunal's findings contained in paragraph 95 of the Judgment since I agree with these findings with regard to their main objective, that is the release of the *Volga*.

2. However, I dissociate myself from all statements or conclusions in the Judgment which are based on the proclaimed exclusive economic zone around Heard Island and the McDonald Islands.

[...]

[461] [...] In the present case, an exclusive economic zone has been proclaimed by Australia off the coasts of two uninhabited islands which are much smaller than the Kerguelen Islands. As I did not do so in my Declaration attached to the Judgment in the *'Monte Confurco' Case*, I feel obliged to explain my position concerning the appropriation of vast areas of the oceans by some States which possess tiny uninhabited islands thousands of miles from their own coasts.

The reasons for the establishment of the exclusive economic zone régime

3. Many coastal States have considered it just and equitable to secure for their coastal population some priority in the fisheries even beyond the outer limits of their territorial sea. As a consequence of such a tendency, a resolution adopted at the 1958 United Nations Conference on the Law of the Sea considered the special situation of countries whose coastal population depended 'upon coastal fisheries for their livelihood or economic development in an area of the high seas adjacent to the territorial sea of the coastal State ...'.[8]

At the Second United Nations Conference on the Law of the Sea (Geneva, 1960) a proposal claiming preferential rights for the fisheries of the coastal State in the high seas adjacent to its waters if 'the exploitation of the living resources of the high seas in that area [was] of fundamental [462] importance to the economic development of the coastal State or the feeding of its population' was widely supported.[9]

4. '[T]he concept of preferential rights of fishing in adjacent waters in favour of the coastal State in a situation of special dependence on its coastal fisheries' was in 1974 confirmed by the International Court of Justice as being a concept crystallized as customary international law.[10]

5. The insistence of developing coastal States to recognize that the preferential fishing rights of their population be recognized in an area beyond their territorial waters – already confirmed by the domestic legislation of some of those States – resulted at UNCLOS III in the adoption of the régime of the exclusive economic zone.

The scope of the creation of this new international régime at sea is clearly stated by René-Jean Dupuy:

---

[8] Resolution VI 'Special situations relating to coastal fisheries', *UN Official Records of the UN Conference on the Law of the Sea*, Vol. II, Doc. A/CONF.13/38, p. 144.

[9] Doc. A/CONF.19/L.12, Brazil, Cuba and Uruguay: Amendments to the second proposal in document A/CONF.19/L.4: *UN Official Records of the Second UN Conference on the Law of the Sea*, Doc. A/CONF.19/8, p. 173.

[10] *Fisheries Jurisdiction (United Kingdom v. Iceland), Merits, Judgment, ICJ Reports 1974*, p. 23 [see p. 33 above].

The notion of an economic zone, in the view of the developing coastal States, has the purpose of helping them gain access to the resources they previously could not claim; it therefore has unquestionable merit from the standpoint of promoting their interests.[11]

Thus, the protection of the economic interests of the coastal States, and in particular of their population in the coastal areas, has been the essential factor in establishing this new régime at sea. This is clear not only from the name of the new legal régime itself, but also from the main provisions on the exclusive economic zone in the LOS Convention. The basic rule (article 56, paragraph 1(a)) proclaims the sovereign rights of coastal States 'for the purpose of exploring and exploiting, conserving and managing the natural resources, whether living or non-living'. The conservation and management measures undertaken for the maintenance of the living resources in the zone, have to take into account, inter alia, 'the economic needs of coastal fishing communities' (article 61, paragraph 3).

[...]

[**463**] [...] *The exclusive economic zone and the preservation of marine resources in the Southern Ocean*

7. In view of the above-mentioned absence of permanent habitation, and the geographical and climatic characteristics of Heard Island and the McDonald Islands, it comes as no surprise that some interests and/or concerns other than economic ones are pointed to as the reason for establishing the exclusive economic zone around these islands. Thus, Dr David Bennett, Solicitor-General of the Respondent, said that the establishment of the exclusive economic zone was useful for the more effective preservation of the marine resources in the rather shallow waters surrounding these islands.[12]

[**464**] Notwithstanding the importance of preservation of marine resources, the argument advanced by Dr Bennett does not sound very convincing, particularly in relation to the sea area in question.

8. There are two sets of international treaty rules generally applicable to the conservation of the living resources of the high seas: the 1958 Convention on Fishing and Conservation of the Living Resources of the High Seas, and Part VII, Section 2, of the LOS Convention, entitled 'Conservation and Management of the Living Resources of the High Seas'. Both Conventions call for cooperation between States whose nationals exploit the same marine areas. One of the best examples of such cooperation is the conclusion of the Convention on the Conservation of Antarctic Marine Living Resources (CCAMLR – Canberra, 20 May 1980). The Commission for the Conservation of Antarctic Marine Living Resources established under the Convention (article VII) has been entrusted with the adoption of conservation measures,

---

[11] René-Jean Dupuy, 'The Sea under National Competence', René-Jean Dupuy and Daniel Vignes (eds.), *A Handbook of the New Law of the Sea 1*, Martinus Nijhoff Publishers, Dordrecht/Boston/Lancaster, 1991, p. 281.

[12] ITLOS/PV.02/02, p. 24.

the establishment and implementation of a system of observation and inspection (article IX, paragraph 1(f) and (g)). This system includes, inter alia,

> procedures for boarding and inspection by observers and inspectors designated by the Members of the Commission and procedures for flag state prosecution and sanctions on the basis of evidence resulting from such boarding and inspections (article XXIV, paragraph 2(a)).

It is therefore unnecessary and confusing if individual States adopt and apply their own measures in the exclusive economic zone they have proclaimed inside the area of application of the CCAMLR. In this sense, referring to the French exclusive economic zone, Bruce W. Davis remarked that 'consistency has had to give way to the requirements for internal acceptance'.[13]

[...]

[466] DECLARATION OF JUDGE MARSIT (EXTRACT)

[Translation]

1. I have voted in favour of this Judgment but I should nevertheless like to give my view on certain aspects of this case or any similar case that might give cause for concern not only to developed countries but in particular the young States which are endeavouring to achieve a higher level of development, especially from the economic point of view.

2. The new law of the sea acknowledges coastal States' exclusive sovereign rights to take advantage of the resources of the maritime areas over which they have sovereignty or jurisdiction. However, this particular case demonstrates, if the charges complained of by the Respondent prove to be true, that it is far from easy to protect those resources from any serious, repeated attack. If a country such as Australia or France is not always able to provide such protection, what about new developing countries, regardless of whether they open onto oceans or smaller seas?

3. It should be noted that a number of people have seen fit to voice their firm support for the right of the coastal State to defend itself in order to preserve its resources from any illegal, unregulated and unreported exploitation having ruinous consequences. Such an attitude reflects the concern of the international community to safeguard the maritime waters within the domestic jurisdiction from reckless action of this kind and seeks to protect the marine environment from an imbalance that will sooner or later prove harmful and may be seriously detrimental to the rights of future generations. It is to be hoped that, on the basis of such an approach, the conduct of fishermen will no longer be guided solely by material interests and a desire for quick profits regardless of the rights of others.

[...]

---

[13] Bruce W. Davis, 'The legitimacy of CCAMLR', Olav Schram Stokke and Davor Vidas (eds.), *Governing the Antarctic*, Cambridge University Press, 1996, p. 244.

SEPARATE OPINION OF JUDGE COT (EXTRACT)

[Translation]

1. I subscribe to the findings of the Judgment. However, I consider it necessary to add some observations on the two questions of the [467] context of illegal fishing and the 'margin of appreciation' of the coastal State.

The context of illegal fishing

2. The Tribunal understands the international concerns about illegal, unregulated and unreported fishing. It appreciates the objectives behind the measures taken by States, including the States Parties to CCAMLR, to deal with the problem (paragraph 68 of the Judgment). I believe that it is necessary to clarify the difficulties encountered by States in combating illegal, unregulated and unreported fishing in the Southern Ocean and the necessary margin of appreciation they must be acknowledged as having in defining and implementing the means for tackling this problem.

[. . .]

5. Russia and Australia are both parties to the Convention on the Conservation of Antarctic Marine Living Resources and Members of CCAMLR. They have pledged to take part in the campaign against illegal fishing as part of their responsibilities as a flag State and coastal State respectively. Russia confirmed at the hearing that it intended to play its part fully in that campaign (statement by Mr Dzubenko, Friday 13 December, p.m., p. 5).

6. CCAMLR's verdict on the devastation caused by illegal fishing in the region is damning. The proceeds of illegal fishing appear to be greater than those of licensed fishing – at least that was CCAMLR's estimate for the 1997/98 season – and therefore more than double the level of catches regarded as the maximum to ensure the preservation of the species. If the parties to the Convention do not manage to put an end to these practices, stocks of Patagonian toothfish will be completely wiped out within about ten years.

[. . .]

[468] [. . .] 10. International organizations have called upon Member States to take measures against illegal fishing. Thus, at its 120th session the Council of the Food and Agriculture Organization adopted the International Plan of Action to Prevent, Deter and Eliminate Illegal, Unreported and Unregulated Fishing. Paragraph 24 of this Plan requires States to adopt sufficiently tough punitive measures to deter potential offenders. For its part, CCAMLR has adopted a number of conservation measures, including the installation of a VMS on board fishing vessels.

11. The measures taken by Australia, both in terms of prevention and enforcement, clearly fall within the scope of the efforts made by international organizations to combat illegal, unreported and unregulated fishing. They come under article 56 of the Convention on the Law of the Sea and have been taken in pursuance of the sovereign rights exercised by coastal States for the purpose of exploring, exploiting, conserving and managing the natural resources of the exclusive economic zone. In

exercising their enforcement powers coastal States may specify monetary penalties they consider appropriate and establish – within the framework of the Convention or other applicable international agreements – their rules on arrest, detention and release upon the posting of a bond. In particular, the Convention does not set any limit on the fines a coastal State may consider appropriate to impose on offenders.[14]

12. The Tribunal has a duty to respect the implementation by the coastal State of its sovereign rights with regard to the conservation of living resources, particularly as these measures should be seen within the context of a concerted effort within the FAO and CCAMLR. In taking these measures, Australia is upholding not only its legitimate right to explore and exploit the resources of its exclusive economic zone. It [469] takes conservation measures within the framework of an international system of authorization in order to protect a common heritage. This is a good example of a plurality of functions. This particular circumstance widens Australia's scope for action. While the coastal State does not have the right to take measures that are arbitrary or would contravene an obligation under international law, it has a considerable margin of appreciation within that framework.

[...]

[473] [...] DISSENTING OPINION OF JUDGE ANDERSON (EXTRACT)

[...]

2. In *paragraph 68*, the Tribunal has gone further than it did in the *'Monte Confurco'* *Case*. Two years ago, the Tribunal simply took note of concerns of the Respondent about the serious situation caused by IUU fishing in the CCAMLR Area without drawing any conclusions. I fully concur, therefore, with the expressions of understanding and appreciation of the international concerns over IUU fishing in the CCAMLR Area. In this connection, I would note that the Respondent submitted to the Tribunal some relevant extracts from the Report of the recent meeting of CCAMLR,[15] as well as diplomatic notes addressed to Australia by several Contracting Parties, including Chile, France (Kerguelen), New Zealand and South Africa from the southern hemisphere, all expressing concern about the conservation and management of the living resources of the CCAMLR Area.[16] Other documentation submitted by the Respondent and not challenged by the Applicant indicates clearly that the *Volga* had been fishing in the Statistical Division 58.5.2 of the CCAMLR Area (including the EEZ around Heard Island)[17] during the greater part of the 2001–2 Austral summer as part of a large fleet of Russian and other vessels. In my opinion, the duty of the coastal State to ensure the conservation of the living resources of the EEZ contained in article 61 of

---

[14] *The Camouco Case*, Dissenting Opinion of Judge Wolfrum, para. 6.

[15] Statement in Response, Annexes 4 and 5.

[16] *Ibid.*, Annex 4 and attachments to the letter of the Agent for the Respondent dated 10 December 2002. There is a precedent for the submission of such diplomatic correspondence in Annex 4 to the Common Rejoinder of Denmark and the Netherlands in the North Sea Continental Shelf Cases: *ICJ Pleadings*, etc., 1968, Vol. I, p. 546.

[17] Heard Island is clearly an island and not a rock. As such, an EEZ can be validly established.

the Convention, as well as the obligations of Contracting [474] Parties to CCAMLR to protect the Antarctic ecosystem, are relevant factors when determining in a case under article 292 whether or not the amount of the bail money demanded for the release of a vessel such as the *Volga* is 'reasonable'.

[...]

[480] [...] DISSENTING OPINION OF JUDGE *AD HOC* SHEARER (EXTRACT)

[...]

[482] [...] *Consideration and substantiation of facts in prompt release cases*

7. The Tribunal in its Judgment has been reluctant to state or enter into an evaluation of the facts other than those directly concerned with the reasonableness of the bond for prompt release. Reference should also be made to the provisions of article 292, paragraph 3, of the Convention which prohibits the Tribunal from prejudicing the merits of any case before the appropriate domestic forum against the vessel, its owner, or its crew. In my opinion the Tribunal erred too much on the side of reticence. [...]

8. I therefore find it necessary to consider to what extent the Tribunal should have regard to facts which nevertheless belong ultimately to the merits of the case, and which might not be substantiated in a hearing on the merits. In my opinion, for the limited purpose of proceedings for prompt release of vessels and crews, facts should be cognisable, and regarded as substantiated, if they are not contested by the opposing party. None of the facts set out above were contested by the Applicant in the present case. The Tribunal should also take into account the obligations [483] of the parties under related international agreements and facts which are public knowledge, such as agreed statistics relating to fish stocks, the findings of respected scientific bodies, and the resolutions of competent international organisations. All of these are in my view examples of relevant surrounding circumstances.

The relevance of the surrounding circumstances

9. The Respondent laid prime emphasis in the present proceedings, as relevant to the bond, on the problem of illegal, unreported and unregulated (IUU) fishing worldwide, and particularly in relation to the Patagonian toothfish in the Southern Ocean. Reference was made not only to the provisions of article 61, paragraph 2, of the Convention, which require States Parties to conserve and manage the living resources of their exclusive economic zones so that they are not endangered through over-exploitation, but also to the Convention for the Conservation of Antarctic Marine Living Resources, 1980 (CCAMLR). Both Australia and the Russian Federation are parties to CCAMLR. The EEZ of Australia generated by Heard Island and the McDonald Islands is within the area covered by CCAMLR. That Convention requires parties to take appropriate measures within its competence to ensure compliance with the Convention and with the conservation measures adopted by the

Commission for the Conservation of Antarctic Marine Living Resources. The Commission has set catch limits and restrictions on fishing seasons. The most recent meeting of the Commission (4 November 2002) noted that illegal fishing had seriously depleted the stocks of Patagonian toothfish, and pointed to the potentially catastrophic effects of the continuation of such fishing.

10. Another important circumstance, pointed out by the Respondent, is the difficulty of enforcement of fisheries laws in the inhospitable environment of the Southern Ocean. The weather is constantly bleak and cold, with high winds and heavy seas. The distances to be covered by fisheries enforcement vessels and aircraft are great. Unlicensed fishing vessels are encouraged to believe that the chances of their detection are small enough, and the potential rewards high enough, to justify taking the risk.

11. A logical conclusion to be drawn from these circumstances is that illegal fishing must be punished with a high and deterrent level of monetary penalty. (Other forms of penalty are precluded by article 73, paragraph 3, of the United Nations Convention on the Law of the Sea.) The necessity of deterrence as an element of the penalty is specifically recognised in the Agreement for the Implementation of the [**484**] United Nations Convention on the Law of the Sea, 1982, Relating to the Conservation and Management of Straddling Fish Stocks and Highly Migratory Species, 1995, article 19, paragraph 2. If deterrence is to be achieved, national courts must take into account the gravity not only of the particular offence but also of the effects of offences generally on the conservation efforts of the international community. This indicates that the penalty should be so set by national courts as to deter further illegal activity. The Tribunal, and other international courts and tribunals, should be fully aware, and supportive, of these aims.

12. I have had the advantage of reading in draft the Separate Opinion of Judge Cot in the present case. I agree fully with the views he has expressed regarding the context of illegal fishing.

13. In the present case, if highly deterrent penalties are required by the circumstances of IUU fishing in areas where fish stocks are endangered, such as in the Southern Ocean, the bond for the release of the vessel and of the crew (or at least of the leading crew members) must reflect the gravity of those offences.

[...]

[Report: 126 *ILR* 439]

Case Concerning Land Reclamation by Singapore in and around the Straits of Johor (Malaysia *v.* Singapore)[1]

International Tribunal for the Law of the Sea, Hamburg

8 October 2003 (Nelson, *President*; Vukas, *Vice-President*; Caminos, Marotta Rangel, Yankov, Yamamoto, Kolodkin, Park, Bamela Engo, Mensah, Chandrasekhara Rao, Akl, Anderson, Wolfrum, Treves, Marsit, Ndiaye, Jesus, Xu, Cot and Lucky, *Judges*; Hossain and Oxman, *Judges* ad hoc)

Waters – marine environment – preservation of marine and coastal environment – maritime access to coastline – effect of land reclamation works on marine environment

Powers and procedures of tribunals – International Tribunal for the Law of the Sea – provisional measures – United Nations Convention on the Law of the Sea, 1982, Article 290 – requirements for order of provisional measures – jurisdiction – Article 288 of Convention – Article 283 of Convention – obligation to exchange views regarding settlement of dispute by negotiation or other peaceful means – whether precondition of exhaustion of diplomatic negotiations before referring dispute to Tribunal

Waters – territorial sea – provisional measures – claim to territorial sea as basis for prescription of provisional measures – insufficient basis for ordering provisional measures

Rights and interests – right to natural resources within territorial sea – estuary – semi-enclosed sea – right to integrity of marine environment – right to be consulted with respect to major land reclamation works – possible impact on maritime transit rights

---

[1] Mr Abdul Gani Patail, Sir Elihu Lauterpacht CBE QC, Mr James Crawford SC FBA and Mr Nico Schrijver acted as Counsel for Malaysia. Mr Sek Keong Chan, Mr Vaughan Lowe and Mr Michael Reisman acted as Counsel for Singapore.

466

International cooperation – duty to cooperate to prevent pollution of marine environment – Part XII of Convention

SUMMARY   *The facts*   On 4 July 2003, Malaysia filed a request for the constitution of an arbitral tribunal under Annex VII of the United Nations Convention on the Law of the Sea, 1982 in relation to a dispute concerning land reclamation by Singapore in and around the Straits of Johor.[2] Both Malaysia and Singapore were State Parties to the Convention. Malaysia claimed that Singapore's land reclamation works were impinging on Malaysia's territorial sea. Provisional measures were sought by Malaysia in a Request made on 5 September 2003.[3] Malaysia sought, *inter alia*, the suspension of all land reclamation activities in the vicinity of the maritime boundary between the two States and in areas claimed as territorial waters by Malaysia. Malaysia claimed that provisional measures were necessary to preserve its rights relating to the preservation of the marine and coastal environment and its rights to maritime access to its coastline, in particular via the eastern entrance to the Straits of Johor. Singapore requested the Tribunal to dismiss Malaysia's Request for Provisional Measures.

Held by the International Tribunal for the Law of the Sea   Provisional measures would be granted in part. Malaysia and Singapore were ordered to cooperate and to jointly establish a group of independent experts with a mandate to study the effects of Singapore's land reclamation, to propose measures to deal with any adverse effects of Singapore's land reclamation and to prepare a report on the infilling works in Area D at Pulau Tekong. The Parties were also ordered to exchange information on Singapore's land reclamation works, to assess the risks or effects of Singapore's land reclamation works and to consult with a view to reaching a prompt agreement on temporary measures with respect to Area D at Pulau Tekong, including suspension or adjustment of land reclamation activities if necessary to ensure that the infilling operations did not prejudice Singapore's ability to carry out the commitments referred to in paragraphs 85 to 87 of the Order of the Tribunal. Finally, the Parties were ordered to avoid any action incompatible with the effective implementation of the provisional measures ordered by the Tribunal.

(1)   Before prescribing provisional measures under Article 290(5) of the Convention, the Tribunal must satisfy itself that *prima facie* it would

---

[2] The relief sought by Malaysia in its Statement of Claim is listed in paragraph 22 of the Order.
[3] The provisional measures sought by Malaysia are listed in paragraph 23 of the Order.

have jurisdiction to decide the claim. There was no requirement in the Convention for State Parties to pursue settlement by negotiation or other peaceful means when the possibilities for settlement through such means were exhausted. International law did not require the exhaustion of diplomatic negotiations as a precondition for a matter to be referred to an international court. The Annex VII arbitral tribunal would *prima facie* have jurisdiction over the dispute.

(2)   The Tribunal might prescribe provisional measures to preserve the respective rights of the parties to a dispute or to prevent serious harm to the marine environment. The urgency of the situation must require the prescription of provisional measures, and such urgency was to be assessed taking into account the period during which an arbitral tribunal was not yet in a position to 'modify, revoke or affirm ... provisional measures', rather than the period until the arbitral tribunal was to be constituted.

(3)   A claim to an area of territorial sea was not, *per se*, a sufficient basis for the prescription of provisional measures under Article 290(5) of the Convention. There must be a situation of urgency or a risk that the rights claimed with respect to an area of territorial sea would suffer irreversible damage pending consideration of the merits of the case by the Annex VII arbitral tribunal.

(4)   The duty on State Parties to cooperate was a fundamental principle in the prevention of pollution of the marine environment. Hitherto cooperation between Malaysia and Singapore had been insufficient. Malaysia and Singapore must establish mechanisms for exchanging information and assessing the risks or effects of land reclamation works and devising ways to deal with them.

Declaration of President Nelson   Singapore had already pledged to undertake seriously to examine its land reclamation works and to consider taking necessary and proper steps, including a suspension, to deal with adverse effects. Good faith was to be presumed by the Tribunal when prescribing provisional measures. Cooperation in the protection and preservation of the marine environment was of central importance to the Tribunal.

Declaration of Judge Anderson   It was doubtful whether the requirement for 'the urgency of the situation' in Article 290, paragraph 5, of the Convention had been satisfied in light of the commitments made by the Parties. The Parties must implement their commitments in good faith, which was to be presumed in international litigation.

Joint Declaration of Judges ad hoc *Hossain and Oxman*   The right of a State to use marine areas and natural resources subject to its sovereignty or jurisdiction was broad, but not unlimited. States had a duty to have due regard to the rights of other States and to the protection and preservation of the marine environment. A joint process for addressing the most urgent concerns of Malaysia and Singapore was needed to build upon the statements already made by both States and implement their duties to cooperate.

Separate Opinion of Judge Chandrasekhara Rao (1) The requirements of Article 283, paragraph 1, of the Convention had *prima facie* been satisfied. The requirement in Article 283, paragraph 1, of the Convention for an exchange of views was not an empty formality. It must be discharged in good faith. It was the Tribunal's duty to examine whether this had been done. In deciding whether it had been done, it was not to be forgotten that the duty to cooperate was a fundamental principle in the preservation of the marine environment under Part XII of the Convention and general international law.

(2) There was no disagreement that the Annex VII arbitral tribunal would *prima facie* have jurisdiction over the dispute and that the Request was admissible. The Tribunal must be satisfied that, on the evidence before it, there was a reasonable possibility of either irreparable damage to the rights of Malaysia or serious harm to the marine environment before a decision of the Annex VII arbitral tribunal was made. The requirement of urgency had not been shown by Malaysia. There was no reason to believe that an arbitral tribunal would not be constituted by 9 October 2003 or that it would not meet shortly thereafter.

Separate Opinion of Judge Ndiaye It was doubtful whether there was a rule of general international law that parties must exhaust the negotiation process prior to seeking compulsory dispute settlement. For such a rule to be applicable, the party invoking the rule (of prior exhaustion of the negotiation process) must provide proof that it was bound to the other party by a specific undertaking to that effect.

Separate Opinion of Judge Jesus Every party was free not to accept a particular settlement procedure, unless bound by a treaty provision or otherwise. There was nothing in the Convention that imposed a general obligation on States to settle a dispute through negotiations instead of another peaceful means. States were only obligated to submit their disputes to negotiation if they had agreed to do so.

Separate Opinion of Judge Cot The appropriate measure in order to protect the rights of Malaysia would have been to prescribe the suspension of the infilling works in Area D at Pulau Tekong pending the results of the scientific study requested by the Parties. In any event, Singapore was bound by this obligation since it resulted from the commitments entered into by Singapore in its diplomatic notes and in the statements made by its Agent at the hearing. It also resulted from the general obligation on parties stated by the Permanent Court of International Justice in *Electricity Company of Sofia and Bulgaria* to 'abstain from any measure capable of exercising a prejudicial effect in regard to the execution of the decision to be given and, in general, not allow any step of any kind to be taken which might aggravate or extend the dispute'.

Separate Opinion of Judge Lucky   (1)   There was a dispute between Malaysia and Singapore and the Parties had complied with the obligation to exchange views provided in Article 283 of the Convention.

(2)   A high burden of proof must be satisfied before the Tribunal would grant provisional measures.

(3)   Because Malaysia shared a common sea and ecosystem with Singapore there should have been consultation, exchange of information and a joint study before the land reclamation works began, to determine whether there would be irreparable harm to the environment by the works.

(4)   In order to show a *prima facie* case that the Tribunal had jurisdiction to decide the claim, the evidence must show that there would be serious harm to the environment and the right of the applicant party would be prejudiced. The Applicant must show a very strong probability upon the facts that serious harm would accrue to the Applicant in the future.

(5)   The Convention required States which border the same maritime areas to cooperate in matters relating to the protection and preservation of the marine environment. Before Singapore had carried out reclamation works in its territorial sea which was shared with Malaysia, it should have consulted Malaysia.

(6)   The evidence disclosed the possibility of serious harm to the environment. The land reclamation works by Singapore could result in an infringement of Malaysia's rights with respect to navigation.

Subsequent facts and settlement   Following a series of meetings in 2004 and 2005, the Parties settled their dispute in this case fully and definitively in accordance with the terms agreed in the Settlement Agreement, which was signed and entered into force on 26 April 2005. On 1 September 2005, in response to a joint request from the Parties, the arbitral tribunal delivered a final award, which was binding upon them in the terms set out in the Settlement Agreement.

There follows

Order of International Tribunal for the Law of the Sea on Request for Provisional Measures, 8 October 2003 (extract)

[. . .]

[**494**] [. . .] 22. *Whereas*, in the Notification and Statement of Claim of 4 July 2003, Malaysia requested the arbitral tribunal to be constituted under Annex VII (hereinafter 'the Annex VII arbitral tribunal'):

  (1) to delimit the boundary between the territorial waters of the two States in the area beyond Points W25 and E47 of the 1995 Agreement;

  (2) [**495**] to declare that Singapore has breached its obligations under the 1982 Convention and under general international law by the initiation and continuation of its land reclamation activities without due notification and full consultation with Malaysia;

  (3) to decide that, as a consequence of the aforesaid breaches, Singapore shall:

    (a) cease its current land reclamation activities in any area forming part of Malaysian waters, and restore those areas to the situation they were in before the works were commenced;

    (b) suspend its current land reclamation activities until it has conducted and published an adequate assessment of their potential effects on the environment and on the affected coastal areas, taking into account representations made by affected parties;

    (c) as an aspect of this assessment process:

      (i) provide Malaysia with full information as to the current and projected works, including in particular their proposed extent, their method of construction, the origin and kind of materials used, and designs for coastal protection and remediation (if any);

---

[4] Only the opinions listed are reproduced in this volume. The declaration of President Nelson can be found at 126 *ILR* 506; the declaration of judge Anderson can be found at 126 *ILR* 508; the joint declaration of Judges *ad hoc* Hossain and Oxman can be found at 126 *ILR* 509; the separate opinion of Judge Ndiaye can be found at 126 *ILR* 521; and the separate opinion of Judge Jesus can be found at 126 *ILR* 524.

[5] The members of the Arbitral Tribunal were Mr Pinto (President), Dr Hossain, Professor Oxman, Professor Shearer and Sir Arthur Watts KCMG QC.

    (ii)   afford Malaysia a full opportunity to comment upon the works and their potential impacts having regard, *inter alia*, to the information provided, and

    (iii)   negotiate with Malaysia concerning any remaining unresolved issues;

(d) in the light of the assessment and of the required processes of consultation and negotiation with Malaysia, revise its reclamation plans so as to minimise or avoid the risks or effects of pollution or of other significant effects of those works on the marine environment (including excessive sedimentation, bed level changes and coastal erosion);

(e) provide adequate and timely information to Malaysia of projected bridges or other works tending to restrict maritime access to coastal areas and port facilities in the Straits of Johor, and take into account any representations of Malaysia so as to ensure that rights of maritime transit and access under international law are not impeded;

(f) to the extent that – notwithstanding the above measures – Malaysia, or persons or entities in Malaysia, are injuriously affected by the reclamation activities, provide full compensation for such injury, the amount of such compensation (if not previously agreed between the parties) to be determined by the Tribunal in the course of the proceedings;

23. *Whereas* the provisional measures requested by Malaysia in the Request to the Tribunal filed on 5 September 2003, and maintained in [**496**] the final submissions read by the Agent of Malaysia at the public sitting held on 27 September 2003, are as follows:

(a) that Singapore shall, pending the decision of the Arbitral Tribunal, suspend all current land reclamation activities in the vicinity of the maritime boundary between the two States or of areas claimed as territorial waters by Malaysia (and specifically around Pulau Tekong and Tuas);

(b) to the extent it has not already done so, provide Malaysia with full information as to the current and projected works, including in particular their proposed extent, their method of construction, the origin and kind of materials used, and designs for coastal protection and remediation (if any);

(c) afford Malaysia a full opportunity to comment upon the works and their potential impacts having regard, *inter alia*, to the information provided; and

(d) agree to negotiate with Malaysia concerning any remaining unresolved issues;

24. *Whereas* the submissions presented by Singapore in its Response, and maintained in the final submissions read by the Agent of Singapore at the public sitting held on 27 September 2003, are as follows:

Singapore requests the International Tribunal for the Law of the Sea to:

(a) dismiss Malaysia's Request for provisional measures; and

(b) order Malaysia to bear the costs incurred by Singapore in these proceedings;

25. *Considering* that, in accordance with article 287 of the Convention, Malaysia has, on 4 July 2003, instituted proceedings under Annex VII to the Convention against Singapore in the dispute concerning land reclamation by Singapore in and around the Straits of Johor;

26. *Considering* that Malaysia sent the notification instituting proceedings under Annex VII to the Convention to Singapore on 4 July 2003, together with a Request for provisional measures;

[...]

[**500**] [...] 59. *Considering* that [...] the Tribunal finds that the Annex VII arbitral tribunal would *prima facie* have jurisdiction over the dispute;

60. *Considering* that Singapore contends that Malaysia's Request (for the prescription of provisional measures) is inadmissible because it 'does not "specify ... the possible consequences ... for the preservation of the respective rights of the parties or for the [prevention] of serious harm to the marine environment", as required by Article 89(3) of the ITLOS Rules'; and further that the Request does not identify '"the urgency of the situation" as required by Article 89(4) of the ITLOS Rules';

61. *Considering* that, in its Request for provisional measures of 5 September 2003, Malaysia stated that the rights which it seeks to preserve by the grant of provisional measures are those relating to the preservation of the marine and coastal environment and the preservation of its rights to maritime access to its coastline, in particular via the eastern entrance of the Straits of Johor, and claimed that these rights are guaranteed by the provisions of the Convention which it specified in the Request;

62. *Considering* that Malaysia states that in the context of the diplomatic correspondence and during the bilateral consultations it has time and again specified which of its rights are at stake and what is their basis in law;

[**501**] [...] 63. *Considering* that, in the view of the Tribunal, the Request of Malaysia has fulfilled the requirements of article 89, paragraphs 3 and 4, of the Rules and therefore the Request is admissible;

64. *Considering* that, in accordance with article 290, paragraph 1, of the Convention, the Tribunal may prescribe measures to preserve the respective rights of the parties to the dispute or to prevent serious harm to the marine environment;

65. *Considering* that, according to article 290, paragraph 5, of the Convention, provisional measures may be prescribed pending the constitution of the Annex VII arbitral tribunal if the Tribunal considers that the urgency of the situation so requires;

66. *Considering* that Singapore contends that, as the Annex VII arbitral tribunal is to be constituted not later than 9 October 2003, there is no need to prescribe provisional measures given the short period of time remaining before that date;

67. *Considering* that, under article 290, paragraph 5, of the Convention, the Tribunal is competent to prescribe provisional measures prior to the constitution of the Annex VII arbitral tribunal, and that there is nothing in article 290 of the Convention to suggest that the measures prescribed by the Tribunal must be confined to that period;

68. *Considering* that the said period is not necessarily determinative for the assessment of the urgency of the situation or the period during which the prescribed measures are applicable and that the urgency of the situation must be assessed taking

into account the period during which the Annex VII arbitral tribunal is not yet in a position to 'modify, revoke or affirm those provisional measures';

69. *Considering* further that the provisional measures prescribed by the Tribunal may remain applicable beyond that period;

70. *Considering* that Malaysia alleges that, contrary to articles 2 and 15 of the Convention, Singapore has impinged on areas of Malaysia's territorial sea by its land reclamation works in the sector of Tuas, in the vicinity of Point 20, and that, for that reason, the Tribunal should prescribe the suspension of the said land reclamation works in that sector;

71. *Considering* that the existence of a claim to an area of territorial sea is not, *per se*, a sufficient basis for the prescription of provisional measures under article 290, paragraph 5, of the Convention;

72. *Considering* that, in the view of the Tribunal, the evidence presented by Malaysia does not show that there is a situation of urgency or that there is a risk that the rights it claims with respect to an area of territorial sea would suffer irreversible damage pending consideration of the merits of the case by the Annex VII arbitral tribunal;

[**502**] 73. *Considering* that the Tribunal, therefore, does not consider it appropriate in the circumstances to prescribe provisional measures with respect to the land reclamation by Singapore in the sector of Tuas;

74. *Considering* that Malaysia has further argued that Singapore has placed itself in breach of its obligations under international law, specifically under articles 123, 192, 194, 198, 200, 204, 205, 206 and 210 of the Convention, and in relation thereto, article 300 of the Convention and the precautionary principle, which under international law must direct any party in the application and implementation of those obligations;

75. *Considering* that Singapore submits that in the present situation there is no room for applying the precautionary principle for the prescription of provisional measures;

76. *Considering* that, at a public sitting held on 26 September 2003, Singapore, in response to Malaysia's second requested measure, cited in paragraph 23(b) above, stated that it had already given an explicit offer to share the information that Malaysia requested in reliance on its rights under the Convention and that this offer had been made in Singapore's Note dated 17 July 2003 and its letter of 21 August 2003;

77. *Considering* that at the same sitting, in response to Malaysia's third requested measure, cited in paragraph 23(c) above, Singapore expressly stated that it would give Malaysia a full opportunity to comment on the reclamation works and their potential impacts, and that it would notify and consult Malaysia before it proceeded to construct any transport links between Pulau Tekong, Pulau Ubin and the main island of Singapore if such links could affect Malaysia's rights of passage;

78. *Considering* that, at the same sitting, in response to Malaysia's fourth requested measure, cited in paragraph 23(d) above, Singapore declared that it had expressly stated its readiness and willingness to enter into negotiations and that it remained ready and willing to do so;

79. *Considering* that, at the public sitting held on 27 September 2003, Malaysia stated that during the hearing, Singapore had provided some further clarifications on the

three requested measures, cited in paragraph 23(b), (c) and (d) above, and that, in the light of this new information, Malaysia would be prepared to accept these assurances if the Tribunal made them a matter of formal judicial record;

80. *Considering* that Malaysia stated that there had been an acceleration of work around Pulau Tekong and that Singapore had solemnly assured the Tribunal that it had not been and was not accelerating its works;

81. *Considering* that the Tribunal places on record the assurances given by Singapore as specified in paragraphs 76 to 80;

[503] 82. *Considering* that Malaysia, in the first measure cited in paragraph 23(a) above, requests that Singapore shall, pending the decision of the Annex VII arbitral tribunal, suspend all current land reclamation activities in the vicinity of the maritime boundary between the two States or of areas claimed as territorial sea by Malaysia (and specifically around Pulau Tekong and Tuas);

83. *Considering* that, at the public sitting held on 27 September 2003, Malaysia stated that it accepts the importance of land reclamation and does not claim a veto over Singapore's activities;

84. *Considering* that, at the same public sitting, Malaysia stressed, however, that in-filling works in Area D at Pulau Tekong was of primary concern and that if Singapore were to give clear undertakings to the Tribunal that no effort would be made to infill Area D pending the decision of the Annex VII arbitral tribunal, and if these under-takings were likewise made a matter of formal judicial record, Malaysia's concerns would be significantly reduced;

85. *Considering* that, in response to Malaysia's first requested measure, as cited in paragraph 23(a) above, the Agent of Singapore, at the public sitting on 27 September 2003, read out a 'commitment' that the Government of Singapore had already made in its Note of 2 September 2003, as follows:

> If, after having considered the material [*that is to say the material we have provided Malaysia with*] Malaysia believes that Singapore had missed some point or misinterpreted some data and can point to a specific and unlawful adverse effect that would be avoided by suspending some part of the present works, Singapore would carefully study Malaysia's evidence. If the evidence were to prove compelling, Singapore would seriously re-examine its works and consider taking such steps as are necessary and proper, including a suspension, [*and I emphasize that*] to deal with the adverse effect in question;

86. *Considering* that Singapore accepted the proposal that Malaysia and Singapore jointly sponsor and fund a scientific study by independent experts on terms of reference to be agreed by the two sides;

87. *Considering* that, when presenting its final submissions during the public sitting held on 27 September 2003, the Agent of Singapore stated:

> Concerning Malaysia's first [requested measure] for Singapore to stop its reclamation works immediately, which was modified by the Malaysian Agent this morning, . . . Singapore is pleased to inform the Tribunal that regarding Area D, no irreversible action

will be taken by Singapore to construct the stone revetment around Area D pending the completion of the joint study, which should be completed within a year;

[504] 88. *Considering* that the Tribunal places on record the commitments referred to in paragraphs 85 to 87;

89. *Considering* that the Agent of Singapore stated that:

> none of the above agreements affect[s] the rights of both Malaysia and Singapore to continue our reclamation works, which, however, must be conducted in accordance with international best practice and the rights and obligations of both parties under international law;

90. *Considering* that, having regard to the obligation of the parties not to aggravate the dispute pending its settlement, the parties have the obligation not to create an irremediable situation and in particular not to frustrate the purpose of the study to be undertaken by a group of independent experts;

91. *Considering* that Malaysia and Singapore share the same marine environment in and around the Straits of Johor;

92. *Considering* that, as this Tribunal has stated:

> the duty to cooperate is a fundamental principle in the prevention of pollution of the marine environment under Part XII of the Convention and general international law and that rights arise therefrom which the Tribunal may consider appropriate to preserve under article 290 of the Convention (*The MOX Plant Case*, Order of 3 December 2001, paragraph 82);[6]

93. *Considering* that Malaysia claims that Singapore, by initiating and carrying on major reclamation works in the areas concerned, has affected Malaysia's rights to the natural resources within its territorial sea and violated its rights to the integrity of the marine environment in those areas;

94. *Considering* that Singapore maintains that the land reclamation works have not caused any significant impact on Malaysia and that the necessary steps were taken to examine possible adverse impacts on the surrounding waters;

95. *Considering* that an assessment concerning the impact of the land reclamation works on waters under the jurisdiction of Malaysia has not been undertaken by Singapore;

96. *Considering* that it cannot be excluded that, in the particular circumstances of this case, the land reclamation works may have adverse effects on the marine environment;

97. *Considering* that, in the view of the Tribunal, the record of this case shows that there was insufficient cooperation between the parties up to the submission of the Statement of Claim on 4 July 2003;

[6 See p. 431 above.]

98. *Considering* that the last public sitting of the hearing showed a change in the attitude of the parties resulting in the commitments [**505**] which the Tribunal has put on record, and that it is urgent to build on the commitments made to ensure prompt and effective cooperation of the parties in the implementation of their commitments;

99. *Considering* that, given the possible implications of land reclamation on the marine environment, prudence and caution require that Malaysia and Singapore establish mechanisms for exchanging information and assessing the risks or effects of land reclamation works and devising ways to deal with them in the areas concerned;

100. *Considering* that Malaysia and Singapore shall ensure that no action is taken which might prejudice the carrying out of any decision on the merits which the Annex VII arbitral tribunal may render;

101. *Considering* that, in accordance with article 89, paragraph 5, of the Rules, the Tribunal may prescribe measures different in whole or in part from those requested;

102. *Considering* that Malaysia and Singapore should each ensure that no action is taken which might aggravate or extend the dispute submitted to the Annex VII arbitral tribunal;

103. *Considering* that, pursuant to article 95, paragraph 1, of the Rules, each party is requested to submit to the Tribunal a report and information on compliance with any provisional measures prescribed;

104. *Considering* that, in the view of the Tribunal, it is consistent with the purpose of proceedings under article 290, paragraph 5, of the Convention that parties submit reports to the Annex VII arbitral tribunal, unless the arbitral tribunal decides otherwise;

105. *Considering* that, in the present case, the Tribunal sees no reason to depart from the general rule, as set out in article 34 of its Statute, that each party shall bear its own costs;

106. *For these reasons,*

THE TRIBUNAL,

1. Unanimously,

Prescribes, pending a decision by the Annex VII arbitral tribunal, the following provisional measures under article 290, paragraph 5, of the Convention:

Malaysia and Singapore shall cooperate and shall, for this purpose, enter into consultations forthwith in order to:

(a)   establish promptly a group of independent experts with the mandate

  (i)   to conduct a study, on terms of reference to be agreed by Malaysia and Singapore, to determine, within a period not exceeding one year from the date of this Order, the effects of Singapore's land [**506**] reclamation and to propose, as appropriate, measures to deal with any adverse effects of such land reclamation;

  (ii)   to prepare, as soon as possible, an interim report on the subject of infilling works in Area D at Pulau Tekong;

(b)   exchange, on a regular basis, information on, and assess risks or effects of, Singapore's land reclamation works;

(c)   implement the commitments noted in this Order and avoid any action incompatible with their effective implementation, and, without prejudice to their positions
on any issue before the Annex VII arbitral tribunal, consult with a view to reaching a prompt agreement on such temporary measures with respect to Area D at
Pulau Tekong, including suspension or adjustment, as may be found necessary to
ensure that the infilling operations pending completion of the study referred to in
subparagraph (a)(i) with respect to that area do not prejudice Singapore's ability
to implement the commitments referred to in paragraphs 85 to 87.

2. Unanimously,

Directs Singapore not to conduct its land reclamation in ways that might cause
irreparable prejudice to the rights of Malaysia or serious harm to the marine environment, taking especially into account the reports of the group of independent
experts.

3. Unanimously,

Decides that Malaysia and Singapore shall each submit the initial report referred to
in article 95, paragraph 1, of the Rules, not later than 9 January 2004 to this Tribunal
and to the Annex VII arbitral tribunal, unless the arbitral tribunal decides otherwise.

4. Unanimously,

Decides that each party shall bear its own costs.

[. . .]

SEPARATE OPINION OF JUDGE CHANDRASEKHARA RAO (EXTRACT)

[. . .]

III. Conclusion

[. . .]

[520] [. . .] 36. As regards the prescription of provisional measures, the limited
question that calls for determination by the Tribunal is whether, on the evidence before
the Tribunal, it can be said that there is a reasonable possibility of either irreparable
damage to the rights of Malaysia or serious harm to the marine environment in the
short period before a decision of the Annex VII arbitral tribunal.

37. Malaysia contends that the Tribunal should not give credence to the argument
of Singapore that Malaysia has delayed its own case for too long to make its claim of
urgency credible, since the case involves the protection of the ecological interests, and
the suspension of certain reclamation works can still make a difference. Assuming for
the sake of argument that this is a valid justification for the delay involved, it would
not absolve Malaysia from supplying proof of the damage alleged. Malaysia further
contends that in matters involving protection of the environment the burden of proof
lies on the State against whose conduct the case is brought. Here too, even if one were
to accept this argument, it has been seen that Singapore has placed materials before

the Tribunal to indicate that there is no likelihood of its actions causing irreparable prejudice to the rights of Malaysia or serious harm to the marine environment before the arbitral tribunal has had occasion to deal with Malaysia's claim. Singapore's assertions have not been seriously challenged. Proof of the damage alleged by Malaysia has not been supplied. In its Request for provisional measures, the only argument advanced in support of the urgency of the situation is that there is little prospect that the Annex VII arbitral tribunal will be established and able to render a decision on provisional measures for some time. This argument too is untenable. In the normal course of events, the arbitral tribunal will be constituted not later than 9 October 2003. There is also no reason to believe that this body will not meet shortly thereafter.

38. It appears that urgency is indeed absent in respect of the substantial relief sought by Malaysia concerning suspension of Singapore's land reclamation activities. The Tribunal observes in paragraphs 72 and 73 of its Order that Malaysia has not proven the existence of a situation of urgency in respect of its claims in relation to Singapore's land reclamation in the sector of Tuas and it accordingly declares that it does not consider it appropriate under the circumstances to prescribe provisional measures with respect to that area. It may be recalled that, at the public sitting held on 27 September 2003, Malaysia stated that its concerns would be 'significantly reduced' if Singapore were to give undertakings to the Tribunal that no effort would be made to infill Area D pending [521] the decision of the merits tribunal. Singapore gave no such undertaking. The Tribunal's Order does not prescribe any measures requiring Singapore to stop infilling Area D, for there is no evidence before the Tribunal that such infilling would lead to irreparable prejudice to the rights of Malaysia or serious harm to the marine environment pending a decision of the arbitral tribunal. Accordingly, Malaysia has failed to prove a situation of urgency in respect of the substantial relief it sought concerning reclamation works even around Pulau Tekong. The operative part of the Order prescribes certain provisional measures which are consistent with that premise; these measures underline a sense of urgency arising out of the duty to cooperate as enshrined in Part XII of the Convention and general international law. The Tribunal is not an innovator of these measures. They emanate from the assurances given by Singapore during the course of the oral proceedings, the agreement of the parties to have a joint study undertaken of the effects of Singapore's land reclamation and the statement of Singapore that if there is compelling evidence that its reclamation works have adverse effects it would re-examine its works and consider taking such steps as are necessary and proper, including a suspension, to deal with them. The Tribunal considered it necessary to underline that, in view of the special concerns expressed by Malaysia, the group of independent experts entrusted with the mandate of determining the effects of Singapore's land reclamation should prepare an interim report on the subject of infilling works in Area D at Pulau Tekong with a view to examining as soon as possible whether Malaysia's concerns in respect of Area D are properly based. The Order further calls upon the parties to enter into consultations with a view to ensuring that the infilling operations do not prejudice Singapore's ability to implement the commitments referred to in paragraphs 85 to 87 of the

Order. It recognizes the basic stand of Singapore that any suspension or adjustment of land reclamation works should follow an objective study by a group of independent experts and that corrective measures would be taken only if such a study provides proof of adverse effects of the type mentioned by Malaysia.

[528] SEPARATE OPINION OF JUDGE COT

[Translation]

1. I subscribe to the operative part of the Order and to the reasons on which it is based. I agree with the view that Malaysia's request for the [529] prescription of provisional measures is admissible and that the Tribunal is competent to entertain that request. I also agree with the Tribunal's view that there is no need to prescribe provisional measures in the western part of the Straits of Johor. It is my opinion that Malaysia has not established the possibility or likelihood of its rights in this area being affected or of serious harm being caused to the marine environment. This finding does not in any way prejudice the merits of the case, in particular the assessment that the Annex VII arbitral tribunal will have to make concerning Malaysia's territorial claim to point 20.

2. Like the Tribunal, I consider that the situation is different in the eastern part of the Straits. It is possible or probable that Malaysia's rights, in particular its rights of navigation and its right to preserve the marine environment falling within its sovereignty, will be affected. It is difficult to deny that land reclamation works in an international waterway up to the boundary of the neighbouring territorial sea may adversely affect the neighbour's rights. In view of the narrowness of the Straits and the proximity of the coastline on either side, the works planned by Singapore will have a drastic affect on the geography and hydrography of the Straits of Johor. If Malaysia were to undertake similar works, the Calder channel would be completely unnavigable. Furthermore, the studies made by the Applicant show that serious harm to the environment in this area is possible. In short, the condition of urgency is satisfied.

3. I believe that in the present case the appropriate measure in order to protect the rights of the Applicant would have been to prescribe the suspension of the infilling works in Area D at Pulau Tekong pending the results of the scientific study requested by the parties. In fact, I believe that this obligation devolves upon Singapore in any case. First, it results from the commitments entered into by the Government of Singapore in its diplomatic notes and in the statements made by its Agent at the hearing, in particular on Saturday, 27 September 2003 (ITLOS/PV.03/05, pp. 37 *et seq.*). Second, it results from the general obligation that parties have to

> abstain from any measure capable of exercising a prejudicial effect in regard to the execution of the decision to be given and, in general, not allow any step of any kind to be taken which might aggravate or extend the dispute ... [*Electricity Company of Sofia and Bulgaria, Order of 5 December 1939, PCIJ, Series A/B, No. 79*, p. 199.]

4. In fact I consider the infilling works in Area D to be an irreparable measure. It is not a question of filling the area with sand which will then be able to be dredged at will, like the sandcastles built by children on the beach that are washed away by the next

tide. The advocate [530] for Singapore, Mrs Cheong, explained the land reclamation process very clearly (ITLOS/PV.03/03, pp. 13–19). The infilling to a depth of 15 metres must be of a sufficiently solid composition to serve as a foundation for buildings some twenty to thirty or more metres high, similar to those that appeared in the video she showed.

5. Singapore referred to the cost of suspending the infilling works but was very careful not to put forward a figure or a rough estimate. Remember that we are talking about a suspension limited in time and affecting only one of the areas in question, viz. Area D at Pulau Tekong. I have no idea of the sums involved but I note that Singapore did indeed consider the possibility of suspending the works – the Agent of Singapore even referred to this possibility at the hearing (ITLOS/PV.03/05, p. 38) – if it felt that Malaysia's rights were at stake. The cost is therefore bearable. It should be added that a financial cost is by definition not irreparable and may result in damages.

6. The provisional measures prescribed by the Tribunal go further than and at the same time fall short of the suspension requested by Malaysia. On the one hand, operative paragraph 1(c) prescribes that the parties should consult with a view to reaching a prompt agreement on measures with respect to Area D at Pulau Tekong; the text therefore adds an obligation of immediate cooperation, so that the parties agree on the measures to be taken. However, on the other hand, the Order does not specify to what extent the infilling works must be suspended or slowed down pending the results of the study referred to. On this point there is a certain degree of uncertainty concerning the precise extent of the obligation devolving upon the parties.

7. However, I believe that the application by the parties of the operative part of the Order, in good faith and with a view to the forthcoming arbitration, must enable the rights of the Applicant to be preserved. That is why I have concurred with the text.

SEPARATE OPINION OF JUDGE LUCKY (EXTRACT)

1. This dispute revolves around complex issues over which the parties are at variance because the pleadings [and] documentary and oral evidence indicate diverse views and opinions.

2. Briefly, Malaysia alleges that reclamation works by Singapore in the eastern and western areas in Singapore's territorial sea are causing and will cause 'serious and irreparable damage to the marine environment and serious prejudice to its rights'. Singapore has responded that the technical reports it has received; careful planning; as well as detailed [531] studies; all show that no significant adverse effects would result from the reclamation works.

[...]

[533] [...] *The degree of proof*

11. The burden of proof required in a case for provisional measures is relatively high. The Tribunal is being asked to make mandatory orders, *inter alia* to cease work on a project which is elaborate, expensive and of considerable magnitude. Therefore, several factors have to be considered: the balance of convenience or inconvenience to each side; the status quo as to whether the works are reversible; whether the decision

would cause prejudice; and, whether there will be serious harm to the environment. Because of the foregoing factors, could and should the matter be deemed urgent? Nevertheless, the question to be posed and answered when considering each factor, and/or all of them jointly, is: whether the decision will be fair to both parties.

Urgency

12. Perhaps, at this juncture it will be convenient to deal with the question of 'urgency' which is a requirement for prescribing provisional measures. This is of particular significance in the special circumstances of this case. The view expressed here is supportive of my reason for recommending the measure in the concluding paragraph of this opinion. The work in progress, specifically in Area D off Pulau Tekong, is part of an ongoing programme of land reclamation by Singapore. Malaysia is a neighbouring coastal State. It shares a common sea and ecosystem with Singapore and it is only fair that there should have been consultation, exchange of information and a joint study before the works began; to determine whether there would be irreparable harm to the environment.

[534] *Is there a* prima facie *case?*

13. In my view the merits of the application have to be considered, but not determined or seemingly determined. The evidence must disclose that there would be serious harm to the environment and the rights of the applicant party would be prejudiced. The possibility or probability of such harm cannot be based on speculation or projections as this is insufficient; because the Applicant must show a very strong probability upon the facts that serious harm will accrue to the Applicant in the future. The degree of probability of future harm is not an absolute standard; what is to be aimed at is justice between the parties having regard to the circumstances. I mean no disrespect to either party because in such applications time constraints are relevant; the full 'pre-trial' processes have not occurred, the defence to the Statement of Claim has not been served and neither side's case has been 'proved' as at a final hearing on the merits. As I alluded to earlier I do not find that the evidential requirements for provisional measures have been met in the western area (Tuas area).

Pulau Tekong – Area D

14. Perhaps, the crucial question could be: What is the extent to which a State can carry out reclamation works in its territorial sea where it shares a common sea with its neighbour? Internal public hearings and reports and studies by the coastal State are not enough. There ought to be consultation with the neighbouring State. There was no meaningful consultation between the parties until the Statement of Claim was filed on 4 July 2003. Singapore's studies focused on Singapore alone.

15. The essence of this claim for relief is protection of the environment and rights of navigation. Article 123 specifies for cooperation of States bordering enclosed or semi-enclosed seas and provides for direct cooperation or through an appropriate regional organisation. The parties did not pursue the direct or regional approach.

The Convention is quite clear at many points in providing that States which border the same maritime areas should cooperate especially in matters relating to the protection and preservation of the marine environment.

16. National coastal reclamation which is crucial and necessary for development and growth ought to be carried out in recognition of the rights of a neighbouring State. It is an equitable maxim that a person or State ought to have his (its) neighbour in mind when directing his (its) mind to any act or action which may affect rights.

[**535**] 17. The position in respect of the areas complained of (off Pulau Tekong) is different to the areas off Tuas in the West. In this area the evidence discloses the possibility of serious harm to the environment. These works could result in an infringement of Malaysia's rights with respect to navigation in that channels are being rearranged so that smaller vessels are diverted to the Johor Channel. It is also my view that the question of irreparable harm or more specifically, 'serious harm to the environment and marine life' has been sufficiently established to accord with the standard of proof required in an application for provisional measures.

18. Singapore suggested that it was prepared to consider suspending works if Malaysia established that its rights are being infringed. But one might ask: if Malaysia says its rights are being infringed and Singapore does not think so, who will determine the issue? An exchange of views took place but this did not result in a settlement and as time elapsed and communication broke down it became necessary to invite a third party to resolve the issue; hence the application for provisional measures before this Tribunal. As I alluded to at the beginning, the work is in progress and while certain assurances have been given and appreciated by both parties and recorded by the Tribunal, the application must be addressed and measures prescribed or denied.

19. After considering the issues and evidence I agree with the Tribunal. Might I humbly suggest that I would have added that specific measures be prescribed with respect to Area D off Pulau Tekong, i.e., that infilling works in Area D off Pulau Tekong be suspended until a joint assessment authority is established to report within three months whether there will be serious harm to the environment and whether the rights of Malaysia with respect to navigation will be infringed.

20. Although there is no international precedent that I can find, I think the time has come to consider whether applicants for provisional measures, as in some municipal systems, should provide a guarantee in their applications that if the measures sought are granted, but discontinued if the substantive matter is determined in the respondent's favour, they will pay damages incurred and costs to the respondents.

21. I have voted in favour of the Order of the Tribunal.

[Report: 126 *ILR* 491]

Award of the Arbitral Tribunal on Agreed Terms, 1 September 2005

1. *Whereas* Malaysia and Singapore are, and at all relevant times were, Parties to the United Nations Convention on the Law of the Sea (the Convention), Part XV of which

obligates them to settle any dispute between them concerning the interpretation or application of the Convention by peaceful means as specified therein;

2. *Whereas* neither Malaysia nor Singapore has made a written declaration pursuant to article 287, paragraph 1 of the Convention, with the result that, pursuant to article 287, paragraph 3, they are deemed to have accepted arbitration in accordance with Annex VII to the Convention as the means of settling their disputes;

3. *Whereas* neither Malaysia nor Singapore has made a written declaration pursuant to article 298 of the Convention;

4. *Whereas* on 4 July 2003 Malaysia transmitted to Singapore the Notification and Statement of Claim instituting arbitral proceedings as provided for in Annex VII to the Convention in a dispute concerning land reclamation by Singapore in and around the Straits of Johor, and a Request for provisional measures in that dispute pending constitution of an arbitral tribunal under Annex VII to the Convention;

5. *Whereas* Malaysia, in the foregoing Notification, on 4 July 2003, appointed Dr Kamal Hossain as a member of the Arbitral Tribunal pursuant to article 3, paragraph (b) of Annex VII to the Convention, and Singapore, on 29 July 2003, appointed Professor Bernard H. Oxman as a member of the Arbitral Tribunal pursuant to article 3, paragraph (c) of Annex VII to the Convention;

6. *Whereas* on 5 September 2003 Malaysia transmitted to the International Tribunal for the Law of the Sea (ITLOS) a Request for the prescription of provisional measures in the said dispute by ITLOS in accordance with article 290, paragraph 5 of the Convention;

7. *Whereas* on 5 September 2003 the Registrar of ITLOS was notified of the appointment of HE Mr Ahmad Fuzi Haji Abdul Razak, the Secretary-General of the Ministry of Foreign Affairs, as Agent for Malaysia;

8. *Whereas* on 6 September 2003 the Registrar of ITLOS was notified of the appointment of HE Professor Tommy Koh, Ambassador-at-Large in the Ministry of Foreign Affairs, as Agent for Singapore;

9. *Whereas* on 20 September 2003 Singapore filed with the Registry of ITLOS its response to Malaysia, a certified copy of which was transmitted to the Agent for Malaysia on the same day;

10. *Whereas* ITLOS did not include upon the bench judges of the nationalities of the Parties, and pursuant to article 17, paragraph 3 of the Statute of ITLOS, Malaysia chose Dr Kamal Hossain, and Singapore chose Professor Bernard H. Oxman to sit as judges *ad hoc* in the case, and they were duly admitted to sit as such on 24 September 2003;

11. *Whereas* after an exchange of written pleadings, and oral statements at public sittings of ITLOS on 25, 26 and 27 September 2003, ITLOS, in an Order dated 8 October 2003, stated:

THE TRIBUNAL

   1. Unanimously,

   Prescribes, pending a decision by the Annex VII arbitral tribunal, the following provisional measures under article 290, paragraph 5, of the Convention:

Malaysia and Singapore shall cooperate and shall, for this purpose, enter into consultations forthwith in order to:

(a) establish promptly a group of independent experts with the mandate

    (i) to conduct a study, on terms of reference to be agreed by Malaysia and Singapore, to determine, within a period not exceeding one year from the date of this Order, the effects of Singapore's land reclamation and to propose, as appropriate, measures to deal with any adverse effects of such land reclamation;

    (ii) to prepare, as soon as possible, an interim report on the subject of infilling works in Area D at Pulau Tekong;

(b) exchange, on a regular basis, information on, and assess risks or effects of, Singapore's land reclamation works;

(c) implement the commitments noted in this Order and avoid any action incompatible with their effective implementation, and, without prejudice to their positions on any issue before the Annex VII arbitral tribunal, consult with a view to reaching a prompt agreement on such temporary measures with respect to Area D at Pulau Tekong, including suspension or adjustment, as may be found necessary to ensure that the infilling operations pending completion of the study referred to in subparagraph (a)(i) with respect to that area do not prejudice Singapore's ability to implement the commitments referred to in paragraphs 85 to 87.

2. Unanimously,

Directs Singapore not to conduct its land reclamation in ways that might cause irreparable prejudice to the rights of Malaysia or serious harm to the marine environment, taking especially into account the reports of the group of independent experts.

3. Unanimously,

Decides that Malaysia and Singapore shall each submit the initial report referred to in article 95, paragraph 1 of the Rules, not later than 9 January 2004 to this Tribunal and to the Annex VII arbitral tribunal, unless the arbitral tribunal decides otherwise.

4. Unanimously,

Decides that each party shall bear its own costs.

12. *Whereas* ITLOS, for the reasons stated in its Order dated 8 October 2003, in determining its jurisdiction to prescribe provisional measures under article 290, paragraph 5 of the Convention pending a decision by this Tribunal, found *inter alia* that there was no controversy between the Parties as to the existence of a dispute, and that this Tribunal would *prima facie* have jurisdiction over the dispute;

13. *Whereas*, for the reasons indicated in its Order of 8 October 2003, ITLOS stated in paragraph 73 of that Order that it did not consider it appropriate in the circumstances to prescribe provisional measures with respect to the land reclamation by Singapore in the sector of Tuas;

14. *Whereas* the President of ITLOS had by his letter dated 10 October 2003 addressed to the President of the Tribunal notified the appointment, pursuant to article 3(e) of Annex VII to the Convention, of the following three members of that Tribunal:

Mr Christopher Pinto (President)
Professor Ivan Shearer
Sir Arthur Watts, KCMG QC;

15. *Whereas* the President of ITLOS by the same letter noted the appointment for the Annex VII arbitration, of HE Mr Tan Sri Ahmad Fuzi Haji Abdul Razak as Agent for Malaysia, and HE Professor Tommy Koh as Agent for Singapore;

16. *Whereas* this Tribunal, having been thus validly constituted, and having consulted extensively with the Parties, by its Order dated 19 July 2004, established its Rules of Procedure, article 2 of which designates the International Bureau of the Permanent Court of Arbitration (PCA) as the Registry for the arbitration;

17. *Whereas* the Secretary-General of the PCA, having consulted the Tribunal and the Parties, designated Ms Anne Joyce, a member of the International Bureau, as the Registrar of the Tribunal;

18. *Whereas* by letters dated 24 September 2004, the Parties notified ITLOS and this Tribunal that the Group of Experts established by them pursuant to paragraph 106(1)(a) of the Order of 8 October 2003, had completed its work on the Interim Report on infilling works required by paragraph 106(1)(a)(ii) of the Order, and transmitted copies thereof both to ITLOS and this Tribunal;

19. *Whereas* the Tribunal, at the request of the Parties, by Order dated 19 October 2004 extended until 8 November 2004 the due date for completion of the Final Report on the study to be carried out by the Group of Experts referred to; and *whereas* the Parties, by their letter dated 8 November 2004, transmitted a copy of the Final Report to the Tribunal, requesting also that arrangements be made for a conference at which the Parties could present to the Tribunal an overview of the Joint Study, and apprise the Tribunal of the progress of consultations that had taken place between them;

20. *Whereas* at the conference referred to in paragraph 19 of this preamble, which took place at The Hague on 10 January 2005, the Parties informed the Tribunal *inter alia* that they had agreed *ad referendum* on the draft of a Settlement Agreement to which it was expected that the Government of Malaysia would give its approval within one month of the conference;

21. *Whereas* the Parties by their letter dated 18 May 2005, notified the Tribunal that the said Settlement Agreement had been signed on 26 April 2005; and *whereas* the Settlement Agreement entered into force in accordance with its terms;

22. *Whereas* the Parties transmitted to the Tribunal duly certified copies of the said Settlement Agreement, as well as the Joint Records of their meetings on 22–23 December 2004, 7–8 January 2005 and 7–8 February 2005 which resulted in that Agreement;

23. *Whereas*, with respect to the dispute submitted by Malaysia to the Arbitral Tribunal on 4 July 2003, the said Settlement Agreement provides:

> 13. This Agreement is in full and definitive settlement of the dispute with respect to the land reclamation and all other issues related thereto. The Parties agree that the issue pertaining to the maritime boundaries be resolved through amicable negotiations,

without prejudice to the existing rights of the Parties under international law to resort to other pacific means of settlement.

14. This Agreement accordingly terminates the *Case Concerning Land Reclamation by Singapore In and Around the Straits of Johor (Malaysia v. Singapore)* upon the agreed terms.

15. The Parties shall forthwith jointly request that the Arbitral Tribunal in the *Case Concerning Land Reclamation by Singapore In and Around the Straits of Johor (Malaysia v. Singapore)* adopt the terms of this Agreement in the form of an agreed Award which is final and binding upon the Parties.

24. *Whereas* the Parties, by their letter dated 18 May 2005, jointly requested the Arbitral Tribunal to deliver a final Award binding upon the Parties in the terms set out in the said Settlement Agreement;

25. *Whereas* the Tribunal has examined the documentation submitted to it by the Parties including the said Settlement Agreement and has concluded that no further proceedings are necessary;

NOW THEREFORE the Tribunal

1. *Decides* in light of the joint request by the Parties referred to in preambular paragraph 24, that it has jurisdiction to render this Award in the *Case Concerning Land Reclamation by Singapore In and Around the Straits of Johor (Malaysia v. Singapore)*;

2. *Decides* to accede to the said joint request by the Parties and deliver a final Award binding upon the Parties in the terms set out in the Settlement Agreement, and does so by attaching the text of the said Settlement Agreement as the Annex to this Award which is issued pursuant to article 18 of the Rules of Procedure;

3. *Decides*, pursuant to article 19 of the Rules of Procedure, that each Party shall bear its own costs in presenting their respective cases;

4. *Decides* in accordance with article 20 of the Rules of Procedure that the expenses of this Tribunal shall be borne by the Parties in equal shares;

5. *Decides* that these proceedings are terminated.

Annex

CASE CONCERNING LAND RECLAMATION BY SINGAPORE IN AND AROUND THE STRAITS OF JOHOR (MALAYSIA V SINGAPORE)

SETTLEMENT AGREEMENT

Whereas paragraph 106(1)(a)(i) of the Order of the International Tribunal for the Law of the Sea in the *Case Concerning Land Reclamation by Singapore In and Around the Straits of Johor (Malaysia v Singapore), Request for Provisional Measures*, dated 8 October 2003, prescribes that the Governments of Malaysia and Singapore (hereafter 'the Parties') shall cooperate and shall, for this purpose, enter into consultations forthwith in order to establish promptly a group of independent experts with the mandate to conduct a study, on terms of reference to be agreed by the Parties, to determine, within a period not exceeding one year from the date of the Order, the effects of Singapore's land reclamation at Pulau Tekong and Tuas View Extension (hereafter 'the reclamation works') and to propose, as appropriate, measures to deal with any adverse effects of such land reclamation;

And whereas the Parties jointly established the Group of Experts (hereafter 'the GOE') to conduct the study on terms of reference agreed by the Parties;

And whereas the Parties jointly appointed DHI Water and Environment (hereafter 'DHI') to carry out detailed studies in order to assist the GOE;

And whereas the GOE completed the study and submitted its Final Report to the Parties on 5 November 2004;

And whereas the Parties have considered and reviewed the GOE's Final Report and accepted its recommendations;

And whereas the Parties are desirous of reaching an amicable, full and final settlement of the dispute submitted by Malaysia to the arbitral procedure provided for in Annex VII to the United Nations Convention on the Law of the Sea by a written notification to Singapore, accompanied by a Statement of Claim and Grounds on Which it is Based, on 4 July 2003;

And whereas the issue of maritime boundaries is to be dealt with in accordance with paragraph 21 of the Joint Record of the Meeting between Senior Officials of the Parties at The Hague on 7–9 January 2005;

And whereas the Parties agree that the recommendations of the GOE provide the basis for an amicable, full and final settlement of the said dispute;

The Parties have agreed as follows:

A. *Implementation of the recommendations of the GOE's Report*
(i) Design of the final shoreline of Area D at Pulau Tekong
    1. Singapore shall modify the final design of the shoreline of its land reclamation at Area D at Pulau Tekong to incorporate a 'bite' and a 'nose' as recommended by the GOE's Final Report as reflected and finalised in the chart at Annex 1.

(ii) Maintenance dredging of the 'bite'
    2. Singapore shall carry out maintenance dredging as is necessary to ensure that the depth of the dredged area of the 'bite' is kept at minus 12 metres Chart Datum.

(iii) Streamlining of Changi Finger
    3. Singapore shall streamline Changi Finger in line with the recommendations of the GOE either by a temporary or permanent structure (which may include a submerged structure) prior to the completion of the reclamation of the south-western bank of Area D of Pulau Tekong. In the event that this is not feasible or practical, or results in significantly increased costs, the rounding off of Changi Finger shall be completed within 12 months of the completion of the south-western reclamation of Area D.

(iv) Replacement of the sheetpile silt curtain at Area D by the final revetment protection

4. Singapore intends to replace the existing sheetpile silt curtain on the eastern side of Area D in Pulau Tekong with the final revetment protection as soon as is practicable and, in any case, within not more than 70 months, subject to the availability of resources for this purpose. Singapore shall endeavour to give priority to the replacement of the sheetpile silt curtain with the final revetment protection at the 'bite' of Area D which the GOE has concluded shall lead to the widening of Calder Harbour Channel, reducing the local velocities across the Channel and secondarily the current velocities in Kuala Johor.

(v) Scour protection

5. Singapore undertakes to pay the full cost of scour protection works at Tanjung Belungkor jetty, which the Parties have agreed amounts to Three Hundred Thousand Singapore Dollars (SGD 300,000).

6. Malaysia shall be responsible for the full cost of scour protection works at Pularek jetty.

(vi) Compensation for fishermen

7. A lump sum of Three Hundred and Seventy-Four Thousand and Four Hundred Malaysian Ringgit (RM 374,400), which is based on a sum of RM 5,200 per fisherman, shall be paid by Singapore to Malaysia to be distributed by Malaysia to its fishermen as full compensation for losses as a result of the reclamation works.

B. *Navigation*

8. Singapore reassures Malaysia that even after the Pulau Tekong reclamation, the safe and smooth passage of ships through Kuala Johor and Calder Harbour will not be adversely affected by the said reclamation.

C. *Joint mechanisms*

9. The Parties agree to expand the terms of reference of the Malaysia–Singapore Joint Committee on the Environment (MSJCE) to include the following:

a. To exchange information on and discuss matters affecting their respective environments in the Straits of Johor.

b. To undertake monitoring activities in relation to their respective environments in the Straits of Johor and address any adverse impacts, if necessary. These monitoring activities shall include:
   (i) monitoring water quality to protect the marine and estuarine environment; and
   (ii) monitoring ecology and morphology.

10.   The Parties agree that for the purposes of matters affecting navigation in the Straits of Johor under paragraph 8 of this Agreement, a representative of the Marine Department, Peninsular Malaysia shall be designated to co-chair the Maritime and Port Authority of Singapore–Johor Port Authority Operational Meeting (MPA–JPA Operational Meeting) on behalf of the Government of Malaysia.

11.   Each Party will keep the other informed, on a regular basis, of the progress of its implementation, pursuant to this Agreement, of the GOE's recommendations through the MSJCE and/or the MPA–JPA Operational Meeting, which shall be the forum for discussions.

12.   Each Party undertakes to observe the confidentiality and secrecy of documents, information and other data received or supplied by the other Party through the MSJCE or the MPA–JPA Operational Meeting pursuant to this Agreement.

D. Settlement of the dispute submitted to the arbitral procedure provided for in Annex VII to the United Nations Convention on the Law of the Sea pursuant to the written notification by Malaysia to Singapore accompanied by the Statement of Claim and Grounds on which it is based dated 4 July 2003

13.   This Agreement is in full and definitive settlement of the dispute with respect to the land reclamation and all other issues related thereto. The Parties agree that the issue pertaining to the maritime boundaries be resolved through amicable negotiations, without prejudice to the existing rights of the Parties under international law to resort to other pacific means of settlement.

14.   This Agreement accordingly terminates the *Case Concerning Land Reclamation by Singapore In and Around the Straits of Johor (Malaysia v Singapore)* upon the agreed terms.

15.   The Parties shall forthwith jointly request that the Arbitral Tribunal in the *Case Concerning Land Reclamation by Singapore In and Around the Straits of Johor (Malaysia v Singapore)* adopt the terms of this Agreement in the form of an agreed Award which is final and binding upon the Parties.

E. Entry into force

16.   This Agreement shall enter into force on the date of its signature.

IN WITNESS WHEREOF the undersigned, being duly authorised by their respective Governments, have signed this Agreement.

Done in duplicate at Singapore, this 26th day of April, two thousand and five, both texts being equally authentic.

[Source: http://www.pca-cpa.org/ENGLISH/RPC/MA51%20Award.pdf]

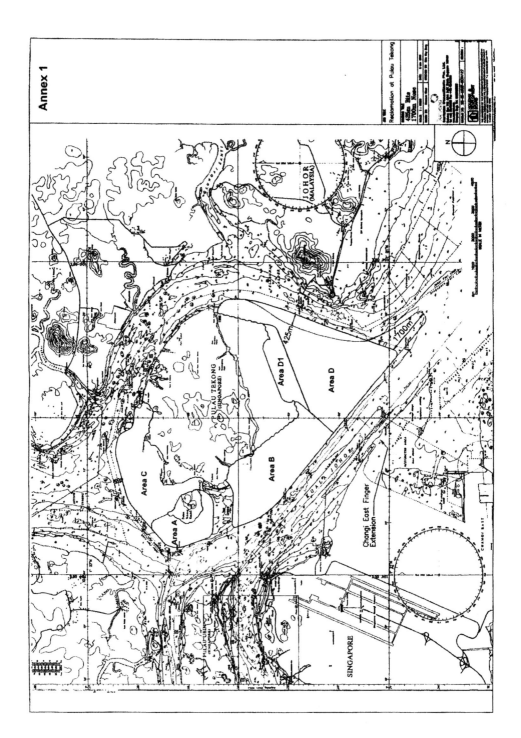

Annex 1

III

DECISIONS OF ARBITRAL TRIBUNALS

Southern Bluefin Tuna Case
(Australia and New Zealand *v.* Japan)[1]

Arbitral Tribunal, Washington DC[2]

4 August 2000 (Schwebel, *President*; Feliciano, Sir Kenneth Keith, Tresselt and Yamada, *Members*)

Conservation – southern bluefin tuna – United Nations Convention on the Law of the Sea, 1982 ('UNCLOS') – Convention for the Conservation of Southern Bluefin Tuna, 1993

Jurisdiction – provision for recourse to arbitration – UNCLOS Article 281 – Convention for the Conservation of Southern Bluefin Tuna, 1993, Article 16 – whether 1993 Convention excludes recourse to UNCLOS dispute settlement provisions

Powers and procedures of tribunals – International Tribunal for the Law of the Sea – provisional measures – legal effects – provisional measures granted pending arbitration – Arbitral Tribunal subsequently holding that it lacked jurisdiction – discharge of provisional measures by Arbitral Tribunal

Treaties – successive treaties – priority – lex specialis – lex posterior – whether specialised agreement supersedes general agreement

SUMMARY   *The facts*   Southern bluefin tuna, a migratory species of pelagic fish, was included on the list of highly migratory species in Annex

---

[1] The related decision on provisional measures of the International Tribunal for the Law of the Sea ('ITLOS') can be found at p. 393 above.

Japan was represented before the Arbitral Tribunal by: Shotaro Yachi, Agent; Nisuke Ando, Sir Elihu Lauterpacht CBE, QC, Shabtai Rosenne and Vaughan Lowe. Australia and New Zealand were represented before the Tribunal by: Bill Campbell, Agent for Australia; Tim Caughley, Agent for New Zealand; James Crawford SC, Bill Mansfield, Henry Burmester QC, Mark Jennings, Elana Geddis, Rebecca Irwin, and Andrew Serdy.

[2] The Arbitral Tribunal was constituted under Annex VII of the United Nations Convention on the Law of the Sea, 1982. It met at the offices of the World Bank in Washington DC and the International Centre for the Settlement of Investment Disputes acted as registrar and provided all secretarial, clerical and other facilities for the Tribunal.

I of the United Nations Convention on the Law of the Sea, 1982 ('UNC-LOS'). In 1982, following a severe decline in stocks as a result of overfishing, Australia, Japan and New Zealand began informally to manage the catching of southern bluefin tuna by setting a total allowable catch and allocating quotas to each of the three States. In 1993, the three States concluded the Convention for the Conservation of Southern Bluefin Tuna ('the 1993 Convention'), which formalised these arrangements and established a Commission for the Conservation of Southern Bluefin Tuna ('the Commission').[3] Article 16 of the 1993 Convention made provision for the settlement of disputes between the Parties regarding the interpretation and implementation of the Convention. Under those provisions, however, recourse to arbitration required the consent of each State. Australia, Japan and New Zealand were also parties to UNCLOS, which also contained provisions regarding the conservation of highly migratory fish stocks and which contained, in Part XV and Annex VII, provision for compulsory arbitration.

In the late 1990s, Japan maintained that, as a result of the conservation measures taken by the three States, there had been a marked improvement in the stock of southern bluefin tuna and that an experimental fishing programme should be permitted in addition to existing commercial fishing. Australia and New Zealand disagreed and the Commission was unable to reach agreement on the Japanese proposal. In June 1999, Japan unilaterally commenced an experimental fishing programme. The three States were unable to agree on arbitration or mediation under Article 16 of the 1993 Convention. In July 1999, Australia and New Zealand invoked the arbitration provisions of Annex VII of UNCLOS and brought proceedings claiming that Japan had violated its obligations under Articles 64 and 116–19 of UNCLOS.[4] On 27 August 1999, the International Tribunal for the Law of the Sea ('ITLOS') indicated provisional measures at the request of Australia and New Zealand. In doing so, ITLOS held that the arbitral tribunal which was to be constituted to hear the cases brought by Australia and New Zealand would *prima facie* have jurisdiction over the dispute.

Before the Arbitral Tribunal, Australia and New Zealand agreed to be treated as a single party. Japan contested the jurisdiction of the Tribunal and the admissibility of the application. Japan maintained that the dispute between the three States was a dispute regarding the 1993 Convention,

---

[3] The relevant provisions of the 1993 Convention are set out in paragraph 23 of the Award.
[4] These articles are set out in paragraph 32 of the Award.

not UNCLOS, and that, in any event, the 1993 Convention, as *lex posterior* and *lex specialis*, governed the relations between the Parties. Accordingly, Article 16 of the 1993 Convention, rather than the provisions of UNCLOS, governed any recourse to arbitration. In the alternative, Japan submitted that Australia and New Zealand had failed to meet the conditions set by UNCLOS for recourse to arbitration. Japan also contended that the case had become moot, because it was now prepared to accept a limit to its catch which had been proposed by Australia and New Zealand during the negotiations. Australia and New Zealand rejected all of these submissions.

Held by the Arbitral Tribunal, 4 August 2000   The Tribunal lacked jurisdiction to rule on the merits of the case; the provisional measures would therefore be discharged.

(1)   The case was not moot. The offer Australia and New Zealand had made during the negotiations was no longer acceptable to them. Even if it had been, the dispute would still not have been moot, because Japan had not undertaken for the future to forgo or restrict what it regarded as its right to fish for southern bluefin tuna in the absence of a decision by the Commission upon a total allowable catch and its allocation among the Parties.

(2)   The dispute between the Parties was not confined to a dispute under the 1993 Convention but also arose under UNCLOS. It was common in international law for more than one treaty to bear upon a particular dispute and the act of a State could violate the obligations of that State under more than one treaty. In some respects, UNCLOS went beyond the provisions of the 1993 Convention and it was not thereby superseded.

(3)   That did not mean, however, that there were distinct disputes under UNCLOS and the 1993 Convention. There was only one dispute, which arose under both Conventions.

(4)   UNCLOS Article 281(1) provided that:

If the States Parties which are parties to a dispute concerning the interpretation or application of this Convention have agreed to seek settlement of the dispute by a peaceful means of their choice, the procedures provided for in this Part apply only where no settlement has been reached by recourse to such means and the agreement between the parties does not exclude any further procedure.

The provisions of Article 16 of the 1993 Convention were an agreement to seek settlement of the dispute. Although Article 16 did not expressly exclude the applicability of any procedure, that was the natural inference to be drawn. Article 16(2) provided that, in the absence of agreement to refer a dispute to arbitration or to the International Court of Justice, there was an express obligation to continue to seek resolution of the dispute by the means listed in Article 16(1). That requirement had the effect of stressing the consensual nature of any reference to judicial settlement or arbitration and of removing proceedings under Article 16 from the reach of the compulsory procedures of Part XV of UNCLOS.

(5)   That conclusion was confirmed by the provisions of Articles 286 and 297 of UNCLOS, which showed that UNCLOS fell significantly short of establishing a comprehensive regime of compulsory jurisdiction entailing binding decisions. In addition, a significant number of international maritime agreements which excluded, with varying degrees of explicitness, unilateral reference to compulsory procedures had entered into force after UNCLOS.

(6)   The ITLOS Order prescribing provisional measures would therefore be revoked. That did not mean, however, that the Parties might disregard the effects of that Order or their own decisions made in conformity with it.

(7)   When it entered into force, the Straddling Stocks Convention, 1995, would go far towards resolving the procedural problems which had come before the Tribunal and, if faithfully and effectively implemented, the substantive issues between the Parties.

Separate Opinion of Sir Kenneth Keith   The Tribunal had jurisdiction under UNCLOS. The objects and purpose of UNCLOS in general and its comprehensive, compulsory dispute settlement provisions, together with the wording of UNCLOS Article 281 and Article 16 of the 1993 Convention, led to the conclusion that Article 16 did not exclude the dispute settlement procedures of UNCLOS.

There follows

Award of Arbitral Tribunal on Jurisdiction and Admissibility, 4 August 2000 (extract)

[. . .]

[514] [. . .] II. BACKGROUND TO THE CURRENT PROCEEDINGS

21. Southern Bluefin Tuna *(Thunnus maccoyi,* hereafter sometimes designated 'SBT') is a migratory species of pelagic fish that is included in the list of highly

migratory species set out in Annex I of the United Nations Convention on the Law of the Sea. Southern Bluefin Tuna range widely through the oceans of the Southern Hemisphere, principally the high seas, but they also traverse the exclusive economic zones and territorial waters of some States, notably Australia, New Zealand [515] and South Africa. They spawn in the waters south of Indonesia. The main market for the sale of Southern Bluefin Tuna is in Japan, where the fish is prized as a delicacy for sashimi.

22. It is common ground between the Parties that commercial harvest of Southern Bluefin Tuna began in the early 1950s and that, in 1961, the global catch peaked at 81,000 metric tons ('mt'). By the early 1980s, the SBT stock had been severely overfished; it was estimated that the parental stock had declined to 23–30% of its 1960 level. In 1982, Australia, New Zealand and Japan began informally to manage the catching of SBT. Japan joined with Australia and New Zealand in 1985 to introduce a global total allowable catch (hereafter, 'TAC') for SBT, initially set at 38,650 mt. In 1989, a TAC of 11,750 tons was agreed, with national allocations of 6,065 tons to Japan, 5,265 tons to Australia and 420 tons to New Zealand; Japan, as the largest harvester of SBT, sustained the greatest cut. But the SBT stock continued to decline. In 1997, it was estimated to be in the order of 7–15% of its 1960 level. Recruitment of SBT stock – the entry of new fish into the fishery – was estimated in 1998 to be about one third of the 1960 level. The institution of total allowable catch restrictions by Japan, Australia and New Zealand to some extent has been offset by the entry into the SBT fishery of fishermen from the Republic of Korea, Taiwan and Indonesia, and some flag-of-convenience States. Whether, in response to TAC restrictions, the stock has in fact begun to recover is at the core of the dispute between Australia and New Zealand, on the one hand, and Japan, on the other. They differ over the current state and recovery prospects of SBT stock and the means by which scientific uncertainty in respect of those matters can best be reduced.

23. In 1993, Australia, Japan and New Zealand concluded the Convention for the Conservation of Southern Bluefin Tuna (hereafter, the '1993 Convention' or 'CCSBT'). The provisions most pertinent to these proceedings are the following:

> Recalling that Australia, Japan and New Zealand have already taken certain measures for the conservation and management of southern bluefin tuna;
>
> Paying due regard to the rights and obligations of the Parties under relevant principles of international law;
>
> Noting the adoption of the United Nations Convention on the Law of the Sea in 1982;
>
> Noting that States have established exclusive economic or fishery zones within which they exercise, in accordance with international law, sovereign rights or jurisdiction for the purpose of exploring and exploiting, conserving and managing the living resources;
>
> Recognising that southern bluefin tuna is a highly migratory species which migrates through such zones;
>
> . . . Recognising that it is essential that they cooperate to ensure the conservation and optimum utilization of southern bluefin tuna;

[516] The Parties agreed *inter alia* that:

Article 3

The objective of this Convention is to ensure, through appropriate management, the conservation and optimum utilisation of southern bluefin tuna.

Article 4

Nothing in this Convention nor any measures adopted pursuant to it shall be deemed to prejudice the positions or views of any Party with respect to its rights and obligations under treaties and other international agreements to which it is party or its positions or views with respect to the law of the sea.

Article 5

1. Each Party shall take all action necessary to ensure the enforcement of this Convention and compliance with measures which become binding under paragraph 7 of Article 8.

2. The Parties shall expeditiously provide to the Commission for the Conservation of Southern Bluefin Tuna scientific information, fishing catch and effort statistics and other data relevant to the conservation of southern bluefin tuna and, as appropriate, ecologically related species.

3. The Parties shall cooperate in collection and direct exchange, when appropriate, of fisheries data, biological samples and other information relevant for scientific research on southern bluefin tuna and ecologically related species.

4. The Parties shall cooperate in the exchange of information regarding any fishing for southern bluefin tuna by nationals, residents and vessels of any State or entity not party to this Convention.

Article 6

1. The Parties hereby establish and agree to maintain the Commission for the Conservation of Southern Bluefin Tuna (hereinafter referred to as 'the Commission').
. . .

Article 7

Each Party shall have one vote in the Commission. Decisions of the Commission shall be taken by a unanimous vote of the Parties present at the Commission meeting.

Article 8

1. The Commission shall collect and accumulate information described below:
a.   scientific information, statistical data and other information relating to southern bluefin tuna and ecologically related species;
b.   information relating to laws, regulations and administrative measures on southern bluefin tuna fisheries;
c.   any other information relating to southern bluefin tuna.
[517] 2. The Commission shall consider matters described below:
a.   interpretation or implementation of this Convention and measures adopted pursuant to it;
b.   regulatory measures for conservation, management and optimum utilisation of southern bluefin tuna;

c.   matters which shall be reported by the Scientific Committee prescribed in Article 9;

d.   matters which may be entrusted to the Scientific Committee prescribed in Article 9;

e.   matters which may be entrusted to the Secretariat prescribed in Article 10;

f.   other activities necessary to carry out the provisions of this Convention.

    3. For the conservation, management and optimum utilisation of southern bluefin tuna:

a.   the Commission shall decide upon a total allowable catch and its allocation among the Parties unless the Commission decides upon other appropriate measures on the basis of the report and recommendations of the Scientific Committee referred to in paragraph 2(c) and (d) of Article 9; and

b.   the Commission may, if necessary, decide upon other additional measures.

    4. In deciding upon allocations among the Parties under paragraph 3 above the Commission shall consider:

a.   relevant scientific evidence;

b.   the need for orderly and sustainable development of southern bluefin tuna fisheries;

c.   the interests of Parties through whose exclusive economic or fishery zones southern bluefin tuna migrates;

d.   the interests of Parties whose vessels engage in fishing for southern bluefin tuna including those which have historically engaged in such fishing and those which have southern bluefin tuna fisheries under development;

e.   the contribution of each Party to conservation and enhancement of, and scientific research on, southern bluefin tuna;

f.   any other factors which the Commission deems appropriate.

    5. The Commission may decide upon recommendations to the Parties in order to further the attainment of the objective of this Convention.

    6. In deciding upon measures under paragraph 3 above and recommendations under paragraph 5 above, the Commission shall take full account of the report and recommendations of the Scientific Committee under paragraph 2(c) and (d) of Article 9.

    7. All measures decided upon under paragraph 3 above shall be binding on the Parties.

    8. The Commission shall notify all Parties promptly of measures and recommendations decided upon by the Commission.

    9. The Commission shall develop, at the earliest possible time and consistent with international law, systems to monitor all fishing activities related to southern bluefin tuna in order to enhance scientific knowledge necessary for conservation and management of southern bluefin tuna and in order to achieve effective implementation of this Convention and measures adopted pursuant to it.

[**518**]   10. The Commission may establish such subsidiary bodies as it considers desirable for the exercise of its duties and functions.

Article 9

    1. The Parties hereby establish the Scientific Committee as an advisory body to the Commission.

    2. The Scientific Committee shall:

a.   assess and analyse the status and trends of the population of southern bluefin tuna;

b.   coordinate research and studies of southern bluefin tuna;

    c.   report to the Commission its findings or conclusions, including consensus, majority and minority views, on the status of the southern bluefin tuna stock and, where appropriate, of ecologically related species;

    d.   make recommendations, as appropriate, to the Commission by consensus on matters concerning the conservation, management and optimum utilisation of southern bluefin tuna;

    e.   consider any matter referred to it by the Commission. . . .

    . . .

5.a. Each Party shall be a member of the Scientific Committee and shall appoint to the Committee a representative with suitable scientific qualifications who may be accompanied by alternates, experts and advisers. . . .

    . . .

Article 13

With a view to furthering the attainment of the objective of this Convention, the Parties shall cooperate with each other to encourage accession by any State to this Convention where the Commission considers this to be desirable.

    . . .

Article 16

1. If any dispute arises between two or more of the Parties concerning the interpretation or implementation of this Convention, those Parties shall consult among themselves with a view to having the dispute resolved by negotiation, inquiry, mediation, conciliation, arbitration, judicial settlement or other peaceful means of their own choice.

2. Any dispute of this character not so resolved shall, with the consent in each case of all parties to the dispute, be referred for settlement to the International Court of Justice or to arbitration; but failure to reach agreement on reference to the International Court of Justice or to arbitration shall not absolve parties to the dispute from the responsibility of continuing to seek to resolve it by any of the various peaceful means referred to in paragraph 1 above.

3. In cases where the dispute is referred to arbitration, the arbitral tribunal shall be constituted as provided in the Annex to this Convention. The Annex forms an integral part of this Convention.

    . . .

[519] Article 20

Any Party may withdraw from this Convention twelve months after the date on which it formally notifies the Depositary of its intention to withdraw.

24. In May 1994, the Commission established by the 1993 Convention set a TAC at 11,750 tons, with the national allocations among Japan, Australia and New Zealand set out above. There has been no agreement in the Commission thereafter to change the TAC level or allotments. Japan from 1994 sought an increase in the TAC and in its allotment but any increase has been opposed by New Zealand and Australia. While the Commission initially maintained the TAC at existing levels due to this impasse, since 1998 it has been unable to agree upon any TAC. In the absence of a Commission decision, the Parties in practice have maintained their TAC as set in 1994. At the same

time, Japan pressed in the Commission not only for a TAC increase, initially of 6,000 tons and then of 3,000 tons in its allotment, but also for agreement upon a joint Experimental Fishing Program ('EFP'), whose particular object would be to gather data in those areas where fishing for SBT no longer took place, with a view to reducing scientific uncertainty about recovery of the stock. Japan sought agreement upon its catching 6,000 EFP tons annually, for three years, for experimental fishing, in addition to its commercial allotment; it subsequently reduced that request to 3,000 tons, also the same amount that it sought by way of increase in its TAC. While the Commission in 1996 adopted a set of 'Objectives and principles for the design and implementation of an experimental fishing program', it proved unable to agree upon the size of the catch that would be allowed under the EFP and on modalities of its execution. However, Australia, Japan and New Zealand are agreed on the objective of restoring the parental stock of Southern Bluefin Tuna to its 1980 level by the year 2020.

25. At a Commission meeting in 1998 Japan stated that, while it would voluntarily adhere to its previous quota for commercial SBT fishing, it would commence a unilateral, three-year EFP as of the summer of 1998. Despite vigorous protests by Australia and New Zealand over pursuance of any unilateral EFP, Japan conducted a pilot program with an estimated catch of 1,464 mt in the summer of 1998.

26. In response, Australia and New Zealand formally requested urgent consultations and negotiations under Article 16(1) of the 1993 Convention. Despite intensive efforts within this framework to reach agreement on an experimental fishing program for 1999, an accord was not achieved. At a meeting in Canberra May 26–28, 1999, Australia was advised that, unless it accepted Japan's proposal for a 1999 joint experimental fishing program, Japan would recommence unilateral experimental fishing on June 1; and New Zealand was similarly so informed. Neither Australia nor New Zealand found Japan's proposal [520] acceptable. While differences about the dimension of EFP tonnage had narrowed, they maintained that Japan's EFP was misdirected and that its design and analysis were fundamentally flawed. In their view, Japan's EFP did not justify what they saw as the significant increased risk to the SBT stock. They informed Japan that, if it recommenced unilateral experimental fishing on June 1, 1999 or thereafter, they would regard such action as a termination by Japan of negotiations under Article 16(1) of the 1993 Convention. Japan, which resumed its EFP on June 1, 1999, replied that it had no intention of terminating those negotiations. It maintained that independent scientific opinion had advised the Commission that Japan's EFP proposals were soundly conceived.

27. On June 23, 1999, Australia restated its position that the dispute did not relate solely to Japan's obligations under the 1993 Convention, but also involved its obligations under UNCLOS and customary international law. It considered that there had been a full exchange of views on the dispute for the purposes of Article 283(1) of UNCLOS, which provides that, 'When a dispute arises between States Parties concerning the interpretation or application of this Convention, the parties to the dispute shall proceed expeditiously to an exchange of views regarding its settlement by negotiation or other peaceful means.'

28. Also on June 23, 1999, Japan stated that it was ready to have the dispute resolved by mediation under the provisions of the 1993 Convention. Australia replied that it was willing to submit the dispute to mediation, provided that Japan agreed to cease its unilateral experimental fishing and that the mediation was expeditious. Japan responded that the question of its unilateral EFP could be discussed in the framework of mediation. On July 14, 1999, Japan reiterated its position that its experimental fishing was consistent with the 1993 Convention and that it could not accept the condition of its cessation in order for mediation to proceed. Japan declared that it was ready to have the dispute resolved by arbitration pursuant to Article 16(2) of the 1993 Convention, indicating however that it was not prepared to halt its unilateral EFP during its pendency though it was prepared to resume consultations about it. Thereafter Australia notified Japan that it viewed Japan's position as a rejection of Australia's conditional acceptance of mediation, and that Australia had decided to commence compulsory dispute resolution under Part XV of UNCLOS. It followed that it did not accept Japan's proposal for arbitration pursuant to Article 16(2) of the Convention. Australia emphasized the centrality of Japan's obligations under UNCLOS and under customary international law to the dispute and the need for those obligations to be addressed if the dispute were to be resolved. Australia reiterated its view that the conduct of Japan under the 1993 Convention was relevant to the issue of its compliance with UNCLOS obligations and may be taken into account in dispute [521] settlement under Part XV of UNCLOS. Pending the constitution of the arbitral tribunal to which the dispute was being submitted under UNCLOS's Annex VII, Australia announced its intention to seek prescription of provisional measures under Article 290(5) of UNCLOS, including the immediate cessation of unilateral experimental fishing by Japan.

29. As the preambular references in the 1993 Convention quoted above confirm, the 1993 Convention was prepared in light of the provisions of the 1982 United Nations Convention on the Law of the Sea and the relevant principles of international law. UNCLOS had not come into force in 1993, and in fact did not come into force for the three Parties to the instant dispute until 1996, but the Parties to the 1993 Convention regarded UNCLOS as an umbrella or framework Convention to be implemented in respect of Southern Bluefin Tuna by the adoption of the 1993 Convention.

30. In reliance upon provisions of UNCLOS and of general international law, including UNCLOS provisions for settlement of disputes (Part XV of UNCLOS), Australia and New Zealand thus sought in 1999 to interdict pursuance of Japan's unilateral EFP. They requested the establishment of an arbitral tribunal pursuant to Annex VII of UNCLOS, and sought provisional measures under Article 290(5) of UNCLOS, which provides:

> Pending constitution of an arbitral tribunal to which a dispute is being submitted under this section, any court or tribunal agreed upon by the parties or, failing such agreement within two weeks from the date of the request for provisional measures, the International Tribunal for the Law of the Sea ... may prescribe ... provisional measures if it

considers that *prima facie* the tribunal which is to be constituted would have jurisdiction and that the urgency of the situation so requires. Once constituted, the tribunal to which the dispute has been submitted may modify, revoke or affirm those provisional measures . . .

31. The Applicants' Statement of Claim filed in invoking arbitration under UNCLOS Annex VII maintained that the dispute turned on what the Applicants described as Japan's failure to conserve, and to cooperate in the conservation of, the SBT stock, as manifested, *inter alia*, by its unilateral experimental fishing for SBT in 1998 and 1999. The Applicants stated that the dispute concerned the interpretation and application of certain provisions of UNCLOS, and that the arbitral tribunal will be asked to take into account provisions of the 1993 Convention and the Parties' practice thereunder, as well as their obligations under general international law, 'in particular the precautionary principle'.

32. The provisions of UNCLOS centrally invoked by Australia and New Zealand were the following:

[**522**] *Article 64*
Highly migratory species

1. The coastal State and other States whose nationals fish in the region for the highly migratory species listed in Annex I shall cooperate directly or through appropriate international organizations with a view to ensuring conservation and promoting the objective of optimum utilization of such species throughout the region, both within and beyond the exclusive economic zone. In regions for which no appropriate international organization exists, the coastal State and other States whose nationals harvest these species in the region shall cooperate to establish such an organization and participate in its work.

2. The provisions of paragraph 1 apply in addition to the other provisions of this Part.

Article 116
Right to fish on the high seas

All States have the right for their nationals to engage in fishing on the high seas subject to:

a.   their treaty obligations;
b.   the rights and duties as well as the interests of coastal States provided for, *inter alia*, in article 63, paragraph 2, and articles 64 to 67; and
c.   the provisions of this section.

Article 117
Duty of States to adopt with respect to their nationals
measures for the conservation of the living resources of the high seas

All States have the duty to take, or to cooperate with other States in taking, such measures for their respective nationals as may be necessary for the conservation of the living resources of the high seas.

Article 118
Cooperation of States in the conservation and
management of living resources

States shall cooperate with each other in the conservation and management of living resources in the areas of the high seas. States whose nationals exploit identical living resources, or different living resources in the same area, shall enter into negotiations with a view to taking the measures necessary for the conservation of the living resources concerned. They shall, as appropriate, cooperate to establish subregional or regional fisheries organizations to this end.

Article 119
Conservation of the living resources of the high seas

1. In determining the allowable catch and establishing other conservation measures for the living resources in the high seas, States shall:

    a. take measures which are designed, on the best scientific evidence available to the States concerned, to maintain or restore populations of harvested species at levels which can produce the maximum sustainable yield, as qualified by relevant environmental and economic factors, including the special requirements of [523] developing States, and taking into account fishing patterns, the interdependence of stocks and any generally recommended international minimum standards, whether subregional, regional or global;

    b. take into consideration the effects on species associated with or dependent upon harvested species with a view to maintaining or restoring populations of such associated or dependent species above levels at which their reproduction may become seriously threatened.

2. Available scientific information, catch and fishing effort statistics, and other data relevant to the conservation of fish stocks shall be contributed and exchanged on a regular basis through competent international organizations, whether subregional, regional or global, where appropriate and with participation by all States concerned.

3. States concerned shall ensure that conservation measures and their implementation do not discriminate in form or in fact against the fishermen of any State.

33. In seeking provisional measures, Australia and New Zealand among other contentions argued that Article 64, read in conjunction with other provisions of UNCLOS, imposes an obligation on Japan, as a distant water State whose nationals fish for SBT, to cooperate with Australia and New Zealand, as coastal States, in the conservation of SBT. The Commission established under the 1993 Convention is 'the appropriate international organization' for the purposes of Article 64. Japan's unilateral actions defeat the object and purpose of the 1993 Convention. In such a case, the underlying obligations of UNCLOS remain. While the 1993 Convention was intended as a means of implementing the obligations imposed by UNCLOS in respect of highly migratory fish species, it is not a means of escaping those

obligations. Australia and New Zealand contended that Japan's conduct also placed it in violation of Articles 116, 117, 118, and 119, *inter alia* by failing to adopt necessary conservation measures for its nationals so as to maintain or restore SBT stock to levels which can produce the maximum sustainable yield, by ignoring credible scientific evidence presented by Australia and New Zealand and by pursuing a course of unilateral action in its exclusive interest contrary to their rights as coastal States while enjoying the benefits of restraint by Australia and New Zealand, with discriminatory effect upon nationals of the Applicants. They requested the prescription of provisional measures requiring that Japan immediately cease experimental fishing for SBT; that Japan restrict its SBT catch to its national allocation as last agreed in the Commission, subject to reduction by the amount of catch taken in pursuance of its unilateral EFP; that the Parties act consistently with the precautionary principle pending a final settlement of the dispute; and that the Parties ensure that no action is taken to aggravate their dispute or prejudice the carrying out of any decision on the merits.

34. Japan challenged the contentions of Australia and New Zealand on the facts and the law. It contended that it was Australia and New Zealand [**524**] who had frustrated the functioning of the CCSBT Commission and regime. It maintained that the gravamen of the claims asserted concern the 1993 Convention, not UNCLOS, and that those claims turned not on issues of law but matters of scientific appreciation. Article 290(5) of UNCLOS contemplates the imposition of provisional measures by the International Tribunal for the Law of the Sea ('ITLOS') only if the arbitral tribunal would have *prima facie* jurisdiction over the underlying dispute. Article 288(1) of UNCLOS gave an arbitral tribunal jurisdiction over any dispute concerning the interpretation or application of UNCLOS, a treaty not actually the basis of the Applicants' claims. The Applicants in August 1998 specifically invoked dispute resolution under the 1993 Convention, not UNCLOS; they had treated the dispute as one arising under the CCSBT, and sought consultations not under UNCLOS but under Article 16 of the 1993 Convention. The procedures under the 1993 Convention had not been exhausted; the Parties were required to continue to seek resolution of their dispute pursuant to those procedures. Nor had the procedural conditions for arbitration under UNCLOS been met; Australia and New Zealand had not attempted to reach a settlement in good faith, or even exchange views, in accordance with the provisions of UNCLOS Part XV. No irreparable damage threatened. Article 64 of UNCLOS merely created an obligation of cooperation, and prescribed no specific principles of conservation or concrete conservation measures. It was doubtful that the precautionary principle had attained the status of a rule of customary international law. The Applicants' actions to thwart settlement under Article 16 of the CCSBT were 'abusive' and 'redolent of bad faith'. For all these reasons, Japan argued that the proposed Annex VII arbitral tribunal lacked jurisdiction *prima facie* and that hence ITLOS lacked authority to prescribe provisional measures. The only remedy that made sense, if there were to be any, would be to call on Australia and New Zealand to resume negotiations

under the 1993 Convention with a view to reaching agreement on the TAC, annual quotas, and the continuation of the EFP on a joint basis, with the assistance of independent scientific advice. In the event that ITLOS should make a finding of *prima facie* jurisdiction, Japan asked for counter-provisional measures prescribing that Australia and New Zealand urgently and in good faith recommence negotiations with Japan for a period of six months to reach a consensus on outstanding issues between them, including a protocol for a continued EFP and the determination of a TAC and national allocations for the year 2000.

III. PROVISIONAL MEASURES PRESCRIBED BY ITLOS

35. Australia and New Zealand requested provisional measures on July 30, 1999. The International Tribunal for the Law of the Sea held initial deliberations on August 16 and 17 and noted points and issues that [525] it wished the Parties specially to address; oral hearings were conducted at five public sittings on August 18, 19 and 20. On August 27, 1999, ITLOS issued an Order prescribing provisional measures.[5]

[...]

[529] [...] 36. It should be observed that, while the Order of ITLOS was not unanimous, no Member of the Tribunal disputed 'the view of the Tribunal' that 'the provisions of the Convention on the Law of the Sea invoked by Australia and New Zealand appear to afford a basis on which the jurisdiction of the arbitral tribunal might be founded' (paragraph 52). It so held despite Japan's contention that recourse to the arbitral tribunal 'is excluded because the Convention of 1993 provides for a dispute settlement procedure' (paragraph 53). It noted the position of Australia and New Zealand 'that they are not precluded from having recourse to the arbitral tribunal since the Convention of 1993 does not provide for a compulsory dispute settlement procedure entailing a binding decision as required under article 282 of the Convention on the Law of the Sea' (paragraph 54). It held that, 'in the view of the Tribunal, the fact that the Convention of 1993 applies between the parties does not preclude recourse to the procedures in Part XV, section 2 of the Convention on the Law of the Sea' (paragraph 55). For the above and other reasons quoted, 'the Tribunal finds that the arbitral tribunal would *prima facie* have jurisdiction over the disputes' (paragraph 62).

37. It is these holdings of the International Tribunal for the Law of the Sea that were the particular focus of controversy in these proceedings. The Agents and counsel of Australia, New Zealand and Japan plumbed the depths of these holdings with a profundity that the time pressures of the ITLOS processes did not permit. In any event, the ITLOS holdings upheld no more than the jurisdiction *prima facie* of this Tribunal. [530] It remains for it to decide whether it has jurisdiction to pass upon the merits of the dispute.

[...]

[5 See p. 397 above.]

44. The Preliminary Objections raised by Japan and the arguments advanced in support of them, and the rejection of those Preliminary Objections by Australia and New Zealand and the arguments advanced in support of that rejection, present this Tribunal with questions of singular complexity and significance. The Tribunal is conscious of its position as the first arbitral tribunal to be constituted under Part XV ('Settlement of Disputes'), Annex VII ('Arbitration') of the United Nations Convention on the Law of the Sea. The Parties, through their written pleadings and the oral arguments so ably presented on their behalf by their distinguished Agents and counsel, have furnished the Tribunal with a comprehensive and searching analysis of issues that are of high importance not only for the dispute that divides them but for the understanding and evolution of the processes of peaceful settlement of disputes embodied in UNCLOS and in treaties implementing or relating to provisions of that great law-making treaty.

45. Having regard to the final Submissions of the Parties, the Tribunal will initially address the contention that the case has become moot and should be discontinued. The relevant arguments of the Parties have been set forth above (in paragraphs 40(c), 41(m) [not reproduced here]). In short, Japan maintains that the essence of the dispute turns on its pursuance of a unilateral experimental fishing program; that the contentious element of that program is its proposal to fish 1,800 mt of Southern Bluefin Tuna; that in the course of exchanges between the Parties in that regard, Australia had in 1999 proposed an EFP limit of 1,500 mt; that Japan is now prepared to limit its EFP catch to 1,500 mt; hence that the Parties are in accord on what had been the focus of their dispute, with the result that it has been rendered moot. Australia and New Zealand reply that the proposed acceptance of an EFP of 1,500 tons of tuna was an offer made in the course of negotiations which is no longer on the table; and that in any event their dispute with Japan over a unilateral EFP is not limited to the quantity of the tonnage to be fished but includes the quality of the program, i.e., the design and modalities for its execution, which they maintain is flawed.

46. In the view of the Tribunal, the case is not moot. If the Parties could agree on an experimental fishing program, an element of which would be to limit catch beyond the de facto TAC limits to 1,500 mt, that salient aspect of their dispute would indeed have been resolved; but Australia and New Zealand do not now accept such an offer or limitation by Japan. Even if that offer were today accepted, it would not be sufficient to dispose of their dispute, which concerns the quality as well as the quantity of the EFP, and perhaps other elements of difference as well, such as the assertion of a right to fish beyond TAC limits that were last agreed. Japan now proposes experimentally to fish for no more [546] than 1,500 mt, but it has not undertaken for the future to forgo or restrict what it regards as a right to fish on the high seas for Southern Bluefin Tuna in the absence of a decision by the Commission for the Conservation of Southern Bluefin Tuna upon a total allowable catch and its allocation among the Parties.

47. The Tribunal will now turn to the fundamental and multifaceted issues of jurisdiction that divide the Parties. Putting aside the question of mootness, it is common ground that there is a dispute, and that the core of that dispute relates to differences about the level of a total allowable catch and to Japan's insistence on conducting, and its conduct of, a unilateral experimental fishing program. What profoundly divides the Parties is whether the dispute arises solely under the 1993 Convention, or whether it also arises under UNCLOS.

48. The conflicting contentions of the Parties on this question are found in paragraphs 38 (a) (d) and 41 [not reproduced here] of this Award. An essential issue is, is the dispute with which the Applicants have seized the Tribunal a dispute over the interpretation of the CCSBT, or UNCLOS, or both? That the Applicants maintain, and the Respondent denies, that the dispute involves the interpretation and application of UNCLOS does not of itself constitute a dispute over the interpretation of UNCLOS over which the Tribunal has jurisdiction. In the words of the International Court of Justice in like circumstances, 'in order to answer that question, the Court cannot limit itself to noting that one of the Parties maintains that such a dispute exists, and the other denies it. It must ascertain whether the violations of the Treaty . . . pleaded . . . do or do not fall within the provisions of the Treaty and whether, as a consequence, the dispute is one which the Court has jurisdiction *ratione materiae* to entertain . . . ' (*Case Concerning Oil Platforms (Islamic Republic of Iran v. United States of America), Preliminary Objections, Judgment, ICJ Reports 1996*, para. 16.) In this and in any other case invoking the compromissory clause of a treaty, the claims made, to sustain jurisdiction, must reasonably relate to, or be capable of being evaluated in relation to, the legal standards of the treaty in point, as determined by the court or tribunal whose jurisdiction is at issue. 'It is for the Court itself, while giving particular attention to the formulation of the dispute chosen by the Applicant, to determine on an objective basis the dispute dividing the parties, by examining the position of both Parties . . . The Court will itself determine the real dispute that has been submitted to it . . . It will base itself not only on the Application and final submissions, but on diplomatic exchanges, public statements and other pertinent evidence . . . ' (*Fisheries Jurisdiction Case (Spain v. Canada), ICJ Reports 1998,*[6] paragraphs 30–1.) In the instant case, it is for this Tribunal to decide whether the 'real dispute' between the Parties does [**547**] or does not reasonably (and not just remotely) relate to the obligations set forth in the treaties whose breach is alleged.

49. From the record placed before the Tribunal by both Parties, it is clear that the most acute elements of the dispute between the Parties turn on their inability to agree on a revised total allowable catch and the related conduct by Japan of unilateral experimental fishing in 1998 and 1999, as well as Japan's announced plans for such fishing thereafter. Those elements of the dispute were clearly within the mandate of the Commission for the Conservation of Southern Bluefin Tuna. It was there that the Parties failed to agree on a TAC. It was there that Japan announced in 1998 that

[6] See p. 363 above.]

it would launch a unilateral experimental fishing program; it was there that that announcement was protested by Australia and New Zealand; and the higher level protests and the diplomatic exchanges that followed refer to the Convention for the Conservation of Southern Bluefin Tuna and to the proceedings in the Commission. The Applicants requested urgent consultations with Japan pursuant to Article 16(1) of the Convention, which provides that, 'if any dispute arises between two or more of the Parties concerning the interpretation or implementation of this Convention, those Parties shall consult among themselves with a view to having the dispute resolved . . . '. Those consultations took place in 1998, and they were pursued in 1999 in the Commission in an effort to reach agreement on a joint EFP. It was in the Commission in 1999 that a proposal by Japan to limit its catch to 1,800 mt under the 1999 EFP was made, and it was in the Commission that Australia indicated that it was prepared to accept a limit of 1,500 mt. It was in the Commission that Japan stated, on May 26 and 28, 1999 that, unless Australia and New Zealand accepted its proposals for a joint EFP, it would launch a unilateral program on June 1. Proposals for mediation and arbitration made by Japan were made in pursuance of provisions of Article 16 of the CCSBT. In short, it is plain that all the main elements of the dispute between the Parties had been addressed within the Commission for the Conservation of Southern Bluefin Tuna and that the contentions of the Parties in respect of that dispute related to the implementation of their obligations under the 1993 Convention. They related particularly to Article 8(3) of the Convention, which provides that, 'For the conservation, management and optimum utilization of southern bluefin tuna: (a) the Commission shall decide upon a total allowable catch and its allocation among the Parties . . . ' and to the powers of a Party in a circumstance where the Commission found itself unable so to decide.

50. There is in fact no disagreement between the Parties over whether the dispute falls within the provisions of the 1993 Convention. The issue rather is, does it also fall within the provisions of UNCLOS? The Applicants maintain that Japan has failed to conserve and to cooperate in the conservation of the SBT stock, particularly by its unilateral experimental **[548]** fishing for SBT in 1998 and 1999. They find a certain tension between cooperation and unilateralism. They contend that Japan's unilateral EFP has placed it in breach of its obligations under Articles 64, 116, 117, 118 and 119 of UNCLOS, for the specific reasons indicated earlier in this Award (in paragraphs 33 and 41 [not reproduced here]). Those provisions, they maintain, lay down applicable norms by which the lawfulness of Japan's conduct can be evaluated. They point out that, once the dispute had ripened, their diplomatic notes and other demarches to Japan made repeated reference to Japan's obligations not only under the 1993 Convention but also under UNCLOS and customary international law.

51. Japan for its part maintains that such references were belated and were made for the purpose of permitting a request to ITLOS for provisional measures. It contends that the invoked articles of UNCLOS are general and do not govern the particular dispute between the Parties. More than that, Japan argues that UNCLOS is a framework or umbrella convention that looks to implementing conventions to give it effect;

that Article 64 provides for cooperation 'through appropriate international organizations' of which the Commission is an exemplar; that any relevant principles and provisions of UNCLOS have been implemented by the establishment of the Commission and the Parties' participation in its work; and that the *lex specialis* of the 1993 Convention and its institutional expression have subsumed, discharged and eclipsed any provisions of UNCLOS that bear on the conservation and optimum utilization of Southern Bluefin Tuna. Thus Japan argues that the dispute falls solely within the provisions of the 1993 Convention and in no measure also within the reach of UNCLOS.

52. The Tribunal does not accept this central contention of Japan. It recognizes that there is support in international law and in the legal systems of States for the application of a *lex specialis* that governs general provisions of an antecedent treaty or statute. But the Tribunal recognizes as well that it is a commonplace of international law and State practice for more than one treaty to bear upon a particular dispute. There is no reason why a given act of a State may not violate its obligations under more than one treaty. There is frequently a parallelism of treaties, both in their substantive content and in their provisions for settlement of disputes arising thereunder. The current range of international legal obligations benefits from a process of accretion and cumulation; in the practice of States, the conclusion of an implementing convention does not necessarily vacate the obligations imposed by the framework convention upon the parties to the implementing convention. The broad provisions for the promotion of universal respect for and observance of human rights, and the international obligation to co-operate for the achievement of those purposes, found in Articles 1, 55 and 56 of the Charter of the United Nations, have not been discharged for States Parties by their ratification of the Human Rights Covenants and other human rights treaties. **[549]** Moreover, if the 1993 Convention were to be regarded as having fulfilled and eclipsed the obligations of UNCLOS that bear on the conservation of SBT, would those obligations revive for a Party to the CCSBT that exercises its right under Article 20 to withdraw from the Convention on twelve months' notice? Can it really be the case that the obligations of UNCLOS in respect of a migratory species of fish do not run between the Parties to the 1993 Convention but do run to third States that are Parties to UNCLOS but not to the 1993 Convention? Nor is it clear that the particular provisions of the 1993 Convention exhaust the extent of the relevant obligations of UNCLOS. In some respects, UNCLOS may be viewed as extending beyond the reach of the CCSBT. UNCLOS imposes obligations on each State to take action in relation to its own nationals: 'All States have the duty to take … such measures for their respective nationals as may be necessary for the conservation of the living resources of the high seas' (Article 117). It debars discrimination 'in form or fact against the fishermen of any State' (Article 119). These provisions are not found in the CCSBT; they are operative even where no TAC has been agreed in the CCSBT and where co-operation in the Commission has broken down. Article 5(1) of the CCSBT provides that, 'Each Party shall take all action necessary to ensure the enforcement of this Convention and compliance with measures which

become binding ...' But UNCLOS obligations may be viewed not only as going beyond this general obligation in the foregoing respects but as in force even where 'measures' being considered under the 1993 Convention have not become binding thereunder. Moreover, a dispute concerning the interpretation and implementation of the CCSBT will not be completely alien to the interpretation and application of UNCLOS for the very reason that the CCSBT was designed to implement broad principles set out in UNCLOS. For all these reasons, the Tribunal concludes that the dispute between Australia and New Zealand, on the one hand, and Japan on the other, over Japan's role in the management of SBT stocks and particularly its unilateral experimental fishing program, while centered in the 1993 Convention, also arises under the United Nations Convention on the Law of the Sea. In its view, this conclusion is consistent with the terms of UNCLOS Article 311(2) and (5), and with the law of treaties, in particular Article 30(3) of the Vienna Convention on the Law of Treaties.[7]

53. This holding, however, while critical to the case of the Applicants, is not dispositive of this case. It is necessary to examine a number of articles of Part XV of UNCLOS. Article 286 introduces section 2 of Part XV, a section entitled, 'Compulsory Procedures Entailing Binding Decisions'. [**550**] Article 286 provides that, 'Subject to section 3, any dispute concerning the interpretation or application of this Convention shall, where no settlement has been reached by recourse to section 1, be submitted at the request of any party to the dispute to the court or tribunal having jurisdiction under this section.' Article 286 must be read in context, and that qualifying context includes Article 281(1) as well as Articles 279 and 280. Under Article 281(1), if the States which are parties to a dispute concerning the interpretation or application of UNCLOS (and the Tribunal has just held that this is such a dispute) have agreed to seek settlement of the dispute 'by a peaceful means of their own choice', the procedures provided for in Part XV of UNCLOS apply only (a) where no settlement has been reached by recourse to such means and (b) the agreement between the parties 'does not exclude any further procedure'.

54. The Tribunal accepts Article 16 of the 1993 Convention as an agreement by the Parties to seek settlement of the instant dispute by peaceful means of their own choice. It so concludes even though it has held that this dispute, while centered in the 1993 Convention, also implicates obligations under UNCLOS. It does so because the Parties to this dispute – the real terms of which have been defined above – are the same Parties grappling not with two separate disputes but with what in fact is a single dispute arising under both Conventions. To find that, in this case, there is a dispute actually arising under UNCLOS which is distinct from the dispute that arose under the CCSBT would be artificial.

---

[7] Article 30(3) of the Vienna Convention on the Law of Treaties provides:

> When all the parties to an earlier treaty are parties also to the later treaty but the earlier treaty is not terminated or suspended in operation under article 59, the earlier treaty applies only to the extent that its provisions are compatible with those of the later treaty.

55. Article 16 is not 'a' peaceful means; it provides a list of various named procedures of peaceful settlement, adding 'or other peaceful means of their own choice'. No particular procedure in this list has thus far been chosen by the Parties for settlement of the instant dispute. Nevertheless – bearing in mind the reasoning of the preceding paragraph – the Tribunal is of the view that Article 16 falls within the terms and intent of Article 281(1), as well as Article 280. That being so, the Tribunal is satisfied about fulfillment of condition (a) of Article 281(1). The Parties have had recourse to means set out in Article 16 of the CCSBT. Negotiations have been prolonged, intense and serious. Since in the course of those negotiations, the Applicants invoked UNCLOS and relied upon provisions of it, while Japan denied the relevance of UNCLOS and its provisions, those negotiations may also be regarded as fulfilling another condition of UNCLOS, that of Article 283, which requires that, when a dispute arises between States Parties concerning UNCLOS' interpretation or application, the parties to the dispute shall proceed expeditiously to an exchange of views regarding its settlement by negotiation or other peaceful means. Manifestly, no settlement has been reached by recourse to such negotiations, at any rate, as yet. It is true that every means listed in Article 16 has not been tried; indeed, the Applicants have not accepted proposals of Japan for mediation and for arbitration under the CCSBT, essentially, it seems, because Japan was [**551**] unwilling to suspend pursuance of its unilateral EFP during the pendency of such recourse. It is also true that Article 16(2) provides that failure to reach agreement on reference of a dispute to the International Court of Justice or to arbitration 'shall not absolve parties to the dispute from the responsibility of continuing to seek to resolve it by any of the various peaceful means referred to in paragraph 1 above'. But in the view of the Tribunal, this provision does not require the Parties to negotiate indefinitely while denying a Party the option of concluding, for purposes of both Articles 281(1) and 283, that no settlement has been reached. To read Article 16 otherwise would not be reasonable.

56. The Tribunal now turns to the second requirement of Article 281(1): that the agreement between the parties 'does not exclude any further procedure'. This is a requirement, it should be recalled, for applicability of 'the procedures provided for in this Part', that is to say, the 'compulsory procedures entailing binding decisions' dealt with in section 2 of UNCLOS Part XV. The terms of Article 16 of the 1993 Convention do not expressly and in so many words exclude the applicability of any procedure, including the procedures of section 2 of Part XV of UNCLOS.

57. Nevertheless, in the view of the Tribunal, the absence of an express exclusion of any procedure in Article 16 is not decisive. Article 16(1) requires the parties to 'consult among themselves with a view to having the dispute resolved by negotiation, inquiry, mediation, conciliation, arbitration, judicial settlement or other peaceful means of their own choice'. Article 16(2), in its first clause, directs the referral of a dispute not resolved by any of the above-listed means of the parties' 'own choice' for settlement 'to the International Court of Justice or to arbitration' but 'with the consent in each case of all parties to the dispute'. The ordinary meaning of these terms of Article 16 makes it clear that the dispute is not referable to adjudication by the International Court of

Justice (or, for that matter, ITLOS), or to arbitration, 'at the request of any party to the dispute' (in the words of UNCLOS Article 286). The consent in each case of all parties to the dispute is required. Moreover, the second clause of Article 16(2) provides that 'failure to reach agreement on reference to the International Court of Justice or to arbitration shall not absolve the parties to the dispute from the responsibility of continuing to seek to resolve it by any of the various peaceful means referred to in paragraph 1 above'. The effect of this express obligation to continue to seek resolution of the dispute by the listed means of Article 16(1) is not only to stress the consensual nature of any reference of a dispute to either judicial settlement or arbitration. That express obligation equally imports, in the Tribunal's view, that the intent of Article 16 is to remove proceedings under that Article from the reach of the compulsory procedures of section 2 of Part XV of UNCLOS, that is, to exclude the application to a specific dispute of any procedure of dispute resolution that is not accepted by all parties to the dispute. Article 16(3) reinforces that intent [552] by specifying that, in cases where the dispute is referred to arbitration, the arbitral tribunal shall be constituted as provided for in an annex to the 1993 Convention, which is to say that arbitration contemplated by Article 16 is not compulsory arbitration under section 2 of Part XV of UNCLOS but rather autonomous and consensual arbitration provided for in that CCSBT annex.

58. It is plain that the wording of Article 16(1) and (2) has its essential origins in the terms of Article XI of the Antarctic Treaty; the provisions are virtually identical. In view of the States that concluded the Antarctic Treaty – divided as they were between some States that adhered to international adjudication and arbitration and a Great Power that then ideologically opposed it – it is obvious that these provisions are meant to exclude compulsory jurisdiction.

59. For all these reasons, the Tribunal concludes that Article 16 of the 1993 Convention 'exclude[s] any further procedure' within the contemplation of Article 281(1) of UNCLOS.

60. There are two other considerations that, to the mind of the Tribunal, sustain this conclusion. The first consideration is the extent to which compulsory procedures entailing binding decisions have in fact been prescribed by Part XV of UNCLOS for all States Parties to UNCLOS. Article 286, in providing that disputes concerning the interpretation or application of UNCLOS 'shall . . . where no settlement has been reached by recourse to section 1, be submitted at the request of any party to the dispute to the court or tribunal having jurisdiction under [Article 287]', states that that apparently broad provision is 'subject to section 3' of Part XV. Examination of the provisions comprising section 3 (and constituting interpretive context for sections 1 and 2 of Part XV) reveals that they establish important limitations and exceptions to the applicability of the compulsory procedures of section 2.

61. Article 297 of UNCLOS is of particular importance in this connection for it provides significant limitations on the applicability of compulsory procedures insofar as coastal States are concerned. Paragraph 1 of Article 297 limits the application of such procedures to disputes concerning the exercise by a coastal State of its sovereign rights

or jurisdiction in certain identified cases only, i.e.: (a) cases involving rights of navigation, overflight, laying of submarine cables and pipelines or other internationally lawful uses of the sea associated therewith; and (b) cases involving the protection and preservation of the marine environment. Paragraph 2 of Article 297, while providing for the application of section 2 compulsory procedures to disputes concerning marine scientific research, exempts coastal States from the obligation of submitting to such procedures in cases involving exercise by a coastal State of its rights or discretionary authority in its exclusive economic zone (EEZ) or its continental shelf, and cases of termination or suspension by the coastal State of a research project in accordance with article 253. Disputes between the researching [553] State and the coastal State concerning a specific research project are subject to conciliation under annex V of UNCLOS. Under paragraph 3 of Article 297, section 2 procedures are applicable to disputes concerning fisheries but, and this is an important 'but', the coastal State is not obliged to submit to such procedures where the dispute relates to its sovereign rights or their exercise with respect to the living resources in its EEZ, including determination of allowable catch, harvesting capacity, allocation of surpluses to other States, and application of its own conservation and management laws and regulations. Complementing the limitative provisions of Article 297 of UNCLOS, Article 298 establishes certain optional exceptions to the applicability of compulsory section 2 procedures and authorizes a State (whether coastal or not), at any time, to declare that it does not accept any one or more of such compulsory procedures in respect of: (a) disputes concerning Articles 15, 74 and 83 relating to sea boundary delimitations or historic bays or titles; (b) disputes concerning military activities, including military activities by government vessels and aircraft engaged in non-commercial service, and disputes concerning law enforcement activities by a coastal State. Finally, Article 299 of UNCLOS provides that disputes excluded by Article 297 or exempted by Article 298 from application of compulsory section 2 procedures may be submitted to such procedures 'only by agreement of the parties to the dispute'.

62. It thus appears to the Tribunal that UNCLOS falls significantly short of establishing a truly comprehensive regime of compulsory jurisdiction entailing binding decisions. This general consideration supports the conclusion, based on the language used in Article 281(1), that States Parties that have agreed to seek settlement of disputes concerning the interpretation or application of UNCLOS by 'peaceful means of their own choice' are permitted by Article 281(1) to confine the applicability of compulsory procedures of section 2 of Part XV to cases where all parties to the dispute have agreed upon submission of their dispute to such compulsory procedures. In the Tribunal's view, Article 281(1), when so read, provides a certain balance in the rights and obligations of coastal and non-coastal States in respect of settlement of disputes arising from events occurring within their respective Exclusive Economic Zones and on the high seas, a balance that the Tribunal must assume was deliberately established by the States Parties to UNCLOS.

63. The second consideration of a general character that the Tribunal has taken into account is the fact that a significant number of international agreements with

maritime elements, entered into after the adoption of UNCLOS, exclude with varying degrees of explicitness unilateral reference of a dispute to compulsory adjudicative or arbitral procedures. Many of these agreements effect such exclusion by expressly requiring disputes to be resolved by mutually agreed procedures, whether by negotiation and consultation or other method acceptable to the parties [554] to the dispute or by arbitration or recourse to the International Court of Justice by common agreement of the parties to the dispute. Other agreements preclude unilateral submission of a dispute to compulsory binding adjudication or arbitration, not only by explicitly requiring disputes to be settled by mutually agreed procedures, but also, as in Article 16 of the 1993 Convention, by requiring the parties to continue to seek to resolve the dispute by any of the various peaceful means of their own choice. The Tribunal is of the view that the existence of such a body of treaty practice – postdating as well as antedating the conclusion of UNCLOS – tends to confirm the conclusion that States Parties to UNCLOS may, by agreement, preclude subjection of their disputes to section 2 procedures in accordance with Article 281(1). To hold that disputes implicating obligations under both UNCLOS and an implementing treaty such as the 1993 Convention – as such disputes typically may – must be brought within the reach of section 2 of Part XV of UNCLOS would be effectively to deprive of substantial effect the dispute settlement provisions of those implementing agreements which prescribe dispute resolution by means of the parties' choice.

64. The Tribunal does not exclude the possibility that there might be instances in which the conduct of a State Party to UNCLOS and to a fisheries treaty implementing it would be so egregious, and risk consequences of such gravity, that a Tribunal might find that the obligations of UNCLOS provide a basis for jurisdiction, having particular regard to the provisions of Article 300 of UNCLOS. While Australia and New Zealand in the proceedings before ITLOS invoked Article 300, in the proceedings before this Tribunal they made clear that they do not hold Japan to any independent breach of an obligation to act in good faith.

65. It follows from the foregoing analysis that this Tribunal lacks jurisdiction to entertain the merits of the dispute brought by Australia and New Zealand against Japan. Having reached this conclusion, the Tribunal does not find it necessary to pass upon questions of the admissibility of the dispute, although it may be observed that its analysis of provisions of UNCLOS that bring the dispute within the substantive reach of UNCLOS suggests that the dispute is not one that is confined to matters of scientific judgment only. It may be added that this Tribunal does not find the proceedings brought before ITLOS and before this Tribunal to be an abuse of process; on the contrary, as explained below, the proceedings have been constructive.

66. In view of this Tribunal's conclusion that it lacks jurisdiction to deal with the merits of the dispute, and in view of the terms of Article 290(5) of UNCLOS providing that, 'Once constituted, the tribunal to which the dispute has been submitted may modify, revoke or affirm those provisional measures . . .', the Order of the International Tribunal for the Law of the Sea of August 27, 1999, prescribing provisional measures, shall cease to have effect as of the date of the signing of this Award.

[555] 67. However, revocation of the Order prescribing provisional measures does not mean that the Parties may disregard the effects of that Order or their own decisions made in conformity with it. The Order and those decisions – and the recourse to ITLOS that gave rise to them – as well as the consequential proceedings before this Tribunal, have had an impact: not merely in the suspension of Japan's unilateral experimental fishing program during the period that the Order was in force, but on the perspectives and actions of the Parties.

68. As the Parties recognized during the oral hearings before this Tribunal, they have increasingly manifested flexibility of approach to the problems that divide them; as the Agent of Japan put it, 'strenuous efforts which both sides have made in the context of the CCSBT have already succeeded in narrowing the gap between the Parties'. An agreement on the principle of having an experimental fishing program and on the tonnage of that program appears to be within reach. The possibility of renewed negotiations on other elements of their differences is real. Japan's counsel, in the course of these hearings, emphasized that Japan remained prepared to submit the differences between the Parties to arbitration under Article 16 of the 1993 Convention; Japan's Agent observed that, 'That would allow the Parties to set up procedures best suited to the nature and the characteristics of the case.' Japan's counsel affirmed Japan's willingness to work with Australia and New Zealand on the formulation of questions to be put to a CCSBT Arbitration Tribunal, and on the procedure that it should adopt in dealing with those questions. He restated Japan's willingness to agree on the simultaneous establishment of a mechanism in which experts and scientists can resume consultation on a joint EFP and related issues. The agent of Japan stated that, not only is its proposal to cap its EFP at 1,500 mt on the negotiating table; negotiations on the appropriate design for the EFP are already underway.

69. Counsel for Australia pointed out that the ITLOS Order already had played a significant role in encouraging the Parties to make progress on the issue of third-party fishing. The Agents of Australia and of New Zealand declared that progress in settling the dispute between the Parties had been made. They expressed the hope that progress would continue and stated that they will make every attempt to ensure that it does; they 'remain ready to explore all productive ways of finding solutions'.

70. The Tribunal recalls that Article 16(2) prescribes that failure to reach agreement on reference to arbitration shall not absolve the parties to the dispute from the responsibility of continuing to seek to resolve it by any of the various peaceful means referred to in paragraph 1; and among those means are negotiation, mediation and arbitration. The Tribunal further observes that, to the extent that the search for resolution of the dispute were to resort to third-party procedures, those listed in Article 16 are labels that conform to traditional diplomatic precedent. Their content and *modus operandi* can be refined and developed by the [556] Parties to meet their specific needs. There are many ways in which an independent body can be configured to interact with the States party to a dispute. For example, there may be a combination or alternation of direct negotiations, advice from expert panels, benevolent supervision and good offices extended by a third-party body, and recourse to a third party for

step-by-step aid in decision-making and for mediation, quite apart from third-party binding settlement rendered in the form of an arbitral award. Whatever the mode or modes of peaceful settlement chosen by the Parties, the Tribunal emphasizes that the prospects for a successful settlement of their dispute will be promoted by the Parties' abstaining from any unilateral act that may aggravate the dispute while its solution has not been achieved.

71. Finally, the Tribunal observes that, when it comes into force, the Agreement for the Implementation of the Provisions of the United Nations Convention on the Law of the Sea of 10 December 1982 Relating to the Conservation and Management of Straddling Fish Stocks and Highly Migratory Fish Stocks, which was adopted on August 4, 1995 and opened for signature December 4, 1995 (and signed by Australia, Japan and New Zealand), should, for States Parties to it, not only go far towards resolving procedural problems that have come before this Tribunal but, if the Convention is faithfully and effectively implemented, ameliorate the substantive problems that have divided the Parties. The substantive provisions of the Straddling Stocks Agreement are more detailed and far-reaching than the pertinent provisions of UNCLOS or even of the CCSBT. The articles relating to peaceful settlement of disputes specify that the provisions relating to the settlement of disputes set out in Part XV of UNCLOS apply *mutatis mutandis* to any dispute between States Parties to the Agreement concerning its interpretation or application. They further specify that the provisions relating to settlement of disputes set out in Part XV of UNCLOS apply *mutatis mutandis* to any dispute between States Parties to the Agreement concerning the interpretation or application of a subregional, regional or global fisheries agreement relating to straddling fish stocks or highly migratory fish stocks to which they are parties, including any dispute concerning the conservation and management of such stocks.

72. FOR THESE REASONS

The Arbitral Tribunal

By vote of 4 to 1,

1. Decides that it is without jurisdiction to rule on the merits of the dispute; and,

Unanimously,

2. Decides, in accordance with Article 290(5) of the United Nations Convention on the Law of the Sea, that provisional measures in force by Order of the International Tribunal for the Law of the Sea prescribed on August 27, 1999 are revoked from the day of the signature of this Award.

[. . .]

[557] [. . .] SEPARATE OPINION OF JUSTICE SIR KENNETH KEITH (EXTRACT)

1. While I agree with much of the Award, I have the misfortune to disagree with my colleagues on one critical issue. I have accordingly prepared this opinion.

Each of the treaties in issue in this case sets up substantive obligations and obligations relating to peaceful settlement. The parallel and overlapping existence of the obligations arising under each treaty is fundamental in this case. I conclude that the one has not excluded or in any relevant way prejudiced the other.

2. This Tribunal has jurisdiction under section 2 of Part XV of UNCLOS 'where no settlement has been reached by recourse to section 1' (Article 286). [. . .]

[565] [. . .] 30. The objects and purposes of UNCLOS in general and its comprehensive, compulsory and where necessary, binding dispute settlement provisions in particular, along with the plain wording of its Article 281(1) and of Article 16 of the CCSBT lead me to the conclusion that the latter does not 'exclude' the jurisdiction of this tribunal in respect of disputes arising under UNCLOS.

31. The possibly quite different subject matter of an arbitration under Article 16 of the CCSBT relating to the 'implementation' of that Convention (see paragraph 15 above)[8] both supports that conclusion and suggests the possible limits on an assessment by a tribunal of a State's actions by reference to its obligations under Articles 64 and 117–19 of UNCLOS and on any relief which might be available were a breach to be established. But such limits do not at this stage, to my mind, affect this tribunal's jurisdiction.

32. I have accordingly voted in favour of holding that this Tribunal has jurisdiction and against the contrary decision of the Tribunal. Given the majority position, I agree of course with the revocation of the order for provisional measures.

[Report: 119 *ILR* 511]

[8 Not reproduced in this volume.]

The MOX Plant Case
(Ireland *v.* United Kingdom)[1]

Arbitral Tribunal, The Hague[2]

24 June 2003 (Mensah, *President*; Crawford, Fortier, Hafner and Sir Arthur Watts, *Members*)

14 November 2003 (Mensah, *President*; Crawford, Fortier, Hafner and Sir Arthur Watts, *Members*)

Jurisdiction – admissibility of claims – applicable law – United Nations Convention on the Law of the Sea, 1982 ('UNCLOS'), Article 288(1) – distinction between Article 288(1) and Article 293 of UNCLOS – claims arising under legal instruments other than UNCLOS inadmissible – European Community law – exclusive jurisdiction of European Court – division of competence – matter of European Community law – jurisdiction not firmly established until competence issues resolved – proceedings suspended

Powers and procedures of tribunals – suspension of proceedings on jurisdiction and merits – Rules of Procedure, Article 8

Powers and procedures of tribunals – provisional measures – conditions to be satisfied for granting provisional measures under UNCLOS Article 290 –

---

[1] Ireland initiated two separate arbitrations against the United Kingdom in relation to the approval of the MOX plant. The first arbitration, commenced on 15 June 2001, resulted in a Final Award of the OSPAR Tribunal of 2 July 2003 and is reported at p. 552 below. Orders Nos. 3 and 4 resulted from the second arbitration (reported here), which was commenced on 25 October 2001. The judgment of the European Court of Justice for which proceedings were suspended is reported at pp. 526 and 539 below. In connection with this second arbitration, Ireland filed a request for provisional measures with the International Tribunal for the Law of the Sea on 9 November 2001. The Order of 3 December 2001 is reported at p. 421 above.

    Ireland was represented before the Arbitral Tribunal by David J. O'Hagan, Agent; Rory Brady SC, Attorney-General; Eoghan Fitzsimons SC, Paul Sreenan SC, Professor Philippe Sands and Professor Vaughan Lowe, Counsel. The United Kingdom was represented before the Arbitral Tribunal by Michael Wood CMG, Agent; Rt Hon. Lord Goldsmith QC, Attorney-General; Richard Plender QC, Daniel Bethlehem QC and Samuel Wordsworth, Counsel.

[2] Constituted pursuant to Article 287, and Article 1 of Annex VII of the United Nations Convention on the Law of the Sea for the Dispute Concerning the MOX Plant, International Movements of Radioactive Materials, and the Protection of the Marine Environment of the Irish Sea.

change of circumstances since ITLOS provisional measures granted – relevant considerations – risk of serious harm to the marine environment – protection of rights of Parties – no urgent and serious risk of irreparable harm

Waters – Irish Sea – protection of the marine environment – UNCLOS – environmental effects of the MOX plant and of international movements of radioactive materials

SUMMARY   *The facts*   The facts of this case can be found at p. 422 above. On 25 October 2001, Ireland commenced proceedings against the United Kingdom by Notification under Part XV of the United Nations Convention on the Law of the Sea ('UNCLOS').

Ireland claimed that the United Kingdom had breached various provisions of Part XII of UNCLOS by failing to protect the marine environment. In particular, Ireland claimed that it had failed to protect the marine environment from radioactive discharges. According to Ireland, the approval of the MOX plant would lead to radioactive discharges from the MOX plant and consequential radioactive discharges from increased operation of the Thermal Oxide Reprocessing Plant ('THORP') at the Sellafield site, the primary source of feedstock for the MOX plant.

Ireland requested the following relief in its Notification:

(a) a declaration that the United Kingdom had breached its obligations under UNCLOS Articles 192, 193, 194, 207, 211 and 213, including by failing to take necessary measures to prevent, reduce and control pollution of the marine environment of the Irish Sea from intended and accidental radioactive discharges from the MOX plant, or from additional consequential discharges from THORP, or from the international movement of radioactive materials associated with the MOX plant and THORP;

(b) a declaration that the United Kingdom had breached its obligations under the same articles of UNCLOS by failing properly to assess and respond to the risk of a terrorist attack on the MOX plant and associated facilities at the Sellafield site;

(c) a declaration that the United Kingdom had breached its obligations under UNCLOS Articles 123 and 197 by failing to cooperate with Ireland;

(d) a declaration that the United Kingdom had breached its obligations under UNCLOS Article 206 by failing properly to assess the direct and indirect effects of the MOX plant; and

(e) that the United Kingdom refrain from authorising the operation of the MOX plant and/or related international movements until a proper assessment of effects had been carried out demonstrating that there would be no discharge of radioactive materials, and until a comprehensive strategy was agreed with Ireland to respond to any terrorist attack.

The United Kingdom contested Ireland's case both as to the jurisdiction of the Tribunal and as to the merits. It maintained that the jurisdiction of the Tribunal was limited or absent altogether on two bases. First, it maintained that Ireland's claim was in large part a claim of breach of instruments other than UNCLOS, notably the 1992 OSPAR Convention and instruments under that Convention, as well as various European Community ('EC') Directives, and that the Tribunal had no jurisdiction to decide claims based on other instruments and/or that such claims were inadmissible. Second, it maintained that pursuant to Annex IX of UNCLOS, and as a matter of EC law, the allegations made by Ireland were a matter within the competence of the EC, and hence the Tribunal lacked jurisdiction altogether. The United Kingdom also challenged Ireland's claims on the merits, in particular claiming that radioactive discharges from the MOX plant were negligible and a minute fraction of those discharges allowed as a matter of EC and domestic law, that the issue of whether there would be additional consequential discharges from THORP was a matter of speculation, but that discharges from THORP were in any event a small fraction of those discharges allowed as a matter of EC and domestic law.

At the commencement of the hearing of 10 June 2003, the Tribunal decided that it would hear argument on the jurisdictional issues before proceeding further. It subsequently decided (on 13 June 2003) to suspend the proceedings, but also that in circumstances where there would be no immediate hearing of the merits it was open to Ireland to make an application for provisional measures further to those ordered by the International Tribunal for the Law of the Sea ('ITLOS')[3] on 3 December 2001.

On 16 June 2003, Ireland submitted a request for provisional measures seeking orders that: (a) the United Kingdom ensure that there be no liquid waste discharges from the MOX plant, and that both aerial discharges from the MOX plant and liquid and aerial discharges from THORP did not exceed 2002 levels; (b) that the United Kingdom provide certain specified information to Ireland and cooperate with Ireland in certain specified respects; (c) that the United Kingdom ensure that no steps be taken or

---

[3] The ITLOS decision on provisional measures is reproduced in this volume at p. 427 above.

implemented which might preclude full effect being given to the results of any environmental assessment that the Tribunal might order pursuant to UNCLOS Article 206. The United Kingdom challenged the grant of any further provisional measures order but did not seek any order lifting the provisional measures ordered by ITLOS on 3 December 2001. In the course of the hearing and in correspondence, the United Kingdom also made certain statements that were noted and placed on the record by the Tribunal in its Decision.

Held by the Arbitral Tribunal   Further proceedings would be suspended, in the first instance until 1 December 2003. The provisional measures ordered by ITLOS on 3 December 2001 were to remain in place.

(1)   There was a cardinal distinction to be drawn between the scope of jurisdiction under UNCLOS Article 288(1) and the law to be applied under UNCLOS Article 293 (which stated that the law to be applied by a court or tribunal having jurisdiction was UNCLOS and other rules of international law not incompatible with UNCLOS). To the extent that any aspects of claims arose directly under legal instruments other than UNCLOS, such claims might be inadmissible. However, it was not accepted that Ireland had failed to plead a case arising substantially under UNCLOS.

(2)   Certain problems had become apparent as to the standing of the Parties, the division of competences between the EC and its Member States, the extent to which provisions and instruments invoked by the Parties could properly be relied on, and as to matters which by agreement of the Parties were subject to the exclusive jurisdiction of the European Court of Justice as a matter of EC law. In circumstances where the EC had indicated that it was examining whether to institute proceedings under Article 226 of the EC Treaty, there was a real possibility that the European Court of Justice might be seised of the question of whether the provisions of UNCLOS on which Ireland relied were matters in relation to which competence had been transferred to the EC, and whether the exclusive jurisdiction of the European Court of Justice extended to the interpretation and application of UNCLOS in its entirety (so far as Ireland and the United Kingdom, as EC Member States, were concerned).

(3)   The determination of jurisdiction and the identification of the treaty provisions and other rules of international law which could be applied were crucially dependent upon the resolution of the problems as to competence. Those problems related to matters essentially concerning the internal operation of the EC legal order which were to be determined within the institutional framework of the EC. Until the problems were

resolved, there remained substantial doubts as to whether jurisdiction could be firmly established in respect of all or any of Ireland's claims.

(4)   The resolution of the issues within the EC legal order might involve decisions that were final and binding. The Tribunal's decision, including on jurisdiction, would be final and binding on the Parties. It was inappropriate to proceed further in the absence of a resolution of the problems identified: a procedure that might result in two conflicting decisions on the same issue would not be helpful to the resolution of the dispute between the Parties. Further proceedings on jurisdiction and the merits were accordingly suspended until not later than 1 December 2003, at which time there would hopefully be a clearer or even definitive picture of the position regarding EC law and possible proceedings thereunder.

(5)   The Tribunal had *prima facie* jurisdiction so as to be able to make an order of provisional measures. The order of provisional measures was governed by UNCLOS Article 290, with the burden of showing that its requirements were met falling on Ireland. In so far as it was relevant, there had been a change in circumstances justifying the modification or revocation of the ITLOS provisional measures (Article 290(2)), namely the constitution of the Tribunal and the delay before a decision could be made on the merits, which was longer than the delay contemplated by ITLOS. Although the language of UNCLOS Article 290 was not identical to that of Article 41 of the Statute of the International Court of Justice, it was right to have regard to the law and practice of that Court as well as ITLOS in considering provisional measures.

(6)   Pursuant to UNCLOS Article 290(1), provisional measures could only be prescribed where these were appropriate in the prevailing circumstances and in the light of the information available 'to preserve the respective rights of the parties to the dispute or to prevent serious harm to the marine environment'. Ireland had not established that any harm which might be caused to the marine environment by virtue of the operation of the MOX plant, pending the determination of the case on the merits, met the serious harm threshold test.

(7)   With respect to the preservation of the respective rights of the Parties, international judicial practice confirmed that a general requirement for the prescription of provisional measures to protect the rights of the Parties was a showing of urgency and of irreparable harm to the claimed rights. Ireland's request seeking restrictions on discharges from the MOX plant and THORP (paragraph (A) of its Request) had to be rejected as it could not be accepted that there was an urgent and serious risk of irreparable harm to Ireland's claimed rights. In addition,

no provisional measure was justified in response to Ireland's request in relation to giving effect to any environmental assessment subsequently ordered by the Tribunal (paragraph (C) of its Request). Further, the text of the measure would not give clear guidance to the United Kingdom on what conduct was required of it pending a final decision.

(8)   So far as concerned Ireland's request on information and co-operation (paragraph (B) of its Request), the ITLOS Order had required cooperation and consultation for specified purposes. Since December 2001 when that Order had been made, there had been an increased measure of cooperation, although this might not always have been as timely or effective as it could have been, and problems had sometimes arisen (both before and since the ITLOS Order) from the absence of secure arrangements, at a suitable inter-governmental level, for coordination of all of the various agencies and bodies involved. The establishment of such arrangements was recommended, as was a review of the inter-governmental systems.

(9)   It followed that no order would be made as to cooperation and provision of information at this stage. The provisional measures ordered by ITLOS on 3 December 2001 would be affirmed. No action was to be taken by either Party which might aggravate or extend the dispute.

Note   On 14 November 2003, the Arbitral Tribunal ordered a further suspension of the proceedings on jurisdiction and merits until the European Court of Justice gave judgment in the proceedings instituted by the European Community against Ireland, or the Tribunal otherwise determined. On 30 May 2006, the European Court of Justice held that Ireland had violated Articles 10 and 292 of the Treaty Establishing the European Community and Articles 192 and 193 of the Treaty Establishing the European Atomic Energy Community by instituting dispute settlement proceedings against the United Kingdom under the United Nations Convention on the Law of the Sea (Case C-459/03 *Commission of the European Communities* v. *Ireland* [2006] ECR I-4635, [2006] 2 CMLR 59).

Order No. 3 of the Arbitral Tribunal, 24 June 2003 (extract)
[...]

[315] [...] THE DISPUTE

9. The dispute brought before the Tribunal by Ireland essentially concerns discharges into the Irish Sea of certain radioactive wastes produced by or as a result of the operation of the MOX plant, which is a new reprocessing plant at Sellafield in the United Kingdom. This reprocessing plant is designed to reprocess spent nuclear fuel into a new fuel (known as mixed oxide fuel, or 'MOX') made from a mixture of **[316]** plutonium dioxide and uranium dioxide. The spent nuclear fuel reprocessed at the MOX plant comes principally from another plant at Sellafield, the Thermal Oxide Reprocessing Plant ('THORP'). The MOX and THORP facilities are operated by British Nuclear Fuels plc ('BNFL'), with the authorisation of the United Kingdom Government. BNFL is a corporation wholly owned by the United Kingdom Government.

10. It is apparent from the nature of operations carried out at the MOX and THORP facilities that they involve quantities of radioactive substances. Sellafield, where the MOX and THORP facilities are located, is on the west coast of Cumbria in the United Kingdom, facing onto the Irish Sea. The United Kingdom forms the eastern and part of the western coast of the Irish Sea, and Ireland forms the rest of that western coast. In the present context, both States clearly have an interest in what happens in the Irish Sea, which is a semi-enclosed sea within the meaning of article 122 of the Convention.

11. In its Notification and Amended Statement of Claim, Ireland asserts that, in respect of the establishment and prospective operation of the MOX plant, there is a risk of harm arising from discharges of radioactive wastes. By the amendment to its Statement of Claim, Ireland made it clear 'that Ireland's claim is not confined to the immediate consequences arising directly from the MOX plant alone, considered in isolation from the rest of the Sellafield complex, but extends to all the consequences that flow from the establishment and operation of the MOX plant, including the consequences flowing from the increased activity at the THORP plant that is supported by the MOX plant'. Ireland also maintains that there are risks arising from transport of radioactive material through the Irish Sea to and from the facilities, and from the storage of such material at those facilities.

12. Ireland considers that, in the circumstances, the Convention imposes on the United Kingdom obligations concerning the protection of the marine environment; the prevention and control of pollution, and co-operation between the two States; and that it gives Ireland corresponding rights. Ireland contends that the United Kingdom is in breach of the obligations under various articles of the Convention (including articles 123, 192, 193, 194, 197, 206, 207, 211, and 213), and Ireland accordingly seeks from the Tribunal appropriate remedies against the United Kingdom.

13. For its part, the United Kingdom raises various questions relating to the jurisdiction of the Tribunal to hear and determine the merits of the dispute submitted to it by

Ireland. In any event, on their merits the United Kingdom rejects Ireland's allegations that the United Kingdom is in breach of any obligations under the Convention.

[317] THE TRIBUNAL'S JURISDICTION TO DECIDE THE MERITS

14. [. . .] [The International Tribunal for the Law of the Sea] found, in its Order, that 'the Annex VII Tribunal would *prima facie* have jurisdiction over the dispute' (ITLOS Order,[4] paragraph 62). The Tribunal sees no reason to disagree with the finding that *prima facie* it has jurisdiction. Ireland and the United Kingdom are both parties to the Convention; the arbitral tribunal has been duly constituted in accordance with Part XV of the Convention and Annex VII to the Convention; it is apparent that Ireland has presented its claims on the basis of various provisions of the Convention; the Parties agree that there is a dispute concerning the MOX plant; that dispute clearly concerns the interpretation and application of the Convention (in that the Parties have adopted different legal positions on that matter); and there is nothing which manifestly and in terms excludes the Tribunal's jurisdiction.

15. However, before proceeding to any final decision on the merits, the Tribunal must satisfy itself that it has jurisdiction in a definitive sense. Moreover, even to proceed to hear argument on the merits of the dispute brought before it, the Tribunal needs to be satisfied at least that there are no substantial doubts as to its jurisdiction.

16. The United Kingdom raises objections to the jurisdiction of the Tribunal, which fall into two categories. First, the United Kingdom raises a number of questions of jurisdiction and admissibility in respect of the Convention itself and other international agreements and instruments invoked by Ireland. The Tribunal will refer to these as the international law issues. Second, certain objections are raised relating to the position of the Parties under the law of the European Communities. The Tribunal will refer to these as the European Community law issues.

17. The Tribunal considers that none of the issues raised casts doubt on its *prima facie* jurisdiction.

18. With regard to the international law issues raised by the United Kingdom, there has clearly been an exchange of views between the Parties, as required under article 283 of the Convention, and the United Kingdom does not now contest this. It is true that the 1992 Convention for the Protection of the Marine Environment of the North-East Atlantic ('the OSPAR Convention') is relevant to some at least of the questions in issue between the Parties,[5] but the Tribunal does not consider that this alters the character of the dispute as one essentially involving the interpretation and application of the Convention. Furthermore, the Tribunal is not persuaded that the OSPAR Convention substantially covers the field of the present dispute so as to trigger the application of articles 281 or 282 of the Convention.

[4 See p. 427 above.]
[5 See p. 558 below.]

[318] 19. The Parties discussed at some length the question of the scope of Ireland's claims, in particular its claims arising under other treaties (e.g. the OSPAR Convention) or instruments (e.g. the Sintra Ministerial Statement, adopted at a meeting of the OSPAR Commission on 23 July 1998), having regard to articles 288 and 293 of the Convention. The Tribunal agrees with the United Kingdom that there is a cardinal distinction between the scope of its jurisdiction under article 288, paragraph 1, of the Convention, on the one hand, and the law to be applied by the Tribunal under article 293 of the Convention, on the other hand. It also agrees that, to the extent that any aspects of Ireland's claims arise directly under legal instruments other than the Convention, such claims may be inadmissible. However, the Tribunal does not agree that Ireland has failed to state and plead a case arising substantially under the Convention.

20. With regard to the European Community law issues, however, certain problems have become apparent to the Tribunal in respect of some important and interrelated areas of European Community law as they appear to affect the dispute between the Parties before this Tribunal. These areas concern in particular:

(i)   the standing of Ireland to institute proceedings before this Tribunal in reliance upon the Convention rights which it invokes;

(ii) the standing of the United Kingdom to respond to such proceedings;

(iii) the division of competences between the European Community (of which both Ireland and the United Kingdom are Member States) and its Member States in respect of the Convention, particularly in the light of the declarations made by the Parties and the European Community pursuant to article 5 of Annex IX to the Convention;[6]

(iv) the extent to which provisions and instruments invoked by the Parties may properly be relied upon before this Tribunal; and

(v)   the matters which, by agreement of the Parties, are subject to the exclusive jurisdiction of the European Court of Justice under European Community law.

21. These problems have become more acute following a Written Answer given by the Commission of the European Communities ('the European Commission') in the European Parliament on 15 May 2003, [319] after the closure of the written pleadings in the present case.[7] This Written Answer was brought to the Tribunal's attention on 5 June 2003, only five days before the commencement of the hearings. The Tribunal notes that the European Commission has indicated in its Written Answer that it is examining the question whether to institute proceedings under article 226 of the European Community Treaty. In these circumstances, there is a real possibility that the European Court of Justice may be seised of the question whether the provisions of the Convention on which Ireland relies are matters in relation to which

---

[6] For the declaration texts, *see* http://www.un.org/Depts/los/convention_agreement/convention_declarations.htm.

[7] The European Parliament Plenary Session, Oral question by Proinsias De Rossa (H-0256/03), Sitting of Thursday, 15 May 2003.

competence has been transferred to the European Community and, indeed, whether the exclusive jurisdiction of the European Court of Justice, with regard to Ireland and the United Kingdom as Member States of the European Community, extends to the interpretation and application of the Convention as such and in its entirety.

22. While neither the United Kingdom nor Ireland sought to sustain the view that the interpretation of the Convention in its entirety fell within the exclusive competence of the European Court of Justice as between Member States of the European Union, it cannot be said with certainty that this view would be rejected by the European Court of Justice. The Parties agreed in argument that, if this view were to be sustained, it would preclude the jurisdiction of the present Tribunal entirely, by virtue of article 282 of the Convention.

23. In these circumstances, the determination of the Tribunal's jurisdiction, particularly in the light of articles 281 and 282 of the Convention, and the identification of the treaty provisions and other rules of international law which the Tribunal could apply to the dispute brought before it by Ireland, are crucially dependent upon the resolution of the problems referred to above.

24. The Tribunal recognizes that the problems referred to above relate to matters which essentially concern the internal operation of a separate legal order (namely the legal order of the European Communities) to which both of the Parties to the present proceedings are subject and which, in the circumstances referred to in paragraph 21 above, are to be determined within the institutional framework of the European Communities. The European Community law issues are still to be resolved, and there is a risk of considerable further delay.

25. Despite this risk, the fact remains that, until these issues are definitively resolved, there remain substantial doubts whether the jurisdiction of the Tribunal can be firmly established in respect of all or any of the claims in the dispute.

[320] 26. Although it is possible that the Tribunal might conclude from the arguments of the Parties that at least certain provisions of the Convention do not fall within the exclusive jurisdiction and competence of the European Communities in the present case, it would still not be appropriate for the Tribunal to proceed with hearings on the merits in respect of any such provisions. For one thing, it is not at all clear at this stage that the Parties are able to identify with any certainty what such provisions might be; and the Tribunal is in no better position. For another, there is no certainty that any such provisions would in fact give rise to a self-contained and distinct dispute capable of being resolved by the Tribunal. Finally, the Tribunal notes that, whatever the Parties may agree in these proceedings as to the scope and effects of European Community law applicable in the present dispute, the question is ultimately not for them to decide but is rather to be decided within the institutions of the European Communities, and particularly by the European Court of Justice.

27. The Tribunal observes that the resolution of the essentially internal problems within the European Community legal order may involve decisions that are final and binding. The Tribunal further observes that its decision, including a decision on jurisdiction, will be final and binding on the Parties by virtue of article 296 of the Convention and article 11 of Annex VII to the Convention.

28. In the circumstances, and bearing in mind considerations of mutual respect and comity which should prevail between judicial institutions both of which may be called upon to determine rights and obligations as between two States, the Tribunal considers that it would be inappropriate for it to proceed further with hearing the Parties on the merits of the dispute in the absence of a resolution of the problems referred to. Moreover, a procedure that might result in two conflicting decisions on the same issue would not be helpful to the resolution of the dispute between the Parties.

SUSPENSION OF FURTHER PROCEEDINGS ON JURISDICTION AND MERITS

29. For these reasons, the Tribunal has decided, in exercise of its powers under article 8 of the Rules of Procedure, that further proceedings on jurisdiction and the merits in this arbitration will be suspended.

30. The Tribunal nevertheless remains seised of the dispute. Unless otherwise agreed or decided, the Tribunal will resume its proceedings not later than 1 December 2003. The Tribunal hopes that it will at that time have a clearer picture of the position regarding European Community law and possible proceedings thereunder insofar as they appertain to the present dispute.

[321] IRELAND'S REQUEST FOR FURTHER PROVISIONAL MEASURES

31. In announcing its decision to suspend further proceedings in the case, the Tribunal stated its willingness, in the circumstances now prevailing, to consider the possibility of prescribing provisional measures if either Party considers that such measures are necessary to preserve the respective rights of the Parties or to prevent serious harm to the marine environment.

32. By communication dated 16 June 2003, Ireland submitted to the Tribunal a Request for Further Provisional Measures ('the Request') pursuant to article 290 of the Convention 'to preserve Ireland's rights under UNCLOS and to prevent harm to the marine environment'.

33. The provisional measures requested by Ireland are as follows:

(A) *Discharges*
   (i) The United Kingdom shall ensure that there are no liquid waste discharges from the MOX Plant at Sellafield into the Irish Sea.
   (ii) The United Kingdom shall ensure that annual aerial waste discharges of radionuclides from MOX, and annual aerial and liquid waste discharges of radionuclides from THORP, do not exceed 2002 levels.
(B) *Co-operation* (Note: the following is on a confidential basis)
   (i) In the event of any proposal for additional reprocessing at THORP or manufacturing at MOX (by reference to existing binding contractual commitments), the United Kingdom will notify Ireland, provide Ireland with full information in relation to the proposal and consult with, and consider and respond to issues raised by, Ireland.
   (ii) The United Kingdom will inform the Irish Government as soon as possible of the precise date and time at which it is expected that any vessel carrying radioactive

substances to or from the MOX or THORP Plant or to a storage facility with the possibility of subsequent reprocessing or manufacture in THORP or MOX will arrive within Ireland's Pollution Response Zone, SAR Zone or within the Irish Sea, and shall inform Ireland on a daily basis as to the intended route and progress of such vessel.

(iii)   The United Kingdom shall ensure that Ireland is promptly provided with:

a.   Monthly information as to the quantity (in becquerels) of specific radionuclide discharges in the form of liquid and aerial waste discharges arising from the MOX Plant and separately from the THORP Plant, and the flow sheets relating to environmental [322] discharges liquid and aerial referred to at paragraphs 118 and 124 of Mr Clarke's first statement;

b.   Monthly information as to the volume of waste in the HAST tanks and the volume vitrified during the previous month;

c.   All research studies carried out or funded in whole or in part by or on behalf of the United Kingdom government or any of its agencies or BNFL into the effect of liquid or aerial discharges, from the MOX or THORP Plant, upon the Irish Sea, its environment or biota;

d.   Full details of any reportable accidents or incidents at the MOX or THORP Plant or associated facilities, that will be the subject of a report to the United Kingdom's Health and Safety Executive (or any other public body with responsibility for health and safety at the Sellafield site);

e.   Access to, and the right and facility to make a copy of Continued Operation Safety Reports (including the Probabilistic Risk Assessments) and associated documents relating to the Sellafield site;

f.   The results of reappraisals since 11 September 2001 of the risks to the MOX Plant and THORP and associated facilities such as the HAST tanks, and of the measures taken to counter any change since 11 September 2001 in the level of the perceived threat.

(iv)   The United Kingdom shall co-operate and co-ordinate with Ireland in respect of emergency planning and preparedness in respect of risks arising out of reprocessing, MOX fuel manufacture and storage of radioactive materials including providing Ireland with such information as is necessary to take appropriate response measures.

(v)   The United Kingdom shall co-operate with Ireland in arranging trilateral liaison between the Irish Coastguard, BNFL/PNTL and the United Kingdom's Maritime and Coastguard Agency in respect of all shipments of radioactive materials to or from the MOX and/or THORP Plants.

(C) *Assessment*

The United Kingdom shall ensure that no steps or decisions are taken or implemented which might preclude full effect being given to the results of any environmental assessment which the Tribunal may order to be carried out in accordance with Article 206 of UNCLOS in respect of the MOX Plant and/or THORP.

(D) *Other Relief*

(i)   Further and other relief;

(ii)   Liberty to apply.

[323] The Tribunal understands that, by the Note in parenthesis to Section (B) of its Request, Ireland intended to indicate that any information provided by the United Kingdom in response to provisional measures would be treated as confidential.

34. In its Request, Ireland states that 'the circumstances justifying this request include the likely duration of the suspension of the hearing and the real possibility of proceedings before the European Court of Justice, and the conduct of the United Kingdom as outlined in the pleadings'.

THE TRIBUNAL'S COMPETENCE WITH REGARD TO PROVISIONAL MEASURES
AND THE APPLICABLE RULES

[. . .]

[**324**] [. . .] 39. Although a provisional measure was prescribed by ITLOS, Ireland's request for additional provisional measures is the first such request to this Tribunal. Hence, the Tribunal's competence to prescribe provisional measures is contained in article 290, paragraph 1, of the Convention, and is subject to the provisions of paragraphs 2 to 4 of that article.

40. To the extent this may be relevant, the Tribunal considers that there has been a change in the circumstances in which ITLOS prescribed its provisional measure. First, this Tribunal has now been constituted. Furthermore, following the suspension of the proceedings, the time that will elapse before the Tribunal can reach a decision on the merits is likely to be greater than was to be expected when ITLOS made its Order. In the view of the Tribunal, the longer delay in reaching a final decision on the merits of the dispute constitutes a change in the circumstances that would, if necessary, warrant modification of the provisional measure prescribed by ITLOS in accordance with article 290, paragraph 5, of the Convention.

[. . .]

[**325**] [. . .] 43. In that connection, the Tribunal notes that according to article 89, paragraph 5, of the ITLOS Rules of Procedure, it is open to ITLOS to prescribe measures different in whole or in part from those requested. A similar provision is contained in article 75, paragraph 2, of the Rules of Court of the International Court of Justice. The Tribunal, having drawn these provisions to the attention of the Parties without comment from either, considers that it is also competent to prescribe provisional measures other than those sought by any Party.

[. . .]

[**326**] [. . .] 47. In a letter to the Agent of Ireland dated 13 June 2003 (which was copied to the Tribunal) the Agent of the United Kingdom stated that 'there are no current proposals for new contracts for reprocessing at THORP or for the modification of existing contracts so as to reprocess further materials. No decision to authorize further reprocessing at THORP would be taken without consultation in which Ireland would be invited to participate.' The Agent of the United Kingdom also made certain statements, on a confidential basis, relating to shipments of MOX fuel.

48. In oral argument, the Attorney-General for the United Kingdom also drew attention to the United Kingdom's earlier offer to engage in a general review with Ireland of the mechanisms for intergovernmental co-operation in respect of the concerns of

Ireland as to the Sellafield plant, including those parts of it comprised in the present dispute.

[...]

[327] [...] THE TRIBUNAL'S CONCLUSIONS ON PROVISIONAL MEASURES

52. As noted already, the Tribunal may only prescribe provisional measures if these are appropriate, in the prevailing circumstances and in the light of the information available, 'to preserve the respective rights of the parties to the dispute or to prevent serious harm to the marine environment'. Furthermore, the relevant period for this purpose is the period 'pending the final decision'. Harm which may be caused thereafter is a matter to be considered in the context of the case on the merits.

A. *Serious harm to the marine environment*

53. For the purposes of provisional measures, the Convention clearly identifies the prevention of serious harm to the marine environment as a special consideration, and it is appropriate to deal with that first.

54. As the Tribunal has already noted, the liquid wastes discharged from the MOX plant into the Irish Sea contain small quantities of radionuclides, some of which (e.g. Cs-137 and Pu-241) have an extremely long half-life. The wastes in question arise not as a direct by-product of reprocessing of spent nuclear fuels, but from ancillary activities such as the cleaning of the plant and sanitary operations. The Attorney-General for Ireland, in opening the case, accepted that '... the level of discharges from the MOX plant ... is not of a significant magnitude...'.

55. Under article 290, paragraph 1, any harm caused, or likely to be caused, to the marine environment must be 'serious' before the Tribunal's power to prescribe provisional measures on that basis arises. In the present state of the evidence, the Tribunal does not consider that Ireland has established that any harm which may be caused to the marine [328] environment by virtue of the operation of the MOX plant, pending the determination of this case on the merits, meets this threshold test.

B. *Protection of the rights of the Parties*

56. Ireland also argues that provisional measures were necessary to protect its rights under the Convention (a) in respect of discharges into the Irish Sea with potential effects on Irish waters, (b) in respect of co-operation with the United Kingdom to minimize harm to the marine environment and (c) in respect of its claimed right that, the potential effects of the MOX plant not having been adequately assessed, either in themselves or in terms of increased discharges resulting from THORP, it was a violation of Ireland's rights in particular under article 206 of the Convention for the discharges to continue, even in the period before the final decision.

57. The United Kingdom, in opposing these measures, notes that some of them at least are capable of having a serious impact on its own rights, in particular to the continued lawful operation of the MOX plant in the period pending a final decision, and it stresses that the rights or interests of both parties have to be taken into account in

any decision on provisional measures. The United Kingdom points out that the MOX plant and related facilities have been approved under a stringent regulatory regime established and operated with full regard to the applicable regional and international norms.

58. International judicial practice confirms that a general requirement for the prescription of provisional measures to protect the rights of the Parties is that there needs to be a showing both of urgency and of irreparable harm to the claimed rights (see, e.g., the Order of 17 June 2003 of the International Court of Justice in the *Case concerning Certain Criminal Proceedings in France (Republic of the Congo* v. *France)*, paragraphs 34–5).

59. The Tribunal notes that ITLOS was requested by way of provisional measures to order that the MOX plant not be approved or commissioned. This ITLOS declined to do, although it did prescribe a different provisional measure focusing on improved co-operation between the Parties and the provision of information.

60. The Tribunal further notes that in the period since it was constituted, Ireland could have sought a modification of the ITLOS Order if it had been dissatisfied with its operation, or it could have sought additional provisional measures if evidence available to it had indicated an urgent need for them in terms of the criteria in article 290, paragraph 1.

[329] 61. Turning first to the question of discharges (paragraph (A) of the Request), the Tribunal has before it a much greater volume of written material than ITLOS had at the time of its Order. But the Tribunal does not consider that this material leads it to reach any different conclusion as to the question of discharges from the MOX plant, so far as concerns the period prior to the decision on the merits. In this respect it notes in particular the statement made by the Agent for the United Kingdom, which the Tribunal has set out in paragraph 47 above, that 'there are no current proposals for new contracts for reprocessing at THORP or for the modification of existing contracts so as to reprocess further materials'. There is thus no clear indication at this stage that there will be additional discharges from THORP arising by reason of the MOX plant and falling within the scope of the present proceedings.

62. For these reasons, the Tribunal is not satisfied that in the present circumstances there is an urgent and serious risk of irreparable harm to Ireland's claimed rights, which would justify it in prescribing provisional measures relating to discharges from the MOX plant.

63. As to the question of assessment (paragraph (C) of the Request), the Tribunal notes that this is presented as a key part of Ireland's case on the merits. In this respect, Ireland emphasised the provisions of article 206 of the Convention. The Tribunal would also draw attention to article 204, paragraph 2. But the Tribunal does not believe that any provisional measure is justified at this stage, in advance of the Tribunal's eventual consideration of the merits, even assuming that the issue of assessment does indeed fall definitively within the Tribunal's jurisdiction. In this context the Tribunal does not consider that paragraph (C) of the Request, in either of its versions, would give any clear guidance to the United Kingdom of what conduct is required of it pending a final decision.

64. Turning to the question of co-operation between the Parties in relation to the preservation of the marine environment of the Irish Sea (paragraph (B) of the Request), the Tribunal first observes that this matter was dealt with, to some extent at least, in the ITLOS Order. Both Parties accept that that Order remains in force and is binding upon them. Moreover Ireland does not seek any modification of the ITLOS Order as such, as distinct from an order requiring further measures of co-operation and exchange of information.

65. The ITLOS Order requires the Parties to co-operate and to enter into consultations forthwith for the purposes specified in the ITLOS Order. In its Reply Ireland acknowledged that since the ITLOS Order, there had been some improvement in the processes of co-operation and the provision of information; but it pointed to a number of continuing [330] difficulties. The United Kingdom provided detailed responses to individual points raised by Ireland.

66. The Tribunal does not need at this stage to resolve the factual issues in dispute between the Parties as to the adequacy and timeliness of the disclosure of certain information and as to the character and extent of co-operation. It is satisfied that since December 2001, there has been an increased measure of co-operation and consultation, as required by the ITLOS Order. On the other hand, the Tribunal is concerned that such co-operation and consultation may not always have been as timely or effective as it could have been. In particular, problems have sometimes arisen, both before and since the ITLOS Order, from the absence of secure arrangements, at a suitable inter-governmental level, for coordination of all of the various agencies and bodies involved. The United Kingdom's offer, referred to in paragraph 48 above, to review with Ireland the whole system of intergovernmental notification and co-operation in this context should once again be recalled.

67. The Tribunal, accordingly, recommends that the Parties should seek to establish arrangements of the kind referred to in the previous paragraph, and to undertake the review of the intergovernmental system referred to in that paragraph.

OTHER MATTERS

68. The Tribunal notes also that it is consistent with the practice of ITLOS that each Party should submit reports and information on compliance with the Tribunal's Order below.

69. In addition, the Tribunal urges both Ireland and the United Kingdom, jointly and separately, to take appropriate steps to expedite the resolution of the outstanding questions of European Community law. In this connection, the Tribunal draws the attention of the Parties to the provisions of article 5, paragraph 5, and article 6, paragraph 2, of Annex IX to the Convention.

70. In making its Request, Ireland did not include any request for costs. The United Kingdom for its part submitted that the Tribunal, in rejecting the Request, should order that Ireland pay the United Kingdom's costs of these proceedings. The Tribunal considers that no order as to costs is appropriate at this stage. In the light of articles 16 and 17 of its Rules of Procedure, the Tribunal reserves until its final Award any decision as to the costs of the Parties and the expenses of the Tribunal.

[331] THE TRIBUNAL'S ORDER

For the foregoing reasons

The Tribunal, unanimously, pursuant to articles 1 and 8 of its Rules of Procedure and article 290 of the Convention, makes the following Order:

1. *Decides* that further proceedings in the case are suspended until not later than 1 December 2003;

2. *Affirms* the provisional measure prescribed by ITLOS in its Order of 3 December 2001;

3. *Rejects* Ireland's Request for Provisional Measures in so far as concerns paragraphs (A) and (C) of the Request;

4. *Decides*, in so far as concerns paragraph (B) of the Request, having regard to the considerations referred to in paragraphs 64 to 67 above, that no further order is required as to co-operation and the provision of information at this stage;

5. *Calls on* the Parties, pending the final decision of the Tribunal, to ensure that no action is taken by either Party which might aggravate or extend the dispute submitted to the Tribunal;

6. *Requests* the Parties to take such steps as are open to them separately or jointly to expedite the resolution of the outstanding issues within the institutional framework of the European Communities; and to notify the Tribunal and each other of all relevant developments;

7. *Decides,*

   (a) that no later than 12 September 2003, Ireland and the United Kingdom shall each submit to the Tribunal and to the other Party an initial report and information on compliance with the provisional measure affirmed, and the recommendations made in paragraph 67 above, by the Tribunal in the present Order;

   (b) that subject to any further order of the Tribunal, not later than 17 November 2003, a further report and information on compliance shall be submitted; and

   (c) to keep under review the possible need for further measures in this connection; and

8. *Instructs* the Registrar to provide a copy of this Order to the European Commission.

[Report: 126 *ILR* 314]

Order No. 4 of the Arbitral Tribunal, 14 November 2003

[332] *The Arbitral Tribunal*

Having regard to articles 1 and 8 of the Rules of Procedure adopted by the Tribunal;

Having regard to *Order No. 3* of 24 June 2003 by which the Tribunal decided to suspend further proceedings in the case until not later than 1 December 2003;

Having regard to the Reports dated 12 September 2003 submitted by Ireland and the United Kingdom, pursuant to *Order No. 3* of 24 June 2003;

Having regard to the letter dated 21 October 2003 from the Agent of Ireland with which Ireland informed the Tribunal that the College of Commissioners of the European Community decided on 15 October 2003 to authorise the institution of proceedings against Ireland in respect of Community law issues, and that Ireland expected that proceedings would accordingly issue within the next week or very shortly thereafter;

Having regard to the statement by the Agent of Ireland that 'it is apparent that the resolution of the Community law issues will have to await a decision of the European Court of Justice';

Having regard to Ireland's application, in the Agent's letter dated 21 October 2003, to the Tribunal to suspend the hearings in the proceedings until the European Court of Justice has given judgment in the matter;

Having ascertained the views of the parties;

1. *Decides* that
   (a)   further proceedings in the case shall remain suspended until the European Court of Justice has given judgment or the Tribunal otherwise determines;
   (b)   the suspension of the proceedings shall be without prejudice to the continuation of the matters ordered in paragraphs 2, 5, 6 and 7 of the *Dispositif* of the Tribunal's *Order No. 3* of 24 June 2003, and the statements made by the United Kingdom as recorded in paragraphs 47 and 48 of that Order;
   (c)   further reports and information to be submitted by the Parties pursuant to paragraph 7(b) of the *Dispositif* of the Tribunal's **[333]** *Order No. 3* of 24 June 2003, shall be submitted not later than 28 November 2003;
   (d)   subject to any further order by the Tribunal, the Parties shall each submit, not later than 31 May 2004 and every six months thereafter, a report and information on compliance with the provisional measure affirmed and recommendations made by the Tribunal in *Order No. 3* of 24 June 2003;
   (e)   subject to any further order by the Tribunal, Ireland shall submit, not later than 30 June 2004 and every six months thereafter, a report to the Tribunal on developments in the proceedings before the European Court of Justice;
   (f)   the Tribunal shall remain seised of the dispute;
2. *Reserves* the subsequent procedure for further decision;
3. *Instructs* the Registrar to transmit a copy of this Order to the European Commission.

[Report: 126 *ILR* 332]

Judgment of European Court of Justice, 30 May 2006 (extract)

1. By its application, the Commission of the European Communities seeks a declaration by the Court that, by instituting dispute-settlement proceedings against the

United Kingdom of Great Britain and Northern Ireland under the United Nations Convention on the Law of the Sea ('the Convention') concerning the MOX plant located at Sellafield (United Kingdom), Ireland has failed to fulfil its obligations under Articles 10 EC and 292 EC and Articles 192 EA and 193 EA.

LEGAL CONTEXT

2. The Convention, which was signed at Montego Bay (Jamaica) on 10 December 1982, came into force on 16 November 1994.

3. The Convention was approved on behalf of the European Community by Council Decision 98/392/EC of 23 March 1998 (OJ 1998 L 179, p. 1). The Convention has also been ratified by all of the Member States of the European Union.

4. On 21 June 1996, at the time when the Convention was being ratified by Ireland, that Member State made the following declaration:

> Ireland recalls that, as a State member of the European Community, it has transferred competence to the Community in regard to certain matters which are governed by the Convention. A detailed declaration on the nature and extent of the competence transferred to the European Community will be made in due course in accordance with the provisions of Annex IX to the Convention.

[...]

BACKGROUND TO THE DISPUTE

[...]

Dispute-settlement proceedings brought by Ireland in regard to the MOX plant
[...]

42. By order of 24 June 2003,[8] notified to the Commission on 27 June 2003, the Arbitral Tribunal decided to suspend the proceedings until 1 De mber 2003 and asked to be more extensively informed, by that date, as to the implications of Community law in regard to the dispute pending before it.

43. In that order, the Arbitral Tribunal noted that problems closely related to Community law had arisen concerning important issues such as the standing of Ireland and the United Kingdom, the division of areas of competence between the Community and its Member States in respect of the Convention, the extent to which the provisions invoked by the parties could be relied upon by the Arbitral Tribunal and the question of the exclusive jurisdiction of the Court of Justice.

44. The Tribunal took the view in this regard that there was a real possibility that the Court of Justice might be seised of the dispute and rule that the dispute was a matter of Community law, thereby precluding the Tribunal's jurisdiction under Article 282 of the Convention.

[8 See p. 527 above.]

45. The Arbitral Tribunal went on to observe that the issues on which its jurisdiction depends concern essentially the internal operation of a separate legal order, namely the legal order of the Community, and that those issues must be resolved within the institutional framework of the Community and, in particular, by the Court of Justice.

46. In that connection, the Arbitral Tribunal took the view that, given the risk of conflicting decisions and bearing in mind considerations of mutual respect and comity between judicial institutions, it would not be appropriate to continue the proceedings without a resolution of the issues touching on Community law. The Arbitral Tribunal also enjoined the parties to take the appropriate steps separately or jointly to expedite resolution of the outstanding issues within the institutional framework of the European Communities.

47. By that order the Arbitral Tribunal also confirmed the provisional measures previously prescribed by the International Tribunal for the Law of the Sea and refused the further provisional measures requested by Ireland.

48. Following the Commission's decision to bring the present action for failure to fulfil obligations, Ireland requested the Arbitral Tribunal to suspend hearings until the Court of Justice has delivered judgment in the present case. The Tribunal acceded to that request by order of 14 November 2004.

[. . .]

THE ACTION

59. The Commission raises three heads of complaint in its action. First, it claims that, by bringing proceedings against the United Kingdom under the Convention, Ireland has failed to respect the exclusive jurisdiction vested in the Court by Article 292 EC to rule on any dispute concerning the interpretation and application of Community law. Second, the Commission argues that Ireland has breached Articles 292 EC and 193 EA by referring to the Arbitral Tribunal a dispute which requires for its resolution the interpretation and application of measures of Community law. Third, the Commission alleges that Ireland has failed to comply with its duty of cooperation under Article 10 EC by exercising a competence which belongs to the Community and that it has failed in that duty under Articles 10 EC and 192 EA by failing first to inform or consult with the competent Community institutions.

The first head of complaint

60. In its first head of complaint, the Commission submits that, by instituting the dispute-settlement proceedings provided for under the Convention for the purpose of resolving its dispute with the United Kingdom concerning the MOX plant, Ireland has failed to respect the exclusive jurisdiction of the Court in regard to disputes concerning the interpretation and application of Community law and has thereby breached Article 292 EC.

[. . .]

Findings of the Court

80. It is necessary to specify at the outset that, by its first head of complaint, the Commission is criticising Ireland for failing to respect the exclusive jurisdiction of the Court by bringing before the Arbitral Tribunal a dispute between it and another Member State concerning the interpretation and application of provisions of the Convention involving obligations assumed by the Community in the exercise of its external competence in regard to protection of the environment, and for thereby breaching Article 292 EC. The articles of the EAEC Treaty to which the Commission refers in its submissions relate to the second and third heads of complaint.

81. Under Article 300(7) EC, '[a]greements concluded under the conditions set out in [that] Article shall be binding on the institutions of the Community and on Member States'.

82. The Convention was signed by the Community and subsequently approved by Decision 98/392. It follows that, according to settled case-law, the provisions of that convention now form an integral part of the Community legal order (see, inter alia, Case C-344/04 *IATA and ELFAA* [2006] 2 CMLR 20 at paragraph 36).

83. The Convention was concluded by the Community and all of its Member States on the basis of shared competence.

84. The Court has already ruled that mixed agreements have the same status in the Community legal order as purely Community agreements, as these are provisions coming within the scope of Community competence (Case C-13/00 *Commission* v. *Ireland*, paragraph 14).

85. From this the Court has concluded that, in ensuring respect for commitments arising from an agreement concluded by the Community institutions, the Member States fulfil, within the Community system, an obligation in relation to the Community, which has assumed responsibility for the due performance of that agreement (Case C-13/00 *Commission* v. *Ireland*, paragraph 15).

86. As the Convention is a mixed agreement, it is for that reason necessary to examine whether the provisions of that agreement relied on by Ireland before the Arbitral Tribunal in connection with the dispute concerning the MOX plant come within the scope of Community competence.

87. It follows from the wording of Ireland's statement of claim (set out in paragraph 35 of the present judgment) that that Member State is essentially criticising the United Kingdom for granting authorisation to operate the MOX plant without having met a number of obligations arising under the Convention.

88. With the exception of Article 123 of the Convention, all of the provisions relied on in that regard feature in Part XII of that Convention, entitled 'Protection and preservation of the marine environment'.

89. Ireland criticises the United Kingdom in particular for having breached, in the first place, Article 206 of the Convention by failing in its obligation to carry out a proper assessment of the environmental impact of all activities associated with the MOX plant on the marine environment of the Irish Sea, secondly, Articles 123 and 197 of the Convention by failing in its obligation to cooperate with Ireland in order to

protect the marine environment of the Irish Sea, a sea which is semi-enclosed, and, finally, Articles 192, 193 and/or 194 and/or 207, 211 and 213 of the Convention by failing to take the measures necessary to prevent, reduce and control pollution of the marine environment of the Irish Sea.

90. The Court has already interpreted Article 175(1) EC as being the appropriate legal basis for conclusion, on behalf of the Community, of international agreements on protection of the environment (see, in this regard, Opinion 2/00 [2001] ECR I-9713, paragraph 44).

91. That conclusion is reinforced by the reading of Article 175(1) EC in conjunction with the fourth indent in Article 174(1) EC, which expressly includes 'promoting measures at international level to deal with regional or worldwide environmental problems' among the objectives to be pursued within the framework of policy on the environment.

92. Admittedly, as indicated in Article 176 EC, that external competence of the Community in regard to the protection of the environment, in this case the marine environment, is not exclusive but rather, in principle, shared between the Community and the Member States (see, to that effect, Opinion 2/00, paragraph 47).

93. However, the question as to whether a provision of a mixed agreement comes within the competence of the Community is one which relates to the attribution and, thus, the very existence of that competence, and not to its exclusive or shared nature.

94. It follows that the existence of the Community's external competence in regard to protection of the marine environment is not, in principle, contingent on the adoption of measures of secondary law covering the area in question and liable to be affected if Member States were to take part in the procedure for concluding the agreement in question, within the terms of the principle formulated by the Court in paragraph 17 of the *AETR* judgment [Case 22/70 *Commission* v. *Council* [1971] ECR 263].

95. The Community can enter into agreements in the area of environmental protection even if the specific matters covered by those agreements are not yet, or are only very partially, the subject of rules at Community level, which, by reason of that fact, are not likely to be affected (see, in that regard, Opinion 2/00, paragraphs 44 to 47, and Case C-239/03 *Commission* v. *France* [2004] ECR I-9325, paragraph 30).

96. That being so, it is necessary to establish whether and to what extent the Community, by becoming a party to the Convention, elected to exercise its external competence in matters of environmental protection.

97. In this regard, the reference, in the first citation in the preamble to Decision 98/392, to Article 130s(1) of the EC Treaty (now, after amendment, Article 175(1) EC) as one of the provisions constituting the legal basis of the decision approving the Convention indicates that this was indeed the case.

98. Furthermore, the fifth recital in the preamble to that decision states that approval of the Convention by the Community is designed to enable it to become a party to it within the limits of its competence.

99. The Declaration of Community competence referred to in Article 1(3) of that decision, which forms part of the Community's instrument of formal confirmation constituting Annex II to the Decision, specifies the extent and the nature of the areas of competence transferred by the Member States to the Community in the matters dealt with by the Convention in respect of which the Community accepts the rights and obligations provided for by that convention.

100. Ireland submits that Article 4(3) of Annex IX to the Convention, in particular the notion of 'transfer of competence' which features there, and the Declaration of Community competence must be construed as meaning that, in regard to shared competence, the only areas of competence transferred and exercised by the Community when it became a party to the Convention are those which have become exclusive as a result of having been affected, within the meaning of the principle set out in paragraph 17 of the *AETR* judgment.

101. This, it claims, is a particular feature of the Convention, which allows only the transfer of exclusive competence of the Community, the other areas of competence and the relevant responsibilities remaining within the purview of the Member States.

102. According to Ireland, as the Community provisions in issue are only minimum rules, they are not in principle affected; consequently, the related areas of shared competence have not been transferred within the framework of the Convention.

103. By contrast, the Commission avers that the Declaration of Community competence must be understood as meaning that the areas of shared competence in question are transferred and exercised by the Community even if they relate to matters in respect of which there are at present no Community rules.

104. It is necessary to point out in this regard that the second sentence of the first paragraph of the second indent of point 2 of the Declaration of Community competence states, with regard to, inter alia, the provisions of the Convention relating to the prevention of marine pollution, that '[w]hen Community rules exist but are not affected, in particular in cases of Community provisions establishing only minimum standards, the Member States have competence, without prejudice to the competence of the Community to act in this field'.

105. Consequently, that declaration confirms that a transfer of areas of shared competence, in particular in regard to the prevention of marine pollution, took place within the framework of the Convention, and without any of the Community rules concerned being affected, within the terms of the principle set out in the *AETR* judgment.

106. However, that passage of the Declaration of Community competence makes the transfer of areas of shared competence subject to the existence of Community rules, even though it is not necessary that those rules be affected.

107. In the other cases, that is to say, those in which there are no Community rules, competence rests with the Member States, in accordance with the third sentence of the first paragraph of the second indent of point 2 of the Declaration of Community competence.

108. It follows that, within the specific context of the Convention, a finding that there has been a transfer to the Community of areas of shared competence is contingent on the existence of Community rules within the areas covered by the Convention provisions in issue, irrespective of what may otherwise be the scope and nature of those rules.

109. In this regard, the appendix to the Declaration of Community competence, while not exhaustive, constitutes a useful reference base.

110. It appears that the matters covered by the provisions of the Convention relied on by Ireland before the Arbitral Tribunal are very largely regulated by Community measures, several of which are mentioned expressly in the appendix to that declaration.

111. Thus, with regard to the head of complaint alleging failure to meet the obligation to carry out a proper assessment of the environmental impact of all of the activities associated with the MOX plant on the marine environment of the Irish Sea, based on Article 206 of the Convention, it must be stated that this matter is the subject of Directive 85/337, which is mentioned in the appendix to the Declaration of Community competence.

112. Ireland also cannot question the relevance of Directive 85/337 since it itself referred to that directive in its statement of claim before the Arbitral Tribunal as a measure which could serve as a reference for the interpretation of the relevant provisions of the Convention.

113. In addition, Ireland derived a number of arguments from that directive in support of its complaint in its pleadings before the Arbitral Tribunal.

114. The same observation also holds true for the complaint which Ireland bases on Articles 192, 193, 194, 207, 211 and 213 of the Convention, in so far as that complaint relates to the obligation to take the measures necessary to prevent, reduce and control pollution in the Irish Sea.

115. In its pleadings before the Arbitral Tribunal, Ireland derived several arguments from Directive 85/337 with a view to supporting that complaint in regard to the obligation to prevent pollution. The relevance of Directive 85/337 to the matter under consideration is therefore manifest.

116. Furthermore, that complaint, in so far as it concerns international transfers of radioactive substances connected to the activity of the MOX plant, is closely linked to Directive 93/75, which is also mentioned in the appendix to the Declaration of Community competence and regulates the minimum requirements for vessels bound for or leaving Community ports and carrying dangerous or polluting goods.

117. Furthermore, with regard to the complaint derived from Articles 123 and 197 of the Convention concerning the lack of cooperation on the part of the United Kingdom and, in particular, its refusal to provide Ireland with certain information, such as the full version of the PA report, it must be held that the provision of information of this kind comes within the scope of Council Directive 90/313/EEC of 7 June 1990 on the freedom of access to information on the environment (OJ 1990 L 158, p. 56).

118. In addition, as has been stated in paragraph 31 of the present judgment, Ireland set out that same head of complaint before the arbitral tribunal established pursuant to the Convention for the Protection of the Marine Environment of the North-East Atlantic on the basis of Article 9 of that convention, a convention which it once again invoked in its application initiating proceedings before the Arbitral Tribunal as a reference base for the interpretation of the Convention provisions in issue. The Convention for the Protection of the Marine Environment of the North-East Atlantic was concluded by the Community and, moreover, replaced the Paris conventions for the prevention of marine pollution from landbased sources, themselves mentioned in the appendix to the Declaration of Community competence.

119. It is also common ground that, in its pleadings before the Arbitral Tribunal, Ireland based its arguments in support of the head of claim in issue simultaneously on Directive 85/337, Directive 90/313 and the Convention for the Protection of the Marine Environment of the North-East Atlantic.

120. Those matters suffice to establish that the Convention provisions on the prevention of marine pollution relied on by Ireland, which clearly cover a significant part of the dispute relating to the MOX plant, come within the scope of Community competence which the Community has elected to exercise by becoming a party to the Convention.

121. It follows that the provisions of the Convention relied on by Ireland in the dispute relating to the MOX plant and submitted to the Arbitral Tribunal are rules which form part of the Community legal order. The Court therefore has jurisdiction to deal with disputes relating to the interpretation and application of those provisions and to assess a Member State's compliance with them (see, in that connection, Case C-13/00 *Commission* v. *Ireland*, paragraph 20, and Case C-239/03 *Commission* v. *France*, paragraph 31).

122. It is, however, necessary to determine whether this jurisdiction of the Court is exclusive, such as to preclude a dispute like that relating to the MOX plant being brought by a Member State before an arbitral tribunal established pursuant to Annex VII to the Convention.

123. The Court has already pointed out that an international agreement cannot affect the allocation of responsibilities defined in the Treaties and, consequently, the autonomy of the Community legal system, compliance with which the Court ensures under Article 220 EC. That exclusive jurisdiction of the Court is confirmed by Article 292 EC, by which Member States undertake not to submit a dispute concerning the interpretation or application of the EC Treaty to any method of settlement other than those provided for therein (see, to that effect, Opinion 1/91 [1991] ECR I-6079, paragraph 35, and Opinion 1/00 [2002] ECR I-3493, paragraphs 11 and 12).

124. It should be stated at the outset that the Convention precisely makes it possible to avoid such a breach of the Court's exclusive jurisdiction in such a way as to preserve the autonomy of the Community legal system.

125. It follows from Article 282 of the Convention that, as it provides for procedures resulting in binding decisions in respect of the resolution of disputes between Member

States, the system for the resolution of disputes set out in the EC Treaty must in principle take precedence over that contained in Part XV of the Convention.

126. It has been established that the provisions of the Convention in issue in the dispute concerning the MOX plant come within the scope of Community competence which the Community exercised by acceding to the Convention, with the result that those provisions form an integral part of the Community legal order.

127. Consequently, the dispute in this case is indeed a dispute concerning the interpretation or application of the EC Treaty, within the terms of Article 292 EC.

128. Furthermore, as it is between two Member States in regard to an alleged failure to comply with Community-law obligations resulting from those provisions of the Convention, this dispute is clearly covered by one of the methods of dispute settlement established by the EC Treaty within the terms of Article 292 EC, namely the procedure set out in Article 227 EC.

129. In addition, it is not open to dispute that proceedings such as those brought by Ireland before the Arbitral Tribunal fall to be described as a method of settlement of a dispute within the terms of Article 292 EC inasmuch as, under Article 296 of the Convention, the decisions delivered by such a tribunal are final and binding on the parties to the dispute.

130. Ireland contends, however, by way of alternative submission, that, if the Court were to conclude that the provisions of the Convention invoked before the Arbitral Tribunal form an integral part of Community law, that conclusion would also be unavoidable with regard to the provisions of the Convention dealing with dispute settlement. Consequently, it submits, the initiation of proceedings before an arbitral tribunal referred to in Article 287(1)(c) of the Convention constitutes a method of dispute settlement provided for in the EC Treaty, within the terms of Article 292 EC.

131. That argument must be rejected.

132. As has been pointed out in paragraph 123 of the present judgment, an international agreement such as the Convention cannot affect the exclusive jurisdiction of the Court in regard to the resolution of disputes between Member States concerning the interpretation and application of Community law. Furthermore, as indicated in paragraphs 124 and 125 of the present judgment, Article 282 of the Convention precisely makes it possible to avoid such a breach occurring, in such a way as to preserve the autonomy of the Community legal system.

133. It follows from all of the foregoing that Articles 220 EC and 292 EC precluded Ireland from initiating proceedings before the Arbitral Tribunal with a view to resolving the dispute concerning the MOX plant.

134. This finding cannot be brought into question by the fact that the application by Ireland instituting proceedings before the Arbitral Tribunal also relates to certain obligations of the United Kingdom concerning the risks connected with terrorism.

135. Without it being necessary to rule on the question as to whether that part of the dispute comes within the scope of Community law, suffice it to hold that, as follows from paragraph 120 of the present judgment, a significant part of the dispute

in this case between Ireland and the United Kingdom relates to the interpretation or application of Community law. It is for the Court, should the need arise, to identify the elements of the dispute which relate to provisions of the international agreement in question which fall outside its jurisdiction.

136. As the jurisdiction of the Court is exclusive and binding on the Member States, the arguments put forward by Ireland concerning the advantages which arbitration proceedings under Annex VII to the Convention would present in comparison with an action brought before the Court under Article 227 EC cannot be accepted.

137. Even if they were assumed to have been demonstrated, such advantages could not in any event justify a Member State in avoiding its Treaty obligations with regard to judicial proceedings intended to rectify an alleged breach of Community law by another Member State (see, to that effect, Case 232/78 *Commission* v. *France* [1979] ECR 2729, paragraph 9).

138. Finally, with regard to the arguments put forward by Ireland concerning urgency and the possibility of obtaining interim measures under Article 290 of the Convention, suffice it to point out that, under Article 243 EC, the Court may prescribe any necessary interim measures in cases before it. It is evident that such measures may therefore be ordered in the context of proceedings brought under Article 227 EC.

139. In the light of all of the foregoing, the first head of complaint must be upheld.

The second head of complaint

140. By its second head of complaint, the Commission contends that the submission by Ireland of instruments of Community law for interpretation and application by the Arbitral Tribunal amounts to a breach of Article 292 EC and, in regard to the measures relied on which come within the ambit of the EAEC Treaty, a breach of Article 193 EA.

[...]

Findings of the Court

146. It is common ground that, in its statement of claim and in its written submissions to the Arbitral Tribunal, Ireland invoked a number of Community measures.

147. In addition to the Convention for the Protection of the Marine Environment of the North-East Atlantic, the measures in question are essentially, in regard to the EC Treaty, Directives 85/337 and 90/313 and, in regard to the EAEC Treaty, Directives 80/836, 92/3 and 96/29.

148. It is also common ground that those Community measures were invoked by Ireland pursuant to Article 293(1) of the Convention, which provides that a tribunal such as the Arbitral Tribunal is to 'apply this Convention and other rules of international law not incompatible with this Convention'.

149. As the Advocate General has noted in points 49 and 50 of his Opinion, it follows from the different passages in the pleadings lodged by Ireland before the Arbitral Tribunal that that Member State presented those Community measures not

only as relevant for the purpose of clarifying the meaning of the general provisions of the Convention in issue in the dispute but also as rules of international law to be applied by the Arbitral Tribunal pursuant to Article 293 of the Convention.

150. Thus, as the United Kingdom Government has submitted without being challenged on this point, Ireland argued inter alia before the Arbitral Tribunal that the 1993 environmental statement did not meet the requirements of Directive 85/337 and that the United Kingdom's refusal to disclose the operating plan for the MOX plant meant that it was not possible to evaluate the justification for that plant, as required under Directive 96/29, in addition to the contention that this refusal amounted to a breach of Article 6 of Directive 80/836 and of Article 6 of Directive 96/29.

151. It thus appears that Ireland submitted instruments of Community law to the Arbitral Tribunal for purposes of their interpretation and application in the context of proceedings seeking a declaration that the United Kingdom had breached the provisions of those instruments.

152. That is at variance with the obligation imposed on Member States by Articles 292 EC and 193 EA to respect the exclusive nature of the Court's jurisdiction to resolve disputes concerning the interpretation and application of provisions of Community law, in particular by having recourse to the procedures set out in Articles 227 EC and 142 EA for the purpose of obtaining a declaration that another Member State has breached those provisions.

153. Therefore, as some of the measures in question come within the scope of the EC Treaty and others within the scope of the EAEC Treaty, it must be held that there has been a breach of Articles 292 EC and 193 EA.

154. It must also be pointed out that the institution and pursuit of proceedings before the Arbitral Tribunal, in the circumstances indicated in paragraphs 146 to 150 of the present judgment, involve a manifest risk that the jurisdictional order laid down in the Treaties and, consequently, the autonomy of the Community legal system may be adversely affected.

155. That risk exists even though, as Ireland avers, it has given a formal assurance that it has not called on, and will not call on, the Arbitral Tribunal to examine or appraise, pursuant to Article 293 of the Convention or any other provision, whether the United Kingdom has breached any rule of Community law.

156. Furthermore, the existence of that risk renders entirely irrelevant the fact that Ireland may have called on the Arbitral Tribunal to apply Community law by way of renvoi or by recourse to any other technique.

157. The second head of complaint must accordingly be regarded as being well founded.

The third head of complaint

158. By its third head of complaint, the Commission submits, first, that Ireland has failed to comply with the duty of cooperation under Article 10 EC inasmuch as, by instituting proceedings under the Convention on the basis of provisions falling within the competence of the Community, Ireland exercised a competence which belongs

to the Community. Second, the Commission contends that Ireland also failed in its duty of cooperation under both Article 10 EC and Article 192 EA by bringing those proceedings unilaterally without having first informed and consulted the competent Community institutions.

[. . .]

Findings of the Court

168. The Commission first of all criticises Ireland for having failed in its duty of cooperation under Article 10 EC inasmuch as, by bringing arbitral proceedings under the Convention, Ireland exercised a competence which belongs to the Community.

169. The obligation devolving on Member States, set out in Article 292 EC, to have recourse to the Community judicial system and to respect the Court's exclusive jurisdiction, which is a fundamental feature of that system, must be understood as a specific expression of Member States' more general duty of loyalty resulting from Article 10 EC.

170. The unavoidable conclusion must also be drawn that this first part of the third head of complaint has the same subject-matter as the first head of complaint since it focuses on the same conduct on the part of Ireland, that is to say, the bringing by that Member State of the proceedings before the Arbitral Tribunal in contravention of Article 292 EC.

171. It is for that reason unnecessary to find that there has been a failure to comply with the general obligations contained in Article 10 EC that is distinct from the failure, already established, to comply with the more specific Community obligations devolving on Ireland pursuant to Article 292 EC.

172. Second, the Commission criticises Ireland for having breached Articles 10 EC and 192 EA by bringing the proceedings before the Arbitral Tribunal without having first informed and consulted the competent Community institutions.

173. This second part of the third head of complaint relates to an alleged omission by Ireland which is distinct from the conduct forming the subject-matter of the first head of complaint. It is for that reason necessary to examine it.

174. The Court has pointed out that, in all the areas corresponding to the objectives of the EC Treaty, Article 10 EC requires Member States to facilitate the achievement of the Community's tasks and to abstain from any measure which could jeopardise the attainment of the objectives of the Treaty (see, inter alia, Opinion 1/03 [2006] ECR I-01145, paragraph 119). The Member States assume similar obligations under the EAEC Treaty by virtue of Article 192 EA.

175. The Court has also emphasised that the Member States and the Community institutions have an obligation of close cooperation in fulfilling the commitments undertaken by them under joint competence when they conclude a mixed agreement (see [Joined Cases C-300/98 and C-392/98] *Dior and Others* [[2000] ECR I-11307], paragraph 36).

176. That is in particular the position in the case of a dispute which, as in the present case, relates essentially to undertakings resulting from a mixed agreement

which relates to an area, namely the protection and preservation of the marine environment, in which the respective areas of competence of the Community and the Member States are liable to be closely interrelated, as is, moreover, evidenced by the Declaration of Community competence and the appendix thereto.

177. The act of submitting a dispute of this nature to a judicial forum such as the Arbitral Tribunal involves the risk that a judicial forum other than the Court will rule on the scope of obligations imposed on the Member States pursuant to Community law.

178. Moreover, in their letter of 8 October 2001, the Commission's services had already contended that the dispute relating to the MOX plant, as referred by Ireland to the arbitral tribunal constituted pursuant to the Convention for the Protection of the Marine Environment of the North-East Atlantic, was a matter falling within the exclusive jurisdiction of the Court.

179. In those circumstances, the obligation of close cooperation within the framework of a mixed agreement involved, on the part of Ireland, a duty to inform and consult the competent Community institutions prior to instituting dispute-settlement proceedings concerning the MOX plant within the framework of the Convention.

180. The same duty of prior information and consultation was also imposed on Ireland by virtue of the EAEC Treaty in so far as that Member State contemplated invoking provisions of that Treaty and measures adopted pursuant to it within the framework of the proceedings which it was proposing to bring before the Arbitral Tribunal.

181. It is common ground that, at the date on which those proceedings were brought, Ireland had not complied with that duty of prior information and consultation.

182. Regard being had to the foregoing, the third head of complaint must be upheld in so far as it seeks a declaration by the Court that, by bringing proceedings under the dispute-settlement system set out in the Convention, without having first informed and consulted the competent Community institutions, Ireland has failed to comply with its duty of cooperation under Articles 10 EC and 192 EA.

183. The action must accordingly be upheld.

COSTS

184. Under Article 69(2) of the Rules of Procedure, the unsuccessful party is to be ordered to pay the costs if they have been applied for in the successful party's pleadings. As the Commission has applied for costs to be awarded against Ireland and the latter has been unsuccessful, Ireland must be ordered to pay the costs. In accordance with Article 69(4) of the Rules of Procedure, the United Kingdom and the Kingdom of Sweden shall bear their own costs.

On those grounds, the Court (Grand Chamber) hereby:

1. Declares that, by instituting dispute-settlement proceedings against the United Kingdom of Great Britain and Northern Ireland under the United Nations Convention on the Law of the Sea concerning the MOX plant located at Sellafield (United Kingdom), Ireland has failed to fulfil its obligations under Articles 10 EC and 292 EC and under Articles 192 EA and 193 EA;
2. Orders Ireland to pay the costs;
3. Orders the United Kingdom of Great Britain and Northern Ireland and the Kingdom of Sweden to bear their own respective costs.

[Report: [2006] 2 CMLR 59]

Dispute Concerning Access to Information under Article 9 of the OSPAR Convention (Ireland v. United Kingdom)[1]

Arbitral Tribunal, The Hague[2]

2 July 2003 (Reisman, *Chairman*; Griffith and Lord Mustill, *Members*)

Sources of international law – Convention for the Protection of the Marine Environment of the North-East Atlantic ('OSPAR Convention') – general international law – sources applicable to extent lex specialis *created by Parties – unilateral declarations – whether create binding obligations – Sintra Ministerial Statement of 1998 – not relevant to access to information – Rio Declaration, Principle 10 – Aarhus Convention on Access to Information, Public Participation in Decision-making and Access to Justice in Environmental Matters, 1998 – concept of 'environmental information' – evolving international law – not applicable by Tribunal*

Relationship between international law and national law – OSPAR Convention – Article 9(1) of Convention – obligation on Contracting Parties to ensure disclosure of information – international obligation – meaning of obligation – obligation of result rather than provision of access to domestic regime obtaining result – no exclusion of responsibility for inadequacy of national

---

[1] Ireland initiated two separate arbitrations against the United Kingdom in relation to the approval of the MOX plant. This Final Award was the result of the first arbitration, which was commenced on 15 June 2001. The second arbitration, commenced on 25 October 2001, resulted in the arbitral Tribunal's Order No. 3 of 24 June 2003 and Order No. 4 of 14 November 2003 and is reported at p. 521 above. On 14 November 2003, the Arbitral Tribunal suspended proceedings until judgment had been given by the European Court of Justice in proceedings instituted by the European Community against Ireland or until the Tribunal otherwise determined (see p. 539 above). In connection with this second arbitration, Ireland filed a request for provisional measures with the International Tribunal for the Law of the Sea on 9 November 2001. The Order of 3 December 2001 is reported at p. 421 above.

Ireland was represented before the Arbitral Tribunal by: Rory Brady, Attorney-General; Eoghan Fitzsimons, Senior Counsel, and Philippe Sands, Counsel. The United Kingdom was represented before the Arbitral Tribunal by: Richard Plender QC; Daniel Bethlehem and Samuel Wordsworth, Counsel.

[2] Constituted pursuant to Article 32 of the Convention for the Protection of the Marine Environment of the North-East Atlantic, 1992.

system or failure of competent authorities to act as prescribed by international obligation

Rights and interests – OSPAR Convention – right to information – Article 9(2) of Convention – scope of Article 9(2) – information sought not within scope

SUMMARY   *The facts*   Ireland requested access to information redacted from two reports (the 'PA report' and the 'ADL report') prepared as part of the approval process for the commissioning of the Mixed Oxide Plant ('the MOX plant'). Ireland relied on Article 9 of the 1992 Convention for the Protection of the Marine Environment of the North-East Atlantic ('the OSPAR Convention'). The United Kingdom declined to provide the information requested. On 15 June 2001, Ireland commenced proceedings under Article 32 of the OSPAR Convention.

In its Request (as amended), Ireland sought: (a) a declaration that the United Kingdom had breached Article 9 of the OSPAR Convention by refusing to make the requested information available; and (b) complete copies of the PA report and the ADL report, alternatively a copy of those reports including all such redacted information that the Tribunal decided was not commercially confidential.

The United Kingdom maintained that: (a) Article 9 of the OSPAR Convention did not establish a direct right to receive information, but rather required Contracting Parties to establish a domestic framework for the disclosure of information, which the United Kingdom had done in accordance with the applicable European Community (EC) legislation, Directive 90/313/EEC; (b) the information requested by Ireland was not in any event information within the scope of Article 9(2) of the Convention; and (c) the United Kingdom had the right pursuant to Article 9(3)(d) of the Convention to provide for a request for information to be refused on grounds of commercial confidentiality, which right had been properly exercised. The United Kingdom also maintained that Ireland's claim was inadmissible as it should have been brought before a different forum, i.e. before the European Court of Justice, and that the corollary of there being no information within the scope of Article 9(2) of the Convention was that the claim fell outside the Convention and the Tribunal lacked jurisdiction altogether.

Held by the Arbitral Tribunal   The Tribunal had jurisdiction to consider Ireland's claims, which were admissible. However, the information requested by Ireland was not information within the scope of Article 9(2) of the Convention.

(1)   The first duty of the Tribunal was to apply the OSPAR Convention. An international tribunal, such as this Tribunal, would also apply customary international law and general principles unless and to the extent that the Parties had created a *lex specialis*. The competence of a tribunal established under the OSPAR Convention was not intended to extend to obligations that the Parties might have under other instruments unless, of course, parts of the OSPAR Convention included a direct *renvoi* to such other instruments.

(2)   Ireland relied on the Sintra Ministerial Statement of 1998, where the Ministers agreed to prevent pollution of the maritime area from ionising radiation through progressive and substantial reductions of discharges, emissions and losses of radioactive substances, with the ultimate aim of concentrations in the environment near background values for naturally occurring radioactive substances and close to zero for artificial radioactive substances. The Statement also welcomed the United Kingdom's announcement that no new commercial contracts would be accepted for reprocessing spent fuel at Dounreay. Although this unilateral declaration might have created binding obligations for the United Kingdom (*Case Concerning Nuclear Tests (Australia v. France),*[3] Judgment of 20 December 1974, 1974 *ICJ Reports* 253, at p. 266, para. 43), it was not relevant to the question of access to information about the activities at Sellafield, and the more general goals of the Sintra Ministerial Statement were plainly exhortatory.

(3)   Article 9(3)(d) of the OSPAR Convention stated that Parties had the right to refuse a request for information that qualified under Article 9(2) 'in accordance with their national legal systems and applicable international regulations' where the information affects 'commercial and industrial confidentiality, including intellectual property . . .'. The United Kingdom submitted that there were no such 'applicable international regulations' other than Directive 90/313/EEC. Ireland contended that 'applicable international regulations' meant 'international law and practice', and relied (in particular) upon the Rio Declaration (Principle 10) and the 1998 Aarhus Convention on Access to Information, Public Participation in Decision-making and Access to Justice in Environmental Matters ('the Aarhus Convention'), which entered into force on 30 October 2001, but had not been ratified by either Party. The Aarhus Convention contained a definition of 'environmental information' within

---

[3]   The related proceedings in the *Nuclear Tests Case* (*New Zealand v. France*) are reported in this volume at p. 88 above.

which it contended the information sought would fall. Ireland said that the instruments on which it relied were to be interpreted in light of the evolving international law and practice on access to environmental information. However, the Tribunal had not been authorised to apply evolving international law and practice and could not do so. A tribunal established under the OSPAR Convention could not go beyond existing law. This is not to say that a tribunal could not apply customary international law of a recent vintage, but that it must in fact be customary international law. Ireland's proposal that the Aarhus Convention or that draft proposals for a new EC Directive be applied was accordingly rejected.

(4)   The question posed with respect to Article 9(1) of the OSPAR Convention was not one of jurisdiction or admissibility, but one of substance: whether, as the United Kingdom contended, the obligation of a Contracting Party under Article 9(1) was completely discharged by putting in place an appropriate domestic regulatory framework so that disputes about specific applications of the obligations under Article 9 were to be exclusively determined within the municipal law of the Contracting Party.

(5)   The obligation expressed in Article 9(1) by the requirement that a Contracting Party 'shall ensure' the stipulated result was a reflection of a deliberate rather than a lax choice of vocabulary. It illustrated the application of a chosen (and strong) level of expression applied by the drafters to the subject matter of disclosure of information to any persons, whether nationals or not, who requested it. Article 9(1) imposed an obligation of result rather than merely to provide access to a domestic regime directed at obtaining the required result. This interpretation was consistent with contemporary principles of State responsibility. Even where international law assigned competence to a national system, there was no exclusion of responsibility of a State for the inadequacy of such a national system or the failure of its competent authorities to act in a way prescribed by an international obligation or implementing legislation.

(6)   The question posed with respect to Article 9(2) was again not one of jurisdiction or admissibility, but one of substance: the issue was whether the fourteen categories of information sought by Ireland (relating to annual production figures, sales volumes, estimated sales demand, etc.) fell within the Article 9(2) definition of 'information in written, visual, aural or data-base form on the state of the maritime area, on activities or measures adversely affecting or likely to affect it and on activities or measures introduced in accordance with the Convention'.

(7)   None of the fourteen categories in Ireland's list could plausibly be characterised as 'information . . . on the state of the maritime area'.

Ireland's submission (which might be called an interpretative theory of 'inclusive causality') was that without the ADL report there would be no discharges from the MOX plant into the Irish Sea and that therefore any test of directness or proximity was satisfied. Under an interpretative theory of inclusive causality, anything, no matter how remote, which facilitated the performance of an activity was to be deemed part of that activity, and the information sought would accordingly fall within Article 9(2). While the drafters sought inclusiveness with respect to some aspects of the information covered by Article 9(2), they had no intention of adopting a theory of inclusive causality. Ireland's submission would anyway founder on the adverbs 'adversely' and 'likely'. By including those two adverbs, the drafters had excluded from the scope of the obligation of Article 9 current activities or measures that affected or were likely to affect the maritime area, but did not affect it *adversely*, and prospective activities that were not likely to affect *adversely* the maritime area. Ireland had failed to demonstrate that the fourteen categories of redacted items in the PA and ADL reports, in so far as they might be taken to be activities or measures with respect to the commissioning and operation of the MOX plant, were 'information . . . on the state of the maritime area' or, even if they were, were likely adversely to affect the maritime area. Hence, Ireland's claim failed.

Declaration of Professor W. Michael Reisman   Ireland's proposed interpretation of Article 9(1) should have been rejected. Ireland's proposed meaning required deletion of a critical phrase in Article 9(1), i.e. it required that the Article read 'The Contracting Parties shall make available the information . . .', instead of the actual wording 'The Contracting Parties shall *ensure that their competent authorities are required to* make available the information . . .'. The Tribunal could not ignore those words. Those words made Article 9(1) an obligation to adjust domestic law in a prescribed way by providing for certain institutional recourses, for which specific criteria were provided. Article 9(1) was not expressed in terms to establish an obligation on the international plane to provide information. This did not mean that Article 9(1) was not subject to international standards. Although such a provision had to allow a certain discretion or 'margin of appreciation' as to its implementation to the Contracting Parties, the national arrangements nonetheless had to meet the objective criteria set out in the provision if they were not to be in breach of the Convention.

Dissenting Opinion of Gavan Griffith QC   The interpretation of applicable law adopted by the majority was unduly restrictive. Other sources of international law had direct relevance through Article 32 of the OSPAR Convention, which required the Tribunal to 'decide according to the rules of international law and, in particular, those of the Convention', as an interpreting agency pursuant to Article 31(3)(c) of the Vienna Convention, and pursuant to Article 9(3) of the OSPAR Convention, which directed the Tribunal to take account of international regulations. The Aarhus Convention had relevant normative and evidentiary value as it fell within the definition of applicable law and also pursuant to Article 31(3)(c) of the Vienna Convention.

As to the correct interpretation of Article 9(2) of the Convention, as a matter of unambiguous grammatical construction, the expression of the second category of information ('on activities or measures adversely affecting or likely to affect it') was incapable of being confined to 'information . . . on the state of the maritime area'. As to the extent and meaning of *adverse effect* as referred to in the second category of information, (a) the majority interpretation failed to address the admitted environmental harm to the marine environment of the Irish Sea, as well as the fact that Article 9(2) referred only to the likelihood of adverse effect (these two factors created a lower threshold of proof for Ireland); (b) in accordance with the precautionary principle, the burden of proof lay with the United Kingdom; (c) the majority conclusion appeared to be unfounded since no factual evidence had been presented in support of its finding; and (d) the available material militated in favour of the conclusion that the probability of adverse effect might be demonstrated.

The correct approach was to identify whether the reports as a whole in principle fell within the scope of the Article 9(2) definition. The production of MOX fuel fell within the scope of the second category of Article 9(2) to the extent that it constituted an activity which had the potential of adversely affecting the maritime area of the Irish Sea, and that, properly characterised, the entire balancing process, including consideration of the economic case in the justification exercise (which involved the production of the PA and ADL reports), was an enquiry concerning information within the terms of Article 9(2). The information contained in the PA and ADL reports also qualified as measures introduced in accordance with the Convention under the third category of information of Article 9(2). The process of justification, including obtaining the PA and ADL reports, was a necessary measure introduced in accordance with the OSPAR Convention designed to protect the marine environment. It followed that the whole of the PA and ADL reports, including the redacted items, was information within Article 9, and that the dispute called for further hearing and consideration of the contention by the United Kingdom that Article 9(3)(d) justified the redactions made to the reports.

There follows

Final Award of Arbitral Tribunal, 2 July 2003 (extract)

[339] I. INTRODUCTION

1. This matter concerns a dispute between Ireland as claimant and the United Kingdom of Great Britain and Northern Ireland ('the United Kingdom') as respondent, determined by a Tribunal constituted pursuant to the 1992 Convention for the Protection of the Marine Environment of the North-East Atlantic ('the OSPAR Convention').[1] The issue concerns access to information as defined by the OSPAR Convention. Ireland has requested access to information redacted from reports prepared as part of the approval process for the commissioning of a Mixed Oxide Plant ('the MOX Plant') in the United Kingdom, based on Ireland's understanding of Article 9 of the OSPAR Convention. The United Kingdom has declined to provide the information requested based on its understanding of the OSPAR Convention.

II. THE OSPAR CONVENTION

2. The OSPAR Convention comprises 34 articles, five annexes and three appendices. Under Article 14(1), '[t]he Annexes and Appendices [340] form an integral part of the OSPAR Convention'. Article 14(2) provides: 'The Appendices shall be of a scientific, technical or administrative nature.'

3. Article 1 sets out definitions, to be considered as necessary in the course of this award. Article 2 provides:

General obligations

1.

(a) The Contracting Parties shall, in accordance with the provisions of the Convention, take all possible steps to prevent and eliminate pollution and shall take the necessary measures to protect the maritime area against the adverse effects of human activities so as to safeguard human health and to conserve marine ecosystems and, when practicable, restore marine areas which have been adversely affected.

(b) To this end Contracting Parties shall, individually and jointly, adopt programmes and measures and shall harmonise their policies and strategies.

2. The Contracting Parties shall apply:

---

[1] Convention for the Protection of the Marine Environment of the North-East Atlantic, 22 September 1992, 32 ILM 1069 (1992). Ireland and the United Kingdom are both Parties to the OSPAR Convention.

(a) the precautionary principle, by virtue of which preventive measures are to be taken when there are reasonable grounds for concern that substances or energy introduced, directly or indirectly, into the marine environment may bring about hazards to human health, harm living resources and marine ecosystems, damage amenities or interfere with other legitimate uses of the sea, even when there is no conclusive evidence of a causal relationship between the inputs and the effects;

(b) the polluter pays principle, by virtue of which the costs of pollution prevention, control and reduction measures are to be borne by the polluter.

    3.

(a) In implementing the Convention, Contracting Parties shall adopt programmes and measures which contain, where appropriate, time limits for their completion and which take full account of the use of the latest technological developments and practices designed to prevent and eliminate pollution fully.

(b) To this end they shall:

    (i) taking into account the criteria set forth in Appendix 1, define with respect to programmes and measures the application of, *inter alia*,

      – best available techniques

      – best environmental practice

    including, where appropriate, clean technology;

    (ii) in carrying out such programmes and measures, ensure the application of best available techniques and best environmental practice as so defined, including, where appropriate, clean technology.

[341] 4. The Contracting Parties shall apply the measures they adopt in such a way as to prevent an increase in pollution of the sea outside the maritime area or in other parts of the environment.

5. No provision of the Convention shall be interpreted as preventing the Contracting Parties from taking, individually or jointly, more stringent measures with respect to the prevention and elimination of pollution of the maritime area or with respect to the protection of the maritime area against the adverse effects of human activities.

4. Article 3 provides:

Pollution from land-based sources

The Contracting Parties shall take, individually and jointly, all possible steps to prevent and eliminate pollution from land-based sources in accordance with the provisions of the Convention, in particular as provided for in Annex I.

5. Article 4 provides:

Pollution by dumping or incineration

The Contracting Parties shall take, individually and jointly, all possible steps to prevent and eliminate pollution by dumping or incineration of wastes or other matter in accordance with the provisions of the Convention, in particular as provided for in Annex II.

6. Article 9 provides:

Access to information

1. The Contracting Parties shall ensure that their competent authorities are required to make available the information described in paragraph 2 of this Article to any natural

or legal person, in response to any reasonable request, without that person's having to prove an interest, without unreasonable charges, as soon as possible and at the latest within two months.

2. The information referred to in paragraph 1 of this Article is any available information in written, visual, aural or data base form on the state of the maritime area, on activities or measures adversely affecting or likely to affect it and on activities or measures introduced in accordance with the Convention.

3. The provisions of this Article shall not affect the right of Contracting Parties, in accordance with their national legal systems and applicable international regulations, to provide for a request for such information to be refused where it affects:

(a) the confidentiality of the proceedings of public authorities, international relations and national defence;
(b) public security;
(c) matters which are, or have been, *sub judice*, or under enquiry (including disciplinary enquiries), or which are the subject of preliminary investigation proceedings;
(d) [**342**] commercial and industrial confidentiality, including intellectual property;
(e) the confidentiality of personal data and/or files;
(f) material supplied by a third party without that party being under a legal obligation to do so;
(g) material, the disclosure of which would make it more likely that the environment to which such material related would be damaged.

4. The reasons for a refusal to provide the information requested must be given.

7. Article 10 establishes a Commission of representatives of each of the Contracting Parties, sets out its duties, and, with respect to those duties, authorizes the Commission to '*inter alia*, adopt decisions and recommendations in accordance with Article 13'. Article 13(1) states that '[d]ecisions and recommendations shall be adopted by unanimous vote of the Contracting Parties'. If unanimity is not attainable, decisions may be taken by a three-quarters majority vote of the Contracting Parties and will become binding on those voting for it, if, at the end of 200 days after its adoption the number of Contracting Parties who have notified the Executive Secretary that they are unable to accept the decision does not reduce the number of those accepting the decision to below three-quarters of the Contracting Parties to the OSPAR Convention.

8. The provisions for amendment of the OSPAR Convention, addition and amendment of annexes, and addition and amendment of appendices are not relevant to the issues in dispute in this case.

9. Article 28 provides that no reservations may be made to the Convention.

10. Article 31 provides for the continuing force of decisions, recommendations, and all other agreements adopted under the Oslo and Paris Conventions[2] to the extent that they are compatible with the OSPAR Convention and have not been terminated by its procedures.

---

[2] The Convention for the Prevention of Marine Pollution by Dumping from Ships and Aircraft (Oslo), 932 UNTS 3 (1972), and the Convention for the Prevention of Marine Pollution from Land-based Sources (Paris), 13 ILM 352 (1974).

11. Article 32 of the OSPAR Convention provides:[3]

[343] *Settlement of disputes*

1. Any disputes between Contracting Parties relating to the interpretation or application of the Convention, which cannot be settled otherwise by the Contracting Parties concerned, for instance by means of inquiry or conciliation within the Commission, shall, at the request of any of those Contracting Parties, be submitted to arbitration under the conditions laid down in this Article.

2. Unless the Parties to the dispute decide otherwise, the procedure of the arbitration referred to in paragraph 1 of this Article shall be in accordance with paragraphs 3 to 10 of this Article.

3.

(a) At the request addressed by one Contracting Party to another Contracting Party in accordance with paragraph 1 of this Article, an arbitral tribunal shall be constituted. The request for arbitration shall state the subject matter of the application including in particular the Articles of the Convention, the interpretation or application of which is in dispute.

(b) The applicant party shall inform the Commission that it has requested the setting up of an arbitral tribunal, stating the name of the other party to the dispute and the Articles of the Convention the interpretation or application of which, in its opinion, is in dispute. The Commission shall forward the information thus received to all Contracting parties to the Convention.

4. The arbitral tribunal shall consist of three members: each of the parties to the dispute shall appoint an arbitrator; the two arbitrators so appointed shall designate by common agreement the third arbitrator who shall be the chairman of the tribunal. The latter shall not be a national of one of the parties to the dispute, nor have his usual place of residence in the territory of one of these parties, nor be employed by any of them, nor have dealt with the case in any other capacity.

5.

(a) If the chairman of the arbitral tribunal has not been designated within two months of the appointment of the second arbitrator, the President of the International Court of Justice shall, at the request of either party, designate him within a further two months' period.

(b) If one of the parties to the dispute does not appoint an arbitrator within two months of receipt of the request, the other party may inform the President of the International Court of Justice who shall designate the chairman of the arbitral tribunal within a further two months' period. Upon designation, the chairman of the arbitral tribunal shall request the party which has not appointed an arbitrator to do so within two months. After such period, he shall inform the President of the

---

[3] It should also be noted that the last preambular paragraph of the Rules of Procedure for this Tribunal (the 'Rules of Procedure for the Tribunal Constituted Under the OSPAR Convention Pursuant to the Request of Ireland dated 15 June 2001') provides:

Whereas the Applicant and the Respondent (together, the 'Parties') have decided that the procedure of the arbitration of the Dispute shall be in accordance with the following rules (the 'Rules'), which shall replace Articles 32(4) to 32(10) of the OSPAR Convention, insofar as they do not impair the rights of other States Parties to the OSPAR Convention.

The OSPAR Tribunal Rules of Procedure may be found on the website of the Permanent Court of Arbitration (hereinafter 'PCA') at www.pca-cpa.org.

International Court of Justice who shall make this appointment within a further two months' period.

[344] 6.

(a)   The arbitral tribunal shall decide according to the rules of international law and, in particular, those of the Convention.

(b)   Any arbitral tribunal constituted under the provisions of this Article shall draw up its own rules of procedure.

(c)   In the event of a dispute as to whether the arbitral tribunal has jurisdiction, the matter shall be decided by the decision of the arbitral tribunal.

7.

(a)   The decisions of the arbitral tribunal, both on procedure and on substance, shall be taken by majority voting of its members.

(b)   The arbitral tribunal may take all appropriate measures in order to establish the facts. It may, at the request of one of the parties, recommend essential interim measures of protection.

(c)   If two or more arbitral tribunals constituted under the provisions of this Article are seized of requests with identical or similar subjects, they may inform themselves of the procedures for establishing the facts and take them into account as far as possible.

(d)   The parties to the dispute shall provide all facilities necessary for the effective conduct of the proceedings.

(e)   The absence or default of a party to the dispute shall not constitute an impediment to the proceedings.

8. Unless the arbitral tribunal determines otherwise because of the particular circumstances of the case, the expenses of the tribunal, including the remuneration of its members, shall be borne by the parties to the dispute in equal shares. The tribunal shall keep a record of all its expenses, and shall furnish a final statement thereof to the parties.

9. Any Contracting Party that has an interest of a legal nature in the subject matter of the dispute which may be affected by the decision in the case, may intervene in the proceedings with the consent of the tribunal.

10.

(a)   The award of the arbitral tribunal shall be accompanied by a statement of reasons. It shall be final and binding upon the parties to the dispute.

(b)   Any dispute which may arise between the parties concerning the interpretation or execution of the award may be submitted by either party to the arbitral tribunal which made the award or, if the latter cannot be seized thereof, to another arbitral tribunal constituted for this purpose in the same manner as the first.

12. Annex I deals with the prevention and elimination of pollution from land-based sources. Article 2 of this annex establishes obligations with respect to them.

[345] 13. Article 3 of Annex II provides:

1. The dumping of all wastes or other matter is prohibited, except for those wastes or other matter listed in paragraphs 2 and 3 of this Article.

2. The list referred to in paragraph 1 of this Article is as follows:

(a)   dredged material;

(b)   inert materials of natural origin, that is solid, chemically unprocessed geological material the chemical constituents of which are unlikely to be released into the marine environment;

(c)   sewage sludge until 31 December 1998;

(d)   fish waste from industrial fish processing operations;

(e)   vessels or aircraft until, at the latest, 31 December 2004.

  3.

(a)   The dumping of low and intermediate level radioactive substances, including wastes, is prohibited.

(b)   As an exception to subparagraph 3(a) of this Article, those Contracting Parties, the United Kingdom and France, who wish to retain the option of an exception to subparagraph 3(a) in any case not before the expiry of a period of 15 years from 1 January 1993, shall report to the meeting of the Commission at Ministerial level in 1997 on the steps taken to explore alternative land-based options.

(c)   Unless, at or before the expiry of this period of 15 years, the Commission decides by a unanimous vote not to continue the exception provided in subparagraph 3(b), it shall take a decision pursuant to Article 13 of the Convention on the prolongation for a period of 10 years after 1 January 2008 of the prohibition, after which another meeting of the Commission at Ministerial level shall be held. Those Contracting Parties mentioned in subparagraph 3(b) of this Article still wishing to retain the option mentioned in subparagraph 3(b) shall report to the Commission meetings to be held at Ministerial level at two yearly intervals from 1999 onwards about the progress in establishing alternative land-based options and on the results of scientific studies which show that any potential dumping operations would not result in hazards to human health, harm to living resources or marine ecosystems, damage to amenities or interference with other legitimate uses of the sea.

14. The United Kingdom's signature was accompanied by the following declaration:[4]

[346] The Government of the United Kingdom of Great Britain and Northern Ireland declares its understanding of the effect of paragraph 3 of Article 3 of Annex II to the Convention to be amongst other things that, where the Commission takes a decision pursuant to Article 13 of the Convention, on the prolongation of the prohibition set out in subparagraph (3)(a), those Contracting Parties who wish to retain the option of the exception to that prohibition as provided for in subparagraph (3)(b) may retain that option, provided that they are not bound, under paragraph 2 of Article 13, by that decision.

III. FACTUAL BACKGROUND

15. British Nuclear Fuels, plc ('BNFL'), a public limited company wholly owned by the United Kingdom, owns and operates a licensed nuclear enterprise at Sellafield in

---

[4]   The declaration may be found at www.ospar.org, where a note from the OSPAR Secretariat follows the declaration:

Following the entry into force of OSPAR Decision 98/2 on Dumping of Radioactive Waste on 9 February 1999, subparagraphs (b) and (c) of paragraph 3 of Article 3 of Annex II to the Convention ceased to have effect.

Cumbria. In 1993, BNFL applied to the local authority for permission to build a MOX Plant to process spent nuclear fuels by retrieving and blending separated plutonium oxide and uranium oxide into pellets to be reused as fuel in nuclear reactors. BNFL prepared and submitted Environmental Statements to the relevant authorities,[5] as required by United Kingdom law.[6] Relevant consents to build the Plant were given in 1994, and construction was completed in 1996.

16. Each of Ireland and the United Kingdom is a Party to the Treaty Establishing the European Atomic Energy Community ('EURATOM'),[7] which includes a comprehensive regulatory system for planning for the disposal of radioactive waste. Article 37 of EURATOM provides:

> Each Member State shall provide the Commission with such general data relating to any plan for the disposal of radioactive waste in whatever form as will make it possible to determine whether the implementation of such plan is liable to result in the radioactive contamination of the water, soil or airspace of another Member State.
>
> The Commission shall deliver its opinion within six months, after consulting the group of experts referred to in Article 31.

In *Saarland* v. *Minister for Industry*, the European Court explained the purpose of the Article 37 procedure as follows:

> [347] [t]he purpose of Article 37, within the context of environmental protection, is to provide the Commission with comprehensive information on every plan for disposal and every activity liable to cause accidental discharges of waste, so that it is in a position to assess the repercussions thereof on the environment in the other Member States.[8]

17. On 2 August 1996, the United Kingdom submitted the data required under Article 37 to the European Commission. On 25 February 1997, the European Commission delivered its opinion under Article 37, including the conclusions:

(a) The distance between the plant and nearest point on the territory of another Member State, in this case Ireland, is 184 km;

(b) Under normal operating conditions, the discharge of liquid and gaseous effluents will be small fractions of present authorized limits and will produce an exposure of the population in other Member States that is negligible from the health point of view;

(c) Low-level solid radioactive waste is to be disposed to the authorized Drigg site operated by BNFL plc. Intermediate level wastes are to be stored at the Sellafield site, pending disposal to an appropriate authorized facility;

---

[5] Ireland's Memorial, Annex 9. The Parties' written pleadings are available at www.pca-cpa.org. Annexes are on file at the offices of the PCA.

[6] UK Town and Country Planning (Assessment of Environmental Effects) Regulations 1988 (SI No. 1199).

[7] Treaty Establishing the European Atomic Energy Community ('EURATOM'), 25 March 1957, 298 UNTS 167.

[8] Case 187/87, *Saarland and Others* v. *Minister for Industry, Post and Telecommunications and Tourism and Others* (reference for a preliminary ruling from the *tribunal administratif*, Strasbourg), [1988] ECR 5013, at p. 5018.

(d) In the event of unplanned discharges of radioactive waste which may follow an accident on the scale considered in the general data, the doses likely to be received by the population in other Member States would not be significant from the health point of view.

In conclusion, the Commission is of the view that the implementation of the plan for the disposal of radioactive wastes arising from the operation of the BNFL Sellafield mixed oxide fuel plant, both in normal operation and in the event of an accident of the type and magnitude considered in the general data, is not liable to result in radioactive contamination, significant from the point of view of health, of the water, soil or airspace of another Member State.[9]

18. Although the Article 37 procedure fulfilled a critical part of the United Kingdom's international legal obligations with respect to the environmental consequences of commissioning, there were further requirements under EURATOM and United Kingdom law to be met before the MOX Plant could be commissioned and operated. Relevantly, the domestic agency approving the Plant was required to ensure whatever environmental detriments it might cause were economically justified. In its most recent formulation, Directive 96/29 EURATOM provided in Article 6(1) that:

[**348**] Member States shall ensure that all new classes or types of practice resulting in exposure to ionizing radiation are justified in advance of being first adopted or first approved by their economic, social or other benefits in relation to the health detriment they may cause.[10]

19. Although the relevant United Kingdom statute, the United Kingdom Radioactive Substances Act 1993, does not, in terms, require such justification, in *R v. Secretary of State for the Environment and others ex parte Greenpeace Ltd*,[11] Potts J held (as explained in a later case) that 'there was a legal obligation to justify any activity resulting in exposure to ionizing radiation in accordance with the then operative Directive, namely Euratom 80/836'.[12]

20. Accordingly, over a period of eight weeks in 1997, the United Kingdom Environment Agency ('the Agency') held a public consultation on the economic justification of the MOX Plant at Sellafield.[13] This initial public consultation emerged as the first of five such consultations.

21. By its letter of 5 February 1997 inviting views, the Agency stated:

The Agency considers that the issues associated with uranium commissioning may be separated from those associated with full operation and are simpler in nature, since no

---

[9] European Commission Opinion under Article 37 EURATOM, 1997 OJ (C 86) 3. *See* United Kingdom's Counter-Memorial, Annex 9 (Vol. II).

[10] Directive 96/29 EURATOM, Article 6(1), 1996 OJ (L 159) 1. Several documents cited below refer instead to an earlier version of this directive – namely, Directive 80/836 EURATOM, 1980 OJ (L 246) 1.

[11] *R v. Secretary of State for the Environment and others ex parte Greenpeace Ltd*, [1994] 4 All ER 352.

[12] *R (Friends of the Earth Ltd and Greenpeace Ltd) v. Secretary of State for the Environment, Food and Rural Affairs and Secretary of State for Health*, [2001] EWHC Admin. 914, at para. 8.

[13] As argued by Counsel for the United Kingdom, Oral Hearing Transcript (hereinafter 'Transcript'), Day 2 Proceedings, pp. 64–6. Transcripts are available at www.pca-cpa.org.

plutonium is involved. BNFL has also stated that the total activity discharged would be very small, amounting to less than 0.0000001% of the total activity discharged from the Sellafield site.[14]

The Agency enclosed a document entitled 'Radioactive Substances Act 1993 Explanatory Memorandum for the Consultation on Justification and Uranium Commissioning of Sellafield MOX Plant (SMP)', which explained in its introduction that:

> [a]ll practices giving rise to radioactive waste must be justified, i.e. the benefits of the practice must outweigh the detriments. The manufacture of fuel in the Sellafield MOX Plant (SMP) is a new practice on the Sellafield site. The [349] need for the Agency to consider justification in advance of the commissioning and operation of SMP arises from EU Council Directive of 15 July 1980, which lays down the basic safety standards for the health protection of the general public and workers against dangers of ionizing radiation (the Euratom Directive). . . [15]

The Agency went on to explain that those issues did not have to be part of the application because no change in the estimated radiological impact of the predicted operational releases was anticipated and no change in permitted levels was being requested. Rather, the focus would be on economic justification.[16] Nonetheless, data on projected aerial and liquid discharges was included.[17]

22. Another enclosure with the 5 February letter was an undated document entitled 'Sellafield MOX Plant (SMP)', which had been transmitted to the Agency by BNFL under a covering letter of 27 January 1997. The transmittal letter identified the document as 'the public consultation document' covering commercial and dose aspects. In discussing waste management, the document referred to 'effluent arisings' which would 'be conditioned as necessary to make them suitable, after monitoring, for discharge to sea'.[18]

23. The Government of Ireland participated in this first of the public consultations as a 'respondent'. In its submission dated 4 April 1997, Ireland stated that it 'opposes the commissioning of the MOX Plant on the grounds that it will perpetuate the nuclear fuel reprocessing industry in Britain', and that it deemed 'objectionable and unacceptable' the 'additional radioactive marine discharges from Sellafield into the Irish Sea arising from MOX production'.[19] Ireland went on to raise several specific concerns about the proposed MOX Plant, including one that 'the quality of information available for consultation is deficient in many respects'.[20]

---

[14] Letter from I. T. Porter, Environment Agency to statutory consultees (5 February 1997), at Tab 1, p. 2, *in* SMP Consultation Documents Bundle ('SMP Bundle'), on file at the offices of the PCA.

[15] 'UK Environment Agency, Radioactive Substances Act 1993, Explanatory Memorandum for the Consultation on Justification and Uranium Commissioning of Sellafield Mox Plant (SMP), British Nuclear Fuels plc at Sellafield', *in* SMP Bundle, at Tab 1, p. 3, para. 1.3 (1997).

[16] *Id.*, at p. 4, para. 1.6.

[17] *Id.*, at p. 11, para. 6.2.

[18] 'Sellafield MOX Plant (SMP)', attachment to Letter from Robert Anderson of BNFL to the UK Environment Agency (27 January 1997), *in* SMP Bundle, at Tab 1, p. 13.

[19] Ireland's Memorial, Annex 4, at No. 2.

[20] *Ibid.*

24. The initial consultations were followed by a further round of public consultations because 'several respondents ... were concerned that BNFL had not provided in the public domain sufficient commercial information to justify the commissioning and operation of the plant'.[21] Further, other respondents had raised concerns about whether [350] 'the movements of MOX fuel from the SMP by air, sea or land'[22] could be carried out safely, and still other respondents raised non-proliferation and other security concerns.[23]

25. In preparation for the second consultation, the Agency asked BNFL to provide additional information in the form of a business case that could be independently examined. It invited prominent financial consultants to tender for the work and selected the PA Consulting Group, London ('PA') to carry out a detailed assessment.[24] As the Agency's Explanatory Memorandum under the Radioactive Substances Act explained, in addition, 'PA was requested to identify if there were areas of the economic case that were not commercially sensitive which could be published in the public domain.'[25]

26. PA submitted the full version of its report ('the PA Report') to BNFL and, pursuant to the Agency's request, then considered what data should be redacted. After consulting with BNFL about redactions, PA made recommendations, which were reviewed and finally determined by the Agency, and reflected in a public version of the PA Report released in December 1997 ('the 1997 PA Report'). PA gave a detailed explanation of the basis for redactions from its full report on commercial confidentiality' grounds under section 4(2) of the United Kingdom's Environmental Information Regulations (1992) ('the 1992 Regulations'),[26] and stated:

> *1.3. Commercial confidentiality issues*
> PA was asked to provide the Agency with an independent view on the validity of BNFL's assertion that elements of the economic case for the SMP are commercially sensitive, and therefore that certain information therein should be withheld from the public domain. The Environmental Information Regulations 1992 (section 4(2)) provide that for the purposes of those regulations 'information relating to matters to which any commercial or industrial confidentiality attaches' may be treated as confidential. PA therefore identified a series of specific criteria to determine the information the placing of which in the public domain could prejudice the commercial interests of BNFL. Information should not be placed in the public domain if it would:
> 1. Allow or assist competitors to build market share or to benchmark their own operations.

---

[21] Letter from UK Environment Agency to Friends of the Earth (14 January 1998), *in* SMP Bundle, at Tab 2.

[22] 'UK Environment Agency, Explanatory Memorandum for a Further Public Consultation on the Application by BNFL for the Commissioning and Operation of the Mixed Oxide Fuel Plant at its Sellafield site in Cumbria', *in* SMP Bundle, at Tab 2, p. 4, para. 2.2 (1998).

[23] *Id.*, at p. 4, para. 2.3.

[24] *Id.*, at pp. 1–2.

[25] *Id.*, at p.2.

[26] UK Environmental Information Regulations 1992 (SI No. 1992/3240).

2.   Allow or assist competitors to attack the BNFL customer base and erode business profitability.
3.   [351] Allow or assist new competitors to enter the market.
4.   Allow customers or competitors to understand the specific economics and processes of the BNFL MOX fuel fabrication business.
5.   Breach contractual confidentiality requirements with customers or vendors.

In addition, information should not be placed in the public domain that would breach security and safeguards requirements with respect to plutonium quantities, locations and movements.

Given the issue of commercial confidentiality, and using the criteria set out above, two parallel reports have been prepared. The version for the Environment Agency contains information commercially confidential to BNFL; in the public domain report PA has replaced this information with a box in which is outlined the nature of the confidential information that has been removed and the reason, in terms of the criteria set out above, for the removal. In addition, in certain instances, specific financial, production or customer data in the full report have been deleted or replaced by a word such as 'significant' or 'minor' in the public domain version. These represent the only differences between the texts of the full version and the public domain version. This approach enables the placing in the public domain of information that allows public review of the robustness of the BNFL economic case, without prejudicing the commercial interests of BNFL.[27]

27. In the second public consultation, Ireland submitted a detailed statement which was critical of parts of the reasoning of the 1997 PA Report. Although it did not then object to or mention any of the redactions from the published version of the PA Report, Ireland's submission concluded:

[T]he PA Consulting report has failed to fulfil the purpose of this further consultation as set out in the Environment Agency's letter of 14 January, 1998, namely, to provide in the public domain sufficient commercial information to justify the commissioning and operation of the plant.[28]

28. After consultations, in October 1998 the Agency released a draft decision which found that '[t]he assessed radiation doses to members of the public as a consequence of discharges from the MOX Plant have negligible radiological significance',[29] and that the balance between benefits and detriments was 'broadly neutral' in terms of radioactive discharges, waste management, health and safety operations on the MOX [352] Plant's transport, safety of the MOX fuel in reactors, radiological impact, sustainable development and proliferation of nuclear weapons and the plutonium

---

[27] 'PA Consulting Group, Environment Agency Final Report – Public Domain Version; Assessment of BNFL's Economic Case for the Sellafield MOX Plant', *in*, SMP Bundle, at Tab 2, pp. 1-1 to 1-6 (1997).

[28] Ireland's Memorial, Annex 4, at No. 3.

[29] 'UK Environment Agency, Radioactive Substances Act 1993, Document Containing the Agency's Proposed Decision on the Justification for the Plutonium Commissioning and Full Operation of the MOX Plant, BNFL plc at Sellafield', *in* SMP Bundle, Tab 2, at para. 22 (1998).

stockpile.[30] The decision then considered the question of economic justification, which it found compelling.

29. Among others, Ireland made further representations,[31] whereafter a decision was taken in June 1999 at the ministerial level to release a new version of the PA Report, with some of the redacted material restored, and to hold a third round of consultations. The Department for the Environment, Transport and the Regions ('DETR') and the Ministry of Agriculture, Fisheries and Food ('MAFF') invited fresh comments 'on the material concerning the economic case for the [MOX] plant'.[32]

30. Ireland again submitted comments. By letter of 30 July 1999, Ireland elaborated upon its earlier objections and requested 'an unedited and full copy of the PA Report'.[33] Among other things, Ireland argued that 'the information made available in the June 1999 version of the PA Report does not provide a basis for concluding that the MOX Plant is "justified" within the meaning of Directive 80/836 EURATOM (as amended)'. Ireland also raised the issue of compliance with EC Directive 90/313/EEC ('Directive 90/313')[34] on Freedom of Access to Environmental Information, and reserved its right

> to invoke – *inter alia* in relation to intensified international transportation associated with the MOX plant – procedures and substantive requirements under *inter alia* . . . the 1992 OSPAR Convention.

31. The process of review was interrupted in 1999 when BNFL discovered that fuel pellet diameter readings at the MOX demonstration facility had been falsified and reported this fact to the nuclear installation inspectorate.

32. The OSPAR Convention was first raised by Ireland in connection with the redacted information in the PA Report on 25 May 2000, when it wrote to DETR, invoking Article 9 in requesting information redacted from the published PA Report.[35] On 27 October 2000, DETR responded that 'the UK Government does not wish to prejudice the commercial interests of an enterprise by disclosing commercially confidential information'.[36]

[353] 33. In March 2001, a fourth consultation process commenced, now under Directive 96/29 EURATOM (*see* para. 18 above), which had come into force in May 2000. In the consultation paper issued by DETR and the Department of Health in March 2001, potential respondents were invited to comment on BNFL's economic case, as revised in light of the data falsification incident, and an updated MOX market review.[37]

34. Ireland filed a detailed submission dated 22 May 2001. Ireland concluded:

[30] *Id.*, at para. 31.
[31] Counsel for the United Kingdom, Transcript, Day 2 Proceedings, p. 69.
[32] Letter from UK DETR & MAFF (June 11, 1999), *in* SMP Bundle, at Tab 3.
[33] Ireland's Memorial, Annex 4, at No. 4.
[34] Directive 90/313/EEC, 1990 OJ (L 158) 56.
[35] Ireland's Memorial, Annex 4, at No. 9.
[36] *Id.*, at No. 10.
[37] 'UK Department of Health and DETR, British Nuclear Fuels plc – Sellafield Mixed Oxide Plant: A Consultation Paper', *in* SMP Bundle, at Tab 4, p. 5, para. 10 (2001).

It is the view of the Irish Government that the information contained in the Consultation Papers and the absence of critical information relating to primary economic factors including critical data relating to other cost factors such as transportation and security, makes it impossible for the reader to assess the justification of the [proposed MOX Plant] . . .

The Irish Government in its submissions in regard to the previous Consultation Rounds sought the unedited and full copy of the then PA Consulting Report. In the absence of this information . . . the Irish Government is reserving its right to pursue legal measures for the release of the information.[38]

35. Further, in the spring of 2001, BNFL prepared a new confidential document for departmental and ministerial consideration setting out the economic justification for the MOX Plant. Following a new public tender in April 2001, the consulting firm Arthur D. Little ('ADL') was appointed 'to analyse the business case and to report on the responses to the public consultation exercise on it'.[39] The terms of reference for ADL also included an instruction to form its own view as to what material should be redacted on the grounds of commercial sensitivity. ADL submitted a full version of its Report to Ministers, along with a proposed redacted public version, to which BNFL objected. The final decision about redactions in the published version was made at the Ministerial level, and the redacted ADL Report was released to the public in July 2001.[40] The transmittal letter from the Department of the Environment, Food and Rural Affairs ('DEFRA') (which had taken over responsibilities in this area from DETR) and the Department of Health stated that '[t]he published version excludes only that information whose publication would cause unreasonable damage to BNFL's commercial operations or to the economic case for the MOX plant'.[41]

[354] 36. A fifth public consultation ensued in August 2001. In a letter dated 7 August 2001, Ireland requested an unredacted version of the ADL Report in order 'to make an independent analysis of the economic justification of the proposed [MOX] plant'.[42] Ireland also restated its opposition to the MOX Plant, but did not comment in detail on the published version of the ADL Report.

37. On 3 October 2001, a decision was issued approving the manufacture of MOX at Sellafield.[43] Greenpeace, a non-governmental organization, challenged the decision in the United Kingdom courts, but its application for review was rejected,[44] and failed on appeal.[45] Ireland separately applied to the International Tribunal for the Law of

---

[38] Ireland's Memorial, Annex 4, at No. 13.

[39] Letter from UK Department of Environment, Food, and Rural Affairs ('DEFRA') and Department of Health (27 July 2001), *in* SMP Bundle, at Tab 5.

[40] United Kingdom's Counter-Memorial, para. 2.22.

[41] *Supra* note 39.

[42] Ireland's Memorial, Annex 4, at No. 15.

[43] Ireland's Memorial, Annex 5.

[44] *See supra* note 12.

[45] *Friends of the Earth Ltd & Another, The Queen on the Application of v. Secretary of State for the Environment, Food and Rural Affairs & Others*, [2001] EWCA Civ. 1847.

the Sea ('ITLOS') for provisional measures restraining the United Kingdom from commissioning the Plant in a request which, after a hearing, was rejected.[46]

38. Against the background of these events, Ireland contended that the United Kingdom was obliged to make the information redacted from the consultation Reports available under Article 9 of the OSPAR Convention. On 15 June 2001 Ireland requested that an arbitral tribunal be constituted under Article 32 to determine its dispute with the United Kingdom concerning the United Kingdom's refusal to make available information redacted from the published versions of the PA Report and relating to the proposed MOX Plant. In its request, Ireland stated that it had previously notified the United Kingdom that a dispute had arisen as to the interpretation and application of the OSPAR Convention and that Ireland had sought to settle the dispute through bilateral diplomatic means and by raising the matter with the OSPAR Commission. A Statement of Claim was also filed.

39. In its letter dated 7 August 2001 (submitted in the context of the fifth consultation), Ireland had stated: 'In the event that a copy of the full [ADL] report is not provided Ireland reserves its right to amend and extend its application in the OSPAR arbitration filed on 15 June last to include the information omitted from the ADL Report.'[47] By letter dated 5 September 2001, DEFRA asserted that the information excised from the public version of the ADL Report did not fall within [355] the scope of Article 9(2).[48] By reply of 26 September 2001, the Agent for Ireland objected to DEFRA's assertion that the ADL Report did not fall within the scope of Article 9(2), and noted its intention to amend the relief sought in the Statement of Claim to include disclosure of the full unredacted ADL Report.[49]

IV. THE CLAIMS AND SUBMISSIONS OF THE PARTIES AND QUESTIONS RAISED FOR DETERMINATION BY THE TRIBUNAL

40. The formal claims of Ireland and the United Kingdom ('the Parties') were set forth in their written pleadings.

41. On the basis of Article 9 of the OSPAR Convention, Ireland, in its Memorial requested

> full disclosure of two reports commissioned by the United Kingdom Government in the context of the authorisation of a new facility at Sellafield for the production of mixed oxide (MOX) fuel ... in order to be in a better position to consider the impacts which the commissioning of the MOX plant will or might have on the marine environment ... [and] to be able to assess the extent of the compliance by the United Kingdom with its obligations under ... the OSPAR Convention, the 1982 United Nations Convention

---

[46] *The MOX Plant Case (Ireland v. United Kingdom)*, Request for Provisional Measures, Order Dated 3 December 2001, International Tribunal for the Law of the Sea, Case No. 10. Available from www.itlos.org [see p. 421 above].

[47] Ireland's Memorial, Annex 4, at No. 15.

[48] *Id.*, at No. 17.

[49] *Id.*, at No. 16.

on the Law of the Sea . . . and various provisions of European Community law, including in particular Council Directive 96/29 Euratom . . .[50]

42. In its final prayer, Ireland requested the Tribunal to order and declare:

    (1)   That the United Kingdom has breached its obligations under Article 9 of the OSPAR Convention by refusing to make available information deleted from the PA Report and ADL Report as requested by Ireland.

    (2)   That, as a consequence of the aforesaid breach of the OSPAR Convention, the United Kingdom shall provide Ireland with a complete copy of both the PA Report and the ADL Report, alternatively a copy of the PA Report and the ADL Report which includes all such information the release of which the arbitration tribunal decides will not affect commercial confidentiality within the meaning of Article 9(3)(d) of the OSPAR Convention.

    (3)   That the United Kingdom pay Ireland's costs of the proceedings.

43. **The United Kingdom refused to disclose the full Reports, contending in its Counter-Memorial that:**

[356] First, Article 9 of the OSPAR Convention does not establish a direct right to receive information. Rather it requires Contracting Parties to establish a domestic framework for the disclosure of information. This the United Kingdom has done . . .

Second, in the event that the United Kingdom is wrong in this reading of Article 9, Ireland must show that the information it requests is information within the scope of Article 9(2) of the Convention. It has failed to show that this is the case . . . the information in question is insufficiently proximate to the state of the maritime area or to measures or activities affecting or likely to affect it. It is not information within the scope of Article 9(2) of the Convention . . .

Third, in the event that the United Kingdom is wrong on this point, Article 9(3)(d) of the Convention affirms the right of the Contracting Parties, in accordance with their national legal systems and applicable international regulations, to provide for a request for information to be refused on grounds of commercial confidentiality. The United Kingdom has legislated to this effect. Its refusal to disclose the particular information requested by Ireland is consistent with both national law and applicable international regulations.[51]

44. In its final prayer, the United Kingdom requested the Tribunal:

    (1)   to adjudge and declare that it lacks jurisdiction over the claims brought against the United Kingdom by Ireland and/or that those are inadmissible;

    (2)   to dismiss the claims brought against the United Kingdom by Ireland;

    (3)   to reject Ireland's request that the United Kingdom pay Ireland's costs, and instead to order Ireland to pay the United Kingdom's costs.

45. **It thus appears to the Tribunal that three sequential questions are raised for determination by the Tribunal, namely:**

---

[50] Ireland's Memorial, para. 2.
[51] United Kingdom's Counter-Memorial, paras. 1.4, 1.5, 1.6.

(1) Does Article 9(1) of the Convention require a Contracting Party to disclose, or to set up a procedure to disclose, 'information' within the meaning of Article 9(2)?

(2) If so, does the material the disclosure of which Ireland has requested constitute 'information' for the purposes of Article 9 of the Convention?

(3) If so, has the United Kingdom redacted and withheld any and what information requested by Ireland contrary to Article 9(3)(d)?

46. After a review of the procedural history of the case and the question of applicable law, the Tribunal will return to consider these questions.

[. . .]

[**362**] [. . .] VI. THE TRIBUNAL'S FINDINGS

78. For the reasons set out below, the Tribunal:

(i) by unanimous decision rejects the United Kingdom's request that the Tribunal find that it lacks jurisdiction over the dispute;

(ii) by unanimous decision rejects the United Kingdom's request that Ireland's claims are inadmissible;

(iii) by majority decision rejects the United Kingdom's submission that the implementation of Article 9(1) is assigned exclusively to the competent authorities in the United Kingdom and not to a tribunal established under the OSPAR Convention;

(iv) by majority decision finds that Ireland's claim for information does not fall within Article 9(2) of the OSPAR Convention; and

(v) by majority decision finds that as a consequence, Ireland's claim – that the United Kingdom has breached its obligations under Article 9 of the OSPAR Convention, by refusing, on the basis of its understanding of the requirements of Article 9(3)(d), to make available information – does not arise.

VII. APPLICABLE LAW

79. This part of the Tribunal's decision is supported by a majority comprising Professor Reisman and Lord Mustill.

[**363**] 1. *Interpretation*

80. The OSPAR Convention has two authentic languages and the United Kingdom made reference to the French text of the OSPAR Convention for clarification of certain provisions. However, neither Party has alleged a discrepancy between the English and French texts for the current dispute.

81. The Parties agree that the OSPAR Convention governs the arbitration. Although the United Kingdom is Party to the Vienna Convention on the Law of Treaties ('Vienna

Convention'),[52] Ireland is not, but, nonetheless, has relied upon its interpretation provisions.[53] The Parties also are agreed that the interpretation provisions of the Vienna Convention govern the construction of the OSPAR Convention.[54]

82. Articles 31 and 32 of the Vienna Convention are relevant:

Article 31 – General rule of interpretation

1. A treaty shall be interpreted in good faith in accordance with the ordinary meaning to be given to the terms of the treaty in their context and in the light of its object and purpose.

2. The context for the purpose of the interpretation of a treaty shall comprise, in addition to the text, including its preamble and annexes:

(a) any agreement relating to the treaty which was made between all the parties in connection with the conclusion of the treaty;

(b) any instrument which was made by one or more parties in connection with the conclusion of the treaty and accepted by the other parties as an instrument related to the treaty.

3. There shall be taken into account, together with the context:

(a) any subsequent agreement between the parties regarding the interpretation of the treaty or the application of its provisions;

(b) any subsequent practice in the application of the treaty which establishes the agreement of the parties regarding its interpretation;

(c) any relevant rules of international law applicable in the relations between the parties.

4. A special meaning shall be given to a term if it is established that the parties so intended.

Article 32 – Supplementary means of interpretation

1. Recourse may be had to supplementary means of interpretation, including the preparatory work of the treaty and the circumstances of its conclusion, [364] in order to confirm the meaning resulting from the application of article 31, or to determine the meaning when the interpretation according to article 31:

(a) leaves the meaning ambiguous or obscure; or

(b) leads to a result which is manifestly absurd or unreasonable.

83. As set out in paragraph 11 above, Article 32(6)(a) of the OSPAR Convention provides that '[t]he arbitral tribunal shall decide according to the rules of international law and, in particular, those of the OSPAR Convention'.[55] In dealing with general obligations, Article 2 of the OSPAR Convention provides in section 2(1)(a) that all possible steps shall be taken, 'in accordance with the provisions of the Convention'.

84. It should go without saying that the first duty of the Tribunal is to apply the OSPAR Convention. An international tribunal, such as this Tribunal, will also apply customary international law and general principles unless and to the extent that the

---

[52] Vienna Convention on the Law of Treaties, 23 May 1969, 1155 UNTS 331.

[53] Counsel for Ireland, Transcript, Day 1 Proceedings, pp. 23–4.

[54] *Id.* and Counsel for the United Kingdom, Transcript, Day 2 Proceedings, p. 75.

[55] Identical language is repeated in Article 19 of the Rules of Procedure for the OSPAR Tribunal.

Parties have created a *lex specialis*. Even then, it must defer to a relevant *jus cogens* with which the Parties' *lex specialis* may be inconsistent.

85. Ireland's submission is of a different order, namely the applicability of other conventional international law. The absence of an additional phrase in Article 2 of the OSPAR Convention (set out in para. 3 above) on the order of 'and in accordance with international law' does not mean that the OSPAR Convention intended to discharge the Parties to it *inter se* from other obligations that they may have assumed under other international instruments or under general international law. However, it does mean that the competence of a tribunal established under the OSPAR Convention was not intended to extend to obligations the Parties might have under other instruments (unless, of course, parts of the OSPAR Convention included a direct *renvoi* to such other instruments). Interpreting Article 32(6)(a) otherwise would transform it into an unqualified and comprehensive jurisdictional regime, in which there would be no limit *ratione materiae* to the jurisdiction of a tribunal established under the OSPAR Convention. Here, there is no indication that the Parties to the OSPAR Convention have, in their individual capacities, submitted themselves to such a comprehensive jurisdictional regime with respect to any other international tribunal. Nor is it reasonable to suppose that they would have accepted such a jurisdictional regime through the vehicle of the OSPAR Convention.

86. The Tribunal's interpretation is reinforced by the explicit reference in Article 9(3) of the OSPAR Convention to 'applicable international regulations'. The explicit incorporation of other regulations in [365] Article 9(3) imports that, when this was not done for other provisions of the OSPAR Convention, there was no implied intention to extend the competence of the Tribunal to other parts of international conventional law.

2. The Sintra Ministerial Statement

87. Beyond the OSPAR Convention, Ireland relied in support of its claims upon the Sintra Ministerial Statement of 1998,[56] where the Ministers agreed:

> to prevent pollution of the maritime area from ionizing radiation through progressive and substantial reductions of discharges, emissions and losses of radioactive substances, with the ultimate aim of concentrations in the environment near background values for naturally occurring radioactive substances and close to zero for artificial radioactive substances.

The Ministers also noted 'the concerns expressed by a number of Contracting Parties about the recent increases in technetium discharges from Sellafield and their view that these discharges should cease'. The Statement continued 'that the United Kingdom Ministers have indicated that such concerns will be addressed in their forthcoming decisions concerning the discharge authorisations for Sellafield'. The Statement welcomed

---

[56] *See* Ireland's Memorial, Annex 8. Also available from www.ospar.org.

The announcement of the UK Government that no new commercial contracts will be accepted for reprocessing spent fuel at Dounreay, with the result of future reductions in radioactive discharges in the maritime area.

88. Subsequently, the OSPAR Commission (with the United Kingdom abstaining) issued its Decisions 2000/1 and 2001/1 with respect to non-reprocessing of spent nuclear fuel. By operation of Article 13, the United Kingdom is not bound by the two Commission decisions. They cannot be considered as governing law for this arbitration.

89. However, for other reasons the Sintra Statement may have created binding obligations for the United Kingdom. The International Court of Justice ('ICJ') held in the *Nuclear Tests* case that unilateral declarations accompanied by an intention to be bound may create binding obligations:

> It is well recognized that declarations made by way of unilateral acts, concerning legal or factual situations, may have the effect of creating legal obligations. Declarations of this kind may be, and often are, very specific. When it is the [**366**] intention of the State making the declaration that it should become bound according to its terms, that intention confers on the declaration the character of a legal undertaking, the State being thenceforth legally required to follow a course of conduct consistent with the declaration. An undertaking of this kind, if given publicly, and with an intent to be bound, even though not made with the context of international negotiations, is binding.[57]

90. It is arguable that the United Kingdom's commitment with respect to reprocessing spent fuel at Dounreay announced in the Sintra Ministerial Statement may have created an international obligation on its part and in relation to the other states represented at the Ministerial meeting. But the question of whether the United Kingdom is under an obligation with respect to reprocessing spent fuel at Dounreay as a consequence of the announcement referred to in the Sintra Ministerial Statement is not relevant to the different question here of access to information about the activities at Sellafield.

91. The more general goals of the Sintra Ministerial Statement were plainly exhortatory. That matter aside, it appears to the Tribunal that the Sintra Ministerial Statement is not a decision or even a recommendation within the meaning of Article 13 of the OSPAR Convention.

92. Neither Article 9(1) nor Article 9(2) refers specifically to any other bodies of substantive conventional international law to which the Tribunal should have recourse.

3. 'Applicable international regulations'

93. Article 9(3)(d) states that Parties have the right to refuse a request for information that qualifies under Article 9(2) 'in accordance with their national legal systems and

---

[57] *Case Concerning Nuclear Tests (Australia v. France)*, Judgment of 20 December 1974, 1974 ICJ Rep. 253, at p. 266, para. 43.

applicable international regulations' where the information affects 'commercial and industrial confidentiality, including intellectual property . . . '.

94. Ireland acknowledged that the relevant national legal system applicable to Article 9(3) was English law.

95. Further, the Parties agreed that the 1992 Regulations (*see* para. 26 above), which give effect to Directive 90/313 (*see* para. 30 above), apply as the legislative component of the relevant national legal system. However, the Parties did not agree on their interpretation.

96. The Parties disagreed, in a number of ways, as to the reference of 'applicable international regulations' in Article 9(3). Ireland contended that 'applicable international regulations' means 'international law and [**367**] practice'.[58] The United Kingdom proposed a strict textual interpretation and submitted that there are no 'applicable international regulations' for Article 9(3)(d) of the OSPAR Convention other than Directive 90/313, which was implemented in UK law.

97. On its broader submission, Ireland relied upon the Rio Declaration,[59] in particular Principle 10, and the 1998 Aarhus Convention on Access to Information, Public Participation in Decision-making and Access to Justice in Environmental Matters (the 'Aarhus Convention'), which entered into force on 30 October 2001.[60] The United Kingdom replied that the Rio Declaration was not a treaty and that the Aarhus Convention has been ratified by neither Ireland nor the United Kingdom.

98. In its Reply, Ireland submitted that ' "regulations" include all the instruments relating to the environment and access to information referred to in detail in Ireland's Memorial . . . ', and that such instruments are to be interpreted in light of 'the evolving international law and practice on access to environmental information'.[61]

99. A jurisdictional clause may incorporate international law *in statu nascendi*. For example, the Special Agreement between Libya and Tunisia of 10 June 1977, submitting to the ICJ their continental shelf boundary dispute, incorporated as applicable law international maritime norms that had not yet become *lex lata*. Article 1 provided that:

> the Court shall take its decision according to equitable principles, and the relevant circumstances which characterize the area, as well as the new accepted trends in the Third Conference on the Law of the Sea.[62]

When the Parties have so empowered an international arbitral tribunal, it may apply norms that are not *lex lata*, if, in the tribunal's judgment, the norms have been accepted and are soon likely to become part of the international *corpus juris*. But the arbitral

---

[58] Ireland's Memorial, para. 117.

[59] Declaration of the UN Conference on Environment and Development, 31 ILM 874 (1992).

[60] Convention on Access to Information, Public Participation in Decision-making and Access to Justice in Environmental Matters, 25 June 1998, 38 ILM 517 (1999).

[61] Ireland's Reply, para. 42.

[62] *Case Concerning the Continental Shelf (Tunisia/Libyan Arab Jamahiriya)*, Judgment of 24 February 1982, 1982 ICJ Rep. 18, at p. 23.

tribunal then applies them because of the Parties' instructions, not because they are 'almost' law.

100. As long as it is not inconsistent with *jus cogens*, Parties may also instruct a tribunal to apply a *lex specialis* that is not part of general international law at the time. But the OSPAR Convention does not incorporate such a reference. Without such an authorization, a tribunal established under the OSPAR Convention cannot go beyond existing [368] law. This is not to say that a tribunal cannot apply customary international law of a recent vintage, but that it must in fact be customary international law.

101. Although the issue does not arise, the Tribunal agrees with Ireland's proposal to 'draw on current international law and practice in considering whether a "commercial confidentiality" exception to a request for information may be invoked', but only insofar as such law and practice are relevant and hence admissible under Article 31(3)(b) and (c) of the Vienna Convention. However, the Tribunal has not been authorized to apply 'evolving international law and practice' and cannot do so. In this regard, the Tribunal would note that the ICJ in its decision in the *Gabčíkovo–Nagymaros* case, was not, as Ireland argued,[63] proposing that it – and arguably other international tribunals – had an inherent authority to apply law *in statu nascendi*. The ICJ said:

> new norms and standards have been developed, set forth in a great number of instru-
> ments during the last two decades. Such new norms have to be taken into consideration,
> and such new standards given proper weight, not only when States contemplate new
> activities but also when continuing with activities begun in the past.[64]

102. The issue here is one of interpretation in good faith, as required by Article 31(1) of the Vienna Convention, if not by an essential ingredient of law itself. A treaty is a solemn undertaking and States Parties are entitled to have applied to them and to their peoples that to which they have agreed and not things to which they have not agreed.

103. Lest it produce anachronistic results that are inconsistent with current international law, a tribunal must certainly engage in *actualization* or contemporization when construing an international instrument that was concluded in an earlier period.[65] Oppenheim, after restating the so-called law of inter-temporality (i.e., that an instrument is to be interpreted in the light of the general rules of international law in force at the time of its conclusion), adds the qualification that 'in some respects the interpretation of a treaty's provisions cannot be divorced from developments in the law subsequent to its adoption'.[66] But the reference in the Court's *dictum* and the doctrinal statement in Oppenheim based [369] upon it is to developments in *law*. Wholly apart from the question of the need for actualization of a treaty made

---

[63] *See* Ireland's Reply, para. 42.

[64] *Case Concerning the Gabcikovo–Nagymaros Project (Hungary v. Slovakia)*, Judgment of 25 September 1997, 1997 ICJ Rep., at p. 7, para. 140 [see p. 311 above].

[65] *Legal Consequences for States of the Continued Presence of South Africa in Namibia (South West Africa) notwithstanding Security Council Resolution 276 (1970)*, Advisory Opinion, 1971 ICJ Rep., at p. 3.

[66] *Oppenheim's International Law*, ninth edition, at 1281–2 (Sir Robert Jennings and Sir Arthur Watts eds., Longman, 1996).

scarcely ten years earlier, the Court's reference in *Gabcíkovo–Nagymaros* is to new *law* 'in a great number of *instruments*' [italics supplied] and not material that has not yet become law. As stated, a tribunal must also adjust application of a treaty insofar as one of its provisions proves inconsistent with a *jus cogens* that subsequently emerged. The present case does not raise questions of *jus cogens*.

104. For these reasons, the Tribunal cannot accept Ireland's proposal that the Aarhus Convention or that 'draft proposals for a new EC Directive' be applied.[67]

105. Nonetheless, the Tribunal may apply, where appropriate, other extant international agreements insofar as they are admissible for purposes of interpretation under Article 31 of the Vienna Convention.

VIII. FINDINGS WITH RESPECT TO ARTICLE 9(I)

[...]

[372] [...] 2. *The Tribunal's decision with respect to jurisdiction under Article 9(1)*

118. The United Kingdom has characterized its objection to Ireland's claim under Article 9(1) as going to the lack of jurisdiction of the Tribunal and/or being inadmissible. However, in the unanimous view of the Tribunal the question posed by Ireland with respect to Article 9(1) is not one of jurisdiction or admissibility, but one of substance, namely what is the purport of Article 9(1) under the facts of this case.

[373] 119. The remaining holding with respect to Article 9(1) is supported by a majority comprising Dr Griffith and Lord Mustill.

120. As noted above (para. 109), Regulation 3 of the 1992 Regulations giving effect to Directive 90/313 is relied upon by the United Kingdom as constituting its compliance under domestic law with the requirements of Article 9(1).[68] The United Kingdom contends that the mandated regime under domestic law is not required to be expressed as being pursuant to the OSPAR Convention obligation.[69] The Tribunal agrees that the standard may be satisfied in a form such as the 1992 Regulations, which are otherwise justified under Directive 90/313.

121. Although, as asserted by the United Kingdom and not contested by Ireland, it would be a proper subject for this Tribunal's jurisdiction, it is no part of Ireland's claims in this dispute that there are defects within the domestic regime to the extent that the 1992 Regulations fall below the standards required by Article 9(1).

122. For the purpose of this issue of construction of Article 9(1), the Tribunal assumes that the redacted information sought by Ireland is of a sort required to be disclosed.

123. The issue remains one of interpretation of public international law, namely whether, as the United Kingdom contends, the obligation of a Contracting Party under Article 9(1) is completely discharged by putting in place an appropriate domestic

---

[67] *See* Ireland's Reply, para. 42.
[68] *See* United Kingdom's Counter-Memorial, para. 3.12.
[69] Counsel for the United Kingdom, Transcript, Day 2 Proceedings, p. 85.

regulatory framework so that disputes about specific applications of the obligations under Article 9 are to be exclusively determined within the municipal law of the Contracting Party. Should this be the case, the appropriate forum for Ireland with respect to its claims that information to which it was entitled under the OSPAR Convention was improperly withheld will be found in the United Kingdom municipal system.

124. If Article 9(1) is to be interpreted as maintained by Ireland, then this Tribunal may exercise its jurisdiction to consider the merits of the refusal of the United Kingdom's competent authorities to disclose information contained in the PA and ADL Reports, provided that such information falls within the definition of Article 9(2) of the OSPAR Convention.

125. Consistently with Article 31 of the Vienna Convention, the Parties have focused their arguments on the treaty text to determine the meaning of the Article 9(1) obligation.[70] The Tribunal applies this [374] approach to examine the terms of Article 9(1) in the context of the entire Article 9 and the OSPAR Convention.

126. The Tribunal first examines the meaning of the obligation in the context of the OSPAR Convention regime, taking into account its objects and purposes and also the fact that a dispute settlement clause is incorporated by Article 32. In confirmation of this analysis the Tribunal also is guided by Article 32(6)(a) to analyse the relevant rules of international law that inform the meaning of the obligation of Article 9(1), and in particular (the now superseded) Directive 90/313.

127. Article 9 is an access to information provision that must be taken to articulate the Contracting Parties' intentions as expressed within the framework of the general objectives and the particular other provisions of the OSPAR Convention. As much as do the other operative articles of the OSPAR Convention, the disputes clause, Article 32, applies Article 9 as an enforceable obligation in its particular subject matter. Its provisions for disclosure of defined information must be taken to have an intended bite beyond being an expression of aspirational objectives for the domestic laws of the Contracting Parties.

128. The main purpose of the OSPAR Convention is the protection of the marine environment and the elimination of the marine pollution in the North-East Atlantic. The objectives of the OSPAR Convention are set out in its Preamble and include, *inter alia*, obligations

- to protect the marine and other environments;
- to prevent and eliminate pollution;
- to prevent and punish infringements;
- to assist a Contracting Party;
- to conduct research; and
- to prevent dumping.

129. For the achievement of these aims the framers of the OSPAR Convention have carefully applied differential language to provide for stipulated levels of engagement

---

[70] *See, e.g.*, United Kingdom's Counter-Memorial, paras. 3.1–3.3; United Kingdom's Rejoinder, para. 14; Counsel for Ireland, Transcript, Day 1 Proceedings, pp. 23–4.

of treaty obligation to achieve these objectives. There is a cascading standard of expression providing for the particular obligations imposed on a Contracting Party. For example, there are mandatory provisions that provide for Contracting Parties:

- to take some act ('shall apply', 'shall include', 'shall undertake', 'shall co-operate' or 'shall keep');
- actively to work towards an objective ('take all possible steps', 'implement programs', 'carry out programs');
- [375] to deal with issues of planning for the objective ('establish programs', 'adopt', 'define', 'draw up', 'develop', 'take account of'); and
- to take measures ('take', 'adopt', 'plan', 'apply', 'introduce', 'prescribe', 'take into account').

At a lesser level of engagement, other provisions provide for information to be dealt with ('collect', 'access information') or that systems be set up ('provide for', 'establish').

130. When read as a whole (including the Annexes), it is plain to the Tribunal that the entire text discloses a carefully crafted hierarchy of obligations or engagement to achieve the disparate objectives of the OSPAR Convention. Those who framed the OSPAR Convention expressed themselves in carefully chosen, rather than in loose and general, terms. They plainly identified matters for mandatory obligation for action by Contracting Parties, as in

- Article 5 ('The Contracting Party shall take');
- Article 6 ('The Contracting Party shall ... undertake');
- Article 7 ('The Contracting Party shall co-operate ...'); and
- Article 8 ('The Contracting Party shall establish ...', 'The Contracting Party shall have regard ...').

131. Further, requirements for Contracting Parties to ensure a result are not confined to Article 9(1). Importantly, the general obligations expressed in Article 8(2) and embraced under Article 2(3)(b)(ii) are that the Contracting Parties shall '... ensure the application of best available techniques and best environmental practice ...'. Similarly, Article 4(1) of Annex II dealing with dumping requires that the Contracting Parties shall 'ensure' the required result and, under Article 10(1), shall 'ensure compliance' by vessels or aircraft. Likewise, Article 5(1) of Annex III demands that the Contracting Parties shall 'ensure' that their competent authorities implement the relevant applicable decisions, recommendations, and all other agreements adopted under the OSPAR Convention.

132. The issue for determination is whether the requirement in Article 9(1) 'to ensure' the obligated result, mandates a result rather than merely a municipal law system directed to obtain the result.

133. In the context of the language used within Article 9, it remains for the Tribunal to discern the extent of the comprised obligation. Whatever its particular replication of Directive 90/313, what does appear plain to the Tribunal is that the obligation expressed in Article 9(1) by the requirement that a Contracting Party 'shall ensure' the [376] stipulated result is a reflection of a deliberate rather than a lax choice of

vocabulary. It illustrates the application of a chosen (and strong) level of expression, deftly applied by the drafters to the particular and, to them, important subject matter of disclosure of information to any persons, whether nationals or not, who request it. It is expressed at the higher level of obligation, and when applying it in the complex of the provisions on disclosure of information embraced by the scheme of Article 9, the Tribunal sees no reason to read its particular language in a way that is discordant with the structure and use of language in the entire OSPAR Convention. The search is for conformity of meaning within the OSPAR Convention.

134. On that approach, the Tribunal finds that the obligation is to be construed as expressed at the mandatory end of the scale. The applied requirement of Article 9(1) is read by the Tribunal as imposing an obligation upon the United Kingdom, as a Contracting Party, to ensure something, namely that its competent authorities 'are required to make available the information described in paragraph 2 ... to any natural legal person, in response to any reasonable request'.

135. It appears to the Tribunal that to accept the expression of the requirement 'to ensure' a result as expressed at the lesser level of setting up a regime or system directed to obtain the stipulated result under the domestic law of the Contracting Party, as is contended by the United Kingdom, would be to apply an impermissible gloss that does not appear as part of the unconditional primary obligation under Article 9(1). In contrast, a limitation of this sort is expressly embraced in the scheme of Article 9(3) providing for exceptions of disclosure expressed by reference to criteria to be imposed by the Contracting Parties 'in accordance with their national legal systems'. The fact that Article 9(3) engages such a limitation by reference to domestic law forecloses the possibility that Article 9(1) silently and similarly limits the obligation upon a Contracting Party to that of putting in place a domestic legal regime providing for disclosure in compliance with the Article 9 obligations.

136. A further matter that militates in favour of this interpretation is the fact that Article 9(1) identifies the objective criteria that should be met when a request to provide information is received by the competent authorities of a Contracting State. Hence, compliance by a Contracting State with these criteria may itself become a separate subject matter of arbitration under Article 32.

137. For these reasons in this aspect it appears to the Tribunal that Article 9(1) is advisedly pitched at a level that imposes an obligation of result rather than merely to provide access to a domestic regime which is directed at obtaining the required result.

[377] 138. In adopting this construction the Tribunal gives full effect to the terms of Article 9(1), including particularly the requirement that as a Contracting Party the United Kingdom 'shall ensure that their competent authorities are required to make available the information'. The Tribunal applies, rather than excises, this clause as the defining part of the obligation.

139. The Tribunal derives further support for its mere textual analysis of Article 9(1) from the relevant rules of international and European Union law.

140. The Parties are in agreement on the origins of Article 9(1) as derived from, and closely following, the language of Directive 90/313.[71] As noted above, in support of its position the United Kingdom refers to the notion of a directive as defined in Article 249 of the EC Treaty as a measure which shall be 'binding as to the result to be achieved, upon each Member State to which it is addressed, but shall leave to the national authorities the choice of form and methods'.[72] The United Kingdom submits that by adopting the language of the Directive, 'the Contracting Parties to the OSPAR Convention evinced their intention to adopt the same approach',[73] namely that a State's only obligation is 'to take such legislative or administrative measures as may be appropriate to achieve the stated objective'.[74]

141. In considering these contentions the Tribunal first notes that the adoption of a similar or identical definition or term in international texts should be distinguished from the intention to bestow the same normative status upon both instruments. The complex of instruments whose wording was used by the drafters may include unilateral statements, position papers, declarations, recommendations, and the like. While the language of such sources might be instrumental to the extent that it allows one to trace and understand the origins of specific treaty terms, their normative value should not be attributed to similarly worded legal obligations imposed by that treaty. As the ITLOS has helpfully observed in its Order of 3 December 2001:

> [E]ven if the OSPAR Convention, the EC Treaty and the Euratom Treaty contain rights or obligations similar to or identical with the rights and obligations set out in [UNCLOS], the rights and obligations under those agreements have a separate existence from those under [UNCLOS].

[378] Further,

> [T]he application of international law rules on interpretation of treaties to identical or similar provisions of different treaties may not yield the same results, having regard to, *inter alia*, differences in the respective contexts, objects and purposes, subsequent practice of parties and *travaux préparatoires*.[75]

142. Each of the OSPAR Convention and Directive 90/313 is an independent legal source that establishes a distinct legal regime and provides for different legal remedies. The United Kingdom recognizes Ireland's right as an EU Member State to challenge the implementation of the Directive in the United Kingdom's domestic legal system before the ECJ.[76] Similarly, a Contracting Party to the OSPAR Convention, with its

---

[71] United Kingdom's Counter-Memorial, para. 3.9. *See also* Counsel for Ireland, Transcript, Day 1 Proceedings, pp. 24–5; Counsel for the United Kingdom, Transcript, Day 2 Proceedings, pp. 78–9; Counsel for Ireland, Transcript, Day 4 Proceedings, p. 21.

[72] *See* Article 249 of the Treaty Establishing the European Community ('EC Treaty'), 2002 OJ (C 325), as cited in the United Kingdom's Counter-Memorial, para. 3.11.

[73] United Kingdom's Counter-Memorial, para. 3.11.

[74] United Kingdom's Rejoinder, para. 13.

[75] *Id.*, para. 51.

[76] United Kingdom's Counter-Memorial, paras. 3.13–3.15.

elaborate dispute settlement mechanism, should be able to question the implementation of a distinct legal obligation imposed by the OSPAR Convention in the arbitral forum, namely this designated Tribunal.[77]

143. Pursuant to Article 4 of Directive 90/313, legal action against a State in breach is to be pursued domestically. However, and in contrast, the OSPAR Convention contains a particular and self-contained dispute resolution mechanism in Article 32, in accordance with which this Tribunal acts. Article 9(1) does not provide for an exception to the OSPAR disputes clause by referring, for instance, to an exclusive municipal remedy, and is therefore as subject to review by an arbitral tribunal as any other provision of the OSPAR Convention. The similar language of the two legal instruments, as well as the fact that the 1992 Regulations are an implementing instrument for both Directive 90/313 and the OSPAR Convention, does not limit a Contracting Party's choice of a legal forum to only one of the two available, i.e. either the ECJ or an OSPAR tribunal. Nor, contrary to the United Kingdom's contention, does it suggest that the only cause of action available to Ireland is confined exclusively to those provided for by Directive 90/313 and implementing legislation. The primary purpose of employing the similar language is to create uniform and consistent legal standards in the field of the protection of the marine environment, and not to create precedence of one set of legal remedies over the other.

[**379**] 144. The proposed reading of Article 9(1) also is consistent with contemporary principles of State responsibility. A State is internationally responsible for the acts of its organs. On conventional principles, a State covenanting with other States to put in place a domestic framework and review mechanisms remains responsible to those other States for the adequacy of this framework and the conduct of its competent authorities who, in the exercise of their executive functions, engage the domestic system.

145. Amongst others, this submission is confirmed by Articles 4 and 5 of the International Law Commission Draft Articles on the Responsibility of States for Internationally Wrongful Acts,[78] providing for rules of attribution of certain acts to States. On the international plane, acts of 'competent authorities' are considered to be attributable to the State as long as such authorities fall within the notion of State organs or entities that are empowered to exercise elements of the governmental authority. As the ICJ stated in the *LaGrand* case, 'the international responsibility of a State is engaged by the action of the competent organs and authorities acting in that State, whatever they may be'.[79]

---

[77] In 2001 the ITLOS was confronted with a similar situation. In response to the jurisdictional objections raised by the United Kingdom, it remarked that 'since the dispute before the Annex VII arbitral tribunal concerns the interpretation or application of the [UNCLOS] and no other agreement, only the dispute settlement procedures under the Convention are relevant to that dispute'. See *The Mox Plant Case, supra* note 46, para. 52.

[78] *Draft Articles on Responsibility of States for Internationally Wrongful Acts*, Report of the International Law Commission, 53rd Session, Supp. No. 10, UN Doc. A/56/10, 44 (2001).

[79] *LaGrand (Germany v. United States of America)*, Provisional Measures, Order of 3 March 1999, 1999 ICJ Rep. 9, at p. 16, para. 28.

146. It follows as an ordinary matter of obligation between States, that even where international law assigns competence to a national system, there is no exclusion of responsibility of a State for the inadequacy of such a national system or the failure of its competent authorities to act in a way prescribed by an international obligation or implementing legislation. Adopting a contrary approach would lead to the deferral of responsibility by States and the frustration of the international legal system.

147. In support of its interpretation of Article 9(1), Ireland invoked the *LaGrand* case, to contend that the ICJ found that Article 36(1)(b) of the Vienna Convention on Consular Relations[80] created an obligation of result, and that 'the failure to provide consular access at the national level gave rise to a dispute over which the International Court of Justice had jurisdiction'.[81] Although there are obvious differences in the direct and indirect references to the relevant competent authorities between Article 9(1) of the OSPAR Convention and Article 36(1)(b) of [**380**] the Vienna Convention on Consular Relations, one Tribunal member (Dr Griffith) finds some independent support in *LaGrand* for these conclusions. However, the Tribunal's position on the more direct issues of textual interpretation make it unnecessary to invoke such other matters of confirmatory support.

148. For these reasons the Tribunal rejects the contention of the United Kingdom based on Article 9(1), and determines that upon its proper construction Article 9(1) requires an outcome of result, namely that information falling within the meaning of Article 9(2) (and not excluded under Article 9(3)) is in fact disclosed in conformity with the Article 9 obligation imposed upon each Contracting Party.

IX. FINDINGS WITH RESPECT TO ARTICLE 9(2)

[. . .]

[**383**] [. . .] 2. *The Tribunal's decision with respect to the claims relating to Article 9(2)*

159. The United Kingdom has characterized its objection to Ireland's claim under Article 9(2) as going to the lack of jurisdiction of the Tribunal and/or being inadmissible. In the unanimous view of the Tribunal, however, the question posed by Ireland with respect to Article 9(2) is not one of jurisdiction or admissibility, but one of substance, viz. what is the purport of Article 9(2) under the facts of this case.

160. The remaining holding with respect to Article 9(2) is supported by a majority comprising Professor Reisman and Lord Mustill.

161. The Tribunal has not been requested to issue an advisory opinion as to the abstract meaning of Article 9(2) of the OSPAR Convention, but rather to apply the provision to a specific controversy about 14 categories of information redacted from

---

[80] Vienna Convention on Consular Relations, 24 April 1963, 596 UNTS 261.
[81] Counsel for Ireland, Transcript, Day 1 Proceedings, p. 43. Ireland also submitted that 'the ICJ made it clear that its function was to review the merits of whether the United States had complied with obligations to ensure consular access to an individual in the United States, a German national'. *Id.*, at p. 35.

the PA and ADL Reports. In its Memorial, Ireland identified those 14 categories as information relating to:

- (A) Estimated annual production capacity of the MOX facility;
- (B) Time taken to reach this capacity;
- (C) [384] Sales volumes;
- (D) Probability of achieving higher sales volumes;
- (E) Probability of being able to win contracts for recycling fuel in 'significant quantities';
- (F) Estimated sales demand;
- (G) Percentage of plutonium already on site;
- (H) Maximum throughput figures;
- (I) Life span of the MOX facility;
- (J) Number of employees;
- (K) Price of MOX fuel;
- (L) Whether, and to what extent, there are firm contracts to purchase MOX from Sellafield;
- (M) Arrangements for transport of plutonium to, and MOX from, Sellafield;
- (N) Likely number of such transports.[82]

It will be recalled that in its Amended Statement of Claim, the first relief which Ireland sought was an order and declaration that the United Kingdom had breached its obligations under Article 9 of the OSPAR Convention 'by refusing to make available information deleted from the PA Report and the ADL Report'. Ireland's second prayer for relief was, in effect, for an order for the provision by the United Kingdom of those parts of the PA and ADL Reports that had been redacted or, contingently, those parts that had been redacted but that did not affect commercial confidentiality within the meaning of Article 9(3)(d). The specific issue before the Tribunal is whether the redacted portions of the PA and ADL Reports, viewed as categories, constitute 'information' within the meaning of Article 9(2). The Tribunal distinguishes here between the categories of redaction and the content of those categories. A determination under Article 9(3)(d) would require a detailed examination of the *content* of the various categories of redaction. A determination under Article 9(2) requires only an examination of the categories of redaction, in order to determine whether they fall within the definition of 'information' in Article 9(2).

162. As will be recalled, Article 9(2) provides:

> The information referred to in paragraph 1 of this Article is any available information in written, visual, aural or data-base form on the state of the maritime area, on activities or measures adversely affecting or likely to affect it and on activities or measures introduced in accordance with the Convention.

[385] 163. Article 9(2), whose chapeau is 'Access to Information', establishes the scope of information to which, subject to specific enumerated rights of refusal in Article 9(3), the obligation in Article 9(1) relates. The scope of the information in

---

[82] Ireland's Memorial, para. 75. Ireland also provided more detailed lists of specific items deleted from the PA and ADL Reports in its Memorial Annexes 3 and 3 B, respectively.

the provision is not environmental, in general, but, in keeping with the focus of the OSPAR Convention, 'the state of the maritime area'. It is manifest to the Tribunal that none of the above 14 categories in Ireland's list can plausibly be characterized as 'information . . . on the state of the maritime area'. The Tribunal could, thus, rest its decision on the fact that none of the material in the 14 categories falls within the definition of 'information' in Article 9(2).

164. In response to this, Ireland's submission of what might be called an interpretative theory of 'inclusive causality' would overcome this difficulty. Ireland argued, it will be recalled,

> without the ADL report there would be no discharges from the MOX plant into the Irish Sea. It is hard to think how that report cannot even according to that test be direct and proximate.[83]

Under an interpretative theory of inclusive causality, anything, no matter how remote, which facilitated the performance of an activity is to be deemed part of that activity. Legislators and drafters of treaties may adopt a theory of inclusive causality. The question is whether the drafters of the OSPAR Convention did. Some parts of Article 9(2) are, indeed, quite expansive, but other parts make abundantly clear that while the drafters sought inclusiveness with respect to some aspects of the information covered by Article 9(2), they had no intention of adopting a theory of inclusive causality. The Tribunal now turns its attention to these matters.

165. Article 9(2) identifies three categories, within each of which 'any available information' falls within the obligations of Article 9, unless that category has a restriction. The drafters' selection of the adjectives 'any' and 'available' in Article 9(2) is significant.

166. The adjective 'available' indicates that the drafters were not imposing an obligation on a Contracting Party to gather and process information of a certain sort upon the request of any natural or legal person, but rather were limiting the obligation of the Contracting Parties under Article 9 to information which had already been gathered and was already available to them. This provision is thus similar, in effect, to Article 14(1) of the Convention on Civil Liability for Damage Resulting from Activities Dangerous to the Environment of 1993,[84] which establishes access to information simply if it is 'held by public authorities'. [386] In this respect, the obligation of Article 9(2) differs from obligations in certain national instruments, under which a claimant with standing may require that a government or its agency or instrumentality gather, process, and make available certain types of information.

167. The adjective 'any' indicates that, unless set out explicitly within the three categories enumerated in Article 9(2), no selections or restrictions are implied. One such explicit class of restrictions is to be found in the rights of refusal to a request for information under the grounds specified in Article 9(3). Apart from exceptions,

---

[83] Counsel for Ireland, Transcript, Day 1 Proceedings, p. 50.

[84] Convention on Civil Liability for Damage Resulting from Activities Dangerous to the Environment, 21 June 1993, ETS 150.

the insertion by the drafters of the adjective 'any' requires an applier to interpret extensively *within* each of the three categories. Once a matter is found to fall within one of the categories of Article 9(2), the presumption is that it is within the scope of the OSPAR Convention. This mandate for an extensive construction of the provision is reinforced by the drafters' selection of the term 'information'.

168. Article 1 does not define 'information' but it is clear that it is a broad and inclusive reference with respect to the state of the maritime area. The point of emphasis, however, is that it is 'information' about the state of the maritime area. The three categories of 'information . . . on the state of the maritime area' in Article 9(2) are

   (i)   'any available information' on 'the state of the maritime area',
   (ii) 'any available information' on 'activities or measures adversely affecting or likely to affect . . . the maritime area',
   (iii) 'any available information' on 'activities or measures introduced in accordance with the Convention'.

169. In their submissions to the Tribunal, both Parties focused attention on the second category of Article 9(2). In their responses to the Tribunal's *Decision No. 5* requesting their views on the third category, both Parties again indicated that the critical category for decision was the second. Accordingly, the Tribunal will direct its attention to this category, relying on the other categories, insofar as appropriate, for purposes of interpreting the second, as did the Parties in their responses.

170. It is clear that Article 9(2) is not a general freedom of information statute. The information here is restricted in a number of ways. First, as noted, it is restricted by the term 'maritime area', which appears in the first and second categories of Article 9(2), and is given a specific definition in Article 1(a) and 1(b), which provide

   (a)   'Maritime area' means the internal waters and the territorial seas of the Contracting Parties, the sea beyond and adjacent to the territorial sea under the jurisdiction of the coastal state to the extent recognised by international [387] law, and the high seas, including the bed of all those waters and its sub-soil, situated within the following limits:
      (i)   those parts of the Atlantic and Arctic Oceans and their dependent seas which lie north of 36° north latitude and between 42° west longitude and 51° east longitude, but excluding:
         (1)   the Baltic Sea and the Belts lying to the south and east of lines drawn from Hasenore Head to Gniben Point, from Korshage to Spodsbjerg and from Gilbjerg Head to Kullen,
         (2)   the Mediterranean Sea and its dependent seas as far as the point of intersection of the parallel of 36° north latitude and the meridian of 5° 36' west longitude;
      (ii) that part of the Atlantic Ocean north of 59° north latitude and between 44° west longitude and 42° west longitude.
   (b)   'Internal waters' means the waters on the landward side of the baselines from which the breadth of the territorial sea is measured, extending [in] the case of watercourses up to the freshwater limit.

As so defined, the area covered by the OSPAR Convention includes the internal waters and territorial seas of Ireland and the United Kingdom as well as the Irish Sea between them, but Article 1 does not indicate whether particular information is relevant to that maritime area.

171. Each of the second and third categories of Article 9(2) relates to 'activities or measures'. Neither of these terms is defined in Article 1 of the Convention, but it is clear from other parts of the OSPAR Convention (e.g., Article 2(1)(a)) that the term 'measures' refers generically to regulatory initiatives by any part of the governmental apparatus of the Contracting Parties with respect to matters covered by the OSPAR Convention, while 'activities' refers to the actions, whether emanating from or effected by governmental or non-governmental entities, that would be the object of the 'measures'.

172. In commenting on identical language in Article 2(a) of Directive 90/313, the ECJ in *Mecklenburg*,[85] remarked on 'the term "measures" as serving merely to make it clear that the acts governed by the directive included all forms of administrative activity'.[86] Plainly, the inclusion of both 'activities' and 'measures' indicates that the drafters intended a regime in the second category covering 'any available information' about a wide, rather than narrow, range of matters relating to the specific subject matter of each of those categories, but the Tribunal notes, once again, that the information must relate to the state of the maritime area.

[388] 173. The second category of Article 9(2) relates to two types of activities or measures. First, activities or measures that are already adversely affecting the maritime area and, second, activities or measures that are likely to affect it. The second type of activity or measure may be underway and already be affecting or likely to affect adversely the maritime area or it may not be underway, but if and when it is, it must be likely to affect adversely the maritime area if it is to fall within the second category. Thus the second category of Article 9(2) includes prospective activities and measures as well as activities and measures already underway.

174. Each of the three categories in Article 9(2) is cast in the broad terms that are consistent with the 'any information' formula. As such, they might warrant an interpretation of inclusive causality. However, it is only the second category that contains an additional threshold of inclusion/exclusion that is manifestly designed by the drafters to be more restrictive than the first and third categories. While the scope of Article 9 covers *simpliciter* 'any available information' 'on the state of the maritime area' (first category) and 'any available information' 'on activities or measures introduced in accordance with the Convention' (third category), the second category of Article 9(2) qualifies the obligation to provide 'any available information' on activities or measures 'adversely affecting or likely to affect' the maritime area.

175. The adverb 'adversely' qualifies both existing and prospective activities and measures and raises the threshold of inclusion, as does the adverb 'likely'. Even

---

[85] [C-321/96, *Mecklenburg v. Kreis Pinneberg – Der Landrat*, [1999] 2 CMLR 418, 435.]
[86] *Id.*, at para. 20.

were the Tribunal to accept, *arguendo*, Ireland's submission of inclusive causality, the submission would founder on the adverbs 'adversely' and 'likely'. Had the adverbs 'adversely' and 'likely' not been inserted in the provision, the scope of that part of Article 9(2) would have included any present or prospective activity or measure having *any* effect on the maritime area and might, as a result, have indicated an intention of inclusive causality. By including those two adverbs, the drafters have excluded from the scope of the obligation of Article 9 current activities or measures that affected or were likely to affect the maritime area, but did not affect it *adversely* and prospective activities that were not likely to affect *adversely* the maritime area.

176. It may be that the object and purpose of this restrictive provision was based on a *de minimis* policy and was intended to preclude claims under Article 9 for available information about activities and measures that did not have adverse impacts on the maritime area. Alternatively, the restrictive character of the language may simply reflect a reluctance on the part of the Contracting Parties, at least at that stage, to undertake a broader obligation. In either case, the restrictive effect of the language [389] in the second category is clear and is the standard which the Tribunal must apply.

177. The relevant parts of the *travaux préparatoires* show that Article 9(2) drew upon Directive 90/313. Article 2(a) of Directive 90/313, which speaks of 'information relating to the environment', also establishes, as the criterion of inclusion, activities and measures 'adversely affecting or likely so to affect ...'.[87] The decision of the ECJ in *Mecklenburg* (para. 150 above),[88] relied upon in this regard by Ireland, is not helpful. The Court was not there concerned with how the word 'adversely' should be interpreted, but with how inclusively the term 'information relating to the environment' should be construed.[89]

178. In fact, the phrase 'information relating to the environment' does not appear in Article 9(2) of the OSPAR Convention. Even if such a phrase did, it is doubtful if that would help Ireland, for it is far from clear that the 14 categories of redacted information identified by Ireland would fall within even that broader class. In any case, even if they did, the ultimate question is not the inclusiveness of the word 'information' in Article 9(2), but the effect to be given to the additional and qualified threshold of adverse effect which is established by the second category of that provision.

179. In the opinion of the Tribunal, Ireland has failed to demonstrate that the 14 categories of redacted items in the PA and ADL Reports, insofar as they may be taken to be activities or measures with respect to the commissioning and operation of a

---

[87] The Tribunal notes a minor discrepancy between the language of the Directive and that of the OSPAR Convention – namely, that the former includes the phrase 'likely *so* to affect' (italics supplied) rather than 'likely to affect'. However, the drafting history in the record gives no indication that the word 'so' was dropped with meaningful intent, and it is the Tribunal's view that the phrases were both intended to express a requirement of adverse effect of potential activities as well as current ones.

[88] Not reproduced in this volume.]

[89] *Supra* note [85], at para. 6. Curiously, the adverb 'adversely' appears to have been dropped in the *Umweltinformationsgesetz* of 8 July 1994 which transposed the Directive into German law.

MOX Plant at Sellafield, are 'information. . . on the state of the maritime area' or, even if they were, are likely adversely to affect the maritime area.

180. Rather than engage the requirement of establishing an adverse effect, Ireland has focused its arguments on the questions of directness of the effect and whether or not the information considered as a whole was 'environmental'. To buttress its arguments, Ireland has sought to rely upon treaties that are as yet unratified and not in force as between the Parties or regional legislative initiatives that have not been finalized nor entered into force for the Parties. Although it is arguable – but in the view of the Tribunal not conclusive – that Ireland's claim might have succeeded under some of these drafts, the Tribunal is not empowered to [**390**] apply legally unperfected instruments. The OSPAR Convention does not adopt a lower threshold requiring no more than an activity or measure that 'affects' rather than one that 'affects adversely' the maritime area.

181. Ireland has also argued that Article 9(2) relates to any environmental information as such. But, wholly aside from the difficult question of whether the PA and ADL Reports dealt with environmental information (as opposed to information about economic justification), the words 'environmental information' do not appear in Article 9(2) nor, indeed, in any part of Article 9. Even if such words did, it is doubtful that the 14 categories listed in paragraph 161 above would come within that class.

182. Hence the Tribunal finds that Ireland has not established that the class of redacted information that it seeks from the PA and ADL Reports under the second category of Article 9(2) falls under Article 9(2).

[. . .]

XI. CONCLUSION

185. For the above reasons, the Tribunal

(i)   by unanimous decision rejects the United Kingdom's request that the Tribunal find that it lacks jurisdiction over the dispute;

(ii) by unanimous decision rejects the United Kingdom's request that Ireland's claims are inadmissible;

(iii) by majority decision rejects the United Kingdom's submission that the implementation of Article 9(1) is assigned exclusively to the competent authorities in the United Kingdom and not to a tribunal established under the OSPAR Convention;

(iv) by majority decision finds that Ireland's claim for information does not fall within Article 9(2) of the OSPAR Convention;

(v)   by majority decision finds that as a consequence, Ireland's claim – that the United Kingdom has breached its obligations under [**391**] Article 9 of the OSPAR Convention, by refusing, on the basis of its understanding of the requirements of Article 9(3)(d), to make available information – does not arise; and

(vi) by unanimous decision decides that each Party will bear its own costs and an equal share of the costs of this arbitration.

DECLARATION OF PROFESSOR W. MICHAEL REISMAN (EXTRACT)

1. I do not concur in the majority's interpretation of Article 9(1) of the 1992 Convention for the Protection of the Marine Environment of the North-East Atlantic ('the OSPAR Convention').[90] In my opinion, Ireland's proposed interpretation of Article 9(1) should have been rejected.

[. . .]

[397] [. . .] DISSENTING OPINION OF GAVAN GRIFFITH QC (EXTRACT)

I here express my reasons for my disagreement with Parts VII and IX of the Majority Opinion and my dissent from the majority's decision to dismiss Ireland's claims.

For the reason that the majority has determined in Part IX that the whole of the redacted material in the PA and ADL Reports is not information within Article 9(2) I have joined in signing the Final Award as dispositive of the dispute.

[. . .]

[405] [. . .] *Findings with respect to Article 9(2) – Part IX Section 2 of the Majority Opinion*
Second category of information

[. . .]

[420] [. . .] *Relationship between the reports and activities likely adversely to affect the marine environment*

93. The defining issue for the Tribunal's consideration is whether a link exists between the harmful activity and the information contained in the PA and ADL Reports.

94. In answering this question, the majority invokes and considers what it calls the 'theory of inclusive causality'. The majority maintains that 'under an interpretative theory of inclusive causality, anything, no matter how remote, which facilitated the performance of an activity is to be deemed part of that activity' (para. 164). This theory is then picked up as the vehicle for denunciation of Ireland's arguments in the following paragraphs of Part IX, with the majority concluding (para. 174) that because Article 9(2) establishes an additional threshold of adversity, the concept of 'inclusive causality' fails.

95. The sources and definition of this 'theory of inclusive causality' embraced by the majority are unknown to me. The expression was not part of either Party's submissions, and it conveys nothing beyond what I discern from the majority's references to it. I have had a nil return on my searches of textbooks on international law, Lexis-Nexis, a bibliography on causation,[91] dictionaries and the like, and I have not found any reference to the semantic linking of the words 'inclusive' and 'causality'. In

---

[90] Convention for the Protection of the Marine Environment of the North-East Atlantic, 22 September 1992, 32 ILM 1069 (1992).

[91] *See* Partial Bibliography on Causation, compiled by Ellery Eels and Dan Hausmann, published at http://www.vanderbilt.edu/quantmetheval/causality.htm.

explanation, it may be that the majority is doing no more than attaching to Ireland's arguments their own creative appellation. If so, such a nomenclature in no way assists in the consideration of the case.

[**421**] 96. Plainly, the PA and ADL Reports are a cause (or, more correctly, one of the causes) necessary for a harmful activity to occur, in the sense that at least the following are demonstrated –

- the submission of the Reports was causally prior to the occurrence of the harmful activity;
- the commissioning of the Reports and the actual harmful activity are two distinct factual events; and that
- in the circumstances, had the Reports not been provided, the harmful activity would not be authorised or occur.

97. I support the United Kingdom's proposition that information falling within the scope of Article 9(2) is required to concern a harmful activity and its effect on the state of the maritime area.[92] However, and contrary to its submissions,[93] I conclude that Article 9(2) does not require this link to be direct and proximate,[94] or even sufficiently proximate.[95] In my opinion, Article 9(2) merely requires the existence of *any* relationship between future negative effects of the MOX Plant operation and the information contained in the PA and ADL Reports. In this regard, the justification exercise carried out by the United Kingdom is of primary importance to establishing this link.

98. The United Kingdom does not contest its obligation to justify the operation of the MOX Plant by a process that 'requires a consideration of whether the benefits of the practice outweigh the detriments'.[96] It also agreed with Ireland that the PA and ADL Report processes were carried out 'within the context of the justification exercise under Euratom Directive 96/29 (replacing Directives 80/836 and 84/467)'.[97]

99. Ireland contended that the obligation to justify requires an identification of the economic costs and benefits of the MOX Plant operation, and that, because of the omission of the economic data from the public domain versions of the PA and ADL Reports, Ireland is unable to assess whether potential negative environmental consequences [**422**] of the MOX Plant operations are justified from the economic standpoint.[98]

---

[92] Counsel for the United Kingdom, Transcript, Day 1 Proceedings, p. 92. United Kingdom's Counter-Memorial, para. 4.12.

[93] *See*, for instance, the following statement: 'the material words of that provision [Article 9(2)] cover only information which is directly and proximately related to the state of the maritime area or to activities or measures adversely affecting or likely to affect the maritime area'. United Kingdom's Counter-Memorial, para. 4.8.

[94] Ireland maintains that even though Article 9(2) does not contain such a condition, both the PA and ADL Reports meet the requirement of directness and proximity. *See* Counsel for Ireland, Transcript, Day 1 Proceedings, pp. 49–50.

[95] United Kingdom's Counter-Memorial, para. 4.12.

[96] *Id.*, footnote 5, at pp. 3–4.

[97] *Id.*, para. 1.3.

[98] Ireland's Memorial, para. 40; Counsel for Ireland, Transcript, Day 1 Proceedings, p. 11 and Day 4 Proceedings, p. 66. *See also* Letter from Renee Dempsey to Michael Wood, 7 August

100. To this extent, it appears that the Parties were agreed that the assessment of benefits, including economic benefits, constitutes an integral part of the justification exercise. They diverged on the issue whether information concerning such benefits in the assessment process may fall within the scope of the definition of Article 9(2).

101. The United Kingdom contended that the information excised from the PA and ADL Reports was of a purely commercial nature[99] and that each of the PA and ADL Reports was an independent review of the business case for the commissioning of the MOX Plant.[100] It submitted that the information ceased to be relevant to the environment[101] upon the Executive concluding that the balance was broadly neutral.

102. Although Ireland accepted that the redacted information related to the commercial activity of the operation of the MOX Plant,[102] it submitted that, nonetheless, such information directly affected the environment[103] and that its commercial character was not determinative of characterisation as information within Article 9(2).[104]

103. Ireland identified that the 'purpose of the PA and ADL Reports is to examine the justification of the MOX Plant, taking into account inter alia the economic costs of its environmental consequences and of measures taken to limit those environmental consequences'.[105] It further submitted that the redacted commercial data is directly related to the environment because it sheds light on –

2001, para. 13. *See also* the Second MacKerron Report which reads: 'This is an admission that without the information sought, the economic case for the SMP cannot be assessed. This goes contrary to Article 6 of the Directive 80/836/EURATOM and Article 6 of Directive 96/269. Ireland, who has a material interest in the environmental consequences of the SMP, is unable to assess without the information sought, whether there ever was an economic justification to the SMP. The statement by David Wadsworth confirms this.' (Appendix B, para. B.1.1.) Ireland's Reply, para. 34.

[99]   United Kingdom's Counter-Memorial, para. 4.10; Counsel for the United Kingdom, Transcript, Day 2 Proceedings, p. 67.

[100] Counsel for the United Kingdom, Transcript, Day 2 Proceedings, p. 96.

[101] *See,* for instance, the following statement: 'given its conclusion on environmental and other issues, that the balance is broadly neutral, the draft decision then went on to consider the economic case concluded that there was a case for approval. This is the point in the stage of consultations at which consideration of the environmental issues was concluded and from this point onwards, essentially, the issues being considered are no longer environmental, ... the issues considered hereafter were the commercial arguments for and against the plant or the process.' Counsel for the United Kingdom, Transcript, Day 2 Proceedings, pp. 68–9.

[102] Counsel for Ireland, Transcript, Day 1 Proceedings, p. 48.

[103] [Counsel for Ireland, Transcript, Day 1 Proceedings, p. 48. *See also* para. 66 of the Written Outline of submissions on behalf of Ireland on file at the Permanent Court of Arbitration (Professor Sands): 'the information relates to commercial activity, but it is (presumably) not in dispute that the consequences of the activity may be harmful to the environment'.]

[104] [Counsel for Ireland, Transcript, Day 1 Proceedings, p. 48. In support of this statement Ireland refers, amongst others, to the case *ex parte Alliance against Birmingham Northern Relief Road:* 'the fact that that Agreement can be described as a commercial document does not mean that it does not contain information which relates to the environment'.]

[105] Written outline of submissions on behalf of Ireland, on file at the offices of the PCA (Professor Sands), para. 62.

[**423**] ... whether all the costs have been properly integrated into the design and operation of the plant; whether best environmental practices are being budgeted for; whether best available technology is being used; whether best available technology will continue to be used in the coming years as technology evolves.[106]

104. The United Kingdom was required to 'justify' the MOX Plant under the applicable approval processes before its operation may be authorised. This relevant obligation first imposed on the United Kingdom in 1980 by Directive 80/836/EURATOM, Article 6, which provided –

> ... the limitation of individual and collective doses resulting from controllable exposures shall be based on the following general principles: (a) every activity resulting in an exposure to ionising radiation shall be justified by the advantages which it produces,[107]

was replaced in 1996 by Directive 96/29/EURATOM, Article 6(1) in terms –

> Member States shall ensure that all new classes or types of practice resulting in exposure to ionising radiation are justified in advance of being adopted by their economic, social or other benefits in relation to the health detriment they may cause.[108]

105. The applicability of these 1996 EURATOM standards to the 'justification test' is accepted by the Parties.[109]

106. The intention and purpose of the United Kingdom to treat economic data as having direct relevance to the environment is discerned from the contents of the DEFRA Decision ('the Decision') on the justification of the MOX Plant, adopted on 3 October 2001,[110] and, in particular, from the circumstances that –

- the essence of the obligation of justification is described by the Decision as: 'the requirement of justification is based on the internationally accepted principle of radiological protection that no practice involving exposure to radiation should be adopted unless [**424**] it produces sufficient benefits to the exposed individuals or to society in general to offset radiation and any other detriment it may cause';[111]

---

[106] Counsel for Ireland, Transcript, Day 1 Proceedings, p. 26. *See also* the following statement: 'the very purpose of the PA and ADL reports is to examine the justification of the MOX plant taking into account all economic costs and those economic costs include the cost of environmental consequences, include the costs of ensuring against environmental damage, include the costs of ensuring against transport accidents, include the costs of ensuring that the plant is safe and complies with all domestic and international environmental standards'. Counsel for Ireland, Transcript, Day 1 Proceedings, p. 46.

[107] Ireland's Memorial, para. 37; United Kingdom's Counter-Memorial, para. 1.13; Counsel for Ireland, Transcript, Day 1 Proceedings, p. 6; Counsel for the United Kingdom, Transcript, Day 2 Proceedings, p. 64.

[108] Ireland's Memorial, para. 38.

[109] *See*, for instance, United Kingdom's Counter-Memorial, paras. 1.3 and 1.11.

[110] [*See* Decision of the Secretary of State for Environment, Food and Rural Affairs and the Secretary of State for Health of 3 October 2001, paras. 56–70. Ireland's Memorial, Annex 5]; United Kingdom's Counter-Memorial, paras. 2.22–2.23; Counsel for the United Kingdom, p. 73.

[111] [*See* Decision of the Secretary of State for Environment, Food and Rural Affairs and the Secretary of State for Health of 3 October 2001, para. 13. Ireland's Memorial, Annex 5.]

- the Decision states that 'the application of the justification test requires the consideration of environmental, safety, economic, social and other benefits and disbenefits';[112]
- the Decision explicitly relies on the EURATOM Regulations as grounds for conclusions regarding the justification of the MOX Plant:[113] paragraph 91 states that 'The Secretaries of State have concluded that the manufacture of MOX fuel is justified in accordance with the requirements of Article 6(1) of Directive 96/26/EURATOM'; and
- paragraphs 56–70 of the Decision extensively analyse environmental detriments that may be caused by the manufacture of MOX fuel as well as safety and security concerns associated with the Plant's operation. These detriments are further balanced against economic and other benefits in paragraphs 71–81. This balance, of environmental concerns *vis-à-vis* future profits, is based primarily on the calculations produced by ADL in its Report.[114]

107. I demur to the contention of the United Kingdom that each of the PA and ADL Reports has nothing to do with the state of the maritime area embraced by the Convention. This is because each was commissioned by the United Kingdom Government in the framework of the mandated justification exercise considering whether economic benefits offset environmental harm.[115] This balancing process was acknowledged in the United Kingdom's Counter-Memorial as requiring 'a consideration of whether the benefits of the practice outweigh the [environmental] detriments'.[116]

108. The significance of the environmental factors during the economic analysis is further confirmed by the explicit language of the ADL Report –

> [*the Plant*] *cannot operate without passing a test of justification*: the benefits of a practice involving ionising radiation need to outweigh any environmental or other detriments.[117]

[**425**] 109. The economic data collected and presented in the PA and ADL Reports was an integral and necessary part of the required process to determine whether the pollution of the marine environment might be legitimised under the nuclear regimes. It was this data that was deployed by the decision-makers (at the executive level of Ministers of State) in the justification exercise for the commissioning of the MOX Plant.

110. At this point, the interdependence between economic data and environmental impacts becomes evident. It is inherent in the justification test that economic analyses may be determinative of whether future environmental harm is legitimate and

---

112 *Id.*, para. 28.
113 *See supra* fn. [111], paras. 13–20.
114 *See*, in particular, paras. 76–7, 85 and 89 of the DEFRA Decision.
115 *Supra* fn. [111], para. 13.
116 United Kingdom's Counter-Memorial, footnote 5, at pp. 3–4.
117 ADL Report, para. 1.

whether the activity that is likely adversely to affect the maritime area should be authorised. Without economic data the exercise of justification becomes meaningless, as the second integral part of the entire test (namely the economic, social, and any other benefits in justification) will be missing.[118]

111. It is the economic analyses that provide the balancing factor to the scales of assessment in a justification process calibrated by the EURATOM Regulations to favour the environment. In the terms of physics, the moment tilting the balance against approval can only be offset by a larger moment arising from the justification exercise. That was the inherent function of the Reports. As information so directly integral to the process of assessment, such information must be characterised as bearing a most direct relevance to the state of the marine environment of the North-East Atlantic. To my mind, it would be futile for the exercise, and also confound the purpose of the justification regime, to qualify by unexpressed limitations the broad definition of information under Article 9(2) (as has the majority) to enable access only to the purely environmental side of the balance and to exclude the information taken into account on the other side of the scale.

112. For these reasons, the fact that the Parties are agreed that the PA and ADL Reports are comprehensive reviews of the business case[119] and contain commercial information,[120] cannot in itself exclude the relevance of the Reports to an activity which is likely to adversely affect the maritime area.

Other considerations

113. Ireland supported its non-restrictive interpretation of Article 9(2) as consistent with international and domestic law and **[426]** practice[121] arising from the Aarhus Convention[122] as confirming the validity of the approach taken by Ireland in its broad definition.[123] It also relied upon cited ECJ jurisprudence,[124] EC legislative proposals and domestic sources.[125]

---

[118] In his testimony, Mr MacKerron alleges that 'justification has been established in prior cases as amounting to net economic advantage which should outweigh any radiological betterment'. *See* Testimony of Mr Gordon MacKerron, Transcript, Day 2 Proceedings, p. 6.

[119] Counsel for the United Kingdom, Transcript, Day 2 Proceedings, p. 96.

[120] Counsel for Ireland, Transcript, Day 1 Proceedings, p. 48.

[121] Ireland's Memorial, para. 100. Counsel for Ireland, Transcript, Day 1 Proceedings, pp. 55–7.

[122] Article 2(3) of the Aarhus Convention reads as follows:

'Environmental information' means any information in written, visual, aural, electronic or any other material form on: . . . (b) Factors, such as substances, energy, noise and radiation, and activities or measures, including administrative measures, environmental agreements, policies, legislation, plans and programmes, affecting or likely to affect the elements of the environment within the scope of subparagraph (a) above, and cost–benefit and other economic analyses and assumptions used in environmental decision-making; . . .

[123] Counsel for Ireland, Transcript, Day 1 Proceedings, p. 52.

[124] *See, e.g., Mecklenburg, supra* note [85], Ireland's Memorial, para. 102. Counsel for Ireland, Transcript, Day 1 Proceedings, p. 55.

[125] Counsel for Ireland, Transcript, Day 1 Proceedings, pp. 56–7

114. The United Kingdom responded that such sources were either irrelevant or inapplicable in the relations between the Parties,[126] or support the United Kingdom's position.[127]

115. Plainly, it is not the function of the Tribunal to consider or determine whether the Aarhus Convention and EC legislation reflect a progressive development of international environmental laws and regulations.[128] Nor to engage in the interpretation of such instruments. The relevant enquiry is whether the terms of these instruments relevantly and permissibly inform the proper interpretation of Article 9(2). In this regard, Article 2(3)(b) of the Aarhus Convention expressly includes in the definition of environmental information 'cost–benefit and other economic analyses and assumptions used in environmental decision-making'.

116. For the reasons stated, I have concluded that the Convention possesses normative and evidentiary value and should be included in the complex of rules of international law in accordance with which the Tribunal is required to resolve the dispute at bar.

117. Further and beyond the Aarhus Convention, other of the materials put before the Tribunal by the Parties confirm regional trends exposing the intention of States and the European Union itself to include economic analyses in the definition of environmental [**427**] information.[129] At the least, these trends appear to broaden the content of the definition of environmental information so as explicitly to include cost–benefit and other economic analyses.

118. Be that as it may, more significantly for the issues of definition arising under the OSPAR Convention, the EU and United Kingdom proposals noted in the previous paragraph refer to the *clarification* of the existing formulation of Directive 90/313

---

[126] United Kingdom's Rejoinder, para. 21. Counsel for the United Kingdom, Transcript, Day 2 Proceedings, p. 51.

[127] *See*, for instance, the United Kingdom's interpretation of the conclusions reached by the ECJ in the *Mecklenburg* case. United Kingdom's Counter-Memorial, para. 4.11.

[128] In the UK's view, the definition of the Aarhus Convention reflects 'an exercise of progressive development of the law relating to "environmental information"'. United Kingdom's Counter-Memorial, para. 4.13.

[129] *See*, in particular, Counsel for Ireland, Transcript, Day 1 Proceedings, pp. 68–71; United Kingdom's Counter-Memorial, para. 4.13. *See also* 'Report from the Commission to the Council and the European Parliament on the experience gained in the application of Council Directive 90/313/EEC on freedom of access to information on the environment' (COM(2000) 400 final). *See* Counsel for the United Kingdom, Transcript, Day 2 Proceedings, p. 87; Outline of written submissions on behalf of the United Kingdom (Mr Wordsworth); the 'Proposal for a Directive of the European Parliament and of the Council on public access to environmental information' (COM(2000) 402 final. Counsel for the United Kingdom, Transcript, Day 2 Proceedings, p. 88); 'Amended Proposal for a Directive of the European Parliament and of the Council on public access to environmental information' (COM(2001) 303 final); Common Position 'with a view to adopting Directive 2003/4/EC on public access to environmental information and repealing Council Directive 90/313/EEC' (Counsel for the United Kingdom, Transcript, Day 2 Proceedings, pp. 88–90); DEFRA 'Proposals for a revised public access to environmental information consultation paper' (Ireland, Authorities Bundle 1, Tab 5, paras. 13–15. *See also* Counsel for Ireland, Transcript, Day 1 Proceedings, pp. 52–3. *But see* Oral Pleadings, Counsel for the United Kingdom, Transcript, Day 2 Proceedings, p. 88).

rather than the adoption of a new definition.[130] This 'clarification' approach also is evident from the unambiguous language of the 2002 EC Common Position[131] expressed by the EU Commission as based on the experience gained by Member States in the operation of Directive 90/313.[132]

119. In its ordinary sense, such a 'clarification' does not so much extend meaning but merely confirms the content of existing meaning, including in the context of definitions within Article 9 of the OSPAR Convention.

120. Directive 2003/4 on public access to environmental information entered into force on 14 February 2003, to replace Directive 90/313,[133] and confirms that its main purpose is to bring EU law in [428] compliance with the Aarhus Convention (para. 5) and environmental information is defined as –

> The definition of environmental information should be *clarified* so as to encompass information in any form on the state of the environment, on factors, measures or activities affecting or likely to affect the environment or designed to protect it, *on cost– benefit and economic analyses used within the framework of such measures* or activities and also information on the state of human health and safety, including the contamination of the food chain, conditions of human life, cultural sites and built structures in as much as they are, or may be, affected by any of those matters.[134] (emphasis added)

121. Again, it is the language of clarification, rather than of extension or substitution, that is invoked. As Article 9(2) is nearly identical to the language of the old Directive, at the least the drafters of the Directive 2003/4 must be taken to have understood the definition of Article 9(2) in the same way. Hence, as much as for Directive 90/313 that it replaced, Directive 2003/4 thereby appears also relevant to understanding the meaning of 'information' under the Article 9(2) definition by making explicit that which already was implicit under the OSPAR Convention.[135]

---

[130] *See*, for instance, para. 14 of the DEFRA 'Proposals for a revised public access to environmental information consultation paper': 'the definition of environmental information is clarified to refer specifically to the atmosphere, landscape, biological diversity etc. It is also defined to include cost benefit economic analyses and other assumptions used in the decision making process.' Para. 15 further states that 'These are minor changes. They are not expected to broaden the practical application of the regime.'

[131] Para. 10 of the Common Position reads: 'The definition of environmental information should be clarified so as to encompass . . .' Common Position 'with a view to adopting Directive 2003/4/EC on public access to environmental information and repealing Council Directive 90/313/EEC' (Counsel for the United Kingdom, Transcript, Day 2, p. 90).

[132] 'Report from the Commission to the Council and the European Parliament on the experience gained in the application of Council Directive 90/313/EEC on freedom of access to information on the environment', COM(2000) 400 final. *See* Counsel for the United Kingdom, Transcript, Day 2 Proceedings, p. 88; Outline of written submissions on behalf of the United Kingdom (Mr Wordsworth).

[133] [Directive 2003/4/EC on Public Access to Environmental Information and Repealing Council Directive 90/313/EEC, 2003 OJ (L41).]

[134] *Id.*, para. 10.

[135] Ireland's Memorial, para. 100. Counsel for Ireland, Transcript, Day 1 Proceedings, p. 52. Counsel for the United Kingdom, Transcript, Day 2 Proceedings, p. 89.

122. It follows that international environmental regulations as binding as Directive 2003 / 4 now define that facts similar in nature to the PA and ADL Reports fall within the definition of disclosable information. Since Directive 2003 / 4 presently is binding on the United Kingdom, it is not amenable to be characterised as soft law or progressive development of law that is irrelevant to the interpretation of Article 9(2). And, contrary to the United Kingdom's view,[136] there is now a clear consensus and practice with the European Union as to the meaning and application of the Aarhus Convention's terms.

123. I regret that I have not had the advantage of the submissions of the Parties as to the relevance of Directive 2003 / 4 that came into force during the pendency of this Tribunal's award. My conditional conclusion is that Directive 2003 / 4 is confirmatory (but certainly not determinative) of the interpretation of Article 9(2).

Conclusion on second category of information

124. For the reasons stated, I am of the opinion that the production of MOX fuel falls within the scope of the second category of Article 9(2) **[429]** to the extent that it constitutes an activity which has potential of adversely affecting the maritime area of the Irish Sea, and that, properly characterised, the entire balancing process, including consideration of the economic case in justification, is an enquiry concerning information within the terms of Article 9(2).

Third category of information

125. The Tribunal's *Decision No. 5*, to which the Parties responded, raised with the Parties the question whether the information contained in the PA and ADL Reports may fall within the third category of information within Article 9(2) as related to an activity or measure introduced in accordance with the OSPAR Convention.

126. Plainly, the three categories of information are not disjunctive, and material may fall within more than one category. For this reason it appears to me appropriate to consider whether the relevant material also constitutes information under the third category. As I am of the opinion that in any event it falls under the second category this enquiry is not essential for my dissent. However, as the majority is of the contrary view on the second category, it appears to me that the majority determination is in error and incomplete by then failing to consider the third category.

127. For information to fall under the third category a relationship has to be established between an activity or measure and a specific provision of the Convention in accordance with which such a measure has been undertaken and activity carried out.

128. In this regard, the third category does not require a direct relationship between the state of the maritime area and information on such activities or measures. I reject the United Kingdom's contention to the contrary as in that case the second and third

---

[136] United Kingdom's Counter-Memorial, para. 4.13.

categories would be otiose as subsumed in the first category. In effect, Article 9(2) then would be read as if it provided for 'any available information . . . on the state of the maritime area, *and in particular* information on activities or measures . . .'. Plainly such a construction is not open to be made.

129. A different issue is whether a measure is directly related to the state of the marine environment. The examples used by the United Kingdom's response to the Tribunal's *Decision No. 5* demonstrate the link between a measure and the state of the marine area. In my view, this is not an absolute requirement for all cases. However, even if one accepts the United Kingdom's proposition that a direct relationship is required in all instances, clearly such relationship is evident here.

130. In the context of the OSPAR Convention, I support the majority's interpretation (para. 171) of the term 'measure' as a regulatory **[430]** initiative 'by any part of the governmental apparatus of the Contracting Parties with respect to matters covered by the OSPAR Convention'. I derive support for this meaning from the ECJ Judgment in the *Mecklenburg* case,[137] where the ECJ has helpfully defined the term 'measure' as an 'act linked to an individual case directed towards a specific aim and having determinative effects'.[138] The ECJ further found that this term serves merely 'to make it clear that the acts governed by the directive [whose language, as recognised by both parties, is nearly identical to Article 9(2)] included all forms of administrative activity'.[139]

131. The authorisation of the MOX Plant undoubtedly qualifies as a measure undertaken in accordance with the OSPAR Convention. It is a form of administrative activity exercised by the United Kingdom government which is directed towards a specific aim and designed to further the disparate objectives of the OSPAR Convention. The relevant provision in accordance with which this complex of measures was introduced, is Article 2(1) of Annex I –

> Point source discharges to the maritime area, and releases into water or air which reach and may affect the maritime area, shall be strictly subject to authorisation or regulation by the competent authorities of the Contracting Parties. Such authorisation or regulation shall, in particular, implement relevant decisions of the Commission which bind the relevant Contracting Party.

132. The justification of the MOX Plant that the United Kingdom undertook by way of arranging public consultations and commissioning and considering the Reports clearly falls within such an authorisation. The process, including obtaining the PA and ADL Reports, was a necessary measure introduced in accordance with the OSPAR Convention designed to protect the marine environment. In its written response to the Decision Ireland has reiterated that the main reason for its enquiry was to assure itself that the authorisation of the MOX Plant was carried out in a manner

---

[137] *See Mecklenburg, supra* note [85].
[138] *See* para. 18 of the Judgment.
[139] *Id.*, para. 20.

consistent with the OSPAR Convention.[140] It sought information on the measures introduced in accordance with the OSPAR Convention that could be found in the Reports.[141]

[...]

[431] [...] *Summary*
In summary, I identify the principal vitiating errors of the majority in finding that none of the redacted items was information within the definition of Article 9(2) arose from its approach of –

(1) interpreting the OSPAR Convention as if it were an isolated legal regime without regard to its context within a continuum of emerged and emerging legal instruments concerning the environment, including those in a relevant sense binding on the Parties;

(2) refusing to examine the PA and ADL Reports as a whole in light of the definition of Article 9(2) and suggesting instead to test each of the 14 categories of redacted items against the definition;

(3) confining, without any textual support, the second and third categories of information of Article 9(2) to being 'on the state of the maritime area';

(4) finding, incorrectly, that future radioactive discharges into the Irish Sea do not constitute an activity which is likely adversely to **[432]** affect the state of the maritime area within the second category of information of Article 9(2);

(5) assuming, incorrectly, for the second category of information the onus of proof was on Ireland to establish that the MOX fuel production is an activity which is likely adversely to affect the maritime area;

(6) failing to characterise, for the second category of information, the justification exercise, of which the PA and ADL Reports were an integral part, as concerning the state of the maritime area; and

(7) failing adequately to examine the relevance of the third category of information of Article 9(2).

Conclusion
For these reasons I dissent from the dispositive conclusion of the majority accepting the United Kingdom's submissions that the whole of the redacted materials in the PA and ADL Reports is not information within Article 9(2) of the OSPAR Convention and that a final award presently should be made dismissing the claims of Ireland.

---

[140] *See* Letter from the Agent for Ireland to the Secretary of the Tribunal (21 February 2003), footnote 4 on p. 2 providing a summary of Ireland's claims to that effect.
[141] *See*, for instance, the following statement: 'what is at issue here is a measure and the measure is the process of justification'. Counsel for Ireland, Transcript, Day 4 Proceedings, p. 56.

I am of the opinion that the whole of the PA and ADL Reports, including the redacted items, is information within Article 9(1) and (2) and that on such finding being made the dispute called for further hearing and consideration of the contention by the United Kingdom that Article 9(3)(d) justified the redactions made to these Reports.

[Report: 126 *ILR* 338]

IV

DECISIONS OF THE UNITED NATIONS COMPENSATION COMMISSION

Report and Recommendations made by the Panel of Commissioners Appointed to Review the Well Blowout Control Claim

United Nations Compensation Commission, Geneva

18 December 1996[1] (Philip, *Chairman*; Ajibola and Antoun, *Members*)

Claims – large claims – United Nations Compensation Commission – claim by the Kuwait Oil Company ('KOC') for the cost of extinguishing fires at the oil well-heads in Kuwait – evidence of cause of damage – costs – evidence that costs actually incurred – attribution of costs to particular claims – use of expert accountancy reports to verify costs

Damage and compensation – damages – principles – claim by KOC for the cost of extinguishing fires at the oil well-heads in Kuwait – heads of damage – general principles of international law – mitigation of damages – interest – date from which interest to be awarded – date taken to be 19 October 1991 – use of different date for calculating interest in other claims

Pollution – environmental damage resulting from Iraq's invasion and occupation of Kuwait – Security Council Resolution 687 – Iraq responsible for such damage – provision for claims by States and international organisations in respect of environmental damage – threat to environment caused by fires at oil well-heads in Kuwait – claim by corporation – whether admissible

International organisations – United Nations – Security Council – powers – affirmation of Iraq's liability to compensate for losses caused by invasion and occupation of Kuwait – Security Council Resolution 687 – establishment of United Nations Compensation Commission – nature and function of Commission – standing of claimants

Powers and procedures of tribunals – international tribunals – United Nations Compensation Commission – nature and functions – hearings before Panel of

---

[1] The Report and Recommendations were signed on 15 November 1996. Governing Council Decision 40 can be found at p. 625 below.

*Commissioners – quasi-judicial character – application of rules of due process –
procedure – consideration of evidence – overlap between different claims*

*Responsibility and liability – State responsibility – losses occasioned by invasion
of another State – Iraqi invasion of Kuwait – Iraqi responsibility for losses
resulting directly from invasion and occupation – proof of causation – damage
to oil wells – allegation by Iraq that damage caused by Coalition armed forces –
whether relieving Iraq of responsibility – application of general principles of
State responsibility by United Nations Compensation Commission*

*War and armed conflict – consequences – responsibility for damage occasioned
by armed conflict – liability of aggressor – Iraqi invasion and occupation of
Kuwait – responsibility of Iraq for losses resulting directly from invasion and
occupation – damage to oil well-heads in Kuwait – whether attributable to
sabotage by Iraqi forces – whether caused by Coalition armed forces' bombing
campaign – whether Iraq responsible if damage caused by military operations
of Coalition – United Nations Compensation Commission*

SUMMARY   *The facts*   This claim was submitted under category 'E' by
the Kuwait Oil Company ('KOC'), a wholly owned subsidiary of Kuwait
Petroleum Corporation ('KPC') which in turn was wholly owned by
the State of Kuwait. KOC sought compensation in the amount of US
$950,715,662[2] for the costs it claimed to have incurred in planning and
executing the work of extinguishing the well-head fires that were burning
upon the withdrawal of Iraqi forces from Kuwait; stopping the flow of
oil and gas from those wells; and making the well-heads safe for the reinstatement of production (the 'Well Blowout Control ("WBC") exercise').
KOC stated that, after the Iraqi invasion of Kuwait, the company became
aware that Iraqi forces were placing explosives around oil installations
in Kuwait. They then devised a plan called 'Al-Awda'[3] ('Al-Awda project')
to cope with the anticipated destruction of the Kuwaiti oil sector. The
WBC exercise was one of the priorities of this plan. Contracts were concluded with various fire fighting and support services companies and a
contract was entered into with the international engineering company
Bechtel Limited ('Bechtel') under which Bechtel agreed to manage the
entire Al-Awda project.

Although the claim was filed by KOC, not all contracts relating to the
WBC exercise were signed by that company; some were concluded by

---

[2] The claimant had originally sought compensation in the amount of US $951,630,871. However,
the amount sought was reduced after the oral proceedings by US $915,209.
[3] 'Al-Awda' means 'the Return'.

the State of Kuwait, KPC or Kuwait Petroleum International Ltd (KPI), another subsidiary of KPC. Funding for the WBC exercise was ultimately provided by the Kuwaiti Ministry of Oil. KOC stated, however, that the contracts referred to above were assigned to KOC and that any payments made by the Government of Kuwait or KPC were charged to KOC, to whom any assets purchased were assigned. KOC claimed for costs incurred by KOC and recorded on the accounting system maintained by KOC Financial Services Department ('KOC costs') as well as costs associated with the Al-Awda project recorded by Bechtel as project managers ('KOC–Al-Awda costs'). All these costs were stated to have been paid for by KOC.

According to KOC, of the 914 operational wells in Kuwait, 798 wellheads were detonated by Iraqi forces during the closing stages of Iraq's occupation of Kuwait, of which 603 were on fire, 45 were gushing oil but not on fire and 150, although damaged, were neither on fire nor gushing oil. KOC alleged that all of this damage was the result of the deliberate firing of the oilfields of Kuwait by retreating Iraqi forces.

In its submissions to the Panel, Iraq denied any responsibility for the oil-well fires. It stated that no explosives had been planted by the Iraqi armed forces and alleged that the fires were the result of bombings by Coalition armed forces. It also challenged the authenticity of documents submitted by KOC, which KOC had alleged were official Iraqi documents left behind by retreating Iraqi forces. These documents, *inter alia*, purported to allocate 'responsibilities for well demolition' among the various units of the Iraqi armed forces. They also contained instructions for 'deferred detonation' of certain oilfields and detailed 'fire plans for the destruction of oil wells'.

Iraq asked that the Governing Council allow payment out of the Compensation Fund for the conduct of Iraq's legal defence and requested that the Panel postpone the oral hearings until the Governing Council had taken a decision on the above request. It also requested the Panel to determine, under Decision 35 of the Governing Council,[4] that it required time in excess of that available under Article 38(d) of the Provisional Rules for Claims Procedure[5] to complete its review of the present claim. After the Panel refused the requests addressed to it, the Iraqi delegation withdrew from the proceedings. However, on 2 September 1996, Iraq requested that the Governing Council grant Iraq additional

---

[4] *Further Procedures for Review of Claims under Article 38*, UN Doc. S/AC.24/Dec.35, reported at 109 *ILR* 655.

[5] Decision 10 of the Governing Council, UN Doc. S/AC.26/1992/10, reported at 109 *ILR* 597.

time 'to produce a Comprehensive Statement of Defence on the WBC Claim'.

Held by the Panel of Commissioners   (1)   Although reference to claims for environmental damage and specifically to claims for 'expenses directly relating to fighting oil fires' (Decision 7 of the Governing Council, paragraph 35)[6] had been made in the context of Category 'F' claims submitted by governments, claims for those sorts of losses could also be filed under category 'E' by a corporation.

(a)   Categorisation of a claim as an 'E' or 'F' claim did not necessarily entail any substantive consequences in terms of the law applicable to such claims. It should be noted that Security Council Resolution 687 (1991)[7] referred, *inter alia*, to 'environmental damage and the depletion of natural resources' as potential heads of claim, without making any qualification as to the legal subject or entity eligible to make such claims.

(b)   It could not have been the intention of the Governing Council when drafting Decision 7 to exclude the applicability of the criteria listed in paragraph 35 to a claim filed by a corporate entity where that entity had suffered the type of losses described in that paragraph.

(c)   In any event, costs incurred in fighting fires at oil wells would be compensable under the general language of paragraph 21(c) of Decision 7, the provision relied upon by the claimant.

(d)   Under general principles of international law concerning the mitigation of damages, the claimant was not only permitted but indeed obligated to take reasonable steps to fight the oil-well fires in order to mitigate losses to property of Kuwaiti oil sector companies and the State of Kuwait.

(2)   In view of the fact that the costs incurred in the WBC exercise had ultimately been borne, or shared, by the Ministry of Oil and KPC, the KOC claim had to be considered to have been made by KOC on behalf of Kuwait's public oil sector as a whole. Consequently, the Government of Kuwait and KPC would be bound by the decision rendered in the claim and would thus be estopped from bringing the same claim before the United Nations Compensation Commission ('UNCC').

(3)   Although part of the damage for which compensation was sought might have been the result of the allied bombing, the bulk of the oil-well fires had been caused by explosives placed on the well-heads and detonated by Iraqi armed forces. In any event, under Decision 7, Iraq was

---

[6] *Criteria for Additional Categories of Claims*, UN Doc. S/AC.26/1991/7/Rev.1, reported at 109 *ILR* 583.

[7] Extracted at 109 *ILR* 553.

responsible for any direct loss, damage or injury suffered as a result of military operations conducted by either side during the Kuwait conflict and was therefore liable to compensate KOC even if the damage had been caused by Coalition armed forces. Decision 7 was in accordance with general principles of international law.

(4)   The task of the Panel was to determine whether all the costs included by KOC in the WBC Claim could be considered to be a direct result of Iraq's invasion and occupation of Kuwait and to verify that these costs had in fact been incurred by KOC in the WBC exercise. Although the function of the Panel was quasi-judicial, rather than judicial (paras. 20 and 25 of the Secretary-General's Report),[8] every effort had to be made to ensure that the requirements of due process were met. Given the time-frames for review of claims, the Panel had not relied solely on the contributions of the Parties, but had assumed an investigative role that went beyond using the adversarial method of verifying claims.

(5)   The Panel was satisfied that the costs forming the subject-matter of the WBC Claim had in fact been incurred by the claimant and that reasonable measures had been taken to ensure that the costs had not exceeded what could have been expected in the circumstances. These findings were without prejudice to the issue of whether all the costs included in the WBC Claim had been incurred in the execution of the WBC exercise and could thus be verified in the WBC Claim, rather than being included in other claims by KOC or other Kuwait public sector claimants. The findings were also without prejudice to the issue whether all the costs were compensable as loss, damage or injury sustained by the claimant as a direct result of Iraq's invasion and occupation of Kuwait.

(6)   The WBC exercise could not have been performed without the purchase of equipment, buildings and other facilities. A certain amount of capital expenditure was, therefore, appropriately included in the WBC Claim. However, in view of the fact that these assets continued to be used after the WBC exercise, in particular for the reinstatement of KOC's assets damaged or destroyed as a result of the invasion and occupation, the Panel was unable to recommend compensation in full for capital expenditure in purchasing such assets in the present claim. A portion of the capital expenditure included in the present claim had to be allocated to the Physical Assets Claim, filed by KOC with the UNCC on 27 June 1994. This allocation was to be done on the basis of the length of time during

---

[8] *Report of the Secretary-General Pursuant to Paragraph 19 of Security Council Resolution 687 (1991)*, UN Doc. S/22559, reported at 109 *ILR* 554.

which the capital assets in question were used. Of the entire period during which the assets in question were used, approximately 22 per cent could be apportioned to the WBC exercise and approximately 78 per cent to the reconstruction effort. The Panel therefore determined that 22 per cent, or US $66,859,457, of the total value of the capital assets (US $303,906,625) purchased could be verified in the present claim. The remaining portion, US $237,047,168, had to be included in KOC's Physical Assets Claim.

(7)   Of the costs common to the WBC exercise and other projects undertaken concurrently by KOC, only that portion that related to the WBC exercise could properly be verified in the present claim. The other portion had to be verified in other KOC claims. Taking into account the manual labour charges, the Panel determined that 80 per cent of these common costs could be verified in this claim and 20 per cent had to be verified in KOC's other claims.

(8)   KOC's costs claimed under the heading 'international fire fighting and support services contractors' were compensable as loss, damage or injury sustained by KOC as a direct result of Iraq's invasion and occupation of Kuwait.

(9)   While it was debatable whether post-capping (making the well-heads permanently safe after the fires had been put out) technically constituted part of the WBC exercise or part of the reconstruction effort, the award of a portion of the post-capping costs in the present claim would not create a risk of double compensation. The post-capping costs included in the WBC Claim were compensable as loss, damage or injury sustained by KOC as a direct result of Iraq's invasion and occupation of Kuwait.

(10)   Costs under the heading 'sundries', including, *inter alia*, 'legal costs' incurred by KOC in the arrangement and control of the WBC contracts and 'consulting costs' in respect of the operation of KOC's accounting system after the liberation, were compensable as loss, damage or injury sustained by KOC as a direct result of Iraq's invasion and occupation of Kuwait. However, in the light of the finding regarding common costs, only 80 per cent of those costs could be verified in the WBC Claim.

(11)   Payments made by KOC to fire fighting personnel that were part of its regular staff could not be regarded as a loss, damage or injury resulting from Iraq's invasion and occupation of Kuwait as KOC would have had to make such salary payments even if there had been no invasion.

(12)   Costs under the heading 'fire fighting support' (the costs of providing the infrastructure within which the WBC exercise was performed) and the heading 'construction equipment' (consisting mainly of the costs incurred in purchasing and renting equipment) were compensable as loss, damage or injury sustained by KOC as a direct result of Iraq's invasion and

occupation of Kuwait. However, a portion of the total amount claimed for capital expenditure under these headings had to be allocated to the Physical Assets Claim.

(13)   Of the amount claimed under the 'project management and related services' heading (expenditure incurred by Bechtel in organising and managing the Al-Awda Project), 20 per cent related to KOC's Physical Assets Claim and other KOC claims and could not, therefore, properly be verified in the present claim. The remaining costs had been incurred by KOC in the execution of the WBC exercise and were a direct result of the Iraqi invasion. They were therefore compensable.

(14)   Costs incurred in removing unexploded ordnance, claimed under the heading 'support facilities', could not properly be verified in the present claim and were to be included in KOC's 'Removal of Unexploded Ordnance Claim'. Furthermore only 22 per cent of capital expenditure under this heading could be verified in the present claim. The remainder was to be verified in the Physical Assets Claim. In addition, all of the costs claimed under this heading were to be considered common costs and only 80 per cent of those costs could be verified in the present claim. The Panel was satisfied, however, that costs under the 'support facilities' heading verified in the present claim had been incurred by KOC in the performance of the WBC exercise and were a direct result of the Iraqi invasion. They were therefore compensable.

(15)   Given that costs claimed under the heading 'freight' (charges made in connection with shipping and handling of supplies and equipment purchased for use in the Al-Awda project) were almost exclusively linked to equipment and other capital assets, they were to be treated like capital expenditure. Accordingly, only 22 per cent of the costs claimed under this heading was to be considered as relating to the WBC exercise and capable of being verified under the present claim. However, that 22 per cent of the freight costs was compensable as loss, damage or injury arising directly from the Iraqi invasion and occupation of Kuwait.

(16)   The heading 'communications' (costs associated with installing temporary communication facilities essential for the WBC exercise) included a substantial amount of capital expenditure, only 22 per cent of which could be verified in the present claim. Furthermore, the revenue expenditure claimed under the 'communications' heading consisted of costs incurred in supporting the Al-Awda project as a whole and therefore common costs, 20 per cent of which were to be verified in KOC's other claims. The Panel determined, however, that the remaining 'communications' costs were necessary to support the execution of the WBC exercise and were therefore compensable.

(17)   Costs claimed under the heading 'Jebel Ali staging area' included capital expenditure and only 22 per cent of this capital expenditure could be verified in the present claim. The revenue expenditure under this heading constituted common costs, only 80 per cent of which could be verified in the present claim. Subject to these determinations, the Panel determined that the costs claimed under this heading were compensable as loss, damage or injury sustained by the claimant as a direct result of Iraq's invasion and occupation of Kuwait.

(18)   Interest should be awarded on the WBC Claim as of 15 October 1991, that date being considered to be the date on which the loss to the claimant occurred.

The Panel recommended that KOC, on behalf of Kuwait's public oil sector as a whole, should be paid US $610,048,547 as compensation for the costs incurred in the execution of the WBC exercise. KOC should be allowed to amend its Physical Assets and Related Damage Claim to include 78 per cent of the capital expenditure claimed in the present claim and to amend its other claims to include 20 per cent of common costs.

Note   By its Decision 40, the Governing Council approved the recommendations made by the Panel.

There follows

Report and Recommendations Made by the Panel of Commissioners Appointed to Review the Well Blowout Control Claim (the 'WBC Claim'), 18 December 1996 (extract)

[...]

[500] [...] III. PRELIMINARY ISSUES

A. Categorization of the claim

47. As noted in paragraph 1,[10] the WBC [Well Blowout Control] Claim is submitted on a category 'E' (corporate) claim form. The Claimant states that, in terms of the

---

[9]   The full text is not reproduced in this volume but can be found at 109 *ILR* 485.

[10   Paragraphs referred to throughout the Report which are not reproduced in this volume can be found at 109 *ILR* 485.]

loss types listed on the category 'E' claim form, the WBC Claim falls within the category of real property claims and is for compensation for losses which are compensable under United Nations Security Council resolution 687 (1991) and sub-paragraph (c) of paragraph 21 of Governing Council decision 7.[11]

48. The issue arose in the course of the proceedings as to whether the WBC Claim is properly categorized as a category 'E' (corporate) claim, or whether it should be more properly submitted as a category 'F' (government) claim. A related question is whether KOC is the proper party to assert the Claim.

49. The proper categorization of the WBC Claim was addressed by the Panel in the interrogatories annexed to the Procedural Order of 27 November 1995 and subsequently also by Iraq. Taking note of the Claimant's argument to the effect that 'the WBC Claim is for compensation for losses which have been specifically identified as compensable by the Governing Council in sub-paragraph (c) of paragraph 21 of decision 7, i.e., direct losses suffered as a result of actions by officials or agents of the Government of Iraq', the Panel put the following questions to the Claimant:

> The Panel notes that the provision cited by the Claimant, sub-paragraph (c) of paragraph 21 of Governing Council decision 7, is part of section II of that **[501]** decision, entitled 'Criteria for processing claims of corporations and other entities', and that the WBC Claim has been brought by KOC, a corporation.
>
> The Panel further notes that paragraph 35 of Governing Council decision 7, which is part of section III of that decision, entitled 'Criteria for processing claims of governments and international organizations', provides that 'payments are available with respect to direct environmental damage and the depletion of natural resources, as a result of Iraq's unlawful invasion and occupation of Kuwait'. Sub-paragraph (a) of paragraph 35 further specifies that '[t]his will include losses or expenses resulting from . . . [a]batement and prevention of environmental damage, including *expenses directly relating to fighting oil fires* and stemming the flow of oil in coastal and international waters; . . .' (Emphasis added.)
>
> It appears to the Panel that, according to its wording, sub-paragraph (a) of paragraph 35 of Governing Council decision 7 was specifically intended to apply, *inter alia*, to the type of losses or expenses for which compensation is being sought in the WBC Claim.
>
> *Question 2.1*: In view of the above, can the Claimant clarify the submission of the WBC Claim as a category 'E' (corporate) claim? [. . .]
>
> *Question 2.2*: More particularly, what is the Claimant's understanding of the relationship between sub-paragraph (c) of paragraph 21 and sub-paragraph (a) of paragraph 35 of decision 7?

50. The Claimant stated in its response that the WBC Claim is properly filed as a category 'E' claim, 'because it seeks to recover compensation for financial costs

---

[11] Governing Council decision 7, 'Criteria for Additional Categories of Claims' (S/AC.26/1991/7/ Rev. 1).

incurred by KOC, a corporation, as a direct result of damage and destruction caused by Iraq in the oil fields operated by KOC'. The Claimant went on to state:

> KOC agrees with the Panel's further assessment that the WBC Claim may be charac-terised as a claim for 'losses or expenses resulting from . . . abatement and prevention of environmental damage, including expenses directly relating to fighting oil fires and stemming the flow of oil'. The WBC Claim arises from KOC's expenses incurred in fighting and extinguishing the oil fires.
>
>   . . .
>
> KOC considers that the types of compensable loss expressly referred to by the Gov-erning Council in decision 7, rev 1, were not intended to be exhaustive, but to comprise illustrations of the types of situation which may give rise to compensable losses, so long as the principal jurisdictional criterion is established: being the basic statement of Iraq's liability contained in paragraph 16 of UNSC resolution 687 (1991).
>
>   . . .
>
> [I]n its categorisation of the various types of payments referred to in decision 7, rev 1, the Governing Council was making a *procedural* distinction, not – it is submitted – a substantive one. Corporations such as KPC can fall into both 'E' and 'F' categories for the purposes of decision 7, rev 1. The fact that paragraph 35 of decision 7, rev 1 is appended to the latter part of the decision dealing with 'F' Claims owes more to the evolution of the drafting of the decision than to any deliberate policy of the Governing Council to [502] *exclude* claimants from being compensated for such losses. Such a policy would have been inconceivable (and beyond the powers of the Governing Council ordained by the Security Council by UNSCR 692). (Emphasis in original.)

51. The issue before the Panel is the apparent inconsistency between the submis-sion of the WBC Claim as a category 'E' claim, on the one hand, and the criteria applicable to the subject matter of the Claim, on the other. While under Governing Council decision 7 'public sector enterprises' such as KOC were envisaged to file their claims under category 'E', the criteria that appear to specifically apply to the WBC Claim are set out under category 'F'. The Panel concurs in the view that the categorization of a claim as an 'E' or 'F' claim does not necessarily entail any substan-tive consequences in terms of the law applicable to such claim. In this connection, it should be noted that paragraph 16 of Security Council resolution 687 (1991) provides for the compensability of, *inter alia*, 'environmental damage and the depletion of natural resources', without making any qualifications as to the legal subject or entity eligible to make such claims.

52. In light of the above, the Panel concludes that it could not have been the Gov-erning Council's intention, when drafting decision 7, to exclude the applicability of the criteria listed under paragraph 35 of decision 7 to a claim filed by a corporate entity, should the types of losses described thereunder, including costs incurred in fighting the oil-well fires, have been sustained by such an entity, or to declare corpo-rations ineligible to seek compensation for such losses. Indeed, paragraphs 17 and 31 of decision 7 specifically state that '[t]he following criteria are not intended to resolve every issue that may arise' with respect to category 'E' and 'F' claims.

53. The Panel is also of the opinion that, even if paragraph 35 of decision 7 were not considered to apply to claims brought by corporations, costs incurred in fighting oil-well fires would in any event be compensable under the general language of sub-paragraph (c) of paragraph 21 of Governing Council decision 7, which is the provision relied on by the Claimant in its Statement of Claim, see *supra* paragraph 47.

54. Furthermore, the Panel notes that under the general principles of international law relating to mitigation of damages, which have also been recognized by the Governing Council[12] the Claimant was not only permitted but indeed obligated to take reasonable steps to fight [**503**] the oil-well fires in order to mitigate the loss, damage or injury being caused by those fires to the property of the Kuwaiti oil sector companies and the State of Kuwait.

B. The Claimant's standing

55. As described in paragraph 41, the Claimant acknowledges that, although the costs incurred in the WBC Exercise were initially expended by KOC, the WBC Exercise was ultimately funded by the Ministry of Oil. Subsequently, according to the Annual Report of KPC for the financial year 1992/1993,

> . . . an agreement was reached [between the Ministry of Oil and KPC] such that part of the costs charged to the Ministry resulting from the Iraqi invasion would be repaid over a period of thirty six months. The repayment takes the form of a monthly deduction from the costs of crude oil charged by the Ministry to the Corporation. At the year end 29 instalments were outstanding amounting to some KD 160 million.

56. Given that the costs incurred in the WBC Exercise were ultimately borne and shared by the Ministry of Oil and KPC, the issue arises whether KOC is the proper claimant in this Claim. In the course of the proceedings, the Panel asked the Claimant to elaborate on this point. The Claimant argued in response as follows:

> The WBC Claim has been made by KOC because it is the entity which initially met the costs when incurred. The Ministry of Oil had to provide the funding for KOC to pay for the WBC exercise (as it does for all of KOC's operations); otherwise KOC would have had to borrow the funds. This is the normal funding mechanism used within Kuwait's Oil Sector, and does not affect the decision that KOC is the appropriate party to make the claim. The financial arrangements in place in Kuwait's Oil Sector will ensure that there is no duplication of compensation and KOC confirms that neither any other Oil Sector entity nor the State of Kuwait/Ministry of Oil has made a claim to the UNCC for the costs included in the WBC Claim.

57. The Panel also asked the Claimant to clarify as to why KOC, the operating company of Kuwait's oil sector, was the claimant in this Claim, and whether KOC

---

[12] See Governing Council decision 15, 'Compensation for Business Losses Resulting from Iraq's Unlawful Invasion and Occupation of Kuwait where the Trade Embargo and Related Measures Were also a Cause' (S/AC.26/1992/15), paragraph 9 (iv); Governing Council decision 9, 'Propositions and Conclusions on Compensation for Business Losses: Types of Damages and Their Valuation' (S/AC.26/1992/9), paragraphs 10, 17 and 19.

was doing so on its own behalf or on behalf of the State. The Claimant stated in reply as follows:

> KOC seeks reimbursement of the costs of fighting the oil fires on its own behalf . . . KOC was the Oil Sector company responsible for bringing the damaged oil wells under control and expended the sums underlying this claim. The costs of the firefighting were charged as extraordinary costs in the KOC accounts. The costs of fighting the oil fires were thus KOC's direct loss. As the operator of all Kuwait's onshore oil fields, it was essential for KOC to **[504]** oversee and organise the WBC exercise. It was inevitable, therefore, that KOC would pay these costs, since it owns the facilities in the oil fields, and has responsibility for oil production and all operations in the field. KOC was thus the only organisation able to direct and manage the well blowout control exercise and make the payments for the work in question. After the task of extinguishing the fires was completed, KOC was the only organisation with the knowledge and records necessary to prepare and present this claim . . . Strictly, in summary, KOC makes the WBC Claim on its own behalf and not on behalf of the State.

58. The Claimant's standing and the related risk of double compensation were further addressed during the oral proceedings. On 2 August 1996, upon the completion of the oral proceedings, the Panel issued a Procedural Order asking the Claimant to 'comment on KOC's standing to pursue a claim for costs part of which ultimately were borne by another entity, particularly in light of the fact that neither the Government of Kuwait nor KPC are co-claimants in this case, and the ensuing risk of double compensation'. In its reply, the Claimant stated as follows:

> All KOC's expenses are met in due course by its parent company, KPC, under the arrangements in place between the companies. The extraordinary losses suffered by KOC (and by other Oil Sector Companies) as a result of Iraq's invasion and occupation, would have caused KPC, the parent company, to be insolvent. Exceptional measures were taken to deal with this situation, and certain specific sums were borne by the Ministry of Oil, and are thus at present carried by the Government. [. . .] In due course, these exceptional charges will need to be resolved. This will depend on many factors. Meanwhile, it is accepted within the Oil Sector that all payments by way of compensation will be credited to whichever body is carrying the loss at the time. [. . .] To the extent that costs included in the WBC Claim are at present borne by either KPC or the Government of the State of Kuwait, KOC . . . has no entitlement to retain compensation awarded by the UNCC in respect of such costs.

59. The letter of 27 August 1996 from Mr Adel Omar Asem, Deputy Chairman and Director General of PAAC, to the Executive Secretary of the UNCC also addressed the issue. In the letter, it was confirmed that

> . . . [KOC] is the only entity within Kuwait which has made a claim in respect of the costs included in the [WBC Claim]. No claim for these costs has been submitted by [KPC], or by the Ministry of Oil or, indeed, by any other entity in Kuwait. Accordingly, there is no risk of the UNCC awarding compensation in relation to any other claim which could potentially duplicate compensation awarded in respect of the [WBC Claim].

60. The Panel finds that the issue concerning the Claimant's standing [**505**] should be resolved, and the related risk of double compensation addressed, in light of the structure of Kuwait's oil sector as a whole, taking into account the respective roles of the companies operating therein and the Claimant's statements and clarifications summarized above. Apart from the Claimant's own acknowledgment that it 'has no entitlement to retain compensation awarded by the UNCC in respect of' costs borne by KPC and the Ministry of Oil, the Panel considers it particularly relevant that, according to KPC's Annual Reports, '[KPC] and its subsidiaries perform certain activities on behalf of the Ministry of Oil primarily in relation to (a) the exploration for and production of crude oil and natural gas in Kuwait . . . The costs and revenues of these activities are accounted for to the Ministry by [KPC].' Given that the exploration for and production of crude oil and natural gas in Kuwait is the function of KOC, the Claimant in this Claim, it appears to the Panel that KOC in all its operations acts, in effect, on behalf of the Ministry of Oil.

61. In view of the above, and taking note of the presence of the representatives of the parent company, KPC, and of the Government of Kuwait at the oral proceedings, the Panel concludes that the WBC Claim must be deemed to have been made by KOC on behalf of Kuwait's public oil sector as a whole. Consequently, the Panel determines that the Government of Kuwait as well as KPC will be bound by the decision to be rendered by the UNCC in this Claim and thus they will be estopped from bringing the same claim before the UNCC.

C. Other preliminary issues

62. As explained in paragraphs 42–6, Iraq objects to the Commission's jurisdiction over the WBC Claim, asserting that the oil-well fires were not a direct result of Iraq's invasion and occupation of Kuwait as required by Security Council resolution 687 (1991). The gist of Iraq's argument is that there was an intervening event between Iraq's invasion and occupation of Kuwait and the oil-well fires – the allied air raids. According to Iraq,

> . . . the bombing was an interrupting event between Iraq's entry and the result, namely the oil well fire, rendering the damage or loss indirect, thus it makes the subject matter fall outside the jurisdiction of paragraph 16 of the Security Council's Resolution 687 and the requirements established by the Governing Council of the UNCC.

63. The issue raised by Iraq is closely related to the substantive aspects of the WBC Claim, in particular the law applicable before the Commission and the legal basis of Iraq's liability. Consequently, the Panel will address the issue *infra*, in connection with these two topics.

[**506**] 64. Iraq also raises the point that, as explained in paragraph 40, some of the contracts relating to the WBC Exercise were initially signed by the Government of Kuwait and KPC and not by KOC, the entity that brings the Claim. According to the Claimant, such contracts were assigned to KOC after the invasion and occupation and any payments which had already been made by the Government of

Kuwait, KPC or KPI were charged to KOC, which was credited with any assets thereby purchased. Iraq suggests that these arrangements involve a risk of double compensation.

65. The Panel agrees that it will be necessary to verify that the costs initially incurred by the Government of Kuwait, KPC or KPI were ultimately borne by KOC. The Panel's findings in this regard are explained in paragraphs 156–60.

IV. LEGAL FRAMEWORK

A. *Applicable law and criteria*

66. The law to be applied by the Commission has been set out in article 31 of the Rules. The article provides as follows:

> In considering the claims, Commissioners will apply Security Council resolution 687 (1991) and other relevant Security Council resolutions, the criteria established by the Governing Council for particular categories of claims, and any pertinent decisions of the Governing Council. In addition, where necessary, Commissioners shall apply other relevant rules of international law.

67. According to paragraph 16 of Security Council resolution 687 (1991), which under article 31 of the Rules forms part of the law applicable before the Commission, 'Iraq . . . is liable under international law for any direct loss, damage, including environmental damage and the depletion of natural resources, or injury to foreign Governments, nationals and corporations, as a result of Iraq's unlawful invasion and occupation of Kuwait.' The Panel notes that, when making resolution 687 (1991), the Security Council acted under Chapter VII of the United Nations Charter, i.e., it exercised its powers under that Chapter to maintain and restore international peace and security.[13]

68. The Security Council having determined, under Chapter VII of the Charter, that compensation in accordance with international law [**507**] should be provided to foreign Governments, nationals and corporations for any direct loss, damage or injury sustained by them as a result of Iraq's unlawful invasion and occupation of Kuwait, in order to restore international peace and security, the issue of Iraq's liability has been resolved by the Security Council and constitutes part of the law applicable before the Commission.[14]

---

[13] The Security Council also acted under Chapter VII when making resolution 692 (1991), in which it decided to establish the Commission and the Compensation Fund referred to in paragraph 18 of resolution 687 (1991). Under article 29 of the Charter, '[t]he Security Council may establish such subsidiary organs as it deems necessary for the performance of its functions'.

[14] Accord 'Report and Recommendations Made by the Panel of Commissioners Concerning the First Instalment of Individual Claims for Damages up to US $100,000 (Category "C" Claims)' (S/AC.26/1994/3), at 9:

> Resolution 687 (1991) reaffirmed that Iraq was liable, under international law, for direct losses, damages or other injuries as a result of its unlawful invasion and occupation of Kuwait. Iraq's liability under international law for such losses having been reaffirmed by

69. Security Council resolution 687 (1991) requires that the loss, damage or injury for which compensation is being sought be a direct result of Iraq's invasion and occupation of Kuwait. This requirement has been further defined in paragraph 21 of Governing Council decision 7. Reaffirming that 'payments are available with respect to any direct loss, damage, or injury to corporations and other entities as a result of Iraq's unlawful invasion and occupation of Kuwait', paragraph 21 goes on to specify that '[t]his will include any loss suffered as a result of . . . [m]ilitary operations or threat of military action by either side during the period 2 August 1990 to 2 March 1991; . . . [and] [a]ctions by officials, employees or agents of the Government of Iraq or its controlled entities during th[e] period [2 August 1990 to 2 March 1991] in connection with the invasion and occupation'.

70. While on its face related to category 'F' claims, paragraph 35 of Governing Council decision 7 is also relevant in this regard, as discussed in paragraphs 49–52, *supra*. Paragraph 35 reads, in relevant part, as follows:

> These payments are available with respect to direct environmental damage and the depletion of natural resources as a result of Iraq's unlawful invasion and occupation of Kuwait. This will include losses or expenses resulting from:
> (a) Abatement and prevention of environmental damage, including expenses directly relating to fighting oil fires and stemming the flow of oil in coastal and international waters;
> . . .

71. The fact that paragraph 35 is contained in the part of Governing Council decision 7 dealing with category 'F' claims does not, in the Panel's view, mean that the principle contained therein cannot be applied to category 'E' claims. As explained in paragraph [508] 51, *supra*, in view of paragraph 16 of Security Council resolution 687 (1991), which provides for the compensability of 'environmental damage and the depletion of natural resources', the distinction between category 'E' and 'F' claims should not be considered as a substantive one entailing consequences in terms of the law to be applied.

72. Applying the law and criteria stated above, the Panel now proceeds to resolve the issue of whether the loss, damage or injury for which compensation is being sought in the WBC Claim can be considered a direct result of Iraq's invasion and occupation of Kuwait.

B. Liability and causation
1. The Claimant's argument
73. The Claimant states that 'the deliberate firing of the oil fields of Kuwait [by the withdrawing Iraqi forces] [was] [p]robably the most graphic effect of the occupation

the Security Council, the issues remaining for the Panel are to determine the proper scope of causality – that is, determining for any particular claim or category of claims whether such loss or losses are a 'direct' result of Iraq's invasion and occupation – and to assess the amount of the losses incurred.

and the ensuing hostilities between Iraq and the coalition forces operating under the auspices of the United Nations'. Consequently, according to the Claimant, '[t]he physical damage giving rise to the necessity to incur the costs concerned having been inflicted deliberately and wantonly by the Iraqi forces, the WBC Claim is for compensation for losses which have been specifically defined as compensable by the Governing Council in sub-paragraph (c) of paragraph 21 of decision 7 rev. 1, i.e., direct losses suffered as a result of actions by officials or agents of the Government of Iraq'.

74. The Statement of Claim contains affidavits by senior officials of Kuwait's oil sector supporting the Claimant's assertion that the Iraqi forces were responsible for the well blowouts. The Claimant also suggests that the fact that the oil fields were set on fire by Iraqi forces is a matter of public knowledge. The Claimant states that '[t]he extent, in general terms, of the devastation wreaked upon the oil fields of Kuwait was the subject of much media coverage during and immediately after the period of hostilities between the coalition forces and those of Iraq in January and February 1991'.

75. From the legal point of view, the Claimant argues that, '[e]ven if the damage had been inflicted otherwise [than by the retreating Iraqi forces], e.g., by bombing from Coalition forces, Iraq would still be liable to compensate Kuwait for the damage caused during Iraq's unlawful occupation of Kuwait, including the full costs incurred by KOC and the subject of the WBC claim'. In support of its argument, the Claimant refers to paragraph 21 (a) of Governing Council decision 7, according to which Iraq is liable for any loss suffered as a result of 'military operations or threat of military action by either side'.

76. In its Supplementary Evidence filed on 7 June 1995 the Claimant submitted additional documentation in support of its claim. This documentation consists of an Introductory Statement and copies, with [509] English translation, of 22 allegedly official Iraqi documents. The documents are of a varying nature, including documents purporting to allocate 'responsibilities for well demolition' among the various units of the Iraqi armed forces, providing instructions for 'deferred detonation' of certain oil fields, detailing 'fire plans for the destruction of oilwells', etc.

77. In support of the above documentation, the Claimant refers to a report by Mr Walter Kälin, Special Rapporteur of the United Nations Commission on Human Rights, who visited Kuwait in the aftermath of the Gulf War.[15] One of the documents presented by the Claimant as part of its Supplementary Evidence was also included in the Special Rapporteur's report. The document, which is dated 2 December 1990 and classified as 'Top-Secret', was issued by the Operational Headquarters of the 18th Battalion of Field Engineers, a unit of the Iraqi Army, and contains 'Directives for the demolition of the wells that are being prepared for eventual sabotage'.

---

[15] See 'Report on the situation of human rights in Kuwait under Iraqi occupation, prepared by Mr Walter Kälin, Special Rapporteur of the Commission on Human Rights, in accordance with Commission Resolution 1991/67' (E/CN.4/1992/26) (the 'Kälin Report').

78. At the oral proceedings the Claimant's witnesses presented further testimony on the subject. Mr Ahmed Murad, Manager, Systems Development, of KOC, who at the relevant time was in Kuwait, testified that he did not witness, nor was aware, of any allied bombing of the oil wells, but that he did see, after the liberation, wellheads with explosives positioned on them. He explained that the explosives were still on the wellheads and had not been detonated because the wires had for some reason been cut. According to Mr Murad, after the liberation there were more than one hundred oil wells in Kuwait on which explosives had been placed but which were still intact.

79. The Claimant also presented at the oral proceedings excerpts from video films showing wellheads with undetonated explosives on them. These films are part of the file in this Claim.

2. Iraq's argument

80. As explained in paragraphs 42–6, Iraq denies any responsibility for the oil-well fires, arguing that the fires were caused by the allied air raids. According to Iraq,

> . . . [t]he decision to pull Iraqi forces out of Kuwait was issued swiftly and immediately. This decision did not refer to any firing of wells at the final stages of withdrawal. On the contrary the destruction and fire of oil wells occurred because of coalition bombing and bombardment whether by direct hits or shrapnel, before the date of withdrawal.

81. In support of its assertion Iraq refers to newspaper and news magazine articles, including an article published in the Middle East [**510**] Economic Survey, vol. XXXIV (No. 22), on 4 March 1991. This article, headed 'All Producing Wells Damaged in Kuwait', states in relevant part:

> A devastating assessment of the war damage to oil wells and other oil installations in Kuwait has emerged from the first on-the-spot report by returning Kuwaiti oil officials. According to initial surveys by the Kuwaiti Oil Company (KOC), the producing arm of the Kuwait Petroleum Corporation (KPC), all Kuwait's producing oil wells have been set ablaze or otherwise damaged by Iraqi sabotage or allied bombing.
>
> Mr Musab al-Yasin, KOC General Superintendent for Oil Reservoirs, told Reuters on 1 March: 'Our provisional assessment is that they have damaged every producing well. Our feeling from checks our personnel have done so far is that all the wells have been exploded.' Wells that had not caught fire when blasted by Iraqi explosives had been badly damaged and were spouting crude oil. Some wells had been destroyed by allied bombing, he said, but the vast majority had been blown up by occupying Iraqi forces. Mr Yasin and other KOC officials were being interviewed at the Ahmadi oil complex in Kuwait.
>
> . . .
>
> KOC executives were quoted as saying that allied bombing had set fire to as many as 34 wells, and had also caused varying degrees of damage, from minor to total loss, to some 13 out of 18 important oil gathering centers in the country.

82. Iraq suggests that the fact that undetonated explosives were found on the wellheads after the liberation resulted from a conspiracy against Iraq. Iraq asserts as follows:

> The Government of Iraq would also like to stress the fact that somebody working for the interest of Iraq's enemies planted explosives in order to incriminate Iraq and throw the responsibility of the firing of the oil wells on the Iraqi Armed Forces which we categorically deny. These explosives could have easily been picked up and planted by Iraq's enemies and this is not an unexpected act from this category of individuals, especially under such circumstances. This could also be an act committed in order to shift the accusation from the coalition forces whose bombing and shelling led to the firing of the wells in the first place.

83. As noted above, Iraq also denies the authenticity of the documents submitted by the Claimant in its Supplementary Evidence. See paragraph 46. According to Iraq, the fact that the documents 'are not consistent with customary regulations of Iraqi military correspondence' suggests that they are forgeries.

84. From the legal point of view, Iraq argues that, '[a]ccording to all known systems of jurisprudence, a (direct loss) is that loss which emanates directly from the act without any interrupting event where the result is directly connected'. (Parenthesis in original.) Consequently, according to Iraq, '[d]irect damage or loss dictates that the link of [511] causation between the (act) and the (loss) must be continuous and uninterrupted'. (Parentheses in original.) Iraq concludes that, '[i]n the case of Kuwait oil wells the chain was broken by the coalition bombing, whether from air or by artillery or rocket bombardment which covered the whole area of the Iraqi defensive positions including the sites of oil wells'.

3. The Panel's findings

85. Based on the evidence and testimony presented, the Panel finds that, although part of the damage for which compensation is being sought in the WBC Claim may be a result of the allied bombing, the bulk of the oil-well fires was directly caused by the explosives placed on the wellheads and detonated by Iraqi armed forces. In this regard the Panel finds the testimony presented by the Claimant's witnesses at the oral proceedings, which included videotapes of explosives placed on the wellheads, as well as the documentation attached to the Kälin Report, *supra* paragraph 77, particularly convincing. The Panel also notes that the evidence referred to by Iraq is consistent with this conclusion. See *supra* paragraph 81 (quoting a news magazine article stating that 'the vast majority [of the oil wells] had been blown up by occupying Iraqi forces').

86. As described above under the section 'Applicable law and criteria', according to paragraph 21 (a) of Governing Council decision 7, Iraq's liability includes any direct loss, damage or injury suffered as a result of '[m]ilitary operations or threat of military action *by either side* during the period 2 August 1990 to 2 March 1991'. (Emphasis added.) This decision is, in the Panel's view, in accordance with the general principles of international law. Consequently, Iraq is liable for any direct loss, damage

or injury whether caused by its own or by the coalition armed forces. Iraq's contention that the allied air raids broke the chain of causation therefore cannot be upheld.

[...]

[*Source:* 109 *ILR* 485; UN Doc. S/AC.26/1996/5/Annex]

Governing Council Decision 40 (UN Doc. S/AC.26/Dec.40 (1996); 17 December 1996)

DECISION CONCERNING THE WELL BLOWOUT CLAIM

The Governing Council,

Recalling that the Panel of Commissioners for the Well Blowout Control Claim was appointed specifically in light of the Claim's special nature and special circumstances,

Having received, in accordance with Article 38 of the Provisional Rules for Claims Procedure, the executive summary of the report and recommendations of the Panel of Commissioners appointed to review the Well Blowout Control Claim (the 'executive summary'),

1. *Approves* the recommendations made by the Panel of Commissioners and, accordingly,

2. *Decides,* pursuant to Article 40 of the Rules, to approve the amount of the recommended award of US $610,048,547, as referred to in paragraph 45(a) of the executive summary, to Kuwait Oil Company on behalf of Kuwait's public oil sector as a whole, without prejudice to adjustments, where necessary, that might be reached concerning allocation of costs after the review of other related Kuwait Oil Company claims,

3. *Decides* that the payment of claims in accordance with paragraph 6 of Decision 17 [S/AC.26/Dec.17 (1994)] and future decisions of the Governing Council on the priority of payment and the payment mechanism are in no way affected by this decision,

4. *Notes* that, to the extent specified in paragraphs 45(e), 45(f), 45(g) and 45(h) of the executive summary, Kuwait Oil Company may amend its other claims before the Commission, for examination by the relevant Panels of Commissioners,

5. *Decides* that no compensation be awarded concerning the claims referred to in paragraphs 45(c) and 45 (d) of the executive summary,

6. *Requests* the Executive Secretary to provide copies of the executive summary and its annex to the Secretary-General, to the Government of the State of Kuwait and to the Government of the Republic of Iraq.

[*Source:* UN Doc. S/AC.26/Dec.40 (1996)]

Report and Recommendations made by the Panel of Commissioners Concerning the First Instalment of 'F4' Claims

United Nations Compensation Commission, Geneva

22 June 2001[1] (Mensah, *Chairman*; Allen and Sand, *Members*)

Damage and compensation – Iraq's invasion and occupation of Kuwait, 1991 – assessment and monitoring claims by six governments – claims for environmental damage – depletion of natural resources – impacts on marine and coastal environment – impacts on terrestrial environment – cultural heritage – public health – impact on environment of influx of refugees and involuntary migration – reasonable monitoring and assessment activities compensable

Air – pollution – transport and dispersion of air pollution – whether claims for reasonable monitoring and assessment activities compensable

Waters – depletion of water resources – damage to groundwater – damage to marine and coastal environment – whether claims for reasonable monitoring and assessment activities compensable

War and armed conflict – Iraq's invasion and occupation of Kuwait, 1991 – environmental damage caused by setting light to oil wells and spilling oil into Persian Gulf – impact on environment of influx of refugees and involuntary migration caused by war

SUMMARY   *The facts*   The United Nations Compensation Commission ('the UNCC'), a subsidiary organ of the United Nations Security Council, was established on 20 May 1991 by the Security Council's Resolution 692 (1991) to process claims and pay compensation for losses resulting from Iraq's invasion and occupation of Kuwait. The UNCC was created after the Security Council adopted Resolution 687 (on 3 April 1991) establishing Iraq's legal responsibility '... for any direct loss, damage, including

---

[1] The Report and Recommendations were signed on 28 March 2001. A note on subsequent instalments of Category 'F4' Claims can be found at p. 632 below.

environmental damage and the depletion of natural resources, or injury to foreign Governments, nationals and corporations, as a result of Iraq's unlawful invasion and occupation of Kuwait'.

Various panels of the UNCC have been established with mandates to review claims and recommend compensation where appropriate. This report addressed the first instalment of claims by governments and international organisations. A total of 107 claims were filed by six governments: the Islamic Republic of Iran ('Iran'), the Hashemite Kingdom of Jordan ('Jordan'), the State of Kuwait ('Kuwait'), the Kingdom of Saudi Arabia ('Saudi Arabia'), the Syrian Arab Republic ('Syria') and the Republic of Turkey ('Turkey').

The Claimants sought compensation for environmental damage, depletion of natural resources and increased health risks caused by damage from air pollution; the depletion of water resources; damage to groundwater and cultural heritage resources; oil pollution; damage to coastlines, fisheries, wetlands, rangelands, forestry, agriculture and livestock; and damage to public health. According to the Claimants, the environmental damage resulted from the release and transport of airborne pollutants caused by oil fires; the formation of oil rivers and lakes from destroyed oil wells; the release of oil into the sea from oil pipelines, offshore terminals and tankers; the disruption of fragile desert and coastal terrain caused by the movement of military vehicles and personnel and the construction of military trenches and the emplacement of mines, weapons and other fortifications; and adverse impacts on the environment resulting from the transit and settlement of persons fleeing Iraq and Kuwait as a result of Iraq's invasion and occupation of Kuwait.[2]

Held by the Panel of Commissioners   The claims were examined on an individual basis by the Panel and compensation was recommended in part.

Iran's claims   The Panel recommended monitoring and assessment claims totalling US $17,007,070.

(1)   The costs of reasonable monitoring and assessment activities relating to the transport and dispersion of air pollution from oil fires in Kuwait and oil spills in the Persian Gulf were compensable. However, there had to be evidence that oil pollutants had actually reached the ground of the territory of a Claimant State.

(2)   Deterioration of indoor and outdoor cultural heritage materials was compensable where it was caused by pollutants from the oil fires.

---

[2] Particulars of the Claimants' allegations are outlined in paragraphs 13 and 14 at pp. 637–8 below.

(3)   Unexcavated archaeological sites were likely to have had significantly less exposure to airborne pollutants from oil fires compared to cultural heritage materials.

(4)   Damage to groundwater could not be ruled out since airborne pollutants from the oil fires had reached Iran. A study of the extent of groundwater pollution was a reasonable monitoring and assessment activity.

(5)   Pollutants from the oil spill and oil fires could have deleterious impacts on the marine and coastal environments, including impacts on wetlands, mangrove forests, coral reefs and seagrass beds. Numerous studies by Iran examining, *inter alia*, the extent of groundwater pollution, the impact of the oil pollution on mangrove forests, the natural recovery and remediation capacities of polluted marine environments, the damage caused by the oil fires and oil spills to coral reefs and their impact on seagrass beds, and the extent to which coastal areas had recovered from pollution, were reasonable monitoring and assessment activities. It was also reasonable for Iran to monitor natural revegetation capacities and production capabilities in areas that might have been polluted. The oil pollution might have affected wetland bird populations and fishing resources. Studies by Iran examining these affects were also reasonable monitoring and assessment activities.

(6)   Oil pollution might have contaminated the soil and natural vegetation (including forests) through the deposition of heavy metals and hydrocarbons from black rain and soot; it was reasonable for Iran to study whether soil and natural vegetation had been contaminated. Some damage might also have resulted from oil pollution to livestock, which was a reasonable assessment activity. However, rehabilitation studies were unlikely to produce information not already available in scientific literature, and were, accordingly, not reasonable assessment activities.

(7)   Losses resulting from the departure of persons from Iraq or Kuwait were compensable if the departure had occurred between 2 August 1990 and 2 March 1991. However, insufficient evidence had been provided by Iran to establish the departure of refugees from the Zagros Mountain range during this period.

(8)   There was no justification for studies purporting to detect effects of smoke inhalation on health by examining mitochondrial function nine to ten years after exposure to smoke. It was highly unlikely that such effects would still be measurable in circulating platelets after such a long time had elapsed. A study investigating possible links between airborne

pollution and the incidence of cancer and haematological disorders was premature and not reasonable. However, a project to investigate the psychiatric effects on the population as a result of trauma experienced during Iraq's invasion and occupation of Kuwait was justified, since scientific literature indicated that psychiatric disorders might result from events such as those that occurred during Iraq's invasion of Kuwait. It was also reasonable for Iran to investigate the effect of airborne pollutants on the respiratory health of young persons in Iran.

Jordan's claims   The Panel recommended monitoring and assessment claims totalling US $7,060,625.

(1)   Environmental damage might have resulted from the population influx into Jordan caused by the departure of persons from Iraq or Kuwait. This might have included degradation of the quality and quantity of water resources, an increase in groundwater pollution down-gradient at the As-Samra Wastewater Treatment Plant, bacterial contamination of freshwater springs in major water extraction areas, degradation in quality and quantity of water resources in Jordan as a result of the use of unlined cesspits at refugee camps and involuntary immigrant settlements in Jordan, and damage to water resources and related infrastructure resulting from the presence in Jordan of refugees and involuntary immigrants.

(2)   Jordan's coastal marine environment, wetland and desert ecosystems, and agricultural resources in the Jordan Valley, might also have been affected by the presence in Jordan of refugees and involuntary immigrants as a result of Iraq's invasion and occupation of Kuwait. Studies to determine the environmental impacts were reasonable monitoring and assessment activities.

Kuwait's claims   The Panel recommended monitoring and assessment claims totalling US $108,908,412.

(1)   Studies of damage to groundwater and surface water, current groundwater quality and an evaluation of technologies for treating contaminated groundwater were reasonable monitoring and assessment activities. Leaks from damaged oil well casings could contaminate groundwater resources over time, therefore Kuwait was entitled to compensation to monitor potential leaks for ten years.

(2)   There was a link between damage to Kuwait's marine environment and the oil released into the Persian Gulf as a result of Iraq's invasion of Kuwait. Studies to monitor and assess the effects of the oil pollution on its marine resources during Iraq's invasion and occupation of Kuwait were reasonable monitoring and assessment activities. However,

compensation was not payable since Kuwait had not provided sufficient evidence of the cost of these activities. Compensation was payable for monitoring programmes that identified and assessed the long-term impacts of the oil spills on the marine environment and for studying technologies to treat contaminated shoreline areas and sunken oil. No compensation was payable for loss of beach use, loss of recreational fishing or loss of desert recreational camping opportunities as a result of Iraq's invasion and occupation of Kuwait.

(3)   Oil lakes created by Iraq's action might pose persistent ecological and human health risks, including risks to scarce groundwater resources. It was appropriate for Kuwait to investigate the nature and extent of the risks caused by the oil lakes. Kuwait was also to be compensated for damage to its desert environment caused by military activities and was entitled to monitor and assess this damage.

(4)   The destruction of large numbers of mines and unexploded ordnance in Kuwait could have led to environmental damage, including soil contamination and loss of vegetation. It was appropriate for Kuwait to undertake studies to assess the extent of such damage.

(5)   Compensation was recommended for Kuwait to undertake programmes and studies on the public health impacts of Iraq's invasion and occupation, for the establishment and operation of the following: a data repository and exposure registry to collect and manage health information and medical records of persons whose health was affected by Iraq's actions; a human health risk assessment programme to identify potential long-term adverse health effects of the war; a clinical monitoring programme to track the health of persons affected by the war; and a public health survey to assess the cost of dealing with increased incidence of disease as a result of the war.

Saudi Arabia's claims   The Panel recommended monitoring and assessment claims totalling US $109,584,660.

(1)   Substantial quantities of oil had entered into and damaged Saudi Arabia's marine and coastal environment. A study was required to determine the existence and nature of potential damage to its marine and coastal environment, including coastal and offshore coral reefs, as a result of the oil spills. Saudi Arabia was also to be compensated to undertake a number of studies, including: a five-year oceanographic survey and sampling project to evaluate long-term adverse effects on its fishery resources of the oil pollution; an assessment of the risks to human health and ecological risks posed by oil pollution of its marine and coastal environment; a survey of the 'oiled shoreline' between Kuwait and Saudi Arabia; and

an evaluation of remediation technologies for treating polluted coastal areas and for the removal of sunken oil.

(2)   Extensive damage was caused in Saudi Arabia as a result of the oil fires in Kuwait and the military activities during the war. Saudi Arabia was to be compensated to undertake, *inter alia*, the following studies which were reasonable monitoring and assessment activities: a monitoring and assessment programme of the impact of Iraq's actions on its terrestrial environment; the development of a Geographic Information System database to facilitate analysis of field observations and data on damage to the terrestrial environment; an assessment of the risks to human health and ecology from damage to its terrestrial environment; an evaluation of remediation and restoration technologies for desert surfaces, vegetation and groundwater resources in its territory which might have been damaged; and field reconnaissance, sampling and satellite and aerial imaging to determine the extent of damage and natural recovery processes in its territory.

(3)   It was possible that pollutants from oil fires had increased the long-term risks of some diseases, including respiratory and pulmonary diseases, in Saudi Arabia. Accordingly, Saudi Arabia was to be compensated to undertake an integrated public health monitoring programme, a data repository and an exposure registry, a programme to monitor and assess risks to human health as a result of Iraq's invasion and occupation of Kuwait, a study determining the long-term health effects on the population, a clinical monitoring programme tracing clinical symptoms and diseases, and a public health survey.

Syria's claims   The Panel recommended monitoring and assessment claims totalling US $674,200.

(1)   Emissions from the oil fires might have reached Syria, albeit infrequently. However, Syria had not provided sufficient evidence to support the expenses it claimed for studies assessing the amount of pollutants transported to Syria from the oil fires, and consequent damage caused, resulting from Iraq's invasion and occupation of Kuwait, so no such compensation was awarded.

(2)   A study already undertaken by Syria to determine whether damage was caused to its cultural heritage sites by pollutants resulting from Iraq's invasion and occupation of Kuwait was reasonable monitoring and assessment. However, Syria had not provided sufficient evidence to support the expenses it claimed for this study, therefore no compensation was recommended. Compensation was, however, recommended for Syria to undertake a project to assess damage that might have

been caused to cultural heritage sites by pollutants from the oil fires in Kuwait.

(3)   A project to assess the pollution of surface water and groundwater that might have been caused by oil pollution was a reasonable monitoring and assessment activity.

(4)   Studies on the effects of the oil fires on (a) Syrian livestock and (b) forest resources were not reasonable monitoring and assessment activities since Syria had failed to provide a proposed methodology to the Panel and had not indicated how the studies would (a) link sheep mortality to air pollution and (b) differentiate between vegetation contaminated as a result of Iraq's actions and vegetation otherwise contaminated.

(5)   Compensation was awarded for a project to assess the state of health of its population before, during and after the oil fires in Kuwait, which was a reasonable monitoring and assessment activity.

Turkey's claims   No monitoring and assessment claims were recommended by the Panel for compensation as Turkey had failed to meet the evidentiary requirements.

Note on subsequent instalments of Category 'F4' Claims   The second, third, fourth and fifth instalments of claims for environmental damage and depletion of natural resources are not reported in full in this volume for reasons of space but are noted below. The report on the fifth instalment completed the work of the Panel on the review of 'F4' claims.

Second Instalment, 3 October 2002 (UN Doc. S/AC.26/2002/26, http://www2. unog.ch/uncc/reports/r02-26.pdf)   The second 'F4' instalment consisted of a total of thirty claims for expenses incurred for measures to abate and prevent environmental damage, to clean and restore the environment, and to monitor public health risks alleged to have resulted from Iraq's invasion and occupation of Kuwait. A total amount of US $872,760,543 was claimed and an award of US $711,087,737 recommended.

Regional Claimants Iran (four claims), Kuwait (one claim) and Saudi Arabia (six claims) sought compensation in the amount of US $829,458,298 for measures to respond to environmental damage and human health risks from: (a) mines, unexploded ordnance and other remnants of war; (b) oil lakes formed by oil released from damaged wells in Kuwait; (c) oil spills in the Persian Gulf caused by oil released from pipelines, offshore terminals and tankers; and (d) pollutants released from oil-well fires in Kuwait. An award of US $702,734,089 was recommended for the Regional Claimants (US $67,587, US $694,375,281 and US $8,291,221 respectively).

Non-Regional Claimants Australia (two claims), Canada (two claims), Germany (four claims), the Netherlands (one claim), the United Kingdom (one claim) and the United States (nine claims) sought compensation in the total amount of US $43,302,236 for expenses incurred in providing assistance to countries in the Persian Gulf region to respond to environmental damage, or threat of damage to the environment or public health, resulting from Iraq's invasion and occupation of Kuwait. A total award of US $8,353,648 was recommended for the Non-Regional Claimants (US $7,777, US $529,923, US $2,038,256, nil, US $1,891,857 and US $3,885,835 respectively).

Third Instalment, 18 December 2003 (UN Doc. S/AC.26/2003/31, http:// www2.unog.ch/uncc/reports/r03-31.pdf) The third 'F4' instalment consisted of a total of five claims for expenses resulting from measures already taken or to be undertaken in the future to clean and restore environment alleged to have been damaged as a direct result of Iraq's invasion and occupation of Kuwait.

The Claimants, Kuwait (three claims) and Saudi Arabia (two claims), sought compensation in the amount of US $10,004,219,582 (US $5,235,325,175 and US $4,768,894,407 respectively) for expenses resulting from cleaning and restoration measures undertaken or to be undertaken by them to remediate damage from: (a) oil released from damaged oil wells in Kuwait; (b) pollutants released from oil-well fires and fire-fighting activities in Kuwait; (c) oil spills into the Persian Gulf from pipelines, offshore terminals and tankers; (d) laying and clearance of mines; (e) movements of military vehicles and personnel; and (f) construction of military fortifications. A total award of US $1,148,701,011 was recommended (US $685,381,727 and US $463,319,284 respectively).

Fourth Instalment, parts one and two, 9 December 2004 (UN Doc. S/AC.26/2004/16, http://www2.unog.ch/uncc/reports/r04-16.pdf and UN Doc. S/AC.26/2004/17, http://www2.unog.ch/uncc/reports/r04-17.pdf)
The fourth instalment of 'F4' claims consisted of a total of nine claims for expenses resulting from measures already taken or to be undertaken to clean and restore environment alleged to have been damaged as a direct result of Iraq's invasion and occupation of Kuwait.

The Claimants, Iran (one claim), Jordan (one claim), Kuwait (three claims in total, one of which was dealt with in part two of the report), Saudi Arabia (two claims), Syria (one claim) and Turkey (one claim), sought compensation in the amount of US $16,305,459,098 (US $2,484,623,669, US $136,761,897, US $729,020,720, US $11,315,164,493, US $1,634,619,154 and US $5,269,165 respectively) for expenses resulting

from measures already taken or to be undertaken by them to reme-
diate damage caused *inter alia* by: (a) oil released from damaged oil
wells in Kuwait; (b) pollutants released from the oil-well fires and fire-
fighting activities in Kuwait; (c) oil released from pipelines onto the land;
(d) oil-filled trenches; (e) oil spills into the Persian Gulf from pipelines,
offshore terminals and tankers; (f) movement and presence of refugees
who departed from Iraq and Kuwait; (g) mines and other remnants of
war; (h) movement of military vehicles and personnel; and (i) construction of military fortifications, encampments and roads. A total award
of US $629,487,878 was recommended (US $188,760, nil, US $4,152,411,
US $625,146,707, nil and nil respectively).

Part two of the report contained the Panel's recommendations on one
of Kuwait's three claims, Claim No. 5000454, in accordance with the
provisions of Governing Council decision 114, which stipulated that a
separate report was to be prepared on each claim with a recommended
award value of 1 billion United States dollars or more. Kuwait claimed a
total amount of US $6,799,491,526 for Claim No. 5000454 and the Panel
recommended an award of US $2,277,206,389.

*Fifth Instalment, 30 June 2005 (UN Doc. S/AC.26/2005/10, http://www2.
unog.ch/uncc/reports/r05-10.pdf)*   The fifth instalment of 'F4' claims
consisted of a total of nineteen claims for damage to or depletion
of natural resources, including cultural heritage resources, measures
to clean and restore damaged environment, and damage to public
health.

The Claimants, Iran (five claims), Jordan (two claims), Kuwait
(four claims), Saudi Arabia (four claims), Syria (three claims)
and Turkey (one claim), sought compensation in the amount of
US $49,936,562,997 (US $11,090,762,249, US $5,217,117,182, US
$2,715,934,222, US $28,742,311,029, US $2,165,021,052 and US $5,417,263
respectively). The claims related to damage resulting from, *inter alia*: (a)
pollutants from the oil-well fires and damaged oil wells in Kuwait; (b) oil
spills into the Persian Gulf from pipelines, offshore terminals and tankers;
(c) influx of refugees into the territories of some of the Claimants; (d)
operations of military personnel and equipment; (e) mines and other
remnants of war; and (f) exposure of the populations of the Claimants
to pollutants from the oil-well fires and oil spills in Kuwait and to hostilities and various acts of violence. A total award of US $252,028,468
was recommended (US $27,780,752, US $161,926,734, US $16,207,276,
US $46,113,706, nil and nil respectively).

There follows
Report and Recommendations Made by the Panel of
Commissioners Concerning the First Instalment of 'F4' claims,
22 June 2001³ (extract)   635

Report and Recommendations Made by the Panel of Commissioners Concerning the First Instalment of 'F4' Claims, 22 June 2001 (extract)

INTRODUCTION

1. At its thirtieth session held from 14 to 16 December 1998, the Governing Council of the United Nations Compensation Commission (the 'Commission') appointed the 'F4' Panel of Commissioners (the 'Panel'), composed of Messrs Thomas A. Mensah (Chairman), José R. Allen and Peter H. Sand, to review claims for losses resulting from environmental damage and the depletion of natural resources submitted by Governments under category 'F' and by public sector enterprises under category 'E' (the ' "F4" claims').

2. This is the first report of the Panel to the Governing Council submitted pursuant to article 38 (e) of the Provisional Rules For Claims Procedure (the 'Rules') (S/AC.26/1992/10).

3. The report addresses the first instalment of 'F4' claims, which includes 107 claims for monitoring and assessment of environmental damage, depletion of natural resources, monitoring of public health, and performing medical screenings for the purposes of investigation and combating increased health risks (the 'monitoring and assessment claims') submitted by the Governments of the Islamic Republic of Iran ('Iran'), the Hashemite Kingdom of Jordan ('Jordan'), the State of Kuwait ('Kuwait'), the Kingdom of Saudi Arabia ('Saudi Arabia'), the Syrian Arab Republic ('Syria') and the Republic of Turkey ('Turkey') (collectively 'the Claimants').

4. A summary of the monitoring and assessment claims submitted by each claimant country appears in table 1 [see p. 636]. The 'amount claimed' column in table 1 shows the amount of compensation requested by the Claimants (including amendments) expressed in United States dollars ('USD') and, where necessary, corrected for arithmetic errors.

I. BACKGROUND

A. Mandate of the Panel
5. The mandate of the Panel is to review the 'F4' claims and recommend compensation, where appropriate.

---

³ The individual sections in the Report that examine the claims for Jordan, Kuwait, Saudi Arabia, Syria and Turkey are not reproduced below. The Report can, however, be found in its entirety online at http://www2.unog.ch/uncc/reports/r01-16.pdf.

Table 1. *Summary of first instalment monitoring and
assessment claims*

Country	Total number of claims	Amount claimed (USD)
Iran	40	42,951,383
Jordan	10	12,488,949
Kuwait	22	460,421,114
Saudi Arabia	24	482,156,943
Syria	10	5,623,885
Turkey	1	3,770,300
Total	107	1,007,412,574

6. Article 31 of the Rules sets out the law to be applied by the Panel in considering claims for compensation. It reads:

> In considering the claims, Commissioners will apply Security Council resolution 687 (1991) and other relevant Security Council resolutions, the criteria established by the Governing Council for particular categories of claims, and any pertinent decisions of the Governing Council. In addition, where necessary, Commissioners shall apply other relevant rules of international law.

7. Paragraph 16 of Security Council resolution 687 (1991) affirms that the Republic of Iraq ('Iraq') is 'liable under international law for any direct loss, damage, including environmental damage and the depletion of natural resources, or injury to foreign Governments, nationals and corporations, as a result of Iraq's unlawful invasion and occupation of Kuwait'.

8. In discharging its mandate, the Panel has borne in mind the statement of the Secretary-General of the United Nations, in his report of 2 May 1991 to the Security Council, that:

> The Commission is not a court or an arbitral tribunal before which the parties appear; it is a political organ that performs an essentially fact-finding function of examining claims, verifying their validity, evaluating losses, assessing payments and resolving disputed claims. It is only in this last respect that a quasi-judicial function may be involved. Given the nature of the Commission, it is all the more important that some element of due process be built into the procedure. It will be the function of the commissioners to provide this element. ((S/22559), para. 20.)

B. *Compensable losses or expenses*

9. Governing Council decision 7 (S/AC.26/1991/7/Rev.1) provides guidance regarding the losses or expenses that may be considered as 'direct loss, damage, or injury' resulting from Iraq's invasion and occupation of Kuwait. Paragraph 34 of the decision states that 'direct loss, damage, or injury' includes any loss suffered as a result of:

(a)   Military operations or threat of military action by either side during the period 2 August 1990 to 2 March 1991;

(b) Departure of persons from or their inability to leave Iraq or Kuwait (or a decision not to return) during that period;

(c) Actions by officials, employees or agents of the Government of Iraq or its controlled entities during that period in connection with the invasion or occupation;

(d) The breakdown of civil order in Kuwait or Iraq during that period; or

(e) Hostage-taking or other illegal detention.

10. Paragraph 35 of Governing Council decision 7 provides that 'direct environmental damage and depletion of natural resources' includes losses or expenses resulting from:

(a) Abatement and prevention of environmental damage, including expenses directly relating to fighting oil fires and stemming the flow of oil in coastal and international waters;

(b) Reasonable measures already taken to clean and restore the environment or future measures which can be documented as reasonably necessary to clean and restore the environment;

(c) Reasonable monitoring and assessment of the environmental damage for the purposes of evaluating and abating the harm and restoring the environment;

(d) Reasonable monitoring of public health and performing medical screenings for the purposes of investigation and combating increased health risks as a result of the environmental damage; and

(e) Depletion of or damage to natural resources.

11. Thus, monitoring and assessment expenses that qualify for compensation are those resulting from:

(a) Monitoring and assessment of environmental damage that is reasonable for any of the purposes specified in sub-paragraph (c) of paragraph 35 of Governing Council decision 7; and

(b) Monitoring of public health and performing medical screenings that is reasonable for any of the purposes set out in sub-paragraph (d) of paragraph 35 of the same decision.

II. OVERVIEW OF THE FIRST INSTALMENT OF 'F4' CLAIMS

A. The claims

12. The first instalment of 'F4' claims consists of monitoring and assessment claims submitted pursuant to paragraph 35 of Governing Council decision 7. A summary of the claims is given in table 1. The total compensation claimed is USD 1,007,412,574.

13. The Claimants seek compensation for expenses resulting from monitoring and assessment activities undertaken or to be undertaken to identify and evaluate damage or loss suffered by them as a result of Iraq's invasion and occupation of

Kuwait. These activities relate to, *inter alia*, damage from air pollution; depletion of water resources; damage to groundwater; damage to cultural heritage resources; oil pollution in the Persian Gulf; damage to coastlines; damage to fisheries; damage to wetlands and rangelands; damage to forestry, agriculture and livestock; and damage or risk of damage to public health.

14. The Claimants allege that environmental damage, depletion of natural resources and increased health risks resulted from, *inter alia*:

(a)   The release and transport, into the Claimants' territories, of airborne pollutants caused by oil fires resulting from the ignition of hundreds of oil wells in Kuwait by Iraqi forces during Iraq's invasion and occupation of Kuwait;

(b)   Numerous oil rivers and lakes formed by oil from the destroyed oil wells that did not ignite;

(c)   The release, by Iraqi forces, of millions of barrels of oil into the sea from oil pipelines, off-shore terminals and oil tankers;

(d)   Disruption of fragile desert and coastal terrain caused by the movement of military vehicles and personnel, coupled with the construction of thousands of kilometres of military trenches and the emplacement of mines, weapons caches and other fortifications; and

(e)   Adverse impacts on the environment resulting from the transit and settlement of the thousands of persons who departed from Iraq and Kuwait as a result of Iraq's invasion and occupation of Kuwait.

B. *Priority given to monitoring and assessment claims*

15. Prior to the expiration of the deadline established by the Governing Council, a number of governments submitted claims for environmental damage and the depletion of natural resources, including claims for compensation for expenses resulting from monitoring and assessment of such damage.

16. At the twenty-eighth session of the Governing Council, held on 29 June to 1 July 1998, Saudi Arabia, on behalf of itself, Iran, Jordan, Kuwait, and Syria, presented a proposal requesting the Governing Council to agree to a procedure under which awards for the monitoring and assessment claims would be made in advance of the review of the related substantive claims. Such advance awards would be made by the Governing Council on the basis of recommendations of the Panel.

17. The Governing Council, at its twenty-ninth session held on 28 to 30 September 1998, requested the Executive Secretary of the Commission (the 'Executive Secretary') to invite the Claimants as well as other similarly situated claimant Governments, if any, to identify and file separately, within the period to be specified by the Executive Secretary, those portions of their claims already filed with the Commission that pertained to the monitoring and assessment of environmental damage. The Governing Council also decided that appropriate priority should be given to the processing of such claims, so that the claims could be resolved quickly and separately from the resolution of the related claims for environmental damage.

18. This report deals with the claims filed by six Governments, as listed in paragraph 3 above.

[. . .]

IV. REVIEW OF MONITORING AND ASSESSMENT CLAIMS

A. *Special aspects of monitoring and assessment claims*

28. The monitoring and assessment claims reviewed in this report relate to expenses resulting from three different categories of activities, namely:

  (a)   Investigations to ascertain whether environmental damage or depletion of natural resources has occurred;

  (b)   Studies to quantify the loss resulting from the damage or depletion; and

  (c)   Assessment of methodologies to abate or mitigate the damage or depletion.

Some of the claims relate to activities falling into more than one of the above categories.

29. The monitoring and assessment claims present special problems in that they are being reviewed before decisions have been taken on the compensability of any substantive claims. Thus, the claims are being reviewed at a point where it may not have been established that environmental damage or depletion of natural resources occurred as a result of Iraq's invasion and occupation of Kuwait. Yet, the results of the monitoring and assessment activities may be critical in enabling claimants to establish the existence of damage and evaluate the quantum of compensation to be claimed. Hence, although it may be correct in some cases to say that a claimant is seeking compensation for monitoring and assessment without prior proof that environmental damage has in fact occurred, it would be both illogical and inequitable to reject a claim for reasonable monitoring and assessment on the sole ground that the claimant did not establish beforehand that environmental damage occurred. To reject a claim for that reason would, in effect, deprive the claimant of the opportunity to generate the very evidence that it needs to demonstrate the nature and extent of damage that may have occurred.

30. For that reason, the Panel does not consider that conclusive proof of environmental damage is a prerequisite for a monitoring and assessment activity to be compensable in accordance with paragraph 35 of Governing Council decision 7. In the view of the Panel, the purpose of monitoring and assessment is to enable a claimant to develop evidence to establish whether environmental damage has occurred and to quantify the extent of the resulting loss.

31. However, the Panel is of the view that compensation should not be awarded for monitoring and assessment activities that are purely theoretical or speculative, or which have only a tenuous link with damage resulting from Iraq's invasion and occupation of Kuwait. There should be a sufficient nexus between the activity and environmental damage or risk of damage that may be attributed directly to Iraq's invasion and occupation of Kuwait. In assessing the strength of the nexus, and hence

the reasonableness of the monitoring and assessment activity, the Panel has taken into account, *inter alia*, the following considerations:

(a) Whether there is a possibility that environmental damage or depletion of natural resources could have been caused as a result of Iraq's invasion and occupation of Kuwait. This entails an inquiry regarding the plausibility that pollutants released as a result of Iraq's invasion and occupation of Kuwait, or other effects of the invasion, could have impacted the territories of the Claimants;

(b) Whether the particular areas or resources in respect of which the monitoring and assessment activity is undertaken could have been affected by pollutants released as a result of Iraq's invasion and occupation of Kuwait, or other effects of the invasion. This entails, in appropriate cases, an examination of the possible pathways and media by which pollutants resulting from Iraq's invasion and occupation of Kuwait could have reached the areas or resources concerned;

(c) Whether there is evidence of environmental damage or risk of such damage as a result of Iraq's invasion and occupation of Kuwait; and

(d) Whether, having regard to the stated purpose of the monitoring and assessment activity and the methodologies to be used, there is a reasonable prospect that the activity will produce results that can assist the Panel in reviewing any related substantive claims.

32. In applying these considerations to determine the appropriateness of monitoring and assessment activities, due account needs to be taken of the particular circumstances of each case. Thus the possibility that a monitoring and assessment activity might not establish conclusively that environmental damage has been caused is not necessarily a valid reason for rejecting a claim for expenses resulting from that activity. In the view of the Panel, a monitoring and assessment activity could be of benefit even if the results generated by the activity establish that no damage has been caused. The same may be the case where the results indicate that damage has occurred but that it is not feasible or advisable to undertake measures of remediation or restoration. Confirmation that no damage has been caused or that measures of remediation or restoration are not possible or advisable in the circumstances could assist the Panel in reviewing related substantive claims. It could also be beneficial in alleviating the concerns of Claimants regarding potential risks of damage, and help to avoid unnecessary and wasteful measures to deal with non-existent or negligible risks.

33. A further complication presented by claims for monitoring and assessment of environmental damage and depletion of natural resources results from the difficulty of ascertaining whether, and if so to what extent, damage identified by a monitoring and assessment activity is attributable to Iraq's invasion and occupation of Kuwait. In each of the claimant countries and in the region as a whole, there are natural and other phenomena that could result in environmental damage, depletion of natural

resources or risks to public health of the same or similar type as those that are the subject of some of the claims. It is, therefore, possible that some of the damage revealed by monitoring and assessment activities resulted from causes other than the effects of Iraq's invasion and occupation of Kuwait. It is also possible that the cause of the damage was a combination of the effects of Iraq's invasion and occupation of Kuwait together with phenomena and activities that occurred before or after that event.

34. Moreover, in some of the countries there may not be adequately documented baseline information on the state of the environment or on conditions and trends regarding natural resources prior to Iraq's invasion and occupation of Kuwait. This may make it difficult in many cases to distinguish between damage attributable to Iraq's invasion and occupation of Kuwait and damage that may be due either to factors unrelated to Iraq's invasion and occupation or only partly attributable to Iraq's invasion and occupation. Where damage revealed by monitoring and assessment was not a direct result of Iraq's invasion and occupation of Kuwait, such damage would not be compensable in accordance with paragraph 35 of Governing Council decision 7. And where damage was caused partly by Iraq's invasion and occupation of Kuwait and partly by other factors, such damage may or may not be compensable. Yet the possibility that damage revealed by a monitoring and assessment activity could have been wholly or partly caused by factors unrelated to Iraq's invasion and occupation of Kuwait does not necessarily rule out compensation for that activity. Nor would monitoring and assessment be unreasonable solely because it might be difficult for the Claimant to differentiate damage resulting from Iraq's invasion and occupation of Kuwait from damage that may have resulted from other factors.

35. In deciding whether expenses incurred for a monitoring and assessment activity are compensable in accordance with paragraph 35 of Governing Council decision 7, the Panel considered, *inter alia*, the circumstances of the claim, including the nature of the damage to be assessed and the location and purpose of the monitoring and assessment activity and the appropriateness of the activity by reference to generally accepted scientific criteria and methodologies. Each claim has been reviewed on its own merits. In particular, the Panel has considered whether there was evidence that the activity proposed or undertaken could produce information that might be helpful in identifying environmental damage and depletion of natural resources, or that could offer a useful basis for taking preventive or remedial measures.

B. Relationship among claims

36. A number of the monitoring and assessment claims are closely related to each other. In some cases, this results from the separation of monitoring and assessment claims from the related substantive claims because, in submitting monitoring and assessment claims separately from the substantive claims, some Claimants have formulated each monitoring and assessment activity as an independent claim with its own budget.

37. The Panel believes that, in some cases, savings can be achieved by co-ordinating activities of a Claimant relating to the same subject matter. In such cases, the Panel has suggested co-ordination of the relevant activities. Where the Panel has found that the costs of a particular activity can be reduced by using personnel or resources available for another activity or information available elsewhere, it has taken the possible savings into account in recommending the compensation to be awarded.

38. Most of the monitoring and assessment claims are related to substantive claims for environmental damage and depletion of natural resources because the Claimants expect to use information obtained from the monitoring and assessment activities to support their substantive claims. The Panel stresses that its recommendations on monitoring and assessment claims do not in any way prejudice its findings on related substantive claims that it may review subsequently. Each substantive claim will be reviewed on its own merits on the basis of the evidence presented to support it.

39. However, the Panel anticipates that the results of some monitoring and assessment activities will assist its review of related substantive claims. It recalls that the Governing Council's decision to authorize expedited review of monitoring and assessment claims was, in large part, intended to make funds available to claimants to finance activities that might produce information to support their substantive 'F4' claims. The Panel, therefore, emphasizes the importance of early submission of the results of monitoring and assessment activities for which compensation is awarded.

40. The Panel also notes that some of the monitoring and assessment activities may need to be conducted for several years. In certain circumstances, the Panel has recommended awards of compensation for monitoring and assessment activities even though the results of the activities may not become available in time for use in the review of any substantive claims or may not be needed for such review. However, where preliminary results of long-term monitoring and assessment that could be helpful in the review of related substantive claims become available, the Claimant should make every effort to bring them to the attention of the Panel as soon as possible.

C. The review process

41. Article 36 of the Rules provides that a panel of Commissioners may '(a) in unusually large or complex cases, request further written submissions and invite individuals, corporations or other entities, Governments or international organizations to present their views in oral proceedings; [and] (b) request additional information from any other source, including expert advice, as necessary'. Article 38 (b) of the Rules provides that a panel of Commissioners 'may adopt special procedures appropriate to the character, amount and subject-matter of the particular types of claims under consideration'.

42. In evaluating the scientific and technical appropriateness of monitoring and assessment activities and assessing the reasonableness of the expenses claimed, the Panel was assisted by expert consultants retained by the Commission. In view of the complexity of the issues and the need to consider scientific, legal, social, commercial

and accounting issues in evaluating the claims and assessing the amounts of compensation, the Panel considered it desirable and necessary to have the assistance of a multidisciplinary team of experts. Expert consultants were retained in, *inter alia*, the following fields: chemistry; toxicology; biology (including microbiology, marine biology, biological oceanography, marine zoology and plant pathology); medicine; epidemiology; environmental, ecological and natural resource economics; geology (including geochemistry, hydrology, geoecology); atmospheric sciences; oil spill assessment and response; rangeland management; and accounting.

43. The expert consultants prepared professional judgement reports on all the monitoring and assessment activities for which compensation was sought. Each report included the opinion of the expert consultants regarding the appropriateness of the activity by reference to generally accepted scientific criteria, standards and methodologies. The reports also contained the expert consultants' evaluation of the reasonableness of the costs claimed, having regard to the results likely to be produced. Where appropriate, the expert consultants suggested modifications to the activities proposed or adjustments to the cost estimates presented.

44. The Panel also requested information from a number of international organizations, agencies and individual experts on issues regarding environmental damage and depletion of natural resources relevant to the claims including compensation for oil pollution damage; air quality monitoring and modelling; hydrogeology and groundwater pollution; soil remediation techniques; public health and epidemiology; and environmental and ecological economics.

45. In addition, the Panel requested additional information from the Claimants in order to clarify ambiguities or to amplify information regarding their claims. At the request of the Panel and in accordance with its instructions, members of the secretariat and, where appropriate, the Panel's expert consultants held discussions with representatives of the Claimants in order to obtain such information.

46. In reaching its findings and formulating its recommendations on the claims, the Panel has taken due account of all the information and evidence made available to it, including the materials provided by the Claimants in the claim documents and in response to requests for additional information; the written responses submitted by Iraq; the views presented by Iraq and the Claimants during the oral proceedings; the reports of the Panel's expert consultants; and information and views received from the experts and organizations referred to in paragraph 44 above.

47. Where the Panel has found that modifications to monitoring and assessment activities are necessary or desirable, it has provided details of those modifications. These details are set out in the relevant parts of this report or in the technical annexes.

48. In the cases where the Panel found the cost estimates to be unreasonable, it made adjustments to the amounts claimed. In determining standard rates, the Panel reviewed information provided by its expert consultants concerning applicable rates, having regard to, *inter alia*, the location and nature of the tasks to be undertaken. In each case, the Panel assured itself that the adjustments would not prejudice the ability of the Claimant to achieve the objectives stated in the claim.

49. The Panel's findings and recommendations on each claim are based on its assessment of the totality of evidence presented.

D. *Evidentiary requirements*

50. Article 35(1) of the Rules provides that '[e]ach claimant is responsible for submitting documents and other evidence which demonstrate satisfactorily that a particular claim or group of claims is eligible for compensation pursuant to Security Council resolution 687 (1991)'. Article 35(1) also provides that it is for each panel to determine 'the admissibility, relevance, materiality and weight of any documents and other evidence submitted'.

51. Article 35(3) of the Rules provides that category 'F' claims 'must be supported by documentary and other appropriate evidence sufficient to demonstrate the circumstances and amount of the claimed loss'. The Governing Council emphasized the mandatory nature of this requirement in paragraph 37 of decision 7: 'Since these [category "F"] claims will be for substantial amounts, they must be supported by documentary and other appropriate evidence sufficient to demonstrate the circumstances and the amount of the claimed loss.' In addition, Governing Council decision 46 states that, for category 'F' claims, 'no loss shall be compensated by the Commission solely on the basis of an explanatory statement provided by the claimant' (S/AC.26/1998/46). In this decision, the Governing Council also reaffirmed that, pursuant to article 31 of the Rules, the amounts recommended by the panels of Commissioners 'can only be approved when they are in accordance with this decision'.

52. In some claims, the Panel has found that a monitoring and assessment activity is reasonable in accordance with paragraph 35 of Governing Council decision 7 but has, nevertheless, recommended either that no compensation should be awarded or that compensation be awarded in an amount less than what was sought by the Claimant. For claims concerning monitoring and assessment activities already completed, no compensation has been recommended if the evidence presented to the Panel was not sufficient to demonstrate that the amounts claimed were in fact expended. For activities that are yet to be undertaken, the Panel has recommended compensation only where sufficient evidence has been provided.

E. *Location of the damage*

53. Some of the monitoring and assessment claims relate to environmental damage alleged to have occurred outside Kuwait or Iraq, specifically in the territories of Iran, Jordan, Saudi Arabia, Syria, and Turkey. Neither Security Council resolution 687 (1991) nor any decision of the Governing Council restricts eligibility for compensation to damage that occurred in Kuwait or Iraq. In this regard, the Panel notes that the 'E2' Panel of Commissioners stated in its second report, that 'the place where the loss or damage was suffered by the claimant is not in itself determinative of the Commission's competence' (Report and Recommendations made by the panel of Commissioners concerning the second instalment of 'E2' claims, S/AC.26/1999/6, para. 54).

54. The Panel agrees with this view. Accordingly, it has concluded that expenses resulting from reasonable monitoring and assessment of loss or damage that may have occurred outside Iraq or Kuwait are, in principle, compensable in accordance with paragraph 35 of Governing Council decision 7.

F. Analysis of claims and recommendations

55. The Panel's analysis of the first instalment claims is set forth in the sections V through X of this report. There are separate sections for each claimant country, which are divided into subsections that describe each of the monitoring and assessment claims in the instalment, review their scientific and technical merits, analyse their cost-reasonableness, and report the Panel's recommendations regarding compensation.[4] Additional technical recommendations are contained in technical annexes at the end of the report.

V. MONITORING AND ASSESSMENT CLAIMS OF THE ISLAMIC REPUBLIC OF IRAN

[. . .]

A. Overview

56. Iran submitted a consolidated claim for monitoring and assessment of environmental damage, depletion of natural resources and public health damage that it alleges it suffered as a result of Iraq's invasion and occupation of Kuwait. It states that Iraq's detonation of oil wells in Kuwait resulted in the release of more than 760,000 tons of smoke into the atmosphere. Over 280,000 tons of highly toxic pollutants were dispersed by air and deposited on Iranian territory, particularly the southern provinces of the country. According to Iran, over 15 million people inhaled the toxic smoke for more than 250 days. Iran further alleges that one third of its freshwater resources, its largest agricultural lands, and its most important archaeological sites are located in those provinces and were affected by the pollutants.

57. Iran further alleges that millions of barrels of crude oil were deliberately released into the Persian Gulf by Iraq's forces, and that this resulted in serious damage to the Persian Gulf's fragile ecosystem and to the natural resources of Iran.

58. Finally, Iran alleges that the damage caused to the environment will continue to have adverse impacts on its marine environment, fisheries, water resources, terrestrial environment, agricultural lands, rangelands and forests, cultural heritage sites and public health. The monitoring and assessment would enable it to evaluate the extent of the damage and to determine the most appropriate measures to abate the harm and restore the environment.

59. Iraq argues in its written response, *inter alia*, that Iran has failed to show that it has suffered any direct damage as a result of Iraq's invasion and occupation of Kuwait. In addition, Iraq contends that, because of the direction of the prevailing winds in

---

[4 The sections for Jordan, Kuwait, Saudi Arabia, Syria and Turkey are not reproduced in this volume.]

the region, the smoke plume rarely reached Iranian territory. It further contends that only the 'thin part' of the plume reached the coast of Iran, and just for a short period. Iraq also argues that because no sampling was conducted in Iran in 1991, Iran has no scientific basis for claiming that any damage is attributable to its actions.

60. Iraq reiterated these contentions during the oral proceedings.

61. The Panel has noted the views of Iraq. However, as indicated in paragraphs 29 and 30, it does not consider that a claimant is required to prove the existence of any specific damage before submitting a claim or claims for monitoring and assessment of environmental damage and depletion of natural resources. Moreover, as noted in the sections that follow, there is ample evidence that pollutants from the oil fires in Kuwait reached some parts of Iran and that the territory of Iran was exposed to the oil spill in the Persian Gulf that resulted from Iraq's invasion and occupation of Kuwait.

B. *Transport and dispersion of pollution*
1. Claim No. 5000329

62. Iran seeks compensation in the amount of USD 432,983 for a completed study that used satellite imagery analysis and related methodologies to track the transport of airborne pollutants from the oil fires in Kuwait and the spilled oil in the Persian Gulf that resulted from Iraq's invasion and occupation of Kuwait. The purpose of the study was to determine whether and to what extent airborne pollutants from the oil fires and spilled oil reached the territory of Iran.

63. There is evidence in the scientific literature that emissions from the oil fires reached some parts of Iran. It is, therefore, likely that some airborne pollutants from the oil fires reached the ground in Iran, mainly through wet deposition. There is also evidence that the territory of Iran was affected by the oil spill in the Persian Gulf. It was, therefore, appropriate for Iran to attempt to determine whether pollutants from the oil fires and the spilled oil reached its territory.

64. Accordingly, the Panel finds that the study constituted reasonable monitoring and assessment, and the expenses qualify for compensation in accordance with paragraph 35 (c) of Governing Council decision 7.

[. . .]

69. The Panel, therefore, recommends compensation in the amount of USD 120,000 for this claim.

[. . .]

2. Claim No. 5000330

71. Iran seeks compensation in the amount of USD 1,984,660 for a project to develop a computer-based model of the transport of air pollutants from the oil fires in Kuwait. The model would use an adjusted meso-scale atmospheric model for the region and a specialized air quality model to analyse atmospheric pollutants. (The term 'meso-scale' refers to models that include effects of smaller meteorological frontal or pressure systems and that evaluate spatial grids ranging from 1 to 100 kilometres.) The project is intended to determine the short-term effects that wet and

dry deposition of pollutants resulting from Iraq's invasion and occupation of Kuwait may have had on various types of vegetation in Iran.

72. The Panel considers that, given the lack of monitoring data collected in Iran at the time of the oil fires, it is reasonable for Iran to attempt to estimate the amount of air pollution that affected ground level receptors in its territory. The Panel appreciates that computer models of atmospheric transport of pollutants can only provide general guidance and cannot be used either to establish that pollution from the oil fires affected ground level receptors or to provide an accurate quantitative estimate of exposure. Nonetheless, these models can provide useful information concerning the transport and dispersion of air pollutants.

73. In the Panel's opinion, a competent computer modelling analysis could provide some useful guidance about the exposure of Iran to pollution from the oil fires. However, to succeed within a period of one to two years, such a modelling analysis would need to build upon existing models, rather than upon a newly constructed computer model. In this regard, the Panel notes that excellent meso-scale models already exist and are available for public use.

74. The Panel finds that a project using analyses of existing computer models is a reasonable attempt to determine the transport and dispersion of pollutants in Iran from the oil fires. Consequently, the expenses qualify for compensation in accordance with paragraph 35 (c) of Governing Council decision 7.

75. However, the Panel considers that the modelling analysis should be supplemented by the collection of additional data, particularly data on 'black rain' and 'black snow'. Such data would enable Iran to verify the results of the modelling effort.

76. In addition, account should be taken of data obtained from soil core samples in other monitoring and assessment projects in Iran, particularly claim Nos. 5000347 and 5000425 (paras. 113–18 and 218–22, respectively). Details of the suggested modifications are set out in annex I to this report.[5]

77. Following a review of the cost estimates presented by Iran, the Panel has concluded that a much smaller amount would be sufficient to enable Iran to undertake a competent computer modelling analysis based on existing computer models, coupled with the collection and analysis of data on black rain and snow. The Panel's estimate of a reasonable cost of the project is USD 672,960.

78. The Panel, therefore, recommends compensation in the amount of USD 672,960 for this claim.

C. *Impacts on cultural heritage materials and sites*
1. Claim No. 5000331

79. Iran seeks compensation in the amount of USD 43,605 for preliminary monitoring studies that were conducted to evaluate damage that might have been caused to cultural relics in Iran by pollutants from the oil fires in Kuwait.

[5 The annexes are not reproduced in this volume.]

80. The only evidence provided by Iran to support the claim was a series of letters ordering individuals to travel to certain areas of the country to undertake a variety of activities in late 1997 and 1998. According to the letters, the purpose of the trips was to study, sample and photograph certain cultural relics and prepare reports on the extent of damage caused to those relics as a result of Iraq's invasion and occupation of Kuwait. Iran did not provide a description of the activities undertaken or the methodologies used for the studies. No reports or other evidence were submitted to show that any work had been undertaken.

81. By Procedural Order No. 2, dated 10 May 2000, the Panel requested Iran to provide, *inter alia*, information regarding the number of preliminary studies conducted, the dates on which they were conducted, their objectives, the reports containing the results of the studies, and documentary and other appropriate evidence in support of the costs claimed. The Panel did not receive this information in time to take it into account during its review of the claim.

82. The Panel, therefore, finds that Iran has failed to meet the evidentiary requirements for compensation specified in article 35(3) of the Rules and Governing Council decision 46.

83. Accordingly, no compensation is recommended for this claim.

2. Claim No. 5000446

84. Iran seeks compensation in the amount of USD 2,734,600 for five studies to determine the extent of deterioration that may have been caused to certain outdoor cultural heritage materials in Iran by pollutants from the oil fires in Kuwait. These cultural heritage materials include stone relics in Persepolis; tilework in Eṣfahan and Kermân; wall paintings in Eṣfahan, Fârs and Yazd; construction materials at the Tchoga Zanbil Ziggurat in Khûzestân; and construction materials, archaeological sites and artefacts in Susa. Some wall paintings referred to herein are located outdoors, while others are indoors.

85. As previously noted (para. 63), there is evidence in the scientific literature that emissions from the oil fires reached some parts of Iran. It is, therefore, likely that some airborne pollutants from the oil fires reached the ground in Iran, mainly through wet deposition. In the Panel's opinion, although the probability of identifying damage to the outdoor cultural heritage materials by airborne pollutants from the oil fires, and differentiating such damage from other sources, is low, this cannot be ruled out completely.

86. The Panel considers that it is appropriate for Iran to attempt to determine whether any damage to outdoor cultural heritage materials occurred as a result of the oil fires. The results of the studies could be useful not only for evaluating the extent of damage suffered by the outdoor cultural heritage materials, but also in determining whether there is any need for abatement or restoration measures.

87. The Panel finds that the studies constitute reasonable monitoring and assessment. Consequently, the expenses qualify for compensation in accordance with paragraph 35(c) of Governing Council decision 7.

88. Following a review of the project as presented by Iran, the Panel suggests certain modifications, details of which are set out in annex II to this report.

89. In addition, the Panel has made adjustments to the cost estimate as follows:

(a)   The number of person-months of labour has been reduced with a consequential decrease in labour costs;

(b)   The number and, therefore, cost of analytic tests has been reduced by 80 per cent; and

(c)   The preparation of educational handbooks and the training of technicians and staff in the field of hazard preparedness and management have been eliminated because these activities are not necessary for the studies.

These adjustments reduce the estimated cost to USD 1,398,100.

90. The Panel, therefore, recommends compensation in the amount of USD 1,398,100 for this claim.

3. Claim No. 5000447

91. Iran seeks compensation in the amount of USD 2,716,200 for four studies to determine the extent of deterioration that may have been caused to certain indoor cultural heritage materials in its territory by pollutants from the oil fires in Kuwait. The cultural heritage materials include manuscripts and books in libraries and museums; bronze and iron objects in museums and collections; textile artefacts in museums and repositories; and easel paintings in museums and repositories.

92. As previously noted (para. 63), there is evidence that pollutants from the oil fires reached the ground in parts of Iran, mainly through wet deposition. However, damage to indoor cultural heritage materials is likely to be much less than damage to outdoor materials, because indoor materials are not exposed to air pollution to the same extent.

93. The Panel notes that, as with the outdoor cultural heritage materials, the probability of identifying damage caused by airborne pollutants from the oil fires and differentiating such damage from damage from other sources is low. Indeed, the probability is even lower in the case of indoor materials.

94. Nonetheless, there is the possibility of some exposure of the material to airborne pollutants from the oil fires; and it is appropriate for Iran to attempt to determine the existence and extent of damage that may have been caused. Moreover, the results of the studies may be useful for establishing the possible need for abatement and restoration measures.

95. For these reasons, the Panel finds that the studies constitute reasonable monitoring and assessment. Consequently, the expenses qualify for compensation in accordance with paragraph 35 (c) of Governing Council decision 7.

96. Following a review of the project as presented by Iran, the Panel suggests certain modifications, details of which are set out in annex III to this report.

97. In addition, the Panel has made adjustments to the cost estimate as follows:

(a)   The overall scope of the studies has been substantially reduced to reflect a more focussed approach in the selection of sites and materials;

(b)   The number of person-months of labour has been substantially reduced with a consequential decrease in labour costs;

(c)   The number and, therefore, cost of analytic tests has been reduced by 80 per cent; and

(d)   The preparation of educational handbooks and the training of technicians and staff in the field of hazard preparedness and management have been eliminated because these activities are not necessary for the studies.

These adjustments reduce the estimated cost to USD 575,000.

98. The Panel, therefore, recommends compensation in the amount of USD 575,000 for this claim.

4. Claim No. 5000341

99. Iran seeks compensation in the amount of USD 783,300 for a study to determine damage that may have been caused to unexcavated archaeological sites in the southern part of its territory by pollutants from the oil fires in Kuwait.

100. In the Panel's opinion, the unexcavated sites are likely to have had significantly less, if any, exposure to airborne pollutants from the oil fires than outdoor or indoor cultural heritage materials. Iran has developed neither a methodology for the study nor a procedure for selecting sites for damage assessment and unaffected control sites.

101. The Panel, therefore, finds that the study does not constitute reasonable monitoring and assessment for the purposes of paragraph 35(c) of Governing Council decision 7.

102. Accordingly, the Panel recommends no compensation for this claim.

5. Claim No. 5000342

103. Iran seeks compensation in the amount of USD 472,800 for a project to assess the susceptibility of museums and archaeological sites to sudden increases of pollutants and to develop strategies for air pollution control in museums and repositories in Iran. According to Iran, the purpose of the project is to prepare a blueprint for measures to protect and preserve historic cultural objects from future pollution.

104. In the opinion of the Panel, the project is intended to establish a system to prevent future damage, rather than to evaluate or abate harm that may have been caused as a result of Iraq's invasion and occupation of Kuwait. Hence this project does not qualify as reasonable monitoring and assessment for the purposes of paragraph 35 (c) of Governing Council decision 7.

105. Accordingly, no compensation is recommended for this claim.

D. *Impacts on groundwater and surface water*
Claim No. 5000343

106. Iran seeks compensation in the amount of USD 785,000 for a project to assess the extent of groundwater pollution by hydrocarbons and related heavy metals that

may have been caused by deposition of pollutants from the oil fires in Kuwait. The project would also estimate costs of groundwater remediation.

107. According to Iran, the project would use a 'tiered approach' in which areas in the southern region of Khûzestân suspected to have been affected by hydrocarbon and heavy metal contamination would be identified, sampled and classified as 'low contamination' or 'high contamination' zones. Groundwater in zones classified as highly contaminated would be further sampled. The data generated by the further sampling would be analysed and mapped with Geographic Information System ('GIS') methods. Transport modelling would be used to verify the results of the sampling and to assess the behaviour of pollutants in groundwater over a given period.

108. As previously noted (para. 63), evidence in the scientific literature indicates that airborne pollutants from the oil fires passed over parts of Iran. It is, therefore, likely that some of these pollutants reached the ground in Iran, mainly through wet deposition. Although the probability of identifying incremental damage to the groundwater aquifers caused specifically by the deposition of pollutants from the oil fires is low, this cannot be ruled out completely.

109. The Panel finds that the project is an appropriate attempt to determine whether pollutants from the oil fires had any adverse effects on the groundwater aquifers in Iran. Thus the project constitutes reasonable monitoring and assessment, and the expenses qualify for compensation in accordance with paragraph 35 (c) of Governing Council decision 7.

110. Following a review of the project as presented by Iran, the Panel suggests certain modifications, details of which are set out in annex IV to this report.

111. In addition, the Panel has adjusted the cost of labour by substantially reducing the number of person-months of labour required. This adjustment reduces the estimated cost to USD 371,656.

112. The Panel, therefore, recommends compensation in the amount of USD 371,656 for this claim.

E. *Impacts on the marine and coastal environment*
1. Claim No. 5000347

113. Iran seeks compensation in the amount of USD 822,400 for a project to investigate the natural revegetation capacities of mangrove trees and bioaccumulation of toxic heavy metals and oil-related hydrocarbons in mangroves in areas of the northern Persian Gulf that may have been affected by pollutants released as a result of Iraq's invasion and occupation of Kuwait.

114. As previously noted (para. 63), there is evidence in the scientific literature that pollutants from the oil spill and oil fires reached parts of Iran. There is also evidence that such pollutants can have deleterious impacts on mangrove trees. These effects can become chronic for all growth stages of the trees if the pollutants permeate soft, anaerobic sediments and are subsequently released. Hence, mangrove trees along the Iranian coast could have been adversely affected by exposure to oil pollution. Therefore, an attempt to ascertain the existence and extent of any such effects is appropriate.

115. The Panel finds that the project constitutes reasonable monitoring and assessment. Consequently, the expenses qualify for compensation in accordance with paragraph 35 (c) of Governing Council decision 7.

116. Following a review of the project as presented by Iran, the Panel suggests certain modifications, details of which are set out in annex V to this report.

117. In addition, the Panel has made adjustments to the cost estimate as follows:

(a)   The costs of certain analytical work have been eliminated because Iran informed the Panel that it will not be undertaken;

(b)   The costs of laboratory services have been adjusted to allow for petroleum fingerprinting analysis using gas chromatography / mass spectrometry;

(c)   The cost of equipment has been reduced because Iran has indicated that some equipment purchased for another project will be used;

(d)   The amount of labour for research personnel has been reduced with a consequential decrease in labour costs; and

(e)   The costs of attendance at seminars have been eliminated because the Panel does not consider that attendance at seminars is necessary. These adjustments reduce the estimated cost to USD 711,200.

118. Accordingly, the Panel recommends compensation in the amount of USD 711,200 for this claim.

2. Claim No. 5000349

119. Iran seeks compensation in the amount of USD 363,537 for a project to determine the current status of indicator microfaunal species and the natural recovery and remediation capacities of polluted marine environments. The purpose of the project would be to determine the extent of long-term damage to the marine environment of Iran that may have resulted from Iraq's invasion and occupation of Kuwait.

120. As previously noted (para. 63), there is evidence that the coast of Iran was exposed to oil pollution resulting from Iraq's invasion and occupation of Kuwait. There is also evidence in the scientific literature that oil pollution can have adverse effects on intertidal organisms and may cause alterations in intertidal communities, including reductions in stocks and changes in trophic structure.

121. The Panel considers that it is appropriate for Iran to attempt to find out whether any long-term damage was caused to its marine environment by the oil pollution.

122. Accordingly, the Panel finds that the project constitutes reasonable monitoring and assessment, and the expenses qualify for compensation in accordance with paragraph 35 (c) of Governing Council decision 7.

123. Following a review of the project as presented by Iran, the Panel suggests certain modifications, details of which are set out in annex VI to this report.

124. In addition, the Panel has made adjustments to the cost estimate as follows:

(a)   The cost of labour has been reduced to take account of the decrease in research work; and

(b)   The amount claimed for the purchase of binocular microscopes has been reduced.

These adjustments reduce the estimated cost to USD 263,037.

125. Accordingly, the Panel recommends compensation in the amount of USD 263,037 for this claim.

3. Claim No. 5000350

126. Iran seeks compensation in the amount of USD 822,500 for a project to assess coral reefs under its jurisdiction that may have been affected by oil pollution resulting from Iraq's invasion and occupation of Kuwait. The project would involve assessment of the current status of these reefs, recovery rate of damaged coral reefs, feasibility studies on restoration techniques and a pilot restoration programme.

127. There is evidence in the scientific literature that coral reefs can be damaged by oil pollution. Iran's marine resources were exposed to pollution resulting from Iraq's invasion and occupation of Kuwait, and Iran's coral reefs may have been affected by either the oil spill or deposition of airborne pollutants from the oil fires, or both. Accordingly, it is appropriate for Iran to attempt to identify and assess damage that may have been caused to the coral reefs.

128. The Panel finds that the project constitutes reasonable monitoring and as-sessment. Consequently, the expenses qualify for compensation in accordance with paragraph 35 (c) of Governing Council decision 7.

129. Following a review of the project as presented by Iran, the Panel suggests certain modifications, details of which are set out in annex VII to this report.

130. In addition, the Panel has adjusted the estimated cost by eliminating the costs of a 'mini transport and a research submarine transport system', scuba diving, and submarine pilot courses because they are unnecessary. These adjustments reduce the estimated cost to USD 661,140.

131. Accordingly, the Panel recommends compensation in the amount of USD 661,140 for this claim.

4. Claim No. 5000351

132. Iran seeks compensation in the amount of USD 454,500 for a project to assess long-term changes to seagrass beds under its jurisdiction in the Persian Gulf that may have been caused by oil pollution resulting from Iraq's invasion and occupation of Kuwait. According to Iran, the project would involve the collection of information on the concentration of pollutants in underlying sediments.

133. There is evidence in the scientific literature that seagrass communities, which constitute an important and productive element of coastal ecosystems, are vulner-able to oil pollution. Oil retained in sediments can have a toxic effect on organisms burrowing in or living on the surface sediment. These organisms are an important component of seagrass ecosystems. As previously noted, there is evidence that the Iranian coastline was exposed to oil pollution resulting from Iraq's invasion and oc-cupation of Kuwait. As a result, seagrass communities along the coastline could have

been damaged. It is, therefore, appropriate for Iran to attempt to assess damage that may have been caused to the seagrass beds.

134. The Panel finds that the project constitutes reasonable monitoring and assessment. Consequently, the expenses qualify for compensation in accordance with paragraph 35(c) of Governing Council decision 7.

135. Following a review of the project as presented by Iran, the Panel suggests certain modifications, details of which are set out in annex VIII to this report.

136. In addition, the Panel has reduced the total amount of labour required with a consequential decrease in labour costs. This adjustment reduces the estimated cost to USD 157,776.

137. Accordingly, the Panel recommends compensation in the amount of USD 157,776 for this claim.

5. Claim No. 5000352

138. Iran seeks compensation in the amount of USD 488,630 for a project to select the most cost-effective method of restoring mangrove forests in its territory that may have been damaged as a result of Iraq's invasion and occupation of Kuwait.

139. As previously noted (para. 114), oil pollution can cause damage to mangrove forests at all growth stages. Such damage can become chronic if oil permeates soft, anaerobic sediments and is subsequently released. In the Panel's view, mangrove forests along the Iranian coast could have been affected by exposure to oil pollution resulting from Iraq's invasion and occupation of Kuwait. It is therefore appropriate for Iran to attempt to assess the means of restoring forests that may have been damaged.

140. In this connection the Panel notes that some of these mangrove forests are located in areas listed as wetlands of international importance under the 1971 Ramsar Convention (Convention on Wetlands of International Importance especially as Waterfowl Habitat, *United Nations Treaty Series*, vol. 996, No. 14583, p. 245).

141. The Panel finds that the project constitutes reasonable monitoring and assessment. Consequently, the expenses qualify for compensation in accordance with paragraph 35(c) of Governing Council decision 7.

142. Following a review of the project as presented by Iran, the Panel suggests certain modifications, details of which are set out in annex IX to this report.

143. In addition, the Panel has made adjustments to the cost estimate as follows:

(a)   The cost of labour has been reduced to reflect a decrease in the amount of labour required;

(b)   The cost of an irrigated nursery has been reduced; and

(c)   The cost of transportation has been corrected as indicated by Iran.

These adjustments reduce the estimated cost to USD 357,730.

144. Accordingly, the Panel recommends compensation in the amount of USD 357,730 for this claim.

6. Claim No. 5000344

145. Iran seeks compensation in the amount of USD 686,100 for a project to monitor plant community characteristics in areas of the Shadegan Wetland in Iran that may have been polluted as a result of Iraq's invasion and occupation of Kuwait. The purpose of the project would be to determine natural revegetation capacities and production capabilities of dominant plant species. It would also provide information that would serve as the basis for restoration activities, quantification of other environmental damage claims and calculation of the economic value of lost ecosystem resources.

146. There is evidence that the Shadegan Wetland was exposed to oil pollution resulting from Iraq's invasion and occupation of Kuwait. Wetlands provide a variety of important ecological functions that can be impaired or destroyed by oil pollution. In particular, oil can have a toxic effect on vegetation and alter an ecosystem's community structure. It is, therefore, appropriate for Iran to attempt to assess the nature of any damage that may have been caused.

147. The Panel notes that the Shadegan Wetland is listed as a wetland of international importance under the 1971 Ramsar Convention (Convention on Wetlands of International Importance especially as Waterfowl Habitat, *United Nations Treaty Series*, vol. 996, No. 14583, p. 245).

148. The Panel finds that the project constitutes reasonable monitoring and assessment. Consequently, the expenses qualify for compensation in accordance with paragraph 35(c) of Governing Council decision 7.

149. Following a review of the project as presented by Iran, the Panel suggests certain modifications, details of which are set out in annex X to this report.

150. In addition, the Panel has made adjustments to the cost estimate as follows:

    (a)   The cost of labour has been reduced to reflect a decrease in the scope of the project indicated by Iran;

    (b)   The cost of the microscope has been eliminated because Iran has stated that it will not be purchased; and

    (c)   A laboratory bench fee has been eliminated because it is unnecessary.

These adjustments reduce the estimated cost to USD 489,750.

151. Accordingly, the Panel recommends compensation in the amount of USD 489,750 for this claim.

7. Claim No. 5000345

152. Iran seeks compensation in the amount of USD 143,600 for a project to assess the impacts of Iraq's invasion and occupation of Kuwait on wetland bird populations in Iran by collecting and comparing current population data with pre-invasion data. The project also would assist efforts to restore wetlands and bird populations that may have been harmed by pollution resulting from Iraq's invasion and occupation of Kuwait.

153. The available evidence suggests that wetland birds in Iran are likely to have been exposed to pollution resulting from Iraq's invasion and occupation of Kuwait. In

the opinion of the Panel, the project is a reasonable attempt to evaluate the reduction in wetland bird populations that may have resulted from the pollution and to identify measures needed to restore the bird populations of Iranian wetland areas.

154. The Panel finds that the project constitutes reasonable monitoring and assessment. Consequently, the expenses qualify for compensation in accordance with paragraph 35(c) of Governing Council decision 7.

155. The Panel finds the amount claimed reasonable and accordingly recommends compensation in the amount of USD 143,600 for this claim.

8. Claim No. 5000346

156. Iran seeks compensation in the amount of USD 4,208,900 for a project to determine the current status of Iranian fishery resources that may have been damaged by pollution resulting from Iraq's invasion and occupation of Kuwait and to provide information that may assist in restoration and rehabilitation of these resources. The project would involve an evaluation of the bioaccumulation rate of pollutants in fishery species and impacts to the fishery stock, and attempt to develop a reliable estimate of recovery rates.

157. As previously noted, there is evidence that Iranian coastal areas, fisheries resources and marine ecosystems were exposed to oil pollution that resulted from Iraq's invasion and occupation of Kuwait. There is evidence in the scientific literature that petroleum hydrocarbons can have many adverse impacts on fish, including mortality, defects in reproduction such as reduced fertility and reduced hatching success, reduced growth rates, and reduced survival of eggs and juveniles. This can have long-term adverse effects on fisheries stocks.

158. In the Panel's view, the objectives of the project are appropriate, given the dearth of information available on the state of Iran's fisheries resources before and after Iraq's invasion and occupation of Kuwait.

159. The Panel finds that the project constitutes reasonable monitoring and assessment. Consequently, expenses of the project qualify for compensation in accordance with paragraph 35 (c) of Governing Council decision 7.

160. Following a review of the project as presented by Iran, the Panel suggests certain modifications, details of which are set out in annex XI to this report.

161. As a result of the modifications, the Panel has adjusted the cost of labour. This adjustment reduces the estimated cost to USD 2,908,274.

162. The Panel, therefore, recommends compensation in the amount of USD 2,908,274 for this claim.

9. Claim No. 5000348

163. Iran seeks compensation in the amount of USD 594,000 for a project to identify and assess the presence of pollutants, such as petroleum hydrocarbons and trace metals, in a variety of fish species in Iranian waters resulting from the pollution from Iraq's invasion and occupation of Kuwait. According to Iran, the project would seek to establish, through chemical analyses and physiological tests, the link between

the concentration of hydrocarbon pollutants in soil sediments and the concentration of such pollutants in fish tissues. In addition, Iran plans to assess the short-term and long-term effects of Kuwait crude oil on selected species in its marine environment.

164. As previously noted, there is evidence that Iran's marine environment was exposed to pollution resulting from Iraq's invasion and occupation of Kuwait. In the Panel's opinion, an attempt by Iran to determine the impact of the oil spill and atmospheric deposition of pollutants on fish species is appropriate. In this connection, the Panel notes that the fish species concerned are of major economic importance for Iran.

165. The Panel finds that the project constitutes reasonable monitoring and assessment. Consequently, the expenses qualify for compensation in accordance with paragraph 35(c) of Governing Council decision 7.

166. Following a review of the project as presented by Iran, the Panel suggests certain modifications, details of which are set out in annex XII to this report.

167. Taking into consideration the suggested modifications and resulting cost adjustments, the Panel has developed what it considers to be a reasonable estimate for the project. The revised estimate amounts to USD 377,900.

168. The Panel, therefore, recommends compensation in the amount of USD 377,900 for this claim.

10. Claim No. 5000386

169. Iran seeks compensation in the amount of USD 826,000 for a study on the use of genetically modified bacteria to combat residual oil pollution that may have resulted from Iraq's invasion and occupation of Kuwait. According to Iran, the study would isolate a number of bacteria from the Persian Gulf, genetically modify them and release them into its marine environment to assist biodegradation of any remaining hydrocarbons and tarballs.

170. There is evidence in the scientific literature that some bacteria are naturally capable of degrading petroleum hydrocarbons. However, the evidence suggests that a more effective way to encourage bacterial biodegradation of oil would be to add nutrients or oxygen to the contaminated area and thus assist naturally occurring bacteria to grow more rapidly, rather than introducing additional bacteria into the environment. The evidence also indicates that bacterial biodegradation of oil is most effective if undertaken soon after an oil spill. Accordingly, the Panel does not consider that the procedure proposed is likely to be effective so long after the oil spill that resulted from Iraq's invasion and occupation of Kuwait.

171. In addition, the Panel has serious reservations about the deliberate release of genetically modified organisms into the environment. It notes that widespread concerns have been expressed that the release of such organisms could pose risks to the environment and to human health. In the absence of reliable scientific knowledge about the threat posed by these organisms, it is not advisable for Iran to undertake such a potentially risky procedure. This is particularly so in view of the low probability that the experiment would have any practical utility.

172. For these reasons, the Panel finds that the proposed study does not constitute reasonable monitoring and assessment for the purposes of paragraph 35 (c) of Governing Council decision 7.

173. The Panel, therefore, recommends no compensation for this claim.

11. Claim No. 5000387

174. Iran seeks compensation in the amount of USD 1,035,000 for a study on use of Persian Gulf algae and cyanobacteria as a tool for bioremediation of marine ecosystems under its jurisdiction that may have been polluted as a result of Iraq's invasion and occupation of Kuwait. According to Iran, the study is intended to help it identify the species of algae and cyanobacteria that would be most effective for removing oil-borne heavy metals from the environment. The organisms so identified would be introduced into the polluted areas in Iran's marine environment to assist bioremediation of the oil-borne heavy metals in those areas.

175. There is evidence in the scientific literature that some algae and cyanobacteria are capable of absorbing metals into their cells. However, available evidence suggests that photosynthetic organisms do not have any significant ability to degrade petroleum hydrocarbons. There is, therefore, no scientific basis for assuming that algae and cyanobacteria can play an effective role in the bioremediation of environment polluted by oil.

176. The Panel finds that the study does not constitute reasonable monitoring and assessment for the purposes of paragraph 35(c) of Governing Council decision 7.

177. The Panel, therefore, recommends no compensation for this claim.

12. Claim No. 5000382

178. Iran seeks compensation in the amount of USD 3,686,520 for a project to develop a 'regional flow and contaminant transport model' for its marine area that may have been affected by the oil spill resulting from Iraq's invasion and occupation of Kuwait. The purpose of the project would be to help establish the extent of pollution of the Iranian coastal areas. Iran has stated that Kuwait would participate in the project and that the two states would work jointly with the Regional Organization for the Protection of the Marine Environment ('ROPME').

179. The project would consist of a modelling component and fieldwork to collect data. The modelling component would involve the development of a three-dimensional hydrodynamic model and an oil transport model for the Persian Gulf. The field effort would be designed to gather information needed to develop, calibrate and validate the model. According to Iran, the project would be used to develop a tool to determine with reasonable accuracy the areas of its marine environment exposed to oil spilled as a result of Iraq's invasion and occupation of Kuwait.

180. As previously noted, Iran's marine environment was exposed to the oil spill that resulted from Iraq's invasion and occupation of Kuwait. A three-dimensional hydrodynamic model, when used with an oil transport model, can provide information about the fate and location of spilled oil. Such information can be used with available

field data to develop a comprehensive historical picture of the spatial extent of pollution, as well as provide guidance for subsequent field investigations and remediation efforts.

181. The Panel finds that the project is an appropriate attempt to assess the extent of pollution that may have been caused by the oil spill. Consequently, it constitutes reasonable monitoring and assessment and the expenses qualify for compensation in accordance with paragraph 35 (c) of Governing Council decision 7.

182. However, the Panel does not consider it necessary for Iran to develop a separate oil transport model. Excellent models capable of performing the analysis intended are available for use by Iran. In the view of the Panel, a competent modelling analysis, building upon existing models, could provide useful guidance on the extent to which Iran's marine environment was exposed to pollution from the oil spill.

183. Following a review of the project as presented by Iran, the Panel suggests certain modifications, details of which are set out in annex XIII to this report.

184. In addition, the Panel has made adjustments to the cost estimate as follows:

(a) The cost of labour has been decreased to take account of the reduction in the work to be undertaken;

(b) The costs of computer hardware and software have been reduced to reflect current prices;

(c) The cost of field data collection has been reduced; and

(d) All costs relating to the participation of Kuwait and ROPME have been eliminated because of uncertainty concerning the arrangement for the participation and the expenses involved.

These adjustments reduce the estimated cost to USD 953,220.

185. The Panel, therefore, recommends compensation in the amount of USD 953,220 for this claim.

186. As previously noted, the Panel emphasizes that savings and scientific benefits can be achieved by co-ordination of monitoring and assessment activities relating to the same subject matter.

13. Claim No. 5000388

187. Iran seeks compensation in the amount of USD 178,400 for a completed study to determine the presence on its shoreline of tarball residues and the extent of oil penetration in its coastal areas that may have resulted from Iraq's invasion and occupation of Kuwait. The study was carried out by the Iranian Department of the Environment between 1995 and 1996. The purpose of the study was to measure the oil pollution concentration along the coastal areas, to map the distribution of oil in the coastal areas, and to provide data for use in evaluation of technologies that could be used for the cleanup of polluted areas.

188. In the opinion of the Panel the study was an appropriate attempt to evaluate the impacts of the oil spill. Thus it constituted reasonable monitoring and assessment,

and the expenses qualify for compensation in accordance with paragraph 35 (c) of Governing Council decision 7.

189. A report and a one-page budget were submitted by Iran. No other appropriate evidence was submitted. Iran was requested to produce further support to demonstrate the circumstances and amount of the claimed expenditures, but failed to do so.

190. The Panel finds that Iran has failed to meet the evidentiary requirements for compensation specified in article 35(3) of the Rules and Governing Council decision 46.

191. The Panel, therefore, recommends no compensation for this claim.

14. Claim No. 5000389

192. Iran seeks compensation in the amount of USD 842,500 for a project to assess the extent to which Iranian coastal areas have recovered from pollution resulting from Iraq's invasion and occupation of Kuwait; and to determine methodologies for the clean-up of areas which have not recovered. According to Iran, the extent of recovery would be assessed by aerial and land surveys along the shoreline. Appropriate clean-up technologies would be selected. These would be tested on small-scale experimental sites.

193. The survey methodology proposed by Iran is consistent with standard practices in the field, and would enable Iran to locate surface oil and collect valuable data. In the Panel's view, Iran's attempt to determine the most cost-effective remedial techniques under different conditions is appropriate.

194. The Panel finds that the project constitutes reasonable monitoring and assessment. Consequently, the expenses qualify for compensation in accordance with paragraph 35(c) of Governing Council decision 7.

195. Following a review of the project as presented by Iran, the Panel suggests certain modifications, details of which are set out in annex XIV to this report.

196. Upon a review of the cost estimates presented, the Panel finds that the amount claimed is reasonable.

197. The Panel recommends compensation in the amount of USD 842,500 for this claim.

198. The Panel notes that several Claimants are undertaking similar projects (paras. 419–25, 426–33, 592–9 and 606–16). The Panel emphasizes that co-ordination of efforts and sharing of information would be beneficial.

15. Claim No. 5000383

199. Iran seeks compensation in the amount of USD 375,700 for a project to monitor the amount, fate, and effects of petroleum and 'black rain' pollutants that may have affected the root-zone soils of the Shadegan Wetland as a result of Iraq's invasion and occupation of Kuwait. According to Iran, the project would also undertake a cost–benefit analysis of the clean-up methodologies that may be required for the preservation of this wildlife habitat.

200. As previously noted (para. 146), the Shadegan Wetland was exposed to oil pollution as a result of Iraq's invasion and occupation of Kuwait. It is possible that this pollution affected the plant communities in the wetland. It is, therefore, appropriate for Iran to attempt to identify and evaluate possible adverse impacts on the wetland. In the Panel's view, the methods proposed by Iran are consistent with standard practices in this field.

201. The Panel finds that the project constitutes reasonable monitoring and assessment. Consequently, the expenses qualify for compensation in accordance with paragraph 35 (c) of Governing Council decision 7.

202. Following a review of the project as presented by Iran, the Panel suggests certain modifications, details of which are set out in annex XV to this report.

203. Upon a review of the cost estimates presented, the Panel finds that the costs claimed are reasonable.

204. The Panel recommends compensation in the amount of USD 375,700 for this claim.

16. Claim No. 5000384

205. Iran seeks compensation in the amount of USD 412,000 for a study on the use of aquatic fungi for biodegradation of oil in its wetland and coastal regions that may have been polluted as a result of Iraq's invasion and occupation of Kuwait. According to Iran, the purpose of the study would be to identify species of local fungi and mixed fungal cultures that are most effective for biodegrading crude oil from Kuwait. The fungi identified would be used for bioremediation of polluted areas in the wetlands.

206. Although there is evidence in the scientific literature that fungi can play an important role in the biodegradation of petroleum hydrocarbons in terrestrial environments, the literature shows that the contribution of fungi to petroleum degradation in marine ecosystems is virtually zero. Accordingly, the Panel does not consider that the procedure proposed is likely to be effective.

207. For this reason, the Panel finds that the study does not constitute reasonable monitoring and assessment for the purposes of paragraph 35 (c) of Governing Council decision 7.

208. Accordingly, no compensation is recommended for this claim.

17. Claim No. 5000385

209. Iran seeks compensation in the amount of USD 865,400 for a study to quantify the nature and extent of potential injury to coastal marine life in the southwestern part of Iran. According to Iran, the biodiversity and population dynamics of these marine areas were affected by pollutants resulting from Iraq's invasion and occupation of Kuwait. Iran proposes to investigate the biological and genotoxic effects of pollutants on various finfish and shellfish indicator species.

210. In the opinion of the Panel, the objectives of the study would duplicate those of claim Nos. 5000346 and 5000348 (paras. 156–62 and 163–8, respectively). Moreover, claim Nos. 5000346 and 5000348 rely on methodologies that would be more suitable to

distinguish the impacts of oil pollution resulting from Iraq's invasion and occupation of Kuwait from damage due to other causes.

211. The Panel finds that the study does not constitute reasonable monitoring and assessment for the purposes of paragraph 35 (c) of Governing Council decision 7.

212. The Panel, therefore, recommends no compensation for this claim.

F. Impacts on the terrestrial environment
1. Claim No. 5000424

213. Iran seeks compensation in the amount of USD 703,870 for a study to investigate the impact of oil pollution from the oil fires in Kuwait on soil fertility and crop yield in the southern and southeastern provinces of Iran. Iran proposes, *inter alia*, to measure the levels of mineralizable carbon and nitrogen that may have been introduced into the soil through soot and black rain resulting from the oil fires.

214. As previously noted, some airborne pollutants from the oil fires reached parts of the territory of Iran. However, the scientific evidence indicates that soil carbon and nitrogen levels are highly variable and that increases in these levels, especially in agricultural soil, may be due to a variety of factors.

215. In the opinion of the Panel, it is unlikely that the study would enable Iran to determine the extent to which pollution from the oil fires contributed to the levels of carbon that may be observed in the soil. Moreover, the objectives of the study appear to duplicate those of claim No. 5000425, paras. 218–22.

216. The Panel, therefore, finds that the study does not constitute reasonable monitoring and assessment for the purposes of paragraph 35 (c) of Governing Council decision 7.

217. Accordingly, the Panel recommends no compensation for this claim.

2. Claim No. 5000425

218. Iran seeks compensation in the amount of USD 431,000 for a project to determine the level of soil contamination in Iran that may have been caused by deposition of heavy metals and hydrocarbons from black rain and soot as a result of the oil fires in Kuwait.

219. As previously noted, some airborne pollutants from the oil fires reached parts of the territory of Iran. In the opinion of the Panel, the project is an appropriate attempt by Iran to determine whether any of the pollutants contaminated the soil in its territory.

220. The Panel finds that the project constitutes reasonable monitoring and assessment. Consequently, the expenses qualify for compensation in accordance with paragraph 35 (c) of Governing Council decision 7.

221. Following a review of the cost estimates presented by Iran, the Panel finds that the amount claimed is reasonable. The Panel, therefore, recommends compensation in the amount of USD 431,000 for this claim.

222. The Panel emphasizes the need for Iran to take appropriate steps to co-ordinate data collection and analysis in all of its projects that involve sampling of soils.

3. Claim No. 5000420

223. Iran seeks compensation in the amount of USD 980,409 for a completed study to assess the short-term effects of the oil fires in Kuwait on natural vegetation cover in Iran, with particular reference to changes in green biomass. The study was completed in 1998.

224. As previously noted, some airborne pollutants from the oil fires reached parts of Iran. It was, therefore, appropriate for Iran to attempt to determine the effects that these pollutants might have had on vegetation and biomass in its territory.

225. The Panel finds that the study constituted reasonable monitoring and assessment. Consequently, the expenses qualify for compensation in accordance with paragraph 35(c) of Governing Council decision 7.

226. Iran presented documentary evidence in support of costs for the purchase of remote sensing images (including 329 photographic enlargements and associated negatives, and Landsat TM and SPOT images) as well as the costs for support and advisory services provided by the International Institute for Aerospace Survey and Earth Sciences. These expenses amount to USD 758,792. The Panel finds that this amount is reasonable.

227. However, Iran presented no documentary or other appropriate evidence in support of the remaining expenses claimed. Iran was requested to produce supporting documentation for the claim, but the information provided was insufficient to demonstrate the circumstances and amount of the claimed expenditures. For these expenses, the Panel finds that Iran has failed to meet the evidentiary requirements for compensation specified in article 35(3) of the Rules and Governing Council decision 46. The Panel, therefore, recommends no compensation for these expenses.

228. Accordingly, the Panel recommends compensation in the amount of USD 758,792 for this claim.

229. The date of loss for this claim (for the purpose explained in para. 777) is 3 November 1995.

4. Claim No. 5000421

230. Iran seeks compensation in the amount of USD 871,930 for seven completed studies to determine the scope of damage that might have been caused to environmental resources in Iran as a result of Iraq's invasion and occupation of Kuwait. The objectives of the studies were to identify polluted areas and sources of pollution, and to determine the economic value of the loss resulting from the damage.

231. In the opinion of the Panel, these objectives were appropriate. The Panel, therefore, finds that the studies constituted reasonable monitoring and assessment, and the expenses qualify for compensation in accordance with paragraph 35(c) of Governing Council decision 7.

232. Iran provided little evidence in support of the costs claimed for the studies. Iran was requested to produce additional evidence, but the information provided was insufficient to demonstrate the circumstances and amount of the claimed expenditures. Consequently, the Panel finds that Iran has failed to meet the evidentiary

requirements for compensation specified in article 35(3) of the Rules and Governing Council decision 46.

233. Accordingly, the Panel recommends no compensation for this claim.

5. Claim No. 5000422

234. Iran seeks compensation in the amount of USD 632,000 for a study to determine the best and most cost-effective method to rehabilitate areas in the southern parts of Iran that may have been polluted as a result of the oil fires in Kuwait. According to Iran, the study would evaluate and compare three restoration methods, namely, land imprinting, direct seeding and transplantation.

235. In the Panel's opinion, this study is unlikely to produce any information that is not already available in the scientific literature. The restoration techniques to be evaluated have all been well studied in other arid and semi-arid regions around the world, and the conditions under which each technique is likely to be most effective have been discussed in detail.

236. The Panel, therefore, finds that the study does not constitute reasonable monitoring and assessment for the purposes of paragraph 35 (c) of Governing Council decision 7.

237. Accordingly, the Panel recommends no compensation for this claim.

6. Claim No. 5000426

238. Iran seeks compensation in the amount of USD 1,037,000 for a study to assess the most effective method of restoring its forest areas in Khûzestân, Bushehr, Hormozgan, Ilam, and Fârs that may have been damaged by pollution resulting from the oil fires in Kuwait. Iran proposes to introduce fast-growing non-native tree species in affected areas in order to evaluate and compare their ability to survive and thrive.

239. In the opinion of the Panel, the study is unlikely to produce results that are significantly different from those already available. Revegetation has been well studied in other arid and semi-arid regions around the world, including the Middle East, and the scientific literature contains extensive information on the specific complexities of different approaches, and the advantages and disadvantages of using various species.

240. In addition, the Panel has concerns about the proposal to introduce non-native tree species into the environment. The uncontrolled release of non-native species into new environments should generally be undertaken with great caution, especially in environments with fragile ecosystems.

241. The Panel finds that the study does not constitute reasonable monitoring and assessment for the purposes of paragraph 35 (c) of Governing Council decision 7.

242. Accordingly, the Panel recommends no compensation for this claim.

7. Claim No. 5000427

243. Iran seeks compensation in the amount of USD 1,489,100 for a project to investigate the impacts that the pollution from the oil fires in Kuwait may have had

on forests in the southern and southwestern areas of Iran. According to Iran, the project consists of two phases, the first of which was completed in 1998.

244. As previously noted, there is evidence that petroleum-related pollutants can have adverse impacts on various plant species. It is, therefore, reasonable for Iran to attempt to evaluate these impacts in regions of its territory that may have been affected by such pollutants.

245. The Panel finds that the project constitutes reasonable monitoring and assessment. Consequently, the expenses qualify for compensation in accordance with paragraph 35(c) of Governing Council decision 7.

246. A report and a one-page budget were presented by Iran to support the first phase of the project. No evidence was presented in support of the expenses alleged to have been incurred. Although Iran was requested to produce additional, appropriate evidence, such as contracts, invoices, receipts, salary vouchers and/or accounting records, it failed to do so.

247. In view of these evidentiary shortcomings, the Panel does not recommend any compensation for the first phase of the project. Elimination of those expenses reduces the amount claimed to USD 663,600.

248. Following a review of the second phase of the project as presented by Iran, the Panel suggests certain modifications, details of which are set out in annex XVI to this report.

249. In addition, the Panel has made adjustments to the cost estimate as follows:

(a) The costs of labour have been reduced to reflect a decrease in the amount of labour required;

(b) The cost of material for DNA analysis has been eliminated;

(c) Savings from eliminated DNA-related labour costs are assumed to become available for the recommended additional enzyme analyses; and

(d) Additional provision has been made for a dendrochronograph to be used for a temporal analysis of tree ring growth.

These adjustments reduce the estimated costs for the second phase of the project to USD 624,600.

250. Accordingly, the Panel recommends compensation in the amount of USD 624,600 for this claim.

251. The Panel emphasizes the need for Iran to take appropriate steps to co-ordinate data collection and analysis in all of its projects that involve sampling of soils.

8. Claim No. 5000428

252. Iran seeks compensation in the amount of USD 2,054,600 for a three-phase monitoring and assessment project to investigate the long-term effects of pollutants from the oil fires in Kuwait on livestock in Iran's territory. According to Iran, the project would enable it to identify trends in the incidence of diseases among the livestock.

253. The first phase of the project would involve the collection and processing of statistical data on the incidence of health disorders among livestock and poultry

from eight provinces of the country. In the second phase Iran would attempt to determine the bioaccumulation rate of oil-related pollutants in the organs of livestock and poultry. The third phase would identify possible correlations between pollutants from the oil fires and adverse health effects that might be observed in livestock. Where possible, suitable preventive or remedial measures would be selected.

254. Iraq argues that diseases in livestock are caused by bacteria, viruses, parasites and other micro-organisms, but not by smoke.

255. As previously noted, some airborne pollutants from the oil fires reached parts of the territory of Iran. Some of the pollutants could have had adverse health effects on livestock. It is therefore appropriate for Iran to attempt to evaluate these impacts in the regions of its territory that may have been affected by such pollutants.

256. The Panel finds that the project constitutes reasonable monitoring and assessment. Consequently, the expenses qualify for compensation in accordance with paragraph 35 (c) of Governing Council decision 7.

257. However, the Panel notes that ten years have elapsed since Iraq's invasion and occupation of Kuwait. Given the typical lifespan of livestock species in Iran, most of the livestock currently in the country are unlikely to have been present during the invasion and occupation of Kuwait. The Panel therefore finds that an attempt to study impacts on livestock by widespread sampling of bioaccumulation levels in organs of livestock alive today is not appropriate. Accordingly, the Panel finds that the second phase of the project does not constitute reasonable monitoring and assessment for the purposes of paragraph 35(c) of Governing Council decision 7.

258. Following a review of the first and third phases of the project as presented by Iran, the Panel suggests certain modifications, details of which are set out in annex XVII to this report.

259. The Panel has made adjustments to the labour costs in the first and third phases of the project to reflect changes in the scope of the project. In addition, the Panel has made adjustments to take into account the elimination of the second phase of the project. These adjustments reduce the estimated cost to USD 1,679,091.

260. The Panel, therefore, recommends compensation in the amount of USD 1,679,091 for this claim.

G. Departure of persons from Iraq or Kuwait
Claim No. 5000423

261. Iran seeks compensation in the amount of USD 678,100 for a study to investigate the nature and extent of damage that may have been caused to the Zagros Mountain range by refugees who camped there with their livestock, and to determine the likely persistence of any such damage. Iran alleges that the majority of the refugees were Kurds who fled from Iraq as a result of Iraq's invasion and occupation of Kuwait.

262. The Panel notes that, pursuant to paragraph 34(b) of Governing Council decision 7, losses resulting from the departure of persons from Iraq or Kuwait are compensable if the departures occurred within the period 2 August 1990 to 2 March 1991.

263. Iran did not provide adequate documentation to establish that the refugees departed Iraq or Kuwait during the period 2 August 1990 to 2 March 1991. The Panel is thus unable to determine if any of the refugees departed from Iraq during the period specified in Governing Council decision 7 and, consequently, whether damage resulting from their presence in Iran would qualify as direct loss.

264. Accordingly, the Panel finds that Iran has failed to meet the evidentiary requirements for compensation specified in article 35(3) of the Rules and Governing Council decision 46.

265. The Panel, therefore, recommends no compensation for this claim.

[. . .]

XI. RELATED ISSUES

A. Currency exchange rate

775. The Commission issues awards in United States dollars. The majority of claims were filed in United States dollars, and therefore these costs do not raise currency exchange rate issues. However, some items of expenditure in some of the claims were presented in other currencies and converted into United States dollars at specified rates. In the course of its review, the Panel determined whether the exchange rates used by the Claimants were reasonable approximations of the applicable rates in the United Nations Monthly Bulletin of Statistics.

776. The Panel accepted the exchange rates used by the Claimants, except where fluctuations in exchange rates would have resulted in an overstatement of the value of the claim. In such cases, the Panel applied the rates in the United Nations Monthly Bulletin of Statistics.

B. Interest

777. Governing Council decision 16 provides that '[i]nterest will be awarded from the date the loss occurred until the date of payment, at a rate sufficient to compensate successful claimants for the loss of use of the principal amount of the award' (S/AC.26/1992/16, para. 1). It also provides that the Governing Council will consider the methods of calculation and payment of interest at the appropriate time, and that interest will be paid after the principal amount of awards. Accordingly, the Panel must determine the date from which interest will run, where relevant.

778. The majority of the monitoring and assessment claims are for financial expenditures that have not yet been incurred. In such cases, no interest is due and, accordingly, no date of loss has been indicated. With respect to completed studies, the Panel has selected the mid-point of the period during which expenses were incurred as the date of loss.

XII. SUMMARY OF RECOMMENDATIONS

779. Based on the foregoing, the Panel recommends that the amounts set out in table 14 below be paid in respect of the claims included in the first instalment of 'F4' claims.

Table 14. *Summary of recommended awards for monitoring and assessment claims*

Country	Total number of claims	Amount claimed (USD)	Amount recommended (USD)
Iran	40	42,951,383	17,007,070
Jordan	10	12,488,949	7,060,625
Kuwait	22	460,421,114	108,908,412
Saudi Arabia	24	482,156,943	109,584,660
Syria	10	5,623,885	674,200
Turkey	1	3,770,300	nil
Total	107	1,007,412,574	243,234,967

[Report: UN Doc. S/AC.26/2001/16]

Index

Note: This index concentrates on legal issues as decided by the relevant judicial or quasi-judicial body. Facts and parties' arguments are very lightly indexed, concentrating on points necessary to an understanding of the legal argument. Summaries are indexed to the extent that they include material not included in the main report. Material relating to treaties and treaty interpretation is usually indexed by concept. For entries by article, readers should consult the Table of Treaties.